Oracle® PL/SQL™
by Example

D1497494

FOURTH EDITION

Oracle® PL/SQL™
by Example

FOURTH EDITION

BENJAMIN ROSENZWEIG
ELENA SILVESTROVA RAKHIMOV

✦✦ Addison-Wesley

Upper Saddle River, NJ • Boston • Indianapolis • San Francisco • New York •
Toronto • Montreal • London • Munich • Paris • Madrid • Cape Town • Sydney •
Tokyo • Singapore • Mexico City

The publisher offers excellent discounts on this book when ordered in quantity for bulk purchases or special sales, which may include electronic versions and/or custom covers and content particular to your business, training goals, marketing focus, and branding interests. For more information, please contact:

U.S. Corporate and Government Sales
800-382-3419
corpsales@pearsontechgroup.com

For sales outside the United States, please contact:

International Sales
international@pearson.com

Visit us on the Web: www.informit.com/ph

Library of Congress Cataloging-in-Publication Data

Rosenzweig, Benjamin.
   Oracle PL/SQL by example / Benjamin Rosenzweig, Elena Silvestrova Rakhimov.
     p. cm.
   ISBN 0-13-714422-9 (pbk. : alk. paper) 1. PL/SQL (Computer program language) 2. Oracle (Computer file) 3. Relational databases. I. Rakhimov, Elena Silvestrova. II. Title.
   QA76.73.P258R68 2008
   005.75'6—dc22

2008022398

For information regarding permissions, write to:

Pearson Education, Inc.
Rights and Contracts Department
501 Boylston Street, Suite 900
Boston, MA 02116
Fax: (617) 671 3447

ISBN-13: 978-0-137-14422-8
ISBN-10: 0-137-14422-9

Text printed in the United States on recycled paper at Edwards Brothers in Ann Arbor, Michigan

First printing August 2008

Editor-in-Chief: Mark Taub
Acquisitions Editor: Trina MacDonald
Development Editor: Songlin Qiu
Managing Editor: Kristy Hart
Project Editor: Todd Taber
Copy Editor: Gayle Johnson
Indexer: Erika Millen
Proofreader: Debbie Williams
Technical Reviewers: Oleg Voskoboynikov, Shahdad Moradi
Publishing Coordinator: Olivia Basegio
Cover Designer: Chuti Prasertsith
Composition: Nonie Ratcliff

To my parents, Rosie and Sandy Rosenzweig, for their love and support.   —Benjamin Rosenzweig

To Sean.   —Elena Silvestrova Rakhimov

Contents

1) Visit www.informit.com/title/0137144229 to learn how to register this product and gain access to additional content.

2) To register this product and gain access to bonus content, go to www.informit.com/register to sign in and enter the ISBN. After you register the product, a link to the additional content will be listed on your Account page, under Registered Products.

ACKNOWLEDGMENTS

Benjamin Rosenzweig: I would like to thank my coauthor, Elena Silvestrova Rakhimov, for being a wonderful and knowledgeable colleague to work with. I would also like to thank Douglas Scherer for giving me the opportunity to work on this book, as well as for providing constant support and assistance through the entire writing process. I am indebted to the team at Prentice Hall, which includes Trina MacDonald, Songlin Qiu, Todd Taber, Shahdad Moradi, and Oleg Voskoboynikov. Their contributions, suggestions, and edits helped improve our original manuscript and make the book what it is today. Finally, I would like to thank my many friends and family, especially Edward Clarin and Edward Knopping, for helping me through the long process of putting the whole book together, which included many late nights and weekends.

Elena Silvestrova Rakhimov: My contribution to this book reflects the help and advice of many people. I am particularly indebted to my coauthor, Benjamin Rosenzweig, for making this project a rewarding and enjoyable experience. Special thanks to Trina MacDonald, Songlin Qiu, Todd Taber, and many others at Prentice Hall who diligently worked to bring this book to market. Thanks to Shahdad Moradi and Oleg Voskoboynikov for their valuable comments and suggestions. Most importantly, to my family, whose excitement, enthusiasm, inspiration, and support encouraged me to work hard to the very end, and were exceeded only by their love.

ABOUT THE AUTHORS

Benjamin Rosenzweig is a software development manager at Misys Treasury & Capital Markets, where he has worked since 2002. Prior to that he was a principal consultant for more than three years at Oracle Corporation in the Custom Development Department. His computer experience ranges from creating an electronic Tibetan–English dictionary in Kathmandu, Nepal, to supporting presentation centers at Goldman Sachs and managing a trading system at TIAA-CREF. Rosenzweig has been an instructor at the Columbia University Computer Technology and Application program in New York City since 1998. In 2002 he was awarded the Outstanding Teaching Award from the chair and director of the CTA program. He holds a B.A. from Reed College and a certificate in database development and design from Columbia University. His previous books with Prentice Hall are *Oracle Forms Developer: The Complete Video Course* (ISBN: 0-13-032124-9) and *Oracle Web Application Programming for PL/SQL Developers* (ISBN: 0-13-047731-1).

Elena Silvestrova Rakhimov has more than 15 years of experience in database development in a wide spectrum of enterprise and business environments, ranging from nonprofit organizations to Wall Street. She currently works at Alea Software, where she serves as Senior Developer and Team Lead. Her determination to stay hands-on notwithstanding, Rakhimov has managed to excel in the academic arena, having taught relational database programming at Columbia University's highly esteemed Computer Technology and Applications program. She was educated in database analysis and design at Columbia University and in applied mathematics at Baku State University in Azerbaijan. She currently resides in Vancouver, Canada.

INTRODUCTION

PL/SQL New Features in Oracle 11g

Oracle 11g has introduced a number of new features and improvements for PL/SQL. This introduction briefly describes features not covered in this book and points you to specific chapters for features that *are* within scope of this book. The list of features described here is also available in the "What's New in PL/SQL?" section of the PL/SQL Language Reference manual offered as part of Oracle help available online.

The new PL/SQL features and enhancements are as follows:

- Enhancements to regular expression built-in SQL functions
- SIMPLE_INTEGER, SIMPLE_FLOAT, and SIMPLE_DOUBLE datatypes
- CONTINUE statement
- Sequences in PL/SQL expressions
- Dynamic SQL enhancements
- Named and mixed notation in PL/SQL subprogram invocations
- Cross-session PL/SQL function result cache
- More control over triggers
- Compound triggers
- Database resident connection pool
- Automatic subprogram inlining
- PL/Scope
- PL/SQL hierarchical profiler
- PL/SQL native compiler generates native code directly

Enhancements to Regular Expression Built-In SQL Functions

In this release Oracle has introduced a new regular expression built-in function, REGEXP_COUNT. It returns the number of times a specified search pattern appears in a source string.

FOR EXAMPLE

```
SELECT
   REGEXP_COUNT ('Oracle PL/SQL By Example Updated for Oracle 11g',
                 'ora', 1, 'i')
   FROM dual;

REGEXP_COUNT('ORACLEPL/SQLBYEXAMPLEUPDATEDFORORACLE11G','ORA',1,'I')
-----------------------------------------------------------------
                                                                2
```

The REGEXP_COUNT function returns how many times the search pattern `'ora'` appears in the source string `'Oracle PL/SQL...'` 1 indicates the position of the source string where the search begins, and `'i'` indicates case-insensitive matching.

The existing regular expression built-in functions, REGEXP_INSTR and REGEXP_SUBSTR, have a new parameter called SUBEXPR. This parameter represents a subexpression in a search pattern. Essentially it is a portion of a search pattern enclosed in parentheses that restricts pattern matching, as illustrated in the following example.

FOR EXAMPLE

```
SELECT
   REGEXP_INSTR ('Oracle PL/SQL By Example Updated for Oracle 11g',
                 '((ora)(cle))', 1, 2, 0, 'i')
   FROM dual;

REGEXP_INSTR('ORACLEPL/SQLBYEXAMPLEUPDATEDFORORACLE11G',...)
---------------------------------------------------------
                                                       38
```

The REGEXP_INSTR function returns the position of the first character in the source string `'Oracle PL/SQL...'` corresponding to the second occurrence of the first subexpression `'ora'` in the seach pattern `(ora)(cle)`. 1 indicates the position of the source string where the search begins, 2 indicates the occurrence of the subexpression in the source string, 0 indicates that the position returned corresponds to the position of the first character where the match occurs, and `'i'` indicates case-insensitive matching and REGEXP_SUBSTR.

SIMPLE_INTEGER, SIMPLE_FLOAT, and SIMPLE_DOUBLE Datatypes

These datatypes are predefined subtypes of the PLS_INTEGER, BINARY_FLOAT, and BINARY_DOUBLE, respectively. As such, they have the same range as their respective base types. In addition, these subtypes have NOT NULL constraints.

These subtypes provide significant performance improvements over their respective base types when the PLSQL_CODE_TYPE parameter is set to NATIVE. This is because arithmetic operations for these subtypes are done directly in the hardware layer. Note that when PLSQL_CODE_TYPE is set to INTERPRETED (the default value), the performance gains are significantly smaller. This is illustrated by the following example.

FOR EXAMPLE

```
SET SERVEROUTPUT ON
DECLARE
   v_pls_value1    PLS_INTEGER := 0;
   v_pls_value2    PLS_INTEGER := 1;

   v_simple_value1 SIMPLE_INTEGER := 0;
   v_simple_value2 SIMPLE_INTEGER := 1;

   -- Following are used for elapsed time calculation
   -- The time is calculated in 100th of a second
   v_start_time    NUMBER;
   v_end_time      NUMBER;

BEGIN
   -- Perform calculations with PLS_INTEGER
   v_start_time := DBMS_UTILITY.GET_TIME;

   FOR i in 1..50000000 LOOP
      v_pls_value1 := v_pls_value1 + v_pls_value2;
   END LOOP;

   v_end_time := DBMS_UTILITY.GET_TIME;
   DBMS_OUTPUT.PUT_LINE ('Elapsed time for PLS_INTEGER: '||
      (v_end_time - v_start_time));

   -- Perform the same calculations with SIMPLE_INTEGER
   v_start_time := DBMS_UTILITY.GET_TIME;

   FOR i in 1..50000000 LOOP
      v_simple_value1 := v_simple_value1 + v_simple_value2;
   END LOOP;

   v_end_time := DBMS_UTILITY.GET_TIME;
   DBMS_OUTPUT.PUT_LINE ('Elapsed time for SIMPLE_INTEGER: '||
      (v_end_time - v_start_time));
END;
```

This script compares the performance of the PLS_INTEGER datatype with its subtype SIMPLE_INTEGER via a numeric FOR loop. Note that for this run the PLSQL_CODE_TYPE parameter is set to its default value, INTERPRETED.

```
Elapsed time for PLS_INTEGER: 147
Elapsed time for SIMPLE_INTEGER: 115

PL/SQL procedure successfully completed.
```

CONTINUE Statement

Similar to the EXIT statement, the CONTINUE statement controls loop iteration. Whereas the EXIT statement causes a loop to terminate and passes control of the execution outside the loop, the CONTINUE statement causes a loop to terminate its current iteration and passes control to the next iteration of the loop. The CONTINUE statement is covered in detail in Chapter 7, "Iterative Control—Part 2."

Sequences in PL/SQL Expressions

Prior to Oracle 11g, the sequence pseudocolumns CURRVAL and NEXTVAL could be accessed in PL/SQL only through queries. Starting with Oracle 11g, these pseudocolumns can be accessed via expressions. This change not only improves PL/SQL source code, it also improves runtime performance and scalability.

FOR EXAMPLE

```
CREATE SEQUENCE test_seq START WITH 1 INCREMENT BY 1;

Sequence created.

SET SERVEROUTPUT ON
DECLARE
   v_seq_value NUMBER;
BEGIN
   v_seq_value := test_seq.NEXTVAL;
   DBMS_OUTPUT.PUT_LINE ('v_seq_value: '||v_seq_value);
END;
```

This script causes an error when executed in Oracle 10g:

```
      v_seq_value := test_seq.NEXTVAL;
                              *
   ERROR at line 4:
   ORA-06550: line 4, column 28:
   PLS-00357: Table,View Or Sequence reference 'TEST_SEQ.NEXTVAL' not
   allowed in this context
   ORA-06550: line 4, column 4:
   PL/SQL: Statement ignored
```

and it completes successfully when executed in Oracle 11g:

```
v_seq_value: 1

PL/SQL procedure successfully completed.
```

Consider another example that illustrates performance improvement when the PL/SQL expression is used to manipulate sequences:

FOR EXAMPLE

```
SET SERVEROUTPUT ON
DECLARE
   v_seq_value  NUMBER;

   -- Following are used for elapsed time calculation
   v_start_time NUMBER;
   v_end_time   NUMBER;

BEGIN
   -- Retrieve sequence via SELECT INTO statement
   v_start_time := DBMS_UTILITY.GET_TIME;

   FOR i in 1..10000 LOOP
      SELECT test_seq.NEXTVAL
        INTO v_seq_value
        FROM dual;
   END LOOP;

   v_end_time := DBMS_UTILITY.GET_TIME;
   DBMS_OUTPUT.PUT_LINE
      ('Elapsed time to retrieve sequence via SELECT INTO: '||
       (v_end_time-v_start_time));

   -- Retrieve sequence via PL/SQL expression
   v_start_time := DBMS_UTILITY.GET_TIME;

   FOR i in 1..10000 LOOP
      v_seq_value := test_seq.NEXTVAL;
   END LOOP;

   v_end_time := DBMS_UTILITY.GET_TIME;
   DBMS_OUTPUT.PUT_LINE
      ('Elapsed time to retrieve sequence via PL/SQL expression: '||
       (v_end_time-v_start_time));
END;
```

```
Elapsed time to retrieve sequence via SELECT INTO: 52
Elapsed time to retrieve sequence via PL/SQL expression: 43

PL/SQL procedure successfully completed.
```

Dynamic SQL Enhancements

In this version, Oracle has introduced a number of enhancements to the native dynamic SQL and DBMS_SQL package.

Native dynamic SQL enables you to generate dynamic SQL statements larger than 32K. In other words, it supports the CLOB datatype. Native dynamic SQL is covered in detail in Chapter 17, "Native Dynamic SQL."

The DBMS_SQL package now supports all datatypes that native dynamic SQL supports. This includes the CLOB datatype. In addition, two new functions, DBMS_SQL.TO_REFCURSOR and DBMS_SQL.TO_CURSOR_NUMBER, enable you to switch between the native dynamic SQL and DBMS_SQL package.

Named and Mixed Notation in PL/SQL Subprogram Invocations

Prior to Oracle 11g, a SQL statement invoking a function had to specify the parameters in positional notation. In this release, mixed and named notations are allowed as well. Examples of positional, named, and mixed notations can be found in Chapter 21, "Packages," and Chapter 23, "Object Types in Oracle."

Consider the following example:

FOR EXAMPLE

```
CREATE OR REPLACE FUNCTION test_function
   (in_val1 IN NUMBER, in_val2 IN VARCHAR2)
RETURN VARCHAR2
IS
BEGIN
   RETURN (in_val1||' - '||in_val2);
END;
```

Function created.

```
SELECT
   test_function(1, 'Positional Notation') col1,
   test_function(in_val1 => 2, in_val2 => 'Named Notation') col2,
   test_function(3, in_val2 => 'Mixed Notation') col3
  FROM dual;
```

```
COL1                    COL2                COL3
----------------------  ------------------  ------------------
1 - Positional Notation 2 - Named Notation  3 - Mixed Notation
```

Note that mixed notation has a restriction: positional notation may not follow named notation. This is illustrated by the following SELECT:

```
SELECT
   test_function(1, 'Positional Notation') col1,
   test_function(in_val1 => 2, in_val2 => 'Named Notation') col2,
   test_function(in_val1 => 3, 'Mixed Notation') col3
  FROM dual;

   test_function(in_val1 => 3, 'Mixed Notation') col3
   *
ERROR at line 4:
ORA-06553: PLS-312: a positional parameter association may not follow
a named association
```

Cross-Session PL/SQL Function Result Cache

A result-cached function is a function whose parameter values and result are stored in the cache. This means that when such a function is invoked with the same parameter values, its result is retrieved from the cache instead of being computed again. This caching mechanism is known as single-session caching because each session requires its own copy of the cache where function parameters and its results are stored.

Starting with Oracle 11, the caching mechanism for result-cached functions has been expanded to cross-session caching. In other words, the parameter values and results of the result-cached function are now stored in the shared global area (SGA) and are available to any session. Note that when an application is converted from single-session caching to cross-session caching, it requires more SGA but considerably less total system memory.

Consider the following example, which illustrates how a result-cached function may be created:

FOR EXAMPLE

```
-- Package specification
CREATE OR REPLACE PACKAGE test_pkg AS

   -- User-defined record type
   TYPE zip_record IS RECORD
      (zip   VARCHAR2(5),
       city  VARCHAR2(25),
       state VARCHAR2(2));

   -- Result-cached function
   FUNCTION get_zip_info (in_zip NUMBER) RETURN zip_record
   RESULT_CACHE;

END test_pkg;
/

-- Package body
CREATE OR REPLACE PACKAGE BODY test_pkg AS

-- Result-cached function
```

```
FUNCTION get_zip_info (in_zip NUMBER) RETURN zip_record
RESULT_CACHE
RELIES_ON (ZIPCODE)
IS
   rec zip_record;
BEGIN
   SELECT zip, city, state
     INTO rec
     FROM zipcode
    WHERE zip = in_zip;
   RETURN rec;

EXCEPTION
   WHEN NO_DATA_FOUND THEN
      RETURN null;
END get_zip_info;

END test_pkg;
/
```

Note the use of the RESULT_CACHE and RELIES_ON clauses. RESULT_CACHE specifies that the function is a result-cached function, and RELIES_ON specifies any tables and/or views that the function results depend on.

More Control over Triggers

Starting with Oracle 11g, the CREATE OR REPLACE TRIGGER clause may include ENABLE, DISABLE, and FOLLOWS options. The ENABLE and DISABLE options allow you to create a trigger in the enabled or disabled state, respectively. The FOLLOWS option allows you to specify the order in which triggers fire. Note that the FOLLOWS option applies to triggers that are defined on the same table and fire at the same timing point. Triggers are covered in detail in Chapter 13, "Triggers."

Compound Triggers

A compound trigger is a new type of trigger that allows you to combine different types of triggers into one trigger. Specifically, you can combine the following:

▶ A statement trigger that fires before the firing statement

▶ A row trigger that fires before each row that the firing statement affects

▶ A row trigger that fires after each row that the firing statement affects

▶ A statement trigger that fires after the firing statement

This means that a single trigger may fire at different times when a transaction occurs. Compound triggers are covered in detail in Chapter 14, "Compound Triggers."

Database Resident Connection Pool

Database Resident Connection Pool (DRCP) provides a connection pool that is shared by various middle-tier processes. The new package, DBMS_CONNECTION_POOL, enables database administrators to start and stop DRCP and configure its parameters.

Automatic Subprogram Inlining

The PL/SQL compiler translates PL/SQL code into machine code. Starting with Oracle 10g, the PL/SQL compiler can use the performance optimizer when compiling PL/SQL code. The performance optimizer enables the PL/SQL compiler to rearrange PL/SQL code to enhance performance. The optimization level used by the PL/SQL compiler is controlled by the PLSQL_OPTIMIZE_LEVEL parameter. Its values range from 0 to 2, where 2 is the default value. This means that the PL/SQL compiler performs optimization by default.

Starting with Oracle 11g, the PL/SQL compiler can perform subprogram inlining. Subprogram inlining substitutes a subprogram invocation with an actual copy of the called subprogram. This is achieved by specifying PRAGMA INLINE or setting the PLSQL_OPTIMIZE_LEVEL parameter to a new value, 3. When PLSQL_OPTIMIZE_LEVEL is set to 3, the PL/SQL compiler performs automatic subprogram inlining where appropriate. However, in some instances, the PL/SQL compiler may choose not to perform subprogram inlining because it believes it is undesirable.

The use of PRAGMA INLINE is illustrated in the following example. Note that in this example, PLSQL_OPTIMIZE_LEVEL has been set to its default value, 2.

FOR EXAMPLE

```
SET SERVEROUTPUT ON
DECLARE
   v_num     PLS_INTEGER := 1;
   v_result PLS_INTEGER;

   -- Following are used for elapsed time calculation
   v_start_time NUMBER;
   v_end_time   NUMBER;

   -- Define function to test PRAGMA INLINE
   FUNCTION test_inline_pragma
      (in_num1 IN PLS_INTEGER, in_num2 IN PLS_INTEGER)
   RETURN PLS_INTEGER
   IS
   BEGIN
      RETURN (in_num1 + in_num2);
   END test_inline_pragma;

BEGIN
   -- Test function with INLINE PRAGMA enabled
   v_start_time := DBMS_UTILITY.GET_TIME;

   FOR i in 1..10000000 LOOP
```

```
   PRAGMA INLINE (test_inline_pragma, 'YES');
   v_result := test_inline_pragma (1, i);
END LOOP;

v_end_time := DBMS_UTILITY.GET_TIME;
DBMS_OUTPUT.PUT_LINE
   ('Elapsed time when PRAGMA INLINE enabled: '||
    (v_end_time-v_start_time));

-- Test function with PRAGMA INLINE disabled
v_start_time := DBMS_UTILITY.GET_TIME;

FOR i in 1..10000000 LOOP
   PRAGMA INLINE (test_inline_pragma, 'NO');
   v_result := test_inline_pragma (1, i);
END LOOP;

v_end_time := DBMS_UTILITY.GET_TIME;
DBMS_OUTPUT.PUT_LINE
   ('Elapsed time when INLINE PRAGMA disabled: '||
    (v_end_time-v_start_time));
END;

Elapsed time when PRAGMA INLINE enabled: 59
Elapsed time when PRAGMA INLINE disabled: 220

PL/SQL procedure successfully completed.
```

Note that PRAGMA INLINE affects every call to the specified subprogram when PRAGMA INLINE is placed immediately before one of the following:

▶ Assignment

▶ Call

▶ Conditional

▶ CASE

▶ CONTINUE-WHEN

▶ EXECUTE IMMEDIATE

▶ EXIT-WHEN

▶ LOOP

▶ RETURN

PL/Scope

PL/Scope gathers and organizes data about user-defined identifiers used in PL/SQL code. This tool is used primarily in interactive development environments such as SQL Developer or Jdeveloper rather than directly in PL/SQL.

PL/SQL Hierarchical Profiler

PL/SQL hierarchical profiler enables you to profile PL/SQL applications. In other words, it gathers statistical information about the application such as execution times for SQL and PL/SQL, the number of calls to a particular subprogram made by the application, and the amount of time spent in the subprogram itself.

The hierarchical profiler is implemented via the Oracle-supplied package DBMS_HPROF, which is covered in Chapter 24, "Oracle Supplied Packages."

PL/SQL Native Compiler Generates Native Code Directly

In this version of Oracle, the PL/SQL native compiler can generate native code directly. Previously, PL/SQL code was translated into C code, which then was translated by the C compiler into the native code. In some cases, this improves performance significantly. The PL/SQL compiler type is controlled via the PLSQL_CODE_TYPE parameter, which can be set to either INTERPRETED (the default value) or NATIVE.

CHAPTER 1

PL/SQL Concepts

CHAPTER OBJECTIVES

In this chapter, you will learn about

- ▶ PL/SQL in client/server architecture
- ▶ PL/SQL in SQL*Plus

PL/SQL stands for Procedural Language Extension to SQL. PL/SQL extends SQL by adding programming structures and subroutines available in any high-level language. In this chapter, you will see examples that illustrate the syntax and rules of the language.

PL/SQL is used for both server-side and client-side development. For example, database triggers (code that is attached to tables, as discussed in Chapter 13, "Triggers") on the server side and logic behind an Oracle Developer tool on the client side can be written using PL/SQL. In addition, PL/SQL can be used to develop applications for browsers such as Netscape and Internet Explorer when used in conjunction with the Oracle Application Server and the PL/SQL Web Development Toolkit.

LAB 1.1
PL/SQL in Client/Server Architecture

LAB OBJECTIVES

After completing this lab, you will be able to

▶ Use PL/SQL anonymous blocks
▶ Understand how PL/SQL gets executed

Many Oracle applications are built using client/server architecture. The Oracle database resides on the server. The program that makes requests against this database resides on the client machine. This program can be written in C, Java, or PL/SQL.

Because PL/SQL is just like any other programming language, it has syntax and rules that determine how programming statements work together. It is important for you to realize that PL/SQL is not a stand-alone programming language. PL/SQL is a part of the Oracle RDBMS, and it can reside in two environments, the client and the server. As a result, it is very easy to move PL/SQL modules between server-side and client-side applications.

In both environments, any PL/SQL block or subroutine is processed by the PL/SQL engine, which is a special component of many Oracle products. Some of these products are Oracle server, Oracle Forms, and Oracle Reports. The PL/SQL engine processes and executes any PL/SQL statements and sends any SQL statements to the SQL statement processor. The SQL statement processor is always located on the Oracle server. Figure 1.1 illustrates the PL/SQL engine residing on the Oracle server.

When the PL/SQL engine is located on the server, the whole PL/SQL block is passed to the PL/SQL engine on the Oracle server. The PL/SQL engine processes the block according to Figure 1.1.

When the PL/SQL engine is located on the client, as it is in Oracle Developer Tools, the PL/SQL processing is done on the client side. All SQL statements that are embedded within the PL/SQL block are sent to the Oracle server for further processing. When the PL/SQL block contains no SQL statements, the entire block is executed on the client side.

Using PL/SQL has several advantages. For example, when you issue a SELECT statement in SQL*Plus against the STUDENT table, it retrieves a list of students. The SELECT statement you issued at the client computer is sent to the database server to be executed. The results of this execution are then sent back to the client. As a result, you see rows displayed on your client machine.

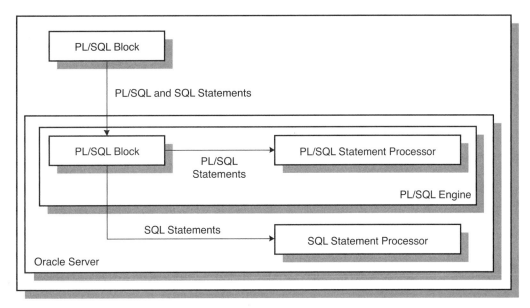

FIGURE 1.1
The PL/SQL engine and Oracle server

Now, assume that you need to issue multiple SELECT statements. Each SELECT statement is a request against the database and is sent to the Oracle server. The results of each SELECT statement are sent back to the client. Each time a SELECT statement is executed, network traffic is generated. Hence, multiple SELECT statements result in multiple round-trip transmissions, adding significantly to the network traffic.

When these SELECT statements are combined into a PL/SQL program, they are sent to the server as a single unit. The SELECT statements in this PL/SQL program are executed at the server. The server sends the results of these SELECT statements back to the client, also as a single unit. Therefore, a PL/SQL program encompassing multiple SELECT statements can be executed at the server and have the results returned to the client in one round trip. This obviously is a more efficient process than having each SELECT statement executed independently. This model is illustrated in Figure 1.2.

Figure 1.2 compares two applications. The first application uses four independent SQL statements that generate eight trips on the network. The second application combines SQL statements into a single PL/SQL block. This PL/SQL block is then sent to the PL/SQL engine. The engine sends SQL statements to the SQL statement processor and checks the syntax of PL/SQL statements. As you can see, only two trips are generated on the network.

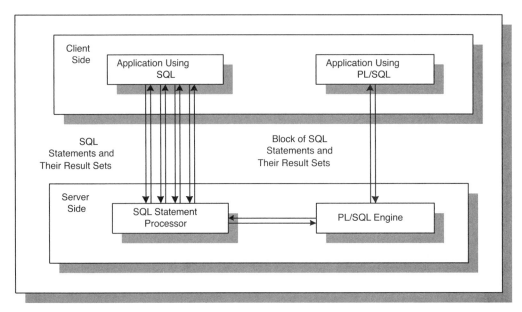

FIGURE 1.2
PL/SQL in client/server architecture

In addition, applications written in PL/SQL are portable. They can run in any environment that Oracle can run in. Because PL/SQL does not change from one environment to the next, different tools can use a PL/SQL script.

PL/SQL BLOCK STRUCTURE

A block is the most basic unit in PL/SQL. All PL/SQL programs are combined into blocks. These blocks can also be nested within each other. Usually, PL/SQL blocks combine statements that represent a single logical task. Therefore, different tasks within a single program can be separated into blocks. As a result, it is easier to understand and maintain the logic of the program.

PL/SQL blocks can be divided into two groups: named and anonymous. Named PL/SQL blocks are used when creating subroutines. These subroutines are procedures, functions, and packages. The subroutines then can be stored in the database and referenced by their names later. In addition, subroutines such as procedures and functions can be defined within the anonymous PL/SQL block. These subroutines exist as long as this block executes and cannot be referenced outside the block. In other words, subroutines defined in one PL/SQL block cannot be called by another PL/SQL block or referenced by their names later. Subroutines are discussed in Chapters 19 through 21. Anonymous PL/SQL blocks, as you probably can guess, do not have names. As a result, they cannot be stored in the database and referenced later.

PL/SQL blocks contain three sections: the declaration section, the executable section, and the exception-handling section. The executable section is the only mandatory section of the block.

The declaration and exception-handling sections are optional. As a result, a PL/SQL block has the following structure:

```
DECLARE
    Declaration statements
BEGIN
    Executable statements
EXCEPTION
    Exception-handling statements
END;
```

DECLARATION SECTION

The declaration section is the first section of the PL/SQL block. It contains definitions of PL/SQL identifiers such as variables, constants, cursors, and so on. PL/SQL identifiers are covered in detail throughout this book.

FOR EXAMPLE

```
DECLARE
   v_first_name  VARCHAR2(35);
   v_last_name   VARCHAR2(35);
   c_counter     CONSTANT NUMBER := 0;
```

This example shows a declaration section of an anonymous PL/SQL block. It begins with the keyword DECLARE and contains two variable declarations and one constant declaration. The names of the variables, v_first_name and v_last_name, are followed by their datatypes and sizes. The name of the constant, $c\_counter$, is followed by the keyword CONSTANT, its datatype, and a value assigned to it. Notice that a semicolon terminates each declaration.

EXECUTABLE SECTION

The executable section is the next section of the PL/SQL block. This section contains executable statements that allow you to manipulate the variables that have been declared in the declaration section.

FOR EXAMPLE

```
BEGIN
   SELECT first_name, last_name
     INTO v_first_name, v_last_name
     FROM student
    WHERE student_id = 123;

   DBMS_OUTPUT.PUT_LINE ('Student name: '||v_first_name||' '||
      v_last_name);
END;
```

This example shows the executable section of the PL/SQL block. It begins with the keyword BEGIN and contains a SELECT INTO statement from the STUDENT table. The first and last names for student ID 123 are selected into two variables: v_first_name and v_last_name. (Chapter 3, "SQL in PL/SQL," contains a detailed explanation of the SELECT INTO statement.) Then the values of the variables, v_first_name and v_last_name, are displayed on the screen with the help of the DBMS_OUTPUT.PUT_LINE statement. This statement is covered in greater detail later in this chapter. The end of the executable section of this block is marked by the keyword END.

BY THE WAY

The executable section of any PL/SQL block always begins with the keyword BEGIN and ends with the keyword END.

EXCEPTION-HANDLING SECTION

The exception-handling section is the last section of the PL/SQL block. This section contains statements that are executed when a runtime error occurs within the block. Runtime errors occur while the program is running and cannot be detected by the PL/SQL compiler. When a runtime error occurs, control is passed to the exception-handling section of the block. The error is then evaluated, and a specific exception is raised or executed. This is best illustrated by the following example.

FOR EXAMPLE

```
BEGIN
   SELECT first_name, last_name
     INTO v_first_name, v_last_name
     FROM student
    WHERE student_id = 123;

   DBMS_OUTPUT.PUT_LINE ('Student name: '||v_first_name||' '||
      v_last_name);
EXCEPTION
   WHEN NO_DATA_FOUND THEN
      DBMS_OUTPUT.PUT_LINE ('There is no student with '||
         'student id 123');
END;
```

This example shows the exception-handling section of the PL/SQL block. It begins with the keyword EXCEPTION. The WHEN clause evaluates which exception must be raised. In this example, there is only one exception, called NO_DATA_FOUND, and it is raised when the SELECT INTO statement does not return any rows. If there is no record for student ID 123 in the STUDENT table, control is passed to the exception-handling section, and the DBMS_OUTPUT.PUT_LINE statement is executed. Chapters 8, 9, and 10 contain more detailed explanations of the exception-handling section.

You have seen examples of the declaration section, executable section, and exception-handling section. Consider combining these examples into a single PL/SQL block.

FOR EXAMPLE

```
DECLARE
   v_first_name VARCHAR2(35);
   v_last_name  VARCHAR2(35);
BEGIN
   SELECT first_name, last_name
     INTO v_first_name, v_last_name
     FROM student
    WHERE student_id = 123;

   DBMS_OUTPUT.PUT_LINE ('Student name: '||v_first_name||' '||
      v_last_name);
EXCEPTION
   WHEN NO_DATA_FOUND THEN
      DBMS_OUTPUT.PUT_LINE ('There is no student with '||
         'student id 123');
END;
```

HOW PL/SQL GETS EXECUTED

Every time an anonymous PL/SQL block is executed, the code is sent to the PL/SQL engine on the server, where it is compiled. A named PL/SQL block is compiled only at the time of its creation, or if it has been changed. The compilation process includes syntax checking, binding, and p-code generation.

Syntax checking involves checking PL/SQL code for syntax or compilation errors. A syntax error occurs when a statement does not exactly correspond to the syntax of the programming language. Errors such as a misspelled keyword, a missing semicolon at the end of the statement, or an undeclared variable are examples of syntax errors.

After the programmer corrects syntax errors, the compiler can assign a storage address to program variables that are used to hold data for Oracle. This process is called binding. It allows Oracle to reference storage addresses when the program is run. At the same time, the compiler checks references to the stored objects such as table names or column names in the SELECT statement, or a call to a named PL/SQL block.

Next, p-code is generated for the PL/SQL block. P-code is a list of instructions to the PL/SQL engine. For named blocks, p-code is stored in the database, and it is used the next time the program is executed. As soon as the process of compilation has completed successfully, the status of a named PL/SQL block is set to VALID, and it is also stored in the database. If the compilation process was unsuccessful, the status of a named PL/SQL block is set to INVALID.

DID YOU KNOW?

Successful compilation of the named PL/SQL block does not guarantee successful execution of this block in the future. At the time of execution, if any one of the stored objects referenced by the block is not present in the database or is inaccessible to the block, execution fails. At such time, the status of the named PL/SQL block is changed to INVALID.

▼ LAB 1.1 EXERCISES

This section provides exercises and suggested answers, with discussion related to how those answers resulted. The most important thing to realize is whether your answer works. You should figure out the implications of the answers and what the effects are of any different answers you may come up with.

1.1.1 Use PL/SQL Anonymous Blocks

Answer the following questions:

A) Why it is more efficient to combine SQL statements into PL/SQL blocks?

ANSWER: It is more efficient to use SQL statements within PL/SQL blocks because network traffic can be decreased significantly, and an application becomes more efficient as well.

When a SQL statement is issued on the client computer, the request is made to the database on the server, and the result set is sent back to the client. As a result, a single SQL statement causes two trips on the network. If multiple SELECT statements are issued, the network traffic can quickly increase significantly. For example, four SELECT statements cause eight network trips. If these statements are part of the PL/SQL block, still only two network trips are made, as in the case of a single SELECT statement.

B) What are the differences between named and anonymous PL/SQL blocks?

ANSWER: Named PL/SQL blocks can be stored in the database and referenced later by their names. Because anonymous PL/SQL blocks do not have names, they cannot be stored in the database and referenced later.

For the next two questions, consider the following code:

```
DECLARE
   v_name   VARCHAR2(50);
   v_total NUMBER;
BEGIN
   SELECT i.first_name||' '||i.last_name, COUNT(*)
     INTO v_name, v_total
     FROM instructor i, section s
    WHERE i.instructor_id = s.instructor_id
      AND i.instructor_id = 102
    GROUP BY i.first_name||' '||i.last_name;

   DBMS_OUTPUT.PUT_LINE
      ('Instructor '||v_name||' teaches '||v_total||' courses');

EXCEPTION
   WHEN NO_DATA_FOUND THEN
      DBMS_OUTPUT.PUT_LINE ('There is no such instructor');
END;
```

BY THE WAY

The SELECT statement in the preceding example is supported by multiple versions of Oracle. However, starting with Oracle 9i, the new ANSI 1999 SQL standard is supported as well, and the SELECT statement can be modified as follows according to this new standard:

```
SELECT i.first_name||' '||i.last_name, COUNT(*)
  INTO v_name, v_total
  FROM instructor i
  JOIN section s
    ON (i.instructor_id = s.instructor_id)
 WHERE i.instructor_id = 102
 GROUP BY i.first_name||' '||i.last_name;
```

Notice that the FROM clause contains only one table, INSTRUCTOR. Following the FROM clause is the JOIN clause that lists the second table, SECTION. Next, the ON clause lists the join condition between the two tables:

```
i.instructor_id = s.instructor_id
```

which has been moved from the WHERE clause.

You will find detailed explanations and examples of the statements using the new ANSI 1999 SQL standard described in Appendix C, "ANSI SQL Standards," and in the Oracle help. Throughout this book we will try to provide examples illustrating both standards; however, our main focus will remain on PL/SQL features rather than SQL.

C) Based on the code example provided, describe the structure of a PL/SQL block.

ANSWER: PL/SQL blocks contain three sections: the declaration section, the executable section, and the exception-handling section. The executable section is the only mandatory section of the PL/SQL block.

The declaration section holds definitions of PL/SQL identifiers such as variables, constants, and cursors. The declaration section starts with the keyword DECLARE:

```
DECLARE
    v_name   VARCHAR2(50);
    v_total  NUMBER;
```

It contains definitions of two variables, v_name and v_total.

The executable section, shown next in bold, holds executable statements. It starts with the keyword BEGIN and ends with the keyword END:

```
BEGIN
   SELECT i.first_name||' '||i.last_name, COUNT(*)
     INTO v_name, v_total
     FROM instructor i, section s
    WHERE i.instructor_id = s.instructor_id
      AND i.instructor_id = 102
   GROUP BY i.first_name||' '||i.last_name;

   DBMS_OUTPUT.PUT_LINE
       ('Instructor '||v_name||' teaches '||v_total||' courses');

EXCEPTION
```

```
      WHEN NO_DATA_FOUND THEN
          DBMS_OUTPUT.PUT_LINE ('There is no such instructor');
END;
```

It contains a SELECT INTO statement that assigns values to the variables v_name and v_total. It also contains a DBMS_OUTPUT.PUT_LINE statement that displays the variables' values on the screen.

The exception-handling section of the PL/SQL block contains statements that are executed only if runtime errors occur in the PL/SQL block:

```
EXCEPTION
    WHEN NO_DATA_FOUND THEN
        DBMS_OUTPUT.PUT_LINE ('There is no such instructor');
```

It also contains the DBMS_OUTPUT.PUT_LINE statement that is executed when the runtime error NO_DATA_FOUND occurs.

D) What happens when the runtime error NO_DATA_FOUND occurs in the PL/SQL block just shown?

ANSWER: When a runtime error occurs in the PL/SQL block, control is passed to the exception-handling section of the block. The exception NO_DATA_FOUND is evaluated then with the help of the WHEN clause.

When the SELECT INTO statement does not return any rows:

```
SELECT i.first_name||' '||i.last_name, COUNT(*)
   INTO v_name, v_total
   FROM instructor i, section s
WHERE i.instructor_id = s.instructor_id
   AND i.instructor_id = 102
GROUP BY i.first_name||' '||i.last_name;
```

control of execution is passed to the exception-handling section of the block. Next, the DBMS_OUTPUT.PUT_LINE statement associated with the exception NO_DATA_FOUND is executed. As a result, the message "There is no such instructor" is displayed on the screen.

1.1.2 Understand How PL/SQL Gets Executed

Answer the following questions:

A) What happens when an anonymous PL/SQL block is executed?

ANSWER: When an anonymous PL/SQL block is executed, the code is sent to the PL/SQL engine on the server, where it is compiled.

B) What steps are included in the compilation process of a PL/SQL block?

ANSWER: The compilation process includes syntax checking, binding, and p-code generation.

Syntax checking involves checking PL/SQL code for compilation errors. After syntax errors have been corrected, a storage address is assigned to the variables that are used to hold data for Oracle. This process is called binding. Next, p-code is generated for the PL/SQL block. P-code is a list of instructions to the PL/SQL engine. For named blocks, p-code is stored in the database, and it is used the next time the program is executed.

C) What is a syntax error?

ANSWER: A syntax error occurs when a statement does not correspond to the syntax rules of the programming language. An undefined variable and a misplaced keyword are examples of syntax errors.

D) How does a syntax error differ from a runtime error?

ANSWER: A syntax error can be detected by the PL/SQL compiler. A runtime error occurs while the program is running and cannot be detected by the PL/SQL compiler.

A misspelled keyword is an example of a syntax error. For example, this script:

```
BEIN
    DBMS_OUTPUT.PUT_LINE ('This is a test');
END;
```

contains a syntax error. Try to find it.

A SELECT INTO statement returning no rows is an example of a runtime error. This error can be handled with the help of the exception-handling section of the PL/SQL block.

LAB 1.2
PL/SQL in SQL*Plus

LAB OBJECTIVES

After completing this lab, you will be able to

- ▶ Use substitution variables
- ▶ Use the DBMS_OUTPUT.PUT_LINE statement

SQL*Plus is an interactive tool that allows you to type SQL or PL/SQL statements at the command prompt. These statements are then sent to the database. After they are processed, the results are sent back from the database and are displayed on the screen. However, there are some differences between entering SQL and PL/SQL statements.

Consider the following example of a SQL statement:

FOR EXAMPLE

```
SELECT first_name, last_name
  FROM student;
```

The semicolon terminates this SELECT statement. Therefore, as soon as you type the semicolon and press Enter, the result set is displayed.

Now, consider the example of the PL/SQL block used in the previous lab:

FOR EXAMPLE

```
DECLARE
   v_first_name VARCHAR2(35);
   v_last_name  VARCHAR2(35);
BEGIN
   SELECT first_name, last_name
     INTO v_first_name, v_last_name
     FROM student
    WHERE student_id = 123;

   DBMS_OUTPUT.PUT_LINE ('Student name: '||v_first_name||' '||
      v_last_name);
EXCEPTION
   WHEN NO_DATA_FOUND THEN
```

```
        DBMS_OUTPUT.PUT_LINE ('There is no student with '||
            'student id 123');
END;
.
/
```

Two additional lines at the end of the block contain . and /. The . marks the end of the PL/SQL block and is optional. The / executes the PL/SQL block and is required.

When SQL*Plus reads a SQL statement, it knows that the semicolon marks the end of the statement. Therefore, the statement is complete and can be sent to the database. When SQL*Plus reads a PL/SQL block, a semicolon marks the end of the individual statement within the block. In other words, it is not a block terminator. Therefore, SQL*Plus needs to know when the block has ended. As you can see here, this can be done with a period and a slash.

SUBSTITUTION VARIABLES

We noted earlier that PL/SQL is not a stand-alone programming language. It exists only as a tool within the Oracle programming environment. As a result, it does not really have capabilities to accept input from a user. However, SQL*Plus allows a PL/SQL block to receive input information with the help of substitution variables. Substitution variables cannot be used to output values, because no memory is allocated for them. SQL*Plus substitutes a variable before the PL/SQL block is sent to the database. Substitution variables usually are prefixed by the ampersand (&) or double ampersand (&&) characters. Consider the following example:

FOR EXAMPLE

```
DECLARE
   v_student_id NUMBER := &sv_student_id;
   v_first_name VARCHAR2(35);
   v_last_name  VARCHAR2(35);
BEGIN
   SELECT first_name, last_name
     INTO v_first_name, v_last_name
     FROM student
    WHERE student_id = v_student_id;

   DBMS_OUTPUT.PUT_LINE ('Student name: '||v_first_name||' '||
      v_last_name);
EXCEPTION
   WHEN NO_DATA_FOUND THEN
      DBMS_OUTPUT.PUT_LINE ('There is no such student');
END;
```

When this example is executed, the user is asked to provide a value for the student ID. The student's name is then retrieved from the STUDENT table if there is a record with the given student ID. If there is no record with the given student ID, the message from the exception-handling section is displayed on the screen.

The preceding example uses a single ampersand for the substitution variable. When a single ampersand is used throughout the PL/SQL block, the user is asked to provide a value for each occurrence of the substitution variable. Consider the following example:

FOR EXAMPLE

```
BEGIN
   DBMS_OUTPUT.PUT_LINE ('Today is '||'&sv_day');
   DBMS_OUTPUT.PUT_LINE ('Tomorrow will be '||'&sv_day');
END;
```

This example produces the following output:

```
Enter value for sv_day: Monday
old    2:    DBMS_OUTPUT.PUT_LINE ('Today is '||'&sv_day');
new    2:    DBMS_OUTPUT.PUT_LINE ('Today is '||'Monday');
Enter value for sv_day: Tuesday
old    3:    DBMS_OUTPUT.PUT_LINE ('Tomorrow will be '||'&sv_day');
new    3:    DBMS_OUTPUT.PUT_LINE ('Tomorrow will be '||'Tuesday');
Today is Monday
Tomorrow will be Tuesday

PL/SQL procedure successfully completed.
```

DID YOU KNOW?

When a substitution variable is used in the script, the output produced by the program contains the statements that show how the substitution was done. For example, consider the following lines of output produced by the preceding example:

```
old    2:    DBMS_OUTPUT.PUT_LINE ('Today is '||  '&sv_day');
new    2:    DBMS_OUTPUT.PUT_LINE ('Today is '||  'Monday');
```

If you do not want to see these lines displayed in the output produced by the script, use the SET command option before you run the script:

```
SET VERIFY OFF;
```

Then the output is as follows:

```
Enter value for sv_day: Monday
Enter value for sv_day: Tuesday
Today is Monday
Tomorrow will be Tuesday

PL/SQL procedure successfully completed.
```

You probably noticed that the substitution variable `sv_day` appears twice in the preceding example. As a result, when this example is run, the user is asked twice to provide a value for the same variable. Now, consider an altered version of the example (changes are shown in bold):

FOR EXAMPLE

```
BEGIN
   DBMS_OUTPUT.PUT_LINE ('Today is '||'&&sv_day');
   DBMS_OUTPUT.PUT_LINE ('Tomorrow will be '||'&sv_day');
END;
```

In this example, the substitution variable sv_day is prefixed by a double ampersand in the first DBMS_OUTPUT.PUT_LINE statement. As a result, this version of the example produces different output:

```
Enter value for sv_day: Monday
old   2:     DBMS_OUTPUT.PUT_LINE ('Today is '||'&&sv_day');
new   2:     DBMS_OUTPUT.PUT_LINE ('Today is '||'Monday');
old   3:     DBMS_OUTPUT.PUT_LINE ('Tomorrow will be '||'&sv_day');
new   3:     DBMS_OUTPUT.PUT_LINE ('Tomorrow will be '||'Monday');
Today is Monday
Tomorrow will be Monday

PL/SQL procedure successfully completed.
```

From this output, it is clear that the user is asked only once to provide the value for the substitution variable sv_day. As a result, both DBMS_OUTPUT.PUT_LINE statements use the value of Monday entered by the user.

When a substitution variable is assigned to the string (text) datatype, it is a good practice to enclose it in single quotes. You cannot always guarantee that a user will provide text information in single quotes. This practice will make your program less error-prone. It is illustrated in the following code fragment:

FOR EXAMPLE

```
v_course_no VARCHAR2(5) := '&sv_course_no';
```

As mentioned earlier, substitution variables usually are prefixed by the ampersand (&) or double ampersand (&&) characters. These are default characters that denote substitution variables. A special SET command option available in SQL*Plus allows you to change the default character (&) to any other character or disable the substitution variable feature. This SET command has the following syntax:

```
SET DEFINE character
```

or

```
SET DEFINE ON
```

or

```
SET DEFINE OFF
```

The first SET command option changes the prefix of the substitution variable from an ampersand to another character. This character cannot be alphanumeric or white space. The second (ON option) and third (OFF option) control whether SQL*Plus looks for substitution variables. In addition, the ON option changes back the value of the character to the ampersand.

DBMS_OUTPUT.PUT_LINE

You already have seen some examples of how the DBMS_OUTPUT.PUT_LINE statement can be used. This statement displays information on the screen. It is very helpful when you want to see how your PL/SQL block is executed. For example, you might want to see how variables change their values throughout the program, in order to debug it.

DBMS_OUTPUT.PUT_LINE is a call to the procedure PUT_LINE. This procedure is a part of the DBMS_OUTPUT package that is owned by the Oracle user SYS.

DBMS_OUTPUT.PUT_LINE writes information to the buffer for storage. When a program has been completed, the information from the buffer is displayed on the screen. The size of the buffer can be set between 2,000 and 1,000,000 bytes. Before you can see the output printed on the screen, one of the following statements must be entered before the PL/SQL block:

```
SET SERVEROUTPUT ON;
```

or

```
SET SERVEROUTPUT ON SIZE 5000;
```

The first SET statement enables the DBMS_OUTPUT.PUT_LINE statement; the default value for the buffer size is used. The second SET statement not only enables the DBMS_OUTPUT. PUT_LINE statement, but also changes the buffer size from its default value to 5,000 bytes.

Similarly, if you do not want the DBMS_OUTPUT.PUT_LINE statement to display information on the screen, you can issue the following SET command prior to the PL/SQL block:

```
SET SERVEROUTPUT OFF;
```

▼ LAB 1.2 EXERCISES

This section provides exercises and suggested answers, with discussion related to how those answers resulted. The most important thing to realize is whether your answer works. You should figure out the implications of the answers and what the effects are of any different answers you may come up with.

1.2.1   Use Substitution Variables

In this exercise, you calculate the square of a number. The value of the number is provided with the help of a substitution variable. Then the result is displayed on the screen.

Create the following PL/SQL script:

```
-- ch01_1a.sql, version 1.0
SET SERVEROUTPUT ON
DECLARE
   v_num    NUMBER := &sv_num;
   v_result NUMBER;
```

```
BEGIN
    v_result := POWER(v_num, 2);
    DBMS_OUTPUT.PUT_LINE ('The value of v_result is: '||
        v_result);
END;
```

Execute the script, and then answer the following questions:

A) If the value of v_num is equal to 10, what output is printed on the screen?

ANSWER: The output should look like the following:

```
Enter value for v_num: 10
old    2:    v_num    NUMBER := &sv_num;
new    2:    v_num    NUMBER := 10;
The value of v_result is: 100

PL/SQL procedure successfully completed.
```

The first line of the output asks you to provide a value for the substitution variable sv_num. The actual substitution is shown in lines 2 and 3. In the second line, you can see the original statement from the PL/SQL block. In the third line, you can see the same statement with the substitution value. The next line shows the output produced by the DBMS_OUTPUT.PUT_LINE statement. Finally, the last line informs you that your PL/SQL block was executed successfully.

B) What is the purpose of using a substitution variable?

ANSWER: A substitution variable allows the PL/SQL block to accept information provided by the user at the time of execution. Substitution variables are used for input purposes only. They cannot be used to output values for a user.

C) Why is it considered a good practice to enclose substitution variables in single quotes for string datatypes?

ANSWER: A program cannot depend wholly on a user to provide text information in single quotes. Enclosing a substitution variable in single quotes helps a program be less error-prone.

1.2.2 Use the DBMS_OUTPUT.PUT_LINE Statement

In this exercise, you determine the day of the week based on today's date. You then display the results on the screen.

Create the following PL/SQL script:

```
-- ch01_2a.sql, version 1.0
SET SERVEROUTPUT ON
DECLARE
    v_day VARCHAR2(20);
BEGIN
    v_day := TO_CHAR(SYSDATE, 'Day');
    DBMS_OUTPUT.PUT_LINE ('Today is '||v_day);
END;
```

Execute the script, and then answer the following questions:

A) What is printed on the screen?

ANSWER: The output should look like the following:

```
Today is Friday

PL/SQL procedure successfully completed.
```

In this example, SQL*Plus does not ask you to enter the value of the v_day variable, because no substitution variable is used. The value of v_day is computed with the help of the TO_CHAR and SYSDATE functions. Then it is displayed on the screen with the help of the DBMS_OUTPUT.PUT_LINE statement.

B) What is printed on the screen if the statement SET SERVEROUTPUT OFF is issued? Why?

ANSWER: If the statement SET SERVEROUTPUT OFF is issued prior to the execution of the PL/SQL block, no output is printed on the screen. The output looks like the following:

```
PL/SQL procedure successfully completed.
```

DID YOU KNOW?

When substitution variables are used, the user is prompted to enter the value for the variable regardless of the SERVEROUTPUT setting. The prompt for the user is provided by SQL*Plus and does not depend on the option chosen for SERVEROUTPUT.

C) How would you change the script to display the time of day as well?

ANSWER: The script should look similar to the following one. Changes are shown in bold.

```
-- ch01_2b.sql, version 2.0
SET SERVEROUTPUT ON
DECLARE
   v_day VARCHAR2(20);
BEGIN
   v_day := TO_CHAR(SYSDATE, 'Day, HH24:MI');
   DBMS_OUTPUT.PUT_LINE ('Today is '|| v_day);
END;
```

The statement shown in bold has been changed to display the time of day as well. The output produced by this PL/SQL block is as follows:

```
Today is Sunday    , 20:39

PL/SQL procedure successfully completed.
```

▼ TRY IT YOURSELF

In this chapter, you have learned about PL/SQL concepts. You've explored PL/SQL block structure, substitution variables, and the DBMS_OUTPUT.PUT_LINE statement. Here are a few exercises that will help you test the depth of your understanding:

1) To calculate the area of a circle, you must square the circle's radius and then multiply it by π. Write a program that calculates the area of a circle. The value for the radius should be provided with the help of a substitution variable. Use 3.14 for the value of π. After the area of the circle is calculated, display it on the screen.

2) Rewrite the script ch01_2b.sql, version 2.0. In the output produced by the script, extra spaces appear after the day of the week. The new script should remove these extra spaces.

   Here's the current output:
   ```
   Today is Sunday    , 20:39
   ```

   The new output should have this format:
   ```
   Today is Sunday, 20:39
   ```

The projects in this section are meant to have you use all the skills you have acquired throughout this chapter. The answers to these projects can be found in Appendix D and on this book's companion Web site. Visit the Web site periodically to share and discuss your answers.

CHAPTER 2

General Programming Language Fundamentals

CHAPTER OBJECTIVES

In this chapter, you will learn about

▶ PL/SQL programming fundamentals

In the Introduction and Chapter 1, "PL/SQL Concepts," you learned about the difference between machine language and a programming language. You have also learned how PL/SQL is different from SQL and about the PL/SQL basic block structure. This is similar to learning the history behind a foreign language and in what context it is used. To use the PL/SQL language, you have to learn the keywords, what they mean, and when and how to use them. First, you will encounter the different types of keywords and then their full syntax. Then you will expand on simple block structure with an exploration of scope and nesting blocks.

LAB 2.1
PL/SQL Programming Fundamentals

LAB OBJECTIVES

After completing this lab, you will be able to

- ▶ Make use of PL/SQL language components
- ▶ Make use of PL/SQL variables
- ▶ Handle PL/SQL reserved words
- ▶ Make use of identifiers in PL/SQL
- ▶ Make use of anchored datatypes
- ▶ Declare and initialize variables
- ▶ Understand the scope of a block, nested blocks, and labels

Most languages have only two sets of characters: numbers and letters. Some languages, such as Hebrew and Tibetan, have specific characters for vowels that are not placed inline with consonants. Other languages, such as Japanese, have three character types: one for words originally taken from the Chinese language, another set for native Japanese words, and a third for other foreign words. To speak any foreign language, you have to begin by learning these character types. Then you learn how to make words from these character types. Finally, you learn the parts of speech, and you can begin talking. You can think of PL/SQL as being a more-complex language, because it has many character types and many types of words or lexical units that are made from these character types. As soon as you learn these, you can begin learning the structure of the PL/SQL language.

CHARACTER TYPES

The PL/SQL engine accepts four types of characters: letters, digits, symbols (*, +, −, =, and so on), and white space. When elements from one or more of these character types are joined, they create a lexical unit (these lexical units can be a combination of character types). The lexical units are the words of the PL/SQL language. First you need to learn the PL/SQL vocabulary, and then you will move on to the syntax, or grammar. Soon you can start talking in PL/SQL.

BY THE WAY

Although PL/SQL can be considered a language, don't try talking to your fellow programmers in PL/SQL. For example, at a dinner table of programmers, if you say, "BEGIN, LOOP FOR PEAS IN PLATE EXECUTE EAT PEAS, END LOOP, EXCEPTION WHEN BROCCOLI FOUND EXECUTE SEND TO PRESIDENT OF THE UNITED STATES, END EAT PEAS," you may not be considered human. This type of language is reserved for Terminators and the like.

LEXICAL UNITS

A language such as English contains different parts of speech. Each part of speech, such as a verb or noun, behaves in a different way and must be used according to specific rules. Likewise, a programming language has lexical units that are the building blocks of the language. PL/SQL lexical units fall within one of the following five groups:

- ▶ Identifiers must begin with a letter and may be up to 30 characters long. See a PL/SQL manual for a more detailed list of restrictions. Generally, if you stay with characters, numbers, and avoid reserved words, you will not run into problems.

- ▶ Reserved words are words that PL/SQL saves for its own use (such as BEGIN, END, and SELECT).

- ▶ Delimiters are characters that have special meaning to PL/SQL, such as arithmetic operators and quotation marks.

- ▶ Literals are values (character, numeric, or Boolean [true/false]) that are not identifiers. 123, "Declaration of Independence," and FALSE are examples of literals.

- ▶ Comments can be either single-line comments (--) or multiline comments (/* */).

See Appendix A, "PL/SQL Formatting Guide," for details on formatting.

In the following exercises, you will practice putting these units together.

▼ LAB 2.1 EXERCISES

This section provides exercises and suggested answers, with discussion related to how those answers resulted. The most important thing to realize is whether your answer works. You should figure out the implications of the answers and what the effects are of any different answers you may come up with.

2.1.1 Make Use of PL/SQL Language Components

Now that you know the character types and the lexical units, this is equivalent to knowing the alphabet and how to spell words.

A) Why does PL/SQL have so many different types of characters? What are they used for?

ANSWER: The PL/SQL engine recognizes different characters as having different meanings and therefore processes them differently. PL/SQL is neither a pure mathematical language nor a spoken language, yet it contains elements of both. Letters form various lexical units such as identifiers or keywords. Mathematic symbols form lexical units called delimiters that perform an operation. Other symbols, such as /*, indicate comments that are ignored by the PL/SQL engine.

B) What are the PL/SQL equivalents of a verb and a noun in English? Do you speak PL/SQL?

ANSWER: A noun is similar to the lexical unit called an identifier. A verb is similar to the lexical unit called a delimiter. Delimiters can simply be quotation marks, but others perform a function such as multiplication (*). You do "speak PL/SQL" to the Oracle server.

2.1.2 Make Use of PL/SQL Variables

Variables may be used to hold a temporary value. The syntax is as follows:

```
Syntax : variable-name data type [optional default assignment]
```

Variables may also be called identifiers. You need to be familiar with some restrictions when naming variables: Variables must begin with a letter and may be up to 30 characters long. Consider the following example, which contains a list of valid identifiers:

FOR EXAMPLE

```
v_student_id
v_last_name
V_LAST_NAME
apt_#
```

Note that the identifiers v_last_name and V_LAST_NAME are considered identical because PL/SQL is not case-sensitive.

Next, consider an example of illegal identifiers:

FOR EXAMPLE

```
X+Y
1st_year
student ID
```

Identifier $X+Y$ is illegal because it contains a + sign. This sign is reserved by PL/SQL to denote an addition operation; it is called a mathematical symbol. Identifier $1st\_year$ is illegal because it starts with a number. Finally, identifier $student\ ID$ is illegal because it contains a space.

Next, consider another example:

FOR EXAMPLE

```
SET SERVEROUTPUT ON;
DECLARE
   first&last_names VARCHAR2(30);
BEGIN
   first&last_names := 'TEST NAME';
   DBMS_OUTPUT.PUT_LINE(first&last_names);
END;
```

In this example, you declare a variable called `first&last_names`. Next, you assign a value to this variable and display the value on the screen. When run, the example produces the following output:

```
Enter value for last_names: Elena
old    2:     first&last_names VARCHAR2(30);
new    2:     firstElena VARCHAR2(30);
Enter value for last_names: Elena
old    4:     first&last_names := 'TEST NAME';
new    4:     firstElena := 'TEST NAME';
Enter value for last_names: Elena
old    5:     DBMS_OUTPUT.PUT_LINE(first&last_names);
new    5:     DBMS_OUTPUT.PUT_LINE(firstElena);
TEST NAME
PL/SQL procedure successfully completed.
```

Consider the output produced. Because an ampersand (`&`) is present in the name of the variable `first&last_names`, a portion of the variable is considered to be a substitution variable (you learned about substitution variables in Chapter 1). In other words, the PL/SQL compiler treats the portion of the variable name after the ampersand (`last_names`) as a substitution variable. As a result, you are prompted to enter the value for the `last_names` variable every time the compiler encounters it.

It is important to realize that although this example does not produce any syntax errors, the variable `first&last_names` is still an invalid identifier, because the ampersand character is reserved for substitution variables. To avoid this problem, change the name of the variable from `first&last_names` to `first_and_last_names`. Therefore, you should use an ampersand in the name of a variable only when you use it as a substitution variable in your program. It is also important to consider what type of program you are developing and that is running your PL/SQL statements. This would be true if the program (or PL/SQL block) were executed by SQL*Plus. Later, when you write stored code, you would not use the ampersand, but you would use parameters.

BY THE WAY

If you are using Oracle SQL Developer, you need to click the leftmost button, Enable DBMS Output, before running this script.

FOR EXAMPLE

```
-- ch02_1a.sql
SET SERVEROUTPUT ON
DECLARE
    v_name        VARCHAR2(30);
    v_dob         DATE;
    v_us_citizen BOOLEAN;
BEGIN
    DBMS_OUTPUT.PUT_LINE(v_name||'born on'||v_dob);
END;
```

A) If you ran this example in a SQL*Plus or Oracle SQL Developer, what would be the result?

ANSWER: Assuming that SET SERVEROUTPUT ON had been issued, you would get only `born on`. The reason is that the variables `v_name` and `v_dob` have no values.

B) Run the example and see what happens. Explain what is happening as the focus moves from one line to the next.

ANSWER: Three variables are declared. When each one is declared, its initial value is null. v_name is set as a VARCHAR2 with a length of 30, v_dob is set as a character type date, and $v\_us\_citizen$ is set to BOOLEAN. When the executable section begins, the variables have no values. Therefore, when DBMS_OUTPUT is told to print their values, it prints nothing.

You can see this if you replace the variables as follows: Instead of v_name, use `COALESCE(v_name, 'No Name')`, and instead of v_dob, use `COALESCE(v_dob, '01-Jan-1999')`.

The COALESCE function compares each expression to NULL from the list of expressions and returns the value of the first non-null expression. In this case, it compares the v_name variable and 'No Name' string to NULL and returns the value of 'No Name'. This is because the v_name variable has not been initialized and as such is NULL. The COALESCE function is covered in Chapter 5, "Conditional Control: CASE Statements."

Then run the same block, and you get the following:

`No Name born on 01-Jan-1999`

To make use of a variable, you must declare it in the declaration section of the PL/SQL block. You have to give it a name and state its datatype. You also have the option to give your variable an initial value. Note that if you do not assign a variable an initial value, it is NULL. It is also possible to constrain the declaration to "not null," in which case you must assign an initial value. Variables must first be declared, and then they can be referenced. PL/SQL does not allow forward references. You can set the variable to be a constant, which means that it cannot change.

2.1.3 **Handle PL/SQL Reserved Words**

Reserved words are ones that PL/SQL saves for its own use (such as BEGIN, END, and SELECT). You cannot use reserved words for names of variables, literals, or user-defined exceptions.

FOR EXAMPLE

```
SET SERVEROUTPUT ON;
DECLARE
    exception VARCHAR2(15);
BEGIN
    exception := 'This is a test';
    DBMS_OUTPUT.PUT_LINE(exception);
END;
```

A) What would happen if you ran this PL/SQL block? Would you receive an error message? If so, what would it say?

ANSWER: In this example, you declare a variable called `exception`. Next, you initialize this variable and display its value on the screen.

This example illustrates an invalid use of reserved words. To the PL/SQL compiler, "exception" is a reserved word that denotes the beginning of the exception-handling section. As a result, it cannot be used to name a variable. Consider the huge error message that this tiny example produces:

```
exception VARCHAR2(15);
    *
ERROR at line 2:
```

```
ORA-06550: line 2, column 4:
PLS-00103: Encountered the symbol "EXCEPTION" when
expecting one of the following:
begin function package pragma procedure subtype type use
<an identifier> <a double-quoted delimited-identifier>
 cursor
form current
The symbol "begin was inserted before "EXCEPTION"
to continue.
ORA-06550: line 4, column 4:
PLS-00103: Encountered the symbol "EXCEPTION" when
expecting one of the following:
begin declare exit for goto if loop mod null pragma
 raise
return select update while <an identifier>
<a double-quoted delimited-identifier> <a bin
ORA-06550: line 5, column 25:
PLS-00103: Encountered the symbol "EXCEPTION" when
expecting one of the following:
( ) - + mod not null others <an identifier>
<a double-quoted delimited-identifier> <a bind variable>
avg
count current exists max min prior sql s
ORA-06550: line 7, column 0:
PLS-00103: Encountered the symbol "end-of-file" when
expecting one of the following:
(  begin declare end exception exit for goto if loop
```

Here is a question you should ask yourself: If you did not know that the word "exception" is a reserved word, do you think you would attempt to debug the preceding script after seeing this error message? I know I wouldn't.

2.1.4 Make Use of Identifiers in PL/SQL

Take a look at the use of identifiers in the following example:

FOR EXAMPLE

```
SET SERVEROUTPUT ON;
DECLARE
   v_var1 VARCHAR2(20);
   v_var2 VARCHAR2(6);
   v_var3 NUMBER(5,3);
BEGIN
   v_var1 := 'string literal';
   v_var2 := '12.345';
   v_var3 := 12.345;
   DBMS_OUTPUT.PUT_LINE('v_var1: '||v_var1);
   DBMS_OUTPUT.PUT_LINE('v_var2: '||v_var2);
   DBMS_OUTPUT.PUT_LINE('v_var3: '||v_var3);
END;
```

In this example, you declare and initialize three variables. The values that you assign to them are literals. The first two values, `'string literal'` and `'12.345'`, are string literals because they are enclosed in single quotes. The third value, 12.345, is a numeric literal. When run, the example produces the following output:

```
v_var1: string literal
v_var2: 12.345
v_var3: 12.345
PL/SQL procedure successfully completed.
```

Consider another example that uses numeric literals:

FOR EXAMPLE

```
SET SERVEROUTPUT ON;
DECLARE
   v_var1 NUMBER(2)  := 123;
   v_var2 NUMBER(3)  := 123;
   v_var3 NUMBER(5,3)  := 123456.123;
BEGIN
   DBMS_OUTPUT.PUT_LINE('v_var1: '||v_var1);
   DBMS_OUTPUT.PUT_LINE('v_var2: '||v_var2);
   DBMS_OUTPUT.PUT_LINE('v_var3: '||v_var3);
END;
```

A) What would happen if you ran this PL/SQL block?

ANSWER: In this example, you declare and initialize three numeric variables. The first declaration and initialization (`v_var1 NUMBER(2)  := 123`) causes an error because the value 123 exceeds the specified precision. The second variable declaration and initialization (`v_var2 NUMBER(3)  := 123`) does not cause any errors because the value 123 corresponds to the specified precision. The last declaration and initialization (`v_var3 NUMBER(5,3)  := 123456.123`) causes an error because the value 123456.123 exceeds the specified precision. As a result, this example produces the following output:

```
ORA-06512: at line 2 ORA-06502: PL/SQL: numeric or value
error: number precision too large
ORA-06512: at line 2
```

2.1.5 **Make Use of Anchored Datatypes**

The datatype that you assign to a variable can be based on a database object. This is called an anchored declaration because the variable's datatype is dependent on that of the underlying object. It is wise to make use of anchored datatypes when possible so that you do not have to update your PL/SQL when the datatypes of base objects change. The syntax is as follows:

```
Syntax: variable_name type-attribute%TYPE
```

The type is a direct reference to a database column.

FOR EXAMPLE

```
-- ch02_2a.sql
SET SERVEROUTPUT ON
DECLARE
   v_name   student.first_name%TYPE;
   v_grade grade.numeric_grade%TYPE;
BEGIN
   DBMS_OUTPUT.PUT_LINE(NVL(v_name,  'No Name ')||
      ' has grade of '||NVL(v_grade, 0));
END;
```

A) In this example, what is declared? State the datatype and value.

ANSWER: The variable v_name is declared with the identical datatype as the column first_name from the database table STUDENT. In other words, the v_name variable is defined as VARCHAR2(25). Additionally, the variable v_grade is declared with the identical datatype as the column grade_numeric from the database table GRADE . That is to say, the v_grade_numeric variable is defined as NUMBER(3). Each variable has a value of NULL.

THE MOST COMMON DATATYPES

When you're a programmer, it is important to know the major datatypes that you can use in a programming language. They determine the various options you have when solving a programmatic problem. Also, you need to keep in mind that some functions work on only certain datatypes. The following are the major datatypes in Oracle that you can use in your PL/SQL:

VARCHAR2(*maximum_length*)

- ▶ Stores variable-length character data.

- ▶ Takes a required parameter that specifies a maximum length up to 32,767 bytes.

- ▶ Does not use a constant or variable to specify the maximum length; an integer literal must be used.

- ▶ The maximum width of a VARCHAR2 database column is 4,000 bytes.

CHAR[(*maximum_length*)]

- ▶ Stores fixed-length (blank-padded if necessary) character data.

- ▶ Takes an optional parameter that specifies a maximum length up to 32,767 bytes.

- ▶ Does not use a constant or variable to specify the maximum length; an integer literal must be used. If the maximum length is not specified, it defaults to 1.

- ▶ The maximum width of a CHAR database column is 2,000 bytes; the default is 1 byte.

NUMBER[(*precision, scale*)]

- ▶ Stores fixed or floating-point numbers of virtually any size.

- ▶ The precision is the total number of digits.

- ▶ The scale determines where rounding occurs.

- ▶ It is possible to specify precision and omit scale, in which case scale is 0 and only integers are allowed.

- Constants or variables cannot be used to specify the precision and scale; integer literals must be used.

- The maximum precision of a NUMBER value is 38 decimal digits.

- The scale can range from 0 to 127. For instance, a scale of 2 rounds to the nearest hundredth (3.456 becomes 3.46).

- The scale can be negative, which causes rounding to the left of the decimal point. For example, a scale of –3 rounds to the nearest thousandth (3,456 becomes 3,000). A scale of 0 rounds to the nearest whole number. If you do not specify the scale, it defaults to 0.

BINARY_INTEGER

- Stores signed integer variables.

- Compares to the NUMBER datatype. BINARY_INTEGER variables are stored in binary format, which takes up less space.

- Calculations are faster.

- Can store any integer value in the range –2,147,483,747 to 2,147,483,747.

- This datatype is used primarily to index a PL/SQL table. This is explained in more depth in Chapter 15, "Collections." You cannot create a column in a regular table of `binary_integer` type.

DATE

- Stores fixed-length date values.

- Valid dates for DATE variables are January 1, 4712 BC to December 31, 9999 AD.

- When stored in a database column, date values include the time of day in seconds since midnight. The date portion defaults to the first day of the current month; the time portion defaults to midnight.

- Dates are actually stored in binary format and are displayed according to the default format.

TIMESTAMP

- This datatype is an extension of the DATE datatype. It stores fixed-length date values with a precision down to a fraction of a second, with up to nine places after the decimal (the default is six). An example of the default for this datatype is 12-JAN-2008 09.51.44.000000 PM.

- The WITH TIME ZONE or WITH LOCAL TIME ZONE option allows the TIMESTAMP to be related to a particular time zone. Then this is adjusted to the time zone of the database. For example, this would allow a global database to have an entry in London and New York recorded as being the same time, even though it would be displayed as noon in New York and 5 p.m. in London.

BOOLEAN

- Stores the values TRUE and FALSE and the nonvalue NULL. Recall that NULL stands for a missing, unknown, or inapplicable value.

- Only the values TRUE and FALSE and the nonvalue NULL can be assigned to a BOOLEAN variable.

- The values TRUE and FALSE cannot be inserted into a database column.

LONG

▶ Stores variable-length character strings.

▶ The LONG datatype is like the VARCHAR2 datatype, except that the maximum length of a LONG value is 2 gigabytes (GB).

▶ You cannot select a value longer than 4,000 bytes from a LONG column into a LONG variable.

▶ LONG columns can store text, arrays of characters, or even short documents. You can reference LONG columns in UPDATE, INSERT, and (most) SELECT statements, but not in expressions, SQL function calls, or certain SQL clauses, such as WHERE, GROUP BY, and CONNECT BY.

LONG RAW

▶ Stores raw binary data of variable length up to 2GB.

LOB (large object)

▶ The four types of LOBs are BLOB, CLOB, NCLOB, and BFILE. These can store binary objects, such as image or video files, up to 4GB in length.

▶ A BFILE is a large binary file stored outside the database. The maximum size is 4GB.

ROWID

▶ Internally, every Oracle database table has a ROWID pseudocolumn, which stores binary values called rowids.

▶ Rowids uniquely identify rows and provide the fastest way to access particular rows.

▶ Use the ROWID datatype to store rowids in a readable format.

▶ When you select or fetch a rowid into a ROWID variable, you can use the function ROWIDTOCHAR, which converts the binary value into an 18-byte character string and returns it in that format.

▶ Extended rowids use base 64 encoding of the physical address for each row. The encoding characters are A to Z, a to z, 0 to 9, +, and /. ROWID is as follows: OOOOOOFFFBBBBBBRRR. Each component has a meaning. The first section, OOOOOO, signifies the database segment. The next section, FFF, indicates the tablespace-relative datafile number of the datafile that contains the row. The following section, BBBBBB, is the data block that contains the row. The last section, RRR, is the row in the block (keep in mind that this may change in future versions of Oracle).

2.1.6 **Declare and Initialize Variables**

In PL/SQL, variables must be declared in order to be referenced. This is done in the initial declarative section of a PL/SQL block. Remember that each declaration must be terminated with a semicolon. Variables can be assigned using the assignment operator $:=$. If you declare a variable to be a constant, it retains the same value throughout the block; to do this, you must give it a value at declaration.

Type the following into a text file, and run the script from a SQL*Plus or Oracle SQL Developer session:

```
-- ch02_3a.sql
SET SERVEROUTPUT ON
DECLARE
   v_cookies_amt        NUMBER := 2;
   v_calories_per_cookie CONSTANT NUMBER := 300;
BEGIN
   DBMS_OUTPUT.PUT_LINE('I ate ' || v_cookies_amt ||
```

```
            ' cookies with ' ||  v_cookies_amt *
            v_calories_per_cookie || ' calories.');
        v_cookies_amt := 3;
        DBMS_OUTPUT.PUT_LINE('I really ate ' ||
            v_cookies_amt
            || ' cookies with ' ||  v_cookies_amt *
            v_calories_per_cookie || ' calories.');
        v_cookies_amt := v_cookies_amt + 5;
        DBMS_OUTPUT.PUT_LINE('The truth is, I actually ate '
            || v_cookies_amt || ' cookies with ' ||
        v_cookies_amt * v_calories_per_cookie
            || ' calories.');
    END;
```

A) What will the output be for this script? Explain what is being declared and what the value of the variable is throughout the scope of the block.

ANSWER: The server output will be as follows:

```
I ate 2 cookies with 600 calories.
I really ate 3 cookies with 900 calories.
The truth is, I actually ate 8 cookies with 2400 calories.
PL/SQL procedure successfully completed.
```

Initially the variable `v_cookies_amt` is declared as a NUMBER with a value of 2, and the variable `v_calories_per_cookie` is declared as a CONSTANT NUMBER with a value of 300. (Because it is declared as a CONSTANT, it does not change its value.) In the course of the procedure, the value of `v_cookies_amt` is later set to 3, and then finally it is set to its current value, 3 plus 5, thus becoming 8.

FOR EXAMPLE

```
-- ch02_3a.sql, version 1.0
SET SERVEROUTPUT ON
DECLARE
    v_lname     VARCHAR2(30);
    v_regdate   DATE;
    v_pctincr   CONSTANT NUMBER(4,2) := 1.50;
    v_counter   NUMBER := 0;
    v_new_cost  course.cost%TYPE;
    v_YorN      BOOLEAN := TRUE;
BEGIN
    DBMS_OUTPUT.PUT_LINE(v_counter);
    DBMS_OUTPUT.PUT_LINE(v_new_cost);
END;
```

B) In the preceding example, add the following expressions to the beginning of the procedure (immediately after the BEGIN). Then explain the values of the variables at the beginning and end of the script.

```
v_counter   := NVL(v_counter, 0) + 1;
v_new_cost  := 800 * v_pctincr;
```

PL/SQL variables are held together with expressions and operators. An expression is a sequence of variables and literals, separated by operators. These expressions are then used to manipulate and compare data and perform calculations.

Expressions are composed of a combination of operands and operators. An operand is an argument to the operator; it can be a variable, a constant, or a function call. An operator is what specifies the action (+, **, /, OR, and so on).

You can use parentheses to control the order in which Oracle evaluates an expression. Continue to add the following to your SQL script:

```
v_counter   := ((v_counter + 5)*2) / 2;
v_new_cost := (v_new_cost * v_counter)/4;
```

ANSWER: The modified version of the script should look similar to the following:

```
-- ch02_3b.sql, version 2.0
SET SERVEROUTPUT ON
DECLARE
    v_lname     VARCHAR2(30);
    v_regdate   DATE;
    v_pctincr   CONSTANT NUMBER(4,2) := 1.50;
    v_counter   NUMBER := 0;
    v_new_cost course.cost%TYPE;
    v_YorN      BOOLEAN := TRUE;
BEGIN
    v_counter   := NVL(v_counter, 0) + 1;
    v_new_cost := 800 * v_pctincr;

    DBMS_OUTPUT.PUT_LINE(v_counter);
    DBMS_OUTPUT.PUT_LINE(v_new_cost);

    v_counter   := ((v_counter + 5)*2) / 2;
    v_new_cost := (v_new_cost * v_counter)/4;

    DBMS_OUTPUT.PUT_LINE(v_counter);
    DBMS_OUTPUT.PUT_LINE(v_new_cost);
END;
```

Initially the variable v_lname is declared as a datatype VARCHAR2 with a length of 30 and a value of NULL. The variable $v\_regdate$ is declared as a datatype date with a value of NULL. The variable $v\_pctincr$ is declared as a CONSTANT NUMBER with a length of 4, a precision of 2, and a value of 1.15. The variable $v\_counter$ is declared as a NUMBER with a value of 0. The variable v_YorN is declared as a variable of the BOOLEAN datatype and has a value of TRUE.

The output of the procedure will be as follows (make sure you have entered SET SERVEROUTPUT ON earlier in your SQL*Plus session):

```
1
1200
PL/SQL procedure successfully completed.
```

When the executable section is complete, the variable $v\_counter$ changes from NULL to 1. The value of v_new_cost changes from NULL to 1200 (800 * 1.50).

Note that a common way to find out the value of a variable at different points in a block is to add a DBMS_OUTPUT.PUT_LINE($v\_variable\_name$); throughout the block.

C) What will the values of the variables be at the end of the script?

ANSWER: The value of $v\_counter$ changes from 1 to 6, which is $((1 + 5) * 2)/2$. The value of new_cost goes from 1200 to 1800, which is $(1200 * 6)/4$. The output from running this procedure is as follows:

```
6
1800
PL/SQL procedure successfully completed.
```

OPERATORS (DELIMITERS): THE SEPARATORS IN AN EXPRESSION

When you're a programmer, it is important to know the operators that you can use in a programming language. They determine your various options for solving a programmatic problem. The following are the operators you can use in PL/SQL:

▶ Arithmetic ($**, *, /, +, -$)

▶ Comparison ($=, <>, !=, <, >, <=, >=$, LIKE, IN, BETWEEN, IS NULL, IS NOT NULL, NOT IN)

▶ Logical (AND, OR, NOT)

▶ String ($||$, LIKE)

▶ Expressions

▶ Operator precedence

▶ $**$, NOT

▶ $+, -$ (arithmetic identity and negation) $*, /, +, -, || =, <>, !=, <=$

▶ $>=, <, >$, LIKE, BETWEEN, IN, IS NULL

▶ AND (logical conjunction)

▶ OR (logical inclusion)

2.1.7 Understand the Scope of a Block, Nested Blocks, and Labels

When you use variables in a PL/SQL block, you must understand their scope. This allows you to understand how and when you can use variables. It also helps you debug the programs you write. The opening section of your PL/SQL block contains the declaration section. This is where you declare the variables that the block will use.

SCOPE OF A VARIABLE

The scope, or existence, of structures defined in the declaration section is local to that block. The block also provides the scope for exceptions that are declared and raised. Exceptions are covered in more detail in Chapters 8, 9, and 10.

The scope of a variable is the portion of the program in which the variable can be accessed, or where the variable is visible. It usually extends from the moment of declaration until the end of the block in which the variable was declared. The visibility of a variable is the part of the program where the variable can be accessed.

```
BEGIN      -- outer block
        BEGIN -- inner block
               ...;
        END;   -- end of inner block
   END;        -- end of outer block
```

LABELS AND NESTED BLOCKS

Labels can be added to a block to improve readability and to qualify the names of elements that exist under the same name in nested blocks. The name of the block must precede the first line of executable code (either the BEGIN or DECLARE), as follows:

FOR EXAMPLE

```
-- ch02_4a.sql
SET SERVEROUTPUT ON
   << find_stu_num >>
   BEGIN
      DBMS_OUTPUT.PUT_LINE('The procedure
                  find_stu_num has been executed.');
   END find_stu_num;
```

The label optionally appears after END. For commenting purposes, you may use either -- or /*, and */. Blocks can be nested in the main section or in an exception handler. A nested block is a block that is placed fully within another block. This has an impact on the scope and visibility of variables. The scope of a variable in a nested block is the period when memory is being allocated for the variable. It extends from the moment of declaration until the END of the nested block from which it was declared. The visibility of a variable is the part of the program where the variable can be accessed.

FOR EXAMPLE

```
-- ch02_4b.sql
SET SERVEROUTPUT ON
<< outer_block >>
DECLARE
   v_test NUMBER := 123;
BEGIN
   DBMS_OUTPUT.PUT_LINE
      ('Outer Block, v_test: '||v_test);
   << inner_block >>
   DECLARE
      v_test NUMBER := 456;
   BEGIN
      DBMS_OUTPUT.PUT_LINE
         ('Inner Block, v_test: '||v_test);
      DBMS_OUTPUT.PUT_LINE
         ('Inner Block, outer_block.v_test: '||
          Outer_block.v_test);
   END inner_block;
END outer_block;
```

This example produces the following output:

```
    Outer Block, v_test: 123
    Inner Block, v_test: 456
    Inner Block, outer_block.v_test: 123
```

A) If the following example were run in SQL*Plus, what do you think would be displayed?

```
-- ch02_5a.sql
SET SERVEROUTPUT ON
DECLARE
    e_show_exception_scope EXCEPTION;
    v_student_id           NUMBER := 123;
BEGIN
  DBMS_OUTPUT.PUT_LINE('outer student id is '
      ||v_student_id);
    DECLARE
      v_student_id    VARCHAR2(8) := 125;
    BEGIN
       DBMS_OUTPUT.PUT_LINE('inner student id is '
          ||v_student_id);
       RAISE e_show_exception_scope;
    END;
EXCEPTION
   WHEN e_show_exception_scope
   THEN
       DBMS_OUTPUT.PUT_LINE('When am I displayed?');
       DBMS_OUTPUT.PUT_LINE('outer student id is '
          ||v_student_id);
END;
```

ANSWER: The following would result:

```
outer student id is 123
inner student id is 125
When am I displayed?
outer student id is 123
PL/SQL procedure successfully completed.
```

B) Now run the example and see if it produces what you expected. Explain how the focus moves from one block to another in this example.

ANSWER: The variable e_Show_Exception_Scope is declared as an exception type in the declaration section of the block. There is also a declaration of the variable called v_student_id of datatype NUMBER that is initialized to the number 123. This variable has a scope of the entire block, but it is visible only outside the inner block. When the inner block begins, another variable, v_student_id, is declared. This time it is of datatype VARCHAR2(8) and is initialized to 125. This variable has scope and visibility only within the inner block. The use of DBMS_OUTPUT helps show which variable is visible. The inner block raises the exception e_Show_Exception_Scope; this means that the focus moves out of the execution section and into the exception section. The focus looks for an exception named e_Show_Exception_Scope. Because the inner block has no exception with this name, the focus moves to the outer block's exception section and finds the exception. The inner variable v_student_id is now out of scope and visibility. The outer variable v_student_id (which has always been in scope) now regains visibility. Because the exception has an IF/THEN construct, it executes the DBMS_ OUTPUT call. This is a simple use of nested blocks. Later in the book you will see more-complex examples. After you learn about exception handling in Chapters 8, 9, and 10, you will see that there is greater opportunity to make use of nested blocks.

▼ TRY IT YOURSELF

Before starting the following projects, take a look at the formatting guidelines in Appendix A. Make your variable names conform to the standard. At the top of the declaration section, put a comment stating which naming standard you are using.

1) Write a PL/SQL block

   A) That includes declarations for the following variables:

   A VARCHAR2 datatype that can contain the string 'Introduction to Oracle PL/SQL'

   A NUMBER that can be assigned 987654.55, but not 987654.567 or 9876543.55

   A CONSTANT (you choose the correct data type) that is auto-initialized to the value '603D'

   A BOOLEAN

   A DATE data type autoinitialized to one week from today

   B) In the body of the PL/SQL block, put a DBMS_OUTPUT.PUT_LINE message for each of the variables that received an autoinitialization value.

   C) In a comment at the bottom of the PL/SQL block, state the value of your NUMBER data type.

2) Alter the PL/SQL block you created in Project 1 to conform to the following specifications:

   A) Remove the DBMS_OUTPUT.PUT_LINE messages.

   B) In the body of the PL/SQL block, write a selection test (IF) that does the following (use a nested IF statement where appropriate):

      I) Checks whether the VARCHAR2 you created contains the course named 'Introduction to Underwater Basketweaving'.

      II) If it does, put a DBMS_OUTPUT.PUT_LINE message on the screen that says so.

      III) If it does not, test to see if the CONSTANT you created contains the room number 603D.

      IV) If it does, put a DBMS_OUTPUT.PUT_LINE message on the screen that states the course name and the room number that you've reached in this logic.

      V) If it does not, put a DBMS_OUTPUT.PUT_LINE message on the screen that states that the course and location could not be determined.

   C) Add a WHEN OTHERS EXCEPTION that puts a DBMS_OUTPUT.PUT_LINE message on the screen that says that an error occurred.

The projects in this section are meant to have you use all the skills you have acquired throughout this chapter. The answers to these projects can be found in Appendix D and on this book's companion Web site.

CHAPTER 3

SQL in PL/SQL

CHAPTER OBJECTIVES

In this chapter, you will learn about

- ▶ Making use of DML in PL/SQL
- ▶ Making use of SAVEPOINT

This chapter is a collection of some fundamental elements of using SQL statements in PL/SQL blocks. In the preceding chapter, you initialized variables with the `:=` syntax. This chapter introduces the method of using a SQL select statement to update the value of a variable. These variables can then be used in data manipulation (DML) statements (Insert, Delete, or Update). Additionally, this chapter demonstrates how you can use a sequence in your DML statements within a PL/SQL block, much as you would in a stand-alone SQL statement.

A transaction in Oracle is a series of SQL statements that the programmer has grouped into a logical unit. A programmer chooses to do this to maintain data integrity. Each application (SQL*Plus, Oracle SQL Developer, Procedure Builder, and so forth) maintains a single database session for each instance of a user login. The changes to the database that have been executed by a single application session are not actually "saved" to the database until a COMMIT occurs. Work within a transaction up to and just before the commit can be rolled back; after a commit has been issued, work within that transaction cannot be rolled back. Note that those SQL statements should be either committed or rejected as a group.

To exert transaction control, a SAVEPOINT can be used to break down large PL/SQL statements into individual units that are easier to manage. This chapter covers the basic elements of transaction control so that you will know how to manage your PL/SQL code by using COMMIT, ROLLBACK, and principally SAVEPOINT.

LAB 3.1
Making Use of DML in PL/SQL

LAB OBJECTIVES

After completing this lab, you will be able to

▶ Use the SELECT INTO syntax for variable initialization

▶ Use DML in a PL/SQL block

▶ Make use of a sequence in a PL/SQL block

VARIABLE INITIALIZATION WITH SELECT INTO

PL/SQL has two main methods of giving value to variables in a PL/SQL block. The first one, which you learned about in Chapter 1, "PL/SQL Concepts," is initialization with the := syntax. In this lab you will learn how to initialize a variable with a select statement by using the SELECT INTO syntax.

A variable that has been declared in the declaration section of the PL/SQL block can later be given a value with a select statement. The syntax is as follows:

```
SELECT item_name
   INTO variable_name
   FROM table_name;
```

It is important to note that any single row function can be performed on the item to give the variable a calculated value.

FOR EXAMPLE

```
--  ch03_1a.sql
SET SERVEROUTPUT ON
DECLARE
   v_average_cost VARCHAR2(10);
BEGIN
   SELECT TO_CHAR(AVG(cost), '$9,999.99')
     INTO v_average_cost
     FROM course;
   DBMS_OUTPUT.PUT_LINE('The average cost of a '||
      'course in the CTA program is '||
      v_average_cost);
END;
```

In this example, a variable is given the value of the average cost of a course in the course table. First, the variable must be declared in the declaration section of the PL/SQL block. In this example, the variable is given the datatype of VARCHAR2(10) because of the functions used on the data. The same select statement that would produce this outcome in SQL*Plus is as follows:

```
SELECT TO_CHAR(AVG(cost), '$9,999.99')
  FROM course;
```

The TO_CHAR function is used to format the cost; in doing this, the number datatype is converted to a character datatype. As soon as the variable has a value, it can be displayed to the screen in SQL*Plus using the PUT_LINE procedure of the DBMS_OUTPUT package.

▼ LAB 3.1 EXERCISES

This section provides exercises and suggested answers, with discussion related to how those answers resulted. The most important thing to realize is whether your answer works. You should figure out the implications of the answers and what the effects are of any different answers you may come up with.

3.1.1 Use the Select INTO Syntax for Variable Initialization

A) Execute the script ch03_1a.sql. What is displayed on the SQL*Plus screen? Explain the results.

ANSWER: You see the following result:

```
The average cost of a course in the CTA program is $1,198.33
PL/SQL procedure successfully completed.
```

In the declaration section of the PL/SQL block, the variable $v\_average\_cost$ is declared as a VARCHAR2. In the executable section of the block, this variable is given the value of the average cost from the course table by means of the SELECT INTO syntax. The SQL function TO_CHAR is issued to format the number. The DBMS_OUTPUT is then used to show the result to the screen.

B) Take the same PL/SQL block, and place the line with the DBMS_OUTPUT before the SELECT INTO statement. What is displayed on the SQL*Plus screen? Explain what the value of the variable is at each point in the PL/SQL block.

ANSWER: You see the following result:

```
The average cost of a course in the CTA program is
PL/SQL procedure successfully completed.
```

The variable $v\_average\_cost$ is set to NULL when it is first declared. Because the DBMS_OUTPUT is placed before the variable is given a value, the output for the variable is NULL. After the SELECT INTO, the variable is given the same value as in the original block described in question A, but it is not displayed because there is no other DBMS_OUTPUT line in the PL/SQL block.

Data Definition Language (DDL) is not valid in a simple PL/SQL block. (More-advanced techniques such as procedures in the DBMS_SQL package enable you to make use of DDL.) However, DML is easily achieved either by use of variables or by simply putting a DML statement into a PL/SQL block. Here is an example of a PL/SQL block that UPDATEs an existing entry in the zip code table:

FOR EXAMPLE

```
--  ch03_2a.sql
DECLARE
   v_city zipcode.city%TYPE;
BEGIN
   SELECT 'COLUMBUS'
     INTO v_city
     FROM dual;
   UPDATE zipcode
     SET city = v_city
   WHERE ZIP = 43224;
END;
```

It is also possible to insert data into a database table in a PL/SQL block, as shown in the following example:

FOR EXAMPLE

```
--  ch03_3a.sql
DECLARE
   v_zip zipcode.zip%TYPE;
   v_user zipcode.created_by%TYPE;
   v_date zipcode.created_date%TYPE;
BEGIN
   SELECT 43438, USER, SYSDATE
     INTO v_zip, v_user, v_date
     FROM dual;
   INSERT INTO zipcode
      (ZIP, CREATED_BY ,CREATED_DATE, MODIFIED_BY,
       MODIFIED_DATE
      )
       VALUES(v_zip, v_user, v_date, v_user, v_date);
END;
```

BY THE WAY

SELECT statements in PL/SQL that return no rows or too many rows cause an error that can be trapped by using an exception. You will learn more about handling exceptions in Chapters 8, 9, and 10.

3.1.2 **Use DML in a PL/SQL Block**

Write a PL/SQL block that inserts a new student in the STUDENT table. Use your own information for the data.

```
   --  ch03_4a.sql
   DECLARE
      v_max_id number;
   BEGIN
```

```
      SELECT MAX(student_id)
        INTO v_max_id
        FROM student;
      INSERT into student
         (student_id, last_name, zip,
          created_by, created_date,
          modified_by, modified_date,
          registration_date
         )
        VALUES (v_max_id + 1, 'Rosenzweig',
               11238, 'BROSENZ ', '01-JAN-99',
               'BROSENZ', '01-JAN-99', '01-JAN-99'
               );
   END;
```

To generate a unique ID, the maximum `student_id` is selected into a variable and then is incremented by 1. It is important to remember in this example that there is a foreign key on the zip item in the student table. This means that the zip code you choose to enter must be in the ZIPCODE table.

USING AN ORACLE SEQUENCE

An Oracle sequence is an Oracle database object that can be used to generate unique numbers. You can use sequences to automatically generate primary key values.

ACCESSING AND INCREMENTING SEQUENCE VALUES

After a sequence has been created, you can access its values in SQL statements with these pseudocolumns:

▶ CURRVAL returns the current value of the sequence.

▶ NEXTVAL increments the sequence and returns the new value.

The following statement creates the sequence ESEQ:

FOR EXAMPLE

```
CREATE SEQUENCE eseq
   INCREMENT BY 10
```

The first reference to ESEQ.NEXTVAL returns 1. The second returns 11. Each subsequent reference returns a value 10 greater than the preceding one.

(Even though you are guaranteed unique numbers, you are not guaranteed contiguous numbers. In some systems this may be a problem, such as when you generate invoice numbers.)

DRAWING NUMBERS FROM A SEQUENCE

Beginning with Oracle v7.3, you can insert a sequence value directly into a table without first selecting it. (Previously you had to use the SELECT INTO syntax and put the new sequence number into a variable before inserting the variable.)

The following example uses a table called test01. First the table test01 is created, and then the sequence `test_seq`, and then the sequence is used to populate the table.

FOR EXAMPLE

```
--  ch03_3a.sql
CREATE TABLE test01 (col1 number);
CREATE SEQUENCE test_seq
   INCREMENT BY 5;
BEGIN
   INSERT INTO test01
     VALUES (test_seq.NEXTVAL);
   END;
   /
Select * FROM test01;
```

In the last exercise for this lab, you will make use of all the material covered so far in this chapter.

3.1.3 Make Use of a Sequence in a PL/SQL Block

Write a PL/SQL block that inserts a new student in the STUDENT table. Use your own information for the data. Create two variables that are used in the SELECT statement. Get the USER and SYSDATE for the variables. Finally, use the existing `student_id_seq` sequence to generate a unique ID for the new student.

ANSWER: The following is one example of how this could be handled:

```
--  ch03_5a.sql
DECLARE
   v_user student.created_by%TYPE;
   v_date student.created_date%TYPE;
BEGIN
   SELECT USER, sysdate
     INTO  v_user, v_date
     FROM dual;
   INSERT INTO student
      (student_id, last_name, zip,
       created_by, created_date, modified_by,
       modified_date, registration_date
      )
      VALUES (student_id_seq.nextval, 'Smith',
             11238, v_user, v_date, v_user, v_date,
              v_date
             );
END;
```

In the declaration section of the PL/SQL block, two variables are declared. They are both set to be datatypes within the student table using the `%TYPE` method of declaration. This ensures that the datatypes match the columns of the tables into which they will be inserted. The two variables `v_user` and `v_date` are given values from the system by means of SELECT INTO. The value of `student_id` is generated by using the next value of the `student_id_seq` sequence.

LAB 3.2
Making Use of SAVEPOINT

LAB OBJECTIVES

After this lab, you will be able to

▶ Make use of COMMIT, ROLLBACK, and SAVEPOINT in a PL/SQL block

Transactions are a means to break programming code into manageable units. Grouping transactions into smaller elements is a standard practice that ensures that an application saves only correct data. Initially, any application must connect to the database to access the data. When a user issues DML statements in an application, the changes are not visible to other users until a COMMIT or ROLLBACK has been issued. Oracle guarantees a read-consistent view of the data. Until that point, all data that has been inserted or updated is held in memory and is available only to the current user. The rows that have been changed are locked by the current user and are not available for other users to update until the locks have been released. A COMMIT or ROLLBACK statement releases these locks. Transactions can be controlled more readily by marking points of the transaction with the SAVEPOINT command.

▶ COMMIT makes events within a transaction permanent.
▶ ROLLBACK erases events within a transaction.

Additionally, you can use a SAVEPOINT to control transactions. Transactions are defined in the PL/SQL block from one SAVEPOINT to another. The use of the SAVEPOINT command allows you to break your SQL statements into units so that in a given PL/SQL block, some units can be *committed* (saved to the database) and some can be *rolled back* (undone), and so forth.

BY THE WAY

Note that there is a distinction between a transaction and a PL/SQL block. The start and end of a PL/SQL block do not necessarily mean the start and end of a transaction.

To demonstrate the need for transaction control, we will examine a two-step data-manipulation process. For example, suppose that the fees for all courses in the Student database that had a prerequisite course needed to be increased by 10 percent. At the same time, all courses that did not have a prerequisite needed to be decreased by 10 percent. This is a two-step process. If one step was successful but the second step was not, the data concerning course cost would be inconsistent in the database. Because this adjustment is based on a change in percentage, there would be no way to track what part of this course adjustment was successful and what was not.

In the next example, you see one PL/SQL block that performs two updates on the cost item in the course table. In the first step (this code is commented to emphasize each update), the cost is updated with a cost that is 10 percent less whenever the course does not have a prerequisite. In the second step, the cost is increased by 10 percent when the course has a prerequisite.

FOR EXAMPLE

```
--  ch03_6a.sql
BEGIN
-- STEP 1
   UPDATE course
      SET cost = cost  - (cost * 0.10)
    WHERE prerequisite IS NULL;
-- STEP 2
   UPDATE course
      SET cost = cost  + (cost * 0.10)
    WHERE prerequisite IS NOT NULL;
END;
```

Let's assume that the first update statement succeeds, but the second update statement fails because the network went down. The data in the course table is now inconsistent, because courses with no prerequisite have had their cost reduced, but courses with prerequisites have not been adjusted. To prevent this sort of situation, statements must be combined into a transaction. So, either both statements will succeed, or both statements will fail.

A transaction usually combines SQL statements that represent a logical unit of work. The transaction begins with the first SQL statement issued after the previous transaction, or the first SQL statement issued after you connect to the database. The transaction ends with the COMMIT or ROLLBACK statement.

COMMIT

When a COMMIT statement is issued to the database, the transaction has ended, and the following results are true:

- ▶ All work done by the transaction becomes permanent.
- ▶ Other users can see changes in data made by the transaction.
- ▶ Any locks acquired by the transaction are released.

A COMMIT statement has the following syntax:

```
COMMIT [WORK];
```

The word WORK is optional and is used to improve readability. Until a transaction is committed, only the user executing that transaction can see changes in the data made by his or her session.

Suppose User A issues the following command on a STUDENT table that exists in another schema but that has a public synonym of student:

FOR EXAMPLE

```
--  ch03_6a.sql
INSERT INTO student
   (student_id, last_name, zip, registration_date,
    created_by, created_date, modified_by,
    modified_date
   )
   VALUES (student_id_seq.nextval, 'Tashi', 10015,
           '01-JAN-99', 'STUDENTA', '01-JAN-99',
           'STUDENTA', '01-JAN-99'
          );
```

Then User B enters the following command to query a table known by its public synonym STUDENT, while logged on to his session:

```
SELECT *
    FROM student
    WHERE last_name = 'Tashi';
```

Then User A issues the following command:

```
COMMIT;
```

If User B enters the same query again, he doesn't see the same results.

In this next example, there are two sessions: User A and User B. User A inserts a record into the STUDENT table. User B queries the STUDENT table but does not get the record that was inserted by User A. User B cannot see the information because User A has not committed the work. When User A commits the transaction, User B, upon resubmitting the query, sees the records inserted by User A.

ROLLBACK

When a ROLLBACK statement is issued to the database, the transaction has ended, and the following results are true:

- ▶ All work done by the transaction is undone, as if it hadn't been issued.
- ▶ Any locks acquired by the transaction are released.

A ROLLBACK statement has the following syntax:

```
ROLLBACK [WORK];
```

The WORK keyword is optional and is available for increased readability.

SAVEPOINT

The ROLLBACK statement undoes all the work done by the user in a specific transaction. With the SAVEPOINT command, however, only part of the transaction can be undone. The SAVEPOINT command has the following syntax:

```
SAVEPOINT name;
```

The word name is the SAVEPOINT's name. As soon as a SAVEPOINT is defined, the program can roll back to the SAVEPOINT. A ROLLBACK statement, then, has the following syntax:

```
ROLLBACK [WORK] to SAVEPOINT name;
```

When a ROLLBACK to SAVEPOINT statement is issued to the database, the following results are true:

▶ Any work done since the SAVEPOINT is undone. The SAVEPOINT remains active, however, until a full COMMIT or ROLLBACK is issued. It can be rolled back to again if desired.

▶ Any locks and resources acquired by the SQL statements since the SAVEPOINT are released.

▶ The transaction is not finished, because SQL statements are still pending.

▼ LAB 3.2 EXERCISES

This section provides exercises and suggested answers, with discussion related to how those answers resulted. The most important thing to realize is whether your answer works. You should figure out the implications of the answers and what the effects are of any different answers you may come up with.

3.2.1 Make Use of COMMIT, ROLLBACK, and SAVEPOINT in a PL/SQL Block

Log into the STUDENT schema and enter the following text exactly as it appears here. (Optionally, you can write the PL/SQL block in a text file and then run the script from the SQL*Plus prompt.)

```
-- ch03_7a.sql
BEGIN
   INSERT INTO student
      ( student_id, Last_name, zip, registration_date,
        created_by, created_date, modified_by,
        modified_date
      )
      VALUES ( student_id_seq.nextval, 'Tashi', 10015,
               '01-JAN-99', 'STUDENTA', '01-JAN-99',
               'STUDENTA','01-JAN-99'
             );
   SAVEPOINT A;
   INSERT INTO student
      ( student_id, Last_name, zip, registration_date,
        created_by, created_date, modified_by,
        modified_date
      )
      VALUES (student_id_seq.nextval, 'Sonam', 10015,
              '01-JAN-99', 'STUDENTB','01-JAN-99',
              'STUDENTB', '01-JAN-99'
             );
   SAVEPOINT B;
   INSERT INTO student
      ( student_id, Last_name, zip, registration_date,
        created_by, created_date, modified_by,
        modified_date
      )
      VALUES (student_id_seq.nextval, 'Norbu', 10015,
```

```
                    '01-JAN-99', 'STUDENTB', '01-JAN-99',
                    'STUDENTB', '01-JAN-99'
                  );
     SAVEPOINT C;
     ROLLBACK TO B;
  END;
```

A) If you tried to issue the following command, what would you expect to see, and why?

```
SELECT *
  FROM student
 WHERE last_name = 'Norbu';
```

ANSWER: You would not be able to see any data, because the ROLLBACK to (SAVEPOINT) B has undone the last insert statement where the student 'Norbu' was inserted.

B) Try issuing this command. What happens, and why?

ANSWER: When you issue this command, you get the message `no rows selected`.

Three students were inserted in this PL/SQL block: first, Tashi in SAVEPOINT A, and then Sonam in SAVEPOINT B, and finally Norbu in SAVEPOINT C. Then, when the command ROLLBACK to B was issued, the insertion of Norbu was undone.

C) Now issue the following command:

```
ROLLBACK to SAVEPOINT A;
```

What happens?

ANSWER: The insert in SAVEPOINT B is undone. This deletes the insert of Sonam, who was inserted in SAVEPOINT B.

D) If you were to issue the following, what would you expect to see?

```
SELECT last_name
  FROM student
 WHERE last_name = 'Tashi';
```

ANSWER: You would see the data for Tashi.

E) Issue the command, and explain your findings.

ANSWER: You see one entry for Tashi, as follows:

```
LAST_NAME
-----------------------
Tashi
```

Tashi was the only student successfully entered into the database. The ROLLBACK to SAVEPOINT A undid the insert statement for Norbu and Sonam.

BY THE WAY

SAVEPOINT is often used before a complicated section of the transaction. If this part of the transaction fails, it can be rolled back, allowing the earlier part to continue.

DID YOU KNOW?

It is important to note the distinction between transactions and PL/SQL blocks. When a block starts, this does not mean that the transaction starts. Likewise, the start of the transaction need not coincide with the start of a block.

A Single PL/SQL block can contain multiple transactions, as shown in this example:

FOR EXAMPLE

```
DECLARE
    v_Counter NUMBER;
BEGIN
    v_counter := 0;
    FOR i IN 1..100
    LOOP
        v_counter := v_counter + 1;
        IF v_counter = 10
        THEN
            COMMIT;
            v_counter := 0;
        END IF;
    END LOOP;
END;
```

In this example, as soon as the value of v_counter becomes equal to 10, the work is committed. So, a total of 10 transactions are contained in this one PL/SQL block.

▼ TRY IT YOURSELF

In this chapter, you've learned how to use numerous SQL techniques in a PL/SQL block. First, you learned how to use SELECT INTO to generate values for a variable. Then you learned the various DML methods, including the use of a sequence. Finally, you learned how to manage transactions by using SAVEPOINTs. Complete the following projects by writing the code for each step, running it, and going on to the next step.

1) Create a table called CHAP4 with two columns; one is ID (a number) and the other is NAME, which is a VARCHAR2(20).

2) Create a sequence called CHAP4_SEQ that increments by units of 5.

3) Write a PL/SQL block that does the following, in this order:

   A) Declares two variables: one for v_name and one for v_id. The v_name variable can be used throughout the block to hold the name that will be inserted; realize that the value will change in the course of the block.

   B) The block inserts into the table the name of the student who is enrolled in the most classes and uses a sequence for the ID. Afterward there is SAVEPOINT A.

   C) The student with the fewest classes is inserted. Afterward there is SAVEPOINT B.

   D) The instructor who is teaching the most courses is inserted in the same way. Afterward there is SAVEPOINT C.

   E) Using a SELECT INTO statement, hold the value of the instructor in the variable v_id.

   F) Undo the instructor insertion by using rollback.

   G) Insert the instructor teaching the fewest courses, but do not use the sequence to generate the ID. Instead, use the value from the first instructor, whom you have since undone.

   H) Insert the instructor teaching the most courses, and use the sequence to populate his or her ID.

   Add DBMS_OUTPUT throughout the block to display the values of the variables as they change. (This is good practice for debugging.)

The answers to these projects can be found in Appendix D and on this book's companion Web site.

CHAPTER 4

Conditional Control: IF Statements

CHAPTER OBJECTIVES

In this chapter, you will learn about

- ▶ IF statements
- ▶ ELSIF statements
- ▶ Nested IF statements

In almost every program you write, you need to make decisions. For example, if it is the end of the fiscal year, bonuses must be distributed to the employees based on their salaries. To compute employee bonuses, a program needs a conditional control. In other words, it needs to employ a selection structure.

Conditional control allows you to control the program's flow of the execution based on a condition. In programming terms, this means that the statements in the program are not executed sequentially. Rather, one group of statements or another is executed, depending on how the condition is evaluated.

PL/SQL has three types of conditional control: IF, ELSIF, and CASE statements. This chapter explores the first two types and shows you how they can be nested inside one another. CASE statements are discussed in the next chapter.

L A B 4 . 1
IF Statements

LAB OBJECTIVES

After completing this lab, you will be able to

▶ Use the IF-THEN statement

▶ Use the IF-THEN-ELSE statement

An IF statement has two forms: IF-THEN and IF-THEN-ELSE. An IF-THEN statement allows you to specify only one group of actions to take. In other words, this group of actions is taken only when a condition evaluates to TRUE. An IF-THEN-ELSE statement allows you to specify two groups of actions. The second group of actions is taken when a condition evaluates to FALSE or NULL.

IF-THEN STATEMENTS

An IF-THEN statement is the most basic kind of a conditional control; it has the following structure:

```
IF CONDITION THEN
   STATEMENT 1;
   ...
   STATEMENT N;
END IF;
```

The reserved word IF marks the beginning of the IF statement. Statements 1 through N are a sequence of executable statements that consist of one or more standard programming structures. The word *CONDITION* between the keywords IF and THEN determines whether these statements are executed. END IF is a reserved phrase that indicates the end of the IF-THEN construct.

Figure 4.1 shows this flow of logic.

When an IF-THEN statement is executed, a condition is evaluated to either TRUE or FALSE. If the condition evaluates to TRUE, control is passed to the first executable statement of the IF-THEN construct. If the condition evaluates to FALSE, control is passed to the first executable statement after the END IF statement.

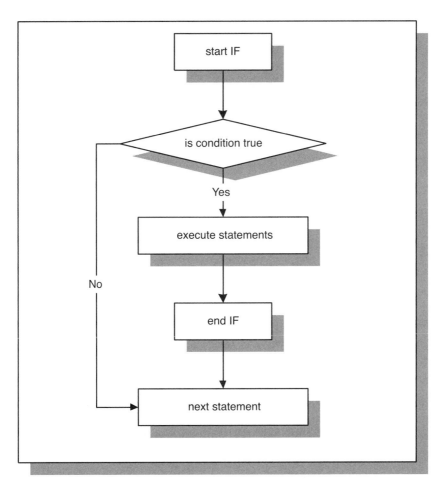

FIGURE 4.1
IF-THEN statement

Consider the following example. Two numeric values are stored in the variables v_num1 and v_num2. You need to arrange their values so that the smaller value is always stored in v_num1 and the larger value is always stored in v_num2.

FOR EXAMPLE

```
DECLARE
    v_num1 NUMBER := 5;
    v_num2 NUMBER := 3;
    v_temp NUMBER;
BEGIN
    -- if v_num1 is greater than v_num2 rearrange their values
    IF v_num1 > v_num2 THEN
        v_temp := v_num1;
```

```
      v_num1 := v_num2;
      v_num2 := v_temp;
   END IF;

   -- display the values of v_num1 and v_num2
   DBMS_OUTPUT.PUT_LINE ('v_num1 = '||v_num1);
   DBMS_OUTPUT.PUT_LINE ('v_num2 = '||v_num2);
END;
```

In this example, condition v_num1 > v_num2 evaluates to TRUE because 5 is greater than 3. Next, the values are rearranged so that 3 is assigned to v_num1 and 5 is assigned to v_num2. This is done with the help of the third variable, v_temp, which is used for temporary storage.

This example produces the following output:

```
   v_num1 = 3
   v_num2 = 5

   PL/SQL procedure successfully completed.
```

IF-THEN-ELSE STATEMENT

An IF-THEN statement specifies the sequence of statements to execute only if the condition evaluates to TRUE. When this condition evaluates to FALSE, there is no special action to take, except to proceed with execution of the program.

An IF-THEN-ELSE statement enables you to specify two groups of statements. One group of statements is executed when the condition evaluates to TRUE. Another group of statements is executed when the condition evaluates to FALSE. This is indicated as follows:

```
   IF CONDITION THEN
      STATEMENT 1;
   ELSE
      STATEMENT 2;
   END IF;
   STATEMENT 3;
```

When *CONDITION* evaluates to TRUE, control is passed to *STATEMENT 1*; when *CONDITION* evaluates to FALSE, control is passed to *STATEMENT 2*. After the IF-THEN-ELSE construct has completed, *STATEMENT 3* is executed. Figure 4.2 illustrates this flow of logic.

DID YOU KNOW?

You should use the IF-THEN-ELSE construct when trying to choose between two mutually exclusive actions. Consider the following example:

```
   DECLARE
      v_num NUMBER := &sv_user_num;
   BEGIN
      -- test if the number provided by the user is even
      IF MOD(v_num,2) = 0  THEN
         DBMS_OUTPUT.PUT_LINE (v_num||
```

```
                ' is even number');
      ELSE
         DBMS_OUTPUT.PUT_LINE (v_num||' is odd number');
      END IF;
      DBMS_OUTPUT.PUT_LINE ('Done');
   END;
```

For any given number, only one of the DBMS_ OUTPUT.PUT_LINE statements is executed. Hence, the IF-THEN-ELSE construct enables you to specify two and only two mutually exclusive actions.

When run, this example produces the following output:

```
   Enter value for v_user_num: 24
   old    2:    v_num  NUMBER := &v_user_num;
   new    2:    v_num  NUMBER := 24;
   24 is even number
   Done


   PL/SQL procedure successfully completed.
```

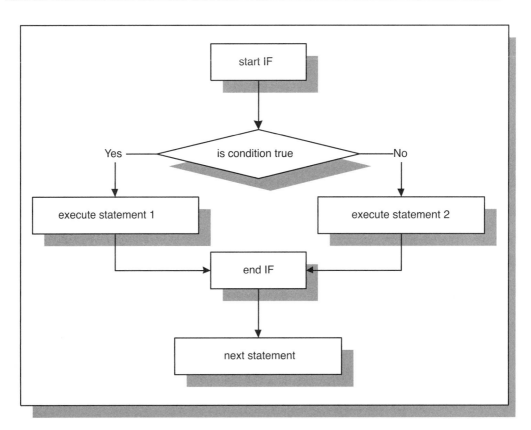

FIGURE 4.2
IF-THEN-ELSE statement

NULL CONDITION

In some cases, a condition used in an IF statement can be evaluated to NULL instead of TRUE or FALSE. For the IF-THEN construct, the statements are not executed if an associated condition evaluates to NULL. Next, control is passed to the first executable statement after END IF. For the IF-THEN-ELSE construct, the statements specified after the keyword ELSE are executed if an associated condition evaluates to NULL.

FOR EXAMPLE

```
DECLARE
   v_num1 NUMBER := 0;
   v_num2 NUMBER;
BEGIN
   IF v_num1 = v_num2 THEN
      DBMS_OUTPUT.PUT_LINE ('v_num1 = v_num2');
   ELSE
      DBMS_OUTPUT.PUT_LINE ('v_num1 != v_num2');
   END IF;
END;
```

This example produces the following output:

```
v_num1 != v_num2

PL/SQL procedure successfully completed.
```

The condition

```
v_num1 = v_num2
```

is evaluated to NULL because a value is not assigned to the variable v_num2. Therefore, variable v_num2 is NULL. Notice that the IF-THEN-ELSE construct is behaving as if the condition evaluated to FALSE, and the second DBMS_ OUTPUT.PUT_LINE statement is executed.

▼ LAB 4.1 EXERCISES

This section provides exercises and suggested answers, with discussion related to how those answers resulted. The most important thing to realize is whether your answer works. You should figure out the implications of the answers and what the effects are of any different answers you may come up with.

4.1.1 Use the IF-THEN Statement

In this exercise, you use the IF-THEN statement to test whether the date provided by the user falls on the weekend (in other words, if the day is Saturday or Sunday).

Create the following PL/SQL script:

```
-- ch04_1a.sql, version 1.0
SET SERVEROUTPUT ON
DECLARE
   v_date DATE := TO_DATE('&sv_user_date', 'DD-MON-YYYY');
```

```
    v_day  VARCHAR2(15);
BEGIN
    v_day := RTRIM(TO_CHAR(v_date, 'DAY'));

    IF v_day IN ('SATURDAY', 'SUNDAY') THEN
       DBMS_OUTPUT.PUT_LINE (v_date||' falls on weekend');
    END IF;

    --- control resumes here
    DBMS_OUTPUT.PUT_LINE ('Done...');
END;
```

To test this script fully, execute it twice. For the first run, enter 09-JAN-2008, and for the second run, enter 13-JAN-2008. Execute the script, and then answer the following questions:

A) What output is printed on the screen (for both dates)?

ANSWER: The first output produced for the date is 09-JAN-2008. The second output produced for the date is 13-JAN-2008.

```
Enter value for sv_user_date: 09-JAN-2008
old   2:     v_date DATE := TO_DATE('&sv_user_date', 'DD-MON-YYYY');
new   2:     v_date DATE := TO_DATE('09-JAN-2008', 'DD-MON-YYYY');
Done...

PL/SQL procedure successfully completed.
```

When the value of 09-JAN-2008 is entered for v_date, the day of the week is determined for the variable v_day with the help of the functions TO_CHAR and RTRIM. Next, the following condition is evaluated:

```
v_day IN ('SATURDAY', 'SUNDAY')
```

Because the value of v_day is 'WEDNESDAY', the condition evaluates to FALSE. Then, control is passed to the first executable statement after END IF. As a result, Done... is displayed on the screen:

```
Enter value for sv_user_date: 13-JAN-2008
old   2:     v_date DATE := TO_DATE('&sv_user_date', 'DD-MON-YYYY');
new   2:     v_date DATE := TO_DATE('13-JAN-2008', 'DD-MON-YYYY');
13-JAN-08 falls on weekend
Done...

PL/SQL procedure successfully completed.
```

As in the previous run, the value of v_day is derived from the value of v_date. Next, the condition of the IF-THEN statement is evaluated. Because it evaluates to TRUE, the statement after the keyword THEN is executed. Therefore, 13-JAN-2008 falls on weekend is displayed on the screen. Next, control is passed to the last DBMS_OUTPUT.PUT_LINE statement, and Done... is displayed on the screen.

B) Explain why the output produced for the two dates is different.

ANSWER: The first date, 09-JAN-2008, is a Wednesday. As a result, the condition v_day IN ('SATURDAY,' 'SUNDAY') does not evaluate to TRUE. Therefore, control is transferred to the statement after END IF, and Done... is displayed on the screen.

The second date, 13-JAN-2008, is a Sunday. Because Sunday falls on a weekend, the condition evaluates to TRUE, and the message `13-JAN-2008 falls on weekend` is displayed on the screen. Next, the last DBMS_OUTPUT.PUT_LINE statement is executed, and `Done . . .` is displayed on the screen.

Remove the RTRIM function from the assignment statement for v_day as follows:

```
v_day := TO_CHAR(v_date, 'DAY');
```

Run the script again, entering `13-JAN-2008` for v_date.

C) What output is printed on the screen? Why?

ANSWER: The script should look similar to the following. Changes are shown in bold.

```
-- ch04_1b.sql, version 2.0
SET SERVEROUTPUT ON
DECLARE
   v_date DATE := TO_DATE('&sv_user_date', 'DD-MON-YYYY');
   v_day  VARCHAR2(15);
BEGIN
   v_day := TO_CHAR(v_date, 'DAY');

   IF v_day IN ('SATURDAY', 'SUNDAY') THEN
      DBMS_OUTPUT.PUT_LINE (v_date||' falls on weekend');
   END IF;

   -- control resumes here
   DBMS_OUTPUT.PUT_LINE ('Done...');
END;
```

This script produces the following output:

```
Enter value for sv_user_date: 13-JAN-2008
old    2:    v_date DATE := TO_DATE('&sv_user_date', 'DD-MON-YYYY');
new    2:    v_date DATE := TO_DATE('13-JAN-2008', 'DD-MON-YYYY');
Done...

PL/SQL procedure successfully completed.
```

In the original example, the variable v_day is calculated with the help of the statement `RTRIM(TO_CHAR(v_date, 'DAY'))`. First, the function TO_CHAR returns the day of the week, padded with blanks. The size of the value retrieved by the function TO_CHAR is always 9 bytes. Next, the RTRIM function removes trailing spaces.

In the statement

```
v_day := TO_CHAR(v_date, 'DAY')
```

the TO_CHAR function is used without the RTRIM function. Therefore, trailing blanks are not removed after the day of the week has been derived. As a result, the condition of the IF-THEN statement evaluates to FALSE even though the given date falls on the weekend, and control is passed to the last DBMS_ OUTPUT.PUT_LINE statement.

D) Rewrite this script using the LIKE operator instead of the IN operator so that it produces the same results for the dates specified earlier.

ANSWER: The script should look similar to the following. Changes are shown in bold.

```
-- ch04_1c.sql, version 3.0
SET SERVEROUTPUT ON
DECLARE
   v_date DATE := TO_DATE('&sv_user_date', 'DD-MON-YYYY');
   v_day  VARCHAR2(15);
BEGIN
   v_day := RTRIM(TO_CHAR(v_date, 'DAY'));

   IF v_day LIKE 'S%' THEN
      DBMS_OUTPUT.PUT_LINE (v_date||' falls on weekend');
   END IF;

   -- control resumes here
   DBMS_OUTPUT.PUT_LINE ('Done...');
END;
```

Saturday and Sunday are the only days of the week that start with S. As a result, there is no need to spell out the names of the days or specify any additional letters for the LIKE operator.

E) Rewrite this script using the IF-THEN-ELSE construct. If the date specified does not fall on the weekend, display a message to the user saying so.

ANSWER: The script should look similar to the following. Changes are shown in bold.

```
-- ch04_1d.sql, version 4.0
SET SERVEROUTPUT ON
DECLARE
   v_date DATE := TO_DATE('&sv_user_date', 'DD-MON-YYYY');
   v_day  VARCHAR2(15);
BEGIN
   v_day := RTRIM(TO_CHAR(v_date, 'DAY'));

   IF v_day IN ('SATURDAY', 'SUNDAY') THEN
      DBMS_OUTPUT.PUT_LINE (v_date||' falls on weekend');
   ELSE
      DBMS_OUTPUT.PUT_LINE
         (v_date||' does not fall on the weekend');
   END IF;

   -- control resumes here
   DBMS_OUTPUT.PUT_LINE('Done...');
END;
```

To modify the script, the ELSE part was added to the IF statement. The rest of the script has not been changed.

4.1.2 **Use the IF-THEN-ELSE Statement**

In this exercise, you use the IF-THEN-ELSE statement to check how many students are enrolled in course number 25, section 1. If 15 or more students are enrolled, section 1 of course number 25 is full. Otherwise, section 1 of course number 25 is not full, and more students can register for it. In both cases, a message should be displayed to the user, indicating whether section 1 is full. Try to answer the questions before you run the script. After you have answered the questions, run the script and check your answers. Note that the SELECT INTO statement uses the ANSI 1999 SQL standard.

Create the following PL/SQL script:

```
-- ch04_2a.sql, version 1.0
SET SERVEROUTPUT ON
DECLARE
   v_total NUMBER;
BEGIN
   SELECT COUNT(*)
     INTO v_total
     FROM enrollment e
     JOIN section s USING (section_id)
    WHERE s.course_no = 25
      AND s.section_no = 1;

   -- check if section 1 of course 25 is full
   IF v_total >= 15 THEN
      DBMS_OUTPUT.PUT_LINE
         ('Section 1 of course 25 is full');
   ELSE
      DBMS_OUTPUT.PUT_LINE
         ('Section 1 of course 25 is not full');
   END IF;
   -- control resumes here
END;
```

Notice that the SELECT INTO statement uses an equijoin. The join condition is listed in the JOIN clause, indicating columns that are part of the primary key and foreign key constraints. In this example, column SECTION_ID of the ENROLLMENT table has a foreign key constraint defined on it. This constraint references column SECTION_ID of the SECTION table, which, in turn, has a primary key constraint defined on it.

BY THE WAY

You will find detailed explanations and examples of the statements using the new ANSI 1999 SQL standard in Appendix C and in the Oracle help. Throughout this book we try to provide examples illustrating both standards; however, our main focus is PL/SQL features rather than SQL.

Try to answer the following questions, and then execute the script:

A) What DBMS_OUTPUT.PUT_LINE statement is displayed if 15 students are enrolled in section 1 of course number 25?

ANSWER: If 15 or more students are enrolled in section 1 of course number 25, the first DBMS_OUTPUT.PUT_LINE statement is displayed on the screen.

The condition
```
v_total >= 15
```

evaluates to TRUE, and as a result, the statement
```
DBMS_OUTPUT.PUT_LINE ('Section 1 of course 25 is full');
```

is executed.

B) What DBMS_OUTPUT.PUT_LINE statement is displayed if three students are enrolled in section 1 of course number 25?

ANSWER: If three students are enrolled in section 1 of course number 25, the second DBMS_OUTPUT.PUT_LINE statement is displayed on the screen.

The condition
```
v_total >= 15
```

evaluates to FALSE, and the ELSE part of the IF-THEN-ELSE statement is executed. As a result, the statement
```
DBMS_OUTPUT.PUT_LINE ('Section 1 of course 25 is not full');
```

is executed.

C) What DBMS_OUTPUT.PUT_LINE statement is displayed if there is no section 1 for course number 25?

ANSWER: If there is no section 1 for course number 25, the ELSE part of the IF-THEN-ELSE statement is executed. So the second DBMS_OUTPUT.PUT_LINE statement is displayed on the screen.

The COUNT function used in the SELECT statement:
```
SELECT COUNT(*)
  INTO v_total
  FROM enrollment e
  JOIN section s USING (section_id)
 WHERE s.course_no = 25
   AND s.section_no = 1;
```

returns 0. The condition of the IF-THEN-ELSE statement evaluates to FALSE. Therefore, the ELSE part of the IF-THEN-ELSE statement is executed, and the second DBMS_OUTPUT.PUT_LINE statement is displayed on the screen.

D) How would you change this script so that the user provides both course and section numbers?

ANSWER: Two additional variables must be declared and initialized with the help of the substitution variables as follows. The script should look similar to the following. Changes are shown in bold.
```
-- ch04_2b.sql, version 2.0
SET SERVEROUTPUT ON
DECLARE
   v_total       NUMBER;
   v_course_no   CHAR(6) := '&sv_course_no';
   v_section_no NUMBER  := &sv_section_no;
BEGIN
   SELECT COUNT(*)
     INTO v_total
     FROM enrollment e
```

```
    JOIN section s USING (section_id)
  WHERE s.course_no  = v_course_no
    AND s.section_no = v_section_no;

  -- check if a specific section of a course is full
  IF v_total >= 15 THEN
     DBMS_OUTPUT.PUT_LINE
        ('Section 1 of course 25 is full');
  ELSE
     DBMS_OUTPUT.PUT_LINE
        ('Section 1 of course 25 is not full');
  END IF;
  -- control resumes here
END;
```

E) How would you change this script so that if fewer than 15 students are enrolled in section 1 of course number 25, a message appears indicating how many students can still enroll?

ANSWER: The script should look similar to the following. Changes are shown in bold.

```
-- ch04_2c.sql, version 3.0
SET SERVEROUTPUT ON
DECLARE
   v_total    NUMBER;
   v_students NUMBER;
BEGIN
   SELECT COUNT(*)
     INTO v_total
     FROM enrollment e
     JOIN section s USING (section_id)
    WHERE s.course_no = 25
      AND s.section_no = 1;

   -- check if section 1 of course 25 is full
   IF v_total >= 15 THEN
      DBMS_OUTPUT.PUT_LINE
         ('Section 1 of course 25 is full');
   ELSE
      v_students := 15 - v_total;
      DBMS_OUTPUT.PUT_LINE (v_students||
         ' students can still enroll into section 1'||
         ' of course 25');
   END IF;
   -- control resumes here
END;
```

Notice that if the IF-THEN-ELSE statement evaluates to FALSE, the statements associated with the ELSE part are executed. In this case, the value of the variable v_total is subtracted from 15. The result of this operation indicates how many more students can enroll in section 1 of course number 25.

LAB 4.2
ELSIF Statements

LAB OBJECTIVES

After completing this lab, you will be able to

▶ Use the ELSIF statement

An ELSIF statement has the following structure:

```
IF CONDITION 1 THEN
    STATEMENT 1;
ELSIF CONDITION 2 THEN
    STATEMENT 2;
ELSIF CONDITION 3 THEN
    STATEMENT 3;
...
ELSE
    STATEMENT N;
END IF;
```

The reserved word IF marks the beginning of an ELSIF construct. *CONDITION 1* through *CONDITION N* are a sequence of the conditions that evaluate to TRUE or FALSE. These conditions are mutually exclusive. In other words, if *CONDITION 1* evaluates to TRUE, *STATEMENT 1* is executed, and control is passed to the first executable statement after the reserved phrase END IF. The rest of the ELSIF construct is ignored. When *CONDITION 1* evaluates to FALSE, control is passed to the ELSIF part and *CONDITION 2* is evaluated, and so forth. If none of the specified conditions yields TRUE, control is passed to the ELSE part of the ELSIF construct. An ELSIF statement can contain any number of ELSIF clauses. Figure 4.3 shows this flow of logic.

Figure 4.3 shows that if condition 1 evaluates to TRUE, statement 1 is executed, and control is passed to the first statement after END IF. If condition 1 evaluates to FALSE, control is passed to condition 2. If condition 2 yields TRUE, statement 2 is executed. Otherwise, control is passed to the statement following END IF, and so forth. Consider the following example.

FOR EXAMPLE

```
DECLARE
    v_num NUMBER := &sv_num;
BEGIN
    IF v_num < 0 THEN
        DBMS_OUTPUT.PUT_LINE (v_num||' is a negative number');
```

```
   ELSIF v_num = 0 THEN
      DBMS_OUTPUT.PUT_LINE (v_num||' is equal to zero');
   ELSE
      DBMS_OUTPUT.PUT_LINE (v_num||' is a positive number');
   END IF;
END;
```

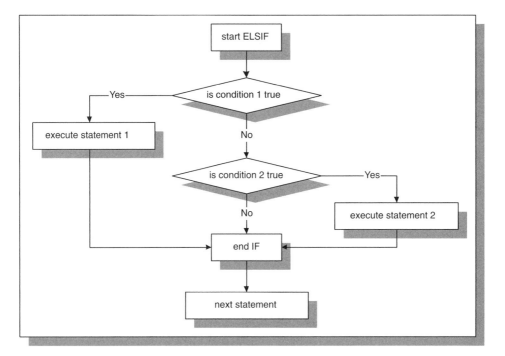

FIGURE 4.3
ELSIF statement

The value of v_num is provided at runtime and is evaluated with the help of the ELSIF state-ment. If the value of v_num is less than 0, the first DBMS_ OUTPUT.PUT_LINE statement executes, and the ELSIF construct terminates. If the value of v_num is greater than 0, both conditions

```
   v_num < 0
```

and

```
   v_num = 0
```

evaluate to FALSE, and the ELSE part of the ELSIF construct executes.

Assume that the value of v_num equals 5 at runtime. This example produces the following output:

```
Enter value for sv_num: 5
old    2:    v_num  NUMBER := &sv_num;
new    2:    v_num  NUMBER := 5;
5 is a positive number

PL/SQL procedure successfully completed.
```

DID YOU KNOW?

Consider the following information about an ELSIF statement:

- ▶ Always match an IF with an END IF.

- ▶ There must be a space between END and IF. If the space is omitted, the compiler produces the following error:
  ```
  ERROR at line 22:
  ORA-06550: line 22, column 4:
  PLS-00103: Encountered the symbol ";" when
  expecting one of the following: if
  ```

  As you can see, this error message is not very clear, and it can take you some time to correct it, especially if you have not encountered it before.

- ▶ There is no second E in ELSIF.

- ▶ Conditions of an ELSIF statement must be mutually exclusive. These conditions are evaluated in sequential order, from the first to the last. When a condition evaluates to TRUE, the remaining conditions of the ELSIF statement are not evaluated. Consider this example of an ELSIF construct:
  ```
  IF v_num >= 0 THEN
      DBMS_OUTPUT.PUT_LINE ('v_num is greater than 0');
  ELSIF v_num =< 10 THEN
      DBMS_OUTPUT.PUT_LINE ('v_num is less than 10');
  ELSE
      DBMS_OUTPUT.PUT_LINE
            ('v_num is less than ? or greater than ?');
  END IF;
  ```

Assume that the value of v_num is equal to 5. Both conditions of the ELSIF statement can evaluate to TRUE because 5 is greater than 0, and 5 is less than 10. However, when the first condition, $v\_num >= 0$, evaluates to TRUE, the rest of the ELSIF construct is ignored.

For any value of v_num that is greater than or equal to 0 and less than or equal to 10, these conditions are not mutually exclusive. Therefore, the DBMS_OUTPUT.PUT_LINE statement associated with the ELSIF clause does not execute for any such value of v_num. For the second condition, $v\_num <= 10$, to yield TRUE, the value of v_num must be less than 0.

How would you rewrite this ELSIF construct to capture any value of v_num between 0 and 10 and display it on the screen with a single condition?

When using an ELSIF construct, it is not necessary to specify what action should be taken if none of the conditions evaluates to TRUE. In other words, an ELSE clause is not required in the ELSIF construct. Consider the following example:

FOR EXAMPLE

```
DECLARE
   v_num NUMBER := &sv_num;
BEGIN
   IF v_num < 0 THEN
      DBMS_OUTPUT.PUT_LINE (v_num||' is a negative number');
   ELSIF v_num > 0 THEN
      DBMS_OUTPUT.PUT_LINE (v_num||' is a positive number');
   END IF;
   DBMS_OUTPUT.PUT_LINE ('Done...');
END;
```

As you can see, no action is specified when v_num is equal to 0. If the value of v_num is equal to 0, both conditions evaluate to FALSE, and the ELSIF statement does not execute. When a value of 0 is specified for v_num, this example produces the following output:

```
Enter value for sv_num: 0
old    2:    v_num  NUMBER := &sv_num;
new    2:    v_num  NUMBER := 0;
Done...

PL/SQL procedure successfully completed.
```

DID YOU KNOW?

You probably noticed that for all IF statement examples, the reserved words IF, ELSIF, ELSE, and END IF are entered on a separate line and are aligned with the word IF. In addition, all executable statements in the IF construct are indented. The format of the IF construct makes no difference to the compiler; however, the meaning of the formatted IF construct becomes obvious to us.

This IF-THEN-ELSE statement:

```
IF x = y THEN v_txt := 'YES'; ELSE v_txt :=
'NO'; END IF;
```

is equivalent to

```
IF x = y THEN
   v_txt := 'YES';
ELSE
   v_txt := 'NO';
END IF;
```

The formatted version of the IF construct is easier to read and understand.

▼ LAB 4.2 EXERCISES

This section provides exercises and suggested answers, with discussion related to how those answers resulted. The most important thing to realize is whether your answer works. You should figure out the implications of the answers and what the effects are of any different answers you may come up with.

4.2.1 **Use the ELSIF Statement**

In this exercise, you use an ELSIF statement to display a letter grade for a student registered for a specific section of course number 25.

Create the following PL/SQL script:

```
-- ch04_3a.sql, version 1.0
SET SERVEROUTPUT ON
DECLARE
    v_student_id    NUMBER := 102;
    v_section_id    NUMBER := 89;
    v_final_grade   NUMBER;
    v_letter_grade CHAR(1);
BEGIN
    SELECT final_grade
      INTO v_final_grade
      FROM enrollment
     WHERE student_id = v_student_id
       AND section_id = v_section_id;

    IF v_final_grade BETWEEN 90 AND 100 THEN
        v_letter_grade := 'A';
    ELSIF v_final_grade BETWEEN 80 AND 89 THEN
        v_letter_grade := 'B';
    ELSIF v_final_grade BETWEEN 70 AND 79 THEN
        v_letter_grade := 'C';
    ELSIF v_final_grade BETWEEN 60 AND 69 THEN
        v_letter_grade := 'D';
    ELSE
        v_letter_grade := 'F';
    END IF;

    -- control resumes here
    DBMS_OUTPUT.PUT_LINE ('Letter grade is: '||
        v_letter_grade);

EXCEPTION
    WHEN NO_DATA_FOUND THEN
        DBMS_OUTPUT.PUT_LINE ('There is no such student or section');
END;
```

Note that you may need to change the values for the variables `v_student_id` and `v_section_id` as you see fit to test some of your answers.

Try to answer the following questions, and then execute the script:

A) What letter grade is displayed on the screen:

   i) if the value of `v_final_grade` is equal to 85?

   ii) if the value of `v_final_grade` is NULL?

   iii) if the value of `v_final_grade` is greater than 100?

ANSWER:

i) If the value of `v_final_grade` is equal to 85, the value "B" of the letter grade is displayed on the screen.

The conditions of the ELSIF statement are evaluated in sequential order. The first condition:

```
v_final_grade BETWEEN 90 AND 100
```

evaluates to FALSE, and control is passed to the first ELSIF part of the ELSIF statement. Then, the second condition:

```
v_final_grade BETWEEN 80 AND 89
```

evaluates to TRUE, and the letter "B" is assigned to the variable `v_letter_grade`. Control is then passed to the first executable statement after END IF, and the message

```
Letter grade is: B
```

is displayed on the screen.

ii) If the value of `v_final_grade` is NULL, value "F" of the letter grade is displayed on the screen.

If the value of the `v_final_grade` is undefined or NULL, all conditions of the ELSIF statement evaluate to NULL (notice that they do not evaluate to FALSE). As a result, the ELSE part of the ELSIF statement is executed, and letter "F" is assigned to the `v_letter_grade`.

iii) If the value of `v_final_grade` is greater than 100, value "F" of the letter grade is displayed on the screen.

The conditions specified for the ELSIF statement cannot handle a value of `v_final_grade` greater than 100. Therefore, any student who should receive a letter grade of A+ will instead receive a letter grade of "F." After the ELSIF statement has terminated, `The letter grade is: F` is displayed on the screen.

B) How would you change this script so that the message `v_final_grade is null` is displayed on the screen if `v_final_grade` is NULL?

ANSWER: The script should look similar to the following. Changes are shown in bold.

```
-- ch04_3b.sql, version 2.0
SET SERVEROUTPUT ON
DECLARE
   v_student_id   NUMBER := 102;
   v_section_id   NUMBER := 89;
   v_final_grade  NUMBER;
   v_letter_grade CHAR(1);
BEGIN
   SELECT final_grade
     INTO v_final_grade
     FROM enrollment
    WHERE student_id = v_student_id
      AND section_id = v_section_id;

   IF v_final_grade IS NULL THEN
      DBMS_OUTPUT.PUT_LINE('v_final_grade is null');
   ELSIF v_final_grade BETWEEN 90 AND 100 THEN
      v_letter_grade := 'A';
```

```
ELSIF v_final_grade BETWEEN 80 AND 89 THEN
    v_letter_grade := 'B';
ELSIF v_final_grade BETWEEN 70 AND 79 THEN
    v_letter_grade := 'C';
ELSIF v_final_grade BETWEEN 60 AND 69 THEN
    v_letter_grade := 'D';
ELSE
    v_letter_grade := 'F';
END IF;

-- control resumes here
DBMS_OUTPUT.PUT_LINE ('Letter grade is: '||
    v_letter_grade);

EXCEPTION
    WHEN NO_DATA_FOUND THEN
        DBMS_OUTPUT.PUT_LINE ('There is no such student or section');
END;
```

One more condition has been added to the ELSIF statement. The condition

`v_final_grade BETWEEN 90 AND 100`

becomes the first ELSIF condition. Now, if the value of `v_final_grade` is NULL, the message `v_final_grade is null` is displayed on the screen. However, no value is assigned to the variable `v_letter_grade`. The message `Letter grade is:` is displayed on the screen as well.

C) How would you change this script so that the user provides the student ID and section ID?

ANSWER: The script should look similar to the following. Changes are shown in bold.

```
-- ch04_3c.sql, version 3.0
SET SERVEROUTPUT ON
DECLARE
    v_student_id    NUMBER := &sv_student_id;
    v_section_id    NUMBER := &sv_section_id;
    v_final_grade  NUMBER;
    v_letter_grade CHAR(1);
BEGIN
    SELECT final_grade
      INTO v_final_grade
      FROM enrollment
     WHERE student_id = v_student_id
       AND section_id = v_section_id;

    IF v_final_grade BETWEEN 90 AND 100 THEN
        v_letter_grade := 'A';
    ELSIF v_final_grade BETWEEN 80 AND 89 THEN
        v_letter_grade := 'B';
    ELSIF v_final_grade BETWEEN 70 AND 79 THEN
        v_letter_grade := 'C';
    ELSIF v_final_grade BETWEEN 60 AND 69 THEN
        v_letter_grade := 'D';
```

```
      ELSE
         v_letter_grade := 'F';
      END IF;

      -- control resumes here
      DBMS_OUTPUT.PUT_LINE ('Letter grade is: '||
         v_letter_grade);

   EXCEPTION
      WHEN NO_DATA_FOUND THEN
         DBMS_OUTPUT.PUT_LINE ('There is no such student or section');
   END;
```

D) How would you change the script to define a letter grade without specifying the upper limit of the final grade? In the statement `v_final_grade BETWEEN 90 and 100`, number 100 is the upper limit.

ANSWER: The script should look similar to the following. Changes are shown in bold.

```
-- ch04_3d.sql, version 4.0
SET SERVEROUTPUT ON
DECLARE
   v_student_id    NUMBER := 102;
   v_section_id    NUMBER := 89;
   v_final_grade   NUMBER;
   v_letter_grade CHAR(1);
BEGIN
   SELECT final_grade
     INTO v_final_grade
     FROM enrollment
    WHERE student_id = v_student_id
      AND section_id = v_section_id;

   IF v_final_grade >= 90 THEN
      v_letter_grade := 'A';
   ELSIF v_final_grade >= 80 THEN
      v_letter_grade := 'B';
   ELSIF v_final_grade >= 70 THEN
      v_letter_grade := 'C';
   ELSIF v_final_grade >= 60 THEN
      v_letter_grade := 'D';
   ELSE
      v_letter_grade := 'F';
   END IF;

   -- control resumes here
   DBMS_OUTPUT.PUT_LINE ('Letter grade is: '||
      v_letter_grade);

EXCEPTION
   WHEN NO_DATA_FOUND THEN
      DBMS_OUTPUT.PUT_LINE ('There is no such student or section');
END;
```

In this example, no upper limit is specified for the variable v_final_grade because the BETWEEN operator has been replaced with the $>=$ operator. Thus, this script can handle a value of v_final_grade that is greater than 100. Instead of assigning letter "F" to v_letter_grade (in version 1.0 of the script), the letter "A" is assigned to the variable v_letter_grade. As a result, this script produces more accurate results.

LAB 4.3
Nested IF Statements

LAB OBJECTIVES

After completing this lab, you will be able to

▶ Use nested IF statements

You have encountered different types of conditional controls: the IF-THEN statement, the IF-THEN-ELSE statement, and the ELSIF statement. These types of conditional controls can be nested inside one another. For example, an IF statement can be nested inside an ELSIF, and vice versa. Consider the following:

FOR EXAMPLE

```
DECLARE
    v_num1  NUMBER := &sv_num1;
    v_num2  NUMBER := &sv_num2;
    v_total NUMBER;
BEGIN
    IF v_num1 > v_num2 THEN
        DBMS_OUTPUT.PUT_LINE ('IF part of the outer IF');
        v_total := v_num1 - v_num2;
    ELSE
        DBMS_OUTPUT.PUT_LINE ('ELSE part of the outer IF');
        v_total := v_num1 + v_num2;

        IF v_total < 0 THEN
            DBMS_OUTPUT.PUT_LINE ('Inner IF');
            v_total := v_total * (-1);
        END IF;

    END IF;
    DBMS_OUTPUT.PUT_LINE ('v_total = '||v_total);
END;
```

The IF-THEN-ELSE statement is called an outer IF statement because it encompasses the IF-THEN statement (shown in bold). The IF-THEN statement is called an inner IF statement because it is enclosed by the body of the IF-THEN-ELSE statement.

Assume that the values for v_num1 and v_num2 are −4 and 3, respectively. First, the condition

```
v_num1 > v_num2
```

of the outer IF statement is evaluated. Because −4 is not greater than 3, the ELSE part of the outer IF statement is executed. As a result, the message

```
ELSE part of the outer IF
```

is displayed, and the value of v_total is calculated. Next, the condition

```
v_total < 0
```

of the inner IF statement is evaluated. Because that value of v_total is equal to −1, the condition yields TRUE, and the message

```
Inner IF
```

is displayed. Next, the value of v_total is calculated again. This logic is demonstrated by the output that the example produces:

```
Enter value for sv_num1: -4
old    2:    v_num1   NUMBER := &sv_num1;
new    2:    v_num1   NUMBER := -4;
Enter value for sv_num2: 3
old    3:    v_num2   NUMBER := &sv_num2;
new    3:    v_num2   NUMBER := 3;
ELSE part of the outer IF
Inner IF
v_total = 1

PL/SQL procedure successfully completed.
```

LOGICAL OPERATORS

So far in this chapter, you have seen examples of different IF statements. All of these examples used test operators, such as >, <, and =, to test a condition. Logical operators can be used to evaluate a condition as well. In addition, they allow a programmer to combine multiple conditions into a single condition if such a need exists.

FOR EXAMPLE

```
DECLARE
   v_letter CHAR(1) := '&sv_letter';
BEGIN
   IF (v_letter >= 'A' AND v_letter <= 'Z') OR
      (v_letter >= 'a' AND v_letter <= 'z')
   THEN
      DBMS_OUTPUT.PUT_LINE ('This is a letter');
   ELSE
      DBMS_OUTPUT.PUT_LINE ('This is not a letter');

      IF v_letter BETWEEN '0' and '9' THEN
```

```
          DBMS_OUTPUT.PUT_LINE ('This is a number');
      ELSE
          DBMS_OUTPUT.PUT_LINE ('This is not a number');
      END IF;

   END IF;
END;
```

In this example, the condition

```
      (v_letter >= 'A' AND v_letter <= 'Z') OR
      (v_letter >= 'a' AND v_letter <= 'z')
```

uses the logical operators AND and OR. Two conditions:

```
      (v_letter >= 'A' AND v_letter <= 'Z')
```

and

```
      (v_letter >= 'a' AND v_letter <= 'z')
```

are combined into one with the help of the OR operator. It is also important to understand the purpose of the parentheses. In this example, they are only used to improve readability, because the AND operator takes precedence over the OR operator.

When the symbol ? is entered at runtime, this example produces the following output:

```
      Enter value for sv_letter: ?
      old   2:    v_letter CHAR(1) := '&sv_letter';
      new   2:    v_letter CHAR(1) := '?';
      This is not a letter
      This is not a number

      PL/SQL procedure successfully completed.
```

▼ LAB 4.3 EXERCISES

This section provides exercises and suggested answers, with discussion related to how those answers resulted. The most important thing to realize is whether your answer works. You should figure out the implications of the answers and what the effects are of any different answers you may come up with.

4.3.1 **Use Nested IF Statements**

In this exercise, you use nested IF statements. This script converts the value of a temperature from one system to another. If the temperature is supplied in Fahrenheit, it is converted to Celsius, and vice versa.

Create the following PL/SQL script:

```
      -- ch04_4a.sql, version 1.0
      SET SERVEROUTPUT ON
      DECLARE
         v_temp_in   NUMBER := &sv_temp_in;
         v_scale_in  CHAR   := '&sv_scale_in';
```

```
    v_temp_out  NUMBER;
    v_scale_out CHAR;
BEGIN
    IF v_scale_in != 'C' AND v_scale_in != 'F' THEN
        DBMS_OUTPUT.PUT_LINE ('This is not a valid scale');
    ELSE
        IF v_scale_in = 'C' THEN
            v_temp_out  := ( (9 * v_temp_in) / 5 ) + 32;
            v_scale_out := 'F';
        ELSE
            v_temp_out  := ( (v_temp_in - 32) * 5 ) / 9;
            v_scale_out := 'C';
        END IF;
        DBMS_OUTPUT.PUT_LINE ('New scale is: '||v_scale_out);
        DBMS_OUTPUT.PUT_LINE ('New temperature is: '||v_temp_out);
    END IF;
END;
```

Execute the script, and then answer the following questions:

A) What output is printed on the screen if the value of 100 is entered for the temperature, and the letter "C" is entered for the scale?

ANSWER: The output should look like the following:

```
Enter value for sv_temp_in: 100
old    2:     v_temp_in    NUMBER := &sv_temp_in;
new    2:     v_temp_in    NUMBER := 100;
Enter value for sv_scale_in: C
old    3:     v_scale_in   CHAR := '&sv_scale_in';
new    3:     v_scale_in   CHAR := 'C';
New scale is: F
New temperature is: 212

PL/SQL procedure successfully completed.
```

After the values for v_temp_in and v_scale_in have been entered, the condition

```
v_scale_in != 'C' AND v_scale_in != 'F'
```

of the outer IF statement evaluates to FALSE, and control is passed to the ELSE part of the outer IF statement. Next, the condition

```
v_scale_in = 'C'
```

of the inner IF statement evaluates to TRUE, and the values of the variables v_temp_out and v_scale_out are calculated. Control is then passed back to the outer IF statement, and the new value for the temperature and the scale are displayed on the screen.

B) Try to run this script without providing a value for the temperature. What message is displayed on the screen? Why?

ANSWER: If the value for the temperature is not entered, the script does not compile.

The compiler tries to assign a value to v_temp_in with the help of the substitution variable. Because the value for v_temp_in has not been entered, the assignment statement fails, and the following error message is displayed:

```
Enter value for sv_temp_in:
old    2:    v_temp_in    NUMBER := &sv_temp_in;
new    2:    v_temp_in    NUMBER := ;
Enter value for sv_scale_in: C
old    3:    v_scale_in    CHAR := '&sv_scale_in';
new    3:    v_scale_in    CHAR := 'C';
   v_temp_in    NUMBER := ;
                          *
ERROR at line 2:
ORA-06550: line 2, column 27:
PLS-00103: Encountered the symbol ";" when expecting one of the
following:
( - + mod not null <an identifier>
<a double-quoted delimited-identifier> <a bind variable> avg
count current exists max min prior sql stddev sum variance
cast <a string literal with character set specification>
<a number> <a single-quoted SQL string>
The symbol "null" was substituted for ";" to continue.
```

You have probably noticed that even though the mistake seems small and insignificant, the error message is fairly long and confusing.

C) Try to run this script providing an invalid letter for the temperature scale, such as "V." What message is displayed on the screen, and why?

ANSWER: If an invalid letter is entered for the scale, the message `This is not a valid scale` is displayed on the screen.

The condition of the outer IF statement evaluates to TRUE. As a result, the inner IF statement is not executed, and the message `This is not a valid scale` is displayed on the screen.

Assume that letter "V" was typed by mistake. This example produces the following output:

```
Enter value for sv_temp_in: 45
old    2:    v_temp_in    NUMBER := &sv_temp_in;
new    2:    v_temp_in    NUMBER := 45;
Enter value for sv_scale_in: V
old    3:    v_scale_in    CHAR := '&sv_scale_in';
new    3:    v_scale_in    CHAR := 'V';
This is not a valid scale

PL/SQL procedure successfully completed.
```

D) Rewrite this script so that if an invalid letter is entered for the scale, `v_temp_out` is initialized to 0 and `v_scale_out` is initialized to C.

ANSWER: The script should look similar to the following. Changes are shown in bold. Notice that the two final DBMS_OUTPUT.PUT_LINE statements have been moved from the body of the outer IF statement.

```
-- ch04_4b.sql, version 2.0
DECLARE
   v_temp_in    NUMBER := &sv_temp_in;
   v_scale_in   CHAR   := '&sv_scale_in';
   v_temp_out   NUMBER;
   v_scale_out  CHAR;
```

```
BEGIN
    IF v_scale_in != 'C' AND v_scale_in != 'F' THEN
        DBMS_OUTPUT.PUT_LINE ('This is not a valid scale');
        v_temp_out  := 0;
        v_scale_out := 'C';
    ELSE
        IF v_scale_in = 'C' THEN
            v_temp_out  := ( (9 * v_temp_in) / 5 ) + 32;
            v_scale_out := 'F';
        ELSE
            v_temp_out  := ( (v_temp_in - 32) * 5 ) / 9;
            v_scale_out := 'C';
        END IF;
    END IF;
    DBMS_OUTPUT.PUT_LINE ('New scale is: '||v_scale_out);
    DBMS_OUTPUT.PUT_LINE ('New temperature is: '||v_temp_out);
END;
```

The preceding script produces the following output:

```
Enter value for sv_temp_in: 100
old   2:    v_temp_in    NUMBER := &sv_temp_in;
new   2:    v_temp_in    NUMBER := 100;
Enter value for sv_scale_in: V
old   3:    v_scale_in   CHAR := '&sv_scale_in';
new   3:    v_scale_in   CHAR := 'V';
This is not a valid scale.
New scale is: C
New temperature is: 0

PL/SQL procedure successfully completed.
```

▼ TRY IT YOURSELF

In this chapter you've learned about different types of IF statements. You've also learned that all these different IF statements can be nested inside one another. Here are some exercises that will help you test the depth of your understanding:

1) Rewrite ch04_1a.sql. Instead of getting information from the user for the variable v_date, define its value with the help of the function SYSDATE. After it has been determined that a certain day falls on the weekend, check to see if the time is before or after noon. Display the time of day together with the day.

2) Create a new script. For a given instructor, determine how many sections he or she is teaching. If the number is greater than or equal to 3, display a message saying that the instructor needs a vacation. Otherwise, display a message saying how many sections this instructor is teaching.

3) Execute the following two PL/SQL blocks, and explain why they produce different output for the same value of the variable v_num. Remember to issue the SET SERVEROUTPUT ON command before running this script.

```
-- Block 1
DECLARE
    v_num NUMBER := NULL;
BEGIN
    IF v_num > 0 THEN
        DBMS_OUTPUT.PUT_LINE ('v_num is greater than 0');
    ELSE
        DBMS_OUTPUT.PUT_LINE ('v_num is not greater than 0');
    END IF;
END;


-- Block 2
DECLARE
    v_num NUMBER := NULL;
BEGIN
    IF v_num > 0 THEN
        DBMS_OUTPUT.PUT_LINE ('v_num is greater than 0');
    END IF;
    IF NOT (v_num > 0) THEN
        DBMS_OUTPUT.PUT_LINE ('v_num is not greater than 0');
    END IF;
END;
```

The projects in this section are meant to have you use all the skills you have acquired throughout this chapter. The answers to these projects can be found in Appendix D and on this book's companion Web site. Visit the Web site periodically to share and discuss your answers.

CHAPTER 5

Conditional Control: CASE Statements

CHAPTER OBJECTIVES

In this chapter, you will learn about

- ▶ CASE statements
- ▶ CASE expressions
- ▶ NULLIF and COALESCE functions

In the preceding chapter, you explored the concept of conditional control via IF and ELSIF statements. In this chapter, you will continue by examining different types of CASE statements and expressions. You will also learn how to use NULLIF and COALESCE functions that are considered an extension of CASE.

LAB 5.1
CASE Statements

LAB OBJECTIVES

After completing this lab, you will be able to

▶ Use the CASE statement
▶ Use the searched CASE statement

A CASE statement has two forms: CASE and searched CASE. A CASE statement allows you to specify a selector that determines which group of actions to take. A searched CASE statement does not have a selector; it has search conditions that are evaluated in order to determine which group of actions to take.

CASE STATEMENTS

A CASE statement has the following structure:

```
CASE SELECTOR
   WHEN EXPRESSION 1 THEN STATEMENT 1;
   WHEN EXPRESSION 2 THEN STATEMENT 2;
   ...
   WHEN EXPRESSION N THEN STATEMENT N;
   ELSE STATEMENT N+1;
END CASE;
```

The reserved word CASE marks the beginning of the CASE statement. A selector is a value that determines which WHEN clause should be executed. Each WHEN clause contains an *EXPRESSION* and one or more executable statements associated with it. The ELSE clause is optional. It works much like the ELSE clause used in the IF-THEN-ELSE statement. END CASE is a reserved phrase that indicates the end of the CASE statement. Figure 5.1 shows the flow of logic from the preceding structure of the CASE statement.

Note that the selector is evaluated only once, and the WHEN clauses are evaluated sequentially. The value of an expression is compared to the value of the selector. If they are equal, the statement associated with a particular WHEN clause is executed, and subsequent WHEN clauses are not evaluated. If no expression matches the value of the selector, the ELSE clause is executed.

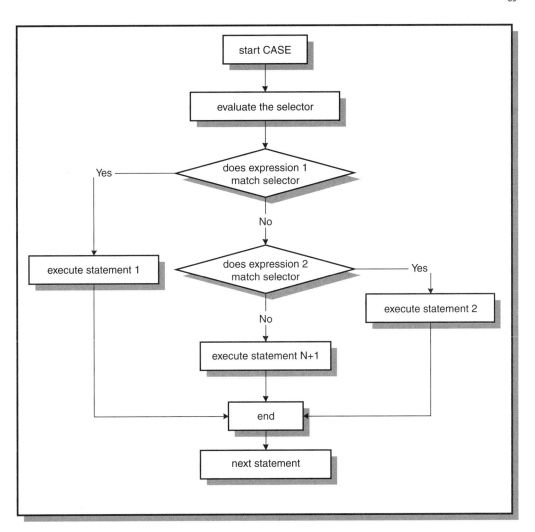

FIGURE 5.1
CASE statement

Recall the example of the IF-THEN-ELSE statement used in the preceding chapter:

FOR EXAMPLE

```
DECLARE
   v_num NUMBER := &sv_user_num;
BEGIN
   -- test if the number provided by the user is even
   IF MOD(v_num,2) = 0  THEN
      DBMS_OUTPUT.PUT_LINE (v_num||' is even number');
```

FOR EXAMPLE (continued)

```
ELSE
    DBMS_OUTPUT.PUT_LINE (v_num||' is odd number');
END IF;
DBMS_OUTPUT.PUT_LINE ('Done');
END;
```

Consider the new version of the same example with the CASE statement instead of the IF-THEN-ELSE statement:

FOR EXAMPLE

```
DECLARE
    v_num      NUMBER := &sv_user_num;
    v_num_flag NUMBER;
BEGIN
    v_num_flag := MOD(v_num,2);

    -- test if the number provided by the user is even
    CASE v_num_flag
       WHEN 0 THEN
           DBMS_OUTPUT.PUT_LINE (v_num||' is even number');
       ELSE
           DBMS_OUTPUT.PUT_LINE (v_num||' is odd number');
    END CASE;
    DBMS_OUTPUT.PUT_LINE ('Done');
END;
```

In this example, a new variable, v_num_flag, is used as a selector for the CASE statement. If the MOD function returns 0, the number is even; otherwise, it is odd. If v_num is assigned the value of 7, this example produces the following output:

```
Enter value for sv_user_num: 7
old    2:    v_num NUMBER := &sv_user_num;
new    2:    v_num NUMBER := 7;
7 is odd number
Done

PL/SQL procedure successfully completed.
```

SEARCHED CASE STATEMENTS

A searched CASE statement has search conditions that yield Boolean values: TRUE, FALSE, or NULL. When a particular search condition evaluates to TRUE, the group of statements associated with this condition is executed. This is indicated as follows:

```
CASE
    WHEN SEARCH CONDITION 1 THEN STATEMENT 1;
    WHEN SEARCH CONDITION 2 THEN STATEMENT 2;
```

```
      . . .
    WHEN SEARCH CONDITION N THEN STATEMENT N;
    ELSE STATEMENT N+1;
END CASE;
```

When a search condition evaluates to TRUE, control is passed to the statement associated with it. If no search condition yields TRUE, statements associated with the ELSE clause are executed. Note that the ELSE clause is optional. Figure 5.2 shows the flow of logic from the preceding structure of the searched CASE statement.

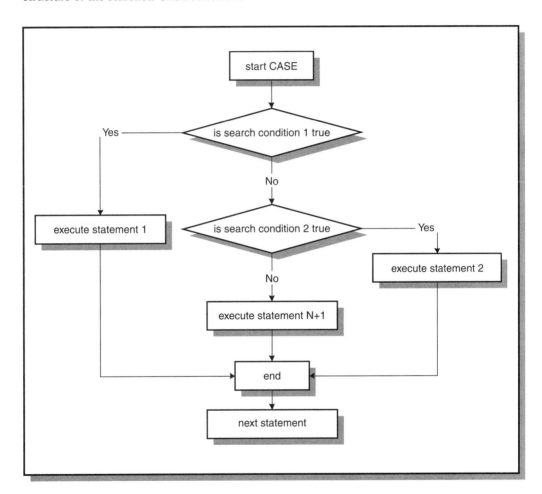

FIGURE 5.2
Searched CASE statement

Consider the modified version of the example that you have seen previously in this lab:

FOR EXAMPLE

```
DECLARE
   v_num NUMBER := &sv_user_num;
BEGIN
   -- test if the number provided by the user is even
   CASE
      WHEN MOD(v_num,2) = 0 THEN
         DBMS_OUTPUT.PUT_LINE (v_num||' is even number');
      ELSE
         DBMS_OUTPUT.PUT_LINE (v_num||' is odd number');
   END CASE;
   DBMS_OUTPUT.PUT_LINE ('Done');
END;
```

Notice that this example is almost identical to the previous example.

In the previous example, the variable v_num_flag was used as a selector, and the result of the MOD function was assigned to it. The value of the selector was then compared to the value of the expression. In this example, you are using a searched CASE statement, so no selector is present. The variable v_num is used as part of the search conditions, so there is no need to declare the variable v_num_flag. This example produces the same output when the same value is provided for v_num:

```
Enter value for sv_user_num: 7
old    2:    v_num NUMBER := &sv_user_num;
new    2:    v_num NUMBER := 7;
7 is odd number
Done

PL/SQL procedure successfully completed.
```

DIFFERENCES BETWEEN CASE AND SEARCHED CASE STATEMENTS

It is important to note the differences between CASE and searched CASE statements. You have seen that the searched CASE statement does not have a selector. In addition, its WHEN clauses contain search conditions that yield a Boolean value similar to the IF statement, not expressions that can yield a value of any type except a PL/SQL record, an index-by-table, a nested table, a vararray, BLOB, BFILE, or an object type. You will encounter some of these types in future chapters. Consider the following two code fragments based on the examples you have seen earlier in this chapter:

FOR EXAMPLE

```
DECLARE
   v_num      NUMBER := &sv_user_num;
   v_num_flag NUMBER;
```

```
BEGIN
    v_num_flag := MOD(v_num,2);

    -- test if the number provided by the user is even
    CASE v_num_flag
        WHEN 0 THEN
            DBMS_OUTPUT.PUT_LINE (v_num||' is even number');
...
And

DECLARE
    v_num NUMBER := &sv_user_num;
BEGIN
    -- test if the number provided by the user is even
    CASE
        WHEN MOD(v_num,2) = 0 THEN
...
```

In the first code fragment, `v_num_flag` is the selector. It is a PL/SQL variable that has been defined as NUMBER. Because the value of the expression is compared to the value of the selector, the expression must return a similar datatype. The expression 0 contains a number, so its datatype is also numeric. In the second code fragment, each searched expression evaluates to TRUE or FALSE, just like conditions of an IF statement.

Next, consider an example of a CASE statement that generates a syntax error because the datatype returned by the expressions does not match the datatype assigned to the selector:

FOR EXAMPLE

```
DECLARE
    v_num       NUMBER := &sv_num;
    v_num_flag NUMBER;
BEGIN
    CASE v_num_flag
        WHEN MOD(v_num,2) = 0 THEN
            DBMS_OUTPUT.PUT_LINE (v_num||' is even number');
        ELSE
            DBMS_OUTPUT.PUT_LINE (v_num||' is odd number');
    END CASE;
    DBMS_OUTPUT.PUT_LINE ('Done');
END;
```

In this example, the variable `v_num_flag` has been defined as a NUMBER. However, the result of each expression yields a Boolean datatype. As a result, this example produces the following syntax error:

```
    Enter value for sv_num: 7
    old   2:    v_num NUMBER := &sv_num;
    new   2:    v_num NUMBER := 7;
```

```
        CASE v_num_flag
              *
    ERROR at line 5:
    ORA-06550: line 5, column 9:
    PLS-00615: type mismatch found at 'V_NUM_FLAG' between CASE
    operand and WHEN operands
    ORA-06550: line 5, column 4:
    PL/SQL: Statement ignored
```

Consider a modified version of this example in which v_num_flag is defined as a Boolean variable:

FOR EXAMPLE

```
DECLARE
   v_num       NUMBER := &sv_num;
   v_num_flag Boolean;
BEGIN
   CASE v_num_flag
      WHEN MOD(v_num,2) = 0 THEN
         DBMS_OUTPUT.PUT_LINE (v_num||' is even number');
      ELSE
         DBMS_OUTPUT.PUT_LINE (v_num||' is odd number');
   END CASE;
   DBMS_OUTPUT.PUT_LINE ('Done');
END;
```

If v_num is assigned a value of 7 again, this example produces the following output:

```
    Enter value for sv_num: 7
    old    2:    v_num NUMBER := &sv_num;
    new    2:    v_num NUMBER := 7;
    7 is odd number
    Done

    PL/SQL procedure successfully completed.
```

At first glance this seems to be the output you would expect. However, consider the output produced by this example when a value of 4 is assigned to the variable v_num:

```
    Enter value for sv_num: 4
    old    2:    v_num NUMBER := &sv_num;
    new    2:    v_num NUMBER := 4;
    4 is odd number
    Done

    PL/SQL procedure successfully completed.
```

Notice that the second run of the example produces incorrect output even though it does not generate any syntax errors. When the value 4 is assigned to the variable v_num, the expression

MOD(v_num,2) = 0 yields TRUE, and it is compared to the selector v_num_flag. However, v_num_flag has not been initialized to any value, so it is NULL. Because NULL does not equal TRUE, the statement associated with the ELSE clause is executed.

▼ LAB 5.1 EXERCISES

This section provides exercises and suggested answers, with discussion related to how those answers resulted. The most important thing to realize is whether your answer works. You should figure out the implications of the answers and what the effects are of any different answers you may come up with.

5.1.1 Use the CASE Statement

In this exercise, you use the CASE statement to display the name of a day on the screen based on the day's number in the week. In other words, if the number of the day of the week is 3, it is Tuesday.

Create the following PL/SQL script:

```
-- ch05_1a.sql, version 1.0
SET SERVEROUTPUT ON
DECLARE
    v_date DATE := TO_DATE('&sv_user_date', 'DD-MON-YYYY');
    v_day  VARCHAR2(1);
BEGIN
    v_day := TO_CHAR(v_date, 'D');
    CASE v_day
        WHEN '1' THEN
            DBMS_OUTPUT.PUT_LINE ('Today is Sunday');
        WHEN '2' THEN
            DBMS_OUTPUT.PUT_LINE ('Today is Monday');
        WHEN '3' THEN
            DBMS_OUTPUT.PUT_LINE ('Today is Tuesday');
        WHEN '4' THEN
            DBMS_OUTPUT.PUT_LINE ('Today is Wednesday');
        WHEN '5' THEN
            DBMS_OUTPUT.PUT_LINE ('Today is Thursday');
        WHEN '6' THEN
            DBMS_OUTPUT.PUT_LINE ('Today is Friday');
        WHEN '7' THEN
            DBMS_OUTPUT.PUT_LINE ('Today is Saturday');
    END CASE;
END;
```

Execute the script, and then answer the following questions:

A) If the value of v_date is 15-JAN-2008, what output is printed on the screen?

ANSWER: The output should look like the following:

```
Enter value for sv_user_date: 15-JAN-2008
old   2:    v_date DATE := TO_DATE('&sv_user_date', 'DD-MON-YYYY');
new   2:    v_date DATE := TO_DATE('15-JAN-2008', 'DD-MON-YYYY');
Today is Tuesday

PL/SQL procedure successfully completed.
```

When the value of $15-JAN-2008$ is entered for v_date, the number of the day of the week is determined for the variable v_day with the help of the TO_CHAR function. Next, each expression of the CASE statement is compared sequentially to the value of the selector. Because the value of the selector is 3, the DBMS_OUTPUT.PUT_LINE statement associated with the third WHEN clause is executed. As a result, the message Today is Tuesday is displayed on the screen. The rest of the expressions are not evaluated, and control is passed to the first executable statement after END CASE.

B) How many times is the CASE selector v_day evaluated?

ANSWER: The CASE selector v_day is evaluated only once. However, the WHEN clauses are checked sequentially. When the value of the expression in the WHEN clause equals the value of the selector, the statements associated with the WHEN clause are executed.

C) Rewrite this script using the ELSE clause in the CASE statement.

ANSWER: The script should look similar to the following. Changes are shown in bold.

```
-- ch05_1b.sql, version 2.0
SET SERVEROUTPUT ON
DECLARE
    v_date DATE := TO_DATE('&sv_user_date', 'DD-MON-YYYY');
    v_day  VARCHAR2(1);
BEGIN
    v_day := TO_CHAR(v_date, 'D');
    CASE v_day
        WHEN '1' THEN
            DBMS_OUTPUT.PUT_LINE ('Today is Sunday');
        WHEN '2' THEN
            DBMS_OUTPUT.PUT_LINE ('Today is Monday');
        WHEN '3' THEN
            DBMS_OUTPUT.PUT_LINE ('Today is Tuesday');
        WHEN '4' THEN
            DBMS_OUTPUT.PUT_LINE ('Today is Wednesday');
        WHEN '5' THEN
            DBMS_OUTPUT.PUT_LINE ('Today is Thursday');
        WHEN '6' THEN
            DBMS_OUTPUT.PUT_LINE ('Today is Friday');
        ELSE
            DBMS_OUTPUT.PUT_LINE ('Today is Saturday');
    END CASE;
END;
```

Notice that the last WHEN clause has been replaced by the ELSE clause. If $19-JAN-2008$ is provided at runtime, the example produces the following output:

```
Enter value for sv_user_date: 19-JAN-2008
old   2:    v_date DATE := TO_DATE('&sv_user_date', 'DD-MON-YYYY');
new   2:    v_date DATE := TO_DATE('19-JAN-2008', 'DD-MON-YYYY');
Today is Saturday

PL/SQL procedure successfully completed.
```

None of the expressions listed in the WHEN clauses is equal to the value of the selector because the date 19-JAN-2008 falls on Saturday, which is the seventh day of the week. As a result, the ELSE clause is executed, and the message Today is Saturday is displayed on the screen.

D) Rewrite this script using the searched CASE statement.

ANSWER: The script should look similar to the following. Changes are shown in bold.

```
-- ch05_1c.sql, version 3.0
SET SERVEROUTPUT ON
DECLARE
    v_date DATE := TO_DATE('&sv_user_date', 'DD-MON-YYYY');
BEGIN
    CASE
        WHEN TO_CHAR(v_date, 'D') = '1' THEN
            DBMS_OUTPUT.PUT_LINE ('Today is Sunday');
        WHEN TO_CHAR(v_date, 'D') = '2' THEN
            DBMS_OUTPUT.PUT_LINE ('Today is Monday');
        WHEN TO_CHAR(v_date, 'D') = '3' THEN
            DBMS_OUTPUT.PUT_LINE ('Today is Tuesday');
        WHEN TO_CHAR(v_date, 'D') = '4' THEN
            DBMS_OUTPUT.PUT_LINE ('Today is Wednesday');
        WHEN TO_CHAR(v_date, 'D') = '5' THEN
            DBMS_OUTPUT.PUT_LINE ('Today is Thursday');
        WHEN TO_CHAR(v_date, 'D') = '6' THEN
            DBMS_OUTPUT.PUT_LINE ('Today is Friday');
        WHEN TO_CHAR(v_date, 'D') = '7' THEN
            DBMS_OUTPUT.PUT_LINE ('Today is Saturday');
    END CASE;
END;
```

Notice that in the new version of the example there is no need to declare the variable `v_day` because the searched CASE statement does not need a selector. The expression that you used to assign a value to the variable `v_day` is now used as part of the searched conditions. When run, this example produces output identical to the output produced by the original version:

```
Enter value for sv_user_date: 15-JAN-2008
old   2:    v_date DATE := TO_DATE('&sv_user_date', 'DD-MON-YYYY');
new   2:    v_date DATE := TO_DATE('15-JAN-2002', 'DD-MON-YYYY');
Today is Tuesday

PL/SQL procedure successfully completed.
```

5.1.2 **Use the Searched CASE Statement**

In this exercise, you modify the script ch04_3d.sql used in the preceding chapter. The original script uses the ELSIF statement to display a letter grade for a student registered for a specific section of course number 25. The new version uses a searched CASE statement to achieve the same result. Try to answer the questions before you run the script. After you have answered the questions, run the script and check your answers. Note that you may need to change the values for the variables `v_student_id` and `v_section_id` as you see fit to test some of your answers.

Create the following PL/SQL script:

```
-- ch05_2a.sql, version 1.0
SET SERVEROUTPUT ON
DECLARE
    v_student_id   NUMBER := 102;
    v_section_id   NUMBER := 89;
```

```
      v_final_grade  NUMBER;
      v_letter_grade CHAR(1);
   BEGIN
      SELECT final_grade
        INTO v_final_grade
        FROM enrollment
       WHERE student_id = v_student_id
         AND section_id = v_section_id;

      CASE
         WHEN v_final_grade >= 90 THEN v_letter_grade := 'A';
         WHEN v_final_grade >= 80 THEN v_letter_grade := 'B';
         WHEN v_final_grade >= 70 THEN v_letter_grade := 'C';
         WHEN v_final_grade >= 60 THEN v_letter_grade := 'D';
         ELSE v_letter_grade := 'F';
      END CASE;
      -- control resumes here
       DBMS_OUTPUT.PUT_LINE ('Letter grade is: '||v_letter_grade);
   END;
```

Try to answer the following questions, and then execute the script:

A) What letter grade is displayed on the screen:

    I) if the value of `v_final_grade` is equal to 60?

    II) if the value of `v_final_grade` is greater than 60 and less than 70?

    III) if the value of `v_final_grade` is NULL?

ANSWER:

    I) If the value of `v_final_grade` is equal to 60, value "D" of the letter grade is displayed on the screen.

    The searched conditions of the CASE statement are evaluated in sequential order. The searched condition

```
WHEN v_final_grade >= 60 THEN
```

    yields TRUE, and as a result, letter "D" is assigned to the variable `v_letter_grade`. Control is then passed to the first executable statement after END IF, and the message `Letter grade is: D` is displayed on the screen.

    II) If the value of `v_final_grade` is greater than 60 and less than 70, value "D" of the letter grade is displayed on the screen.

    If the value of `v_final_grade` falls between 60 and 70, the searched condition

```
WHEN v_final_grade >= 70 THEN
```

    yields FALSE because the value of the variable `v_final_grade` is less than 70. However, the next searched condition

```
WHEN v_final_grade >= 60 THEN
```

    of the CASE statement evaluates to TRUE, and letter "D" is assigned to the variable `v_letter_grade`.

    III) If the value of `v_final_grade` is NULL, value "F" of the letter grade is displayed on the screen.

All searched conditions of the CASE statement evaluate to FALSE because NULL cannot be compared to a value. Such a comparison always yields FALSE, and as a result, the ELSE clause is executed.

B) How would you change this script so that the message There is no final grade is displayed if v_final_grade is null? In addition, make sure that the message Letter grade is: is not displayed on the screen.

ANSWER: The script should look similar to the following. Changes are shown in bold.

```
-- ch05_2b.sql, version 2.0
SET SERVEROUTPUT ON
DECLARE
   v_student_id    NUMBER := &sv_student_id;
   v_section_id    NUMBER := 89;
   v_final_grade  NUMBER;
   v_letter_grade CHAR(1);
BEGIN
   SELECT final_grade
     INTO v_final_grade
     FROM enrollment
    WHERE student_id = v_student_id
      AND section_id = v_section_id;

   CASE -- outer CASE
      WHEN v_final_grade IS NULL THEN
         DBMS_OUTPUT.PUT_LINE ('There is no final grade.');
      ELSE
         CASE -- inner CASE
            WHEN v_final_grade >= 90 THEN v_letter_grade := 'A';
            WHEN v_final_grade >= 80 THEN v_letter_grade := 'B';
            WHEN v_final_grade >= 70 THEN v_letter_grade := 'C';
            WHEN v_final_grade >= 60 THEN v_letter_grade := 'D';
            ELSE v_letter_grade := 'F';
         END CASE;
         -- control resumes here after inner CASE terminates
         DBMS_OUTPUT.PUT_LINE ('Letter grade is: '||v_letter_grade);
   END CASE;
   -- control resumes here after outer CASE terminates
END;
```

To achieve the desired results, you nest CASE statements inside one another, as you did with IF statements in the preceding chapter. The outer CASE statement evaluates the value of the variable v_final_grade. If the value of v_final_grade is NULL, the message There is no final grade. is displayed on the screen. If the value of v_final_grade is not NULL, the ELSE part of the outer CASE statement is executed.

Notice that to display the letter grade only when there is a final grade, you have associated the statement

```
DBMS_OUTPUT.PUT_LINE ('Letter grade is: '||v_letter_grade);
```

with the ELSE clause of the outer CASE statement. This guarantees that the message Letter grade... is displayed on the screen only when the variable v_final_grade is not NULL.

To test this script fully, you have also introduced a substitution variable. This enables you to run the script for the different values of $v\_student\_id$. For the first run, enter a value of 136, and for the second run, enter a value of 102.

The first output displays the message There is no final grade. and does not display the message Letter grade...:

```
Enter value for sv_student_id: 136
old    2:    v_student_id NUMBER := &sv_student_id;
new    2:    v_student_id NUMBER := 136;
There is no final grade.

PL/SQL procedure successfully completed.
```

The second run produces output similar to the output produced by the original version:

```
Enter value for sv_student_id: 102
old    2:    v_student_id NUMBER := &sv_student_id;
new    2:    v_student_id NUMBER := 102;
Letter grade is: A

PL/SQL procedure successfully completed.
```

C) Rewrite this script, changing the order of the searched conditions as shown here. Execute the script and explain the output produced.

```
CASE
    WHEN v_final_grade >= 60 THEN v_letter_grade := 'D';
    WHEN v_final_grade >= 70 THEN v_letter_grade := 'C';
    WHEN v_final_grade >= 80 THEN ...
    WHEN v_final_grade >= 90 THEN ...
    ELSE ...
```

ANSWER: The script should look similar to the following. Changes are shown in bold.

```
-- ch05_2c.sql, version 3.0
SET SERVEROUTPUT ON
DECLARE
    v_student_id    NUMBER := 102;
    v_section_id    NUMBER := 89;
    v_final_grade   NUMBER;
    v_letter_grade CHAR(1);
BEGIN
    SELECT final_grade
      INTO v_final_grade
      FROM enrollment
     WHERE student_id = v_student_id
       AND section_id = v_section_id;

    CASE
        WHEN v_final_grade >= 60 THEN v_letter_grade := 'D';
        WHEN v_final_grade >= 70 THEN v_letter_grade := 'C';
        WHEN v_final_grade >= 80 THEN v_letter_grade := 'B';
```

```
      WHEN v_final_grade >= 90 THEN v_letter_grade := 'A';
      ELSE v_letter_grade := 'F';
   END CASE;
   -- control resumes here
    DBMS_OUTPUT.PUT_LINE ('Letter grade is: '||v_letter_grade);
END;
```

This script produces the following output:

```
Letter grade is: D

PL/SQL procedure successfully completed.
```

The first searched condition of the CASE statement evaluates to TRUE, because the value of v_final_grade equals 92, and it is greater than 60.

You learned earlier that the searched conditions are evaluated sequentially. Therefore, the statements associated with the first condition that yields TRUE are executed, and the rest of the searched conditions are discarded. In this example, the searched condition

```
WHEN v_final_grade >= 60 THEN
```

evaluates to TRUE, and the value of "D" is assigned to the variable v_letter_grade. Then control is passed to the first executable statement after END CASE, and the message Letter grade is: D is displayed on the screen. For this script to assign the letter grade correctly, the CASE statement may be modified as follows:

```
CASE
   WHEN v_final_grade < 60  THEN v_letter_grade := 'F';
   WHEN v_final_grade < 70  THEN v_letter_grade := 'D';
   WHEN v_final_grade < 80  THEN v_letter_grade := 'C';
   WHEN v_final_grade < 90  THEN v_letter_grade := 'B';
   WHEN v_final_grade < 100 THEN v_letter_grade := 'A';
END CASE;
```

However, there is a small problem with this CASE statement. What do you think happens when v_final_grade is greater than 100?

DID YOU KNOW?

With the CASE constructs, as with the IF constructs, a group of statements that is executed generally depends on the order in which its condition is listed.

LAB 5.2
CASE Expressions

LAB OBJECTIVES

After completing this lab, you will be able to

▶ Use CASE expressions

In Chapter 2, "General Programming Language Fundamentals," you encountered various PL/SQL expressions. You will recall that the result of an expression yields a single value that is assigned to a variable. In a similar manner, a CASE expression evaluates to a single value that then may be assigned to a variable.

A CASE expression has a structure almost identical to a CASE statement. Thus, it also has two forms: CASE and searched CASE. Consider an example of a CASE statement used in the preceding lab:

FOR EXAMPLE

```
DECLARE
    v_num      NUMBER := &sv_user_num;
    v_num_flag NUMBER;
BEGIN
    v_num_flag := MOD(v_num,2);

    -- test if the number provided by the user is even
    CASE v_num_flag
        WHEN 0 THEN
            DBMS_OUTPUT.PUT_LINE (v_num||' is even number');
        ELSE
            DBMS_OUTPUT.PUT_LINE (v_num||' is odd number');
    END CASE;
    DBMS_OUTPUT.PUT_LINE ('Done');
END;
```

Consider the new version of the same example, with the CASE expression instead of the CASE statement. Changes are shown in bold.

FOR EXAMPLE

```
DECLARE
    v_num       NUMBER := &sv_user_num;
    v_num_flag NUMBER;
    v_result    VARCHAR2(30);
BEGIN
    v_num_flag := MOD(v_num,2);

    v_result :=
      CASE v_num_flag
        WHEN 0 THEN v_num||' is even number'
        ELSE v_num||' is odd number'
      END;
    DBMS_OUTPUT.PUT_LINE (v_result);
    DBMS_OUTPUT.PUT_LINE ('Done');
END;
```

In this example, a new variable, v_result, is used to hold the value returned by the CASE expression. If v_num is assigned the value of 8, this example produces the following output:

```
Enter value for sv_user_num: 8
old    2:    v_num NUMBER := &sv_user_num;
new    2:    v_num NUMBER := 8;
8 is even number
Done

PL/SQL procedure successfully completed.
```

It is important to note some syntax differences between a CASE statement and a CASE expression. Consider the following code fragments:

```
CASE Statement                      CASE Expression
CASE v_num_flag                     CASE v_num_flag
   WHEN 0 THEN                         WHEN 0 THEN
      DBMS_OUTPUT.PUT_LINE                 v_num||' is even number'ELSE
         (v_num||' is even number');
   ELSE                               ELSE
      DBMS_OUTPUT.PUT_LINE                 (v_num||' is odd number');
         v_num||' is odd number'
END CASE;                           END;
```

In the CASE statement, the WHEN and ELSE clauses each contain a single executable statement. Each executable statement is terminated by a semicolon. In the CASE expression, the WHEN and ELSE clauses each contain an expression that is not terminated by a semicolon. One semicolon is present after the reserved word END, which terminates the CASE expression. Finally, the CASE statement is terminated by the reserved phrase END CASE.

Next, consider another version of the previous example, with the searched CASE expression:

FOR EXAMPLE

```
DECLARE
    v_num    NUMBER := &sv_user_num;
    v_result VARCHAR2(30);
BEGIN
    v_result :=
        CASE
            WHEN MOD(v_num,2) = 0 THEN v_num||' is even number'
            ELSE v_num||' is odd number'
        END;
    DBMS_OUTPUT.PUT_LINE (v_result);
    DBMS_OUTPUT.PUT_LINE ('Done');
END;
```

In this example, there is no need to declare the variable v_num_flag because the searched CASE expression does not need a selector value, and the result of the MOD function is incorporated into the search condition. When run, this example produces output identical to the previous version:

```
Enter value for sv_user_num: 8
old    2:    v_num NUMBER := &sv_user_num;
new    2:    v_num NUMBER := 8;
8 is even number
Done

PL/SQL procedure successfully completed.
```

You learned earlier that a CASE expression returns a single value that is then assigned to a variable. In the examples you saw earlier, this assignment operation was accomplished via the assignment operator, :=. You may recall that there is another way to assign a value to a PL/SQL variable—via a SELECT INTO statement. Consider an example of the CASE expression used in a SELECT INTO statement:

FOR EXAMPLE

```
DECLARE
    v_course_no    NUMBER;
    v_description VARCHAR2(50);
    v_prereq       VARCHAR2(35);
BEGIN
    SELECT course_no, description,
           CASE
               WHEN prerequisite IS NULL THEN
                   'No prerequisite course required'
               ELSE TO_CHAR(prerequisite)
```

```
        END prerequisite
  INTO v_course_no, v_description, v_prereq
  FROM course
 WHERE course_no = 20;

DBMS_OUTPUT.PUT_LINE ('Course: '||v_course_no);
DBMS_OUTPUT.PUT_LINE ('Description: '||v_description);
DBMS_OUTPUT.PUT_LINE ('Prerequisite: '||v_prereq);
END;
```

This example displays the course number, a description, and the number of a prerequisite course on the screen. Furthermore, if a given course does not have a prerequisite course, a message saying so is displayed on the screen. To achieve the desired results, a CASE expression is used as one of the columns in the SELECT INTO statement. Its value is assigned to the variable v_prereq. Notice that there is no semicolon after the reserved word END of the CASE expression.

This example produces the following output:

```
Course: 20
Description: Intro to Information Systems
Prerequisite: No prerequisite course required

PL/SQL procedure successfully completed.
```

Course 20 does not have a prerequisite course. As a result, the searched condition

```
WHEN prerequisite IS NULL THEN
```

evaluates to TRUE, and the value No prerequisite course required is assigned to the variable v_prereq.

It is important to note why the function TO_CHAR is used in the ELSE clause of the CASE expression:

```
CASE
    WHEN prerequisite IS NULL THEN
        'No prerequisite course required'
    ELSE TO_CHAR(prerequisite)
END
```

A CASE expression returns a single value and thus a single datatype. Therefore, it is important to ensure that regardless of what part of a CASE expression is executed, it always returns the same datatype. In the preceding CASE expression, the WHEN clause returns the VARCHAR2 datatype. The ELSE clause returns the value of the PREREQUISITE column of the COURSE table. This column has been defined as NUMBER, so it is necessary to convert it to the string datatype.

When the TO_CHAR function is not used, the CASE expression causes the following syntax error:

```
                ELSE prerequisite
                     *
ERROR at line 9:
ORA-06550: line 9, column 19:
PL/SQL: ORA-00932: inconsistent datatypes
ORA-06550: line 6, column 4:
PL/SQL: SQL Statement ignored
```

▼ LAB 5.2 EXERCISES

This section provides exercises and suggested answers, with discussion related to how those answers resulted. The most important thing to realize is whether your answer works. You should figure out the implications of the answers and what the effects are of any different answers you may come up with.

5.2.1 Use the CASE Expression

In this exercise, you modify the script ch05_2a.sql. Instead of using a searched CASE statement, you use a searched CASE expression to display a letter grade for a student registered for a specific section of course number 25.

Answer the following questions:

A) Modify the script ch05_2a.sql. Substitute the searched CASE expression for the CASE statement, and assign the value returned by the expression to the variable `v_letter_grade`.

ANSWER: The script should look similar to the following. Changes are shown in bold.

```
-- ch05_3a.sql, version 1.0
SET SERVEROUTPUT ON
DECLARE
    v_student_id    NUMBER := 102;
    v_section_id    NUMBER := 89;
    v_final_grade   NUMBER;
    v_letter_grade CHAR(1);
BEGIN
    SELECT final_grade
      INTO v_final_grade
      FROM enrollment
     WHERE student_id = v_student_id
       AND section_id = v_section_id;

    v_letter_grade :=
        CASE
            WHEN v_final_grade >= 90 THEN 'A'
            WHEN v_final_grade >= 80 THEN 'B'
            WHEN v_final_grade >= 70 THEN 'C'
            WHEN v_final_grade >= 60 THEN 'D'
            ELSE 'F'
        END;
    -- control resumes here
    DBMS_OUTPUT.PUT_LINE ('Letter grade is: '||v_letter_grade);
END;
```

In the original version of the script (ch05_2a.sql), you used a searched CASE statement to assign a value to the variable `v_letter_grade` as follows:

```
CASE
    WHEN v_final_grade >= 90 THEN v_letter_grade := 'A';
    WHEN v_final_grade >= 80 THEN v_letter_grade := 'B';
    WHEN v_final_grade >= 70 THEN v_letter_grade := 'C';
    WHEN v_final_grade >= 60 THEN v_letter_grade := 'D';
    ELSE v_letter_grade := 'F';
END CASE;
```

Notice that the variable `v_letter_grade` is used as part of the CASE statement. In the new version of the script, the CASE expression

```
CASE
    WHEN v_final_grade >= 90 THEN 'A'
    WHEN v_final_grade >= 80 THEN 'B'
    WHEN v_final_grade >= 70 THEN 'C'
    WHEN v_final_grade >= 60 THEN 'D'
    ELSE 'F'
END;
```

does not contain any references to the variable `v_letter_grade`. Each search condition is evaluated. As soon as a particular condition evaluates to TRUE, its corresponding value is returned and then assigned to the variable `v_letter_grade`.

B) Run the script you just created, and explain the output produced.

ANSWER: The output should look similar to the following:

```
Letter grade is: A

PL/SQL procedure successfully completed.
```

The SELECT INTO statement returns a value of 92 that is assigned to the variable `v_final_grade`. As a result, the first searched condition of the CASE expression evaluates to TRUE and returns a value of A. This value is then assigned to the variable `v_letter_grade` and is displayed on the screen via the DBMS_OUTPUT.PUT_LINE statement.

C) Rewrite the script you created in part A) so that the result of the CASE expression is assigned to the `v_letter_grade` variable via a SELECT INTO statement.

ANSWER: The script should look similar to the following. Changes are shown in bold.

```
-- ch05_3b.sql, version 2.0
SET SERVEROUTPUT ON
DECLARE
    v_student_id   NUMBER := 102;
    v_section_id   NUMBER := 89;
    v_letter_grade CHAR(1);
BEGIN
    SELECT CASE
              WHEN final_grade >= 90 THEN 'A'
              WHEN final_grade >= 80 THEN 'B'
              WHEN final_grade >= 70 THEN 'C'
              WHEN final_grade >= 60 THEN 'D'
```

```
                ELSE 'F'
            END
    INTO v_letter_grade
    FROM enrollment
  WHERE student_id = v_student_id
    AND section_id = v_section_id;
```

```
    -- control resumes here
    DBMS_OUTPUT.PUT_LINE ('Letter grade is: '||v_letter_grade);
END;
```

In the previous version of the script, the variable v_final_grade was used to hold the value of the numeric grade:

```
SELECT final_grade
  INTO v_final_grade
  FROM enrollment
 WHERE student_id = v_student_id
   AND section_id = v_section_id;
```

The CASE expression used this value to assign the proper letter grade to the variable v_letter_grade:

```
CASE
    WHEN v_final_grade >= 90 THEN 'A'
    WHEN v_final_grade >= 80 THEN 'B'
    WHEN v_final_grade >= 70 THEN 'C'
    WHEN v_final_grade >= 60 THEN 'D'
    ELSE 'F'
END;
```

In the current version of the script, the CASE expression is used as part of the SELECT INTO statement. As a result, the CASE expression can use the column FINAL_GRADE:

```
CASE
    WHEN final_grade >= 90 THEN 'A'
    WHEN final_grade >= 80 THEN 'B'
    WHEN final_grade >= 70 THEN 'C'
    WHEN final_grade >= 60 THEN 'D'
    ELSE 'F'
END
```

as part of the searched conditions to assign a value to the variable v_letter_grade.

LAB 5.3
NULLIF and COALESCE Functions

LAB OBJECTIVES

After completing this lab, you will be able to

- ▶ Use the NULLIF function
- ▶ Use the COALESCE function

The NULLIF and COALESCE functions are defined by the ANSI 1999 standard as "CASE abbreviations." Both functions can be used as a variation on the CASE expression.

THE NULLIF FUNCTION

The NULLIF function compares two expressions. If they are equal, the function returns NULL; otherwise, it returns the value of the first expression. NULLIF has the following structure:

```
NULLIF (expression1, expression2)
```

If *expression1* is equal to *expression2*, NULLIF returns NULL. If *expression1* does not equal *expression2*, NULLIF returns *expression1*. Note that the NULLIF function does the opposite of the NVL function. If the first expression is NULL, NVL returns the second expression. If the first expression is not NULL, NVL returns the first expression.

The NULLIF function is equivalent to the following CASE expression:

```
CASE
    WHEN expression1 = expression2 THEN NULL
    ELSE expression1
END
```

Consider the following example of NULLIF:

FOR EXAMPLE

```
DECLARE
    v_num       NUMBER := &sv_user_num;
    v_remainder NUMBER;
```

FOR EXAMPLE (continued)

```
BEGIN
   -- calculate the remainder and if it is zero return NULL
   v_remainder := NULLIF(MOD(v_num,2),0);
   DBMS_OUTPUT.PUT_LINE ('v_remainder: '||v_remainder);
END;
```

This example is somewhat similar to an example you saw earlier in this chapter. A value is assigned to the variable v_num at runtime. Then this value is divided by 2, and its remainder is compared to 0 via the NULLIF function. If the remainder equals 0, the NULLIF function returns NULL; otherwise, it returns the remainder. The value returned by the NULLIF function is stored in the variable v_remainder and is displayed on the screen via the DBMS_OUTPUT.PUT_LINE statement. When run, the example produces the following output:

For the first run, 5 is assigned to the variable v_num:

```
Enter value for sv_user_num: 5
old    2:    v_num NUMBER := &sv_user_num;
new    2:    v_num NUMBER := 5;
v_remainder: 1

PL/SQL procedure successfully completed.
```

For the second run, 4 is assigned to the variable v_num:

```
Enter value for sv_user_num: 4
old    2:    v_num NUMBER := &sv_user_num;
new    2:    v_num NUMBER := 4;
v_remainder:

PL/SQL procedure successfully completed.
```

In the first run, 5 is not divisible by 2, so the NULLIF function returns the value of the remainder. In the second run, 4 is divisible by 2, so the NULLIF function returns NULL as the value of the remainder.

WATCH OUT!

The NULLIF function has a restriction: *You cannot assign a literal NULL to expression1*. You learned about literals in Chapter 2. Consider another output produced by the preceding example. For this run, the variable v_num is assigned NULL:

```
Enter value for sv_user_num: NULL
old    2:    v_num NUMBER := &sv_user_num;
new    2:    v_num NUMBER := NULL;
v_remainder:

PL/SQL procedure successfully completed.
```

When NULL is assigned to the variable v_num, both the MOD and NULLIF functions return NULL. This example does not produce any errors, because the literal NULL is assigned to the variable v_num, and it is not used as the first expression of the NULLIF function. Next, consider this modified version of the preceding example:

```
DECLARE
    v_remainder NUMBER;
BEGIN
    -- calculate the remainder and if it is zero return NULL
    v_remainder := NULLIF(NULL,0);
    DBMS_OUTPUT.PUT_LINE ('v_remainder: '||v_remainder);
END;
```

In the previous version of this example, the MOD function is used as *expression1*. In this version, the literal NULL is used in place of the MOD function, and as a result, this example produces the following syntax error:

```
    v_remainder := NULLIF(NULL,0);
                         *

ERROR at line 5:
ORA-06550: line 5, column 26:
PLS-00619: the first operand in the NULLIF expression must not be NULL
ORA-06550: line 5, column 4:
PL/SQL: Statement ignored
```

THE COALESCE FUNCTION

The COALESCE function compares each expression to NULL from the list of expressions and returns the value of the first non-null expression. The COALESCE function has the following structure:

```
COALESCE (expression1, expression2, ..., expressionN)
```

If *expression1* evaluates to NULL, *expression2* is evaluated. If *expression2* does not evaluate to NULL, the function returns *expression2*. If *expression2* also evaluates to NULL, the next expression is evaluated. If all expressions evaluate to NULL, the function returns NULL.

Note that the COALESCE function is like a nested NVL function:

```
NVL(expression1, NVL(expression2, NVL(expression3,...)))
```

The COALESCE function can also be used as an alternative to a CASE expression. For example,

```
COALESCE (expression1, expression2)
```

is equivalent to

```
CASE
    WHEN expression1 IS NOT NULL THEN expression1
    ELSE expression2
END
```

If more than two expressions need to be evaluated,

```
COALESCE (expression1, expression2, ..., expressionN)
```

is equivalent to

```
CASE
    WHEN expression1 IS NOT NULL THEN expression1
    ELSE COALESCE (expression2, ..., expressionN)
END
```

which in turn is equivalent to

```
CASE
    WHEN expression1 IS NOT NULL THEN expression1
    WHEN expression2 IS NOT NULL THEN expression2
    ...
    ELSE expressionN
END
```

Consider the following example of the COALESCE function:

FOR EXAMPLE

```
SELECT e.student_id, e.section_id, e.final_grade, g.numeric_grade,
       COALESCE(e.final_grade, g.numeric_grade, 0) grade
  FROM enrollment e, grade g
 WHERE e.student_id = g.student_id
   AND e.section_id = g.section_id
   AND e.student_id = 102
   AND g.grade_type_code = 'FI';
```

This SELECT statement returns the following output:

```
STUDENT_ID SECTION_ID FINAL_GRADE NUMERIC_GRADE      GRADE
---------- ---------- ----------- ------------- ----------
       102         86                        85         85
       102         89          92            92         92
```

The value of GRADE equals the value of the NUMERIC_GRADE in the first row. The COALESCE function compares the value of FINAL_GRADE to NULL. If it is NULL, the value of NUMERIC_GRADE is compared to NULL. Because the value of NUMERIC_GRADE is not NULL, the COALESCE function returns the value of NUMERIC_GRADE. The value of GRADE equals the value of FINAL_GRADE in the second row. The COALESCE function returns the value of FINAL_GRADE because it is not NULL.

The COALESCE function shown in the preceding example is equivalent to the following NVL statement and CASE expressions:

```
NVL(e.final_grade, NVL(g.numeric_grade, 0))

CASE
    WHEN e.final_grade IS NOT NULL THEN e.final_grade
```

```
    ELSE COALESCE(g.numeric_grade, 0)
END
```

and

```
CASE
    WHEN e.final_grade   IS NOT NULL THEN e.final_grade
    WHEN g.numeric_grade IS NOT NULL THEN g.numeric_grade
    ELSE 0
END
```

▼ LAB 5.3 EXERCISES

This section provides exercises and suggested answers, with discussion related to how those answers resulted. The most important thing to realize is whether your answer works. You should figure out the implications of the answers and what the effects are of any different answers you may come up with.

5.3.1 The NULLIF Function

In this exercise, you will modify the following script. Instead of using the searched CASE expression, you use the NULLIF function. Note that the SELECT INTO statement uses the ANSI 1999 SQL standard.

BY THE WAY

You will find detailed explanations and examples of the statements using the new ANSI 1999 SQL standard in Appendix C and in Oracle help. Throughout this book we try to provide you with examples illustrating both standards; however, our main focus is on PL/SQL features rather than SQL.

```
-- ch05_4a.sql, version 1.0
SET SERVEROUTPUT ON
DECLARE
    v_final_grade NUMBER;
BEGIN
    SELECT CASE
                WHEN e.final_grade = g.numeric_grade THEN NULL
                ELSE g.numeric_grade
            END
        INTO v_final_grade
        FROM enrollment e
        JOIN grade g
          ON (e.student_id = g.student_id
          AND e.section_id = g.section_id)
       WHERE e.student_id = 102
         AND e.section_id = 86
         AND g.grade_type_code = 'FI';

    DBMS_OUTPUT.PUT_LINE ('Final grade: '||v_final_grade);
END;
```

In the preceding script, the value of the final grade is compared to the value of the numeric grade. If these values are equal, the CASE expression returns NULL. In the opposite case, the CASE expression returns the numeric grade. The result of the CASE expression is then displayed on the screen via the DBMS_OUTPUT.PUT_LINE statement.

Answer the following questions:

A) Modify script ch05_4a.sql. Substitute the NULLIF function for the CASE expression.

ANSWER: The script should look similar to the following. Changes are shown in bold.

```
-- ch05_4b.sql, version 2.0
SET SERVEROUTPUT ON
DECLARE
    v_final_grade NUMBER;
BEGIN
    SELECT NULLIF(g.numeric_grade, e.final_grade)
      INTO v_final_grade
      FROM enrollment e
      JOIN grade g
        ON (e.student_id = g.student_id
        AND e.section_id = g.section_id)
     WHERE e.student_id = 102
       AND e.section_id = 86
       AND g.grade_type_code = 'FI';

    DBMS_OUTPUT.PUT_LINE ('Final grade: '||v_final_grade);
END;
```

In the original version of the script, you used the CASE expression to assign a value to the variable v_final_grade as follows:

```
CASE
   WHEN e.final_grade = g.numeric_grade THEN NULL
   ELSE g.numeric_grade
END
```

The value stored in the column FINAL_GRADE is compared to the value stored in the column NUMERIC_GRADE. If these values are equal, NULL is assigned to the variable v_final_grade; otherwise, the value stored in the column NUMERIC_GRADE is assigned to the variable v_final_grade.

In the new version of the script, you substitute the CASE expression with the NULLIF function as follows:

```
NULLIF(g.numeric_grade, e.final_grade)
```

It is important to note that the NUMERIC_GRADE column is referenced first in the NULLIF function. You will recall that the NULLIF function compares *expression1* to *expression2*. If *expression1* equals *expression2*, the NULLIF function returns NULL. If *expression1* does not equal *expression2*, the NULLIF function returns *expression1*. To return the value stored in the column NUMERIC_GRADE, you must reference it first in the NULLIF function.

B) Run the modified version of the script, and explain the output produced.

ANSWER: The output should look similar to the following:

```
Final grade: 85


PL/SQL procedure successfully completed.
```

The NULLIF function compares values stored in the columns NUMERIC_GRADE and FINAL_GRADE. Because the column FINAL_GRADE is not populated, the NULLIF function returns the value stored in the column NUMERIC_GRADE. This value is assigned to the variable v_final_grade and is displayed on the screen with the help of the DBMS_OUTPUT.PUT_LINE statement.

C) Change the order of columns in the NULLIF function. Run the modified version of the script, and explain the output produced.

ANSWER: The script should look similar to the following. Changes are shown in bold.

```
-- ch05_4c.sql, version 3.0
SET SERVEROUTPUT ON
DECLARE
   v_final_grade NUMBER;
BEGIN
   SELECT NULLIF(e.final_grade, g.numeric_grade)
     INTO v_final_grade
     FROM enrollment e
     JOIN grade g
       ON (e.student_id = g.student_id
       AND e.section_id = g.section_id)
    WHERE e.student_id = 102
      AND e.section_id = 86
      AND g.grade_type_code = 'FI';

   DBMS_OUTPUT.PUT_LINE ('Final grade: '||v_final_grade);
END;
```

The example produces the following output:

```
Final grade:

PL/SQL procedure successfully completed.
```

In this version of the script, the columns NUMERIC_GRADE and FINAL_GRADE are listed in the opposite order, as follows:

```
NULLIF(e.final_grade, g.numeric_grade)
```

The value stored in the column FINAL_GRADE is compared to the value stored in the column NUMERIC_GRADE. Because these values are not equal, the NULLIF function returns the value of the column FINAL_GRADE. This column is not populated, so NULL is assigned to the variable v_final_grade.

5.3.2 **Use the COALESCE Function**

In this exercise, you modify the following script. Instead of using the searched CASE expression, you use the COALESCE function.

```
-- ch05_5a.sql, version 1.0
SET SERVEROUTPUT ON
DECLARE
    v_num1    NUMBER := &sv_num1;
    v_num2    NUMBER := &sv_num2;
    v_num3    NUMBER := &sv_num3;
    v_result NUMBER;
BEGIN
```

```
    v_result := CASE
                    WHEN v_num1 IS NOT NULL THEN v_num1
                    ELSE
                        CASE
                            WHEN v_num2 IS NOT NULL THEN v_num2
                            ELSE v_num3
                        END
                    END;
    DBMS_OUTPUT.PUT_LINE ('Result: '||v_result);
END;
```

In the preceding script, the list consisting of three numbers is evaluated as follows: If the value of the first number is not NULL, the outer CASE expression returns the value of the first number. Otherwise, control is passed to the inner CASE expression, which evaluates the second number. If the value of the second number is not NULL, the inner CASE expression returns the value of the second number; in the opposite case, it returns the value of the third number.

The preceding CASE expression is equivalent to the following two CASE expressions:

```
CASE
    WHEN v_num1 IS NOT NULL THEN v_num1
    WHEN v_num2 IS NOT NULL THEN v_num2
    ELSE v_num3
END

CASE
    WHEN v_num1 IS NOT NULL THEN v_num1
    ELSE COALESCE(v_num2, v_num3)
END
```

Answer the following questions:

A) Modify script ch05_5a.sql. Substitute the COALESCE function for the CASE expression.

ANSWER: The script should look similar to the following. Changes are shown in bold.

```
-- ch05_5b.sql, version 2.0
SET SERVEROUTPUT ON
DECLARE
    v_num1   NUMBER := &sv_num1;
    v_num2   NUMBER := &sv_num2;
    v_num3   NUMBER := &sv_num3;
    v_result NUMBER;
BEGIN
    v_result := COALESCE(v_num1, v_num2, v_num3);
    DBMS_OUTPUT.PUT_LINE ('Result: '||v_result);
END;
```

In the original version of the script you used a nested CASE expression to assign a value to the variable v_result as follows:

```
CASE
    WHEN v_num1 IS NOT NULL THEN v_num1
    ELSE
        CASE
            WHEN v_num2 IS NOT NULL THEN v_num2
```

```
        ELSE v_num3
    END
END;
```

In the new version of the script, you substitute the COALESCE function for the CASE expression, as follows:

```
COALESCE(v_num1, v_num2, v_num3)
```

Based on the values stored in the variables v_num1, v_num2, and v_num3, the COALESCE function returns the first non-null variable.

B) Run the modified version of the script, and explain the output produced. Use the following values for the list of numbers: NULL, 1, 2.

ANSWER: The output should look similar to the following:

```
Enter value for sv_num1: null
old   2:    v_num1 NUMBER := &sv_num1;
new   2:    v_num1 NUMBER := null;
Enter value for sv_num2: 1
old   3:    v_num2 NUMBER := &sv_num2;
new   3:    v_num2 NUMBER := 1;
Enter value for sv_num3: 2
old   4:    v_num3 NUMBER := &sv_num3;
new   4:    v_num3 NUMBER := 2;
Result: 1

PL/SQL procedure successfully completed.
```

The COALESCE function evaluates its expressions in sequential order. The variable v_num1 is evaluated first. Because the variable v_num1 is NULL, the COALESCE function evaluates the variable v_num2 next. Because the variable v_num2 is not NULL, the COALESCE function returns the value of the variable v_num2. This value is assigned to the variable v_result and is displayed on the screen via a DBMS_OUTPUT.PUT_LINE statement.

C) What output is produced by the modified version of the script if NULL is provided for all three numbers? Try to explain your answer before you run the script.

ANSWER: The variables v_num1, v_num2, and v_num3 are evaluated in sequential order by the COALESCE function. When NULL is assigned to these variables, none of the evaluations produces a non-null result. So the COALESCE function returns NULL when all expressions evaluate to NULL.

The output should look similar to the following:

```
Enter value for sv_num1: null
old   2:    v_num1 NUMBER := &sv_num1;
new   2:    v_num1 NUMBER := null;
Enter value for sv_num2: null
old   3:    v_num2 NUMBER := &sv_num2;
new   3:    v_num2 NUMBER := null;
Enter value for sv_num3: null
old   4:    v_num3 NUMBER := &sv_num3;
new   4:    v_num3 NUMBER := null;
Result:

PL/SQL procedure successfully completed.
```

▼ TRY IT YOURSELF

In this chapter you've learned about different types of CASE statements and expressions. You've also learned about NULLIF and COALESCE functions. Here are some exercises based on the scripts you created in the "Try It Yourself" section in Chapter 4, "Conditional Control: IF Statements" that will help you test the depth of your understanding:

1) Create the following script. Modify the script you created in Chapter 4, project 1 of the "Try It Yourself" section. You can use either the CASE statement or the searched CASE statement. The output should look similar to the output produced by the example you created in Chapter 4.

2) Create the following script. Modify the script you created in Chapter 4, project 2. You can use either the CASE statement or the searched CASE statement. The output should look similar to the output produced by the example you created in Chapter 4.

3) Execute the following two SELECT statements, and explain why they produce different output:

```
SELECT e.student_id, e.section_id, e.final_grade, g.numeric_grade,
       COALESCE(g.numeric_grade, e.final_grade) grade
  FROM enrollment e, grade g
 WHERE e.student_id = g.student_id
   AND e.section_id = g.section_id
   AND e.student_id = 102
   AND g.grade_type_code = 'FI';


SELECT e.student_id, e.section_id, e.final_grade, g.numeric_grade,
       NULLIF(g.numeric_grade, e.final_grade) grade
  FROM enrollment e, grade g
 WHERE e.student_id = g.student_id
   AND e.section_id = g.section_id
   AND e.student_id = 102
   AND g.grade_type_code = 'FI';
```

The projects in this section are meant to have you use all the skills you have acquired throughout this chapter. The answers to these projects can be found in Appendix D and on this book's companion Web site. Visit the Web site periodically to share and discuss your answers.

CHAPTER 6

Iterative Control: Part I

CHAPTER OBJECTIVES

In this chapter, you will learn about

- ▶ Simple loops
- ▶ WHILE loops
- ▶ Numeric FOR loops

Generally, computer programs are written because certain tasks must be executed a number of times. For example, many companies need to process transactions on a monthly basis. A program allows the completion of this task by being executed at the end of each month.

Similarly, programs incorporate instructions that need to be executed repeatedly. For example, a program may need to write a number of records to a table. By using a loop, the program can write the desired number of records to a table. In other words, loops are programming facilities that allow a set of instructions to be executed repeatedly.

PL/SQL has four types of loops: simple loops, WHILE loops, numeric FOR loops, and cursor FOR loops. This chapter explores the first three kinds of loops. The next chapter explores how these types of loops can be nested within each other. In addition, you will learn about the CONTINUE and CONTINUE WHEN statements, introduced in Oracle 11g. Cursor FOR loops are discussed in Chapters 11 and 12.

LAB 6.1
Simple Loops

LAB OBJECTIVES

After completing this lab, you will be able to

▶ Use simple loops with EXIT conditions

▶ Use simple loops with EXIT WHEN conditions

A simple loop, as you can tell from its name, is the most basic kind of loop. It has the following structure:

```
LOOP
    STATEMENT 1;
    STATEMENT 2;
    . . .
    STATEMENT N;
END LOOP;
```

The reserved word LOOP marks the beginning of the simple loop. Statements 1 through N are a sequence of statements that is executed repeatedly. These statements consist of one or more standard programming structures. END LOOP is a reserved phrase that indicates the end of the loop construct.

This flow of logic is illustrated in Figure 6.1.

Every time the loop iterates, a sequence of statements is executed, and then control is passed back to the top of the loop. The sequence of statements is executed an infinite number of times, because no statement specifies when the loop must terminate. Hence, a simple loop is called an infinite loop because there is no means to exit the loop. A properly constructed loop needs an exit condition that determines when the loop is complete. This exit condition has two forms: EXIT and EXIT WHEN.

EXIT STATEMENT

The EXIT statement causes a loop to terminate when the EXIT condition evaluates to TRUE. The EXIT condition is evaluated with the help of an IF statement. When the EXIT condition is evaluated to TRUE, control is passed to the first executable statement after the END LOOP statement. This is indicated by the following:

```
LOOP
    STATEMENT 1;
    STATEMENT 2;
```

```
    IF CONDITION THEN
        EXIT;
    END IF;
END LOOP;
STATEMENT 3;
```

In this example, you can see that after the EXIT condition evaluates to TRUE, control is passed to *STATEMENT 3*, which is the first executable statement after the END LOOP statement.

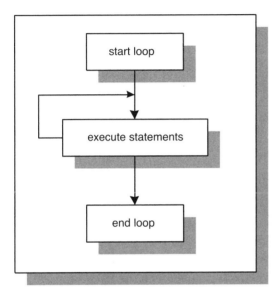

FIGURE 6.1
A simple loop

DID YOU KNOW?

The EXIT statement is valid only when placed inside a loop. When placed outside a loop, it causes a syntax error. To avoid this error, use the RETURN statement to terminate a PL/SQL block before its normal end is reached:

```
BEGIN
    DBMS_OUTPUT.PUT_LINE ('Line 1');
    RETURN;
    DBMS_OUTPUT.PUT_LINE ('Line 2');
END;
```

This example produces the following output:

```
Line 1
PL/SQL procedure successfully completed.
```

Because the RETURN statement terminates the PL/SQL block, the second DBMS_OUTPUT.PUT_LINE statement is never executed.

EXIT WHEN STATEMENT

The EXIT WHEN statement causes a loop to terminate only if the EXIT WHEN condition evaluates to TRUE. Control is then passed to the first executable statement after the END LOOP statement. The structure of a loop using an EXIT WHEN clause is as follows:

```
LOOP
    STATEMENT 1;
    STATEMENT 2;
    EXIT WHEN CONDITION;
END LOOP;
STATEMENT 3;
```

Figure 6.2 shows this flow of logic from the EXIT and EXIT WHEN statements.

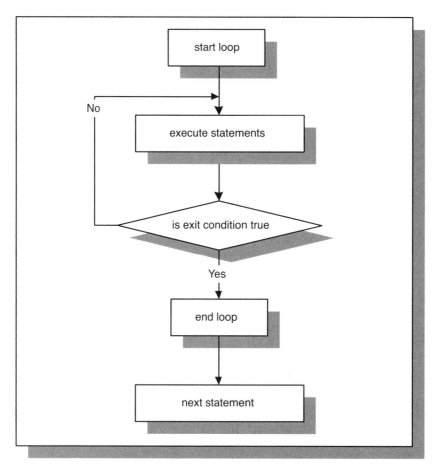

FIGURE 6.2
A simple loop with the EXIT condition

Figure 6.2 shows that during each iteration, the loop executes a sequence of statements. Control is then passed to the loop's EXIT condition. If the EXIT condition evaluates to FALSE, control is passed to the top of the loop. The sequence of statements is executed repeatedly until the EXIT condition evaluates to TRUE. When the EXIT condition evaluates to TRUE, the loop is terminated, and control is passed to the next executable statement following the loop.

Figure 6.2 also shows that the EXIT condition is included in the body of the loop. Therefore, the decision about loop termination is made inside the body of the loop, and the body of the loop, or a part of it, is always executed at least once. However, the number of iterations of the loop depends on the evaluation of the EXIT condition and is not known until the loop completes.

As mentioned earlier, Figure 6.2 illustrates that the flow of logic for the structure of EXIT and EXIT WHEN statements is the same even though two different forms of the EXIT condition are used. In other words,

```
IF CONDITION THEN
    EXIT;
END IF;
```

is equivalent to

```
EXIT WHEN CONDITION;
```

WATCH OUT!

It is important to note that when the EXIT statement is used without an EXIT condition, the simple loop executes only once. Consider the following example.

```
DECLARE
    v_counter NUMBER := 0;
BEGIN
    LOOP
        DBMS_OUTPUT.PUT_LINE ('v_counter = '||v_counter);
        EXIT;
    END LOOP;
END;
```

This example produces the following output:

```
v_counter = 0
PL/SQL procedure successfully completed.
```

Because the EXIT statement is used without an EXIT condition, the loop is terminated as soon as the EXIT statement is executed.

▼ LAB 6.1 EXERCISES

This section provides exercises and suggested answers, with discussion related to how those answers resulted. The most important thing to realize is whether your answer works. You should figure out the implications of the answers and what the effects are of any different answers you may come up with.

6.1.1 **Use Simple Loops with EXIT Conditions**

In this exercise, you use the EXIT condition to terminate a simple loop, and a special variable, $v\_counter$, which keeps count of the loop iterations. With each iteration of the loop, the value of $v\_counter$ is incremented and displayed on the screen.

Create the following PL/SQL script:

```
-- ch06_1a.sql, version 1.0
SET SERVEROUTPUT ON
DECLARE
   v_counter BINARY_INTEGER := 0;
BEGIN
   LOOP
      -- increment loop counter by one
      v_counter := v_counter + 1;
      DBMS_OUTPUT.PUT_LINE ('v_counter = '||v_counter);

      -- if EXIT condition yields TRUE exit the loop
      IF v_counter = 5 THEN
         EXIT;
      END IF;

   END LOOP;
   -- control resumes here
   DBMS_OUTPUT.PUT_LINE ('Done...');
END;
```

The statement

```
v_counter := v_counter + 1;
```

is used often when working with a loop. Variable $v\_counter$ is a loop counter that tracks the number of times the statements in the body of the loop are executed. You will notice that for each iteration of the loop, its value is incremented by 1. However, it is very important to initialize the variable $v\_counter$ for successful termination of the loop. If $v\_counter$ is not initialized, its value is NULL. Then, the statement

```
v_counter := v_counter + 1;
```

never increments the value of $v\_counter$ by 1, because NULL + 1 evaluates to NULL. As a result, the EXIT condition never yields TRUE, and the loop becomes infinite.

Execute the script, and then answer the following questions.

A) What output appears on the screen?

ANSWER: The output should look like the following:

```
v_counter = 1
v_counter = 2
v_counter = 3
v_counter = 4
v_counter = 5
Done...

PL/SQL procedure successfully completed.
```

Every time the loop is run, the statements in the body of the loop are executed. In this script, the value of $v\_counter$ is incremented by 1 and displayed on the screen. The EXIT condition is evaluated for each value of $v\_counter$. When the value of $v\_counter$ increases to 5, the loop is terminated. For the first iteration of the loop, the value of $v\_counter$ is equal to 1, and it is displayed on the screen, and so forth. After the loop has terminated, $Done\ .\ .\ .$ is displayed on the screen.

B) How many times did the loop execute?

ANSWER: The loop executed five times.

When the value of $v\_counter$ increases to 5, the IF statement

```
IF v_counter = 5 THEN
    EXIT;
END IF;
```

evaluates to TRUE, and the loop is terminated.

The loop counter tracks how many times the loop is executed. You will notice that in this exercise, the maximum value of $v\_counter$ is equal to the number of times the loop is iterated.

C) What is the EXIT condition for this loop?

ANSWER: The EXIT condition for this loop is $v\_counter = 5$.

The EXIT condition is used as a part of an IF statement. The IF statement evaluates the EXIT condition to TRUE or FALSE, based on the current value of $v\_counter$.

D) How many times is the value of the variable $v\_counter$ displayed if the DBMS_OUTPUT.PUT_LINE statement is used after the END IF statement?

ANSWER: The value of $v\_counter$ is displayed four times.

```
LOOP
    v_counter := v_counter + 1;
    IF v_counter = 5 THEN
        EXIT;
    END IF;
    DBMS_OUTPUT.PUT_LINE ('v_counter = '||v_counter);
END LOOP;
```

Assume that the loop has already iterated four times. Then the value of $v\_counter$ is incremented by 1, so $v\_counter$ is equal to 5. Next, the IF statement evaluates the EXIT condition. The EXIT condition yields TRUE, and the loop is terminated. The DBMS_OUTPUT.PUT_LINE statement is not executed for the fifth iteration of the loop, because control is passed to the next executable statement after the END LOOP statement. Thus, only four values of $v\_counter$ are displayed on the screen.

E) Why does the number of times the loop counter value is displayed on the screen differ when the DBMS_OUTPUT.PUT_LINE statement is placed after the END IF statement?

ANSWER: When the DBMS_OUTPUT.PUT_LINE statement is placed before the IF statement, the value of $v\_counter$ is displayed on the screen first. Then the IF statement evaluates it. The fifth iteration of the loop $v\_counter = 5$ is displayed first, and then the EXIT condition yields TRUE, and the loop is terminated.

When the DBMS_OUTPUT.PUT_LINE statement is placed after the END IF statement, the EXIT condition is evaluated before the DBMS_OUTPUT.PUT_LINE statement is executed. Thus, for the fifth iteration of the loop, the EXIT condition evaluates to TRUE before the value of $v\_counter$ is displayed on the screen by the DBMS_OUTPUT.PUT_LINE statement.

F) Rewrite this script using the EXIT WHEN condition instead of the EXIT condition so that it produces the same result.

ANSWER: The script should look similar to the following. Changes are shown in bold.

```
-- ch06_1b.sql, version 2.0
SET SERVEROUTPUT ON
DECLARE
    v_counter BINARY_INTEGER := 0;
BEGIN
    LOOP
        -- increment loop counter by one
        v_counter := v_counter + 1;
        DBMS_OUTPUT.PUT_LINE ('v_counter = '||v_counter);

        -- if EXIT WHEN condition yields TRUE exit the loop
        EXIT WHEN v_counter = 5;
    END LOOP;

    -- control resumes here
    DBMS_OUTPUT.PUT_LINE ('Done...');
END;
```

Notice that the IF statement has been replaced by the EXIT WHEN statement. The rest of the statements in the body of the loop do not need to be changed.

6.1.2 Use Simple Loops with EXIT WHEN Conditions

In this exercise, you use the EXIT WHEN condition to terminate the loop. You add a number of sections for a given course number. Try to answer the questions before you run the script. After you have answered the questions, run the script and check your answers.

Create the following PL/SQL script:

```
-- ch06_2a.sql, version 1.0
SET SERVEROUTPUT ON
DECLARE
    v_course        course.course_no%type := 430;
    v_instructor_id instructor.instructor_id%type := 102;
    v_sec_num       section.section_no%type := 0;
BEGIN
    LOOP
        -- increment section number by one
        v_sec_num := v_sec_num + 1;
        INSERT INTO section
            (section_id, course_no, section_no, instructor_id,
             created_date, created_by, modified_date,
             modified_by)
        VALUES
            (section_id_seq.nextval, v_course, v_sec_num,
             v_instructor_id, SYSDATE, USER, SYSDATE, USER);

        -- if number of sections added is four exit the loop
        EXIT WHEN v_sec_num = 4;
```

```
    END LOOP;

    -- control resumes here
    COMMIT;
END;
```

Notice that the INSERT statement contains an Oracle built-in function called USER. At first glance, this function looks like a variable that has not been declared. This function returns the name of the current user. In other words, it returns the login name that you use when connecting to Oracle.

Try to answer the following questions, and then execute the script:

A) How many sections will be added for the specified course number?

ANSWER: Four sections will be added for the given course number.

B) How many times will the loop be executed if the course number is invalid?

ANSWER: The loop will be partially executed once.

If the course number is invalid, the INSERT statement

```
INSERT INTO section
    (section_id, course_no, section_no, instructor_id,
     created_date, created_by, modified_date, modified_by)
VALUES
    (section_id_seq.nextval, v_course, v_sec_num,
     v_instructor_id, SYSDATE, USER, SYSDATE, USER);
```

causes the integrity constraint violation error shown next. As soon as this error occurs, the program terminates. This termination causes partial execution of the loop because the EXIT WHEN statement does not execute even once.

```
DECLARE
*
ERROR at line 1:
ORA-02291: integrity constraint (STUDENT.SECT_CRSE_FK) violated -
parent key not found
ORA-06512: at line 9
```

Note that `line 9` refers to the INSERT statement inside the body of the loop. Therefore, if the course number is invalid, the loop partially executes once.

C) How would you change this script to add ten sections for the specified course number?

ANSWER: The script should look similar to the following script. Changes are shown in bold.

```
-- ch06_2b.sql, version 2.0
DECLARE
    v_course        course.course_no%type := 430;
    v_instructor_id instructor.instructor_id%type := 102;
    v_sec_num       section.section_no%type := 0;
BEGIN
    LOOP
        -- increment section number by one
        v_sec_num := v_sec_num + 1;
        INSERT INTO section
            (section_id, course_no, section_no, instructor_id,
             created_date, created_by, modified_date,
```

```
        modified_by)
    VALUES
        (section_id_seq.nextval, v_course, v_sec_num,
            v_instructor_id, SYSDATE, USER, SYSDATE, USER);

        -- if number of sections added is ten exit the loop
        EXIT WHEN v_sec_num = 10;
    END LOOP;

    -- control resumes here
    COMMIT;
END;
```

To add ten sections for the given course number, the test value of v_sec_num in the EXIT condition is changed to 10.

Note that before you execute this version of the script you need to delete records from the SECTION table that were added when you executed the original example. If you did not run the original script, you do not need to delete records from the SECTION table.

The SECTION table has a unique constraint defined on the COURSE_NO and SECTION_NO columns. In other words, the combination of course and section numbers allows you to uniquely identify each row of the table. When the original script is executed, it creates four records in the SECTION table for course number 430, section numbers 1, 2, 3, and 4. When the new version of this script is executed, the unique constraint defined on the SECTION table is violated because there already are records corresponding to course number 430 and section numbers 1, 2, 3, and 4. Therefore, these rows must be deleted from the SECTION table as follows:

```
DELETE FROM section
 WHERE course_no = 430
   AND section_no <= 4;

COMMIT;
```

As soon as these records are deleted from the SECTION table, you can execute the new version of the script.

D) How would you change the script to add only even-numbered sections (the maximum section number is 10) for the specified course number?

ANSWER: The script should look similar to the following script. Changes are shown in bold. To run this script, you need to delete records from the SECTION table that were added by the previous version. With each iteration of the loop, the value of v_sec_num should be incremented by two, as shown:

```
-- ch06_2c.sql, version 3.0
SET SERVEROUTPUT ON
DECLARE
    v_course        course.course_no%type := 430;
    v_instructor_id instructor.instructor_id%type := 102;
    v_sec_num       section.section_no%type := 0;
BEGIN
    LOOP
        -- increment section number by two
        v_sec_num := v_sec_num + 2;
        INSERT INTO section
```

```
        (section_id, course_no, section_no, instructor_id,
         created_date, created_by, modified_date,
         modified_by)
    VALUES
        (section_id_seq.nextval, v_course, v_sec_num,
         v_instructor_id, SYSDATE, USER, SYSDATE, USER);

    -- if number of sections added is ten exit the loop
    EXIT WHEN v_sec_num = 10;
  END LOOP;

  -- control resumes here
  COMMIT;
END;
```

E) How many times does the loop execute in this case?

ANSWER: The loop executes five times when even-numbered sections are added for the given course number.

LAB 6.2
WHILE Loops

LAB OBJECTIVES

After completing this lab, you will be able to

▶ Use WHILE loops

A WHILE loop has the following structure:

```
WHILE CONDITION LOOP
    STATEMENT 1;
    STATEMENT 2;
    ...
    STATEMENT N;
END LOOP;
```

The reserved word WHILE marks the beginning of a loop construct. The word CONDITION is the test condition of the loop that evaluates to TRUE or FALSE. The result of this evaluation determines whether the loop is executed. Statements 1 through N are a sequence of statements that is executed repeatedly. The END LOOP is a reserved phrase that indicates the end of the loop construct.

This flow of logic is illustrated in Figure 6.3.

Figure 6.3 shows that the test condition is evaluated prior to each iteration of the loop. If the test condition evaluates to TRUE, the sequence of statements is executed, and control is passed to the top of the loop for the next evaluation of the test condition. If the test condition evaluates to FALSE, the loop is terminated, and control is passed to the next executable statement following the loop.

As mentioned earlier, before the body of the loop can be executed, the test condition must be evaluated. The decision as to whether to execute the statements in the body of the loop is made prior to entering the loop. As a result, the loop is not executed if the test condition yields FALSE.

FOR EXAMPLE

```
DECLARE
   v_counter NUMBER := 5;
BEGIN
   WHILE v_counter < 5 LOOP
      DBMS_OUTPUT.PUT_LINE ('v_counter = '||v_counter);
```

```
        -- decrement the value of v_counter by one
        v_counter := v_counter - 1;
    END LOOP;
END;
```

In this example, the body of the loop is not executed at all because the test condition of the loop evaluates to FALSE.

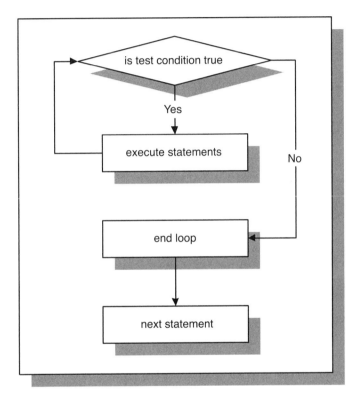

FIGURE 6.3
WHILE loop

The test condition must evaluate to TRUE at least once for the statements in the loop to execute. However, it is important to ensure that the test condition will eventually evaluate to FALSE, as well. Otherwise, the WHILE loop executes continually.

FOR EXAMPLE

```
DECLARE
    v_counter NUMBER := 1;
BEGIN
    WHILE v_counter < 5 LOOP
```

```
      DBMS_OUTPUT.PUT_LINE('v_counter = '||v_counter);

      -- decrement the value of v_counter by one
      v_counter := v_counter - 1;
   END LOOP;
END;
```

This is an example of an infinite WHILE loop. The test condition always evaluates to TRUE, because the value of v_counter is decremented by 1 and is always less than 5.

DID YOU KNOW?

Boolean expressions can also be used to determine when the loop should terminate.

```
DECLARE
   v_test BOOLEAN := TRUE;
BEGIN
   WHILE v_test LOOP
      STATEMENTS;
      IF TEST_CONDITION THEN
         v_test := FALSE;
      END IF;
   END LOOP;
END;
```

When using a Boolean expression as a test condition of a loop, you must make sure that a different value is eventually assigned to the Boolean variable to exit the loop. Otherwise, the loop becomes infinite.

PREMATURE TERMINATION OF THE LOOP

The EXIT and EXIT WHEN statements can be used inside the body of a WHILE loop. If the EXIT condition evaluates to TRUE before the test condition evaluates to FALSE, the loop is terminated prematurely. If the test condition yields FALSE before the EXIT condition yields TRUE, there is no premature termination of the loop. This is indicated as follows:

```
WHILE TEST_CONDITION LOOP
   STATEMENT 1;
   STATEMENT 2;

   IF EXIT_CONDITION THEN
      EXIT;
   END IF;
END LOOP;
STATEMENT 3;
```

or

```
WHILE TEST_CONDITION LOOP
   STATEMENT 1;
   STATEMENT 2;
```

```
      EXIT WHEN EXIT_CONDITION;
   END LOOP;
   STATEMENT 3;
```

Consider the following example.

FOR EXAMPLE

```
DECLARE
   v_counter NUMBER := 1;
BEGIN
   WHILE v_counter <= 5 LOOP
      DBMS_OUTPUT.PUT_LINE ('v_counter = '||v_counter);

      IF v_counter = 2 THEN
         EXIT;
      END IF;

      v_counter := v_counter + 1;
   END LOOP;
END;
```

Before the statements in the body of the WHILE loop are executed, the test condition

```
   v_counter <= 5
```

must evaluate to TRUE. Then, the value of v_counter is displayed on the screen and incremented by one. Next, the EXIT condition

```
   v_counter = 2
```

is evaluated, and as soon as the value of v_counter reaches 2, the loop is terminated.

Notice that according to the test condition, the loop should execute five times. However, the loop is executed only twice, because the EXIT condition is present inside the body of the loop. Therefore, the loop terminates prematurely.

Now try to reverse the test condition and EXIT condition as shown in the following example.

FOR EXAMPLE

```
DECLARE
   v_counter NUMBER := 1;
BEGIN
   WHILE v_counter <= 2 LOOP
      DBMS_OUTPUT.PUT_LINE ('v_counter = '||v_counter);
      v_counter := v_counter + 1;

      IF v_counter = 5 THEN
         EXIT;
      END IF;
   END LOOP;
END;
```

In this example, the test condition is

```
v_counter <= 2
```

and the EXIT condition is

```
v_counter = 5
```

In this case, the loop is executed twice as well. However, it does not terminate prematurely, because the EXIT condition never evaluates to TRUE. As soon as the value of `v_counter` reaches 3, the test condition evaluates to FALSE, and the loop is terminated.

Both examples, when run, produce the following output:

```
v_counter = 1
v_counter = 2

PL/SQL procedure successfully completed.
```

These examples demonstrate not only the use of the EXIT statement inside the body of the WHILE loop, but also a bad programming practice. In the first example, the test condition can be changed so that there is no need to use an EXIT condition, because essentially they both are used to terminate the loop. In the second example, the EXIT condition is useless, because its terminal value is never reached. You should never use unnecessary code in your program.

▼ LAB 6.2 EXERCISES

This section provides exercises and suggested answers, with discussion related to how those answers resulted. The most important thing to realize is whether your answer works. You should figure out the implications of the answers and what the effects are of any different answers you may come up with.

6.2.1 Use WHILE Loops

In this exercise, you use a WHILE loop to calculate the sum of the integers between 1 and 10.

Create the following PL/SQL script:

```
-- ch06_3a.sql, version 1.0
SET SERVEROUTPUT ON
DECLARE
   v_counter BINARY_INTEGER := 1;
      v_sum NUMBER := 0;
BEGIN
   WHILE v_counter <= 10 LOOP
      v_sum := v_sum + v_counter;
      DBMS_OUTPUT.PUT_LINE ('Current sum is: '||v_sum);

      -- increment loop counter by one
      v_counter := v_counter + 1;
   END LOOP;

   -- control resumes here
```

```
        DBMS_OUTPUT.PUT_LINE ('The sum of integers between 1 '||
                       'and 10 is: '||v_sum);
    END;
```

Execute the script, and then answer the following questions:

A) What output appears on the screen?

ANSWER: The output should look like the following:

```
Current sum is: 1
Current sum is: 3
Current sum is: 6
Current sum is: 10
Current sum is: 15
Current sum is: 21
Current sum is: 28
Current sum is: 36
Current sum is: 45
Current sum is: 55
The sum of integers between 1 and 10 is: 55

PL/SQL procedure successfully completed.
```

Every time the loop is run, the value of $v\_counter$ is checked in the test condition. While the value of $v\_counter$ is less than or equal to 10, the statements inside the body of the loop are executed. In this script, the value of v_sum is calculated and displayed on the screen. Next, the value of $v\_counter$ is incremented, and control is passed to the top of the loop. When the value of $v\_counter$ increases to 11, the loop is terminated.

For the first iteration of the loop, the value of v_sum is equal to 1, according to the statement

```
v_sum := v_sum + v_counter
```

After the value of v_sum is calculated, the value of $v\_counter$ is incremented by 1. Then, for the second iteration of the loop, the value of v_sum is equal to 3, because 2 is added to the old value of v_sum.

After the loop has terminated, "The sum of integers..." is displayed on the screen.

B) What is the test condition for this loop?

ANSWER: The test condition for this loop is $v\_counter <= 10$.

C) How many times did the loop execute?

ANSWER: The loop executed 10 times.

As soon as the value of $v\_counter$ reaches 11, the test condition

```
v_counter <= 10
```

evaluates to FALSE, and the loop is terminated.

As mentioned earlier, the loop counter tracks the number of times the loop is executed. You will notice that in this exercise, the maximum value of $v\_counter$ is equal to the number of times the loop is iterated.

D) How many times will the loop execute

  I) if $v\_counter$ is not initialized?

  II) if $v\_counter$ is initialized to 0?

  III) if $v\_counter$ is initialized to 10?

ANSWER:

  I) If the value of $v\_counter$ is not initialized to a value, the loop does not execute.

  For the loop to execute at least once, the test condition must evaluate to TRUE at least once. If the value of $v\_counter$ is only declared and not initialized, it is NULL. It is important to remember that null variables cannot be compared to other variables or values. Therefore, the test condition

```
v_counter <= 10
```

  never evaluates to TRUE, and the loop is not executed.

  II) If $v\_counter$ is initialized to 0, the loop executes 11 times instead of 10, because the minimum value of $v\_counter$ has decreased by 1.

  When $v\_counter$ is initialized to 0, the range of integers for which the test condition of the loop evaluates to TRUE becomes 0 to 10. The given range of the integers has 11 numbers. As a result, the loop iterates 11 times.

  III) If $v\_counter$ is initialized to 10, the loop executes once.

  When the initial value of $v\_counter$ equals 10, the test condition evaluates to TRUE for the first iteration of the loop. Inside the body of the loop, the value of $v\_counter$ is incremented by 1. As a result, for the second iteration of the loop, the test condition evaluates to FALSE, because 11 is not less than or equal to 10, and control is passed to the next executable statement after the loop.

E) How does the value of v_sum change based on the initial value of $v\_counter$ from the preceding question?

  ANSWER: When $v\_counter$ is not initialized, the loop is not executed. Therefore, the value of v_sum does not change from its initial value; it stays 0.

  When $v\_counter$ is initialized to 0, the loop is executed 11 times. The value of v_sum is calculated 11 times as well. However, after the loop completes, the value of v_sum is 55, because 0 is added to v_sum during the first iteration of the loop.

  When $v\_counter$ is initialized to 10, the loop is executed once. As a result, the value of v_sum is incremented only once by 10. After the loop is complete, the value of v_sum is equal to 10.

F) What is the value of v_sum if it is not initialized?

  ANSWER: The value of v_sum is NULL if it is not initialized to some value.

  The value of v_sum in the statement

```
v_sum := v_sum + 1
```

  is always equal to NULL, because NULL + 1 is NULL. It was mentioned previously that NULL variables cannot be compared to other variable or values. Similarly, calculations cannot be performed on null variables.

G) How would you change the script to calculate the sum of the even integers between 1 and 100?

  ANSWER: The script should be similar to the following. Changes are shown in bold.

  Notice that the value of $v\_counter$ is initialized to 2, and with each iteration of the loop, the value of $v\_counter$ is incremented by 2 as well.

```
-- ch06_3b.sql, version 2.0
SET SERVEROUTPUT ON
DECLARE
   v_counter BINARY_INTEGER := 2;
   v_sum      NUMBER := 0;
BEGIN
   WHILE v_counter <= 100 LOOP
      v_sum := v_sum + v_counter;
      DBMS_OUTPUT.PUT_LINE ('Current sum is: '||v_sum);

      -- increment loop counter by two
      v_counter := v_counter + 2;
   END LOOP;

   -- control resumes here
   DBMS_OUTPUT.PUT_LINE ('The sum of even integers between '||
                    '1 and 100 is: '||v_sum);
END;
```

LAB 6.3
Numeric FOR Loops

LAB OBJECTIVES

After completing this lab, you will be able to

▶ Use numeric FOR loops with the IN option
▶ Use numeric FOR loops with the REVERSE option

A numeric FOR loop is called numeric because it requires an integer as its terminating value. Its structure is as follows:

```
FOR loop_counter IN [REVERSE] lower_limit..upper_limit LOOP
    STATEMENT 1;
    STATEMENT 2;
    ...
    STATEMENT N;
END LOOP;
```

The reserved word FOR marks the beginning of a FOR loop construct. The variable `loop_counter` is an implicitly defined index variable. There is no need to define the loop counter in the declaration section of the PL/SQL block. This variable is defined by the loop construct. `lower_limit` and `upper_limit` are two integer numbers or expressions that evaluate to integer values at runtime, and the double dot (..) serves as the range operator. `lower_limit` and `upper_limit` define the number of iterations for the loop, and their values are evaluated once, for the first iteration of the loop. At this point, it is determined how many times the loop will iterate. Statements 1 through N are a sequence of statements that is executed repeatedly. END LOOP is a reserved phrase that marks the end of the loop construct.

The reserved word IN or IN REVERSE must be present when the loop is defined. If the REVERSE keyword is used, the loop counter iterates from the upper limit to the lower limit. However, the syntax for the limit specification does not change. The lower limit is always referenced first. This flow of logic is illustrated in Figure 6.4.

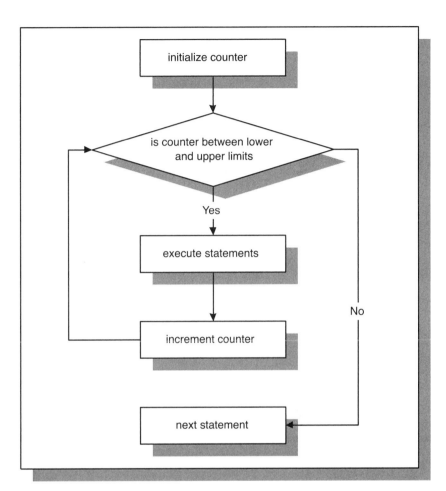

FIGURE 6.4
Numeric FOR loop

Figure 6.4 shows that the loop counter is initialized to the lower limit for the first iteration of the loop only. However, the value of the loop counter is tested for each iteration of the loop. As long as the value of v_counter ranges from the lower limit to the upper limit, the statements inside the body of the loop are executed. When the value of the loop counter does not satisfy the range specified by the lower limit and the upper limit, control is passed to the first executable statement outside the loop.

FOR EXAMPLE

```
BEGIN
   FOR v_counter IN 1..5 LOOP
      DBMS_OUTPUT.PUT_LINE ('v_counter = '||v_counter);
   END LOOP;
END;
```

In this example, there is no declaration section for the PL/SQL block because the only variable used, v_counter, is the loop counter. Numbers 1..5 specify the range of the integer numbers for which this loop is executed.

Notice that there is no statement

```
   v_counter := v_counter + 1;
```

anywhere, inside or outside the body of the loop. The value of v_counter is incremented implicitly by the FOR loop itself.

This example produces the following output when run:

```
   v_counter = 1
   v_counter = 2
   v_counter = 3
   v_counter = 4
   v_counter = 5

   PL/SQL procedure successfully completed.
```

As a matter of fact, if you include the statement

```
   v_counter := v_counter + 1;
```

in the body of the loop, the PL/SQL script compiles with errors. Consider the following example:

FOR EXAMPLE

```
BEGIN
   FOR v_counter IN 1..5 LOOP
      v_counter := v_counter + 1;
      DBMS_OUTPUT.PUT_LINE ('v_counter = '|| v_counter);
   END LOOP;
END;
```

When this example is run, the following error message is produced:

```
   BEGIN
   *
   ERROR at line 1:
   ORA-06550: line 3, column 7:
```

```
PLS-00363: expression 'V_COUNTER' cannot be used as an assignment
target
ORA-06550: line 3, column 7:
PL/SQL: Statement ignored
```

WATCH OUT!

It is important to remember that the loop counter is implicitly defined and incremented when a numeric FOR loop is used. As a result, it cannot be referenced outside the body of the FOR loop. Consider the following example:

```
BEGIN
    FOR v_counter IN 1..5 LOOP
        DBMS_OUTPUT.PUT_LINE ('v_counter = '||v_counter);
    END LOOP;
    DBMS_OUTPUT.PUT_LINE
        ('Counter outside the loop is '||v_counter);
END;
```

When this example is run, the following error message is produced:

```
        ('Counter outside the loop is '||v_counter);
                                           *
ERROR at line 6:
ORA-06550: line 6, column 40:
PLS-00201: identifier 'V_COUNTER' must be declared
ORA-06550: line 5, column 4:
PL/SQL: Statement ignored
```

Because the loop counter is declared implicitly by the loop, the variable v_counter cannot be referenced outside the loop. As soon as the loop completes, the loop counter ceases to exist.

USING THE REVERSE OPTION IN THE LOOP

Earlier in this section, you encountered two options that are available when the value of the loop counter is evaluated, IN and IN REVERSE. You have seen examples that demonstrate the usage of the IN option for the loop. The next example demonstrates the usage of the IN REVERSE option for the loop.

FOR EXAMPLE

```
BEGIN
    FOR v_counter IN REVERSE 1..5 LOOP
        DBMS_OUTPUT.PUT_LINE ('v_counter = '||v_counter);
    END LOOP;
END;
```

When this example is run, the following output is produced:

```
    v_counter = 5
    v_counter = 4
    v_counter = 3
```

```
v_counter = 2
v_counter = 1

PL/SQL procedure successfully completed.
```

As mentioned, even though the REVERSE keyword is present, the lower limit of the loop is referenced first. However, it is important to note that the loop counter is evaluated from the upper limit to the lower limit. For the first iteration of the loop, v_counter (in our case it is a loop counter) is initialized to 5 (upper limit). Then its value is displayed on the screen. For the second iteration of the loop, the value of v_counter is decreased by 1 and displayed on the screen.

Notice that the number of times the body of the loop is executed is not affected by the option used, IN or IN REVERSE. Only the values assigned to the lower limit and the upper limit determine how many times the body of the loop is executed.

PREMATURE TERMINATION OF THE LOOP

The EXIT and EXIT WHEN statements covered in the previous labs can be used inside the body of a numeric FOR loop as well. If the EXIT condition evaluates to TRUE before the loop counter reaches its terminal value, the FOR loop is terminated prematurely. If the loop counter reaches its terminal value before the EXIT condition yields TRUE, the FOR loop doesn't terminate prematurely. Consider the following:

```
FOR LOOP_COUNTER IN LOWER_LIMIT..UPPER_LIMIT LOOP
    STATEMENT 1;
    STATEMENT 2;
    IF EXIT_CONDITION THEN
        EXIT;
    END IF;
END LOOP;
STATEMENT 3;
```

or

```
FOR LOOP_COUNTER IN LOWER_LIMIT..UPPER_LIMIT LOOP
    STATEMENT 1;
    STATEMENT 2;
    EXIT WHEN EXIT_CONDITION;
END LOOP;
STATEMENT 3;
```

Consider the following example of a FOR loop that uses the EXIT WHEN condition. This condition causes the loop to terminate prematurely.

FOR EXAMPLE

```
BEGIN
   FOR v_counter IN 1..5 LOOP
      DBMS_OUTPUT.PUT_LINE ('v_counter = '||v_counter);
      EXIT WHEN v_counter = 3;
   END LOOP;
END;
```

Notice that according to the range specified, the loop should execute five times. However, the loop is executed only three times because the EXIT condition is present inside the body of the loop. Thus, the loop terminates prematurely.

▼ LAB 6.3 EXERCISES

This section provides exercises and suggested answers, with discussion related to how those answers resulted. The most important thing to realize is whether your answer works. You should figure out the implications of the answers and what the effects are of any different answers you may come up with.

6.3.1 Use Numeric FOR Loops with the IN Option

In this exercise, you use a numeric FOR loop to calculate a factorial of 10 (10! = 1*2*3...*10).

Create the following PL/SQL script:

```
-- ch06_4a.sql, version 1.0
SET SERVEROUTPUT ON
DECLARE
   v_factorial NUMBER := 1;
BEGIN
   FOR v_counter IN 1..10 LOOP
      v_factorial := v_factorial * v_counter;
   END LOOP;

   -- control resumes here
   DBMS_OUTPUT.PUT_LINE
      ('Factorial of ten is: '||v_factorial);
END;
```

Execute the script, and then answer the following questions:

A) What output appears on the screen?

ANSWER: The output should look like the following:

```
Factorial of ten is: 3628800

PL/SQL procedure successfully completed.
```

Every time the loop is run, the value of $v\_counter$ is incremented by 1 implicitly, and the current value of the factorial is calculated. As soon as the value of $v\_counter$ increases to 10, the loop is run for the last time. At this point, the final value of the factorial is calculated, and the loop is terminated. After the loop has terminated, control is passed to the first statement outside the loop—in this case, DBMS_OUTPUT.PUT_LINE.

B) How many times did the loop execute?

ANSWER: The loop executed ten times according to the range specified by the loop's lower and upper limits. In this example, the lower limit equals 1, and the upper limit equals 10.

C) What is the value of the loop counter before the loop?

ANSWER: The loop counter is defined implicitly by the loop. Therefore, before the loop, the loop counter is undefined and has no value.

D) What is the value of the loop counter after the loop?

ANSWER: Similarly, after the loop has completed, the loop counter is undefined again and can hold no value.

E) How many times does the loop execute if the value of $v\_counter$ is incremented by 5 inside the body of the loop?

ANSWER: If the value of $v\_counter$ is incremented by 5 inside the body of the loop, the PL/SQL block does not compile successfully. As a result, it does not execute.

In this example, variable $v\_counter$ is a loop counter. Therefore, its value can be incremented only implicitly by the loop. Any executable statement that causes $v\_counter$ to change its current value leads to compilation errors.

F) Rewrite this script using the REVERSE option. What will the value of $v\_factorial$ be after the loop is completed?

ANSWER: The script should look similar to the following. Changes are shown in bold.

The value of $v\_factorial$ equals 3628800 after the loop is completed.

```
-- ch06_4b.sql, version 2.0
SET SERVEROUTPUT ON
DECLARE
   v_factorial NUMBER := 1;
BEGIN
   FOR v_counter IN REVERSE 1..10 LOOP
      v_factorial := v_factorial * v_counter;
   END LOOP;
   -- control resumes here
   DBMS_OUTPUT.PUT_LINE
      ('Factorial of ten is: '||v_factorial);
END;
```

This script produces the following output:

```
Factorial of ten is: 3628800

PL/SQL procedure successfully completed.
```

The value of $v\_factorial$ computed by this loop is equal to the value of $v\_factorial$ computed by the original loop. You will notice that in some cases it does not matter which option, IN or REVERSE, you use to obtain the final result. You will also notice that in other cases, the result produced by the loop can differ significantly.

6.3.2 **Use Numeric FOR Loops with the REVERSE Option**

In this exercise, you use the REVERSE option to specify the range of numbers used by the loop to iterate. You display a list of even numbers starting from 10 and going to 0. Try to answer the questions before you run the script. After you have answered the questions, run the script and check your results.

Create the following PL/SQL script:

```
-- ch06_5a.sql, version 1.0
SET SERVEROUTPUT ON
BEGIN
   FOR v_counter IN REVERSE 0..10 LOOP
      -- if v_counter is even, display its value on the
      -- screen
      IF MOD(v_counter, 2) = 0 THEN
         DBMS_OUTPUT.PUT_LINE ('v_counter = '||v_counter);
      END IF;
   END LOOP;
   -- control resumes here
   DBMS_OUTPUT.PUT_LINE ('Done...');
END;
```

As in the previous exercises, answer the following questions, and then execute the script:

A) What output appears on the screen?

ANSWER: The output should look like the following:

```
v_counter = 10
v_counter = 8
v_counter = 6
v_counter = 4
v_counter = 2
v_counter = 0
Done...

PL/SQL procedure successfully completed.
```

Notice that the values of $v\_counter$ are displayed in decreasing order from 10 to 0 because the REVERSE option is used. Remember that, regardless of the option used, the lower limit is referenced first.

B) How many times does the body of the loop execute?

ANSWER: The body of the loop executes 11 times, because the range of the integer numbers specified varies from 0 to 10.

C) How many times is the value of $v\_counter$ displayed on the screen?

ANSWER: The value of $v\_counter$ is displayed on the screen six times, because the IF statement evaluates to TRUE only for even integers.

D) How would you change this script to start the list from 0 and go up to 10?

ANSWER: The script should look similar to the following. Changes are shown in bold.

To start the list of integers from 0 and go up to 10, the IN option needs to be used in the loop:

```
-- ch06_5b.sql, version 2.0
SET SERVEROUTPUT ON
```

```
BEGIN
    FOR v_counter IN 0..10 LOOP
        -- if v_counter is even, display its value on the
        -- screen
        IF MOD(v_counter, 2) = 0 THEN
            DBMS_OUTPUT.PUT_LINE ('v_counter = '||v_counter);
        END IF;
    END LOOP;
    -- control resumes here
    DBMS_OUTPUT.PUT_LINE ('Done...');
END;
```

This example produces the following output:

```
v_counter = 0
v_counter = 2
v_counter = 4
v_counter = 6
v_counter = 8
v_counter = 10
Done...

PL/SQL procedure successfully completed.
```

Notice that when the IN option is used, the value of v_counter is initialized to 0, and, with each iteration of the loop, it is incremented by 1. When the REVERSE option is used, v_counter is initialized to 10, and its value is decremented by 1 with each iteration of the loop.

E) How would you change the script to display only odd numbers on the screen?

ANSWER: The script should look similar to the following. Changes are shown in bold.

```
-- ch06_5c.sql, version 3.0
SET SERVEROUTPUT ON
BEGIN
    FOR v_counter IN REVERSE 0..10 LOOP
        -- if v_counter is odd, display its value on the
        -- screen
        IF MOD(v_counter, 2) != 0 THEN
            DBMS_OUTPUT.PUT_LINE ('v_counter = '||v_counter);
        END IF;
    END LOOP;
    -- control resumes here
    DBMS_OUTPUT.PUT_LINE ('Done...');
END;
```

Notice that only the test condition of the IF statement is changed to display the list of odd integers, and the following output is produced:

```
v_counter = 9
v_counter = 7
v_counter = 5
v_counter = 3
v_counter = 1
Done...

PL/SQL procedure successfully completed.
```

F) How many times does the loop execute in this case?

ANSWER: In this case the loop executes 11 times.

Based on the test condition used in the IF statement, even or odd integers are displayed on the screen. Depending on the test condition, the number of times `v_counter` is displayed on the screen varies. However, the loop is executed 11 times as long as the number range specified is 0 to 10.

▼ TRY IT YOURSELF

In this chapter you've learned about simple loops, WHILE loops, and numeric FOR loops. Here are some projects that will help you test the depth of your understanding:

1) Rewrite script ch06_1a.sql using a WHILE loop instead of a simple loop. Make sure that the output produced by this script does not differ from the output produced by the script ch06_1a.sql.

2) Rewrite script ch06_3a.sql using a numeric FOR loop instead of a WHILE loop. Make sure that the output produced by this script does not differ from the output produced by the script ch06_3a.sql.

3) Rewrite script ch06_4a.sql using a simple loop instead of a numeric FOR loop. Make sure that the output produced by this script does not differ from the output produced by the script ch06_4a.sql.

The projects in this section are meant to have you use all the skills you have acquired throughout this chapter. The answers to these projects can be found in Appendix D and on this book's companion Web site. Visit the Web site periodically to share and discuss your answers.

CHAPTER 7

Iterative Control: Part II

CHAPTER OBJECTIVES

In this chapter, you will learn about

▶ The CONTINUE statement
▶ Nested loops

In the preceding chapter you explored three types of loops: simple loops, WHILE loops, and numeric FOR loops. You also learned that these types of loops can be terminated with the EXIT condition. In this chapter you will learn about a new PL/SQL feature introduced in Oracle 11g called the CONTINUE condition. Similar to the EXIT condition, the CONTINUE condition has two forms, CONTINUE and CONTINUE WHEN, and it may be used inside the body of the loop only. You will also learn how to nest these types of loops inside one another.

LAB 7.1
The CONTINUE Statement

LAB OBJECTIVES

After completing this lab, you will be able to

▶ Use the CONTINUE statement
▶ Use the CONTINUE WHEN statement

As mentioned previously, the CONTINUE condition has two forms: CONTINUE and CONTINUE WHEN.

THE CONTINUE STATEMENT

The CONTINUE statement causes a loop to terminate its current iteration and pass control to the next iteration of the loop when the CONTINUE condition evaluates to TRUE. The CONTINUE condition is evaluated with the help of an IF statement. When the CONTINUE condition evaluates to TRUE, control is passed to the first executable statement in the body of the loop. This is indicated by the following:

```
LOOP
    STATEMENT 1;
    STATEMENT 2;
    IF CONTINUE_CONDITION THEN
        CONTINUE;
    END IF;

    EXIT WHEN EXIT_CONDITION;
END LOOP;
STATEMENT 3;
```

In this example, you can see that after the CONTINUE condition evaluates to TRUE, control is passed to STATEMENT 1, which is the first executable statement inside the body of the loop. In this case, it causes partial execution of the loop as the statements following the CONTINUE condition inside the body of the loop are not executed.

WATCH OUT!

It is important to note that when the CONTINUE statement is used without a CONTINUE condition, the current iteration of the loop terminates unconditionally, and control of the execution is passed to the first executable statement in the body of the loop. Consider the following example:

```
DECLARE
    v_counter NUMBER := 0;
```

```
BEGIN
    LOOP
        DBMS_OUTPUT.PUT_LINE ('v_counter = '||v_counter);
        CONTINUE;

        v_counter := v_counter + 1;
        EXIT WHEN v_counter = 5;
    END LOOP;
END;
```

Because the CONTINUE statement is used without a CONTINUE condition, this loop never reaches its EXIT WHEN condition and, as a result, never terminates.

THE CONTINUE WHEN STATEMENT

The CONTINUE WHEN statement causes a loop to terminate its current iteration and pass control to the next iteration of the loop only if the CONTINUE WHEN condition evaluates to TRUE. Control is then passed to the first executable statement inside the body of the loop. The structure of a loop using a CONTINUE WHEN clause is as follows:

```
LOOP
    STATEMENT 1;
    STATEMENT 2;
    CONTINUE WHEN CONTINUE_CONDITION;

    EXIT WHEN EXIT_CONDITION;
END LOOP;
STATEMENT 3;
```

Figure 7.1 shows the flow of logic from the CONTINUE and CONTINUE WHEN statements.

Figure 7.1 shows that during each iteration, the loop executes a sequence of statements. Control is then passed to the CONTINUE condition of the loop. If the CONTINUE condition evaluates to TRUE, control is passed to the top of the loop. The sequence of statements is executed repeatedly until the CONTINUE condition evaluates to FALSE. When the CONTINUE condition evaluates to FALSE, control is passed to the next executable statement in the body of the loop, which in this case evaluates the EXIT condition.

As mentioned earlier, Figure 7.1 illustrates that the flow of logic for the CONTINUE and CONTINUE WHEN statements is the same. In other words,

```
IF CONDITION THEN
    CONTINUE;
END IF;
```

is equivalent to

```
CONTINUE WHEN CONDITION;
```

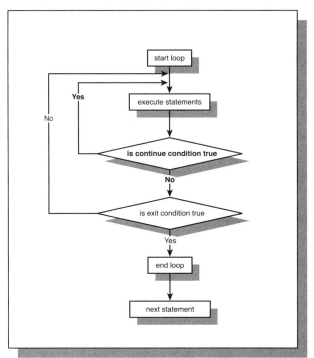

FIGURE 7.1
A simple loop with the CONTINUE condition

WATCH OUT!

The CONTINUE and CONTINUE WHEN statements are valid only when placed inside a loop. When placed outside a loop, they cause a syntax error. To avoid this error, use the RETURN statement, as shown in the preceding chapter.

DID YOU KNOW?

That CONTINUE and CONTINUE WHEN statements can be used with all types of loops.

▼ LAB 7.1 EXERCISES

This section provides exercises and suggested answers, with discussion related to how those answers resulted. The most important thing to realize is whether your answer works. You should figure out the implications of the answers and what the effects are of any different answers you may come up with.

7.1.1 **Use the CONTINUE Statement**

In this exercise, you use a modified version of the ch06_1a.sql script you created in the previous chapter. The original script uses the EXIT condition to terminate a simple loop, and a special variable, `v_counter`, which keeps count of the loop iterations. With each iteration of the loop, the value of `v_counter` is incremented and displayed on the screen. The newly created script adds the CONTINUE condition, which affects the output produced by the script.

Create the following PL/SQL script:

```
-- ch07_1a.sql, version 1.0
SET SERVEROUTPUT ON
DECLARE
   v_counter BINARY_INTEGER := 0;
BEGIN
   LOOP
      -- increment loop counter by one
      v_counter := v_counter + 1;
      DBMS_OUTPUT.PUT_LINE
         ('before continue condition, v_counter = '||
         v_counter);

      -- if CONTINUE condition yields TRUE pass control to the
      -- first executable statement of the loop
      IF v_counter < 3 THEN
         CONTINUE;
      END IF;

      DBMS_OUTPUT.PUT_LINE
         ('after  continue condition, v_counter = '||
         v_counter);

      -- if EXIT condition yields TRUE exit the loop
      IF v_counter = 5 THEN
         EXIT;
      END IF;

   END LOOP;
   -- control resumes here
   DBMS_OUTPUT.PUT_LINE ('Done...');
END;
```

Execute the script, and then answer the following questions:

A) What output appears on the screen?

ANSWER: The output should look like the following:

```
before continue condition, v_counter = 1
before continue condition, v_counter = 2
before continue condition, v_counter = 3
after  continue condition, v_counter = 3
before continue condition, v_counter = 4
after  continue condition, v_counter = 4
before continue condition, v_counter = 5
after  continue condition, v_counter = 5
Done...

PL/SQL procedure successfully completed.
```

B) Explain the output produced by the script.

ANSWER: For the first two iterations of the loop (the values of v_counter are 1 and 2), the CONTINUE condition

```
IF v_counter < 3 THEN
   CONTINUE;
END IF;
```

evaluates to TRUE, and control of the execution is passed to the first statement inside the body. As a result, only the first DBMS_OUTPUT.PUT_LINE statement is executed:

```
before continue condition, v_counter = 1
before continue condition, v_counter = 2
```

In other words, for the first two iterations, only part of the loop before the CONTINUE statement is executed.

For the last three iterations of the loops (the values of v_counter are 3, 4, and 5) the CONTINUE condition evaluates to FALSE, and the second DBMS_OUTPUT.PUT_LINE is executed:

```
before continue condition, v_counter = 3
after  continue condition, v_counter = 3
before continue condition, v_counter = 4
after  continue condition, v_counter = 4
before continue condition, v_counter = 5
after  continue condition, v_counter = 5
```

In this case, all statements inside the body of the loop are executed.

Finally, for the last iteration of the loop, the EXIT condition evaluates to TRUE and the loop terminates, and the last DBMS_OUTPUT.PUT_LINE statement is executed as well.

C) How many times does the loop execute?

ANSWER: The loop executes five times.

Remember that the number of executions is controlled by the EXIT condition, not by the CONTINUE condition.

DID YOU KNOW?

What is the difference between the EXIT and CONTINUE conditions? The EXIT condition terminates the loop, whereas the CONTINUE condition terminates the current iteration of the loop.

D) Explain how each iteration of the loop is affected if the CONTINUE condition is changed to

    I) v_counter = 3

    II) v_counter > 3.

ANSWER:

    I) Changing the CONTINUE condition to

```
IF v_counter = 3 THEN
   CONTINUE;
END IF;
```

affects only the third iteration of the loop.

As long as the value of v_counter is not equal to 3, the CONTINUE condition evaluates to FALSE. As a result, for the first, second, fourth, and fifth iterations of the loop, all statements inside the body of the loop are executed. For the third iteration of the loop, the CONTINUE condition evaluates to TRUE, causing partial execution of the loop. Thus, control of the execution is passed to the first statement inside the body of the loop, as shown in this output:

```
before continue condition, v_counter = 1
after  continue condition, v_counter = 1
before continue condition, v_counter = 2
after  continue condition, v_counter = 2
before continue condition, v_counter = 3
before continue condition, v_counter = 4
after  continue condition, v_counter = 4
before continue condition, v_counter = 5
after  continue condition, v_counter = 5
Done...

PL/SQL procedure successfully completed.
```

II) Changing the CONTINUE condition to

```
IF v_counter > 3 THEN
   CONTINUE;
END IF;
```

affects all iterations of the loop after the third iteration.

As long as the value of v_counter is less than or equal to 3, the CONTINUE condition evaluates to FALSE. As a result, for the first three iterations of the loop, all statements inside the body of the loop are executed. Starting with the fourth iteration of the loop, the CONTINUE condition evaluates to TRUE, causing partial execution. Note that due to this partial execution, the EXIT condition is never reached, causing this loop to become infinite.

WATCH OUT!

When working with the EXIT and CONTINUE conditions, the execution of a loop and the number of iterations are affected by the placement of those conditions inside the body of the loop.

E) How would you modify the script so that the CONTINUE condition v_counter > 3 does not cause an infinite loop?

ANSWER: The script should look similar to the following. Changes are shown in bold.

```
-- ch07_1b.sql, version 2.0
SET SERVEROUTPUT ON
DECLARE
   v_counter BINARY_INTEGER := 0;
BEGIN
   LOOP
      -- if EXIT condition yields TRUE exit the loop
      IF v_counter = 5 THEN
         EXIT;
      END IF;
```

```
            -- if CONTINUE condition yields TRUE pass control to the
            -- first executable statement of the loop
            IF v_counter > 3 THEN
               CONTINUE;
            END IF;

            DBMS_OUTPUT.PUT_LINE
               ('after  continue condition, v_counter = '||
               v_counter);
      END LOOP;
      -- control resumes here
      DBMS_OUTPUT.PUT_LINE ('Done...');
END;
```

In this version of the script, the EXIT condition is moved to the top of the loop, and the placement of the CONTINUE condition remains as is. Note that as long as the EXIT condition is placed before the CONTINUE condition, the loop terminates. In other words, the EXIT condition can be placed anywhere in the loop as long as it is placed before the CONTINUE condition, as shown in a different version of the script:

```
-- ch07_1c.sql, version 3.0
SET SERVEROUTPUT ON
DECLARE
   v_counter BINARY_INTEGER := 0;
BEGIN
   LOOP
      -- increment loop counter by one
      v_counter := v_counter + 1;
      DBMS_OUTPUT.PUT_LINE
         ('before continue condition, v_counter = '||
         v_counter);

      -- if EXIT condition yields TRUE exit the loop
      IF v_counter = 5 THEN
         EXIT;
      END IF;


      -- if CONTINUE condition yields TRUE pass control to the
      -- first executable statement of the loop
      IF v_counter > 3 THEN
         CONTINUE;
      END IF;

      DBMS_OUTPUT.PUT_LINE
         ('after  continue condition, v_counter = '||
         v_counter);
   END LOOP;
   -- control resumes here
   DBMS_OUTPUT.PUT_LINE ('Done...');
END;
```

Both versions of the script produce the following output:

```
before continue condition, v_counter = 1
after  continue condition, v_counter = 1
before continue condition, v_counter = 2
after  continue condition, v_counter = 2
before continue condition, v_counter = 3
after  continue condition, v_counter = 3
before continue condition, v_counter = 4
before continue condition, v_counter = 5
Done...

PL/SQL procedure successfully completed.
```

F) Rewrite the first version of the script using the CONTINUE WHEN condition instead of the CONTINUE condition so that it produces the same result.

ANSWER: The script should look similar to the following. Changes are shown in bold.

```
-- ch07_1d.sql, version 4.0
SET SERVEROUTPUT ON
DECLARE
   v_counter BINARY_INTEGER := 0;
BEGIN
   LOOP
      -- increment loop counter by one
      v_counter := v_counter + 1;
      DBMS_OUTPUT.PUT_LINE
         ('before continue condition, v_counter = '||
         v_counter);

      -- if CONTINUE condition yields TRUE pass control to the
      -- first executable statement of the loop
      CONTINUE WHEN v_counter < 3;

      DBMS_OUTPUT.PUT_LINE
         ('after  continue condition, v_counter = '||
         v_counter);

      -- if EXIT condition yields TRUE exit the loop
      IF v_counter = 5 THEN
         EXIT;
      END IF;

   END LOOP;
   -- control resumes here
   DBMS_OUTPUT.PUT_LINE ('Done...');
END;
```

Notice that the IF statement has been replaced by the CONTINUE WHEN statement. The rest of the statements in the body of the loop do not need to be changed.

7.1.2 **Use the CONTINUE WHEN Condition**

In this exercise, you use the CONTINUE WHEN condition with the numeric FOR loop to calculate to the sum of even integers between 1 and 10.

Create the following PL/SQL script:

```
-- ch07_2a.sql, version 1.0
SET SERVEROUTPUT ON
DECLARE
   v_sum NUMBER := 0;
BEGIN
   FOR v_counter in 1..10 LOOP

       -- if v_counter is odd, pass control to the top of the loop
       CONTINUE WHEN mod(v_counter, 2) != 0;

       v_sum := v_sum + v_counter;
       DBMS_OUTPUT.PUT_LINE ('Current sum is: '||v_sum);
   END LOOP;

   -- control resumes here
   DBMS_OUTPUT.PUT_LINE ('Final sum is:   '||v_sum);
END;
```

Execute the script, and then answer the following questions:

A) What output is printed on the screen?

ANSWER: The output should look similar to the following:

```
Current sum is: 2
Current sum is: 6
Current sum is: 12
Current sum is: 20
Current sum is: 30
Final sum is:   30

PL/SQL procedure successfully completed.
```

For each iteration of the loop, the value of $v\_counter$ is evaluated in the CONTINUE WHEN condition. When the value of $v\_counter$ is even, the CONTINUE WHEN condition yields FALSE, and the current value of the sum is calculated and displayed on the screen. When the value of $v\_counter$ is odd, the CONTINUE WHEN condition yields TRUE, and control of the execution is passed to the top of the loop, causing partial execution of the loop. In this case, the statements following the WHEN CONTINUE condition are not executed.

After the loop has terminated, the final sum is displayed on the screen.

B) How many times did the loop execute?

ANSWER: The loop executed ten times because the number of iterations is controlled by the loop's lower and upper limits, which are 1 and 10.

C) How many iterations of the loop were partial iterations?

ANSWER: Five iterations of the loop were partial iterations.

The CONTINUE WHEN condition evaluates to TRUE for the odd values of $v\_counter$, which are 1, 3, 5, 7, and 9. These values correspond to the loop's iterations. In other words, the first, third, fifth, seventh, and ninth iterations of the loop are partial iterations because for these iterations the CONTINUE WHEN condition yields TRUE.

D) How would you change the script to calculate the sum of odd integers between 1 and 10?

ANSWER: The script should look similar to the following. Changes are shown in bold. Note that only the CONTINUE WHEN condition is modified; the rest of the script remains unchanged.

```
-- ch07_2b.sql, version 2.0
SET SERVEROUTPUT ON
DECLARE
   v_sum NUMBER := 0;
BEGIN
   FOR v_counter in 1..10 LOOP

      -- if v_counter is even, pass control to the top of the loop
      CONTINUE WHEN mod(v_counter, 2) = 0;

      v_sum := v_sum + v_counter;
      DBMS_OUTPUT.PUT_LINE ('Current sum is: '||v_sum);
   END LOOP;

   -- control resumes here
   DBMS_OUTPUT.PUT_LINE ('Final sum is:   '||v_sum);
END;
```

This version of the script produces the following output:

```
Current sum is: 1
Current sum is: 4
Current sum is: 9
Current sum is: 16
Current sum is: 25
Final sum is:   25

PL/SQL procedure successfully completed.
```

In this version of the script, the CONTINUE WHEN condition yields FALSE for the odd values of $v\_counter$, causing the current value of v_sum to be calculated and displayed on the screen. For the even values of $v\_counter$, the CONTINUE WHEN condition evaluates to TRUE, causing control of the execution to be passed to the top of the loop.

LAB 7.2
Nested Loops

LAB OBJECTIVES

After completing this lab, you will be able to

▶ Use nested loops

You have explored three types of loops: simple loops, WHILE loops, and numeric FOR loops. Any of these three types of loops can be nested inside one another. For example, a simple loop can be nested inside a WHILE loop, and vice versa. Consider the following example:

FOR EXAMPLE

```
DECLARE
   v_counter1 INTEGER := 0;
   v_counter2 INTEGER;
BEGIN
   WHILE v_counter1 < 3 LOOP
      DBMS_OUTPUT.PUT_LINE ('v_counter1: '||v_counter1);
      v_counter2 := 0;
      LOOP
         DBMS_OUTPUT.PUT_LINE ('v_counter2: '||v_counter2);
         v_counter2 := v_counter2 + 1;
         EXIT WHEN v_counter2 >= 2;
      END LOOP;
      v_counter1 := v_counter1 + 1;
   END LOOP;
END;
```

In this example, the WHILE loop is called an outer loop because it encompasses the simple loop. The simple loop is called an inner loop because it is enclosed by the body of the WHILE loop.

The outer loop is controlled by the loop counter, **v_counter1**, and it executes if the value of **v_counter1** is less than 3. With each iteration of the loop, the value of **v_counter1** is displayed on the screen. Next, the value of **v_counter2** is initialized to 0. It is important to note that **v_counter2** is not initialized at the time of the declaration. The simple loop is placed inside the body of the WHILE loop, and the value of **v_counter2** must be initialized every time before control is passed to the simple loop.

As soon as control is passed to the inner loop, the value of **v_counter2** is displayed on the screen and incremented by 1. Next, the EXIT WHEN condition is evaluated. If the EXIT WHEN condition evaluates to FALSE, control is passed back to the top of the simple loop. If the EXIT WHEN condition evaluates to TRUE, control is passed to the first executable statement outside the loop. In our case, control is passed back to the outer loop, the value of **v_counter1** is incremented by 1, and the test condition of the WHILE loop is evaluated again.

This logic is demonstrated by the output produced by the example:

```
v_counter1: 0
v_counter2: 0
v_counter2: 1
v_counter1: 1
v_counter2: 0
v_counter2: 1
v_counter1: 2
v_counter2: 0
v_counter2: 1

PL/SQL procedure successfully completed.
```

Notice that for each value of **v_counter1**, two values of **v_counter2** are displayed. For the first iteration of the outer loop, the value of **v_counter1** is equal to 0. After control is passed to the inner loop, the value of **v_counter2** is displayed on the screen twice, and so forth.

LOOP LABELS

Earlier in the book, you read about labeling PL/SQL blocks. Loops can be labeled in a similar manner, as follows:

```
<<label_name>>
FOR LOOP_COUNTER IN LOWER_LIMIT..UPPER_LIMIT LOOP
    STATEMENT 1;
    ...
    STATEMENT N;
END LOOP label_name;
```

The label must appear right before the beginning of the loop. This syntax example shows that the label can optionally be used at the end of the loop statement. It is very helpful to label nested loops, because labels improve readability. Consider the following example:

FOR EXAMPLE

```
BEGIN
   <<outer_loop>>
   FOR i IN 1..3 LOOP
      DBMS_OUTPUT.PUT_LINE ('i = '||i);
      <<inner_loop>>
      FOR j IN 1..2 LOOP
         DBMS_OUTPUT.PUT_LINE ('j = '||j);
```

```
      END LOOP inner_loop;
   END LOOP outer_loop;
END;
```

For both outer and inner loops, the statement END LOOP must be used. If the loop label is added to each END LOOP statement, it is easier to understand which loop is being terminated.

Loop labels can also be used when referencing loop counters.

FOR EXAMPLE

```
BEGIN
   <<outer>>
   FOR v_counter IN 1..3 LOOP
      <<inner>>
      FOR v_counter IN 1..2 LOOP
         DBMS_OUTPUT.PUT_LINE ('outer.v_counter '||outer.v_counter);
         DBMS_OUTPUT.PUT_LINE ('inner.v_counter '||inner.v_counter);
      END LOOP inner;
   END LOOP outer;
END;
```

In this example, both the inner and outer loops use the same loop counter, **v_counter**. To reference both the outer and inner values of **v_counter**, loop labels are used. This example produces the following output:

```
   outer.v_counter 1
   inner.v_counter 1
   outer.v_counter 1
   inner.v_counter 2
   outer.v_counter 2
   inner.v_counter 1
   outer.v_counter 2
   inner.v_counter 2
   outer.v_counter 3
   inner.v_counter 1
   outer.v_counter 3
   inner.v_counter 2

   PL/SQL procedure successfully completed.
```

Your program can differentiate between two variables that have the same name because loop labels are used when the variables are referenced. If no loop labels are used when **v_counter** is referenced, the output produced by this script changes significantly. Basically, after control is passed to the inner loop, the value of **v_counter** from the outer loop is unavailable. When control is passed back to the outer loop, the value of **v_counter** becomes available again.

In this example, the same name is used for two different loop counters to demonstrate another use of loop labels. However, it is not considered good programming practice to use the same name for different variables.

▼ LAB 7.2 EXERCISES

This section provides exercises and suggested answers, with discussion related to how those answers resulted. The most important thing to realize is whether your answer works. You should figure out the implications of the answers and what the effects are of any different answers you may come up with.

7.2.1 **Use Nested Loops**

In this exercise, you use nested numeric FOR loops.

Create the following PL/SQL script:

```
-- ch07_3a.sql, version 1.0
SET SERVEROUTPUT ON
DECLARE
   v_test NUMBER := 0;
BEGIN
   <<outer_loop>>
   FOR i IN 1..3 LOOP
      DBMS_OUTPUT.PUT_LINE('Outer Loop');
      DBMS_OUTPUT.PUT_LINE('i = '||i);
      DBMS_OUTPUT.PUT_LINE('v_test = '||v_test);
      v_test := v_test + 1;

      <<inner_loop>>
      FOR j IN 1..2 LOOP
         DBMS_OUTPUT.PUT_LINE('Inner Loop');
         DBMS_OUTPUT.PUT_LINE('j = '||j);
         DBMS_OUTPUT.PUT_LINE('i = '||i);
         DBMS_OUTPUT.PUT_LINE('v_test = '||v_test);
      END LOOP inner_loop;
   END LOOP outer_loop;
END;
```

Execute the script, and then answer the following questions:

A) What output is printed on the screen?

ANSWER: The output should look like the following:

```
Outer Loop
i = 1
v_test = 0
Inner Loop
j = 1
i = 1
v_test = 1
Inner Loop
j = 2
i = 1
```

```
v_test = 1
Outer Loop
i = 2
v_test = 1
Inner Loop
j = 1
i = 2
v_test = 2
Inner Loop
j = 2
i = 2
v_test = 2
Outer Loop
i = 3
v_test = 2
Inner Loop
j = 1
i = 3
v_test = 3
Inner Loop
j = 2
i = 3
v_test = 3

PL/SQL procedure successfully completed.
```

Every time the outer loop is run, the value of the loop counter is implicitly incremented by 1 and displayed on the screen. In addition, the value of v_test is displayed on the screen and is incremented by 1. Next, control is passed to the inner loop.

Every time the inner loop is run, the value of the inner loop counter is incremented by 1 and displayed on the screen, along with the value of the outer loop counter and the variable v_test.

B) How many times did the outer loop execute?

ANSWER: The outer loop executed three times, according to the range specified by the loop's lower and upper limits. In this example, the lower limit is equal to 1 and the upper limit is equal to 3.

C) How many times did the inner loop execute?

ANSWER: The inner loop executed six times.

For each iteration of the outer loop, the inner loop executed twice. However, the outer loop executed three times. Overall, the inner loop executed six times.

D) What are the values of the loop counters, i and j, after both loops terminate?

ANSWER: After both loops terminate, both loop counters are undefined again and can hold no values. As mentioned earlier, the loop counter ceases to exist as soon as the numeric FOR loop is terminated.

E) Rewrite this script using the REVERSE option for both loops. How many times is each loop executed in this case?

ANSWER: The script should be similar to the following. Changes are shown in bold.

The outer loop executes three times, and the inner loop executes six times.

```
-- ch07_3b.sql, version 2.0
SET SERVEROUTPUT ON
DECLARE
   v_test NUMBER := 0;
BEGIN
   <<outer_loop>>
   FOR i IN REVERSE 1..3 LOOP
      DBMS_OUTPUT.PUT_LINE('Outer Loop');
      DBMS_OUTPUT.PUT_LINE('i = '||i);
      DBMS_OUTPUT.PUT_LINE('v_test = '||v_test);
      v_test := v_test + 1;

      <<inner_loop>>
      FOR j IN REVERSE 1..2 LOOP
         DBMS_OUTPUT.PUT_LINE('Inner Loop');
         DBMS_OUTPUT.PUT_LINE('j = '||j);
         DBMS_OUTPUT.PUT_LINE('i = '||i);
         DBMS_OUTPUT.PUT_LINE('v_test = '||v_test);
      END LOOP inner_loop;
   END LOOP outer_loop;
END;
```

This script produces the following output:

```
Outer Loop
i = 3
v_test = 0
Inner Loop
j = 2
i = 3
v_test = 1
Inner Loop
j = 1
i = 3
v_test = 1
Outer Loop
i = 2
v_test = 1
Inner Loop
j = 2
i = 2
v_test = 2
Inner Loop
j = 1
i = 2
v_test = 2
Outer Loop
i = 1
v_test = 2
Inner Loop
j = 2
```

```
i = 1
v_test = 3
Inner Loop
j = 1
i = 1
v_test = 3
```

```
PL/SQL procedure successfully completed.
```

Notice that the output produced by this example has changed significantly from the output shown in the preceding example. The values of the loop counters are decremented because the REVERSE option is used. However, the value of the variable `v_test` is unaffected by using the REVERSE option.

▼ TRY IT YOURSELF

In this chapter you learned about CONTINUE and CONTINUE WHEN statements. You also learned how to nest different loops inside one another. Here are some projects that will help you test the depth of your understanding:

1) Rewrite script ch06_4a.sql to calculate the factorial of even integers only between 1 and 10. The script should use a CONTINUE or CONTINUE WHEN statement.

2) Rewrite script ch07_3a.sql using a simple loop instead of the outer FOR loop, and a WHILE loop for the inner FOR loop. Make sure that the output produced by this script does not differ from the output produced by the original script.

The projects in this section are meant to have you use all the skills you have acquired throughout this chapter. The answers to these projects can be found in Appendix D and on this book's companion Web site. Visit the Web site periodically to share and discuss your answers.

CHAPTER 8

Error Handling and Built-in Exceptions

CHAPTER OBJECTIVES

In this chapter, you will learn about

- ▶ Handling errors
- ▶ Built-in exceptions

In Chapter 1, "PL/SQL Concepts," you encountered two types of errors that can be found in a program: compilation errors and runtime errors. You will recall that a special section in a PL/SQL block handles runtime errors. This is called the exception-handling section, and in it, runtime errors are called exceptions. The exception-handling section allows programmers to specify what actions should be taken when a specific exception occurs.

PL/SQL has two types of exceptions: built-in and user-defined. In this chapter, you will learn how to handle certain kinds of runtime errors with the help of built-in exceptions. User-defined exceptions are discussed in Chapters 9 and 10.

LAB 8.1
Handling Errors

LAB OBJECTIVES

After completing this lab, you will be able to

▶ Understand the importance of error handling

The following example illustrates some of the differences between compilation and runtime errors:

FOR EXAMPLE

```
DECLARE
   v_num1   INTEGER := &sv_num1;
   v_num2   INTEGER := &sv_num2;
   v_result NUMBER;
BEGIN
   v_result = v_num1 / v_num2;
   DBMS_OUTPUT.PUT_LINE ('v_result: '||v_result);
END;
```

This example is a very simple program. It has two variables, v_num1 and v_num2. A user supplies values for these variables. Next, v_num1 is divided by v_num2, and the result of this division is stored in the third variable, v_result. Finally, the value of v_result is displayed on the screen.

Now, assume that a user supplies values of 3 and 5 for the variables v_num1 and v_num2, respectively. As a result, the example produces the following output:

```
Enter value for sv_num1: 3
old    2:    v_num1 INTEGER := &sv_num1;
new    2:    v_num1 INTEGER := 3;
Enter value for sv_num2: 5
old    3:    v_num2 INTEGER := &sv_num2;
new    3:    v_num2 INTEGER := 5;
   v_result = v_num1 / v_num2;
            *
ERROR at line 6:
ORA-06550: line 6, column 13:
PLS-00103: Encountered the symbol "=" when expecting one of the
following:
```

```
:= . ( @ % ;
The symbol ":= was inserted before "=" to continue.
```

You have probably noticed that the example did not execute successfully. A syntax error was encountered at line 6. Close inspection of the example shows that the statement

```
v_result = v_num1 / v_num2;
```

contains an equals-sign operator where an assignment operator should be used. The statement should be rewritten as follows:

```
v_result := v_num1 / v_num2;
```

After the corrected example is run again, the following output is produced:

```
Enter value for sv_num1: 3
old   2:    v_num1 integer := &sv_num1;
new   2:    v_num1 integer := 3;
Enter value for sv_num2: 5
old   3:    v_num2 integer := &sv_num2;
new   3:    v_num2 integer := 5;
v_result: .6

PL/SQL procedure successfully completed.
```

As you can see, the example now executes successfully because the syntax error has been corrected.

Next, if you change the values of the variables v_num1 and v_num2 to 4 and 0, respectively, the following output is produced:

```
Enter value for sv_num1: 4
old   2:    v_num1 integer := &sv_num1;
new   2:    v_num1 integer := 4;
Enter value for sv_num2: 0
old   3:    v_num2 integer := &sv_num2;
new   3:    v_num2 integer := 0;
DECLARE
*
ERROR at line 1:
ORA-01476: divisor is equal to zero
ORA-06512: at line 6
```

Even though this example does not contain syntax errors, it was terminated prematurely because the value entered for v_num2, the divisor, was 0. As you may recall, division by 0 is undefined and thus leads to an error.

This example illustrates a runtime error that the compiler cannot detect. For some of the values entered for the variables v_num1 and v_num2, this example executes successfully. For other values entered for the variables v_num1 and v_num2, this example cannot execute. As a result, the runtime error occurs. You will recall that the compiler cannot detect runtime errors. In this case, a runtime error occurs because the compiler does not know the result of the division of v_num1 by v_num2. This result can be determined only at runtime. Hence, this error is called a runtime error.

To handle this type of error in the program, you must add an exception handler. The exception-handling section has the following structure:

```
EXCEPTION
    WHEN EXCEPTION_NAME THEN
        ERROR-PROCESSING STATEMENTS;
```

The exception-handling section is placed after the executable section of the block. The preceding example can be rewritten in the following manner:

FOR EXAMPLE

```
DECLARE
    v_num1   INTEGER := &sv_num1;
    v_num2   INTEGER := &sv_num2;
    v_result NUMBER;
BEGIN
    v_result := v_num1 / v_num2;
    DBMS_OUTPUT.PUT_LINE ('v_result: '||v_result);
EXCEPTION
    WHEN ZERO_DIVIDE THEN
        DBMS_OUTPUT.PUT_LINE ('A number cannot be divided by zero.');
END;
```

The section of the example in bold shows the exception-handling section of the block. When this version of the example is executed with the values of 4 and 0 for variables v_num1 and v_num2, respectively, the following output is produced:

```
Enter value for sv_num1: 4
old   2:    v_num1 integer := &sv_num1;
new   2:    v_num1 integer := 4;
Enter value for sv_num2: 0
old   3:    v_num2 integer := &sv_num2;
new   3:    v_num2 integer := 0;
A number cannot be divided by zero.

PL/SQL procedure successfully completed.
```

This output shows that as soon as an attempt to divide v_num1 by v_num2 is made, the exception-handling section of the block is executed. Therefore, the error message specified by the exception-handling section is displayed on the screen.

This version of the output illustrates several advantages of using an exception-handling section. You have probably noticed that the output looks cleaner compared to the preceding version. Even though the error message is still displayed on the screen, the output is more informative. In short, it is oriented more toward a user than a programmer.

WATCH OUT!

Often a user does not have access to the code. Therefore, references to line numbers and keywords in a program are not significant to most users.

An exception-handling section allows a program to execute to completion, instead of terminating prematurely. Another advantage offered by the exception-handling section is isolation of error-handling routines. In other words, all error-processing code for a specific block is located in a single section. As a result, the program's logic is easier to follow and understand. Finally, adding an exception-handling section enables event-driven processing of errors. As in the example shown earlier, in the case of a specific exception event, such as division by 0, the exception-handling section is executed, and the error message specified by the DBMS_OUTPUT. PUT_LINE statement is displayed on the screen.

▼ LAB 8.1 EXERCISES

This section provides exercises and suggested answers, with discussion related to how those answers resulted. The most important thing to realize is whether your answer works. You should figure out the implications of the answers and what the effects are of any different answers you may come up with.

8.1.1 Understand the Importance of Error Handling

In this exercise, you calculate the value of the square root of a number and display it on the screen.

Create the following PL/SQL script:

```
-- ch08_1a.sql, version 1.0
SET SERVEROUTPUT ON;
DECLARE
    v_num NUMBER := &sv_num;
BEGIN
    DBMS_OUTPUT.PUT_LINE ('Square root of '||v_num||
        ' is '||SQRT(v_num));
EXCEPTION
    WHEN VALUE_ERROR THEN
        DBMS_OUTPUT.PUT_LINE ('An error has occurred');
END;
```

In this script, the exception VALUE_ERROR is raised when conversion or type mismatch errors occur. This exception is covered in greater detail in Lab 8.2.

To test this script fully, execute it twice. For the first run, enter a value of 4 for the variable v_num. For the second run, enter a value of –4 for the variable v_num. Execute the script, and then answer the following questions:

A) What output is printed on the screen (for both runs)?

ANSWER: The first version of the output is produced when v_num equals 4. The output should look like the following:

```
Enter value for sv_num: 4
old    2:    v_num NUMBER := &sv_num;
new    2:    v_num NUMBER := 4;
```

```
Square root of 4 is 2

PL/SQL procedure successfully completed.
```

The second version of the output is produced when v_num equals –4. The output should look like the following:

```
Enter value for sv_num: -4
old    2:    v_num NUMBER := &sv_num;
new    2:    v_num NUMBER := -4;
An error has occurred

PL/SQL procedure successfully completed.
```

B) Why do you think an error message was generated when the script was run a second time?

ANSWER: The error message An error has occurred is generated for the second run of the example because a runtime error occurred. The built-in function SQRT is unable to accept a negative number as its argument. Therefore, the exception VALUE_ERROR was raised, and the error message was displayed.

C) Assume that you are unfamiliar with the exception VALUE_ERROR. How would you change this script to avoid this runtime error?

ANSWER: The new version of the program should look similar to the following. All changes are shown in bold.

```
-- ch08_1b.sql, version 2.0
SET SERVEROUTPUT ON;
DECLARE
    v_num NUMBER := &sv_num;
BEGIN
    IF v_num >= 0 THEN
        DBMS_OUTPUT.PUT_LINE ('Square root of '||v_num||
            ' is '||SQRT(v_num));
    ELSE
        DBMS_OUTPUT.PUT_LINE ('A number cannot be negative');
    END IF;
END;
```

Notice that before you calculate the square root of a number, you can check to see if the number is greater than or equal to 0 with the help of the IF-THEN-ELSE statement. If the number is negative, the message A number cannot be negative is displayed on the screen. When a value of –4 is entered for the variable v_num, this script produces the following output:

```
Enter value for sv_num: -4
old    2:    v_num NUMBER := &sv_num;
new    2:    v_num NUMBER := -4;
A number cannot be negative

PL/SQL procedure successfully completed.
```

LAB 8.2
Built-in Exceptions

LAB OBJECTIVES

After completing this lab, you will be able to

▶ Use built-in exceptions

As mentioned earlier, a PL/SQL block has the following structure:

```
DECLARE
   ...
BEGIN
   EXECUTABLE STATEMENTS;
EXCEPTION
   WHEN EXCEPTION_NAME THEN
      ERROR-PROCESSING STATEMENTS;
END;
```

When an error occurs that raises a built-in exception, the exception is said to be raised implicitly. In other words, if a program breaks an Oracle rule, control is passed to the exception-handling section of the block. At this point, the error-processing statements are executed. It is important to realize that after the exception-handling section of the block has executed, the block terminates. Control does not return to the executable section of the block. The following example illustrates this point:

FOR EXAMPLE

```
DECLARE
   v_student_name VARCHAR2(50);
BEGIN
   SELECT first_name||' '||last_name
     INTO v_student_name
     FROM student
    WHERE student_id = 101;

   DBMS_OUTPUT.PUT_LINE ('Student name is '||v_student_name);
EXCEPTION
   WHEN NO_DATA_FOUND THEN
      DBMS_OUTPUT.PUT_LINE ('There is no such student');
END;
```

This example produces the following output:

```
There is no such student

PL/SQL procedure successfully completed.
```

Because there is no record in the STUDENT table with student ID 101, the SELECT INTO statement does not return any rows. As a result, control passes to the exception-handling section of the block, and the error message There is no such student is displayed. Even though there is a DBMS_OUTPUT.PUT_LINE statement right after the SELECT statement, it is not executed, because control has been transferred to the exception-handling section. Control never returns to the executable section of this block, which contains the first DBMS_OUTPUT.PUT_LINE statement.

You have probably noticed that, although every Oracle runtime error has a number associated with it, it must be handled by its name in the exception-handling section. One of the outputs from the example used in the previous lab in this chapter has the following error message:

```
ORA-01476: divisor is equal to zero
```

where ORA-01476 is the error number. This error number refers to the error named ZERO_DIVIDE. Some common Oracle runtime errors are predefined in PL/SQL as exceptions.

The following list describes some commonly used predefined exceptions and how they are raised:

▸ NO_DATA_FOUND: This exception is raised when a SELECT INTO statement that makes no calls to group functions, such as SUM or COUNT, does not return any rows. For example, suppose you issue a SELECT INTO statement against the STUDENT table where student ID equals 101. If there is no record in the STUDENT table passing this criteria (student ID equals 101), the NO_DATA_FOUND exception is raised.

When a SELECT INTO statement calls a group function, such as COUNT, the result set is never empty. When used in a SELECT INTO statement against the STUDENT table, function COUNT returns 0 for the value of student ID 123. Hence, a SELECT statement that calls a group function never raises the NO_DATA_FOUND exception.

▸ TOO_MANY_ROWS: This exception is raised when a SELECT INTO statement returns more than one row. By definition, a SELECT INTO can return only a single row. If a SELECT INTO statement returns more than one row, the definition of the SELECT INTO statement is violated. This causes the TOO_MANY_ROWS exception to be raised.

For example, suppose you issue a SELECT INTO statement against the STUDENT table for a specific zip code. There is a good chance that this SELECT statement will return more than one row, because many students can live in the same zip code area.

▸ ZERO_DIVIDE: This exception is raised when a division operation is performed in the program and a divisor is equal to 0. An example in the previous lab of this chapter illustrated how this exception is raised.

▶ LOGIN_DENIED: This exception is raised when a user tries to log in to Oracle with an invalid username or password.

▶ PROGRAM_ERROR: This exception is raised when a PL/SQL program has an internal problem.

▶ VALUE_ERROR: This exception is raised when a conversion or size mismatch error occurs. For example, suppose you select a student's last name into a variable that has been defined as VARCHAR2(5). If the student's last name contains more than five characters, the VALUE_ERROR exception is raised.

▶ DUP_VALUE_ON_INDEX: This exception is raised when a program tries to store a duplicate value in the column or columns that have a unique index defined on them. For example, suppose you are trying to insert a record into the SECTION table for course number 25, section 1. If a record for the given course and section number already exists in the SECTION table, the DUP_VAL_ON_INDEX exception is raised, because these columns have a unique index defined on them.

So far, you have seen examples of programs that can handle only a single exception. For example, a PL/SQL block contains an exception handler with a single exception ZERO_DIVIDE. However, many times you need to handle different exceptions in the PL/SQL block. Moreover, often you need to specify different actions that must be taken when a particular exception is raised, as the following example illustrates:

FOR EXAMPLE

```
DECLARE
   v_student_id NUMBER := &sv_student_id;
   v_enrolled   VARCHAR2(3) := 'NO';
BEGIN
   DBMS_OUTPUT.PUT_LINE ('Check if the student is enrolled');
   SELECT 'YES'
     INTO v_enrolled
     FROM enrollment
    WHERE student_id = v_student_id;

   DBMS_OUTPUT.PUT_LINE ('The student is enrolled into one course');
EXCEPTION
   WHEN NO_DATA_FOUND THEN
      DBMS_OUTPUT.PUT_LINE ('The student is not enrolled');

   WHEN TOO_MANY_ROWS THEN
       DBMS_OUTPUT.PUT_LINE
          ('The student is enrolled in too many courses');
END;
```

Notice that this example contains two exceptions in a single exception-handling section. The first exception, NO_DATA_FOUND, is raised if there are no records in the ENROLLMENT table for a particular student. The second exception, TOO_MANY_ROWS, is raised if a particular student is enrolled in more than one course.

Consider what happens if you run this example for three different values of student ID: 102, 103, and 319.

The first run of the example (student ID is 102) produces the following output:

```
Enter value for sv_student_id: 102
old   2:    v_student_id NUMBER := &sv_student_id;
new   2:    v_student_id NUMBER := 102;
Check if the student is enrolled
Student is enrolled in too many courses

PL/SQL procedure successfully completed.
```

The first time, a user entered 102 for the value of student ID. Next, the first DBMS_OUTPUT. PUT_LINE statement is executed, and the message Check if the ... is displayed on the screen. Then the SELECT INTO statement is executed. You probably noticed that the DBMS_OUTPUT.PUT_LINE statement following the SELECT INTO statement was not executed. When the SELECT INTO statement is executed for student ID 102, multiple rows are returned. Because the SELECT INTO statement can return only a single row, control is passed to the exception-handling section of the block. Next, the PL/SQL block raises the proper exception. As a result, the message Student is enrolled in too many courses is displayed on the screen, and this message is specified by the exception TOO_MANY_ROWS.

DID YOU KNOW?

Built-in exceptions are raised implicitly. Therefore, you only need to specify what action must be taken in the case of a particular exception.

A second run of the example (student ID is 103) produces the following output:

```
Enter value for sv_student_id: 103
old   2:    v_student_id NUMBER := &sv_student_id;
new   2:    v_student_id NUMBER := 103;
Check if the student is enrolled
The student is enrolled into one course

PL/SQL procedure successfully completed.
```

In this second run, a user entered 103 for the value of student ID. As a result, the first DBMS_OUTPUT.PUT_LINE statement is executed, and the message Check if the ... is displayed on the screen. Then the SELECT INTO statement is executed. When the SELECT INTO statement is executed for student ID 103, a single row is returned. Next, the DBMS_OUTPUT.PUT_LINE statement following the SELECT INTO statement is executed. As a result, the message The student is enrolled into one course is displayed on the screen. Notice that for this value of the variable v_student_id, no exception has been raised.

A third run of the example (student ID is 319) produces the following output:

```
Enter value for sv_student_id: 319
old    2:    v_student_id NUMBER := &sv_student_id;
new    2:    v_student_id NUMBER := 319;
Check if the student is enrolled
The student is not enrolled


PL/SQL procedure successfully completed.
```

This time, a user entered 319 for the value of student ID. The first DBMS_OUTPUT.PUT_LINE statement is executed, and the message Check if the ... is displayed on the screen. Then the SELECT INTO statement is executed. When the SELECT INTO statement is executed for student ID 319, no rows are returned. As a result, control is passed to the exception-handling section of the PL/SQL block, and the proper exception is raised. In this case, the NO_DATA_FOUND exception is raised because the SELECT INTO statement failed to return a single row. Thus, the message The student is not enrolled is displayed on the screen.

So far, you have seen examples of exception-handling sections that have particular exceptions, such as NO_DATA_FOUND and ZERO_DIVIDE. However, you cannot always predict what exception might be raised by your PL/SQL block. For cases like this, there is a special exception handler called OTHERS. All predefined Oracle errors (exceptions) can be handled with the use of the OTHERS handler.

Consider the following:

FOR EXAMPLE

```
DECLARE
    v_instructor_id    NUMBER := &sv_instructor_id;
    v_instructor_name VARCHAR2(50);
BEGIN
    SELECT first_name||' '||last_name
      INTO v_instructor_name
      FROM instructor
     WHERE instructor_id = v_instructor_id;

    DBMS_OUTPUT.PUT_LINE ('Instructor name is '||v_instructor_name);
EXCEPTION
    WHEN OTHERS THEN
        DBMS_OUTPUT.PUT_LINE ('An error has occurred');
END;
```

When run, this example produces the following output:

```
Enter value for sv_instructor_id: 100
old    2:    v_instructor_id NUMBER := &sv_instructor_id;
new    2:    v_instructor_id NUMBER := 100;
An error has occurred
PL/SQL procedure successfully completed.
```

This demonstrates not only the use of the OTHERS exception handler, but also a bad programming practice. The exception OTHERS has been raised because there is no record in the INSTRUCTOR table for instructor ID 100.

This is a simple example, where it is possible to guess what exception handlers should be used. However, in many instances you may find a number of programs that have been written with a single exception handler, OTHERS. This is a bad programming practice, because such use of this exception handler does not give you or your user good feedback. You do not really know what error has occurred. Your user does not know whether he or she entered some information incorrectly. Two special error-reporting functions, SQLCODE and SQLERRM, are very useful when used with the OTHERS handler. You will learn about them in Chapter 10, "Exceptions: Advanced Concepts."

▼ LAB 8.2 EXERCISES

This section provides exercises and suggested answers, with discussion related to how those answers resulted. The most important thing to realize is whether your answer works. You should figure out the implications of the answers and what the effects are of any different answers you may come up with.

8.2.1 Use Built-in Exceptions

In this exercise, you learn more about some built-in exceptions discussed earlier in this chapter.

Create the following PL/SQL script:

```
-- ch08_2a.sql, version 1.0
SET SERVEROUTPUT ON
DECLARE
    v_exists         NUMBER(1);
    v_total_students NUMBER(1);
    v_zip            CHAR(5):= '&sv_zip';
BEGIN
    SELECT count(*)
      INTO v_exists
      FROM zipcode
     WHERE zip = v_zip;

    IF v_exists != 0 THEN
       SELECT COUNT(*)
         INTO v_total_students
         FROM student
        WHERE zip = v_zip;

       DBMS_OUTPUT.PUT_LINE
           ('There are '||v_total_students||' students');
    ELSE
       DBMS_OUTPUT.PUT_LINE (v_zip||' is not a valid zip');
    END IF;
```

```
EXCEPTION
   WHEN VALUE_ERROR OR INVALID_NUMBER THEN
      DBMS_OUTPUT.PUT_LINE ('An error has occurred');
END;
```

This script contains two exceptions, VALUE_ERROR and INVALID_NUMBER. However, only one exception handler is written for both exceptions. You can combine different exceptions in a single exception handler when you want to handle both exceptions in a similar way. Often the exceptions VALUE_ERROR and INVALID_NUMBER are used in a single exception handler because these Oracle errors refer to the conversion problems that may occur at runtime.

To test this script fully, execute it three times. For the first run, enter 07024, for the second run, enter 00914, and for the third run, enter 12345 for the variable v_zip. Execute the script, and then answer the following questions:

A) What output is printed on the screen (for all values of zip)?

ANSWER: The first version of the output is produced when the value of zip is 07024. The second version of the output is produced when the value of zip is 00914. The third version of the output is produced when the value of zip is 12345.

The output should look like the following:

```
Enter value for sv_zip: 07024
old   4:    v_zip CHAR(5):= '&sv_zip';
new   4:    v_zip CHAR(5):= '07024';
There are 9 students


PL/SQL procedure successfully completed.
```

When you enter 07024 for the variable v_zip, the first SELECT INTO statement is executed. This SELECT INTO statement checks whether the value of zip is valid, or, in other words, if a record exists in the ZIPCODE table for a given value of zip. Next, the value of the variable v_exists is evaluated with the help of the IF statement. For this run of the example, the IF statement evaluates to TRUE, and as a result, the SELECT INTO statement against the STUDENT table is evaluated. Next, the DBMS_OUTPUT.PUT_LINE following the SELECT INTO statement is executed, and the message There are 9 students is displayed on the screen.

The output should look like the following:

```
Enter value for sv_zip: 00914
old   4:    v_zip CHAR(5):= '&sv_zip';
new   4:    v_zip CHAR(5):= '00914';
There are 0 students


PL/SQL procedure successfully completed.
```

For the second run, the value 00914 is entered for the variable v_zip. The SELECT INTO statement against the STUDENT table returns one record, and the message There are 0 students is displayed on the screen.

Because the SELECT INTO statement against the STUDENT table uses a group function, COUNT, there is no reason to use the exception NO_DATA_FOUND, because the COUNT function will always return data.

The output should look like the following:

```
Enter value for sv_zip: 12345
old   4:    v_zip CHAR(5):= '&sv_zip';
new   4:    v_zip CHAR(5):= '12345';
12345 is not a valid zip

PL/SQL procedure successfully completed.
```

For the third run, the value 12345 is entered for the variable v_zip. The SELECT INTO statement against the ZIPCODE table is executed. Next, the variable v_exists is evaluated with the help of the IF statement. Because the value of v_exists equals 0, the IF statement evaluates to FALSE. As a result, the ELSE part of the IF statement is executed. The message 12345 is not a valid zip is displayed on the screen.

B) Explain why no exception was raised for these values of the variable v_zip.

ANSWER: The exceptions VALUE_ERROR and INVALID_NUMBER were not raised because no conversion or type mismatch error occurred. Both variables, v_exists and $v\_total\_students$, were defined as NUMBER(1).

The group function COUNT used in the SELECT INTO statement returns a NUMBER datatype. Moreover, on both occasions, the COUNT function returns a single-digit number. As a result, neither exception was raised.

C) Insert a record into the STUDENT table with a zip having the value of 07024.

```
INSERT INTO student (student_id, salutation, first_name,
    last_name, zip, registration_date, created_by, created_date,
    modified_by, modified_date)
VALUES (STUDENT_ID_SEQ.NEXTVAL, 'Mr.', 'John', 'Smith', '07024',
    SYSDATE, 'STUDENT', SYSDATE, 'STUDENT', SYSDATE);

COMMIT;
```

Run the script again for the same value of zip (07024). What output is printed on the screen? Why?

ANSWER: After a student has been added, the output should look like the following:

```
Enter value for sv_zip: 07024
old   4:    v_zip CHAR(5):= '&sv_zip';
new   4:    v_zip CHAR(5):= '07024';
An error has occurred

PL/SQL procedure successfully completed.
```

After the student has been inserted into the STUDENT table with a zip having a value of 07024, the total number of students changes to 10 (remember, previously this number was 9). As a result, the SELECT INTO statement against the STUDENT table causes an error, because the variable $v\_total\_students$ has been defined as NUMBER(1). This means that only a single-digit number can be stored in this variable. The number 10 is a two-digit number, so the exception INVALID_NUMBER is raised. As a result, the message An error has occurred is displayed on the screen.

D) How would you change the script to display a student's first name and last name instead of displaying the total number of students for any given value of a zip? Remember, the SELECT INTO statement can return only one record.

ANSWER: The new version of the script should look similar to the following. All changes are shown in bold.

```
-- ch08_2b.sql, version 2.0
SET SERVEROUTPUT ON
DECLARE
    v_exists        NUMBER(1);
    v_student_name VARCHAR2(30);
    v_zip           CHAR(5):= '&sv_zip';
BEGIN
    SELECT count(*)
      INTO v_exists
      FROM zipcode
     WHERE zip = v_zip;

    IF v_exists != 0 THEN
        SELECT first_name||' '||last_name
          INTO v_student_name
          FROM student
         WHERE zip = v_zip
           AND rownum = 1;
        DBMS_OUTPUT.PUT_LINE ('Student name is '||v_student_name);
    ELSE
        DBMS_OUTPUT.PUT_LINE (v_zip||' is not a valid zip');
    END IF;

EXCEPTION
    WHEN VALUE_ERROR OR INVALID_NUMBER THEN
        DBMS_OUTPUT.PUT_LINE ('An error has occurred');

    WHEN NO_DATA_FOUND THEN
        DBMS_OUTPUT.PUT_LINE
            ('There are no students for this value of zip code');
END;
```

This version of the program contains several changes. The variable `v_total_students` has been replaced by the variable `v_student_name`. The SELECT INTO statement against the STUDENT table has been changed as well. Another condition has been added to the WHERE clause:

```
rownum = 1
```

You have seen in the previous runs of this script that for any given value of zip there could be multiple records in the STUDENT table. Because a SELECT INTO statement returns only a single row, the condition `rownum = 1` has been added to it. Another way to deal with multiple rows returned by the SELECT INTO statement is to add the exception TOO_MANY_ROWS.

Finally, another exception has been added to the program. The SELECT INTO statement against the STUDENT table does not contain any group functions. Therefore, for any given value of zip, the SELECT INTO statement might not return any data and might cause an error. As a result, the exception NO_DATA_FOUND might be raised.

▼ TRY IT YOURSELF

In this chapter you've learned about built-in exceptions. Here are some projects that will help you test the depth of your understanding:

1) Create the following script: Check to see whether there is a record in the STUDENT table for a given student ID. If there is not, insert a record into the STUDENT table for the given student ID.

2) Create the following script: For a given instructor ID, check to see whether it is assigned to a valid instructor. Then check to see how many sections this instructor teaches, and display this information on the screen.

The projects in this section are meant to have you use all the skills you have acquired throughout this chapter. The answers to these projects can be found in Appendix D and on this book's companion Web site. Visit the Web site periodically to share and discuss your answers.

CHAPTER 9

Exceptions

CHAPTER OBJECTIVES

In this chapter, you will learn about

- ▶ Exception scope
- ▶ User-defined exceptions
- ▶ Exception propagation

In the preceding chapter, you explored the concept of error handling and built-in exceptions. In this chapter you continue by examining whether an exception can catch a runtime error occurring in the declaration, executable, or exception-handling section of a PL/SQL block. You also will learn how to define your own exceptions and how to reraise an exception.

LAB 9.1
Exception Scope

LAB OBJECTIVE

After completing this lab, you will be able to

▶ Understand the scope of an exception

You are already familiar with the term scope—for example, the scope of a variable. Even though variables and exceptions serve different purposes, the same scope rules apply to them. Now examine the scope of an exception by means of an example:

FOR EXAMPLE

```
DECLARE
    v_student_id NUMBER := &sv_student_id;
    v_name        VARCHAR2(30);
BEGIN
    SELECT RTRIM(first_name)||' '||RTRIM(last_name)
      INTO v_name
      FROM student
     WHERE student_id = v_student_id;

    DBMS_OUTPUT.PUT_LINE ('Student name is '||v_name);
EXCEPTION
    WHEN NO_DATA_FOUND THEN
       DBMS_OUTPUT.PUT_LINE ('There is no such student');
END;
```

In this example, you display the student's name on the screen. If no record in the STUDENT table corresponds to the value of $v\_student\_id$ provided by the user, the exception NO_DATA_FOUND is raised. Therefore, you can say that the exception NO_DATA_FOUND covers this block, or that this block is the scope of this exception. In other words, *the scope of an exception is the portion of the block that is covered by this exception.*

Now, you can expand on that:

FOR EXAMPLE

```
DECLARE
    v_student_id NUMBER := &sv_student_id;
    v_name       VARCHAR2(30);
    v_total      NUMBER(1);

-- outer block
BEGIN
    SELECT RTRIM(first_name)||' '||RTRIM(last_name)
      INTO v_name
      FROM student
     WHERE student_id = v_student_id;
    DBMS_OUTPUT.PUT_LINE ('Student name is '||v_name);

    -- inner block
    BEGIN
        SELECT COUNT(*)
          INTO v_total
          FROM enrollment
         WHERE student_id = v_student_id;
        DBMS_OUTPUT.PUT_LINE ('Student is registered for '||
            v_total||' course(s)');
    EXCEPTION
        WHEN VALUE_ERROR OR INVALID_NUMBER THEN
            DBMS_OUTPUT.PUT_LINE ('An error has occurred');
    END;

EXCEPTION
    WHEN NO_DATA_FOUND THEN
        DBMS_OUTPUT.PUT_LINE ('There is no such student');
END;
```

The part of the example shown in bold has been added to the original version of the example. The new version of the example has an inner block added to it. This block has a structure similar to the outer block. It has a SELECT INTO statement and an exception section to handle errors. When a VALUE_ERROR or INVALID_NUMBER error occurs in the inner block, the exception is raised.

It is important that you realize that the exceptions VALUE_ERROR and INVALID_ NUMBER have been defined for the inner block only. Therefore, they can be handled only if they are raised in the inner block. If one of these errors occurs in the outer block, the program is unable to terminate successfully.

On the other hand, the exception NO_DATA_FOUND has been defined in the outer block; therefore, it is global to the inner block. This version of the example never raises the exception NO_DATA_FOUND in the inner block. Why do you think this is the case?

DID YOU KNOW?

If you define an exception in a block, it is local to that block. However, it is global to any blocks enclosed by that block. In other words, in the case of nested blocks, any exception defined in the outer block becomes global to its inner blocks.

Note what happens when the example is changed so that the exception NO_DATA_FOUND can be raised by the inner block:

FOR EXAMPLE

```
DECLARE
    v_student_id NUMBER := &sv_student_id;
    v_name        VARCHAR2(30);
    v_registered CHAR;

-- outer block
BEGIN
    SELECT RTRIM(first_name)||' '||RTRIM(last_name)
      INTO v_name
      FROM student
     WHERE student_id = v_student_id;
    DBMS_OUTPUT.PUT_LINE ('Student name is '||v_name);

    -- inner block
    BEGIN
        SELECT 'Y'
          INTO v_registered
          FROM enrollment
         WHERE student_id = v_student_id;
        DBMS_OUTPUT.PUT_LINE ('Student is registered');
    EXCEPTION
        WHEN VALUE_ERROR OR INVALID_NUMBER THEN
            DBMS_OUTPUT.PUT_LINE ('An error has occurred');
    END;

EXCEPTION
    WHEN NO_DATA_FOUND THEN
        DBMS_OUTPUT.PUT_LINE ('There is no such student');
END;
```

The part of the example shown in bold has been added to the original version of the example. The new version of the example has a different SELECT INTO statement. To answer the question posed a moment ago, the exception NO_DATA_FOUND can be raised by the inner block because the SELECT INTO statement does not contain a group function, COUNT(). This function always returns a result, so when no rows are returned by the SELECT INTO statement, the value returned by COUNT(*) equals 0.

Now, run this example with a value of 284 for the student ID. The following output is produced:

```
Enter value for sv_student_id: 284
old    2:    v_student_id NUMBER := &sv_student_id;
new    2:    v_student_id NUMBER := 284;
Student name is Salewa Lindeman
There is no such student

PL/SQL procedure successfully completed.
```

You have probably noticed that this example produces only a partial output. Even though you can see the student's name, an error message is displayed, saying that this student does not exist. This error message is displayed because the exception NO_DATA_FOUND is raised in the inner block.

The SELECT INTO statement of the outer block returns the student's name, and it is displayed on the screen by the DBMS_OUTPUT.PUT_LINE statement. Next, control is passed to the inner block. The SELECT INTO statement of the inner block does not return any rows. As a result, the error occurs, and the NO_DATA_FOUND exception is raised.

Next, PL/SQL tries to find a handler for the exception NO_DATA_FOUND in the inner block. Because there is no such handler in the inner block, control is transferred to the exception section of the outer block. The exception section of the outer block contains the handler for the exception NO_DATA_FOUND. This handler executes, and the message There is no such student is displayed on the screen. This process is called exception propagation, and it is discussed in detail in Lab 9.3.

This example has been shown for illustrative purposes only. In its current version, it is not very useful. The SELECT INTO statement of the inner block is prone to another exception, TOO_MANY_ROWS, that this example does not handle. In addition, the error message There is no such student is not very descriptive when the inner block raises the exception NO_DATA_FOUND.

▼ LAB 9.1 EXERCISES

This section provides exercises and suggested answers, with discussion related to how those answers resulted. The most important thing to realize is whether your answer works. You should figure out the implications of the answers and what the effects are of any different answers you may come up with.

9.1.1 Understand the Scope of an Exception

In this exercise, you display the number of students for a given zip code. You use nested PL/SQL blocks to achieve the desired results. The original PL/SQL script does not contain any exception handlers. Therefore, you are asked to identify possible errors that may occur and define exception handlers for them.

Create the following PL/SQL script:

```
-- ch9_1a.sql, version 1.0
SET SERVEROUTPUT ON
DECLARE
   v_zip   VARCHAR2(5) := '&sv_zip';
   v_total NUMBER(1);

-- outer block
BEGIN
   DBMS_OUTPUT.PUT_LINE ('Check if provided zipcode is valid');
   SELECT zip
     INTO v_zip
     FROM zipcode
    WHERE zip = v_zip;

   -- inner block
   BEGIN
      SELECT count(*)
        INTO v_total
        FROM student
       WHERE zip = v_zip;

      DBMS_OUTPUT.PUT_LINE ('There are '||v_total||
         ' students for zipcode '||v_zip);
   END;
   DBMS_OUTPUT.PUT_LINE ('Done...');
END;
```

Execute the script, providing 07024 for the value of the zip code, and then answer the following questions:

A) What output is printed on the screen?

ANSWER: The output should look like the following:

```
Enter value for sv_zip: 07024
old   2:   v_zip   VARCHAR2(5) := '&sv_zip';
new   2:   v_zip   VARCHAR2(5) := '07024';
Check if provided zip code is valid
There is(are) 9 student(s) for zipcode 07024
Done...

PL/SQL procedure successfully completed.
```

B) The first run of this example succeeds. The output produced by the example shows that there are nine students for zip code 07024. What happens if there are ten students with the zip code 07024? What output is produced? To answer this question, you need to add a record to the STUDENT table:

```
INSERT INTO student (student_id, salutation, first_name, last_name,
   street_address, zip, phone, employer, registration_date,
   created_by, created_date, modified_by, modified_date)
VALUES (STUDENT_ID_SEQ.NEXTVAL, 'Mr.', 'John', 'Smith',
```

```
    '100 Main St.', '07024', '718-555-5555', 'ABC Co.', SYSDATE,
    USER, SYSDATE, USER, SYSDATE);


COMMIT;
```

ANSWER: The example produces partial output only. When the total number of students is calculated for zip code 07024, the following error occurs:

```
Enter value for sv_zip: 07024
old   2:    v_zip   VARCHAR2(5) := '&sv_zip';
new   2:    v_zip   VARCHAR2(5) := '07024';
Check if provided zipcode is valid
DECLARE
*
ERROR at line 1:
ORA-06502: PL/SQL: numeric or value error: number precision too large
ORA-06512: at line 15
```

The SELECT INTO statement returns a value of 10. However, the variable v_total has been defined so that it can hold only single-digit numbers. Because 10 is a two-digit number, the error occurs during the execution of the SELECT INTO statement. As a result, an error message is displayed.

Notice that as soon as the error occurs, the example terminates because there is no exception handler for this error.

C) Based on the error message produced by the example in the preceding question, what exception handler must be added to the script?

ANSWER: The newly created script should look similar to one of the following two scripts. The error message produced by the example in the preceding question refers to a numeric or value error. Therefore, an exception VALUE_ERROR or INVALID_NUMBER must be added to the script. Changes are shown in bold:

```
-- ch9_1b.sql, version 2.0
SET SERVEROUTPUT ON
DECLARE
    v_zip   VARCHAR2(5) := '&sv_zip';
    v_total NUMBER(1);

-- outer block
BEGIN
    DBMS_OUTPUT.PUT_LINE ('Check if provided zipcode is valid');
    SELECT zip
      INTO v_zip
      FROM zipcode
     WHERE zip = v_zip;

    -- inner block
    BEGIN
       SELECT count(*)
         INTO v_total
         FROM student
        WHERE zip = v_zip;
```

```
        DBMS_OUTPUT.PUT_LINE ('There are '||v_total||
            ' students for zipcode '||v_zip);
    EXCEPTION
        WHEN VALUE_ERROR OR INVALID_NUMBER THEN
            DBMS_OUTPUT.PUT_LINE ('An error has occurred');
    END;
    DBMS_OUTPUT.PUT_LINE ('Done...');
END;

-- ch9_1c.sql, version 3.0
SET SERVEROUTPUT ON
DECLARE
    v_zip    VARCHAR2(5) := '&sv_zip';
    v_total NUMBER(1);

-- outer block
BEGIN
    DBMS_OUTPUT.PUT_LINE ('Check if provided zipcode is valid');
    SELECT zip
      INTO v_zip
      FROM zipcode
     WHERE zip = v_zip;

    -- inner block
    BEGIN
        SELECT count(*)
          INTO v_total
          FROM student
         WHERE zip = v_zip;

        DBMS_OUTPUT.PUT_LINE ('There are '||v_total||
            ' students for zipcode '||v_zip);
    END;
    DBMS_OUTPUT.PUT_LINE ('Done...');

EXCEPTION
    WHEN VALUE_ERROR OR INVALID_NUMBER THEN
        DBMS_OUTPUT.PUT_LINE ('An error has occurred');
END;
```

In the second version of the script (ch09_1b.sql), the exception-handling section is added to the inner block. In the third version of the script (ch09_1c.sql), the exception-handling section is added to the outer block. Both versions of the script are similar in their behavior of catching the error and terminating successfully. However, there is a slight difference, as shown in the outputs. The first output corresponds to version 2, and the second output corresponds to version 3:

```
Enter value for sv_zip: 07024
old   2:    v_zip    VARCHAR2(5) := '&sv_zip';
new   2:    v_zip    VARCHAR2(5) := '07024';
Check if provided zipcode is valid
```

```
An error has occurred
Done...

PL/SQL procedure successfully completed.

Enter value for sv_zip: 07024
old    2:     v_zip    VARCHAR2(5) := '&sv_zip';
new    2:     v_zip    VARCHAR2(5) := '07024';
Check if provided zipcode is valid
An error has occurred

PL/SQL procedure successfully completed.
```

D) Explain the difference in the outputs produced by versions 2 and 3 of the script.

ANSWER: Version 2 of the script has an exception-handling section in the inner block, where the exception actually occurs. When the exception is encountered, control of the execution is passed to this exception-handling section, and the message An error has occurred is displayed on the screen. Because the exception was handled successfully, control of the execution is then passed to the outer block, and Done . . . is displayed on the screen. Version 3 of the script has an exception-handling section in the outer block. In this case, when the exception occurs in the inner block, control of the execution is passed to the exception-handling section of the outer block, because the inner block does not have its own exception-handling section. As a result, the message Done . . . is not displayed on the screen. As mentioned earlier, this behavior is called exception propagation, and it is discussed in detail in Lab 9.3.

LAB 9.2
User-Defined Exceptions

LAB OBJECTIVE

After completing this lab, you will be able to

▶ Use user-defined exceptions

Often in your programs you may need to handle problems that are specific to the program you write. For example, your program asks a user to enter a value for student ID. This value is then assigned to the variable $v\_student\_id$ that is used later in the program. Generally, you want a positive number for an ID. By mistake, the user enters a negative number. However, no error occurs, because the variable $v\_student\_id$ has been defined as a number, and the user has supplied a legitimate numeric value. Therefore, you may want to implement your own exception to handle this situation.

This type of exception is called a user-defined exception because the programmer defines it. As a result, before the exception can be used, it must be declared. A user-defined exception is declared in the declaration section of a PL/SQL block:

```
DECLARE
    exception_name EXCEPTION;
```

Notice that this declaration looks similar to a variable declaration. You specify an exception name followed by the keyword EXCEPTION. Consider the following code fragment:

FOR EXAMPLE

```
DECLARE
   e_invalid_id EXCEPTION;
```

In this example, the name of the exception is prefixed by the letter e. This syntax is not required, but it allows you to differentiate between variable names and exception names.

After an exception has been declared, the executable statements associated with this exception are specified in the exception-handling section of the block. The format of the exception-handling section is the same as for built-in exceptions. Consider the following code fragment:

FOR EXAMPLE

```
DECLARE
   e_invalid_id EXCEPTION;
BEGIN
   ...
EXCEPTION
   WHEN e_invalid_id THEN
      DBMS_OUTPUT.PUT_LINE ('An id cannot be negative');
END;
```

You already know that built-in exceptions are raised implicitly. In other words, when a certain error occurs, a built-in exception associated with this error is raised. Of course, you are assuming that you have included this exception in the exception-handling section of your program. For example, a TOO_MANY_ROWS exception is raised when a SELECT INTO statement returns multiple rows. Next, you will explore how a user-defined exception is raised.

A user-defined exception must be raised explicitly. In other words, you need to specify in your program under what circumstances an exception must be raised:

```
DECLARE
   exception_name EXCEPTION;
BEGIN
   ...
   IF CONDITION THEN
      RAISE exception_name;
   ELSE
      ...
   END IF;
EXCEPTION
   WHEN exception_name THEN
      ERROR-PROCESSING STATEMENTS;
END;
```

In this structure, the circumstances under which a user-defined exception must be raised are determined with the help of the IF-THEN-ELSE statement. If *CONDITION* evaluates to TRUE, a user-defined exception is raised. If *CONDITION* evaluates to FALSE, the program proceeds with its normal execution. In other words, the statements associated with the ELSE part of the IF-THEN-ELSE statement are executed. Any form of the IF statement can be used to check when a user-defined exception must be raised.

In the next modified version of the earlier example used in this lab, you will see that the exception e_invalid_id is raised when a negative number is entered for the variable v_student_id:

FOR EXAMPLE

```
DECLARE
   v_student_id      student.student_id%type := &sv_student_id;
   v_total_courses NUMBER;
   e_invalid_id     EXCEPTION;
BEGIN
   IF v_student_id < 0 THEN
      RAISE e_invalid_id;
   ELSE
      SELECT COUNT(*)
        INTO v_total_courses
        FROM enrollment
       WHERE student_id = v_student_id;

      DBMS_OUTPUT.PUT_LINE ('The student is registered for '||
          v_total_courses||' courses');
   END IF;
   DBMS_OUTPUT.PUT_LINE ('No exception has been raised');
EXCEPTION
   WHEN e_invalid_id THEN
      DBMS_OUTPUT.PUT_LINE ('An id cannot be negative');
END;
```

In this example, the exception e_invalid_id is raised with the help of the IF-THEN-ELSE statement. After the user supplies a value for v_student_id, the sign of this numeric value is checked. If the value is less than 0, the IF-THEN-ELSE statement evaluates to TRUE, and the exception e_invalid_id is raised. Therefore, control transfers to the exception-handling section of the block. Next, statements associated with this exception are executed. In this case, the message An id cannot be negative is displayed on the screen. If the value entered for v_student_id is positive, the IF-THEN-ELSE statement yields FALSE, and the ELSE part of the IF-THEN-ELSE statement is executed.

Run this example for two values of v_student_id: 102 and −102.

A first run of the example (student ID is 102) produces this output:

```
Enter value for sv_student_id: 102
old    2:    v_student_id STUDENT.STUDENT_ID%TYPE := &sv_student_id;
new    2:    v_student_id STUDENT.STUDENT_ID%TYPE := 102;
The student is registered for 2 courses
No exception has been raised

PL/SQL procedure successfully completed.
```

For this run, you entered a positive value for the variable v_student_id. As a result, the IF-THEN-ELSE statement evaluates to FALSE, and the ELSE part of the statement executes. The SELECT INTO statement determines how many records are in the ENROLLMENT table for a given student ID. Next, the message The student is registered for 2 courses is displayed on the screen. At this point, the IF-THEN-ELSE statement is complete. So control is transferred to the DBMS_OUTPUT.PUT_LINE statement that follows END IF. As a result, another message is displayed on the screen.

A second run of the example (student ID is –102) produces the following output:

```
Enter value for sv_student_id: -102
old    2:    v_student_id STUDENT.STUDENT_ID%TYPE := &sv_student_id;
new    2:    v_student_id STUDENT.STUDENT_ID%TYPE := -102;
An id cannot be negative

PL/SQL procedure successfully completed.
```

For the second run, a negative value was entered for the variable v_student_id. The IF-THEN-ELSE statement evaluates to TRUE, and the exception e_invalid_id is raised. As a result, control is transferred to the exception-handling section of the block, and the error message An id cannot be negative is displayed on the screen.

WATCH OUT!

It is important for you to note that the RAISE statement should be used in conjunction with an IF statement. Otherwise, control of the execution is transferred to the exception-handling section of the block for every execution. Consider the following example:

```
DECLARE
    e_test_exception EXCEPTION;
BEGIN
    DBMS_OUTPUT.PUT_LINE ('Exception has not been raised');
    RAISE e_test_exception;
    DBMS_OUTPUT.PUT_LINE ('Exception has been raised');
EXCEPTION
    WHEN e_test_exception THEN
        DBMS_OUTPUT.PUT_LINE ('An error has occurred');
END;
```

Every time this example is run, the following output is produced:

```
Exception has not been raised
An error has occurred

PL/SQL procedure successfully completed.
```

Even though no error has occurred, control is transferred to the exception-handling section. It is important for you to check to see if the error has occurred before raising the exception associated with that error.

The same scope rules apply to user-defined exceptions that apply to built-in exceptions. An exception declared in the inner block must be raised in the inner block and defined in the exception-handling section of the inner block. Consider the following example:

FOR EXAMPLE

```
-- outer block
BEGIN
    DBMS_OUTPUT.PUT_LINE ('Outer block');

    -- inner block
    DECLARE
        e_my_exception EXCEPTION;
    BEGIN
        DBMS_OUTPUT.PUT_LINE ('Inner block');
    EXCEPTION
        WHEN e_my_exception THEN
            DBMS_OUTPUT.PUT_LINE ('An error has occurred');
    END;

    IF 10 > &sv_number THEN
        RAISE e_my_exception;
    END IF;
END;
```

In this example, the exception, $e\_my\_exception$, is declared in the inner block. However, you are trying to raise this exception in the outer block. This example causes a syntax error because the exception declared in the inner block ceases to exist as soon as the inner block terminates. As a result, this example produces the following output:

```
Enter value for sv_number: 11
old   12:    IF 10 > &sv_number THEN
new   12:    IF 10 > 11 THEN
        RAISE e_my_exception;
            *
ERROR at line 13:
ORA-06550: line 13, column 13:
PLS-00201: identifier 'E_MY_EXCEPTION' must be declared
ORA-06550: line 13, column 7:
PL/SQL: Statement ignored
```

Notice that the error message

```
PLS-00201: identifier 'E_MY_EXCEPTION' must be declared
```

is the same error message you get when trying to use a variable that has not been declared.

▼ LAB 9.2 EXERCISES

This section provides exercises and suggested answers, with discussion related to how those answers resulted. The most important thing to realize is whether your answer works. You should figure out the implications of the answers and what the effects are of any different answers you may come up with.

9.2.1 **Use User-Defined Exceptions**

In this exercise, you define an exception that allows you to raise an error if an instructor teaches ten or more sections.

Create the following PL/SQL script:

```
-- ch9_2a.sql, version 1.0
SET SERVEROUTPUT ON
DECLARE
    v_instructor_id     NUMBER := &sv_instructor_id;
    v_tot_sections      NUMBER;
    v_name              VARCHAR2(30);
    e_too_many_sections EXCEPTION;
BEGIN
    SELECT COUNT(*)
      INTO v_tot_sections
      FROM section
     WHERE instructor_id = v_instructor_id;

    IF v_tot_sections >= 10 THEN
       RAISE e_too_many_sections;
    ELSE
       SELECT RTRIM(first_name)||' '||RTRIM(last_name)
         INTO v_name
         FROM instructor
        WHERE instructor_id = v_instructor_id;

       DBMS_OUTPUT.PUT_LINE ('Instructor, '||v_name||', teaches '||
          v_tot_sections||' sections');
    END IF;
EXCEPTION
    WHEN e_too_many_sections THEN
       DBMS_OUTPUT.PUT_LINE ('This instructor teaches too much');
END;
```

Execute the script twice, providing 101 and 102 for the values of instructor ID, and then answer the following questions:

A) What output is printed on the screen? Explain the difference in the outputs produced.

ANSWER: The outputs should look like the following:

```
Enter value for sv_instructor_id: 101
old   2:     v_instructor_id     NUMBER := &sv_instructor_id;
new   2:     v_instructor_id     NUMBER := 101;
Instructor, Fernand Hanks, teaches 9 sections

PL/SQL procedure successfully completed.

Enter value for sv_instructor_id: 102
old   2:     v_instructor_id     NUMBER := &sv_instructor_id;
new   2:     v_instructor_id     NUMBER := 102;
This instructor teaches too much

PL/SQL procedure successfully completed.
```

The first output is produced when value 101 is provided for the instructor ID. Because the number of sections taught by this instructor is less than 10, the ELSE part of the IF-THEN-ELSE statement is executed, and the instructor's name is displayed on the screen.

The second output is produced when value 102 is provided for the instructor ID. In this case, the number of sections taught by the instructor is 10. As a result, the IF part of the IF-THEN-ELSE statement is executed, and the user-defined exception is raised. After the exception is raised, control of the execution is transferred to the exception-handling section of the block, and the message `This instructor teaches too much` is displayed on the screen.

B) What condition causes the user-defined exception to be raised?

ANSWER: The user-defined exception is raised if the condition

```
v_tot_sections >= 10
```

evaluates to TRUE. In other words, if an instructor teaches ten or more sections, the exception `e_too_many_sections` is raised.

C) How would you change the script to display an instructor's name in the error message as well?

ANSWER: The script should look similar to the following. All changes are shown in bold.

```
-- ch9_2b.sql, version 2.0
SET SERVEROUTPUT ON
DECLARE
    v_instructor_id      NUMBER := &sv_instructor_id;
    v_tot_sections       NUMBER;
    v_name               VARCHAR2(30);
    e_too_many_sections EXCEPTION;
BEGIN
    SELECT COUNT(*)
      INTO v_tot_sections
      FROM section
     WHERE instructor_id = v_instructor_id;

    SELECT RTRIM(first_name)||' '||RTRIM(last_name)
      INTO v_name
      FROM instructor
     WHERE instructor_id = v_instructor_id;

    IF v_tot_sections >= 10 THEN
       RAISE e_too_many_sections;
    ELSE
       DBMS_OUTPUT.PUT_LINE ('Instructor, '||v_name||', teaches '||
          v_tot_sections||' sections');
    END IF;

EXCEPTION
    WHEN e_too_many_sections THEN
       DBMS_OUTPUT.PUT_LINE ('Instructor, '||v_name||
          ', teaches too much');
END;
```

The new version of this script has only two changes. First, the SELECT INTO statement that returns the instructor name has been moved from the ELSE part of the IF-THEN-ELSE statement immediately after the first SELECT INTO statement. Second, the error message in the exception-handling section has been modified to include the instructor name.

The new version of this script produces the following output:

```
Enter value for sv_instructor_id: 102
old   2:     v_instructor_id      NUMBER := &sv_instructor_id;
new   2:     v_instructor_id      NUMBER := 102;
Instructor, Tom Wojick, teaches too much

PL/SQL procedure successfully completed.
```

In the version of the script shown next, the DBMS_OUTPUT.PUT_LINE statement displaying how many sections are taught by the instructor has been moved from the ELSE portion of the IF-THEN-ELSE statement as well. This eliminates the ELSE portion of the IF-THEN-ELSE statement. In this case, the output produced by the script contains the number of sections for the instructor even when the e_too_many_sections exception occurs.

```
-- ch9_2c.sql, version 3.0
SET SERVEROUTPUT ON
DECLARE
    v_instructor_id     NUMBER := &sv_instructor_id;
    v_tot_sections      NUMBER;
    v_name              VARCHAR2(30);
    e_too_many_sections EXCEPTION;
BEGIN
    SELECT COUNT(*)
      INTO v_tot_sections
      FROM section
     WHERE instructor_id = v_instructor_id;

    SELECT RTRIM(first_name)||' '||RTRIM(last_name)
      INTO v_name
      FROM instructor
     WHERE instructor_id = v_instructor_id;

    DBMS_OUTPUT.PUT_LINE ('Instructor, '||v_name||', teaches '||
       v_tot_sections||' sections');

    IF v_tot_sections >= 10 THEN
       RAISE e_too_many_sections;
    END IF;

EXCEPTION
    WHEN e_too_many_sections THEN
       DBMS_OUTPUT.PUT_LINE ('Instructor, '||v_name||
          ', teaches too much');
END;
```

```
Enter value for sv_instructor_id: 102
old    2:    v_instructor_id     NUMBER := &sv_instructor_id;
new    2:    v_instructor_id     NUMBER := 102;
Instructor, Tom Wojick, teaches 10 sections
Instructor, Tom Wojick, teaches too much

PL/SQL procedure successfully completed.
```

L A B 9 . 3
Exception Propagation

LAB OBJECTIVES

After completing this lab, you will be able to

- ▶ Understand how exceptions propagate
- ▶ Reraise exceptions

You already have seen how different types of exceptions are raised when a runtime error occurs in the executable portion of the PL/SQL block. However, a runtime error also may occur in the declaration section or exception-handling section of the block. The rules that govern how exceptions are raised in these situations are called exception propagation.

Consider the first case: A runtime error occurs in the executable section of the PL/SQL block. This case should be treated as a review, because the examples you have seen so far in this chapter show how an exception is raised when an error occurs in the executable section of the block.

If an exception is associated with a particular error, control is passed to the exception-handling section of the block. After the statements associated with the exception are executed, control is passed to the host environment or to the enclosing block. If there is no exception handler for this error, the exception is propagated to the enclosing block (outer block). Then the steps just described are repeated again. If no exception handler is found, execution of the program halts, and control is transferred to the host environment.

Next, take a look at a second case: A runtime error occurs in the declaration section of the block. If there is no outer block, execution of the program halts, and control is passed to the host environment. Consider the following script:

FOR EXAMPLE

```
DECLARE
   v_test_var CHAR(3):= 'ABCDE';
BEGIN
   DBMS_OUTPUT.PUT_LINE ('This is a test');
EXCEPTION
   WHEN INVALID_NUMBER OR VALUE_ERROR THEN
      DBMS_OUTPUT.PUT_LINE ('An error has occurred');
END;
```

When executed, this example produces the following output:

```
DECLARE
*
ERROR at line 1:
ORA-06502: PL/SQL: numeric or value error: character string buffer
too small
ORA-06512: at line 2
```

As you can see, the assignment statement in the declaration section of the block causes an error. Even though there is an exception handler for this error, the block cannot execute successfully. Based on this example, you may conclude that *when a runtime error occurs in the declaration section of the PL/SQL block, the exception-handling section of this block cannot catch the error.*

Next, consider an example with nested PL/SQL blocks:

FOR EXAMPLE

```
--outer block
BEGIN
   -- inner block
   DECLARE
      v_test_var CHAR(3):= 'ABCDE';
   BEGIN
      DBMS_OUTPUT.PUT_LINE ('This is a test');
   EXCEPTION
      WHEN INVALID_NUMBER OR VALUE_ERROR THEN
         DBMS_OUTPUT.PUT_LINE ('An error has occurred in '||
            'the inner block');
   END;
EXCEPTION
   WHEN INVALID_NUMBER OR VALUE_ERROR THEN
      DBMS_OUTPUT.PUT_LINE ('An error has occurred in the '||
         'program');
END;
```

When executed, this example produces the following output:

```
An error has occurred in the program

PL/SQL procedure successfully completed.
```

In this example, the PL/SQL block is enclosed in another block, and the program can complete. This is possible because the exception defined in the outer block is raised when the error occurs in the declaration section of the inner block. Therefore, you can conclude that *when a runtime error occurs in the declaration section of the inner block, the exception immediately propagates to the enclosing (outer) block.*

Finally, consider a third case: A runtime error occurs in the exception-handling section of the block. Just like the previous case, if there is no outer block, execution of the program halts, and control is passed to the host environment. Consider the following script:

FOR EXAMPLE

```
DECLARE
   v_test_var CHAR(3) := 'ABC';
BEGIN
   v_test_var := '1234';
   DBMS_OUTPUT.PUT_LINE ('v_test_var: '||v_test_var);
EXCEPTION
   WHEN INVALID_NUMBER OR VALUE_ERROR THEN
      v_test_var := 'ABCD';
      DBMS_OUTPUT.PUT_LINE ('An error has occurred');
END;
```

When executed, this example produces the following output:

```
DECLARE
*
ERROR at line 1:
ORA-06502: PL/SQL: numeric or value error: character string buffer
 too small
ORA-06512: at line 8
ORA-06502: PL/SQL: numeric or value error: character string buffer
 too small
```

As you can see, the assignment statement in the executable section of the block causes an error. Therefore, control is transferred to the exception-handling section of the block. However, the assignment statement in the exception-handling section of the block raises the same error. As a result, the output of this example contains the same error message twice. The first message is generated by the assignment statement in the executable section of the block, and the second message is generated by the assignment statement of the exception-handling section of this block. Based on this example, you may conclude that *when a runtime error occurs in the exception-handling section of the PL/SQL block, the exception-handling section of this block cannot prevent the error.*

Next, consider an example with nested PL/SQL blocks:

FOR EXAMPLE

```
--outer block
BEGIN
   -- inner block
   DECLARE
      v_test_var CHAR(3) := 'ABC';
   BEGIN
      v_test_var := '1234';
      DBMS_OUTPUT.PUT_LINE ('v_test_var: '||v_test_var);
```

```
   EXCEPTION
      WHEN INVALID_NUMBER OR VALUE_ERROR THEN
         v_test_var := 'ABCD';
         DBMS_OUTPUT.PUT_LINE ('An error has occurred in '||
            'the inner block');
   END;
EXCEPTION
   WHEN INVALID_NUMBER OR VALUE_ERROR THEN
      DBMS_OUTPUT.PUT_LINE ('An error has occurred in the '||
         'program');
END;
```

When executed, this example produces the following output:

```
   An error has occurred in the program

   PL/SQL procedure successfully completed.
```

In this example, the PL/SQL block is enclosed by another block, and the program can complete. This is possible because the exception defined in the outer block is raised when the error occurs in the exception-handling section of the inner block. Therefore, you can conclude that *when a runtime error occurs in the exception-handling section of the inner block, the exception immediately propagates to the enclosing block.*

In the previous two examples, an exception is raised implicitly by a runtime error in the exception-handling section of the block. However, the RAISE statement can explicitly raise an exception in the exception-handling section of the block. Consider the following example:

FOR EXAMPLE

```
--outer block
DECLARE
   e_exception1 EXCEPTION;
   e_exception2 EXCEPTION;
BEGIN
   -- inner block
   BEGIN
      RAISE e_exception1;
   EXCEPTION
      WHEN e_exception1 THEN
         RAISE e_exception2;
      WHEN e_exception2 THEN
         DBMS_OUTPUT.PUT_LINE ('An error has occurred in '||
            'the inner block');
   END;
EXCEPTION
   WHEN e_exception2 THEN
      DBMS_OUTPUT.PUT_LINE ('An error has occurred in '||
         'the program');
END;
```

This example produces the following output:

```
An error has occurred in the program

PL/SQL procedure successfully completed.
```

Here two exceptions are declared: $e\_exception1$ and $e\_exception2$. Exception $e\_exception1$ is raised in the inner block via the RAISE statement. In the exception-handling section of the block, exception $e\_exception1$ tries to raise $e\_exception2$. Even though there is an exception handler for the exception $e\_exception2$ in the inner block, control is transferred to the outer block. This happens because only one exception can be raised in the exception-handling section of the block. Only after one exception has been handled can another be raised, but two or more exceptions cannot be raised simultaneously.

When a PL/SQL block is not enclosed by another block, control is transferred to the host environment, and the program cannot complete successfully. This is illustrated by the following example:

FOR EXAMPLE

```
DECLARE
    e_exception1 EXCEPTION;
BEGIN
    RAISE e_exception1;
END;
```

The following error message is displayed:

```
DECLARE
*
ERROR at line 1:
ORA-06510: PL/SQL: unhandled user-defined exception
ORA-06512: at line 4
```

RERAISING AN EXCEPTION

On some occasions you may want to be able to stop your program if a certain type of error occurs. In other words, you may want to handle an exception in the inner block and then pass it to the outer block. This process is called reraising an exception. The following example helps illustrate this point:

FOR EXAMPLE

```
-- outer block
DECLARE
    e_exception EXCEPTION;
BEGIN
    -- inner block
    BEGIN
        RAISE e_exception;
```

```
    EXCEPTION
        WHEN e_exception THEN
            RAISE;
    END;
EXCEPTION
    WHEN e_exception THEN
        DBMS_OUTPUT.PUT_LINE ('An error has occurred');
END;
```

In this example, the exception $e\_exception$ is declared in the outer block. Then it is raised in the inner block. As a result, control is transferred to the exception-handling section of the inner block. The RAISE statement in the exception-handling section of the block causes the exception to propagate to the exception-handling section of the outer block.

Notice that when the RAISE statement is used in the exception-handling section of the inner block, it is not followed by the exception name.

When run, this example produces the following output:

```
    The error has occurred

    PL/SQL procedure successfully completed.
```

WATCH OUT!

It is important to note that when an exception is reraised in the block that is not enclosed by any other block, the program is unable to complete successfully. Consider the following example:

```
    DECLARE
        e_exception EXCEPTION;
    BEGIN
        RAISE e_exception;
    EXCEPTION
        WHEN e_exception THEN
            RAISE;
    END;
```

When run, this example produces the following output:

```
    DECLARE
    *
    ERROR at line 1:
    ORA-06510: PL/SQL: unhandled user-defined exception
    ORA-06512: at line 7
```

▼ LAB 9.3 EXERCISES

This section provides exercises and suggested answers, with discussion related to how those answers resulted. The most important thing to realize is whether your answer works. You should figure out the implications of the answers and what the effects are of any different answers you may come up with.

9.3.1 Understand How Exceptions Propagate

In this exercise, you use nested PL/SQL blocks to practice exception propagation. You are asked to experiment with the script via exceptions. Try to answer the questions before you run the script. After you have answered the questions, run the script and check your answers.

Create the following PL/SQL script:

```
-- ch9_3a.sql, version 1.0
SET SERVEROUTPUT ON
DECLARE
    v_my_name VARCHAR2(15) := 'ELENA SILVESTROVA';
BEGIN
    DBMS_OUTPUT.PUT_LINE ('My name is '||v_my_name);

    DECLARE
        v_your_name VARCHAR2(15);
    BEGIN
        v_your_name := '&sv_your_name';
        DBMS_OUTPUT.PUT_LINE ('Your name is '||v_your_name);
    EXCEPTION
        WHEN VALUE_ERROR THEN
            DBMS_OUTPUT.PUT_LINE ('Error in the inner block');
            DBMS_OUTPUT.PUT_LINE ('This name is too long');
    END;

EXCEPTION
    WHEN VALUE_ERROR THEN
        DBMS_OUTPUT.PUT_LINE ('Error in the outer block');
        DBMS_OUTPUT.PUT_LINE ('This name is too long');
END;
```

Answer the following questions, and then execute the script:

A) What exception is raised by the assignment statement in the declaration section of the outer block?

ANSWER: The exception VALUE_ERROR is raised by the assignment statement of the outer block.

The variable v_my_name is declared as VARCHAR2(15). However, the value that is assigned to this variable contains 17 letters. As a result, the assignment statement causes a runtime error.

B) After this exception (based on the preceding question) is raised, will the program terminate successfully? Explain why or why not.

ANSWER: When the exception VALUE_ERROR is raised, the script cannot complete successfully because the error occurs in the declaration section of the outer block. Because the outer block is not enclosed by any other block, control is transferred to the host environment. As a result, an error message is generated when this example is run.

C) How would you change this script so that the exception can handle an error caused by the assignment statement in the declaration section of the outer block?

ANSWER: For the exception to handle the error generated by the assignment statement in the declaration section of the outer block, the assignment statement must be moved to the executable section of this block. All changes are shown in bold.

```
-- ch9_3b.sql, version 2.0
SET SERVEROUTPUT ON
DECLARE
   v_my_name VARCHAR2(15);
BEGIN
   v_my_name := 'ELENA SILVESTROVA';
   DBMS_OUTPUT.PUT_LINE ('My name is '||v_my_name);

   DECLARE
      v_your_name VARCHAR2(15);
   BEGIN
      v_your_name := '&sv_your_name';
      DBMS_OUTPUT.PUT_LINE ('Your name is '||v_your_name);
   EXCEPTION
      WHEN VALUE_ERROR THEN
         DBMS_OUTPUT.PUT_LINE ('Error in the inner block');
         DBMS_OUTPUT.PUT_LINE ('This name is too long');
   END;

EXCEPTION
   WHEN VALUE_ERROR THEN
      DBMS_OUTPUT.PUT_LINE ('Error in the outer block');
      DBMS_OUTPUT.PUT_LINE ('This name is too long');
END;
```

The new version of this script produces the following output:

```
Enter value for sv_your_name: TEST A NAME
old    9:          v_your_name := '&sv_your_name';
new    9:          v_your_name := 'TEST A NAME';
Error in the outer block
This name is too long

PL/SQL procedure successfully completed.
```

D) Change the value of the variable from "Elena Silvestrova" to "Elena." Then change the script so that if the assignment statement of the inner block causes an error, it is handled by the exception-handling section of the outer block.

ANSWER: The script should look similar to the following. All changes are shown in bold.

```
-- ch9_3c.sql, version 3.0
SET SERVEROUTPUT ON
DECLARE
   v_my_name VARCHAR2(15) := 'ELENA';
BEGIN
   DBMS_OUTPUT.PUT_LINE ('My name is '||v_my_name);
```

```
DECLARE
    v_your_name VARCHAR2(15) := '&sv_your_name';
BEGIN
    DBMS_OUTPUT.PUT_LINE ('Your name is '||v_your_name);
EXCEPTION
    WHEN VALUE_ERROR THEN
        DBMS_OUTPUT.PUT_LINE ('Error in the inner block');
        DBMS_OUTPUT.PUT_LINE ('This name is too long');
    END;

EXCEPTION
    WHEN VALUE_ERROR THEN
        DBMS_OUTPUT.PUT_LINE ('Error in the outer block');
        DBMS_OUTPUT.PUT_LINE ('This name is too long');
END;
```

In this version of the example, the assignment statement has been moved from the executable section of the inner block to the declaration section of this block. As a result, if the assignment statement of the inner block raises an exception, control is transferred to the exception section of the outer block.

You can modify this example in a different manner that allows you to achieve the same result.

```
-- ch9_3d.sql, version 4.0
SET SERVEROUTPUT ON
DECLARE
    v_my_name VARCHAR2(15) := 'ELENA';
BEGIN
    DBMS_OUTPUT.PUT_LINE ('My name is '||v_my_name);

    DECLARE
        v_your_name VARCHAR2(15);
    BEGIN
        v_your_name := '&sv_your_name';
        DBMS_OUTPUT.PUT_LINE ('Your name is '||v_your_name);
    EXCEPTION
        WHEN VALUE_ERROR THEN
            RAISE;
    END;

EXCEPTION
    WHEN VALUE_ERROR THEN
        DBMS_OUTPUT.PUT_LINE ('Error in the outer block');
        DBMS_OUTPUT.PUT_LINE ('This name is too long');
END;
```

In this version of the example, the RAISE statement is used in the exception-handling section of the inner block. As a result, the exception is reraised in the outer block.

Both versions of this example produce very similar output. The first output is generated by the third version of the example, and the second output is generated by the fourth version of the example.

```
Enter value for sv_your_name: THIS NAME MUST BE REALLY LONG
old   6:         v_your_name VARCHAR2(15) := '&sv_your_name';
new   6:         v_your_name VARCHAR2(15) := 'THIS NAME MUST BE
                                             REALLY LONG';
My name is ELENA
Error in the outer block
This name is too long

PL/SQL procedure successfully completed.

Enter value for sv_your_name: THIS NAME MUST BE REALLY LONG
old   8:         v_your_name := '&sv_your_name';
new   8:         v_your_name := 'THIS NAME MUST BE REALLY LONG';
My name is ELENA
Error in the outer block
This name is too long

PL/SQL procedure successfully completed.
```

Notice that the only difference between the two versions of the output is the line number of the substitution variable. In the first version of the output, the assignment statement takes place in the declaration section of the inner block. In the second version of the output, the assignment statement occurs in the executable section of the inner block. However, all messages displayed on the screen are identical in both versions of the output.

9.3.2 Reraise Exceptions

In this exercise, you check the number of sections for a course. If a course does not have a section associated with it, you raise an exception, e_no_sections. Again, try to answer the questions before you run the script. After you have answered the questions, run the script and check your answers.

Create the following PL/SQL script:

```
-- ch9_4a.sql, version 1.0
SET SERVEROUTPUT ON
DECLARE
   v_course_no   NUMBER := 430;
   v_total       NUMBER;
   e_no_sections EXCEPTION;
BEGIN
   BEGIN
      SELECT COUNT(*)
        INTO v_total
        FROM section
       WHERE course_no = v_course_no;

      IF v_total = 0 THEN
         RAISE e_no_sections;
      ELSE
         DBMS_OUTPUT.PUT_LINE ('Course, '||v_course_no||
            ' has '||v_total||' sections');
      END IF;
```

```
      EXCEPTION
         WHEN e_no_sections THEN
            DBMS_OUTPUT.PUT_LINE ('There are no sections for course '||
               v_course_no);
      END;
      DBMS_OUTPUT.PUT_LINE ('Done...');
   END;
```

Answer the following questions, and then execute the script:

A) What exception is raised if there are no sections for a given course number?

ANSWER: If there are no sections for a given course number, the exception `e_no_sections` is raised.

B) If the exception `e_no_sections` is raised, how does the control of execution flow? Explain your answer.

ANSWER: If the exception `e_no_sections` is raised, control of the execution is passed from the inner block to the exception-handling section of that inner block. This is possible because the inner block has the exception-handling section, in which the exception is raised and handled. This is illustrated in the following output:

```
There are no sections for course 430
Done...


PL/SQL procedure successfully completed.
```

C) Change this script so that the exception `e_no_sections` is reraised in the outer block.

```
-- ch9_4b.sql, version 2.0
SET SERVEROUTPUT ON
DECLARE
   v_course_no   NUMBER := 430;
   v_total       NUMBER;
   e_no_sections EXCEPTION;
BEGIN
   BEGIN
      SELECT COUNT(*)
        INTO v_total
        FROM section
       WHERE course_no = v_course_no;

      IF v_total = 0 THEN
         RAISE e_no_sections;
      ELSE
         DBMS_OUTPUT.PUT_LINE ('Course, '||v_course_no||
            ' has '||v_total||' sections');
      END IF;
   EXCEPTION
      WHEN e_no_sections THEN
         RAISE;
   END;
   DBMS_OUTPUT.PUT_LINE ('Done...');
```

```
EXCEPTION
   WHEN e_no_sections THEN
      DBMS_OUTPUT.PUT_LINE ('There are no sections for course '||
         v_course_no);
END;
```

In this version of the example, the exception-handling section of the inner block has been modified. The DBMS_OUTPUT.PUT_LINE statement has been replaced with the RAISE statement. In addition, the exception-handling section is included in the outer block.

▼ TRY IT YOURSELF

In this chapter you've learned about built-in exceptions. Here are some projects that will help you test the depth of your understanding:

1) Create the following script: For a course section provided at runtime, determine the number of students registered. If this number is equal to or greater than 10, raise the user-defined exception `e_too_many_students` and display an error message. Otherwise, display how many students are in a section.

2) Modify the script you just created. After the exception `e_too_many_students` has been raised in the inner block, reraise it in the outer block.

The projects in this section are meant to have you use all the skills you have acquired throughout this chapter. The answers to these projects can be found in Appendix D and on this book's companion Web site. Visit the Web site periodically to share and discuss your answers.

CHAPTER 10

Exceptions: Advanced Concepts

CHAPTER OBJECTIVES

In this chapter, you will learn about

- ▶ RAISE_APPLICATION_ERROR
- ▶ EXCEPTION_INIT pragma
- ▶ SQLCODE and SQLERRM

In Chapters 8 and 9, you encountered the concepts of error handling, built-in exceptions, and user-defined exceptions. You also learned about the scope of an exception and how to reraise an exception.

In this chapter you conclude your exploration of error handling and exceptions with a study of advanced topics. After working through this chapter, you will be able to associate an error number with an error message. You also will be able to trap a runtime error that has an Oracle error number but no name by which it can be referenced.

LAB 10.1
RAISE_APPLICATION_ERROR

LAB OBJECTIVE

After completing this lab, you will be able to

▶ Use RAISE_APPLICATION_ERROR

RAISE_APPLICATION_ERROR is a special built-in procedure provided by Oracle. It allows programmers to create meaningful error messages for a specific application. The RAISE_APPLICATION_ERROR procedure works with user-defined exceptions; its syntax is

```
RAISE_APPLICATION_ERROR(error_number, error_message);
```

or

```
RAISE_APPLICATION_ERROR(error_number, error_message, keep_errors);
```

As you can see, the RAISE_APPLICATION_ERROR procedure has two forms. The first form contains only two parameters: $error\_number$ and $error\_message$. $error\_number$ is a number that a programmer associates with a specific error message. It can be any number between –20,999 and –20,000. $error\_message$ is the text of the error; it can contain up to 2,048 characters.

The second form of RAISE_APPLICATION_ERROR contains one additional parameter: `keep_errors`, which is an optional Boolean parameter. If `keep_errors` is set to TRUE, the new error is added to the list of errors that have been raised already. This list of errors is called the error stack. If `keep_errors` is set to FALSE, the new error replaces the error stack that has been raised already. The default value for the parameter `keep_errors` is FALSE.

It is important to note that the RAISE_APPLICATION_ERROR procedure works with unnamed user-defined exceptions. It associates the number of the error with the text of the error. Therefore, the user-defined exception does not have a name associated with it.

Consider the following example used in Chapter 9, "Exceptions." It illustrates the use of the named user-defined exception and the RAISE statement. Within the example you can compare a modified version using the unnamed user-defined exception and the RAISE_APPLICATION_ERROR procedure.

First, view the original example from Chapter 9. The named user-defined exception and the RAISE statement are shown in bold.

FOR EXAMPLE

```
DECLARE
    v_student_id     student.student_id%type := &sv_student_id;
    v_total_courses NUMBER;
    e_invalid_id     EXCEPTION;
BEGIN
    IF v_student_id < 0 THEN
        RAISE e_invalid_id;
    ELSE
        SELECT COUNT(*)
          INTO v_total_courses
          FROM enrollment
         WHERE student_id = v_student_id;
         DBMS_OUTPUT.PUT_LINE ('The student is registered for '||
             v_total_courses||' courses');
    END IF;
    DBMS_OUTPUT.PUT_LINE ('No exception has been raised');
EXCEPTION
    WHEN e_invalid_id THEN
        DBMS_OUTPUT.PUT_LINE ('An id cannot be negative');
END;
```

Now, compare this to the modified example (changes are shown in bold):

FOR EXAMPLE

```
DECLARE
    v_student_id     student.student_id%type := &sv_student_id;
    v_total_courses NUMBER;
BEGIN
    IF v_student_id < 0 THEN
        RAISE_APPLICATION_ERROR (-20000, 'An id cannot be negative');
    ELSE
        SELECT COUNT(*)
          INTO v_total_courses
          FROM enrollment
         WHERE student_id = v_student_id;
         DBMS_OUTPUT.PUT_LINE ('The student is registered for '||
             v_total_courses||' courses');
    END IF;
END;
```

The second version of the example does not contain the name of the exception, the RAISE statement, or the error-handling section of the PL/SQL block. Instead, it has a single RAISE_APPLICATION_ERROR statement.

DID YOU KNOW?

Even though the RAISE_APPLICATION_ERROR is a built-in procedure, it can be referred to as a statement when used in the PL/SQL block.

Both versions of the example achieve the same result: The processing stops if a negative number is provided for v_student_id. However, the second version of this example produces output that has the look and feel of an error message. Now, run both versions of the example with a value of –4 for the variable v_student_id.

The first version of the example produces the following output:

```
Enter value for sv_student_id: -4
old   2: v_student_id student.student_id%type := &sv_student_id;
new   2: v_student_id student.student_id%type := -4;
An id cannot be negative

PL/SQL procedure successfully completed.
```

The second version of the example produces the following output:

```
Enter value for sv_student_id: -4
old    2:    v_student_id student.student_id%type := &sv_student_id;
new    2:    v_student_id student.student_id%type := -4;
DECLARE
*
ERROR at line 1:
ORA-20000: An id cannot be negative
ORA-06512: at line 6
```

The output produced by the first version of the example contains the error message An id cannot be negative and the message PL/SQL procedure successfully completed. The error message An id cannot be negative in the output generated by the second version of the example looks like the error message generated by the system, because the error number ORA-20000 precedes the error message.

The RAISE_APPLICATION_ERROR procedure can work with built-in exceptions as well. Consider the following example:

FOR EXAMPLE

```
DECLARE
   v_student_id student.student_id%type := &sv_student_id;
   v_name        varchar2(50);
BEGIN
   SELECT first_name||' '||last_name
     INTO v_name
     FROM student
    WHERE student_id = v_student_id;
   DBMS_OUTPUT.PUT_LINE (v_name);
EXCEPTION
   WHEN NO_DATA_FOUND THEN
      RAISE_APPLICATION_ERROR (-20001, 'This ID is invalid');
END;
```

When a value of 100 is entered for the student ID, the example produces the following output:

```
Enter value for sv_student_id: 100
old    2:    v_student_id student.student_id%type := &sv_student_id;
new    2:    v_student_id student.student_id%type := 100;
DECLARE
*
ERROR at line 1:
ORA-20001: This ID is invalid
ORA-06512: at line 12
```

The built-in exception NO_DATA_FOUND is raised because no record in the STUDENT table corresponds to this value of the student ID. However, the number of the error message does not refer to the exception NO_DATA_FOUND. It refers to the error message This ID is invalid.

The RAISE_APPLICATION_ERROR procedure allows programmers to return error messages in a manner that is consistent with Oracle errors. However, it is up to a programmer to maintain the relationship between the error numbers and the error messages. For example, you have designed an application to maintain enrollment information on students. In this application you have associated the error text This ID is invalid with the error number ORA-20001. This error message can be used by your application for any invalid ID. After you have associated the error number (ORA-20001) with a specific error message (This ID is invalid), you should not assign this error number to another error message. If you do not maintain the relationship between error numbers and error messages, the error-handling interface of your application might become very confusing to the users and to yourself.

▼ LAB 10.1 EXERCISES

This section provides exercises and suggested answers, with discussion related to how those answers resulted. The most important thing to realize is whether your answer works. You should figure out the implications of the answers and what the effects are of any different answers you may come up with.

10.1.1 Use RAISE_APPLICATION_ERROR

In this exercise, you calculate how many students are registered for a given section of a given course. You then display a message on the screen that contains the course number and the number of students registered for it. The original PL/SQL script does not contain any exception handlers, so you are asked to add the RAISE_APPLICATION_ERROR statements.

Create the following PL/SQL script:

```
-- ch10_1a.sql, version 1.0
SET SERVEROUTPUT ON
DECLARE
   v_students NUMBER(3) := 0;
BEGIN
   SELECT COUNT(*)
     INTO v_students
     FROM enrollment e, section s
    WHERE e.section_id = s.section_id
      AND s.course_no  = 25
```

```
        AND s.section_id = 89;

    DBMS_OUTPUT.PUT_LINE ('Course 25, section 89 has '||v_students||
        ' students');
END;
```

Execute the script, and then answer the following questions:

A) What output is printed on the screen?

ANSWER: The output should look similar to the following:

```
Course 25, section 89 has 12 students

PL/SQL procedure successfully completed.
```

B) Modify this script so that if a section of a course has more than ten students enrolled in it, an error message is displayed, indicating that this course has too many students enrolled.

ANSWER: The script should look similar to the following. All changes are shown in bold.

```
-- ch10_1b.sql, version 2.0
SET SERVEROUTPUT ON
DECLARE
    v_students NUMBER(3) := 0;
BEGIN
    SELECT COUNT(*)
      INTO v_students
      FROM enrollment e, section s
     WHERE e.section_id = s.section_id
       AND s.course_no  = 25
       AND s.section_id = 89;

    IF v_students > 10 THEN
       RAISE_APPLICATION_ERROR
          (-20002, 'Course 25, section 89 has more than 10 students');
    END IF;

    DBMS_OUTPUT.PUT_LINE ('Course 25, section 89 has '||v_students||
        ' students');

END;
```

Consider the result if you were to add an IF statement to this script that checks whether the value of the variable $v\_students$ exceeds 10. If the value of the variable does exceed 10, the RAISE_APPLICATION_ERROR statement executes, and the error message is displayed on the screen.

C) Execute the new version of the script. What output is printed on the screen?

ANSWER: The output should look similar to the following:

```
DECLARE
*
ERROR at line 1:
ORA-20002: Course 25, section 89 has more than 10 students
ORA-06512: at line 12
```

LAB 10.2
EXCEPTION_INIT Pragma

LAB OBJECTIVE

After completing this lab, you will be able to

▶ Use the EXCEPTION_INIT pragma

Often your programs need to handle an Oracle error that has a particular number associated with it, but no name by which it can be referenced. As a result, you are unable to write a handler to trap this error. In a case like this, you can use a construct called a pragma. A pragma is a special instruction to the PL/SQL compiler. It is important to note that pragmas are processed at the time of the compilation. The EXCEPTION_INIT pragma allows you to associate an Oracle error number with the name of a user-defined error. After you associate an error name with an Oracle error number, you can reference the error and write a handler for it.

The EXCEPTION_INIT pragma appears in the declaration section of a block as shown:

```
DECLARE
   exception_name EXCEPTION;
   PRAGMA EXCEPTION_INIT(exception_name, error_code);
```

Notice that the declaration of the user-defined exception appears before the EXCEPTION_INIT pragma where it is used. The EXCEPTION_INIT pragma has two parameters: *exception_name* and *error_code*. *exception_name* is the name of your exception, and *error_code* is the number of the Oracle error you want to associate with your exception. Consider the following:

FOR EXAMPLE

```
DECLARE
   v_zip zipcode.zip%type := '&sv_zip';
BEGIN
   DELETE FROM zipcode
    WHERE zip = v_zip;
   DBMS_OUTPUT.PUT_LINE ('Zip '||v_zip||' has been deleted');
   COMMIT;
END;
```

In this example, the record corresponding to the value of a zip code provided by the user is deleted from the ZIPCODE table. Next, the message that a specific zip code has been deleted is displayed on the screen.

Compare the results when you run this example using 06870 for the value of v_zip. The example produces the following output:

```
Enter value for sv_zip: 06870
old   2:     v_zip zipcode.zip%type := '&sv_zip';
new   2:     v_zip zipcode.zip%type := '06870';
DECLARE
*
ERROR at line 1:
ORA-02292: integrity constraint (STUDENT.STU_ZIP_FK) violated -
           child record found
ORA-06512: at line 4
```

The error message generated by this example occurs because you are trying to delete a record from the ZIPCODE table while its child records exist in the STUDENT table. This violates the referential integrity constraint STU_ZIP_FK. In other words, a record with a foreign key (STU_ZIP_FK) in the STUDENT table (child table) references a record in the ZIPCODE table (parent table).

Notice that this error has Oracle error number ORA-02292 assigned to it, but it does not have a name. As a result, you need to associate this error number with a user-defined exception so that you can handle this error in the script.

Contrast the example if you modify it as follows (all changes are shown in bold):

FOR EXAMPLE

```
DECLARE
   v_zip            zipcode.zip%type := '&sv_zip';
   e_child_exists EXCEPTION;
   PRAGMA EXCEPTION_INIT(e_child_exists, -2292);
BEGIN
   DELETE FROM zipcode
    WHERE zip = v_zip;
    DBMS_OUTPUT.PUT_LINE ('Zip '||v_zip||' has been deleted');
   COMMIT;
EXCEPTION
   WHEN e_child_exists THEN
      DBMS_OUTPUT.PUT_LINE ('Delete students for this '||
         'zipcode first');
END;
```

In this example, you declare the exception e_child_exists. Then you associate the exception with error number –2292. It is important to note that you do not use ORA-02292 in the EXCEPTION_INIT pragma. Next, you add the exception-handling section to the PL/SQL block so that you trap this error. Notice that even though the exception e_child_exists is user-defined, you do not use the RAISE statement, as you saw in Chapter 9. Why do you think you don't use the RAISE statement?

When you run this example using the same value for the zip code, the following output is produced:

```
Enter value for sv_zip: 06870
old    2:    v_zip zipcode.zip%type := '&sv_zip';
new    2:    v_zip zipcode.zip%type := '06870';
Delete students for this zipcode first

PL/SQL procedure successfully completed.
```

Notice that this output contains a new error message displayed by the DBMS_OUTPUT. PUT_LINE statement. This version of the output is more descriptive than the previous version. Remember that the user of the program probably does not know about the referential integrity constraints existing in the database. Therefore, the EXCEPTION_INIT pragma improves the readability of your error-handling interface. If the need arises, you can use multiple EXCEPTION_INIT pragmas in your program.

▼ LAB 10.2 EXERCISES

This section provides exercises and suggested answers, with discussion related to how those answers resulted. The most important thing to realize is whether your answer works. You should figure out the implications of the answers and what the effects are of any different answers you may come up with.

10.2.1 USE the EXCEPTION_INIT Pragma

In this exercise, you insert a record in the COURSE table. The original PL/SQL script does not contain any exception handlers, so you are asked to define an exception and add the EXCEPTION_INIT pragma.

Create the following PL/SQL script:

```
-- ch10_2a.sql, version 1.0
SET SERVEROUTPUT ON
BEGIN
    INSERT INTO course (course_no, description, created_by,
                        created_date)
    VALUES (COURSE_NO_SEQ.NEXTVAL, 'TEST COURSE', USER, SYSDATE);
    COMMIT;
    DBMS_OUTPUT.PUT_LINE ('One course has been added');
END;
```

Execute the script, and then answer the following questions:

A) What output is printed on the screen?

ANSWER: The output should look like the following:

```
BEGIN
*
ERROR at line 1:
ORA-01400: cannot insert NULL into ("STUDENT"."COURSE"."MODIFIED_BY")
ORA-06512: at line 2
```

B) Explain why the script does not execute successfully.

ANSWER: The script does not execute successfully because a NULL is inserted for the MODIFIED_BY and MODIFIED_DATE columns.

The MODIFIED_BY and MODIFIED_DATE columns have check constraints defined on them. You can view these constraints by querying one of the data dictionary tables. The data dictionary comprises tables owned by the user SYS. These tables provide the database with information that it uses to manage itself.

Consider the following SELECT statement against one of Oracle's data dictionary tables, USER_CONSTRAINTS. This table contains information on various constraints defined on each table of the STUDENT schema.

```
SELECT constraint_name, search_condition
  FROM user_constraints
WHERE table_name = 'COURSE';
```

```
CONSTRAINT_NAME              SEARCH_CONDITION
-----------------------     ---------------------------
CRSE_CREATED_DATE_NNULL     "CREATED_DATE" IS NOT NULL
CRSE_MODIFIED_BY_NNULL      "MODIFIED_BY" IS NOT NULL
CRSE_MODIFIED_DATE_NNULL    "MODIFIED_DATE" IS NOT NULL
CRSE_DESCRIPTION_NNULL      "DESCRIPTION" IS NOT NULL
CRSE_COURSE_NO_NNULL        "COURSE_NO" IS NOT NULL
CRSE_CREATED_BY_NNULL       "CREATED_BY" IS NOT NULL
CRSE_PK
CRSE_CRSE_FK

8 rows selected.
```

Notice that the last two rows refer to the primary and foreign key constraints, so no search conditions are specified.

Based on the results produced by the preceding SELECT statement, six columns have a NOT NULL constraint. However, the INSERT statement

```
INSERT INTO course (course_no, description, created_by,
                    created_date)
VALUES (COURSE_NO_SEQ.NEXTVAL, 'TEST COURSE', USER, SYSDATE);
```

has only four columns that have NOT NULL constraints. The columns MODIFIED_BY and MODIFIED_DATE are not included in the INSERT statement. Any column of a table not listed in the INSERT statement has NULL assigned to it when a new record is added to the table. If a column has a NOT NULL constraint and is not listed in the INSERT statement, the INSERT statement fails and causes an error.

C) Add a user-defined exception to the script so that the error generated by the INSERT statement is handled.

ANSWER: The script should look similar to the following. All changes are shown in bold.

```
-- ch10_2b.sql, version 2.0
SET SERVEROUTPUT ON
DECLARE
   e_constraint_violation EXCEPTION;
   PRAGMA EXCEPTION_INIT(e_constraint_violation, -1400);
```

```
BEGIN
    INSERT INTO course (course_no, description, created_by,
                        created_date)
    VALUES (COURSE_NO_SEQ.NEXTVAL, 'TEST COURSE', USER, SYSDATE);
    COMMIT;
    DBMS_OUTPUT.PUT_LINE ('One course has been added');
EXCEPTION
    WHEN e_constraint_violation THEN
        DBMS_OUTPUT.PUT_LINE ('INSERT statement is '||
            'violating a constraint');
END;
```

In this script, you declare the `e_constraint_violation` exception. Then, using the EXCEPTION_INIT pragma to associate the exception with Oracle error number ORA-02290, the handler is written for the new exception `e_constraint_violation`.

D) Run the new version of the script and explain its output.

ANSWER: The output should look similar to the following:

```
INSERT statement is violating a constraint

PL/SQL procedure successfully completed.
```

After you define an exception and associate an Oracle error number with it, you can write an exception handler for it. As a result, as soon as the INSERT statement causes an error, control of the execution is transferred to the exception-handling section of the block. Then the message `INSERT statement` ... is displayed on the screen. Notice that when an exception is raised and processed, the execution of the program does not halt. The script completes successfully.

LAB 10.3
SQLCODE and SQLERRM

LAB OBJECTIVE

After completing this lab, you will be able to

- ▶ Use SQLCODE and SQLERRM

In Chapter 8, "Error Handling and Built-in Exceptions," you learned about the Oracle exception OTHERS. Recall that all Oracle errors can be trapped with the help of the OTHERS exception handler, as illustrated in the following example:

FOR EXAMPLE

```
DECLARE
   v_zip   VARCHAR2(5) := '&sv_zip';
   v_city  VARCHAR2(15);
   v_state CHAR(2);
BEGIN
   SELECT city, state
     INTO v_city, v_state
     FROM zipcode
    WHERE zip = v_zip;

   DBMS_OUTPUT.PUT_LINE (v_city||', '||v_state);

EXCEPTION
   WHEN OTHERS THEN
       DBMS_OUTPUT.PUT_LINE ('An error has occurred');
END;
```

When 07458 is entered for the value of the zip code, this example produces the following output:

```
Enter value for sv_zip: 07458
old    2:    v_zip VARCHAR2(5) := '&sv_zip';
new    2:    v_zip VARCHAR2(5) := '07458';
An error has occurred

PL/SQL procedure successfully completed.
```

This output informs you that an error occurred at runtime. However, you do not know what the error is and what caused it. Maybe no record in the ZIPCODE table corresponds to the value provided at runtime, or maybe a datatype mismatch was caused by the SELECT INTO statement. As you can see, even though this is a simple example, a number of possible runtime errors can occur.

Of course, you cannot always know all the possible runtime errors that may occur when a program is running. Therefore, it is a good practice to have the OTHERS exception handler in your script. To improve the error-handling interface of your program, Oracle gives you two built-in functions, SQLCODE and SQLERRM, used with the OTHERS exception handler. The SQLCODE function returns the Oracle error number, and the SQLERRM function returns the error message. The maximum length of a message returned by the SQLERRM function is 512 bytes.

Consider what happens if you modify the preceding by adding the SQLCODE and SQLERRM functions as follows (all changes are shown in bold):

FOR EXAMPLE

```
DECLARE
   v_zip       VARCHAR2(5) := '&sv_zip';
   v_city      VARCHAR2(15);
   v_state     CHAR(2);
   v_err_code NUMBER;
   v_err_msg  VARCHAR2(200);
BEGIN
   SELECT city, state
     INTO v_city, v_state
     FROM zipcode
    WHERE zip = v_zip;

   DBMS_OUTPUT.PUT_LINE (v_city||', '||v_state);

EXCEPTION
   WHEN OTHERS THEN
      v_err_code := SQLCODE;
      v_err_msg  := SUBSTR(SQLERRM, 1, 200);
      DBMS_OUTPUT.PUT_LINE ('Error code: '||v_err_code);
      DBMS_OUTPUT.PUT_LINE ('Error message: '||v_err_msg);
END;
```

When executed, this example produces the following output:

```
Enter value for sv_zip: 07458
old   2:    v_zip       VARCHAR2(5) := '&sv_zip';
new   2:    v_zip       VARCHAR2(5) := '07458';
Error code: -6502
Error message: ORA-06502: PL/SQL: numeric or value error:
```

```
character string buffer too small

PL/SQL procedure successfully completed.
```

In this example, you declare two variables: v_err_code and v_err_msg. Then, in the exception-handling section of the block, you assign SQLCODE to the variable v_err_code and SQLERRM to the variable v_err_msg. Next, you use the DBMS_OUTPUT.PUT_LINE statements to display the error number and the error message on the screen.

Notice that this output is more informative than the output produced by the previous version of the example, because it displays the error message. As soon as you know which runtime error has occurred in your program, you can take steps to prevent this error's recurrence.

Generally, the SQLCODE function returns a negative number for an error number. However, there are a few exceptions:

▶ When SQLCODE is referenced outside the exception section, it returns 0 for the error code. The value of 0 means successful completion.

▶ When SQLCODE is used with the user-defined exception, it returns +1 for the error code.

▶ SQLCODE returns a value of 100 when the NO_DATA_FOUND exception is raised.

The SQLERRM function accepts an error number as a parameter, and it returns an error message corresponding to the error number. Usually, it works with the value returned by SQLCODE. However, you can provide the error number yourself if such a need arises. Consider the following example:

FOR EXAMPLE

```
BEGIN
   DBMS_OUTPUT.PUT_LINE ('Error code: '||SQLCODE);
   DBMS_OUTPUT.PUT_LINE ('Error message1: '||SQLERRM(SQLCODE));
   DBMS_OUTPUT.PUT_LINE ('Error message2: '||SQLERRM(100));
   DBMS_OUTPUT.PUT_LINE ('Error message3: '||SQLERRM(200));
   DBMS_OUTPUT.PUT_LINE ('Error message4: '||SQLERRM(-20000));
END;
```

In this example, SQLCODE and SQLERRM are used in the executable section of the PL/SQL block. The SQLERRM function accepts the value of the SQLCODE in the second DBMS_OUTPUT.PUT_LINE statement. In the following DBMS_OUPUT.PUT_LINE statements, SQLERRM accepts the values of 100, 200, and –20,000 respectively. When executed, this example produces the following output:

```
Error code: 0
Error message1: ORA-0000: normal, successful completion
Error message2: ORA-01403: no data found
Error message3:  -200: non-ORACLE exception
Error message4: ORA-20000:

PL/SQL procedure successfully completed.
```

The first DBMS_OUTPUT.PUT_LINE statement displays the value of the SQLCODE function. Because no exception is raised, it returns 0. Next, SQLERRM accepts as a parameter the value returned by the SQLCODE function. This function returns the message ORA-0000: normal, ... Next, SQLERRM accepts 100 as its parameter and returns ORA-01403: no data found. Notice that when SQLERRM accepts 200 as its parameter, it cannot find an Oracle exception that corresponds to the error number 200. Finally, when SQLERRM accepts –20,000 as its parameter, no error message is returned. Remember that –20,000 is an error number that can be associated with a named user-defined exception.

▼ LAB 10.3 EXERCISES

This section provides exercises and suggested answers, with discussion related to how those answers resulted. The most important thing to realize is whether your answer works. You should figure out the implications of the answers and what the effects are of any different answers you may come up with.

10.3.1 Use SQLCODE and SQLERRM

In this exercise, you add a new record to the ZIPCODE table. The original PL/SQL script does not contain any exception handlers. You are asked to add an exception-handling section to this script.

Create the following PL/SQL script:

```
-- ch10_3a.sql, version 1.0
SET SERVEROUTPUT ON
BEGIN
   INSERT INTO ZIPCODE (zip, city, state, created_by, created_date,
      modified_by, modified_date)
   VALUES ('10027', 'NEW YORK', 'NY', USER, SYSDATE, USER, SYSDATE);
   COMMIT;
END;
```

Execute the script, and answer the following questions:

A) What output is printed on the screen?

ANSWER: The output should look like the following:

```
BEGIN
*
ERROR at line 1:
ORA-00001: unique constraint (STUDENT.ZIP_PK) violated
ORA-06512: at line 2
```

The INSERT statement

```
INSERT INTO ZIPCODE (zip, city, state, created_by, created_date,
   modified_by, modified_date)
VALUES ('10027', 'NEW YORK', 'NY', USER, SYSDATE, USER, SYSDATE);
```

causes an error because a record with zip code 10027 already exists in the ZIPCODE table. Column ZIP of the ZIPCODE table has a primary key constraint defined on it. Therefore, when you try to insert another record when the value of ZIP already exists in the ZIPCODE table, the error message ORA-00001: unique constraint ... is generated.

B) Modify the script so that it completes successfully and so that the error number and message are displayed on the screen.

ANSWER: The script should resemble the script shown. All changes are shown in bold.

```
-- ch10_3b.sql, version 2.0
SET SERVEROUTPUT ON
BEGIN
    INSERT INTO ZIPCODE (zip, city, state, created_by, created_date,
        modified_by, modified_date)
    VALUES ('10027', 'NEW YORK', 'NY', USER, SYSDATE, USER, SYSDATE);
    COMMIT;
EXCEPTION
    WHEN OTHERS THEN
        DECLARE
            v_err_code NUMBER := SQLCODE;
            v_err_msg VARCHAR2(100) := SUBSTR(SQLERRM, 1, 100);
        BEGIN
            DBMS_OUTPUT.PUT_LINE ('Error code: '||v_err_code);
            DBMS_OUTPUT.PUT_LINE ('Error message: '||v_err_msg);
        END;
END;
```

In this script, you add an exception-handling section with the OTHERS exception handler. Notice that two variables, v_err_code and v_err_msg, are declared in the exception-handling section of the block, adding an inner PL/SQL block.

C) Run the new version of the script and explain the output it produces.

ANSWER: The output should look similar to the following:

```
Error code: -1
Error message: ORA-00001: unique constraint (STUDENT.ZIP_PK)
               violated

PL/SQL procedure successfully completed.
```

Because the INSERT statement causes an error, control is transferred to the OTHERS exception handler. The SQLCODE function returns –1, and the SQLERRM function returns the text of the error corresponding to the error code –1. After the exception-handling section completes its execution, control is passed to the host environment.

▼ TRY IT YOURSELF

In this chapter you've learned about advanced concepts of exception-handling techniques. Here are some projects that will help you test the depth of your understanding:

1) Modify the script you created in project 1 of the "Try It Yourself" section in Chapter 9. Raise a user-defined exception with the RAISE_APPLICATION_ERROR statement. Otherwise, display how many students are in a section. Make sure your program can process all sections.

2) Create the following script: Try to add a record to the INSTRUCTOR table without providing values for the columns MODIFIED_BY and MODIFIED_DATE. Define an exception and associate it with the Oracle error number so that the error generated by the INSERT statement is handled.

3) Modify the script you just created. Instead of declaring a user-defined exception, add the OTHERS exception handler to the exception-handling section of the block. Then display the error number and the error message on the screen.

The projects in this section are meant to have you use all the skills you have acquired throughout this chapter. The answers to these projects can be found in Appendix D and on this book's companion Web site. Visit the Web site periodically to share and discuss your answers.

CHAPTER 11

Introduction to Cursors

CHAPTER OBJECTIVES

In this chapter, you will learn about

▶ Cursor manipulation
▶ Using cursor FOR loops and nested cursors

Cursors are memory areas where Oracle executes SQL statements. In database programming cursors are internal data structures that allow processing of SQL query results. For example, you use a cursor to operate on all the rows of the STUDENT table for students who are taking a particular course (having associated entries in the ENROLLMENT table). In this chapter, you will learn to declare an explicit cursor that enables a user to process many rows returned by a query and allows the user to write code that processes each row one at a time.

LAB 11.1
Cursor Manipulation

LAB OBJECTIVES

After completing this lab, you will be able to

- ▶ Make use of record types
- ▶ Process an explicit cursor
- ▶ Make use of cursor attributes
- ▶ Put it all together

For Oracle to process a SQL statement, it needs to create an area of memory known as the context area; this will have the information needed to process the statement. This information includes the number of rows processed by the statement and a pointer to the parsed representation of the statement. (Parsing a SQL statement is the process whereby information is transferred to the server, at which point the SQL statement is evaluated as being valid.) In a query, the active set refers to the rows that are returned.

A cursor is a handle, or pointer, to the context area. Through the cursor, a PL/SQL program can control the context area and what happens to it as the statement is processed. Cursors have two important features:

- ▶ Cursors allow you to fetch and process rows returned by a SELECT statement one row at a time.

- ▶ A cursor is named so that it can be referenced.

TYPES OF CURSORS

There are two types of cursors:

- ▶ Oracle automatically declares an *implicit* cursor every time a SQL statement is executed. The user is unaware of this and cannot control or process the information in an implicit cursor.

- ▶ The program defines an *explicit* cursor for any query that returns more than one row of data. This means that the programmer has declared the cursor within the PL/SQL code block. This declaration allows the application to sequentially process each row of data as the cursor returns it.

IMPLICIT CURSOR

To better understand the capabilities of an explicit cursor, you first need to understand the process of an implicit cursor:

▶ Any given PL/SQL block issues an implicit cursor whenever a SQL statement is executed, as long as an explicit cursor does not exist for that SQL statement.

▶ A cursor is automatically associated with every DML (data manipulation) statement (UPDATE, DELETE, INSERT).

▶ All UPDATE and DELETE statements have cursors that identify the set of rows that will be affected by the operation.

▶ An INSERT statement needs a place to receive the data that is to be inserted into the database; the implicit cursor fulfills this need.

▶ The most recently opened cursor is called the SQL cursor.

The implicit cursor is used to process INSERT, UPDATE, DELETE, and SELECT INTO statements. During the processing of an implicit cursor, Oracle automatically performs the OPEN, FETCH, and CLOSE operations.

BY THE WAY

An implicit cursor can tell you how many rows were affected by an update. Cursors have attributes such as ROWCOUNT. SQL%ROWCOUNT returns the number of rows updated. It can be used as follows:

```
SET SERVEROUTPUT ON
BEGIN
    UPDATE student
       SET first_name = 'B'
     WHERE first_name LIKE 'B%';
     DBMS_OUTPUT.PUT_LINE(SQL%ROWCOUNT);
  END;
```

Consider the following example of an implicit cursor:

FOR EXAMPLE

```
SET SERVEROUTPUT ON;
DECLARE
   v_first_name VARCHAR2(35);
   v_last_name VARCHAR2(35);
BEGIN
   SELECT first_name, last_name
     INTO v_first_name, v_last_name
     FROM student
    WHERE student_id = 123;
   DBMS_OUTPUT.PUT_LINE ('Student name: '||
```

```
        v_first_name||' '||v_last_name);
EXCEPTION
   WHEN NO_DATA_FOUND THEN
      DBMS_OUTPUT.PUT_LINE
      ('There is no student with student ID 123');
END;
```

Oracle automatically associates an implicit cursor with the SELECT INTO statement and fetches the values for the variables v_first_name and v_last_name. After the SELECT INTO statement completes, Oracle closes the implicit cursor.

Unlike with an implicit cursor, the program defines an explicit cursor for any query that returns more than one row of data. To process an explicit cursor, first you declare it, and then you open it. Then you fetch it, and finally you close it.

EXPLICIT CURSOR

The only means of generating an explicit cursor is to name the cursor in the DECLARE section of the PL/SQL block.

The advantage of declaring an explicit cursor over an indirect implicit cursor is that the explicit cursor gives the programmer more programmatic control. Also, implicit cursors are less efficient than explicit cursors, so it is harder to trap data errors.

The process of working with an explicit cursor consists of the following steps:

1. *Declaring* the cursor. This initializes the cursor into memory.

2. *Opening* the cursor. The declared cursor is opened, and memory is allotted.

3. *Fetching* the cursor. The declared and opened cursor can now retrieve data.

4. *Closing* the cursor. The declared, opened, and fetched cursor must be closed to release the memory allocation.

DECLARING A CURSOR

Declaring a cursor defines the cursor's name and associates it with a SELECT statement. You declare a cursor using the following syntax:

```
CURSOR c_cursor_name IS select statement
```

DID YOU KNOW?

We advise you to always begin a cursor name with c_. When you do so, it will always be clear that the name refers to a cursor.

You can't use a cursor unless the complete cycle of declaring, opening, fetching, and closing has been performed. To explain these four steps, the following examples show code fragments for each step. After that, you are shown the complete process.

FOR EXAMPLE

```
DECLARE
   CURSOR c_MyCursor IS
      SELECT *
        FROM zipcode
        WHERE state = 'NY';
...
      -- code would continue here with opening, fetching
      -- and closing of the cursor>
```

This PL/SQL fragment demonstrates the first step of declaring a cursor. A cursor named c_MyCursor is declared as a select statement of all the rows in the zipcode table that have the item state equal to NY.

BY THE WAY

Cursor names follow the same rules of scope and visibility that apply to the PL/SQL identifiers. Because the cursor name is a PL/SQL identifier, it must be declared before it is referenced. Any valid select statement can be used to define a cursor, including joins and statements with the UNION or MINUS clause.

RECORD TYPES

A record is a composite data structure, which means that it is composed of one or more elements. Records are very much like a row of a database table, but each element of the record does not stand on its own. PL/SQL supports three kinds of records: table-based, cursor-based, and programmer-defined.

A table-based record is one whose structure is drawn from the list of columns in the table. A cursor-based record is one whose structure matches the elements of a predefined cursor. To create a table-based or cursor-based record, use the %ROWTYPE attribute:

```
    record_name table_name or cursor_name%ROWTYPE
```

FOR EXAMPLE

```
-- ch11_1a.sql
SET SERVEROUTPUT ON
DECLARE
   vr_student student%ROWTYPE;
BEGIN
   SELECT *
     INTO vr_student
     FROM student
    WHERE student_id = 156;
   DBMS_OUTPUT.PUT_LINE (vr_student.first_name||' '
      ||vr_student.last_name||' has an ID of 156');
EXCEPTION
   WHEN no_data_found
```

```
        THEN
                RAISE_APPLICATION_ERROR(-2001,'The Student '||
                    'is not in the database');
END;
```

The variable vr_student is a record type of the existing database table student. In other words, it has the same components as a row in the student table. A cursor-based record is much the same, except that it is drawn from the select list of an explicitly declared cursor. When referencing elements of the record, you use the same syntax that you use with tables:

```
    record_name.item_name
```

To define a variable that is based on a cursor record, first you must declare the cursor. In the following lab, you will start by declaring a cursor and then open the cursor, fetch from the cursor, and close the cursor.

A table-based record is drawn from a particular table structure. Consider the following code fragment:

FOR EXAMPLE

```
DECLARE
    vr_zip ZIPCODE%ROWTYPE;
    vr_instructor INSTRUCTOR%ROWTYPE;
```

Record vr_zip has a structure similar to a row of the ZIPCODE table. Its elements are CITY, STATE, and ZIP. It is important to note that if the CITY column of the ZIPCODE table has been defined as VARCHAR2(15), the attribute CITY of the vr_zip record has the same datatype structure. Similarly, record vr_instructor is based on the row of the INSTRUCTOR table.

▼ LAB 11.1 EXERCISES

This section provides exercises and suggested answers, with discussion related to how those answers resulted. The most important thing to realize is whether your answer works. You should figure out the implications of the answers and what the effects are of any different answers you may come up with.

11.1.1 **Make Use of Record Types**

Here is an example of a record type in an anonymous PL/SQL block:

FOR EXAMPLE

```
SET SERVEROUTPUT ON;
DECLARE
 vr_zip ZIPCODE%ROWTYPE;
BEGIN
    SELECT *
      INTO vr_zip
      FROM zipcode
```

```
    WHERE rownum < 2;
  DBMS_OUTPUT.PUT_LINE('City: '||vr_zip.city);
  DBMS_OUTPUT.PUT_LINE('State: '||vr_zip.state);
  DBMS_OUTPUT.PUT_LINE('Zip: '||vr_zip.zip);
END;
```

A) What happens when the preceding example is run in a SQL*Plus session?

ANSWER: In this example, you select a single row for the ZIPCODE table into the vr_zip record. Next, you display each element of the record on the screen. Notice that to reference each attribute of the record, dot notation is used. When run, the example produces the following output:

```
City: Santurce
State: PR
Zip: 00914
PL/SQL procedure successfully completed.
```

A cursor-based record is based on the list of elements of a predefined cursor.

B) Explain how the record type $vr\_student\_name$ is being used in the following example:

FOR EXAMPLE

```
DECLARE
   CURSOR c_student_name IS
      SELECT first_name, last_name
        FROM student;
   vr_student_name c_student_name%ROWTYPE;
```

ANSWER: Record $vr\_student\_name$ has a structure similar to a row returned by the SELECT statement defined in the cursor. It contains two attributes—the student's first and last names.

It is important to note that a cursor-based record can be declared only after its corresponding cursor has been declared; otherwise, a compilation error will occur.

In the next lab you will learn how to process an explicit cursor. Then you will address record types within that process.

11.1.2 **Process an Explicit Cursor**

To use a cursor, you must make use of the complete cycle of declaring, opening, fetching, and closing the cursor. To help you learn these four steps, this lab covers them one at a time.

A) Write the declaration section of a PL/SQL block. It should define a cursor named $c\_student$ based on the student table, with $last\_name$ and $first\_name$ concatenated into one item called name. It also should omit the $created\_by$ and $modified\_by$ columns. Then declare a record based on this cursor.

ANSWER:

```
DECLARE
   CURSOR c_student is
      SELECT first_name||' '||Last_name name
        FROM student;
   vr_student c_student%ROWTYPE;
```

OPENING A CURSOR

The next step in controlling an explicit cursor is to open it. When the OPEN cursor statement is processed, the following four actions take place automatically:

1. The variables (including bind variables) in the WHERE clause are examined.
2. Based on the values of the variables, the active set is determined, and the PL/SQL engine executes the query for that cursor. Variables are examined at cursor open time only.
3. The PL/SQL engine identifies the active set of data—the rows from all the involved tables that meet the WHERE clause criteria.
4. The active set pointer is set to the first row.

The syntax for opening a cursor is

```
OPEN cursor_name;
```

DID YOU KNOW?

A pointer into the active set is also established at cursor open time. The pointer determines which row is the next to be fetched by the cursor. More than one cursor can be open at a time.

B) Add the necessary lines to the PL/SQL block that you just wrote to open the cursor.

ANSWER: The following lines should be added to the lines in A):

```
BEGIN
    OPEN c_student;
```

FETCHING ROWS IN A CURSOR

After the cursor has been declared and opened, you can retrieve data from the cursor. The process of getting data from the cursor is called fetching the cursor. There are two ways to fetch a cursor:

```
FETCH cursor_name INTO PL/SQL variables;
```

or

```
FETCH cursor_name INTO PL/SQL record;
```

When the cursor is fetched, the following occurs:

1. The FETCH command is used to retrieve one row at a time from the active set. This is generally done inside a loop. The values of each row in the active set can then be stored in the corresponding variables or PL/SQL record one at a time, performing operations on each one successively.
2. After each FETCH, the active set pointer is moved forward to the next row. Thus, each FETCH returns successive rows of the active set, until the entire set is returned. The last FETCH does not assign values to the output variables; they still contain their prior values.

FOR EXAMPLE

```
-- ch11_2a.sql
SET SERVEROUTPUT ON
DECLARE
    CURSOR c_zip IS
        SELECT *
          FROM zipcode;
    vr_zip c_zip%ROWTYPE;
```

```
BEGIN
   OPEN c_zip;
   LOOP
      FETCH c_zip INTO vr_zip;
      EXIT WHEN c_zip%NOTFOUND;
      DBMS_OUTPUT.PUT_LINE(vr_zip.zip||
         ' '||vr_zip.city||' '||vr_zip.state);
   END LOOP;
END;
```

The line in italic has not yet been covered but is essential for the code to run correctly. It is explained later in this chapter.

C) In Chapter 6, "Iterative Control: Part I," you learned how to construct a loop. For the PL/SQL block that you have been writing, add a loop. Inside the loop, fetch the cursor into the record. Include a DBMS_OUTPUT line inside the loop so that each time the loop iterates, all the information in the record is displayed in a SQL*Plus session.

ANSWER: The following lines should be added:

```
LOOP
      FETCH c_student INTO vr_student;
      DBMS_OUTPUT.PUT_LINE(vr_student.name);
```

CLOSING A CURSOR

As soon as all the rows in the cursor have been processed (retrieved), the cursor should be closed. This tells the PL/SQL engine that the program is finished with the cursor, and the resources associated with it can be freed. The syntax for closing the cursor is

```
CLOSE cursor_name;
```

BY THE WAY

After a cursor is closed, you no longer can fetch from it. Likewise, it is not possible to close an already closed cursor. Trying to perform either of these actions would result in an Oracle error.

D) Continue with the code you have developed by adding a CLOSE statement to the cursor. Is your code complete now?

ANSWER: The following line should be added:

```
CLOSE c_student;
```

The code is not complete because there is not a proper way to exit the loop.

E) Explain what is occurring in the following PL/SQL block. What will be the output from this example?

FOR EXAMPLE

```
SET SERVEROUTPUT ON;
DECLARE
   CURSOR c_student_name IS
      SELECT first_name, last_name
         FROM student
```

```
      WHERE rownum <= 5;
   vr_student_name c_student_name%ROWTYPE;
BEGIN
   OPEN c_student_name;
   LOOP
      FETCH c_student_name INTO vr_student_name;
      EXIT WHEN c_student_name%NOTFOUND;
      DBMS_OUTPUT.PUT_LINE('Student name: '||
         vr_student_name.first_name
         ||' '||vr_student_name.last_name);
   END LOOP;
   CLOSE c_student_name;
END;
```

ANSWER: In this example, you declare a cursor that returns five student names. Next, you declare a cursor-based record. In the body of the program, you process explicit cursors via the cursor loop. In the body of the loop, you assign each record returned by the cursor to the cursor-based record, `vr_student_name`. Next, you display its contents on the screen. When run, the example produces the following output:

```
Student name: Austin V. Cadet
Student name: Frank M. Orent
Student name: Yvonne Winnicki
Student name: Mike Madej
Student name: Paula Valentine
PL/SQL procedure successfully completed.
```

F) Consider the same example with a single modification. Notice that the DBMS_OUTPUT.PUT_LINE statement (shown in bold) has been moved outside the loop. Execute this example, and try to explain why this version of the script produces different output.

FOR EXAMPLE

```
SET SERVEROUTPUT ON;
DECLARE
   CURSOR c_student_name IS
      SELECT first_name, last_name
        FROM student
       WHERE rownum <= 5;
   vr_student_name c_student_name%ROWTYPE;
BEGIN
   OPEN c_student_name;
   LOOP
      FETCH c_student_name INTO vr_student_name;
      EXIT WHEN c_student_name%NOTFOUND;
   END LOOP;
   CLOSE c_student_name;
   DBMS_OUTPUT.PUT_LINE('Student name: '||
      vr_student_name.first_name||' '
      ||vr_student_name.last_name);
END;
```

ANSWER: The DBMS_OUTPUT.PUT_LINE has been moved outside the loop. First the loop processes the five student records. The values for each record are placed in the record `vr_student_`
`name`, but each time the loop iterates, it replaces the value in the record with a new value. When the five iterations of the loop are finished, it exits because of the EXIT WHEN condition, leaving the `vr_student_name` record with the last value that was in the cursor. This is the only value that is displayed via the DBMS_OUTPUT.PUT_LINE, which comes after the loop is closed.

A user-defined record is based on the record type defined by a programmer. First you declare a record type, and then you declare a record variable based on the record type defined in the preceding step:

```
TYPE type_name IS RECORD
    (field_name 1 DATATYPE 1,
     field_name 2 DATATYPE 2,
     . . .
     field_name N DATATYPE N);


 record_name TYPE_NAME%ROWTYPE;
```

Consider the following code fragment:

FOR EXAMPLE

```
SET SERVEROUTPUT ON;
DECLARE
   -- declare user-defined type
   TYPE instructor_info IS RECORD
      (instructor_id instructor.instructor_id%TYPE,
       first_name instructor.first_name%TYPE,
       last_name instructor.last_name%TYPE,
       sections NUMBER(1));
   -- declare a record based on the type defined above
   rv_instructor instructor_info;
```

In this code fragment, you define your own type, `instructor_info`. This type contains four attributes: the instructor's ID, the instructor's first and last names, and the number of sections taught by this instructor. Next, you declare a record based on the type just described. As a result, this record has a structure similar to the type `instructor_info`.

G) Explain what is declared in the following example. Describe what is happening to the record, and explain how this results in the output:

FOR EXAMPLE

```
SET SERVEROUTPUT ON;
DECLARE
   TYPE instructor_info IS RECORD
      (first_name instructor.first_name%TYPE,
       last_name instructor.last_name%TYPE,
       sections NUMBER);
   rv_instructor instructor_info;
BEGIN
   SELECT RTRIM(i.first_name),
```

```
        RTRIM(i.last_name), COUNT(*)
    INTO rv_instructor
    FROM instructor i, section s
  WHERE i.instructor_id = s.instructor_id
    AND i.instructor_id = 102
  GROUP BY i.first_name, i.last_name;
  DBMS_OUTPUT.PUT_LINE('Instructor, '||
    rv_instructor.first_name||
    ' '||rv_instructor.last_name||
    ', teaches '||rv_instructor.sections||
      ' section(s)');
EXCEPTION
  WHEN NO_DATA_FOUND THEN
    DBMS_OUTPUT.PUT_LINE
        ('There is no such instructor');
END;
```

ANSWER: In this example, you declare a record called `vr_instructor`. This record is based on the type you defined previously. In the body of the PL/SQL block, you initialize this record with the help of the SELECT INTO statement and display its value on the screen. It is important to note that the columns of the SELECT INTO statement are listed in the same order that the attributes are defined in the `instructor_info` type. So there is no need to use dot notation for this record initialization. When run, this example produces the following output:

```
Instructor, Tom Wojick, teaches 9 section(s)
PL/SQL procedure successfully completed.
```

11.1.3 **Make Use of Cursor Attributes**

Table 11.1 lists the attributes of a cursor, which determine the result of a cursor operation when fetched or opened.

TABLE 11.1
Explicit Cursor Attributes

CURSOR ATTRIBUTE	SYNTAX	DESCRIPTION
%NOTFOUND	*cursor_name*%NOTFOUND	A Boolean attribute that returns TRUE if the previous FETCH did not return a row and FALSE if it did.
%FOUND	*cursor_name*%FOUND	A Boolean attribute that returns TRUE if the previous FETCH returned a row and FALSE if it did not.
%ROWCOUNT	*cursor_name*%ROWCOUNT	The number of records fetched from a cursor at that point in time.
%ISOPEN	*cursor_name*%ISOPEN	A Boolean attribute that returns TRUE if the cursor is open and FALSE if it is not.

A) Now that you know about cursor attributes, you can use one of them to exit the loop within the code you developed in the previous example. Can you make a fully executable block now? Why or why not?

ANSWER: You can make use of the attribute %NOTFOUND to close the loop. It would also be wise to add an exception clause to the end of the block to close the cursor if it is still open. If you add the following statements to the end of your block, it will be complete:

```
        EXIT WHEN c_student%NOTFOUND;
    END LOOP;
    CLOSE c_student;
EXCEPTION
    WHEN OTHERS
    THEN
       IF c_student%ISOPEN
       THEN
          CLOSE c_student;
       END IF;
END;
```

Cursor attributes can be used with implicit cursors by using the prefix SQL, such as SQL%ROWCOUNT.

If you use SELECT INTO syntax in your PL/SQL block, you will create an implicit cursor. You can then use these attributes on the implicit cursor.

B) What will happen if the following code is run? Describe what is happening in each phase of the example.

FOR EXAMPLE

```
-- ch11_3a.sql
SET SERVEROUTPUT ON
DECLARE
    v_city zipcode.city%type;
BEGIN
    SELECT city
      INTO v_city
      FROM zipcode
     WHERE zip = 07002;
    IF SQL%ROWCOUNT = 1
    THEN
      DBMS_OUTPUT.PUT_LINE(v_city ||' has a '||
         'zipcode of 07002');
    ELSIF SQL%ROWCOUNT = 0
    THEN
       DBMS_OUTPUT.PUT_LINE('The zipcode 07002 is '||
          ' not in the database');
    ELSE
       DBMS_OUTPUT.PUT_LINE('Stop harassing me');
    END IF;
END;
```

ANSWER: The preceding code displays the following output:

```
Bayonne has a zipcode of 07002
PL/SQL procedure successfully completed.
```

The declaration section declares a variable, v_city, anchored to the datatype of the city item in the zipcode table. The SELECT statement causes an implicit cursor to be opened, fetched, and then closed. The IF clause uses the attribute %ROWCOUNT to determine if the implicit cursor has a row count of 1. If it does, the first DBMS_OUTPUT line is displayed. Note that this example does not handle a situation in which the row count is greater than 1. Because the zipcode table's primary key is the zip code, this could happen.

C) Rerun this block, changing 07002 to 99999. What do you think will happen? Explain.

ANSWER: The PL/SQL block displays the following:

```
DECLARE
ERROR at line 1:
ORA-01403: no data found
ORA-06512: at line 4
```

A select statement in a PL/SQL block that does not return any rows raises a `no data found` exception. Because there is no exception handler, the preceding error is displayed.

D) Try running this file. Does it run as you expected? Why or why not? What could be done to improve how it handles a possible error condition?

ANSWER: You may have expected the second and third condition of the IF statement to capture the instance of a %ROWCOUNT equal to 0. Now that you understand that a SELECT statement that returns no rows raises a WHEN NO_DATA_FOUND exception, it would be a good idea to handle this by adding a WHEN NO_DATA_FOUND exception to the existing block. You can add a %ROWCOUNT in the exception, either to display the row count in a DBMS_OUTPUT or to put an IF statement to display various possibilities.

11.1.4 **Put It All Together**

The following is an example of the complete cycle of declaring, opening, fetching, and closing a cursor, including the use of cursor attributes.

A) Describe what is happening in each phase of the following code. Use the line numbers as a reference.

```
-- ch11_4a.sql
1> DECLARE
2>    v_sid      student.student_id%TYPE;
3>    CURSOR c_student IS
4>       SELECT student_id
5>         FROM student
6>        WHERE student_id < 110;
7> BEGIN
8>    OPEN c_student;
9>    LOOP
10>      FETCH c_student INTO v_sid;
11>      EXIT WHEN c_student%NOTFOUND;
12>         DBMS_OUTPUT.PUT_LINE('STUDENT ID : '||v_sid);
13>    END LOOP;
14>    CLOSE c_student;
15> EXCEPTION
```

```
16>    WHEN OTHERS
17>    THEN
18>       IF c_student%ISOPEN
19>       THEN
20>          CLOSE c_student;
21>       END IF;
22> END;
```

ANSWER: This example illustrates a cursor fetch loop, in which multiple rows of data are returned from the query. The cursor is declared in the declaration section of the block (lines 1 through 6), just like other identifiers. In the executable section of the block (lines 7 through 15), a cursor is opened using the OPEN statement (line 8). Because the cursor returns multiple rows, a loop is used to assign returned data to the variables with a FETCH statement (line 10). Because the loop statement has no other means of termination, an exit condition must be specified. In this case, one of the cursor's attributes is %NOTFOUND (line 11). The cursor is then closed to free the memory allocation (line 14). Additionally, if the exception handler is called, there is a check to see if the cursor is open (line 18). If it is, it is closed (line 20).

B) Modify the example to make use of the cursor attributes %FOUND and %ROWCOUNT.

ANSWER: Your modification should look like this:

```
-- ch11_5a.sql
SET SERVEROUTPUT ON
DECLARE
    v_sid        student.student_id%TYPE;
    CURSOR c_student IS
       SELECT student_id
         FROM student
        WHERE student_id < 110;
 BEGIN
    OPEN c_student;
    LOOP
       FETCH c_student INTO v_sid;
       IF c_student%FOUND THEN
       DBMS_OUTPUT.PUT_LINE
          ('Just FETCHED row '
            ||TO_CHAR(c_student%ROWCOUNT)||
            ' Student ID: '||v_sid);
       ELSE
         EXIT;
       END IF;
    END LOOP;
    CLOSE c_student;
 EXCEPTION
    WHEN OTHERS
    THEN
       IF c_student%ISOPEN
       THEN
          CLOSE c_student;
       END IF;
 END;
```

The loop structure has been modified. Instead of an exit condition, an IF statement is used. The IF statement uses the cursor attribute %FOUND. This attribute returns true when a row is "found" in the cursor and false when it is not. The next attribute, %ROWCOUNT, returns a number, which is the cursor's current row number.

C) Demonstrate how to fetch a cursor that has data from the student table into a %ROWTYPE. Select only students who have a `student_id` of less than 110. The columns are STUDENT_ID, LAST_NAME, FIRST_NAME, and a count of the number of classes they are enrolled in (using the enrollment table). Fetch the cursor with a loop, and then output all the columns. You will have to use an alias for the enrollment count.

ANSWER: One method of doing this is as follows:

```
-- ch11_6a.sql
SET SERVEROUTPUT ON
DECLARE
   CURSOR c_student_enroll IS
      SELECT s.student_id, first_name, last_name,
             COUNT(*) enroll,
             (CASE
                   WHEN count(*) = 1 Then ' class.'
                   WHEN count(*) is null then
                                   ' no classes.'
                   ELSE ' classes.'
              END) class
        FROM student s, enrollment e
       WHERE s.student_id = e.student_id
         AND s.student_id <110
       GROUP BY s.student_id, first_name, last_name;
   r_student_enroll    c_student_enroll%ROWTYPE;
BEGIN
   OPEN c_student_enroll;
   LOOP
      FETCH c_student_enroll INTO r_student_enroll;
      EXIT WHEN c_student_enroll%NOTFOUND;
      DBMS_OUTPUT.PUT_LINE('Student INFO: ID '||
         r_student_enroll.student_id||' is '||
         r_student_enroll.first_name|| ' ' ||
         r_student_enroll.last_name||
         ' is enrolled in '||r_student_enroll.enroll||
         r_student_enroll.class);
   END LOOP;
   CLOSE c_student_enroll;
EXCEPTION
   WHEN OTHERS
   THEN
    IF c_student_enroll %ISOPEN
      THEN
    CLOSE c_student_enroll;
    END IF;
END;
```

WATCH OUT!

Remember that the CASE syntax was introduced in Oracle 9i. This means that the preceding statement will not run in Oracle 8 or 8i. You can change the CASE statement to a DECODE statement as follows:

```
DECODE( count(*), 1, ' class. ', null, 'no classes.',
'classes') class
```

In the declaration section, the cursor $c\_student\_enroll$ is defined, as well as a record, which is the type of a row of the cursor. The cursor loop structure uses an exit condition with the %NOTFOUND cursor attribute. When there are no more rows, %NOTFOUND is true and causes the loop to exit. While the cursor is open and the loop is processing, it fetches a row of the cursor in a record one at a time. The DBMS output causes each row to be displayed to the screen. Finally, the cursor is closed, and an exception clause also closes the cursor if any error is raised.

ASSORTED TIPS ON CURSORS

Cursor SELECT LIST

Match the SELECT list with PL/SQL variables or PL/SQL record components.

The number of variables must be equal to the number of columns or expressions in the SELECT list. The number of components in a record must match the columns or expressions in the SELECT list.

Cursor Scope

The scope of a cursor declared in the main block (or an enclosing block) extends to the subblocks.

Expressions in a Cursor SELECT List

PL/SQL variables, expressions, and even functions can be included in the cursor SELECT list.

Column Aliases in Cursors

An alias is an alternative name you provide to a column or expression in the SELECT list. In an explicit cursor column, aliases are required for calculated columns when

▶ You FETCH into a record declared with a %ROWTYPE declaration against that cursor.

▶ You want to reference the calculated column in the program.

LAB 11.2
Using Cursor FOR Loops and Nested Cursors

LAB OBJECTIVES

After completing this lab, you will be able to

▶ Use a cursor FOR loop
▶ Process nested cursors

There is an alternative way to handle cursors. It is called the cursor FOR loop because of the simplified syntax that is used. With a cursor FOR loop, the process of opening, fetching, and closing is handled implicitly. This makes the blocks much easier to code and maintain.

The cursor FOR loop specifies a sequence of statements to be repeated once for each row returned by the cursor. Use the cursor FOR loop if you need to FETCH and PROCESS every record from a cursor until you want to stop processing and exit the loop.

To use this column, you need to create a new table called table_log with the following script:

FOR EXAMPLE

```
create table table_log
      (description VARCHAR2(250));
```

Then run this script:

```
-- ch11_7a.sql
DECLARE
   CURSOR c_student IS
      SELECT student_id, last_name, first_name
        FROM student
        WHERE student_id < 110;
BEGIN
   FOR r_student IN c_student
   LOOP
      INSERT INTO table_log
         VALUES(r_student.last_name);
   END LOOP;
END;
```

▼ LAB 11.2 EXERCISES

This section provides exercises and suggested answers, with discussion related to how those answers resulted. The most important thing to realize is whether your answer works. You should figure out the implications of the answers and what the effects are of any different answers you may come up with.

11.2.1 **Use a Cursor FOR Loop**

A) Write a PL/SQL block that reduces the cost of all courses by 5 percent for courses having an enrollment of eight students or more. Use a cursor FOR loop that updates the course table.

ANSWER: Your block should look like this:

```
-- ch11_7b.sql
DECLARE
    CURSOR c_group_discount IS
        SELECT DISTINCT s.course_no
          FROM section s, enrollment e
         WHERE s.section_id = e.section_id
          GROUP BY s.course_no, e.section_id, s.section_id
          HAVING COUNT(*)>=8;
BEGIN
    FOR r_group_discount IN c_group_discount    LOOP
        UPDATE course
           SET cost = cost * .95
         WHERE course_no = r_group_discount.course_no;
    END LOOP;
    COMMIT;
END;
```

The cursor `c_group_discount` is declared in the declaration section. The proper SQL is used to generate the SELECT statement to answer the question given. The cursor is processed in a FOR loop. In each iteration of the loop, the SQL update statement is executed. This means that it does not have to be opened, fetched, and closed. This also means that a cursor attribute does not have to be used to create an exit condition for the loop that is processing the cursor.

11.2.2 **Process Nested Cursors**

Cursors can be nested inside each other. Although this may sound complex, it is really just a loop inside a loop, much like nested loops, which were covered in previous chapters. If you have one parent cursor and two child cursors, each time the parent cursor makes a single loop, it loops through each child cursor once and then begins a second round. The following two examples show a nested cursor with a single child cursor.

FOR EXAMPLE

```
SET SERVEROUTPUT ON
-- ch11_8a.sql
1    DECLARE
2        v_zip zipcode.zip%TYPE;
3        v_student_flag CHAR;
4        CURSOR c_zip IS
5           SELECT zip, city, state
6              FROM zipcode
```

```
7                WHERE state = 'CT';
8          CURSOR c_student IS
9             SELECT first_name, last_name
10              FROM student
11             WHERE zip = v_zip;
12    BEGIN
13       FOR r_zip IN c_zip
14       LOOP
15          v_student_flag := 'N';
16          v_zip := r_zip.zip;
17          DBMS_OUTPUT.PUT_LINE(CHR(10));
18          DBMS_OUTPUT.PUT_LINE('Students living in '||
19             r_zip.city);
20          FOR r_student in c_student
21          LOOP
22             DBMS_OUTPUT.PUT_LINE(
23                r_student.first_name||
24                ' '||r_student.last_name);
25             v_student_flag := 'Y';
26          END LOOP;
27          IF v_student_flag = 'N'
28             THEN
29             DBMS_OUTPUT.PUT_LINE
                  ('No Students for this zipcode');
30          END IF;
31       END LOOP;
32    END;
```

This example has two cursors. The first is a cursor of the zip codes, and the second is a list of students. The variable v_zip is initialized in line 16 to be the zip code of the current record of the c_zip cursor. The $c\_$ student cursor ties in the c_zip cursor by means of this variable. Thus, when the cursor is processed in lines 20 through 26, it is retrieving students who have the zip code of the current record for the parent cursor. The parent cursor is processed from lines 13 through 31. Each iteration of the parent cursor will execute the DBMS_OUTPUT in lines 16 and 17 only once. The DBMS_OUTPUT in line 22 will be executed once for each iteration of the child loop, producing a line of output for each student. The DBMS_OUTPUT.PUT_LINE statement in line 29 will only execute if the inner loop did not execute. This was accomplished by setting a variable $v\_student\_flag$. The variable is set to N in the beginning of the parent loop. If the child loop executes at least once, the variable is set to Y. After the child loop has closed, a check is made with an IF statement to determine the value of the variable. If it is still N, it can be safely concluded that the inner loop did not process. This will then allow the last DBMS_OUTPUT.PUT_LINE statement to execute. Nested cursors are more often parameterized. You will see parameters in cursors explained in depth in Lab 12.2, "Using Parameters with Cursors and Nested Cursors."

A) Write a PL/SQL block with two cursor for loops. The parent cursor will call the $student\_id$, $first\_name$, and $last\_name$ from the student table for students with a $student\_id$ less than 110 and output one line with this information. For each student, the child cursor will loop through all the courses that the student is enrolled in, outputting the $course\_no$ and the description.

ANSWER: Your block should look similar to this:

```
-- ch11_09a.sql
SET SERVEROUTPUT ON
```

```
DECLARE
    v_sid student.student_id%TYPE;
    CURSOR c_student IS
        SELECT student_id, first_name, last_name
          FROM student
         WHERE student_id < 110;
    CURSOR c_course IS
        SELECT c.course_no, c.description
          FROM course c, section s, enrollment e
         WHERE c.course_no = s.course_no
           AND s.section_id = e.section_id
           AND e.student_id = v_sid;
BEGIN
    FOR r_student IN c_student
    LOOP
        v_sid := r_student.student_id;
        DBMS_OUTPUT.PUT_LINE(chr(10));
        DBMS_OUTPUT.PUT_LINE(' The Student '||
            r_student.student_id||' '||
            r_student.first_name||' '||
            r_student.last_name);
        DBMS_OUTPUT.PUT_LINE(' is enrolled in the '||
            'following courses: ');
        FOR r_course IN c_course
        LOOP
            DBMS_OUTPUT.PUT_LINE(r_course.course_no||
                '    '||r_course.description);
        END LOOP;
    END LOOP;
END;
```

The select statements for the two cursors are defined in the declaration section of the PL/SQL block. A variable to store the `student_id` from the parent cursor is also declared. The course cursor is the child cursor, and because it uses the variable `v_sid`, the variable must be declared first. Both cursors are processed with a FOR loop, which eliminates the need for OPEN, FETCH, and CLOSE. When the parent student loop is processed, the first step is to initialize the variable `v_sid`, and the value is then used when the child loop is processed. DBMS_OUTPUT is used so that display is generated for each cursor loop. The parent cursor displays the student name once, and the child cursor displays the name of each course in which the student is enrolled.

B) The following is another example of a nested cursor. Before you run this code, analyze what it does, and determine what you think the result will be. Explain what happens in each phase of the PL/SQL block and what happens to the variables as control passes through the parent and child cursors.

FOR EXAMPLE

```
-- ch11_10a.sql
SET SERVEROUTPUT ON
DECLARE
    v_amount course.cost%TYPE;
    v_instructor_id  instructor.instructor_id%TYPE;
```

```
   CURSOR c_inst IS
      SELECT first_name, last_name, instructor_id
        FROM instructor;
   CURSOR c_cost IS
      SELECT c.cost
        FROM course c, section s, enrollment e
       WHERE s.instructor_id = v_instructor_id
         AND c.course_no = s.course_no
         AND s.section_id = e.section_id;
BEGIN
   FOR r_inst IN c_inst
   LOOP
      v_instructor_id := r_inst.instructor_id;
      v_amount := 0;
      DBMS_OUTPUT.PUT_LINE(
         'Amount generated by instructor '||
          r_inst.first_name||' '||r_inst.last_name
         ||' is');
      FOR r_cost IN c_cost
      LOOP
         v_amount := v_amount + NVL(r_cost.cost, 0);
      END LOOP;
      DBMS_OUTPUT.PUT_LINE
      ('       '||TO_CHAR(v_amount,'$999,999'));
   END LOOP;
END;
```

ANSWER: The declaration section contains a declaration for two variables. The first is v_amount of the datatype matching that of the cost in the course table. The second is v_instructor_id of the datatype matching the instructor_id in the instructor table. There are also two declarations for two cursors. The first is for c_inst, which is composed of the first_name, last_name, and instructor_id for an instructor from the instructor table. The second cursor, c_cost, produces a result set of the cost of a course. This is the course taken for each enrolled student. That course is taught by the instructor who matches the variable v_instructor_id. These two cursors are run in nested fashion. First, the cursor c_inst is opened in a FOR loop. The value of the variable v_instructor_id is initialized to match the instructor_id of the current row of the c_inst cursor. The variable v_amount is initialized to 0. The second cursor is open within the loop for the first cursor. This means that for each iteration of the cursor c_inst, the second cursor is opened, fetched, and closed. The second cursor loops through each student enrolled in a course for the instructor, which is current of the c_inst cursor. It adds the cost of the course one time for each enrolled student. Each time the nest loop iterates, it increases the variable v_amount by adding the current cost in the c_cost loop. Before the c_cost loop is opened, a DBMS_OUTPUT displays the instructor name. After the c_cost cursor loop is closed, it displays the total amount generated by all the enrollments of the current instructor.

C) Run the code and see what the result is. Is it what you expected? Explain the difference.

ANSWER: The result set is as follows:

```
Amount generated by instructor Fernand Hanks is
$49,110
Amount generated by instructor Tom Wojick is
$24,582
Amount generated by instructor Nina Schorin is
$43,319
Amount generated by instructor Gary Pertez is
$29,317
Amount generated by instructor Anita Morris is
$18,662
Amount generated by instructor Todd Smythe is
$21,092
Amount generated by instructor Marilyn Frantzen is
$34,311
Amount generated by instructor Charles Lowry is
$37,512
Amount generated by instructor Rick Chow is
$0
Amount generated by instructor Irene Willig is
$0
```

In this example, the nested cursor is tied to the current row of the outer cursor by means of the variable `v_instructor_id`. A more common way of doing this is to pass a parameter to a cursor. You will learn more about how to do this in Chapter 12, "Advanced Cursors."

▼ TRY IT YOURSELF

In this chapter, you've learned how to process data with a cursor. Additionally, you've learned how to simplify the code by using a cursor FOR loop. You've also encountered the more complex example of nesting cursors within cursors. Here are some projects that will help you test the depth of your understanding:

1) Write a nested cursor in which the parent cursor gathers information about each section of a course. The child cursor counts the enrollment. The only output is one line for each course, with the course name, section number, and total enrollment.

2) Write an anonymous PL/SQL block that finds all the courses that have at least one section that is at its maximum enrollment. If no courses meet that criterion, pick two courses and create that situation for each.

   a) For each of those courses, add another section. The instructor for the new section should be taken from the existing records in the instructor table. Use the instructor who is signed up to teach the fewest courses. Handle the fact that, during the execution of your program, the instructor teaching the most courses may change.

   b) Use any exception-handling techniques you think are useful to capture error conditions.

The projects in this section are meant to have you use all the skills you have acquired throughout this chapter. The answers to these projects can be found in Appendix D and on this book's companion Web site. Visit the Web site periodically to share and discuss your answers.

Advanced Cursors

CHAPTER OBJECTIVES

In this chapter, you will learn about

- ▶ Using parameters with cursors and complex nested cursors
- ▶ FOR UPDATE and WHERE CURRENT cursors

In the preceding chapter you mastered basic cursor concepts. In this chapter you will learn how to dynamically alter a cursor's WHERE clause by passing parameters when you call the cursor. Chapter 21 takes cursors to another level. In the context of a package you will also learn to implement cursor variables.

LAB 12.1
Using Parameters with Cursors and Complex Nested Cursors

LAB OBJECTIVES

After completing this lab, you will be able to

- ▶ Use parameters in a cursor
- ▶ Use complex nested cursors

CURSORS WITH PARAMETERS

A cursor can be declared with parameters. This enables a cursor to generate a specific result set that is narrow but also reusable. A cursor of all the data from the zipcode table may be very useful, but it would be more useful for certain data processing if it held information for only one state. At this point, you know how to create such a cursor. But wouldn't it be more useful if you could create a cursor that could accept a parameter of a state and then run through only the city and zip for that state?

FOR EXAMPLE

```
CURSOR c_zip (p_state IN zipcode.state%TYPE) IS
    SELECT zip, city, state
      FROM zipcode
     WHERE state = p_state;
```

Here are the main points to keep in mind for parameters in cursors:

- ▶ Cursor parameters make the cursor more reusable.
- ▶ Cursor parameters can be assigned default values.
- ▶ The scope of the cursor parameters is local to the cursor.
- ▶ The mode of the parameters can only be IN.

When a cursor has been declared as taking a parameter, it must be called with a value for that parameter. The c_zip cursor declared in the preceding example is called as follows:

```
OPEN c_zip (parameter_value)
```

The same cursor could be opened with a CURSOR FOR loop as follows:

```
FOR r_zip IN c_zip('NY')
LOOP  ...
```

▼ LAB 12.1 EXERCISES

This section provides exercises and suggested answers, with discussion related to how those answers resulted. The most important thing to realize is whether your answer works. You should figure out the implications of the answers and what the effects are of any different answers you may come up with.

12.1.1 Use Parameters in a Cursor

A) Complete the code for the parameter cursor that was begun in the preceding example. Include a DBMS_OUTPUT line that displays the zip code, city, and state. This is identical to the process you have already used in a CURSOR FOR loop, only now, when you open the cursor, you pass a parameter.

ANSWER: Your block should look like this:

```
-- ch12_17a.sql
DECLARE
    CURSOR c_zip (p_state IN zipcode.state%TYPE) IS
        SELECT zip, city, state
          FROM zipcode
         WHERE state = p_state
BEGIN
    FOR r_zip IN c_zip('NJ')
    LOOP  ...
       DBMS_OUTPUT.PUT_LINE(r_zip.city||
          ' '||r_zip.zip');
    END LOOP;
END;
```

To complete the block, the cursor declaration must be surrounded by DECLARE and BEGIN. The cursor is opened by passing the parameter NJ. Then, for each iteration of the cursor loop, the zip code and the city are displayed using the built-in package DBMS_OUTPUT.

12.1.2 Use Complex Nested Cursors

Nesting cursors allows for looping through data at various stages. For example, one cursor could loop through zip codes. When it hits a zip code, a second, nested cursor would loop through students who live in that zip code. Working through a specific example will help you understand this in more detail.

A) The following PL/SQL code is complex. It involves all the topics covered so far in this chapter. It has a nested cursor with three levels, meaning a grandparent cursor, a parent cursor, and a child cursor. Before running this script, review the code and identify its levels of nesting. When you describe each level of the code, explain what parameters are passed into the cursor and why. What do you think the result of running this statement will be?

```
-- ch12_1a.sql
SET SERVEROUTPUT ON
   1    DECLARE
   2        CURSOR c_student IS
   3            SELECT first_name, last_name, student_id
```

```
4              FROM student
5             WHERE last_name LIKE 'J%';
6         CURSOR c_course
7              (i_student_id IN
                         student.student_id%TYPE)
8         IS
9           SELECT c.description, s.section_id sec_id
10            FROM course c, section s, enrollment e
11           WHERE e.student_id = i_student_id
12             AND c.course_no = s.course_no
13             AND s.section_id = e.section_id;
14         CURSOR c_grade(i_section_id IN
                         section.section_id%TYPE,
15                     i_student_id IN
                         student.student_id%TYPE)
16           IS
17           SELECT gt.description grd_desc,
18             TO_CHAR
19               (AVG(g.numeric_grade), '999.99')
                                    num_grd
20            FROM enrollment e,
21                 grade g, grade_type gt
22           WHERE e.section_id = i_section_id
23             AND e.student_id = g.student_id
24             AND e.student_id = i_student_id
25             AND e.section_id = g.section_id
26             AND g.grade_type_code =
                            gt.grade_type_code
27           GROUP BY gt.description ;
28     BEGIN
29       FOR r_student IN c_student
30       LOOP
31         DBMS_OUTPUT.PUT_LINE(CHR(10));
32         DBMS_OUTPUT.PUT_LINE(r_student.first_name||
33           ' '||r_student.last_name);
34         FOR r_course IN
                 c_course(r_student.student_id)
35         LOOP
36           DBMS_OUTPUT.PUT_LINE
                 ('Grades for course :'||
37             r_course.description);
38           FOR r_grade IN c_grade(r_course.sec_id,
39                           r_student.student_id)
40           LOOP
41             DBMS_OUTPUT.PUT_LINE(r_grade.num_grd||
42               ' '||r_grade.grd_desc);
43           END LOOP;
44         END LOOP;
45       END LOOP;
46     END;
```

ANSWER: The grandparent cursor, `c_student`, is declared in lines 2 through 5. It takes no parameters and is a collection of students with a last name beginning with J. The parent cursor, `c_course`, is declared in lines 6 through 13. It takes in the parameter of `student_ID` to generate a list of courses that student is taking. The child cursor, `c_grade`, is declared in lines 14 through 27. It takes in two parameters, `section_id` and `student_id`. In this way it can generate an average of the different grade types (quizzes, homework, final, etc.) for that student for that course. The grandparent cursor loop begins on line 29, and only the student name is displayed with DBMS_OUTPUT. The parent cursor loop begins on line 35. It takes the parameter of `student_id` from the grandparent cursor. Only the description of the course is displayed. The child cursor loop begins on line 40. It takes in the parameter of `section_id` from the parent cursor and `student_id` from the grandparent cursor. The grades are then displayed. The grandparent cursor loop ends on line 45, the parent cursor loop on line 44, and the child cursor loop on line 43.

B) Now run the code. Analyze it line by line, and explain what is processed and then displayed for each line.

ANSWER: The output is a student name, followed by the courses he or she is taking and the average grade he or she has earned for each grade type. If you did not guess the correct answer, try commenting out different sections of the block and see what happens. This helps you understand what is happening in each step.

LAB 12.2
FOR UPDATE and WHERE CURRENT Cursors

LAB OBJECTIVES

After completing this lab, you will be able to

▶ Use a FOR UPDATE and WHERE CURRENT in a cursor

The cursor FOR UPDATE clause is used only with a cursor when you want to update tables in the database. Generally, when you execute a SELECT statement, you are not locking any rows. The purpose of using the FOR UPDATE clause is to lock the rows of the tables you want to update so that another user cannot perform an update until you perform your update and release the lock. The next COMMIT or ROLLBACK statement releases the lock. The FOR UPDATE clause changes the manner in which the cursor operates in only a few respects. When you open a cursor, all rows that meet the restriction criteria are identified as part of the active set. Using the FOR UPDATE clause locks these rows that have been identified in the active set. If the FOR UPDATE clause is used, rows may not be fetched from the cursor until a COMMIT has been issued. It is important to think about where to place the COMMIT. Be sure to consider the transaction management issues covered in Chapter 3, "SQL in PL/SQL."

The syntax is simply to add FOR UPDATE to the end of the cursor definition. If several items are being selected, but you want to lock only one of them, end the cursor definition with the following syntax:

```
FOR UPDATE OF <item_name>
```

▼ LAB 12.2 EXERCISES

This section provides exercises and suggested answers, with discussion related to how those answers resulted. The most important thing to realize is whether your answer works. You should figure out the implications of the answers and what the effects are of any different answers you may come up with.

12.2.1 For UPDATE and WHERE CURRENT Cursors

The following example shows how to update the cost of all courses that cost less than $2,500. It increments them by 10.

FOR EXAMPLE

```
-- ch12_2a.sql
DECLARE
  CURSOR c_course IS
     SELECT course_no, cost
       FROM course FOR UPDATE;
BEGIN
   FOR r_course IN c_course
   LOOP
      IF r_course.cost < 2500
      THEN
         UPDATE course
            SET cost = r_course.cost + 10
          WHERE course_no = r_course.course_no;
      END IF;
   END LOOP;
END;
```

A) In this example, where should the COMMIT be placed? What issues are involved in deciding where to place a COMMIT in this example?

ANSWER: Placing a COMMIT after each update can be costly. But if there are a lot of updates and the COMMIT comes after the block loop, the rollback segment might not be large enough. Normally, the COMMIT would go after the loop, except when the transaction count is high. In that case you might want to code something that does a COMMIT for every 10,000 records. If this were part of a large procedure, you may want to put a SAVEPOINT after the loop. Then, if you needed to roll back this update later, this would be easy.

B) What do you think will happen if you run the code in the following example? After making your analysis, run the code, and then perform a SELECT statement to determine if your guess is correct.

FOR EXAMPLE

```
-- ch12_3a.sql
DECLARE
   CURSOR c_grade(
      i_student_id IN enrollment.student_id%TYPE,
      i_section_id IN enrollment.section_id%TYPE)
   IS
      SELECT final_grade
        FROM enrollment
       WHERE student_id = i_student_id
         AND section_id = i_section_id
       FOR UPDATE;
   CURSOR c_enrollment IS
      SELECT e.student_id, e.section_id
        FROM enrollment e, section s
       WHERE s.course_no = 135
         AND e.section_id = s.section_id;
BEGIN
   FOR r_enroll IN c_enrollment
   LOOP
      FOR r_grade IN c_grade(r_enroll.student_id,
                             r_enroll.section_id)
```

```
      LOOP
         UPDATE enrollment
            SET final_grade  = 90
          WHERE student_id = r_enroll.student_id
            AND section_id = r_enroll.section_id;
      END LOOP;
   END LOOP;
END;
```

ANSWER: The `final_grade` for all students enrolled in course 135 is updated to 90. There are two cursors. One cursor captures the students who are enrolled in course 135 into the active set. The other cursor takes the `student_id` and `section_id` from this active set, selects the corresponding `final_grade` from the enrollment table, and locks the entire enrollment table. The enrollment cursor loop occurs first. It passes the `student_id` and `section_id` as IN parameters for the second cursor loop of the `c_grade` cursor, which performs the update.

C) Where should the COMMIT go in the preceding example? Explain the considerations.

ANSWER: The COMMIT should go immediately after the update to ensure that each update is committed into the database.

FOR UPDATE OF can be used when creating a cursor FOR UPDATE that is based on multiple tables. FOR UPDATE OF locks the rows of a table that both contain one of the specified columns and are members of the active set. In other words, it is the means of specifying which table you want to lock. If the FOR UPDATE OF clause is used, rows may not be fetched from the cursor until a COMMIT has been issued.

D) What changes to the database take place if the following example is run? Explain specifically what is being locked, as well as when it is locked and when it is released.

FOR EXAMPLE

```
-- ch12_4a.sql
DECLARE
   CURSOR c_stud_zip IS
      SELECT s.student_id, z.city
        FROM student s, zipcode z
       WHERE z.city = 'Brooklyn'
         AND s.zip = z.zip
        FOR UPDATE OF phone;
BEGIN
  FOR r_stud_zip IN c_stud_zip
  LOOP
     UPDATE student
        SET phone = '718'||SUBSTR(phone,4)
      WHERE student_id = r_stud_zip.student_id;
  END LOOP;
END;
```

ANSWER: The phone numbers of students living in Brooklyn are being updated to change the area code to 718. The cursor declaration only locks the phone column of the student table. The lock is never released because there is no COMMIT or ROLLBACK statement.

Use WHERE CURRENT OF when you want to update the most recently fetched row. WHERE CURRENT OF can be used only with a FOR UPDATE OF cursor. The advantage of the WHERE CURRENT OF clause is that it enables you to eliminate the WHERE clause in the UPDATE statement:

FOR EXAMPLE

```
-- ch12_5a.sql
DECLARE
   CURSOR c_stud_zip IS
      SELECT s.student_id, z.city
        FROM student s, zipcode z
       WHERE z.city = 'Brooklyn'
         AND s.zip = z.zip
       FOR UPDATE OF phone;
BEGIN
   FOR r_stud_zip IN c_stud_zip
   LOOP
      DBMS_OUTPUT.PUT_LINE(r_stud_zip.student_id);
      UPDATE student
         SET phone = '718'||SUBSTR(phone,4)
       WHERE CURRENT OF c_stud_zip;
   END LOOP;
END;
```

E) Compare the two preceding examples. Explain their similarities and differences. What has been altered by using the WHERE CURRENT OF clause? What is the advantage of doing this?

ANSWER: These two statements perform the same update. The WHERE CURRENT OF clause allows you to eliminate a match in the UPDATE statement, because the update is being performed for the cursor's current record only.

DID YOU KNOW?

The FOR UPDATE and WHERE CURRENT OF syntax can be used with cursors that are performing a delete as well as an update.

BY THE WAY

This chapter has no "Try it Yourself" section.

CHAPTER 13

Triggers

CHAPTER OBJECTIVES

In this chapter, you will learn about

- ▶ What triggers are
- ▶ Types of triggers

In Chapter 1, "PL/SQL Concepts," you encountered the concept of named PL/SQL blocks such as procedures, functions, and packages that can be stored in the database. In this chapter, you will learn about another type of named PL/SQL block called a database trigger. You will also learn about different characteristics of triggers and their usage in the database.

LAB 13.1
What Triggers Are

LAB OBJECTIVES

After completing this lab, you will be able to

▶ Understand what a trigger is
▶ Use BEFORE and AFTER triggers

A database trigger is a named PL/SQL block stored in a database and executed implicitly when a *triggering event* occurs. The act of executing a trigger is called firing the trigger. A triggering event can be one of the following:

▶ A DML statement (such as INSERT, UPDATE, or DELETE) executed against a database table. Such a trigger can fire before or after a triggering event. For example, if you have defined a trigger to fire before an INSERT statement on the STUDENT table, this trigger fires each time before you insert a row in the STUDENT table.

▶ A DDL statement (such as CREATE or ALTER) executed either by a particular user against a schema or by any user. Such triggers are often used for auditing purposes and are specifically helpful to Oracle DBAs. They can record various schema changes, when they were made, and by which user.

▶ A system event such as startup or shutdown of the database.

▶ A user event such as logon and logoff. For example, you can define a trigger that fires after database logon that records the username and time of logon.

BY THE WAY

In this chapter you will explore triggers associated with DML statements. Triggers associated with other triggering events are not covered in this book. You can find detailed information about them in the Oracle help.

The general syntax for creating a trigger is as follows (the reserved words and phrases in brackets are optional):

```
CREATE [OR REPLACE] TRIGGER Ttrigger_name
{BEFORE|AFTER} Triggering_event ON table_name
[FOR EACH ROW]
[FOLLOWS another_trigger]
```

```
[ENABLE/DISABLE]
[WHEN condition]
DECLARE
    declaration statements
BEGIN
    executable statements
EXCEPTION
    exception-handling statements
END;
```

The reserved word CREATE specifies that you are creating a new trigger. The reserved word REPLACE specifies that you are modifying an existing trigger. REPLACE is optional. However, note that both CREATE and REPLACE are present most of the time. Consider the following situation. You create a trigger as follows:

```
CREATE TRIGGER Trigger_name
...
```

In a few days you decide to modify this trigger. If you do not include the reserved word REPLACE in the CREATE clause of the trigger, an error message will be generated when you compile the trigger. The error message states that the name of your trigger is already being used by another object. When REPLACE is included in the CREATE clause of the trigger, there is less chance of an error because, if this is a new trigger, it is created, and if it is an old trigger, it is replaced.

The *trigger_name* is the trigger's name. BEFORE or AFTER specifies when the trigger fires (before or after the triggering event). The *triggering_event* is a DML statement issued against the table. *table_name* is the name of the table associated with the trigger. The clause FOR EACH ROW specifies that a trigger is a row trigger and fires once for each row that is inserted, updated, or deleted. You will encounter row and statement triggers in Lab 13.2. A WHEN clause specifies a condition that must evaluate to TRUE for the trigger to fire. For example, this condition may specify a certain restriction on the column of a table. *This portion of the trigger is often called the trigger header*. Next, the trigger body is defined.

Note the three clauses, FOLLOWS, ENABLE, and DISABLE. These were added to the CREATE OR REPLACE TRIGGER clause in Oracle 11g. Prior to Oracle 11g, you needed to issue the ALTER TRIGGER command to enable or disable a trigger after it was created. The ENABLE and DISABLE clauses specify whether the trigger is created in the enabled or disabled state. When the trigger is enabled, it fires when a triggering event occurs. Similarly, when a trigger is disabled, it does not fire when a triggering event occurs. Note that when trigger is first created without an ENABLE or DISABLE clause, it is enabled by default. To disable the trigger, you need to issue the ALTER TRIGGER command as follows:

```
ALTER TRIGGER trigger_name DISABLE;
```

Similarly, to enable a trigger that was disabled previously, you issue the ALTER TRIGGER command as follows:

```
ALTER TRIGGER trigger_name ENABLE;
```

The FOLLOWS option allows you to specify the order in which triggers should fire. This applies to triggers that are defined on the same table and that fire at the same timing point. For example, if you defined two triggers on the STUDENT table that fire before the insert occurs, Oracle does not guarantee the order in which these triggers will fire unless you specify it with the FOLLOWS clause. Note that the trigger referenced in the FOLLOWS clause must already exist and have been successfully compiled.

It is important for you to realize that if you drop a table, the table's database triggers are dropped as well.

You should be careful when using the reserved word REPLACE for a number of reasons. First, if you happen to use REPLACE and the name of an existing stored function, procedure, or package, you will end up with different database objects that have the same name. This occurs because triggers have separate naming space in the database. Although a trigger and a procedure, function, or package sharing the same name does not cause errors, potentially it might become confusing. As a result, it is not considered a good programming practice. Second, when you use the reserved word REPLACE and decide to associate a different table with your trigger, an error message is generated. For example, assume that you created a trigger STUDENT_BI on the STUDENT table. Next, you decide to modify this trigger and associate it with the ENROLL-MENT table. As a result, the following error message is generated:

```
ERROR at line 1:
ORA-04095: trigger 'STUDENT_BI' already exists on another table,
cannot replace it
```

Triggers are used for different purposes:

- ▶ Enforcing complex business rules that cannot be defined by using integrity constraints
- ▶ Maintaining complex security rules
- ▶ Automatically generating values for derived columns
- ▶ Collecting statistical information on table accesses
- ▶ Preventing invalid transactions
- ▶ Providing value auditing

The body of a trigger is a PL/SQL block. However, you need to know about several restrictions before creating a trigger:

- ▶ A trigger may not issue a transactional control statement such as COMMIT, SAVEPOINT, or ROLLBACK. When the trigger fires, all operations performed become part of a transaction. When this transaction is committed or rolled back, the operations performed by the trigger are committed or rolled back as well. An exception to this rule is a trigger that contains an autonomous transaction. Autonomous transactions are discussed in detail later in this lab.

▶ Any function or procedure called by a trigger may not issue a transactional control statement unless it contains an autonomous transaction.

▶ It is not permissible to declare LONG or LONG RAW variables in the body of a trigger.

BEFORE TRIGGERS

Consider the following example of a trigger on the STUDENT table mentioned earlier in this chapter. This trigger fires before the INSERT statement on the STUDENT table and populates the STUDENT_ID, CREATED_DATE, MODIFIED_DATE, CREATED_BY, and MODIFIED_BY columns. Column STUDENT_ID is populated with the number generated by the STUDENT_ID_SEQ sequence, and columns CREATED_DATE, MODIFIED_DATE, CREATED_USER, and MODIFIED_USER are populated with the current date and the current username information.

FOR EXAMPLE

```
CREATE OR REPLACE TRIGGER student_bi
BEFORE INSERT ON student
FOR EACH ROW
BEGIN
    :NEW.student_id    := STUDENT_ID_SEQ.NEXTVAL;
    :NEW.created_by    := USER;
    :NEW.created_date  := SYSDATE;
    :NEW.modified_by   := USER;
    :NEW.modified_date := SYSDATE;
END;
```

This trigger fires for each row before the INSERT statement on the STUDENT table. Notice that the name of the trigger is STUDENT_BI, where STUDENT is the name of the table on which the trigger is defined, and BI means BEFORE INSERT. There is no specific requirement for naming triggers; however, this approach to naming a trigger is descriptive. The name of the trigger contains the name of the table affected by the triggering event, the time of the triggering event (before or after), and the triggering event itself.

In the body of the trigger is a pseudorecord, :NEW, allowing you to access a row currently being processed. In other words, a row is being inserted into the STUDENT table. The :NEW pseudorecord is of type TRIGGERING_TABLE%TYPE, so, in this case, it is of the STUDENT%TYPE type. To access individual members of the pseudorecord :NEW, dot notation is used. In other words, :NEW.CREATED_BY refers to the member CREATED_BY of the :NEW pseudorecord, and the name of the record is separated from the name of its member by a dot.

Take a closer look at the statement that assigns a sequence value to the STUDENT_ID column. The ability to access a sequence via PL/SQL expression is a new feature in Oracle 11g. Prior to Oracle 11g, sequences could be accessed only via queries.

FOR EXAMPLE

```
CREATE OR REPLACE TRIGGER student_bi
BEFORE INSERT ON student
FOR EACH ROW
DECLARE
   v_student_id STUDENT.STUDENT_ID%TYPE;
BEGIN
   SELECT STUDENT_ID_SEQ.NEXTVAL
     INTO v_student_id
     FROM dual;
   :NEW.student_id    := v_student_id;
   :NEW.created_by    := USER;
   :NEW.created_date  := SYSDATE;
   :NEW.modified_by   := USER;
   :NEW.modified_date := SYSDATE;
END;
```

Before you create this trigger, consider the following INSERT statement on the STUDENT table:

```
INSERT INTO student (student_id, first_name, last_name, zip,
   registration_date, created_by, created_date, modified_by,
   modified_date)
VALUES (STUDENT_ID_SEQ.NEXTVAL, 'John', 'Smith', '00914', SYSDATE,
   USER, SYSDATE, USER, SYSDATE);
```

This INSERT statement contains values for the columns STUDENT_ID, CREATED_BY, CREATED_DATE, MODIFIED_BY, and MODIFIED_DATE. It is important to note that for every row you insert into the STUDENT table, the values for these columns must be provided, and they are always derived in the same fashion. Why do you think the values for these columns must be provided when you insert a record into the STUDENT table?

When the trigger shown earlier is created, there is no need to include these columns in the INSERT statement, because the trigger populates them with the required information. Therefore, the INSERT statement can be modified as follows:

```
INSERT INTO student (first_name, last_name, zip, registration_date)
VALUES ('John', 'Smith', '00914', SYSDATE);
```

Notice that this version of the INSERT statement looks significantly shorter than the previous version. The columns STUDENT_ID, CREATED_BY, CREATED_DATE, MODIFIED_BY, and MODIFIED_DATE are not present. However, the trigger provides their values. As a result, there is no need to include them in the INSERT statement, and there is less chance of a transaction error.

You should use BEFORE triggers in the following situations:

▶ When a trigger provides values for derived columns before an INSERT or UPDATE statement is completed. For example, the column FINAL_GRADE in the ENROLLMENT table holds the value of the student's final grade for a specific course. This value is calculated based on the student's performance for the duration of the course.

▶ When a trigger determines whether an INSERT, UPDATE, or DELETE statement should be allowed to complete. For example, when you insert a record into the INSTRUCTOR table, a trigger can verify whether the value provided for the column ZIP is valid, or, in other words, if a record in the ZIPCODE table corresponds to the value of zip that you provided.

AFTER TRIGGERS

Assume that a table called STATISTICS has the following structure:

```
Name                                     Null?    Type
---------------------------------- -------- ----
TABLE_NAME                                        VARCHAR2(30)
TRANSACTION_NAME                                  VARCHAR2(10)
TRANSACTION_USER                                  VARCHAR2(30)
TRANSACTION_DATE                                  DATE
```

This table is used to collect statistical information on different tables of the database. For example, you can record who deleted records from the INSTRUCTOR table and when they were deleted.

Consider the following example of a trigger on the INSTRUCTOR table. This trigger fires after an UPDATE or DELETE statement is issued on the INSTRUCTOR table.

FOR EXAMPLE

```
CREATE OR REPLACE TRIGGER instructor_aud
AFTER UPDATE OR DELETE ON INSTRUCTOR
DECLARE
   v_type VARCHAR2(10);
BEGIN
   IF UPDATING THEN
      v_type := 'UPDATE';

   ELSIF DELETING THEN
      v_type := 'DELETE';
   END IF;

   UPDATE statistics
      SET transaction_user = USER,
          transaction_date = SYSDATE
    WHERE table_name       = 'INSTRUCTOR'
      AND transaction_name = v_type;

   IF SQL%NOTFOUND THEN
      INSERT INTO statistics
      VALUES ('INSTRUCTOR', v_type, USER, SYSDATE);
   END IF;
END;
```

This trigger fires after an UPDATE or DELETE statement on the INSTRUCTOR table. In the body of the trigger are two Boolean functions, UPDATING and DELETING. The function UPDATING evaluates to TRUE if an UPDATE statement is issued on the table, and the function DELETING evaluates to TRUE if a DELETE statement is issued on the table. There is another Boolean function called INSERTING. As you probably can guess, this function evaluates to TRUE when an INSERT statement is issued against the table.

This trigger updates a record or inserts a new record into the STATISTICS table when an UPDATE or DELETE operation is issued against the INSTRUCTOR table. First, the trigger determines the type of the DML statement issued against the INSTRUCTOR table. This determination is made with the help of the UPDATING and DELETING functions.

Next, the trigger tries to update a record in the STATISTICS table where TABLE_NAME is equal to INSTRUCTOR and TRANSACTION_NAME is equal to the current transaction (UPDATE or DELETE). Then the status of the UPDATE statement is checked with the help of the SQL%NOTFOUND constructor. The SQL%NOTFOUND constructor evaluates to TRUE if the UPDATE statement does not update any rows and evaluates to FALSE otherwise. So if SQL%NOTFOUND evaluates to TRUE, a new record is added to the STATISTICS table.

After this trigger is created on the INSTRUCTOR table, any UPDATE or DELETE operation causes modification of old records or creation of new records in the STATISTICS table. Furthermore, you can enhance this trigger by calculating how many rows are updated or deleted from the INSTRUCTOR table.

You should use AFTER triggers in the following situations:

▶ When a trigger should fire after a DML statement is executed

▶ When a trigger performs actions not specified in a BEFORE trigger

AUTONOMOUS TRANSACTION

An autonomous transaction is an independent transaction started by another transaction that is usually called the main transaction. In other words, the autonomous transaction may issue various DML statements and commit or roll them back, without committing or rolling back the DML statements issued by the main transaction.

For example, consider the trigger created earlier that fires after the UPDATE or DELETE statement is issued on the INSTRUCTOR table where you record auditing data. Suppose you want to record auditing data even when the main transaction fails (in this case, the main transaction is the UPDATE or DELETE statement issued on the INSTRUCTOR table). You need to define an autonomous transaction that can be committed independently of the main transaction.

To define an autonomous transaction, you employ the AUTONOMOUS_TRANSACTION pragma. You encountered the EXCEPTION_INIT pragma in Chapter 10, "Exceptions: Advanced Concepts." Recall that a pragma is a special instruction to the PL/SQL compiler that is processed at the time of compilation. The AUTONOMOUS_TRANSACTION pragma appears in the declaration section of a block:

```
DECLARE
    PRAGMA AUTONOMOUS_TRANSACTION;
```

Consider a modified version of INSTRUCTOR_AUD with the autonomous transaction. Changes are shown in bold:

FOR EXAMPLE

```
CREATE OR REPLACE TRIGGER instructor_aud
AFTER UPDATE OR DELETE ON INSTRUCTOR
DECLARE
    v_type VARCHAR2(10);
    PRAGMA AUTONOMOUS_TRANSACTION;
BEGIN
    IF UPDATING THEN
        v_type := 'UPDATE';

    ELSIF DELETING THEN
        v_type := 'DELETE';
    END IF;

    UPDATE statistics
        SET transaction_user = USER,
            transaction_date = SYSDATE
      WHERE table_name       = 'INSTRUCTOR'
        AND transaction_name = v_type;

    IF SQL%NOTFOUND THEN
        INSERT INTO statistics
        VALUES ('INSTRUCTOR', v_type, USER, SYSDATE);
    END IF;

    COMMIT;
END;
```

In this version of the trigger, you add the AUTONOMOUS_TRANSACTION pragma to the declaration portion of the trigger and the COMMIT statement to the executable portion.

Next, consider the UPDATE statement on the INSTRUCTOR table that is rolled back, and the SELECT against the STATISTICS table:

```
UPDATE instructor
    SET phone = '7181234567'
  WHERE instructor_id = 101;
```

1 row updated.

```
ROLLBACK;

SELECT *
  FROM statistics;


TABLE_NAME   TRANSACTIO TRANSACTION_USER TRANSACTI
-----------  ---------- ---------------- ---------
INSTRUCTOR   UPDATE     STUDENT          09-MAR-08
```

Notice that even though you roll the UPDATE statement against the INSTRUCTOR table, the record is inserted in the STATISTICS table due to the autonomous transaction specified in the trigger body.

▼ LAB 13.1 EXERCISES

This section provides exercises and suggested answers, with discussion related to how those answers resulted. The most important thing to realize is whether your answer works. You should figure out the implications of the answers and what the effects are of any different answers you may come up with.

13.1.1 Understand What a Trigger Is

In this exercise, you need to determine the trigger firing event, its type, and so on based on the trigger's CREATE clause.

Consider the following CREATE clause:

```
CREATE TRIGGER student_au
AFTER UPDATE ON STUDENT
FOR EACH ROW
WHEN (NVL(NEW.ZIP, ' ') <> OLD.ZIP)
    Trigger Body...
```

In the WHEN statement of the CREATE clause, the pseudorecord :OLD allows you to access a row currently being processed. It is important to note that neither :NEW nor :OLD is prefixed by a colon (:) when it is used in the condition of the WHEN statement.

You are already familiar with the pseudorecord :NEW. The :OLD pseudorecord allows you to access the current information of the record being updated. In other words, it is information currently present in the STUDENT table for a specified record. The :NEW pseudorecord allows you to access the new information for the current record. In other words, :NEW indicates the updated values. For example, consider the following UPDATE statement:

```
UPDATE student
   SET zip = '01247'
 WHERE zip = '02189';
```

The value 01247 of the ZIP column is a new value, and the trigger references it as :NEW.ZIP. The value 02189 in the ZIP column is the previous value and is referenced as :OLD.ZIP.

DID YOU KNOW?

:OLD is undefined for INSERT statements, and :NEW is undefined for DELETE statements. However, the PL/SQL compiler does not generate syntax errors when :OLD or :NEW is used in triggers where the triggering event is an INSERT or DELETE operation, respectively. In this case, the field values are set to NULL for :OLD and :NEW pseudorecords.

Answer the following questions:

A) Assume that a trigger named STUDENT_AU already exists in the database. If you use the CREATE clause to modify the existing trigger, what error message is generated? Explain your answer.

ANSWER: You see an error message stating that the STUDENT_AU name is already being used by another object. The CREATE clause can create new objects in the database, but it is unable to handle modifications. To modify the existing trigger, you must add the REPLACE statement to the CREATE clause. In this case, the old version of the trigger is dropped without warning, and the new version of the trigger is created.

B) If an update statement is issued on the STUDENT table, how many times does this trigger fire?

ANSWER: The trigger fires as many times as there are rows affected by the triggering event, because the FOR EACH ROW statement is present in the CREATE trigger clause.

When the FOR EACH ROW statement is not present in the CREATE trigger clause, the trigger fires once for the triggering event. In this case, if the following UPDATE statement

```
UPDATE student
   SET zip = '01247'
 WHERE zip = '02189';
```

is issued against the STUDENT table, it updates as many records as there are students with a zip code of 02189.

C) How many times does this trigger fire if an update statement is issued against the STUDENT table but the ZIP column is not changed?

ANSWER: The trigger does not fire, because the condition of the WHEN statement evaluates to FALSE.

The condition

```
(NVL(NEW.ZIP, ' ') <> OLD.ZIP)
```

of the WHEN statement compares the new value of the zip code to the old value of the zip code. If the value of the zip code is not changed, this condition evaluates to FALSE. As a result, this trigger does not fire if an UPDATE statement does not modify the value of the zip code for a specified record.

D) Why do you think an NVL function is present in the WHEN statement of the CREATE clause?

ANSWER: If an UPDATE statement does not modify the column ZIP, the value of the field NEW.ZIP is undefined. In other words, it is NULL. A NULL value of ZIP cannot be compared with a non-NULL value of ZIP. Therefore, the NVL function is present in the WHEN condition.

Because the column ZIP has a NOT NULL constraint defined, there is no need to use the NVL function for the OLD.ZIP field. An UPDATE statement issued against the STUDENT table always has a value of ZIP present in the table.

13.1.2 **Use BEFORE and AFTER Triggers**

In this exercise, you create a trigger on the INSTRUCTOR table that fires before an INSERT statement is issued against the table. The trigger determines the values for the columns CREATED_BY, MODIFIED_BY, CREATED_DATE, and MODIFIED_DATE. In addition, it determines if the value of zip provided by an INSERT statement is valid.

Create the following trigger:

```
-- ch13_1a.sql, version 1.0
CREATE OR REPLACE TRIGGER instructor_bi
BEFORE INSERT ON INSTRUCTOR
FOR EACH ROW
DECLARE
    v_work_zip CHAR(1);
BEGIN
    :NEW.CREATED_BY     := USER;
    :NEW.CREATED_DATE   := SYSDATE;
    :NEW.MODIFIED_BY    := USER;
    :NEW.MODIFIED_DATE  := SYSDATE;

    SELECT 'Y'
      INTO v_work_zip
      FROM zipcode
     WHERE zip = :NEW.ZIP;
EXCEPTION
    WHEN NO_DATA_FOUND THEN
        RAISE_APPLICATION_ERROR (-20001, 'Zip code is not valid!');
END;
```

Answer the following questions:

A) If an INSERT statement issued against the INSTRUCTOR table is missing a value for the column ZIP, does the trigger raise an exception? Explain your answer.

ANSWER: Yes, the trigger raises an exception. When an INSERT statement does not provide a value for the column ZIP, the value of :NEW.ZIP is NULL. This value is used in the WHERE clause of the SELECT INTO statement. As a result, the SELECT INTO statement is unable to return data. Therefore, the trigger raises a NO_DATA_FOUND exception.

B) Modify this trigger so that another error message is displayed when an INSERT statement is missing a value for the column ZIP.

ANSWER: The script should look similar to the following. All changes are shown in bold.

```
-- ch13_1b.sql, version 2.0
CREATE OR REPLACE TRIGGER instructor_bi
BEFORE INSERT ON INSTRUCTOR
FOR EACH ROW
DECLARE
    v_work_zip CHAR(1);
BEGIN
    :NEW.CREATED_BY     := USER;
    :NEW.CREATED_DATE   := SYSDATE;
```

```
:NEW.MODIFIED_BY   := USER;
:NEW.MODIFIED_DATE := SYSDATE;

IF :NEW.ZIP IS NULL THEN
    RAISE_APPLICATION_ERROR (-20002, 'Zip code is missing!');
ELSE
    SELECT 'Y'
      INTO v_work_zip
      FROM zipcode
     WHERE zip = :NEW.ZIP;
END IF;
EXCEPTION
   WHEN NO_DATA_FOUND THEN
       RAISE_APPLICATION_ERROR (-20001, 'Zip code is not valid!');
END;
```

Notice that an IF-ELSE statement is added to the body of the trigger. This IF-ELSE statement evaluates the value of :NEW.ZIP. If the value of :NEW.ZIP is NULL, the IF-ELSE statement evaluates to TRUE, and another error message is displayed, stating that the value of ZIP is missing. If the IF-ELSE statement evaluates to FALSE, control is passed to the ELSE part of the statement, and the SELECT INTO statement is executed.

C) Modify this trigger so that there is no need to supply the value for the instructor's ID at the time of the INSERT statement.

ANSWER: The version of the trigger should look similar to the following. All changes are shown in bold.

```
-- ch13_1c.sql, version 3.0
CREATE OR REPLACE TRIGGER instructor_bi
BEFORE INSERT ON INSTRUCTOR
FOR EACH ROW
DECLARE
   v_work_zip CHAR(1);
BEGIN
   :NEW.CREATED_BY    := USER;
   :NEW.CREATED_DATE  := SYSDATE;
   :NEW.MODIFIED_BY   := USER;
   :NEW.MODIFIED_DATE := SYSDATE;

   SELECT 'Y'
     INTO v_work_zip
     FROM zipcode
    WHERE zip = :NEW.ZIP;

   :NEW.INSTRUCTOR_ID := INSTRUCTOR_ID_SEQ.NEXTVAL;
EXCEPTION
   WHEN NO_DATA_FOUND THEN
       RAISE_APPLICATION_ERROR (-20001, 'Zip code is not valid!');
END;
```

The original version of this trigger does not derive a value for the instructor's ID. Therefore, an INSERT statement issued against the INSTRUCTOR table has to populate the INSTRUCTOR_ID column as well. The new version of the trigger populates the value of the INSTRUCTOR_ID column so that the INSERT statement does not have to do it.

Generally, it is a good idea to populate columns holding IDs in the trigger, because when a user issues an INSERT statement, he or she might not know that an ID must be populated at the time of the insert. Furthermore, a user may not know—more than likely does not know—how to operate sequences to populate the ID.

As mentioned previously, the ability to access a sequence via a PL/SQL expression is a new feature introduced in Oracle 11g. Prior to Oracle 11g, you needed to employ the SELECT INTO statement in the body of the trigger to populate the INSTRUCTOR_ID column.

```
CREATE OR REPLACE TRIGGER instructor_bi
BEFORE INSERT ON INSTRUCTOR
FOR EACH ROW
DECLARE
   v_work_zip      CHAR(1);
   v_instructor_id INSTRUCTOR.INSTRUCTOR_ID%TYPE;
BEGIN
   :NEW.CREATED_BY     := USER;
   :NEW.CREATED_DATE   := SYSDATE;
   :NEW.MODIFIED_BY    := USER;
   :NEW.MODIFIED_DATE  := SYSDATE;

   SELECT 'Y'
     INTO v_work_zip
     FROM zipcode
    WHERE zip = :NEW.ZIP;

   SELECT INSTRUCTOR_ID_SEQ.NEXTVAL
     INTO v_instructor_id
     FROM dual;

   :NEW.INSTRUCTOR_ID := v_instructor_id;
EXCEPTION
   WHEN NO_DATA_FOUND THEN
      RAISE_APPLICATION_ERROR (-20001, 'Zip code is not valid!');
END;
```

LAB 13.2
Types of Triggers

LAB OBJECTIVES

After completing this lab, you will be able to

▶ Use row and statement triggers
▶ Use INSTEAD OF triggers

In the preceding lab you encountered the term row trigger. A row trigger is fired as many times as there are rows affected by the triggering statement. When the statement FOR EACH ROW is present in the CREATE TRIGGER clause, the trigger is a row trigger. Consider the following code:

FOR EXAMPLE

```
CREATE OR REPLACE TRIGGER course_au
AFTER UPDATE ON COURSE
FOR EACH ROW
...
```

In this code fragment, the statement FOR EACH ROW is present in the CREATE TRIGGER clause. Therefore, this trigger is a row trigger. If an UPDATE statement causes 20 records in the COURSE table to be modified, this trigger fires 20 times.

A statement trigger is fired once for the triggering statement. In other words, a statement trigger fires once, regardless of the number of rows affected by the triggering statement. To create a statement trigger, you omit the FOR EACH ROW in the CREATE TRIGGER clause. Consider the following code fragment:

FOR EXAMPLE

```
CREATE OR REPLACE TRIGGER enrollment_ad
AFTER DELETE ON ENROLLMENT
...
```

This trigger fires once after a DELETE statement is issued against the ENROLLMENT table. Whether the DELETE statement removes one row or five rows from the ENROLLMENT table, this trigger fires only once.

Statement triggers should be used when the operations performed by the trigger do not depend on the data in the individual records. For example, if you want to limit access to a table to business hours only, a statement trigger is used. Consider the following example:

FOR EXAMPLE

```
CREATE OR REPLACE TRIGGER instructor_biud
BEFORE INSERT OR UPDATE OR DELETE ON INSTRUCTOR
DECLARE
   v_day VARCHAR2(10);
BEGIN
   v_day := RTRIM(TO_CHAR(SYSDATE, 'DAY'));

   IF v_day LIKE ('S%') THEN
      RAISE_APPLICATION_ERROR
         (-20000, 'A table cannot be modified during off hours');
   END IF;
END;
```

This is a statement trigger on the INSTRUCTOR table, and it fires before an INSERT, UPDATE, or DELETE statement is issued. First, the trigger determines the day of the week. If the day is Saturday or Sunday, an error message is generated. When the following UPDATE statement on the INSTRUCTOR table is issued on Saturday or Sunday:

```
UPDATE instructor
   SET zip = 10025
 WHERE zip = 10015;
```

the trigger generates this error message:

```
update INSTRUCTOR
*
ERROR at line 1:
ORA-20000: A table cannot be modified during off hours
ORA-06512: at "STUDENT.INSTRUCTOR_BIUD", line 6
ORA-04088: error during execution of trigger
           'STUDENT.INSTRUCTOR_BIUD'
```

Notice that this trigger checks for a specific day of the week. However, it does not check the time of day. You can create a more sophisticated trigger that checks what day of the week it is and if the current time is between 9 a.m. and 5 p.m. If the day is during the business week but the time of day is not between 9 a.m. and 5 p.m., the error is generated.

INSTEAD OF TRIGGERS

So far you have seen triggers that are defined on database tables. PL/SQL provides another kind of trigger that is defined on database views. A view is a custom representation of data and can be called a *stored query*. Consider the following example of the view created against the COURSE table:

FOR EXAMPLE

You may find that you do not have privileges to create a view when logged in as STUDENT. If this is so, you need to log in as SYS and grant a CREATE VIEW privilege as follows:

```
GRANT CREATE VIEW TO student;
```

As soon as the privilege has been granted, the view on the COURSE table may be created as follows:

```
CREATE VIEW course_cost AS
    SELECT course_no, description, cost
      FROM course;
```

DID YOU KNOW?

When a view is created, it does not contain or store any data. The data is derived from the SELECT statement associated with the view. Based on the preceding example, the COURSE_COST view contains three columns that are selected from the COURSE table.

Similar to tables, views can be manipulated via INSERT, UPDATE, or DELETE statements, with some restrictions. However, it is important to note that when any of these statements are issued against a view, the corresponding data is modified in the underlying tables. For example, consider an UPDATE statement against the COURSE_COST view:

FOR EXAMPLE

```
UPDATE course_cost
   SET cost = 2000
 WHERE course_no = 450;

COMMIT;
```

After the UPDATE statement is executed, both SELECT statements against the COURSE_COST view and the COURSE table return the same value of the cost for course number 450:

```
SELECT *
  FROM course_cost
 WHERE course_no = 450;


COURSE_NO  DESCRIPTION                       COST
---------- ------------------------- ----------
       450 DB Programming in Java        2000

SELECT course_no, cost
  FROM course
 WHERE course_no = 450;


COURSE_NO       COST
---------- ----------
       450       2000
```

As mentioned earlier, some views are restricted as to whether they can be modified by INSERT, UPDATE, or DELETE statements. Specifically, these restrictions apply to the underlying SELECT statement, which is also called a *view query*. Thus, if a view query performs any of the operations or contains any of the following constructs, a view cannot be modified by an UPDATE, INSERT, or DELETE statement:

- ▶ Set operations such as UNION, UNION ALL, INTERSECT, and MINUS

- ▶ Group functions such as AVG, COUNT, MAX, MIN, and SUM

- ▶ GROUP BY or HAVING clauses

- ▶ CONNECT BY or START WITH clauses

- ▶ The DISTINCT operator

- ▶ The ROWNUM pseudocolumn

Consider the following view created on the INSTRUCTOR and SECTION tables:

FOR EXAMPLE

```
CREATE VIEW instructor_summary_view AS
   SELECT i.instructor_id, COUNT(s.section_id) total_courses
     FROM instructor i
     LEFT OUTER JOIN section s
       ON (i.instructor_id = s.instructor_id)
   GROUP BY i.instructor_id;
```

Note that the SELECT statement is written in the ANSI 1999 SQL standard. It uses the outer join between the INSTRUCTOR and SECTION tables. The LEFT OUTER JOIN indicates that an instructor record in the INSTRUCTOR table that does not have a corresponding record in the SECTION table is included in the result set with TOTAL_COURSES equal to 0.

BY THE WAY

You will find detailed explanations and examples of the statements using the new ANSI 1999 SQL standard in Appendix C, "ANSI SQL Standards," and in the Oracle help. Throughout this book we try to provide examples illustrating both standards; however, our main focus is on PL/SQL features rather than SQL.

In the previous versions of Oracle, this statement would look as follows:

```
SELECT i.instructor_id, COUNT(s.section_id) total_courses
  FROM instructor i, section s
 WHERE i.instructor_id = s.instructor_id (+)
 GROUP BY i.instructor_id;
```

This view is not updatable, because it contains the group function, COUNT(). As a result, the following DELETE statement

```
DELETE FROM instructor_summary_view
  WHERE instructor_id = 109;
```

causes the error shown:

```
DELETE FROM instructor_summary_view
        *
ERROR at line 1:
ORA-01732: data manipulation operation not legal on this view
```

You will recall that PL/SQL provides a special kind of trigger that can be defined on database views. This trigger is called an INSTEAD OF trigger and is created as a row trigger. An INSTEAD OF trigger fires instead of the triggering statement (INSERT, UPDATE, DELETE) that has been issued against a view and directly modifies the underlying tables.

Consider an INSTEAD OF trigger defined on the INSTRUCTOR_SUMMARY_VIEW created earlier. This trigger deletes a record from the INSTRUCTOR table for the corresponding value of the instructor's ID.

FOR EXAMPLE

```
CREATE OR REPLACE TRIGGER instructor_summary_del
INSTEAD OF DELETE ON instructor_summary_view
FOR EACH ROW
BEGIN
   DELETE FROM instructor
    WHERE instructor_id = :OLD.INSTRUCTOR_ID;
END;
```

After the trigger is created, the DELETE statement against the INSTRUCTOR_SUMMARY_VIEW does not generate any errors:

```
DELETE FROM instructor_summary_view
  WHERE instructor_id = 109;
```

   1 row deleted.

When the DELETE statement is issued, the trigger deletes a record from the INSTRUCTOR table corresponding to the specified value of INSTRUCTOR_ID. Consider the same DELETE statement with a different instructor ID:

```
DELETE FROM instructor_summary_view
  WHERE instructor_id = 101;
```

When this DELETE statement is issued, it causes the error shown:

```
DELETE FROM instructor_summary_view
*
ERROR at line 1:
```

```
ORA-02292: integrity constraint (STUDENT.SECT_INST_FK) violated -
           child record found
ORA-06512: at "STUDENT.INSTRUCTOR_SUMMARY_DEL", line 2
ORA-04088: error during execution of trigger -
           'STUDENT.INSTRUCTOR_SUMMARY_DEL'
```

The INSTRUCTOR_SUMMARY_VIEW joins the INSTRUCTOR and SECTION tables based on the INSTRUCTOR_ID column that is present in both tables. The INSTRUCTOR_ID column in the INSTRUCTOR table has a primary key constraint defined on it. The INSTRUCTOR_ID column in the SECTION table has a foreign key constraint that references the INSTRUCTOR_ID column of the INSTRUCTOR table. Thus, the SECTION table is considered a child table of the INSTRUCTOR table.

The original DELETE statement does not cause any errors because no record in the SECTION table corresponds to the instructor ID of 109. In other words, the instructor with the ID of 109 does not teach any courses.

The second DELETE statement causes an error because the INSTEAD OF trigger tries to delete a record from the INSTRUCTOR table, the parent table. However, a corresponding record in the SECTION table, the child table, has the instructor ID of 101. This causes an integrity constraint violation error. It may seem that one more DELETE statement should be added to the INSTEAD OF trigger, as shown here:

FOR EXAMPLE

```
CREATE OR REPLACE TRIGGER instructor_summary_del
INSTEAD OF DELETE ON instructor_summary_view
FOR EACH ROW
BEGIN
   DELETE FROM section
    WHERE instructor_id = :OLD.INSTRUCTOR_ID;
   DELETE FROM instructor
    WHERE instructor_id = :OLD.INSTRUCTOR_ID;
END;
```

Notice that the new DELETE statement removes records from the SECTION table before the INSTRUCTOR table because the SECTION table contains child records of the INSTRUCTOR table. However, the DELETE statement against the INSTRUCTOR_SUMMARY_VIEW causes another error:

```
DELETE FROM instructor_summary_view
 WHERE instructor_id = 101;

DELETE FROM instructor_summary_view
               *
ERROR at line 1:
ORA-02292: integrity constraint (STUDENT.GRTW_SECT_FK) violated -
           child record found
```

```
ORA-06512: at "STUDENT.INSTRUCTOR_SUMMARY_DEL", line 2
ORA-04088: error during execution of trigger -
          'STUDENT.INSTRUCTOR_SUMMARY_DEL'
```

This time, the error refers to a different foreign key constraint that specifies the relationship between the SECTION and the GRADE_TYPE_WEIGHT tables. In this case, the child records are found in the GRADE_TYPE_WEIGHT table. This means that before deleting records from the SECTION table, the trigger must delete all corresponding records from the GRADE_TYPE_WEIGHT table. However, the GRADE_TYPE_WEIGHT table has child records in the GRADE table, so the trigger must delete records from the GRADE table first.

This example illustrates the complexity of designing an INSTEAD OF trigger. To design such a trigger, you must be aware of two important factors: the relationship among tables in the database, and the ripple effect that a particular design may introduce. This example suggests deleting records from four underlying tables. However, it is important to realize that those tables contain information that relates not only to the instructors and the sections they teach, but also to the students and the sections they are enrolled in.

▼ LAB 13.2 EXERCISES

This section provides exercises and suggested answers, with discussion related to how those answers resulted. The most important thing to realize is whether your answer works. You should figure out the implications of the answers and what the effects are of any different answers you may come up with.

13.2.1 Use Row and Statement Triggers

In this exercise, you create a trigger that fires before an INSERT statement is issued against the COURSE table.

Create the following trigger:

```
-- ch13_2a.sql, version 1.0
CREATE OR REPLACE TRIGGER course_bi
BEFORE INSERT ON COURSE
FOR EACH ROW
BEGIN
    :NEW.COURSE_NO      := COURSE_NO_SEQ.NEXTVAL;
    :NEW.CREATED_BY     := USER;
    :NEW.CREATED_DATE   := SYSDATE;
    :NEW.MODIFIED_BY    := USER;
    :NEW.MODIFIED_DATE  := SYSDATE;
END;
```

As mentioned, the ability to access sequence via a PL/SQL expression is a new feature introduced in Oracle 11g. Prior to Oracle 11g, you would have needed to employ the SELECT INTO statement in the body of the trigger to populate the COURSE_NO column.

```
CREATE OR REPLACE TRIGGER course_bi
BEFORE INSERT ON COURSE
FOR EACH ROW
DECLARE
    v_course_no COURSE.COURSE_NO%TYPE;
```

```
BEGIN
    SELECT COURSE_NO_SEQ.NEXTVAL
      INTO v_course_no
      FROM DUAL;

    :NEW.COURSE_NO       := v_course_no;
    :NEW.CREATED_BY      := USER;
    :NEW.CREATED_DATE    := SYSDATE;
    :NEW.MODIFIED_BY     := USER;
    :NEW.MODIFIED_DATE   := SYSDATE;
END;
```

Answer the following questions:

A) What type of trigger is created on the COURSE table—row or statement? Explain your answer.

ANSWER: The trigger created on the COURSE table is a row trigger because the CREATE TRIGGER clause contains the statement FOR EACH ROW. This means that this trigger fires every time a record is added to the COURSE table.

B) Based on the answer you just provided, explain why this particular type is chosen for the trigger.

ANSWER: This trigger is a row trigger because its operations depend on the data in the individual records. For example, for every record inserted into the COURSE table, the trigger calculates the value for the column COURSE_NO. All values in this column must be unique, because it is defined as a primary key. A row trigger guarantees that every record added to the COURSE table has a unique number assigned to the COURSE_NO column.

C) When an INSERT statement is issued against the COURSE table, which actions does the trigger perform?

ANSWER: First, the trigger assigns a unique number derived from the sequence COURSE_NO_SEQ to the filed COURSE_NO_SEQ to the filed COURSE_NO OF THE :NEW PSEUDORECORD. Then, the values containing the current user's name and date are assigned to the fields CREATED_BY, MODIFIED_BY, CREATED_DATE, and MODIFIED_DATE of the :NEW pseudorecord.

D) Modify this trigger so that if a prerequisite course is supplied at the time of the insert, its value is checked against the existing courses in the COURSE table.

ANSWER: The trigger you created should look similar to the following. All changes are shown in bold.

```
-- ch13_2b.sql, version 2.0
CREATE OR REPLACE TRIGGER course_bi
BEFORE INSERT ON COURSE
FOR EACH ROW
DECLARE
    v_prerequisite COURSE.COURSE_NO%TYPE;
BEGIN
    IF :NEW.PREREQUISITE IS NOT NULL THEN
       SELECT course_no
         INTO v_prerequisite
         FROM course
        WHERE course_no = :NEW.PREREQUISITE;
    END IF;
```

```
:NEW.COURSE_NO      := COURSE_NO_SEQ.NEXTVAL;
:NEW.CREATED_BY     := USER;
:NEW.CREATED_DATE   := SYSDATE;
:NEW.MODIFIED_BY    := USER;
:NEW.MODIFIED_DATE  := SYSDATE;
EXCEPTION
   WHEN NO_DATA_FOUND THEN
       RAISE_APPLICATION_ERROR (-20002, 'Prerequisite is not
                                valid!');
END;
```

Notice that because PREREQUISITE is not a required column (in other words, no NOT NULL constraint is defined against it), the IF statement validates the existence of the incoming value. Next, the SELECT INTO statement validates that the prerequisite already exists in the COURSE table. If no record corresponds to the prerequisite course, the NO_DATA_FOUND exception is raised, and the error message `Prerequisite is not valid!` is displayed on the screen.

After this version of the trigger is created, the INSERT statement

```
INSERT INTO COURSE (description, cost, prerequisite)
VALUES ('Test Course', 0, 999);
```

causes the following error:

```
INSERT INTO COURSE (description, cost, prerequisite)
*
ERROR at line 1:
ORA-20002: Prerequisite is not valid!
ORA-06512: at "STUDENT.COURSE_BI", line 21
ORA-04088: error during execution of trigger 'STUDENT.COURSE_BI'
```

13.2.2 **Use INSTEAD OF Triggers**

In this exercise, you create a view STUDENT_ADDRESS and an INSTEAD OF trigger that fires instead of an INSERT statement issued against the view.

Create the following view:

```
CREATE VIEW student_address AS
   SELECT s.student_id, s.first_name, s.last_name,
          s.street_address, z.city, z.state, z.zip
     FROM student s
     JOIN zipcode z
       ON (s.zip = z.zip);
```

Note that the SELECT statement is written in the ANSI 1999 SQL standard.

BY THE WAY

You will find detailed explanations and examples of the statements using the new ANSI 1999 SQL standard in Appendix C and in the Oracle help. Throughout this book we try to provide examples illustrating both standards; however, our main focus is on PL/SQL features rather than SQL.

Create the following INSTEAD OF trigger:

```
-- ch13_3a.sql, version 1.0
CREATE OR REPLACE TRIGGER student_address_ins
INSTEAD OF INSERT ON student_address
FOR EACH ROW
BEGIN
   INSERT INTO STUDENT
      (student_id, first_name, last_name, street_address, zip,
       registration_date, created_by, created_date, modified_by,
       modified_date)
   VALUES
      (:NEW.student_id, :NEW.first_name, :NEW.last_name,
       :NEW.street_address, :NEW.zip, SYSDATE, USER, SYSDATE, USER,

       SYSDATE);
END;
```

Issue the following INSERT statements:

```
INSERT INTO student_address
VALUES (STUDENT_ID_SEQ.NEXTVAL, 'John', 'Smith', '123 Main Street',
        'New York', 'NY', '10019');


INSERT INTO student_address
VALUES (STUDENT_ID_SEQ.NEXTVAL, 'John', 'Smith', '123 Main Street',
        'New York', 'NY', '12345');
```

Answer the following questions:

A) What output is produced after each INSERT statement is issued?

ANSWER: The output should look similar to the following:

```
INSERT INTO student_address
VALUES (STUDENT_ID_SEQ.NEXTVAL, 'John', 'Smith', '123 Main Street',
        'New York', 'NY', '10019');
```

1 row created.

```
INSERT INTO student_address
VALUES (STUDENT_ID_SEQ.NEXTVAL, 'John', 'Smith', '123 Main Street',
   'New York', 'NY', '12345');
```

**VALUES (STUDENT_ID_SEQ.NEXTVAL, 'John', 'Smith', '123 Main Street',
   'New York',**
          *****
ERROR at line 2:
ORA-02291: integrity constraint (STUDENT.STU_ZIP_FK) violated -
**   parent key not found**
ORA-06512: at "STUDENT.STUDENT_ADDRESS_INS", line 2
ORA-04088: error during execution of trigger
**   'STUDENT.STUDENT_ADDRESS_INS'**

B) Explain why the second INSERT statement causes an error.

ANSWER: The second INSERT statement causes an error because it violates the foreign key constraint on the STUDENT table. The value of the zip code provided at the time of an insert does not have a corresponding record in the ZIPCODE table.

The ZIP column of the STUDENT table has a foreign key constraint STU_ZIP_FK defined on it. This means that each time a record is inserted into the STUDENT table, the system checks the incoming value of the zip code in the ZIPCODE table. If there is a corresponding record, the INSERT statement against the STUDENT table does not cause errors. For example, the first INSERT statement is successful because the ZIPCODE table contains a record corresponding to the value of zip code 10019. The second insert statement causes an error because no record in the ZIPCODE table corresponds to the value of zip code 12345.

C) Modify the trigger so that it checks the value of the zip code provided by the INSERT statement against the ZIPCODE table and raises an error if there is no such value.

ANSWER: The trigger should look similar to the following. All changes are shown in bold.

```
-- ch13_3b.sql, version 2.0
CREATE OR REPLACE TRIGGER student_address_ins
INSTEAD OF INSERT ON student_address
FOR EACH ROW
DECLARE
    v_zip VARCHAR2(5);
BEGIN
    SELECT zip
      INTO v_zip
      FROM zipcode
     WHERE zip = :NEW.ZIP;

    INSERT INTO STUDENT
        (student_id, first_name, last_name, street_address, zip,
         registration_date, created_by, created_date, modified_by,
         modified_date)
    VALUES
        (:NEW.student_id, :NEW.first_name, :NEW.last_name,
         :NEW.street_address, :NEW.zip, SYSDATE, USER, SYSDATE, USER,
SYSDATE);

EXCEPTION
    WHEN NO_DATA_FOUND THEN
        RAISE_APPLICATION_ERROR (-20002, 'Zip code is not valid!');
END;
```

In this version of the trigger, the incoming value of zip code is checked against the ZIPCODE table via the SELECT INTO statement. If the SELECT INTO statement does not return any rows, the NO_DATA_FOUND exception is raised, and the error message stating Zip code is not valid! is displayed on the screen.

After this trigger is created, the second INSERT statement produces the following output:
```
INSERT INTO student_address
VALUES (STUDENT_ID_SEQ.NEXTVAL, 'John', 'Smith', '123 Main Street',
   'New York', 'NY', '12345');


VALUES (STUDENT_ID_SEQ.NEXTVAL, 'John', 'Smith', '123 Main Street',
   'New York',
          *
ERROR at line 2:
ORA-20002: Zip code is not valid!
ORA-06512: at "STUDENT.STUDENT_ADDRESS_INS", line 18
ORA-04088: error during execution of trigger
'STUDENT.STUDENT_ADDRESS_INS'
```

D) Modify the trigger so that it checks the value of the zip code provided by the INSERT statement against the ZIPCODE table. If the ZIPCODE table has no corresponding record, the trigger should create a new record for the given value of zip before adding a new record to the STUDENT table.

ANSWER: The trigger should look similar to the following. All changes are shown in bold.
```
-- ch13_3c.sql, version 3.0
CREATE OR REPLACE TRIGGER student_address_ins
INSTEAD OF INSERT ON student_address
FOR EACH ROW
DECLARE
   v_zip VARCHAR2(5);
BEGIN
   BEGIN
      SELECT zip
        INTO v_zip
        FROM zipcode
       WHERE zip = :NEW.zip;
   EXCEPTION
      WHEN NO_DATA_FOUND THEN
         INSERT INTO ZIPCODE
            (zip, city, state, created_by, created_date,
             modified_by, modified_date)
         VALUES
            (:NEW.zip, :NEW.city, :NEW.state, USER, SYSDATE, USER,
             SYSDATE);
   END;
   INSERT INTO STUDENT
      (student_id, first_name, last_name, street_address, zip,
       registration_date, created_by, created_date, modified_by,
       modified_date)
   VALUES
      (:NEW.student_id, :NEW.first_name, :NEW.last_name,
       :NEW.street_address, :NEW.zip, SYSDATE, USER, SYSDATE, USER,
       SYSDATE);
END;
```

As in the previous version, the existence of the incoming value of the zip code is checked against the ZIPCODE table via the SELECT INTO statement. When a new value of zip code is provided by the INSERT statement, the SELECT INTO statement does not return any rows. As a result, the NO_DATA_FOUND exception is raised, and the INSERT statement against the ZIPCODE table is executed. Next, control is passed to the INSERT statement against the STUDENT table.

It is important to realize that the SELECT INTO statement and the exception-handling section have been placed in the inner block. This placement ensures that after the exception NO_DATA_FOUND is raised, the trigger does not terminate but proceeds with its normal execution.

After this trigger is created, the second INSERT statement completes successfully:

```
INSERT INTO student_address
VALUES (STUDENT_ID_SEQ.NEXTVAL, 'John', 'Smith', '123 Main Street',
    'New York', 'NY', '12345');
```

1 row created.

▼ TRY IT YOURSELF

In this chapter you've learned about triggers. Here are some projects that will help you test the depth of your understanding:

1) Create or modify a trigger on the ENROLLMENT table that fires before an INSERT statement. Make sure that all columns that have NOT NULL and foreign key constraints defined on them are populated with their proper values.

2) Create or modify a trigger on the SECTION table that fires before an UPDATE statement. Make sure that the trigger validates incoming values so that there are no constraint violation errors.

The projects in this section are meant to have you use all the skills you have acquired throughout this chapter. The answers to these projects can be found in Appendix D and on this book's companion Web site. Visit the Web site periodically to share and discuss your answers.

CHAPTER 14

Compound Triggers

CHAPTER OBJECTIVES

In this chapter, you will learn about

- ▶ Mutating table issues
- ▶ Compound triggers

In the preceding chapter, you explored the concept of triggers. You learned about using triggers in the database, events that cause triggers to fire, and different types of triggers. In this chapter, you will continue exploring triggers. You will learn about mutating table issues and how triggers can be used to resolve these issues.

In Lab 14.1 you will see how to resolve mutating table issues in the Oracle database prior to version 11g. In Lab 14.2 you will learn about compound triggers, which were introduced in Oracle 11g, and how they can be used to resolve mutating table issues.

LAB 14.1
Mutating Table Issues

LAB OBJECTIVE

After completing this lab, you will be able to

▶ Understand mutating tables

A table that has a DML statement issued against it is called a mutating table. For a trigger, it is the table on which this trigger is defined. If a trigger tries to read or modify such a table, it causes a mutating table error. As a result, a SQL statement issued in the body of the trigger may not read or modify a mutating table. Note that this restriction applies to row-level triggers.

Note that prior to Oracle 8i, another restriction on the SQL statement issued in the body of a trigger caused a different type of error called a constraining table error. A table read from for a referential integrity constraint is called a constraining table. So a SQL statement issued in the body of a trigger could not modify the columns of a constraining table having primary, foreign, or unique constraints defined on them. However, staring with Oracle 8i, there is no such restriction.

Consider the following example of a trigger causing a mutating table error.

WATCH OUT!

A mutating table error is a runtime error. In other words, this error occurs not at the time of trigger creation (compilation), but when the trigger fires.

FOR EXAMPLE

```
CREATE OR REPLACE TRIGGER section_biu
BEFORE INSERT OR UPDATE ON section
FOR EACH ROW
DECLARE
   v_total NUMBER;
   v_name  VARCHAR2(30);
BEGIN
   SELECT COUNT(*)
     INTO v_total
     FROM section  -- SECTION is MUTATING
    WHERE instructor_id = :NEW. instructor_id;
```

```
   -- check if the current instructor is overbooked
   IF v_total >= 10 THEN
      SELECT first_name||' '||last_name
        INTO v_name
        FROM instructor
       WHERE instructor_id = :NEW.instructor_id;

      RAISE_APPLICATION_ERROR
         (-20000, 'Instructor, '||v_name||', is overbooked');
   END IF;
EXCEPTION
   WHEN NO_DATA_FOUND THEN
      RAISE_APPLICATION_ERROR
         (-20001, 'This is not a valid instructor');
END;
```

This trigger fires before an INSERT or UPDATE statement is issued on the SECTION table. The trigger checks whether the specified instructor is teaching too many sections. If the number of sections taught by an instructor is equal to or greater than 10, the trigger issues an error message stating that this instructor teaches too much.

Now, consider the following UPDATE statement issued against the SECTION table:

```
UPDATE section
   SET instructor_id = 101
 WHERE section_id = 80;
```

When this UPDATE statement is issued against the SECTION table, the following error message is displayed:

```
UPDATE section
*
ERROR at line 1:
ORA-04091: table STUDENT.SECTION is mutating, trigger/function
           may not see it
ORA-06512: at "STUDENT.SECTION_BIU", line 5
ORA-04088: error during execution of trigger 'STUDENT.SECTION_BIU'
```

Notice that the error message states that the SECTION table is mutating and that the trigger may not see it. This error message is generated because a SELECT INTO statement

```
SELECT COUNT(*)
   INTO v_total
   FROM section
   WHERE instructor_id = :NEW.INSTRUCTOR_ID;
```

issued against the SECTION table that is being modified and therefore is mutating.

To correct this problem, you must follow these steps when using a version of Oracle prior to 11g:

1. To record the instructor's ID and name as described in the preceding example, you must declare two global variables with the help of a PL/SQL package. You will learn about global variables and packages in Chapter 21, "Packages."

2. You must modify an existing trigger so that it records the instructor's ID, queries the INSTRUCTOR table, and records the instructor's name.

3. You must create a new trigger on the SECTION table. This trigger should be a statement-level trigger that fires after the INSERT or UPDATE statement has been issued. It checks the number of courses that are taught by a particular instructor and raises an error if the number is equal to or greater than 10.

BY THE WAY

As stated, these steps are used to resolve mutating table errors in versions of Oracle prior to 11g. Starting with Oracle 11g, compound triggers are used to resolve this error. Compound triggers are covered in the next lab.

Consider the following package:

```
CREATE OR REPLACE PACKAGE instructor_adm AS
    v_instructor_id   instructor.instructor_id%TYPE;
    v_instructor_name varchar2(50);
END;
```

This package declares two global variables, `v_instructor_id` and `v_instructor_name`. Note that the CREATE OR REPLACE clause is similar to that of a trigger.

Next, the existing trigger SECTION_BIU is modified as follows:

```
CREATE OR REPLACE TRIGGER section_biu
BEFORE INSERT OR UPDATE ON section
FOR EACH ROW
BEGIN
    IF :NEW. instructor_id IS NOT NULL THEN
       BEGIN
          instructor_adm.v_instructor_id := :NEW.INSTRUCTOR_ID;

          SELECT first_name||' '||last_name
            INTO instructor_adm.v_instructor_name
            FROM instructor
           WHERE instructor_id = instructor_adm.v_instructor_id;

       EXCEPTION
          WHEN NO_DATA_FOUND THEN
             RAISE_APPLICATION_ERROR
                (-20001, 'This is not a valid instructor');
       END;
    END IF;
END;
```

In this version of the trigger, the global variables v_instructor_id and v_instructor_name are initialized if the incoming value of the instructor's ID is not null. Notice that the variable names are prefixed by the package name. This type of notation is called dot notation.

Finally, a new trigger is created on the SECTION table:

```
CREATE OR REPLACE TRIGGER section_aiu
AFTER INSERT OR UPDATE ON section
DECLARE
   v_total INTEGER;
BEGIN
   SELECT COUNT(*)
     INTO v_total
     FROM section
    WHERE instructor_id = instructor_adm.v_instructor_id;

   -- check if the current instructor is overbooked
   IF v_total >= 10 THEN
      RAISE_APPLICATION_ERROR
         (-20000, 'Instructor, '||instructor_adm.v_instructor_name||
          ', is overbooked');
   END IF;
END;
```

This trigger checks the number of courses that are taught by a particular instructor and raises an error if the number is equal to or greater than 10. This is accomplished with the help of the global variables v_instructor_id and v_instructor_name. As mentioned, these variables are populated by the SECTION_BIU trigger that fires before the UPDATE statement is issued against the SECTION table.

As a result, the UPDATE statement used earlier

```
UPDATE section
   SET instructor_id = 101
 WHERE section_id = 80;
```

causes a different error:

```
UPDATE section
*
ERROR at line 1:
ORA-20000: Instructor, Fernand Hanks, is overbooked
ORA-06512: at "STUDENT.SECTION_AIU", line 11
ORA-04088: error during execution of trigger 'STUDENT.SECTION_AIU'
```

Notice that this error was generated by the trigger SECTION_AIU and does not contain any message about a mutating table. Next, consider a similar UPDATE statement for a different instructor ID that does not cause any errors:

```
UPDATE section
   SET instructor_id = 110
 WHERE section_id = 80;
```

1 row updated.

▼ LAB 14.1 EXERCISES

This section provides exercises and suggested answers, with discussion related to how those answers resulted. The most important thing to realize is whether your answer works. You should figure out the implications of the answers and what the effects are of any different answers you may come up with.

14.1.1 Understand Mutating Tables

In this exercise, you modify a trigger that causes a mutating table error when an INSERT statement is issued against the ENROLLMENT table.

Create the following trigger:

```
-- ch14_1a.sql, version 1.0
CREATE OR REPLACE TRIGGER enrollment_biu
BEFORE INSERT OR UPDATE ON enrollment
FOR EACH ROW
DECLARE
   v_total NUMBER;
   v_name  VARCHAR2(30);
BEGIN
   SELECT COUNT(*)
     INTO v_total
     FROM enrollment
    WHERE student_id = :NEW. student_id;

   -- check if the current student is enrolled in too
   -- many courses
   IF v_total >= 3 THEN
      SELECT first_name||' '||last_name
        INTO v_name
        FROM student
       WHERE student_id = :NEW.STUDENT_ID;

      RAISE_APPLICATION_ERROR (-20000, 'Student, '||v_name||
         ', is registered for 3 courses already');
   END IF;
EXCEPTION
   WHEN NO_DATA_FOUND THEN
       RAISE_APPLICATION_ERROR
          (-20001, 'This is not a valid student');
END;
```

Issue the following INSERT and UPDATE statements:

```
INSERT INTO ENROLLMENT
   (student_id, section_id, enroll_date, created_by, created_date,
    modified_by, modified_date)
VALUES (184, 98, SYSDATE, USER, SYSDATE, USER, SYSDATE);

INSERT INTO ENROLLMENT
   (student_id, section_id, enroll_date, created_by, created_date,
    modified_by, modified_date)
VALUES (399, 98, SYSDATE, USER, SYSDATE, USER, SYSDATE);
```

```
UPDATE ENROLLMENT
    SET student_id = 399
 WHERE student_id = 283;
```

Answer the following questions:

A) What output is produced after the INSERT and UPDATE statements are issued?

ANSWER: The output should look like this:

```
INSERT INTO ENROLLMENT
    (student_id, section_id, enroll_date, created_by, created_date,
     modified_by, modified_date)
VALUES (184, 98, SYSDATE, USER, SYSDATE, USER, SYSDATE);
```

```
INSERT INTO ENROLLMENT
            *
ERROR at line 1:
ORA-20000: Student, Salewa Zuckerberg, is registered for 3 courses
already
ORA-06512: at "STUDENT.ENROLLMENT_BIU", line 17
ORA-04088: error during execution of trigger
           'STUDENT.ENROLLMENT_BIU'
```

```
INSERT INTO ENROLLMENT
    (student_id, section_id, enroll_date, created_by, created_date,
     modified_by, modified_date)
VALUES (399, 98, SYSDATE, USER, SYSDATE, USER, SYSDATE);
```

```
1 row created.
```

```
UPDATE enrollment
    SET student_id = 399
WHERE student_id = 283;
```

```
UPDATE enrollment
*
ERROR at line 1:
ORA-04091: table STUDENT.ENROLLMENT is mutating, trigger/function
           may not see it
ORA-06512: at "STUDENT.ENROLLMENT_BIU", line 5
ORA-04088: error during execution of trigger
           'STUDENT.ENROLLMENT_BIU'
```

B) Explain why two of the statements did not succeed.

ANSWER: The INSERT statement does not succeed because it tries to create a record in the ENROLLMENT table for a student who is already registered for three courses.

The IF statement

```
IF v_total >= 3 THEN
    SELECT first_name||' '||last_name
        INTO v_name
        FROM student
        WHERE student_id = :NEW.STUDENT_ID;
```

```
RAISE_APPLICATION_ERROR (-20000, 'Student, '||v_name||
   ', is registered for 3 courses already');
END IF;
```

in the body of the trigger evaluates to TRUE. As a result, the RAISE_APPLICATION_ERROR statement raises a user-defined exception.

The UPDATE statement does not succeed because a trigger tries to read data from the mutating table.

The SELECT INTO statement

```
SELECT COUNT(*)
  INTO v_total
  FROM enrollment
 WHERE student_id = :NEW.STUDENT_ID;
```

is issued against the ENROLLMENT table that is being modified and therefore is mutating.

C) Modify the trigger so that it does not cause a mutating table error when an UPDATE statement is issued against the ENROLLMENT table.

ANSWER: First, create a package to hold the student's ID and name:

```
CREATE OR REPLACE PACKAGE student_adm AS
   v_student_id   student.student_id%TYPE;
   v_student_name varchar2(50);
END;
```

Next, modify the existing trigger, ENROLLMENT:

```
CREATE OR REPLACE TRIGGER enrollment_biu
BEFORE INSERT OR UPDATE ON enrollment
FOR EACH ROW
BEGIN
   IF :NEW.STUDENT_ID IS NOT NULL THEN
      BEGIN
         student_adm.v_student_id := :NEW. student_id;

         SELECT first_name||' '||last_name
            INTO student_adm.v_student_name
            FROM student
            WHERE student_id = student_adm.v_student_id;
      EXCEPTION
         WHEN NO_DATA_FOUND THEN
            RAISE_APPLICATION_ERROR
               (-20001, 'This is not a valid student');
      END;
   END IF;
END;
```

Finally, create a new statement-level trigger on the ENROLLMENT table:

```
CREATE OR REPLACE TRIGGER enrollment_aiu
AFTER INSERT OR UPDATE ON enrollment
DECLARE
   v_total INTEGER;
```

```
BEGIN
   SELECT COUNT(*)
     INTO v_total
     FROM enrollment
    WHERE student_id = student_adm.v_student_id;

   -- check if the current student is enrolled in too
   -- many courses
   IF v_total >= 3 THEN
      RAISE_APPLICATION_ERROR (-20000, 'Student, '||
         student_adm.v_student_name||
         ', is registered for 3 courses already ');
   END IF;
END;
```

After the package and two triggers have been created, the UPDATE statement does not cause a mutating table error. However, the UPDATE statement

```
UPDATE enrollment
   SET student_id = 399
WHERE student_id = 283;
```

causes a different kind of error. Why do you think this error occurs, and how would you go about fixing it?

LAB 14.2
Compound Triggers

LAB OBJECTIVE

After completing this lab, you will be able to

▶ Understand compound triggers

In the preceding lab you learned about mutating table issues and how they can be resolved in Oracle versions prior to 11g. In this lab, you learn how to resolve mutating table issues using compound triggers, which were introduced in Oracle 11g.

A compound trigger allows you to combine different types of triggers into one. Specifically, you can combine

▶ A statement trigger that fires before the firing statement

▶ A statement trigger that fires after the firing statement

▶ A row trigger that fires before each row that the firing statement affects

▶ A row trigger that fires after each row that the firing statement affects

For example, you can create a compound trigger on the STUDENT table with portions of code that will fire once before the insert, before the insert for each affected row, after the insert for each affected row, and after the insert.

The structure of the compound trigger is as follows:

```
CREATE [OR REPLACE] TRIGGER trigger_name
triggering_event ON table_name
COMPOUND TRIGGER

declaration statements

BEFORE STATEMENT IS
BEGIN
    executable statements
END BEFORE STATEMENT;

BEFORE EACH ROW IS
BEGIN
    executable statements
END BEFORE EACH ROW;
```

```
AFTER EACH ROW IS
BEGIN
    executable statements
END AFTER EACH ROW;

AFTER STATEMENT IS
BEGIN
    executable statements
END AFTER STATEMENT;

END trigger_name;
```

First, you specify the trigger header that includes the CREATE OR REPLACE clause, the triggering event, the table name for which the trigger is defined, and the COMPOUND TRIGGER clause, which specifies that this is a compound trigger. Note the absence of the BEFORE or AFTER clause in the header of the compound trigger.

Next, you specify the declaration section, which is common to all executable sections. In other words, any variable declared in this section can be referenced in any of the executable sections.

Finally, you specify the executable sections that fire at different timing points. Note that each of these sections is optional. For example, if no action takes place after the firing statement, no AFTER STATEMENT section is needed.

WATCH OUT!

Compound triggers have several restrictions:

▶ A compound trigger may be defined on a table or view only.

▶ A triggering event of a compound trigger is limited to the DML statements.

▶ A compound trigger may not contain an autonomous transaction. In other words, its declaration portion cannot include PRAGMA AUTONOMOUS_TRANSACTION.

▶ An exception that occurs in one executable section must be handled within that section. For example, if an exception occurs in the AFTER EACH ROW section, it cannot propagate to the AFTER STATEMENT section. It must be handled in the AFTER EACH ROW section.

▶ References to :OLD and :NEW pseudocolumns cannot appear in the declaration, BEFORE STATEMENT, and AFTER STATEMENT sections.

▶ The value :NEW pseudocolumn can be changed in the BEFORE EACH ROW section only.

▶ The firing order of the compound and simple triggers is not guaranteed. In other words, the firing of the compound trigger may interleave with the firing of the simple triggers.

▶ If a DML statement issued on a table that has a compound trigger defined on it fails (rolls back) due to an exception:

Variables declared in the compound trigger sections are reinitialized. In other words, any values assigned to those variable are lost.

DML statements issued by the compound trigger are not rolled back.

Consider the following example of the compound trigger on the STUDENT table that has BEFORE STATEMENT and BEFORE EACH ROW sections only:

FOR EXAMPLE

```
CREATE OR REPLACE TRIGGER student_compound
FOR INSERT ON STUDENT
COMPOUND TRIGGER

   -- Declaration section
   v_day  VARCHAR2(10);
   v_date DATE;
   v_user VARCHAR2(30);

BEFORE STATEMENT IS
BEGIN
   v_day := RTRIM(TO_CHAR(SYSDATE, 'DAY'));

   IF v_day LIKE ('S%') THEN
      RAISE_APPLICATION_ERROR
         (-20000, 'A table cannot be modified during off hours');
   END IF;

   v_date := SYSDATE;
   v_user := USER;
END BEFORE STATEMENT;

BEFORE EACH ROW IS
BEGIN
   :NEW.student_id    := STUDENT_ID_SEQ.NEXTVAL;
   :NEW.created_by    := v_user;
   :NEW.created_date  := v_date;
   :NEW.modified_by   := v_user;
   :NEW.modified_date := v_date;
END BEFORE EACH ROW;

END student_compound;
```

This trigger has a declaration section and two executable sections only. As mentioned earlier, each of the executable sections is optional and is specified only when an action is associated with it.

First, the declaration section declares four variables used in the BEFORE STATEMENT and BEFORE EACH ROW sections. Second, the BEFORE STATEMENT section initializes the variables and contains an IF statement that prevents modification of the STUDENT table during off hours. This section fires once before the INSERT statement. Next, the BEFORE EACH ROW section initializes some of the columns of the STUDENT table to their default values.

Note that all references to the :NEW pseudocolumns are placed in the BEFORE EACH ROW section of the trigger. However, the values for the majority of those columns are calculated in the BEFORE STATEMENT section.

As mentioned, one of the reasons to use compound triggers is to avoid mutating table errors. Recall from Lab 14.1 the example of the trigger on the SECTION table that causes a mutating table error:

FOR EXAMPLE

```
CREATE OR REPLACE TRIGGER section_biu
BEFORE INSERT OR UPDATE ON section
FOR EACH ROW
DECLARE
   v_total NUMBER;
   v_name  VARCHAR2(30);
BEGIN
   SELECT COUNT(*)
     INTO v_total
     FROM section  -- SECTION is MUTATING
    WHERE instructor_id = :NEW.instructor_id;

   -- check if the current instructor is overbooked
   IF v_total >= 10 THEN
      SELECT first_name||' '||last_name
        INTO v_name
        FROM instructor
       WHERE instructor_id = :NEW.instructor_id;

      RAISE_APPLICATION_ERROR
          (-20000, 'Instructor, '||v_name||', is overbooked');
   END IF;
EXCEPTION
   WHEN NO_DATA_FOUND THEN
      RAISE_APPLICATION_ERROR
          (-20001, 'This is not a valid instructor');
END;
```

To correct this problem, you followed these steps:

1. You created a package in which you declared two global variables:

```
CREATE OR REPLACE PACKAGE instructor_adm AS
    v_instructor_id   instructor.instructor_id%TYPE;
    v_instructor_name varchar2(50);
END;
```

2. You modified the existing trigger to record the instructor's ID and name:

```
CREATE OR REPLACE TRIGGER section_biu
BEFORE INSERT OR UPDATE ON section
FOR EACH ROW
BEGIN
    IF :NEW. instructor_id IS NOT NULL THEN
        BEGIN
            instructor_adm.v_instructor_id := :NEW.INSTRUCTOR_ID;

            SELECT first_name||' '||last_name
              INTO instructor_adm.v_instructor_name
              FROM instructor
             WHERE instructor_id = instructor_adm.v_instructor_id;

        EXCEPTION
           WHEN NO_DATA_FOUND THEN
              RAISE_APPLICATION_ERROR
                 (-20001, 'This is not a valid instructor');
        END;
    END IF;
END;
```

3. You created a new statement trigger that fires after the INSERT or UPDATE statement has been issued:

```
CREATE OR REPLACE TRIGGER section_aiu
AFTER INSERT OR UPDATE ON section
DECLARE
    v_total INTEGER;
BEGIN
    SELECT COUNT(*)
      INTO v_total
      FROM section
     WHERE instructor_id = instructor_adm.v_instructor_id;

    -- check if the current instructor is overbooked
    IF v_total >= 10 THEN
       RAISE_APPLICATION_ERROR
           (-20000, 'Instructor, '||instructor_adm.v_instructor_name||
            ', is overbooked');
    END IF;
END;
```

Now consider a compound trigger on the SECTION table that fires on INSERT or UPDATE:

FOR EXAMPLE

```
CREATE OR REPLACE TRIGGER section_compound
FOR INSERT OR UPDATE ON SECTION
COMPOUND TRIGGER
```

```
    -- Declaration Section
    v_instructor_id    INSTRUCTOR.INSTRUCTOR_ID%TYPE;
    v_instructor_name VARCHAR2(50);
    v_total            INTEGER;

BEFORE EACH ROW IS
BEGIN
    IF :NEW. instructor_id IS NOT NULL THEN
        BEGIN
            v_instructor_id := :NEW. instructor_id;

            SELECT first_name||' '||last_name
              INTO instructor_adm.v_instructor_name
              FROM instructor
             WHERE  instructor_id = instructor_adm.v_instructor_id;

        EXCEPTION
            WHEN NO_DATA_FOUND THEN
                RAISE_APPLICATION_ERROR
                    (-20001, 'This is not a valid instructor');
        END;
    END IF;
END BEFORE EACH ROW;

AFTER STATEMENT IS
BEGIN
    SELECT COUNT(*)
      INTO v_total
      FROM section
     WHERE instructor_id = v_instructor_id;

    -- check if the current instructor is overbooked
    IF v_total >= 10 THEN
        RAISE_APPLICATION_ERROR
            (-20000, 'Instructor, '||instructor_adm.v_instructor_name||
            ', is overbooked');
    END IF;
END AFTER STATEMENT;

END section_compound;
```

In this trigger, you declare three variables, two of which were previously declared in the package. Next, you place statements from two simple triggers into two corresponding sections of a compound trigger.

Notice that by using a compound trigger you can resolve the mutating table issue with a simpler approach. You eliminated the need for a package that is used as a link between two triggers that fire at different times in a transaction.

Note that the UPDATE statement used earlier

```
UPDATE section
   SET instructor_id = 101
 WHERE section_id = 80;
```

produces the same output:

```
UPDATE section
*
ERROR at line 1:
ORA-20000: Instructor, Fernand Hanks, is overbooked
ORA-06512: at "STUDENT.SECTION_COMPOUND", line 38
ORA-04088: error during execution of trigger 'STUDENT.SECTION_COMPOUND'
```

▼ LAB 14.2 EXERCISES

This section provides exercises and suggested answers, with discussion related to how those answers resulted. The most important thing to realize is whether your answer works. You should figure out the implications of the answers and what the effects are of any different answers you may come up with.

14.2.1 Understand Compound Triggers

In this exercise, you modify the trigger you created in Lab 14.1 that causes a mutating table error when an INSERT statement is issued against the ENROLLMENT table.

Before starting this exercise, we suggest that you drop the triggers and package you created in Lab 14.1 and delete the records you added and/or updated in the ENROLLMENT table as follows:

```
DROP TRIGGER enrollment_biu;
DROP TRIGGER enrollment_aiu;
DROP PACKAGE student_adm;

DELETE FROM enrollment
 WHERE student_id = 399;

COMMIT;
```

Recall the ENROLLMENT_BIU trigger you created in Lab 14.1:

```
-- ch14_1a.sql, version 1.0
CREATE OR REPLACE TRIGGER enrollment_biu
BEFORE INSERT OR UPDATE ON enrollment
FOR EACH ROW
DECLARE
   v_total NUMBER;
   v_name VARCHAR2(30);
BEGIN
   SELECT COUNT(*)
     INTO v_total
     FROM enrollment
    WHERE student_id = :NEW.student_id;
```

```
   -- check if the current student is enrolled in too
   -- many courses
   IF v_total >= 3 THEN
      SELECT first_name||' '||last_name
        INTO v_name
        FROM student
       WHERE student_id = :NEW.STUDENT_ID;

      RAISE_APPLICATION_ERROR (-20000, 'Student, '||v_name||
         ', is registered for 3 courses already');
   END IF;
EXCEPTION
   WHEN NO_DATA_FOUND THEN
       RAISE_APPLICATION_ERROR
           (-20001, 'This is not a valid student');
END;
```

Recall the following INSERT and UPDATE statements and the errors they produced:

```
INSERT INTO ENROLLMENT
    (student_id, section_id, enroll_date, created_by, created_date,
     modified_by, modified_date)
VALUES (184, 98, SYSDATE, USER, SYSDATE, USER, SYSDATE);


INSERT INTO ENROLLMENT
            *
ERROR at line 1:
ORA-20000: Student, Salewa Zuckerberg, is registered for 3 courses
already
ORA-06512: at "STUDENT.ENROLLMENT_BIU", line 17
ORA-04088: error during execution of trigger
           'STUDENT.ENROLLMENT_BIU'


INSERT INTO ENROLLMENT
    (student_id, section_id, enroll_date, created_by, created_date,
     modified_by, modified_date)
VALUES (399, 98, SYSDATE, USER, SYSDATE, USER, SYSDATE);


1 row created.


UPDATE ENROLLMENT
   SET student_id = 399
 WHERE student_id = 283;


UPDATE enrollment
*
ERROR at line 1:
ORA-04091: table STUDENT.ENROLLMENT is mutating, trigger/function
           may not see it
ORA-06512: at "STUDENT.ENROLLMENT_BIU", line 5
ORA-04088: error during execution of trigger
           'STUDENT.ENROLLMENT_BIU'
```

Complete the following tasks:

A) Create a new compound trigger so that it does not cause a mutating table error when an UPDATE
statement is issued against the ENROLLMENT table.

ANSWER: The newly created compound trigger should look similar to the following:

```
-- ch14_2a.sql, version 1.0
CREATE OR REPLACE TRIGGER enrollment_compound
FOR INSERT OR UPDATE ON enrollment
COMPOUND TRIGGER
    v_student_id    STUDENT.STUDENT_ID%TYPE;
    v_student_name VARCHAR2(50);
    v_total         INTEGER;

BEFORE EACH ROW IS
BEGIN
    IF :NEW. student_id IS NOT NULL THEN
        BEGIN
            v_student_id := :NEW.student_id;

            SELECT first_name||' '||last_name
                INTO v_student_name
                FROM student
              WHERE student_id = v_student_id;
        EXCEPTION
            WHEN NO_DATA_FOUND THEN
                RAISE_APPLICATION_ERROR
                    (-20001, 'This is not a valid student');
        END;
    END IF;
END BEFORE EACH ROW;

AFTER STATEMENT IS
BEGIN
    SELECT COUNT(*)
      INTO v_total
      FROM enrollment
     WHERE student_id = v_student_id;

    -- check if the current student is enrolled in too
    -- many courses
    IF v_total >= 3 THEN
        RAISE_APPLICATION_ERROR (-20000, 'Student, '||v_student_name||
            ', is registered for 3 courses already ');
    END IF;
END AFTER STATEMENT;

END enrollment_compound;
```

In this trigger, you declare variables to record student ID and name that were previously declared
in the package STUDENT_ADM. You also declare variable v_total, which was previously
declared in the ENROLLMENT_AIU trigger. Next, you create BEFORE EACH ROW and AFTER STATE-

MENT sections in the body of the trigger. Note that the statements in those sections are copies of the executable sections of the ENROLLMENT_BIU and ENROLLMENT_AIU triggers, respectively.

B) Run the UPDATE statement listed in the exercise text again. Explain the output produced.

ANSWER: The output should look like this:

```
SQL> UPDATE ENROLLMENT
  2     SET student_id = 399
  3   WHERE student_id = 283;


UPDATE ENROLLMENT
*
ERROR at line 1:
ORA-02292: integrity constraint (STUDENT.GR_ENR_FK) violated -
           child record found
```

Note that the error generated by the UPDATE statement is not a mutating table error. This error refers to the integrity constraint violation, because there is a child record in the GRADE table with a student ID of 283.

C) Modify the compound trigger so that the trigger populates the values for the CREATED_BY, CREATED_DATE, MODIFIED_BY, and MODIFIED_DATE columns.

ANSWER: The newly created trigger should look similar to the following. Changes are shown in bold.

```
-- ch14_2b.sql, version 2.0
CREATE OR REPLACE TRIGGER enrollment_compound
FOR INSERT OR UPDATE ON enrollment
COMPOUND TRIGGER
    v_student_id    STUDENT.STUDENT_ID%TYPE;
    v_student_name VARCHAR2(50);
    v_total         INTEGER;
    v_date          DATE;
    v_user          STUDENT.CREATED_BY%TYPE;

BEFORE STATEMENT IS
BEGIN
    v_date := SYSDATE;
    v_user := USER;
END BEFORE STATEMENT;

BEFORE EACH ROW IS
BEGIN
    IF INSERTING THEN
       :NEW.created_date := v_date;
       :NEW.created_by   := v_user;
    ELSIF UPDATING THEN
       :NEW.created_date := :OLD.created_date;
       :NEW.created_by   := :OLD.created_by;
    END IF;
    :NEW.MODIFIED_DATE := v_date;
    :NEW.MODIFIED_BY   := v_user;
```

```
        IF :NEW.STUDENT_ID IS NOT NULL THEN
           BEGIN
              v_student_id := :NEW.STUDENT_ID;

              SELECT first_name||' '||last_name
                 INTO v_student_name
                 FROM student
                 WHERE student_id = v_student_id;
           EXCEPTION
              WHEN NO_DATA_FOUND THEN
                 RAISE_APPLICATION_ERROR
                    (-20001, 'This is not a valid student');
           END;
        END IF;
END BEFORE EACH ROW;

AFTER STATEMENT IS
BEGIN
    SELECT COUNT(*)
      INTO v_total
      FROM enrollment
     WHERE student_id = v_student_id;

    -- check if the current student is enrolled in too
    -- many courses
    IF v_total >= 3 THEN
       RAISE_APPLICATION_ERROR (-20000, 'Student, '||v_student_name||
          ', is registered for 3 courses already ');
    END IF;
END AFTER STATEMENT;

END enrollment_compound;
```

In this version of the trigger, you define two new variables, `v_date` and `v_user`, in the trigger's declaration section. You add a BEFORE STATEMENT section to initialize these variables. You also modify the BEFORE EACH ROW section, where you initialize the CREATED_BY, CREATED_DATE, MODIFIED_BY, and MODIFIED_DATE columns. Note that the ELSIF statement

```
IF INSERTING THEN
   :NEW.CREATED_DATE := v_date;
   :NEW.CREATED_BY   := v_user;
ELSIF UPDATING THEN
   :NEW.created_date := :OLD.created_date;
   :NEW.created_by   := :OLD.created_by;
END IF;
```

checks whether the current operation is INSERT or UPDATE to determine how to populate the CREATED_DATE and CREATED_BY columns. For the INSERT operation, these columns are assigned values based on the `v_date` and `v_user` variables. For the UPDATE operation, the CREATED_BY and CREATED_DATE columns do not change their values. As a result, the values are copied from the OLD pseudorecord. Because the MODIFIED_BY and MODIFIED_DATE columns are always populated with the new values, there is no need to evaluate whether the current record is being inserted or updated.

This version of the trigger may be tested as follows:

```
INSERT INTO enrollment
   (student_id, section_id, enroll_date, final_grade)
VALUES (102, 155, sysdate, null);
```

INSERT INTO enrollment
            *

ERROR at line 1:
ORA-20000: Student, Fred Crocitto, is registered for 3 courses
            already
ORA-06512: at "STUDENT.ENROLLMENT_COMPOUND", line 48
ORA-04088: error during execution of trigger
            'STUDENT.ENROLLMENT_COMPOUND'

```
INSERT INTO enrollment
   (student_id, section_id, enroll_date, final_grade)
VALUES (103, 155, sysdate, null);
```

1 row created.

```
UPDATE ENROLLMENT
   SET final_grade = 85
 WHERE student_id = 105
   AND section_id = 155;
```

1 row updated.

ROLLBACK;

Rollback complete.

It is important to note that when the CREATED_DATE and CREATED_BY columns are not initialized to any values in the body of the trigger for the UPDATE operation, the trigger causes a NOT NULL constraint violation. In other words, the CREATED_DATE and CREATED_BY columns should be reinitialized to their original values explicitly in the BEFORE EACH ROW section of the trigger. Consider a modified version of the BEFORE EACH ROW section that causes a NOT NULL constraint violation error for the UPDATE operation:

```
BEFORE EACH ROW IS
BEGIN
    IF INSERTING THEN
        :NEW.created_date := v_date;
        :NEW.created_by   := v_user;
    END IF;
    :NEW.modified_date := v_date;
    :NEW.modified_by   := v_user;

    IF :NEW.STUDENT_ID IS NOT NULL THEN
        BEGIN
            v_student_id := :NEW.student_id;

            SELECT first_name||' '||last_name
```

```
                INTO v_student_name
                FROM student
               WHERE student_id = v_student_id;
          EXCEPTION
             WHEN NO_DATA_FOUND THEN
                RAISE_APPLICATION_ERROR
                    (-20001, 'This is not a valid student');
          END;
       END IF;
   END BEFORE EACH ROW;
```

Note that in this version, the ELSIF statement has been replaced by the IF statement that initializes the CREATED_DATE and CREATED_BY columns for the INSERT operation only. In this case, the trigger causes the following error when an UPDATE is issued against the ENROLLMENT table:

```
UPDATE enrollment
*
ERROR at line 1:
ORA-01407: cannot update ("STUDENT"."ENROLLMENT"."CREATED_DATE")
           to NULL
```

▼ TRY IT YOURSELF

In this chapter you've learned about mutating table issues and compound triggers. Here are some projects that will help you test the depth of your understanding:

1) Create a compound trigger on the INSTRUCTOR table that fires on the INSERT and UPDATE statements. The trigger should not allow an insert on the INSTRUCTOR table during off hours. Off hours are weekends and times of day outside the 9 a.m. to 5 p.m. window. The trigger should also populate the INSTRUCTOR_ID, CREATED_BY, CREATED_DATE, MODIFIED_BY, and MODIFIED_DATE columns with their default values.

2) Create a compound trigger on the ZIPCODE table that fires on the INSERT and UPDATE statements. The trigger should populate the MODIFIED_BY and MODIFIED_DATE columns with their default values. In addition, it should record in the STATISTICS table the type of the transaction, the name of the user who issued the transaction, the date of the transaction, and how many records are affected by the transaction. Assume that the STATISTICS table has the following structure:

```
Name                            Null?     Type
------------------------------- --------- ----
TABLE_NAME                                VARCHAR2(30)
TRANSACTION_NAME                          VARCHAR2(10)
TRANSACTION_USER                          VARCHAR2(30)
TRANSACTION_DATE                          DATE
```

The projects in this section are meant to have you use all the skills you have acquired throughout this chapter. The answers to these projects can be found in Appendix D and on this book's companion Web site. Visit the Web site periodically to share and discuss your answers.

CHAPTER 15

Collections

CHAPTER OBJECTIVES

In this chapter, you will learn about

- ▶ PL/SQL tables
- ▶ Varrays
- ▶ Multilevel collections

Throughout this book you have explored different types of PL/SQL identifiers or variables that represent individual elements, such as a variable that represents a student's grade. However, often in your programs you want to represent a group of elements such as the grades for a class of students. To support this technique, PL/SQL provides collection datatypes that work just like arrays available in other third-generation programming languages.

A collection is a group of elements of the same datatype. Each element is identified by a unique subscript that represents its position in the collection. In this chapter you will learn about two collection datatypes: tables and varrays. In addition, you will learn about multilevel collections that were introduced in Oracle 9i and that are not supported by the previous releases.

LAB 15.1
PL/SQL Tables

LAB OBJECTIVES

After completing this lab, you will be able to

▶ Use associative arrays
▶ Use nested tables

A PL/SQL table is similar to a one-column database table. The rows of a PL/SQL table are not stored in any predefined order, yet when they are retrieved in a variable, each row is assigned a consecutive subscript starting at 1, as shown in Figure 15.1.

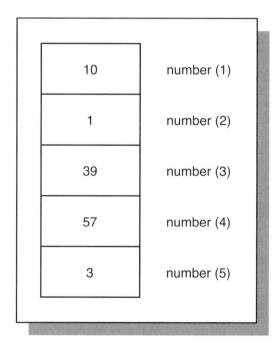

FIGURE 15.1
PL/SQL table

Figure 15.1 shows a PL/SQL table consisting of integers. Each number is assigned a unique subscript that corresponds to its position in the table. For example, number 3 has subscript 5 assigned to it because it is stored in the fifth row of the PL/SQL table.

The two types of PL/SQL tables are associative tables (formerly called index-by tables) and nested tables. They have the same structure, and their rows are accessed in the same way using subscript notation, as shown in Figure 15.1. The main difference between these two types is that nested tables can be stored in a database column, and associative arrays cannot.

ASSOCIATIVE ARRAYS

The general syntax for creating an associative array is as follows (the reserved words and phrases in brackets are optional):

```
TYPE type_name IS TABLE OF element_type [NOT NULL]
    INDEX BY element_type;
table_name TYPE_NAME;
```

Notice that declaring an associative array has two steps. First, a table structure is defined using the TYPE statement, where $type\_name$ is the name of the type that is used in the second step to declare an actual table. An $element\_type$ is any PL/SQL datatype, such as NUMBER, VARCHAR2, or DATE, with some restrictions. The majority of restricted datatypes are beyond the scope of this book and are not mentioned in this chapter. You can find the complete list in the online Oracle help. Second, the actual table is declared based on the type specified in the first step. Consider the following code fragment:

FOR EXAMPLE

```
DECLARE
    TYPE last_name_type IS TABLE OF student.last_name%TYPE
        INDEX BY BINARY_INTEGER;
    last_name_tab last_name_type;
```

In this example, type `last_name_type` is declared based on the column LAST_NAME of the STUDENT table. Next, the actual associative array `last_name_tab` is declared as `last_name_type`.

As mentioned, the individual elements of a PL/SQL table are referenced using subscript notation as follows:

```
table_name(subscript)
```

This technique is demonstrated in the following example:

FOR EXAMPLE

```
DECLARE
    CURSOR name_cur IS
        SELECT last_name
        FROM student
```

FOR EXAMPLE (continued)

```
        WHERE rownum <= 10;

   TYPE last_name_type IS TABLE OF student.last_name%TYPE
      INDEX BY BINARY_INTEGER;
   last_name_tab last_name_type;

   v_counter INTEGER := 0;
BEGIN
   FOR name_rec IN name_cur LOOP
      v_counter := v_counter + 1;
      last_name_tab(v_counter) := name_rec.last_name;
      DBMS_OUTPUT.PUT_LINE ('last_name('||v_counter||'): '||
         last_name_tab(v_counter));
   END LOOP;
END;
```

In this example, the associative array `last_name_tab` is populated with last names from the STUDENT table. Notice that the variable `v_counter` is used as a subscript to reference individual table elements. This example produces the following output:

```
   last_name(1): Crocitto
   last_name(2): Landry
   last_name(3): Enison
   last_name(4): Moskowitz
   last_name(5): Olvsade
   last_name(6): Mierzwa
   last_name(7): Sethi
   last_name(8): Walter
   last_name(9): Martin
   last_name(10): Noviello

   PL/SQL procedure successfully completed.
```

WATCH OUT!

It is important to note that referencing a nonexistent row raises the NO_DATA_FOUND exception as follows:

```
   DECLARE
      CURSOR name_cur IS
         SELECT last_name
           FROM student
          WHERE rownum <= 10;

      TYPE last_name_type IS TABLE OF student.last_name%TYPE
         INDEX BY BINARY_INTEGER;
      last_name_tab last_name_type;
```

```
      v_counter INTEGER := 0;
   BEGIN
      FOR name_rec IN name_cur LOOP
         v_counter := v_counter + 1;
         last_name_tab(v_counter) := name_rec.last_name;
         DBMS_OUTPUT.PUT_LINE ('last_name('||v_counter||
            '): '||last_name_tab(v_counter));
      END LOOP;
      DBMS_OUTPUT.PUT_LINE ('last_name(11): '||
         last_name_tab(11));
   END;
```

This example produces the following output:

```
last_name(1): Crocitto
last_name(2): Landry
last_name(3): Enison
last_name(4): Moskowitz
last_name(5): Olvsade
last_name(6): Mierzwa
last_name(7): Sethi
last_name(8): Walter
last_name(9): Martin
last_name(10): Noviello
DECLARE
*
ERROR at line 1:
ORA-01403: no data found
ORA-06512: at line 19
```

Notice that the DBMS_OUTPUT.PUT_LINE statement shown in bold raises the NO_DATA_FOUND exception because it references the eleventh row of the table, even though the table contains only ten rows.

NESTED TABLES

The general syntax for creating a nested table is as follows (the reserved words and phrases in brackets are optional):

```
TYPE type_name IS TABLE OF element_type [NOT NULL];
table_name TYPE_NAME;
```

Notice that this declaration is very similar to the declaration of an associative array, except that it has no INDEX BY BINARY_INTEGER clause. As in the case of an associative array, restrictions apply to an $element\_type$ of a nested table. These restrictions are listed in the Oracle online help.

It is important to note that a nested table must be initialized before its individual elements can be referenced. Consider a modified version of the example used earlier. Notice that the $last\_name\_type$ is defined as a nested table (there is no INDEX BY clause):

FOR EXAMPLE

```
DECLARE
    CURSOR name_cur IS
        SELECT last_name
          FROM student
         WHERE rownum <= 10;

    TYPE last_name_type IS TABLE OF student.last_name%TYPE;
    last_name_tab last_name_type;

    v_counter INTEGER := 0;
BEGIN
    FOR name_rec IN name_cur LOOP
        v_counter := v_counter + 1;
        last_name_tab(v_counter) := name_rec.last_name;
        DBMS_OUTPUT.PUT_LINE ('last_name('||v_counter||'): '||
            last_name_tab(v_counter));
    END LOOP;
END;
```

This example causes the following error:

```
DECLARE
*
ERROR at line 1:
ORA-06531: Reference to uninitialized collection
ORA-06512: at line 14
```

This example causes an error because a nested table is automatically NULL when it is declared. In other words, no individual elements exist yet because the nested table itself is NULL. For you to reference the individual elements of the nested table, it must be initialized with the help of a system-defined function called a constructor. The constructor has the same name as the nested table type.

For example, the statement

```
last_name_tab := last_name_type('Rosenzweig', 'Silvestrova');
```

initializes the last_name_tab table to two elements. Note that most of the time, it is not known in advance what values should constitute a particular nested table. So, the following statement produces an empty but non-null nested table:

```
last_name_tab := last_name_type();
```

Notice that no arguments are passed to a constructor. Now, consider a modified version of the example shown previously:

FOR EXAMPLE

```
DECLARE
   CURSOR name_cur IS
      SELECT last_name
        FROM student
       WHERE rownum <= 10;

   TYPE last_name_type IS TABLE OF student.last_name%TYPE;
   last_name_tab last_name_type := last_name_type();

   v_counter INTEGER := 0;
BEGIN
   FOR name_rec IN name_cur LOOP
      v_counter := v_counter + 1;
      last_name_tab.EXTEND;
      last_name_tab(v_counter) := name_rec.last_name;

      DBMS_OUTPUT.PUT_LINE ('last_name('||v_counter||'): '||
         last_name_tab(v_counter));
   END LOOP;
END;
```

In this version, the nested table is initialized at the time of declaration. This means that it is empty, but non-null. In the cursor loop is a statement with one of the collection methods, EXTEND. This method allows you to increase the size of the collection. Note that the EXTEND method cannot be used with associative arrays. You will read detailed explanations of various collection methods later in this chapter.

Next, the nested table is assigned values just like the associative array in the original version of the example. When run, the script produces the following output:

```
last_name(1): Crocitto
last_name(2): Landry
last_name(3): Enison
last_name(4): Moskowitz
last_name(5): Olvsade
last_name(6): Mierzwa
last_name(7): Sethi
last_name(8): Walter
last_name(9): Martin
last_name(10): Noviello

PL/SQL procedure successfully completed.
```

DID YOU KNOW?

What is the difference between a NULL collection and an empty collection? If a collection has not been initialized, referencing its individual elements causes the following error:

```
DECLARE
    TYPE integer_type IS TABLE OF INTEGER;
    integer_tab integer_type;

    v_counter integer := 1;
BEGIN
    DBMS_OUTPUT.PUT_LINE (integer_tab(v_counter));
END;
```

DECLARE
*
ERROR at line 1:
ORA-06531: Reference to uninitialized collection
ORA-06512: at line 7

If a collection has been initialized so that it is empty, referencing its individual elements causes a different error:

```
DECLARE
    TYPE integer_type IS TABLE OF INTEGER;
    integer_tab integer_type := integer_type();

    v_counter integer := 1;
BEGIN
    DBMS_OUTPUT.PUT_LINE (integer_tab(v_counter));
END;
```

DECLARE
*
ERROR at line 1:
ORA-06533: Subscript beyond count
ORA-06512: at line 7

COLLECTION METHODS

In the previous examples, you have seen one of the collection methods, EXTEND. A collection method is a built-in function that is called using dot notation as follows:

```
collection_name.method_name
```

The following list explains collection methods that allow you to manipulate or gain information about a particular collection:

- ▶ EXISTS returns TRUE if a specified element exists in a collection. This method can be used to avoid SUBSCRIPT_OUTSIDE_LIMIT exceptions.

- ▶ COUNT returns the total number of elements in a collection.

▶ EXTEND increases the size of a collection.

▶ DELETE deletes either all elements, elements in the specified range, or a particular element from a collection. Note that PL/SQL keeps placeholders of the deleted elements.

▶ FIRST and LAST return subscripts of the first and last elements of a collection. Note that if the first elements of a nested table are deleted, the FIRST method returns a value greater than 1. If elements have been deleted from the middle of a nested table, the LAST method returns a value greater than the COUNT method.

▶ PRIOR and NEXT return subscripts that precede and succeed a specified collection subscript.

▶ TRIM removes either one or a specified number of elements from the end of a collection. Note that PL/SQL does not keep placeholders for the trimmed elements.

BY THE WAY

EXTEND and TRIM methods cannot be used with index-by tables.

Consider the following example, which illustrates the use of various collection methods:

FOR EXAMPLE

```
DECLARE
    TYPE index_by_type IS TABLE OF NUMBER
        INDEX BY BINARY_INTEGER;
    index_by_table index_by_type;

    TYPE nested_type IS TABLE OF NUMBER;
    nested_table nested_type :=
        nested_type(1, 2, 3, 4, 5, 6, 7, 8, 9, 10);

BEGIN
    -- Populate index by table
    FOR i IN 1..10 LOOP
        index_by_table(i) := i;
    END LOOP;

    IF index_by_table.EXISTS(3) THEN
        DBMS_OUTPUT.PUT_LINE ('index_by_table(3) =
                            '||index_by_table(3));
    END IF;

    -- delete 10th element from a collection
    nested_table.DELETE(10);
    -- delete elements 1 through 3 from a collection
    nested_table.DELETE(1,3);
    index_by_table.DELETE(10);
```

FOR EXAMPLE (continued)

```
DBMS_OUTPUT.PUT_LINE ('nested_table.COUNT =
                      '||nested_table.COUNT);
DBMS_OUTPUT.PUT_LINE ('index_by_table.COUNT = '||
   index_by_table.COUNT);

DBMS_OUTPUT.PUT_LINE ('nested_table.FIRST =
                      '||nested_table.FIRST);
DBMS_OUTPUT.PUT_LINE ('nested_table.LAST = '||nested_table.LAST);
DBMS_OUTPUT.PUT_LINE ('index_by_table.FIRST = '||
   index_by_table.FIRST);
DBMS_OUTPUT.PUT_LINE ('index_by_table.LAST =
                      '||index_by_table.LAST);

DBMS_OUTPUT.PUT_LINE ('nested_table.PRIOR(2) = '||
   nested_table. PRIOR(2));
DBMS_OUTPUT.PUT_LINE ('nested_table.NEXT(2) = '||
   nested_table.NEXT(2));
DBMS_OUTPUT.PUT_LINE ('index_by_table.PRIOR(2) = '||
   index_by_table.PRIOR(2));
DBMS_OUTPUT.PUT_LINE ('index_by_table.NEXT(2) = '||
   index_by_table.NEXT(2));

-- Trim last two elements
nested_table.TRIM(2);
-- Trim last element
nested_table.TRIM;

DBMS_OUTPUT.PUT_LINE('nested_table.LAST = '||nested_table.LAST);
END;
```

Consider the output returned by this example:

```
index_by_table(3) = 3
nested_table.COUNT = 6
index_by_table.COUNT = 9
nested_table.FIRST = 4
nested_table.LAST = 9
index_by_table.FIRST = 1
index_by_table.LAST = 9
nested_table.PRIOR(2) =
nested_table.NEXT(2) = 4
index_by_table.PRIOR(2) = 1
index_by_table.NEXT(2) = 3
nested_table.LAST = 7

PL/SQL procedure successfully completed.
```

The first line of the output

```
index_by_table(3) = 3
```

is produced because the EXISTS method returns TRUE. As a result, the IF statement

```
IF index_by_table.EXISTS(3) THEN
    DBMS_OUTPUT.PUT_LINE ('index_by_table(3) = '||index_by_table(3));
END IF;
```

evaluates to TRUE as well.

The second and third lines of the output

```
nested_table.COUNT = 6
index_by_table.COUNT = 9
```

show the results of method COUNT after some elements were deleted from the associative array and nested table.

Next, lines four through seven of the output

```
nested_table.FIRST = 4
nested_table.LAST = 9
index_by_table.FIRST = 1
index_by_table.LAST = 9
```

show the results of the FIRST and LAST methods. Notice that the FIRST method applied to the nested table returns 4 because the first three elements were deleted earlier.

Next, lines eight through eleven of the output

```
nested_table.PRIOR(2) =
nested_table.NEXT(2) = 4
index_by_table.PRIOR(2) = 1
index_by_table.NEXT(2) = 3
```

show the results of the PRIOR and NEXT methods. Notice that the PRIOR method applied to the nested table returns NULL because the first element was deleted earlier.

Finally, the last line of the output

```
nested_table.LAST = 7
```

shows the value of the last subscript after the last three elements were removed. As mentioned earlier, as soon as the DELETE method is issued, PL/SQL keeps placeholders of the deleted elements. Therefore, the first call of the TRIM method removes the ninth and tenth elements of the nested table, and the second call of the TRIM method removes the eighth element of the nested table. As a result, the LAST method returns value 7 as the last subscript of the nested table.

▼ LAB 15.1 EXERCISES

This section provides exercises and suggested answers, with discussion related to how those answers resulted. The most important thing to realize is whether your answer works. You should figure out the implications of the answers and what the effects are of any different answers you may come up with.

15.1.1 Use Associative Arrays

In this exercise, you learn more about associative arrays.

Create the following PL/SQL script:

```
-- ch15_1a.sql, version 1.0
SET SERVEROUTPUT ON
DECLARE
    CURSOR course_cur IS
        SELECT description
          FROM course;

    TYPE course_type IS TABLE OF course.description%TYPE
        INDEX BY BINARY_INTEGER;
    course_tab course_type;

    v_counter INTEGER := 0;
BEGIN
    FOR course_rec IN course_cur LOOP
        v_counter := v_counter + 1;
        course_tab(v_counter) := course_rec.description;
    END LOOP;
END;
```

Answer the following questions, and complete the following tasks:

A) Explain the preceding script.

ANSWER: The declaration section of the script defines the associative array type, `course_type`. This type is based on the column DESCRIPTION of the table COURSE. Next, the actual associative array is declared as `course_tab`.

The executable section of the script populates the `course_tab` table in the cursor FOR loop. Each element of the associative array is referenced by its subscript, `v_counter`. For each iteration of the loop, the value of `v_counter` is incremented by 1 so that each new description value is stored in the new row of the associative array.

B) Modify the script so that rows of the associative array are displayed on the screen.

ANSWER: The script should look similar to the following. Changes are shown in bold.

```
-- ch15_1b.sql, version 2.0
SET SERVEROUTPUT ON
DECLARE
    CURSOR course_cur IS
        SELECT description
          FROM course;
```

```
   TYPE course_type IS TABLE OF course.description%TYPE
      INDEX BY BINARY_INTEGER;
   course_tab course_type;

   v_counter INTEGER := 0;
BEGIN
   FOR course_rec IN course_cur LOOP
      v_counter := v_counter + 1;
      course_tab(v_counter):= course_rec.description;
      DBMS_OUTPUT.PUT_LINE('course('||v_counter||'): '||
         course_tab(v_counter));
   END LOOP;
END;
```

Consider another version of the same script:

```
-- ch15_1c.sql, version 3.0
SET SERVEROUTPUT ON
DECLARE
   CURSOR course_cur IS
      SELECT description
        FROM course;

   TYPE course_type IS TABLE OF course.description%TYPE
      INDEX BY BINARY_INTEGER;
   course_tab course_type;

   v_counter INTEGER := 0;
BEGIN
   FOR course_rec IN course_cur LOOP
      v_counter := v_counter + 1;
      course_tab(v_counter):= course_rec.description;
   END LOOP;

   FOR i IN 1..v_counter LOOP
      DBMS_OUTPUT.PUT_LINE('course('||i||'): '||course_tab(i));
   END LOOP;
END;
```

When run, both versions produce the same output:

```
course(1): DP Overview
course(2): Intro to Computers
course(3): Intro to Programming
course(4): Structured Programming Techniques
course(5): Hands-On Windows
course(6): Intro to Java Programming
course(7): Intermediate Java Programming
course(8): Advanced Java Programming
course(9): JDeveloper
course(10): Intro to Unix
course(11): Basics of Unix Admin
course(12): Advanced Unix Admin
```

```
course(13): Unix Tips and Techniques
course(14): Structured Analysis
course(15): Project Management
course(16): Database Design
course(17): Internet Protocols
course(18): Java for C/C++ Programmers
course(19): GUI Programming
course(20): Intro to SQL
course(21): Oracle Tools
course(22): PL/SQL Programming
course(23): Intro to Internet
course(24): Intro to the Basic Language
course(25): Operating Systems
course(26): Network Administration
course(27): JDeveloper Lab
course(28): Database System Principles
course(29): JDeveloper Techniques
course(30): DB Programming in Java

PL/SQL procedure successfully completed.
```

C) Modify the script so that only first and last rows of the associative array are displayed on the screen.

ANSWER: The script should look similar to the following. Changes are shown in bold.

```
-- ch15_1d.sql, version 4.0
SET SERVEROUTPUT ON
DECLARE
   CURSOR course_cur IS
      SELECT description
        FROM course;

   TYPE course_type IS TABLE OF course.description%TYPE
      INDEX BY BINARY_INTEGER;
   course_tab course_type;

   v_counter INTEGER := 0;
BEGIN
   FOR course_rec IN course_cur LOOP
      v_counter := v_counter + 1;
      course_tab(v_counter) := course_rec.description;
   END LOOP;
   DBMS_OUTPUT.PUT_LINE('course('||course_tab.FIRST||'): '||
      course_tab(course_tab.FIRST));
   DBMS_OUTPUT.PUT_LINE('course('||course_tab.LAST||'): '||
      course_tab(course_tab.LAST));
END;
```

Consider the statements

```
course_tab(course_tab.FIRST)
```

and

```
course_tab(course_tab.LAST)
```

used in this example. Although these statements look somewhat different from the statements you have seen so far, they produce the same effect as the

```
course_tab(1)
```

and

```
course_tab(30)
```

statements. As mentioned earlier, the FIRST and LAST methods return the subscripts of the first and last elements of a collection, respectively. In this example, the associative array contains 30 elements, where the first element has a subscript of 1, and the last element has a subscript of 30.

This version of the script produces the following output:

```
course(1): DP Overview
course(30): DB Programming in Java

PL/SQL procedure successfully completed.
```

D) Modify the script by adding the following statements, and explain the output produced:

   I) Display the total number of elements in the associative array after it has been populated on the screen.

   II) Delete the last element, and display the total number of elements of the associative array again.

   III) Delete the fifth element, and display the total number of elements and the subscript of the last element of the associative array again.

   ANSWER: The script should look similar to the following. All changes are shown in bold.

```
-- ch15_1e.sql, version 5.0
SET SERVEROUTPUT ON
DECLARE
    CURSOR course_cur IS
        SELECT description
        FROM course;

    TYPE course_type IS TABLE OF course.description%TYPE
        INDEX BY BINARY_INTEGER;
    course_tab course_type;

    v_counter INTEGER := 0;
BEGIN
    FOR course_rec IN course_cur LOOP
        v_counter := v_counter + 1;
        course_tab(v_counter) := course_rec.description;
    END LOOP;

    -- Display the total number of elements in the associative array
    DBMS_OUTPUT.PUT_LINE ('1. Total number of elements: '||
        course_tab.COUNT);
```

```
-- Delete the last element of the associative array
-- Display the total number of elements in the associative array
course_tab.DELETE(course_tab.LAST);
DBMS_OUTPUT.PUT_LINE ('2. Total number of elements: '||
   course_tab.COUNT);

-- Delete the fifth element of the associative array
-- Display the total number of elements in the associative array
-- Display the subscript of the last element of the associative
-- array
course_tab.DELETE(5);
DBMS_OUTPUT.PUT_LINE ('3. Total number of elements: '||
   course_tab.COUNT);
DBMS_OUTPUT.PUT_LINE ('3. The subscript of the last element: '||
   course_tab.LAST);
END;
```

When run, this example produces the following output:

```
1. Total number of elements: 30
2. Total number of elements: 29
3. Total number of elements: 28
3. The subscript of the last element: 29

PL/SQL procedure successfully completed.
```

First, the total number of elements in the associative array is calculated using the COUNT method and displayed on the screen. Second, the last element is deleted using the DELETE and LAST methods, and the total number of elements in the associative array is displayed on the screen again. Third, the fifth element is deleted, and the total number of elements in the associative array and the subscript of the last element are displayed on the screen.

Consider the last two lines of output. After the fifth element of the associative array is deleted, the COUNT method returns the value 28, and the LAST method returns the value 29. Usually, the values returned by the COUNT and LAST methods are equal. However, when an element is deleted from the middle of the associative array, the value returned by the LAST method is greater than the value returned by the COUNT method, because the LAST method ignores deleted elements.

15.1.2 Use Nested Tables

In this exercise, you learn more about nested tables.

Complete the following tasks:

A) Modify script ch15_1a.sql, used in Exercise 15.1.1. Instead of using an associative array, use a nested table.

ANSWER: The script should look similar to the following. Changes are shown in bold.

```
-- ch15_2a.sql, version 1.0
SET SERVEROUTPUT ON
DECLARE
   CURSOR course_cur IS
      SELECT description
        FROM course;
```

```
    TYPE course_type IS TABLE OF course.description%TYPE;
    course_tab course_type := course_type();

    v_counter INTEGER := 0;
BEGIN
    FOR course_rec IN course_cur LOOP
        v_counter := v_counter + 1;
        course_tab.EXTEND;
        course_tab(v_counter) := course_rec.description;
    END LOOP;
END;
```

B) Modify the script by adding the following statements, and explain the output produced:

   I) Delete the last element of the nested table, and then assign a new value to it. Execute the script.

   II) Trim the last element of the nested table, and then assign a new value to it. Execute the script.

ANSWER:

   I) The script should look similar to the following. Changes are shown in bold.

```
-- ch15_2b.sql, version 2.0
SET SERVEROUTPUT ON
DECLARE
    CURSOR course_cur IS
        SELECT description
          FROM course;

    TYPE course_type IS TABLE OF course.description%TYPE;
    course_tab course_type := course_type();

    v_counter INTEGER := 0;
BEGIN
    FOR course_rec IN course_cur LOOP
        v_counter := v_counter + 1;
        course_tab.EXTEND;
        course_tab(v_counter) := course_rec.description;
    END LOOP;

    course_tab.DELETE(30);
    course_tab(30) := 'New Course';
END;
```

   II) The script should look similar to the following. Changes are shown in bold.

```
-- ch15_2c.sql, version 3.0
SET SERVEROUTPUT ON
DECLARE
    CURSOR course_cur IS
        SELECT description
        FROM course;
```

```
      TYPE course_type IS TABLE OF course.description%TYPE;
      course_tab course_type := course_type();

      v_counter INTEGER := 0;
   BEGIN
      FOR course_rec IN course_cur LOOP
         v_counter := v_counter + 1;
         course_tab.EXTEND;
         course_tab(v_counter) := course_rec.description;
      END LOOP;

      course_tab.TRIM;
      course_tab(30) := 'New Course';
   END;
```

When run, this version of the script produces the following error:

```
DECLARE
*
ERROR at line 1:
ORA-06533: Subscript beyond count
ORA-06512: at line 18
```

In the previous version of the script, the last element of the nested table was removed using the DELETE method. As mentioned earlier, when the DELETE method is used, PL/SQL keeps a placeholder of the deleted element. Therefore, the statement

```
course_tab(30) := 'New Course';
```

does not cause any errors.

In the current version of the script, the last element of the nested table is removed using the TRIM method. In this case, PL/SQL does not keep a placeholder of the trimmed element, because the TRIM method manipulates the internal size of a collection. As a result, the reference to the trimmed elements causes a `Subscript beyond count` error.

C) How would you modify the script created so that no error is generated when a new value is assigned to the trimmed element?

ANSWER: The script should look similar to the following. Changes are shown in bold.

```
-- ch15_2d.sql, version 4.0
SET SERVEROUTPUT ON
DECLARE
   CURSOR course_cur IS
      SELECT description
        FROM course;

   TYPE course_type IS TABLE OF course.description%TYPE;
   course_tab course_type := course_type();

   v_counter INTEGER := 0;
BEGIN
   FOR course_rec IN course_cur LOOP
      v_counter := v_counter + 1;
      course_tab.EXTEND;
```

```
        course_tab(v_counter) := course_rec.description;
    END LOOP;

    course_tab.TRIM;
    course_tab.EXTEND;
    course_tab(30) := 'New Course';
END;
```

To reference the trimmed element, the EXTEND method is used to increase the size on the collection. As a result, the assignment statement

```
course_tab(30) := 'New Course';
```

does not cause any errors.

LAB 15.2
Varrays

LAB OBJECTIVE

After completing this lab, you will be able to

▶ Use varrays

As mentioned earlier, a varray is another collection type. This term stands for "variable-size array." Similar to PL/SQL tables, each element of a varray is assigned a consecutive subscript starting at 1, as shown in Figure 15.2.

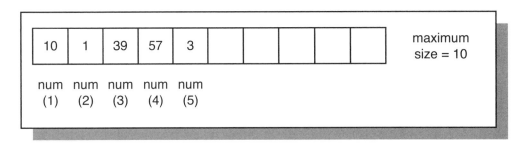

FIGURE 15.2
A varray

Figure 15.2 shows a varray consisting of five integers. Each number is assigned a unique subscript that corresponds to its position in the varray.

It is important to note that a varray has a maximum size. In other words, a subscript of a varray has a fixed lower bound equal to 1, and an upper bound that is extensible if such a need arises. In Figure 15.2, the upper bound of a varray is 5, but it can be extended to 6, 7, 8, and so on up to 10. Therefore, a varray can contain a number of elements, varying from 0 (an empty array) to its maximum size. You will recall that PL/SQL tables do not have a maximum size that must be specified explicitly.

The general syntax for creating a varray is as follows (the reserved words and phrases in square brackets are optional):

```
TYPE type_name IS {VARRAY | VARYING ARRAY} (size_limit) OF
   element_type [NOT NULL];
varray_name TYPE_NAME;
```

First, a varray structure is defined using the TYPE statement, where *type_name* is the name of the type that is used in the second step to declare an actual varray. Notice that there are two variations of the type, VARRAY and VARYING ARRAY. A *size_limit* is a positive integer literal that specifies the upper bound of a varray. As in the case of PL/SQL tables, restrictions apply to an *element_type* of a varray. These restrictions are listed in the online Oracle help. Second, the actual varray is declared based on the type specified in the first step.

Consider the following code fragment:

FOR EXAMPLE

```
DECLARE
   TYPE last_name_type IS VARRAY(10) OF student.last_name%TYPE;
   last_name_varray last_name_type;
```

In this example, type `last_name_type` is declared as a varray of ten elements based on the column LAST_NAME of the STUDENT table. Next, the actual varray `last_name_varray` is declared based on the `last_name_type`.

Similar to nested tables, a varray is automatically NULL when it is declared and must be initialized before its individual elements can be referenced. Consider a modified version of the example used in the preceding lab. Instead of using a nested table, this version uses a varray (changes are highlighted in bold).

FOR EXAMPLE

```
DECLARE
   CURSOR name_cur IS
      SELECT last_name
        FROM student
       WHERE rownum <= 10;

   TYPE last_name_type IS VARRAY(10) OF student.last_name%TYPE;
   last_name_varray last_name_type := last_name_type();

   v_counter INTEGER := 0;
BEGIN
   FOR name_rec IN name_cur LOOP
      v_counter := v_counter + 1;
      last_name_varray.EXTEND;
      last_name_varray(v_counter) := name_rec.last_name;
      DBMS_OUTPUT.PUT_LINE ('last_name('||v_counter||'): '||
         last_name_varray(v_counter));
   END LOOP;
END;
```

This example produces the following output:

```
last_name(1): Crocitto
last_name(2): Landry
last_name(3): Enison
last_name(4): Moskowitz
last_name(5): Olvsade
last_name(6): Mierzwa
last_name(7): Sethi
last_name(8): Walter
last_name(9): Martin
last_name(10): Noviello

PL/SQL procedure successfully completed.
```

Based on this example, you may realize that the collection methods you saw in the preceding lab can be used with varrays as well. Consider the following example, which illustrates the use of various collection methods when applied to a varray:

FOR EXAMPLE

```
DECLARE
   TYPE varray_type IS VARRAY(10) OF NUMBER;
   varray varray_type := varray_type(1, 2, 3, 4, 5, 6);

BEGIN
   DBMS_OUTPUT.PUT_LINE ('varray.COUNT = '||varray.COUNT);
   DBMS_OUTPUT.PUT_LINE ('varray.LIMIT = '||varray.LIMIT);

   DBMS_OUTPUT.PUT_LINE ('varray.FIRST = '||varray.FIRST);
   DBMS_OUTPUT.PUT_LINE ('varray.LAST = '||varray.LAST);

   varray.EXTEND(2, 4);
   DBMS_OUTPUT.PUT_LINE ('varray.LAST = '||varray.LAST);
   DBMS_OUTPUT.PUT_LINE ('varray('||varray.LAST||') = '||
      varray(varray.LAST));

   -- Trim last two elements
   varray.TRIM(2);
   DBMS_OUTPUT.PUT_LINE('varray.LAST = '||varray.LAST);
END;
```

Consider the output returned by this example:

```
varray.COUNT = 6
varray.LIMIT = 10
varray.FIRST = 1
varray.LAST = 6
varray.LAST = 8
```

```
varray(8) = 4
varray.LAST = 6

PL/SQL procedure successfully completed.
```

The first two lines of output

```
varray.COUNT = 6
varray.LIMIT = 10
```

show the results of the COUNT and LIMIT methods, respectively. You will recall that the COUNT method returns the number of elements that a collection contains. The collection has been initialized to six elements, so the COUNT method returns a value of 6.

The next line of output corresponds to another collection method, LIMIT. This method returns the maximum number of elements that a collection can contain. It usually is used with varrays only because varrays have an upper bound specified at the time of declaration. The collection VARRAY has an upper bound of 10, so the LIMIT method returns a value of 10. When used with nested tables, the LIMIT method returns NULL, because nested tables do not have a maximum size.

The third and fourth lines of the output

```
varray.FIRST = 1
varray.LAST = 6
```

show the results of the FIRST and LAST methods.

The fifth and six lines of the output

```
varray.LAST = 8
varray(8) = 4
```

show the results of the LAST method. The value of the eighth element of the collection after the EXTEND method increased the size of the collection. Notice that the EXTEND method

```
varray.EXTEND(2, 4);
```

appends two copies on the fourth element to the collection. As a result, the seventh and eighth elements both contain a value of 4.

The last line of output

```
varray.LAST = 6
```

shows the value of the last subscript after the last two elements were removed using the TRIM method.

WATCH OUT!

You cannot use the DELETE method with a varray to remove its elements. Unlike PL/SQL tables, varrays are dense, and using the DELETE method causes an error, as shown in the following example:

```
DECLARE
   TYPE varray_type IS VARRAY(3) OF CHAR(1);
```

```
      varray varray_type := varray_type('A', 'B', 'C');

BEGIN
   varray.DELETE(3);
END;
```

varray.DELETE(3);
   *****
ERROR at line 6:
ORA-06550: line 6, column 4:
PLS-00306: wrong number or types of arguments in call to
          'DELETE'
ORA-06550: line 6, column 4:
PL/SQL: Statement ignored

▼ LAB 15.2 EXERCISES

This section provides exercises and suggested answers, with discussion related to how those answers resulted. The most important thing to realize is whether your answer works. You should figure out the implications of the answers and what the effects are of any different answers you may come up with.

15.2.1 Use Varrays

In this exercise, you learn more about varrays. You will debug the following script, which populates `city_varray` with ten cities selected from the ZIPCODE table and displays its individual elements on the screen.

Create the following PL/SQL script:

```
-- ch15_3a.sql, version 1.0
SET SERVEROUTPUT ON
DECLARE
   CURSOR city_cur IS
      SELECT city
        FROM zipcode
       WHERE rownum <= 10;

   TYPE city_type IS VARRAY(10) OF zipcode.city%TYPE;
   city_varray city_type;

   v_counter INTEGER := 0;
BEGIN
   FOR city_rec IN city_cur LOOP
      v_counter := v_counter + 1;
      city_varray(v_counter) := city_rec.city;
      DBMS_OUTPUT.PUT_LINE('city_varray('||v_counter||'): '||
         city_varray(v_counter));
   END LOOP;
END;
```

Execute the script, and then answer the following questions and complete the following tasks:

A) What output is printed on the screen? Explain it.

ANSWER: The output should look similar to the following:

```
DECLARE
*
ERROR at line 1:
ORA-06531: Reference to uninitialized collection
ORA-06512: at line 14
```

You will recall that when a varray is declared, it is automatically NULL. In other words, the collection itself is NULL, not its individual elements. Therefore, before it can be used, it must be initialized using the constructor function with the same name as the varray type. Furthermore, after the collection is initialized, the EXTEND method must be used before its individual elements can be referenced in the script.

B) Modify the script so that no errors are returned at runtime.

ANSWER: The script should look similar to the following. Changes are shown in bold.

```
-- ch15_3b.sql, version 2.0
SET SERVEROUTPUT ON
DECLARE
    CURSOR city_cur IS
        SELECT city
          FROM zipcode
         WHERE rownum <= 10;

    TYPE city_type IS VARRAY(10) OF zipcode.city%TYPE;
    city_varray city_type := city_type();

    v_counter INTEGER := 0;
BEGIN
    FOR city_rec IN city_cur LOOP
        v_counter := v_counter + 1;
        city_varray.EXTEND;
        city_varray(v_counter) := city_rec.city;
        DBMS_OUTPUT.PUT_LINE('city_varray('||v_counter||'): '||
            city_varray(v_counter));
    END LOOP;
END;
```

When run, this script produces the following output:

```
city_varray(1): Santurce
city_varray(2): North Adams
city_varray(3): Dorchester
city_varray(4): Tufts Univ. Bedford
city_varray(5): Weymouth
city_varray(6): Sandwich
city_varray(7): Ansonia
city_varray(8): Middlefield
```

```
city_varray(9): Oxford
city_varray(10): New Haven

PL/SQL procedure successfully completed.
```

C) Modify the script as follows: Double the size of the varray, and populate the last ten elements with the first ten elements. In other words, the value of the eleventh element should be equal to the value of the first element, the value of the twelfth element should be equal to the value of the second element, and so forth.

ANSWER: The script should look similar to the following. Changes are shown in bold.

```
-- ch15_3c.sql, version 3.0
SET SERVEROUTPUT ON
DECLARE
   CURSOR city_cur IS
      SELECT city
        FROM zipcode
       WHERE rownum <= 10;

   TYPE city_type IS VARRAY(20) OF zipcode.city%TYPE;
   city_varray city_type := city_type();

   v_counter INTEGER := 0;
BEGIN
   FOR city_rec IN city_cur LOOP
      v_counter := v_counter + 1;
      city_varray.EXTEND;
      city_varray(v_counter) := city_rec.city;
   END LOOP;

   FOR i IN 1..v_counter LOOP
      -- extend the size of varray by 1 and copy the
      -- current element to the last element
      city_varray.EXTEND(1, i);
   END LOOP;

   FOR i IN 1..20 LOOP
      DBMS_OUTPUT.PUT_LINE('city_varray('||i||'): '||
         city_varray(i));
   END LOOP;
END;
```

In the preceding script, you increase the maximum size of the varray to 20 at the time of the `city_type` declaration. After the first ten elements of the varray are populated, the last ten elements are populated using the numeric FOR loop and the EXTEND method:

```
FOR i IN 1..v_counter LOOP
   -- extend the size of varray by 1 and copy the current
   -- element to the last element
   city_varray.EXTEND(1, i);
END LOOP;
```

In this loop, the loop counter is implicitly incremented by 1. So for the first iteration of the loop, the size of the varray is increased by 1, and the first element of the varray is copied to the eleventh element. In the same manner, the second element of the varray is copied to the twelfth element, and so forth.

To display all elements of the varray, the DBMS_OUTPUT.PUT_LINE statement has been moved to its own numeric FOR loop that iterates 20 times.

When run, this script produces the following output:

```
city_varray(1):  Santurce
city_varray(2):  North Adams
city_varray(3):  Dorchester
city_varray(4):  Tufts Univ. Bedford
city_varray(5):  Weymouth
city_varray(6):  Sandwich
city_varray(7):  Ansonia
city_varray(8):  Middlefield
city_varray(9):  Oxford
city_varray(10): New Haven
city_varray(11): Santurce
city_varray(12): North Adams
city_varray(13): Dorchester
city_varray(14): Tufts Univ. Bedford
city_varray(15): Weymouth
city_varray(16): Sandwich
city_varray(17): Ansonia
city_varray(18): Middlefield
city_varray(19): Oxford
city_varray(20): New Haven

PL/SQL procedure successfully completed.
```

LAB 15.3
Multilevel Collections

LAB OBJECTIVE

After completing this lab, you will be able to

▶ Use multilevel collections

So far you have seen various examples of collections with the element type based on a scalar type, such as NUMBER and VARCHAR2. Starting with Oracle 9i, PL/SQL lets you create collections whose element type is based on a collection type. Such collections are called multilevel collections.

Consider the varray of varrays, also called a nested varray, shown in Figure 15.3.

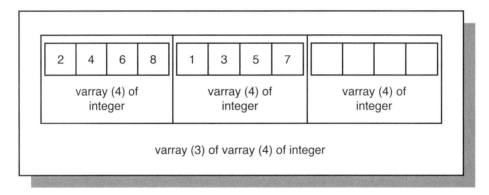

FIGURE 15.3
A varray of varrays

A varray of varrays consists of three elements, where each element is a varray consisting of four integers. To reference an individual element of a varray of varrays, you use the following syntax:

        varray_name(subscript of the outer varray)(subscript of the inner
                varray)

For example, the varray(1)(3) shown in Figure 15.3 equals 6; similarly, varray(2)(1) equals 1.

Consider an example based on Figure 15.3:

FOR EXAMPLE

```
DECLARE
   TYPE varray_type1 IS VARRAY(4) OF INTEGER;
   TYPE varray_type2 IS VARRAY(3) OF varray_type1;

   varray1 varray_type1 := varray_type1(2, 4, 6, 8);
   varray2 varray_type2 := varray_type2(varray1);
BEGIN
   DBMS_OUTPUT.PUT_LINE ('Varray of integers');
   FOR i IN 1..4 LOOP
      DBMS_OUTPUT.PUT_LINE ('varray1('||i||'): '||varray1(i));
   END LOOP;

   varray2.EXTEND;
   varray2(2) := varray_type1(1, 3, 5, 7);

   DBMS_OUTPUT.PUT_LINE (chr(10)||'Varray of varrays of integers');
   FOR i IN 1..2 LOOP
      FOR j IN 1..4 LOOP
         DBMS_OUTPUT.PUT_LINE
            ('varray2('||i||')('||j||'): '||varray2(i)(j));
      END LOOP;
   END LOOP;
END;
```

The declaration portion of this example defines two varray types. The first, `varray_type1`, is based on the INTEGER datatype and can contain up to four elements. The second, `varray_type2`, is based on `varray_type1` and can contain up to three elements where each individual element may contain up to four elements. Next, you declare two varrays based on the types just described. The first varray, `varray1`, is declared as `varray_type1` and is initialized so that its four elements are populated with the first four even numbers. The second varray, `varray2`, is declared as `varray_type2` so that each element is a varray consisting of four integers and is initialized so that its first varray element is populated.

In the executable portion of the example, you display the values of `varray1` on the screen. Next, you extend the upper bound of `varray2` by 1 and populate its second element as follows:

```
   varray2(2) := varray_type1(1, 3, 5, 7);
```

Notice that you are using a constructor corresponding to `varray_type1` because each element of `varray2` is based on the `varray1` collection. In other words, the same result could be achieved using the following two statements:

```
   varray1(2) := varray_type1(1, 3, 5, 7);
   varray2(2) := varray_type2(varray1);
```

After the second element of `varray2` is populated, you display the results on the screen using nested numeric FOR loops.

This example produces the following output:

```
Varray of integers
varray1(1): 2
varray1(2): 4
varray1(3): 6
varray1(4): 8

Varray of varrays of integers
varray2(1)(1): 2
varray2(1)(2): 4
varray2(1)(3): 6
varray2(1)(4): 8
varray2(2)(1): 1
varray2(2)(2): 3
varray2(2)(3): 5
varray2(2)(4): 7

PL/SQL procedure successfully completed.
```

▼ LAB 15.3 EXERCISES

This section provides exercises and suggested answers, with discussion related to how those answers resulted. The most important thing to realize is whether your answer works. You should figure out the implications of the answers and what the effects are of any different answers you may come up with.

15.3.1 Use Multilevel Collections

In this exercise, you learn more about multilevel collections.

Create the following PL/SQL script:

```
-- ch15_4a.sql, version 1.0
SET SERVEROUTPUT ON
DECLARE
    TYPE table_type1 IS TABLE OF INTEGER
       INDEX BY BINARY_INTEGER;
    TYPE table_type2 IS TABLE OF TABLE_TYPE1
       INDEX BY BINARY_INTEGER;

    table_tab1 table_type1;
    table_tab2 table_type2;

BEGIN
   FOR i IN 1..2 LOOP
      FOR j IN 1..3 LOOP
         IF i = 1 THEN
            table_tab1(j) := j;
         ELSE
```

```
                table_tab1(j) := 4 - j;
            END IF;
            table_tab2(i)(j) := table_tab1(j);
            DBMS_OUTPUT.PUT_LINE ('table_tab2('||i||')('||j||'): '||
                table_tab2(i)(j));
        END LOOP;
    END LOOP;
END;
```

Complete the following tasks:

A) Execute the preceding script, and explain the output produced.

ANSWER: The output should look similar to the following:

```
table_tab2(1)(1): 1
table_tab2(1)(2): 2
table_tab2(1)(3): 3
table_tab2(2)(1): 3
table_tab2(2)(2): 2
table_tab2(2)(3): 1


PL/SQL procedure successfully completed.
```

The preceding script uses multilevel associative arrays, or an associative array of associative arrays. The declaration portion of the script defines the multilevel associative array `table_tab2`. Each row of this table is an associative array consisting of multiple rows. The executable portion of the script populates the multilevel table using nested numeric FOR loops. In the first iteration of the outer loop, the inner loop populates the associative array `table_tab1` with values 1, 2, and 3 and the first row of the multilevel table `table_tab2`. In the second iteration of the outer loop, the inner loop populates the associative array `table_tab1` with values 3, 2, and 1 and the second row of the multilevel table `table_tab2`.

B) Modify the script so that instead of using multilevel associative arrays, it uses a nested table of associative arrays.

ANSWER: The script should look similar to the following. Changes are shown in bold.

```
-- ch15_4b.sql, version 2.0
SET SERVEROUTPUT ON
DECLARE
    TYPE table_type1 IS TABLE OF INTEGER INDEX BY BINARY_INTEGER;
    TYPE table_type2 IS TABLE OF TABLE_TYPE1;

    table_tab1 table_type1;
    table_tab2 table_type2 := table_type2();

BEGIN
    FOR i IN 1..2 LOOP
        table_tab2.EXTEND;
        FOR j IN 1..3 LOOP
            IF i = 1 THEN
                table_tab1(j) := j;
            ELSE
                table_tab1(j) := 4 - j;
```

```
         END IF;
         table_tab2(i)(j) := table_tab1(j);
         DBMS_OUTPUT.PUT_LINE ('table_tab2('||i||')('||j||'): '||
            table_tab2(i)(j));
      END LOOP;
   END LOOP;
END;
```

In this version of the script, `table_type2` is declared as a nested table of associative arrays. Next, `table_tab2` is initialized prior to its use, and its size is extended before a new element is assigned a value.

C) Modify the script so that instead of using multilevel associative arrays, it uses a nested table of varrays.

ANSWER: The script should look similar to the following. Changes are shown in bold.

```
-- ch15_4c.sql, version 3.0
SET SERVEROUTPUT ON
DECLARE
   TYPE table_type1 IS VARRAY(3) OF INTEGER;
   TYPE table_type2 IS TABLE      OF TABLE_TYPE1;

   table_tab1 table_type1 := table_type1();
   table_tab2 table_type2 := table_type2(table_tab1);

BEGIN
   FOR i IN 1..2 LOOP
      table_tab2.EXTEND;
      table_tab2(i) := table_type1();
      FOR j IN 1..3 LOOP
         IF i = 1 THEN
            table_tab1.EXTEND;
            table_tab1(j) := j;
         ELSE
            table_tab1(j) := 4 - j;
         END IF;
         table_tab2(i).EXTEND;
         table_tab2(i)(j):= table_tab1(j);
         DBMS_OUTPUT.PUT_LINE ('table_tab2('||i||')('||j||'): '||
            table_tab2(i)(j));
      END LOOP;
   END LOOP;
END;
```

In the declaration section of this script, `table_type1` is defined as a varray with a maximum of three integer elements, and `table_type2` is declared as a nested table of varrays. Next, `table_tab1` and `table_tab2` are initialized prior to their use.

In the executable portion of the script, the size of `table_tab2` is incremented using the EXTEND method, and its individual elements are initialized as follows:

```
table_tab2(i) := table_type1();
```

Notice that each element is initialized using the constructor associated with the varray type `table_type1`. Furthermore, to populate a nested table, a new varray element must be added to each nested table element as shown:

```
table_tab2(i).EXTEND;
```

In other words, for the first iteration of the outer loop, three varray elements are added to the first element of the nested table. Without this statement, the script causes the following error:

```
DECLARE
*
ERROR at line 1:
ORA-06533: Subscript beyond count
ORA-06512: at line 20
```

When run, this script produces output identical to the original example:

```
table_tab2(1)(1): 1
table_tab2(1)(2): 2
table_tab2(1)(3): 3
table_tab2(2)(1): 3
table_tab2(2)(2): 2
table_tab2(2)(3): 1

PL/SQL procedure successfully completed.
```

▼ TRY IT YOURSELF

In this chapter, you've learned about collections and multilevel collections. Here are some projects that will help you test the depth of your understanding.

1) Create the following script: Create an associative array, and populate it with the instructor's full name. In other words, each row of the associative array should contain the first name, middle initial, and last name. Display this information on the screen.

2) Modify the script you just created. Instead of using an associative array, use a varray.

3) Modify the script you just created. Create an additional varray, and populate it with unique course numbers for the courses that each instructor teaches. Display the instructor's name and the list of courses he or she teaches.

4) Find and explain the errors in the following script:

```
DECLARE
    TYPE varray_type1 IS VARRAY(7) OF INTEGER;
    TYPE table_type2 IS TABLE OF varray_type1 INDEX BY
        BINARY_INTEGER;

    varray1 varray_type1 := varray_type1(1, 2, 3);
    table2 table_type2 := table_type2(varray1,
                                      varray_type1(8, 9, 0));

BEGIN
    DBMS_OUTPUT.PUT_LINE ('table2(1)(2): '||table2(1)(2));

    FOR i IN 1..10 LOOP
        varray1.EXTEND;
        varray1(i) := i;
        DBMS_OUTPUT.PUT_LINE ('varray1('||i||'): '||varray1(i));
    END LOOP;
END;
```

The projects in this section are meant to have you use all the skills you have acquired throughout this chapter. The answers to these projects can be found in Appendix D and on this book's companion Web site. Visit the Web site periodically to share and discuss your answers.

CHAPTER 16

Records

CHAPTER OBJECTIVES

In this chapter, you will learn about

- ▶ Record types
- ▶ Nested records
- ▶ Collections of records

Chapter 11, "Introduction to Cursors," introduced the concept of a record type. You have learned that a record is a composite data structure that allows you to combine various yet related data into a logical unit. You have also learned that PL/SQL supports three kinds of record types: table-based, cursor-based, and user-defined. In this chapter, you will revisit table-based and cursor-based record types and learn about user-defined record types. In addition, you will learn about records that contain collections and other records (called nested records) and collections of records.

LAB 16.1
Record Types

LAB OBJECTIVES

After completing this lab, you will be able to

▶ Use table-based and cursor-based records
▶ Use user-defined records

A record structure is somewhat similar to a row of a database table. Each data item is stored in a field with its own name and datatype. For example, suppose you have various data about a company, such as its name, address, and number of employees. A record containing a field for each of these items allows you to treat the company as a logical unit, making it easier to organize and represent the company's information.

TABLE-BASED AND CURSOR-BASED RECORDS

The %ROWTYPE attribute enables you to create table-based and cursor-based records. It is similar to the %TYPE attribute that is used to define scalar variables. Consider the following example of a table-based record:

FOR EXAMPLE

```
DECLARE
   course_rec course%ROWTYPE;
BEGIN
   SELECT *
     INTO course_rec
     FROM course
    WHERE course_no = 25;

   DBMS_OUTPUT.PUT_LINE ('Course No: '||course_rec.course_no);
   DBMS_OUTPUT.PUT_LINE ('Course Description: '||
      course_rec.description);
   DBMS_OUTPUT.PUT_LINE ('Prerequisite: '||
      course_rec.prerequisite);
END;
```

The course_rec record has the same structure as a row from the COURSE table. As a result, there is no need to reference individual record fields when the SELECT INTO statement populates the course_rec record. However, note that a record does not have a value of its own;

rather, each individual field holds a value. Therefore, to display record information on the screen, individual fields are referenced using dot notation, as shown in the DBMS_OUTPUT. PUT_LINE statements.

When run, this example produces the following output:

```
Course No: 25
Course Description: Intro to Programming
Prerequisite: 140

PL/SQL procedure successfully completed.
```

WATCH OUT!

As mentioned previously, a record does not have a value of its own. For this reason, you cannot test records for nullity, equality, or inequality. In other words, the statements

```
IF course_rec IS NULL THEN ...
IF course_rec1 = course_rec2 THEN ...
```

are illegal and will cause syntax errors.

Next, consider an example of a cursor-based record:

FOR EXAMPLE

```
DECLARE
   CURSOR student_cur IS
      SELECT first_name, last_name, registration_date
        FROM student
       WHERE rownum <= 4;

   student_rec student_cur%ROWTYPE;
BEGIN
   OPEN student_cur;
   LOOP
      FETCH student_cur INTO student_rec;
      EXIT WHEN student_cur%NOTFOUND;

      DBMS_OUTPUT.PUT_LINE ('Name: '||
         student_rec.first_name||' '||student_rec.last_name);
      DBMS_OUTPUT.PUT_LINE ('Registration Date: '||
         student_rec.registration_date);
   END LOOP;
END;
```

The student_rec record has the same structure as the rows returned by the STUDENT_CUR cursor. As a result, similar to the previous example, there is no need to reference individual fields when data is fetched from the cursor to the record.

When run, this example produces the following output:

```
Name: Austin V. Cadet
Registration Date: 17-FEB-03
Name: Frank M. Orent
Registration Date: 17-FEB-03
Name: Yvonne Winnicki
Registration Date: 17-FEB-03
Name: Mike Madej
Registration Date: 17-FEB-03

PL/SQL procedure successfully completed.
```

Note that because a cursor-based record is defined based on the rows returned by a cursor's select statement, its declaration must be preceded by a cursor declaration. In other words, *a cursor-based record is dependent on a particular cursor and cannot be declared before its cursor.*

Consider a modified version of the preceding example (changes are shown in bold). The cursor-based record variable is declared before the cursor. As a result, when run, this example causes a syntax error.

FOR EXAMPLE

```
DECLARE
   student_rec student_cur%ROWTYPE;

   CURSOR student_cur IS
      SELECT first_name, last_name, registration_date
      FROM student
      WHERE rownum <= 4;

BEGIN
   OPEN student_cur;
   LOOP
      FETCH student_cur INTO student_rec;
      EXIT WHEN student_cur%NOTFOUND;

      DBMS_OUTPUT.PUT_LINE ('Name: '||
         student_rec.first_name||' '||student_rec.last_name);
      DBMS_OUTPUT.PUT_LINE ('Registration Date: '||
         student_rec.registration_date);
   END LOOP;
END;
```

When run, the example produces the following output:

```
        student_rec student_cur%ROWTYPE;
              *
ERROR at line 2:
ORA-06550: line 2, column 16:
```

```
PLS-00320: the declaration of the type of this expression is
           incomplete or malformed
ORA-06550: line 2, column 16:
PL/SQL: Item ignored
ORA-06550: line 12, column 30:
PLS-00320: the declaration of the type of this expression is
           incomplete or malformed
ORA-06550: line 12, column 7:
PL/SQL: SQL Statement ignored
ORA-06550: line 16, column 10:
PLS-00320: the declaration of the type of this expression is
           incomplete or malformed
ORA-06550: line 15, column 7:
PL/SQL: Statement ignored
ORA-06550: line 17, column 52:
PLS-00320: the declaration of the type of this expression is
           incomplete or malformed
ORA-06550: line 17, column 7:
PL/SQL: Statement ignored
```

USER-DEFINED RECORDS

So far, you have seen how to create records based on a table or cursor. However, you may need to create a record that is not based on any table or any one cursor. For such situations, PL/SQL provides a user-defined record type that gives you complete control over the record structure.

The general syntax for creating a user-defined record is as follows (the reserved words and phrases in brackets are optional):

```
TYPE type_name IS RECORD
   (field_name1 datatype1 [NOT NULL] [ := DEFAULT EXPRESSION],
    field_name2 datatype2 [NOT NULL] [ := DEFAULT EXPRESSION],
    ...
    field_nameN datatypeN [NOT NULL] [ := DEFAULT EXPRESSION]);

record_name TYPE_NAME;
```

First, a record structure is defined using the TYPE statement, where *type_name* is the name of the record type that is used in the second step to declare the actual record. Enclosed in parentheses are declarations of each record field, with its name and datatype. You may also specify a NOT NULL constraint and/or assign a default value. Second, the actual record is declared based on the type specified in the preceding step. Consider the following example:

FOR EXAMPLE

```
DECLARE
   TYPE time_rec_type IS RECORD
      (curr_date DATE,
       curr_day  VARCHAR2(12),
       curr_time VARCHAR2(8) := '00:00:00');
```

FOR EXAMPLE (continued)

```
   time_rec TIME_REC_TYPE;
BEGIN
   SELECT sysdate
     INTO time_rec.curr_date
     FROM dual;

   time_rec.curr_day  := TO_CHAR(time_rec.curr_date, 'DAY');
   time_rec.curr_time := TO_CHAR(time_rec.curr_date, 'HH24:MI:SS');

   DBMS_OUTPUT.PUT_LINE ('Date: '||time_rec.curr_date);
   DBMS_OUTPUT.PUT_LINE ('Day:  '||time_rec.curr_day);
   DBMS_OUTPUT.PUT_LINE ('Time: '||time_rec.curr_time);
END;
```

In this example, `time_rec_type` is a user-defined record type that contains three fields. Notice that the last field, `curr_time`, has been initialized to a particular value. `time_rec` is a user-defined record based on `time_rec_type`. Notice that, in contrast to the previous examples, each record field is assigned a value individually. When run, the script produces the following output:

```
   Date: 30-MAR-08
   Day: SUNDAY
   Time: 18:12:59

   PL/SQL procedure successfully completed.
```

As mentioned, when declaring a record type, you may specify a NOT NULL constraint for individual fields. It is important to note that such fields must be initialized. Consider an example that causes a syntax error because a record field has not been initialized after a NOT NULL constraint has been defined on it:

FOR EXAMPLE

```
DECLARE
   TYPE sample_type IS RECORD
      (field1 NUMBER(3),
       field2 VARCHAR2(3) NOT NULL);

   sample_rec sample_type;

BEGIN
   sample_rec.field1 := 10;
   sample_rec.field2 := 'ABC';

   DBMS_OUTPUT.PUT_LINE ('sample_rec.field1 = '||sample_rec.field1);
   DBMS_OUTPUT.PUT_LINE ('sample_rec.field2 = '||sample_rec.field2);
END;
```

This example produces the following output:

```
field2 VARCHAR2(3) NOT NULL);
          *
ERROR at line 4:
ORA-06550: line 4, column 8:
PLS-00218: a variable declared NOT NULL must have an initialization
            assignment
```

Next, consider the correct version of the preceding example and its output:

FOR EXAMPLE

```
DECLARE
   TYPE sample_type IS RECORD
      (field1 NUMBER(3),
       -- initialize a NOT NULL field
       field2 VARCHAR2(3) NOT NULL := 'ABC');

   sample_rec sample_type;

BEGIN
   sample_rec.field1 := 10;

   DBMS_OUTPUT.PUT_LINE ('sample_rec.field1 = '||sample_rec.field1);
   DBMS_OUTPUT.PUT_LINE ('sample_rec.field2 = '||sample_rec.field2);
END;
```

The output is as follows:

```
sample_rec.field1 = 10
sample_rec.field2 = ABC

PL/SQL procedure successfully completed.
```

RECORD COMPATIBILITY

You have seen that a record is defined by its name, structure, and type. However, it is important to realize that two records may have the same structure yet be of a different type. As a result, certain restrictions apply to the operations between different record types. Consider the following example:

FOR EXAMPLE

```
DECLARE
   TYPE name_type1 IS RECORD
      (first_name VARCHAR2(15),
       last_name  VARCHAR2(30));
```

FOR EXAMPLE (continued)

```
   TYPE name_type2 IS RECORD
      (first_name VARCHAR2(15),
       last_name  VARCHAR2(30));

   name_rec1 name_type1;
   name_rec2 name_type2;
BEGIN
   name_rec1.first_name := 'John';
   name_rec1.last_name  := 'Smith';
   name_rec2 := name_rec1; -- illegal assignment
END;
```

In this example, both records have the same structure; however, each record is of a different type. As a result, these records are incompatible with each other on the record level. In other words, an aggregate assignment statement causes an error:

```
       name_rec2 := name_rec1; -- illegal assignment
                  *
   ERROR at line 15:
   ORA-06550: line 15, column 17:
   PLS-00382: expression is of wrong type
   ORA-06550: line 15, column 4:
   PL/SQL: Statement ignored
```

To assign name_rec1 to name_rec2, you can assign each field of name_rec1 to the corresponding field of name_rec2, or you can declare name_rec2 so that it has the same datatype as name_rec1, as follows:

FOR EXAMPLE

```
DECLARE
   TYPE name_type1 IS RECORD
      (first_name VARCHAR2(15),
       last_name  VARCHAR2(30));

   name_rec1 name_type1;
   name_rec2 name_type1;
BEGIN
   name_rec1.first_name := 'John';
   name_rec1.last_name  := 'Smith';
   name_rec2 := name_rec1; -- no longer illegal assignment
END;
```

It is important to note that the assignment restriction just mentioned applies to user-defined records. In other words, *you can assign a table-based or cursor-based record to a user-defined record as long as they have the same structure.* Consider the following example:

FOR EXAMPLE

```
DECLARE
   CURSOR course_cur IS
      SELECT *
        FROM course
       WHERE rownum <= 4;

   TYPE course_type IS RECORD
      (course_no       NUMBER(38),
       description     VARCHAR2(50),
       cost            NUMBER(9,2),
       prerequisite    NUMBER(8),
       created_by      VARCHAR2(30),
       created_date    DATE,
       modified_by     VARCHAR2(30),
       modified_date   DATE);

   course_rec1 course%ROWTYPE;        -- table-based record
   course_rec2 course_cur%ROWTYPE;    -- cursor-based record
   course_rec3 course_type;           -- user-defined record
BEGIN
   -- Populate table-based record
   SELECT *
     INTO course_rec1
     FROM course
    WHERE course_no = 10;

   -- Populate cursor-based record
   OPEN course_cur;
   LOOP
      FETCH course_cur INTO course_rec2;
      EXIT WHEN course_cur%NOTFOUND;
   END LOOP;

   course_rec1 := course_rec2;
   course_rec3 := course_rec2;
END;
```

In this example, each record is a different type; however, they are compatible with each other because all records have the same structure. As a result, this example does not cause any syntax errors.

▼ LAB 16.1 EXERCISES

This section provides exercises and suggested answers, with discussion related to how those answers resulted. The most important thing to realize is whether your answer works. You should figure out the implications of the answers and what the effects are of any different answers you may come up with.

16.1.1 Use Table-Based and Cursor-Based Records

In this exercise, you will learn more about table-based and cursor-based records.

Create the following PL/SQL script:

```
-- ch16_1a.sql, version 1.0
SET SERVEROUTPUT ON
DECLARE
    zip_rec zipcode%ROWTYPE;

BEGIN
    SELECT *
      INTO zip_rec
      FROM zipcode
     WHERE rownum < 2;
END;
```

Answer the following questions, and complete the following tasks:

A) Explain the preceding script.

ANSWER: The declaration portion of the script contains a declaration of the table-based record, `zip_rec`, that has the same structure as a row from the ZIPCODE table. The executable portion of the script populates the `zip_rec` record using the SELECT INTO statement with a row from the ZIPCODE table. Notice that a restriction applied to the ROWNUM enforces the SELECT INTO statement and always returns a random single row. As mentioned earlier, there is no need to reference individual record fields when the SELECT INTO statement populates the `zip_rec` record, because `zip_rec` has a structure identical to a row of the ZIPCODE table.

B) Modify the script so that `zip_rec` data is displayed on the screen.

ANSWER: The script should look similar to the following. Changes are shown in bold.

```
-- ch16_1b.sql, version 2.0
SET SERVEROUTPUT ON
DECLARE
    zip_rec zipcode%ROWTYPE;

BEGIN
    SELECT *
      INTO zip_rec
      FROM zipcode
     WHERE rownum < 2;

    DBMS_OUTPUT.PUT_LINE ('Zip:           '||zip_rec.zip);
    DBMS_OUTPUT.PUT_LINE ('City:          '||zip_rec.city);
    DBMS_OUTPUT.PUT_LINE ('State:         '||zip_rec.state);
    DBMS_OUTPUT.PUT_LINE ('Created By:    '||zip_rec.created_by);
    DBMS_OUTPUT.PUT_LINE ('Created Date:  '||zip_rec.created_date);
    DBMS_OUTPUT.PUT_LINE ('Modified By:   '||zip_rec.modified_by);
    DBMS_OUTPUT.PUT_LINE ('Modified Date: '||zip_rec.modified_date);
END;
```

When run, this version of the script produces the following output:

```
Zip:            00914
City:           Santurce
State:          PR
Created By:     AMORRISO
Created Date:   03-AUG-07
Modified By:    ARISCHER
Modified Date: 24-NOV-07


PL/SQL procedure successfully completed.
```

C) Modify the script created in the preceding exercise (ch16_1b.sql) so that zip_rec is defined as a cursor-based record.

ANSWER: The script should look similar to the following. Changes are shown in bold.

```
-- ch16_1c.sql, version 3.0
SET SERVEROUTPUT ON
DECLARE
    CURSOR zip_cur IS
        SELECT *
          FROM zipcode
         WHERE rownum < 4;

    zip_rec zip_cur%ROWTYPE;
BEGIN
    OPEN zip_cur;
    LOOP
        FETCH zip_cur INTO zip_rec;
        EXIT WHEN zip_cur%NOTFOUND;

        DBMS_OUTPUT.PUT_LINE ('Zip:            '||zip_rec.zip);
        DBMS_OUTPUT.PUT_LINE ('City:           '||zip_rec.city);
        DBMS_OUTPUT.PUT_LINE ('State:          '||zip_rec.state);
        DBMS_OUTPUT.PUT_LINE ('Created By:     '||zip_rec.created_by);
        DBMS_OUTPUT.PUT_LINE ('Created Date:
                              '||zip_rec.created_date);
        DBMS_OUTPUT.PUT_LINE ('Modified By:
                              '||zip_rec.modified_by);
        DBMS_OUTPUT.PUT_LINE ('Modified Date:
                              '||zip_rec.modified_date);
    END LOOP;
END;
```

The declaration portion of the script contains a definition of the ZIP_CUR cursor that returns three records from the ZIPCODE table. In this case, the number of records returned by the cursor has been chosen for one reason only—so that the cursor loop iterates more than once. Next, it contains the definition of the cursor-based record, zip_rec.

The executable portion of the script populates the zip_rec record and displays its data on the screen using the simple cursor loop.

This version of the script produces the following output:

```
Zip:           00914
City:          Santurce
State:         PR
Created By:    AMORRISO
Created Date:  03-AUG-07
Modified By:   ARISCHER
Modified Date: 24-NOV-07
Zip:           01247
City:          North Adams
State:         MA
Created By:    AMORRISO
Created Date:  03-AUG-07
Modified By:   ARISCHER
Modified Date: 24-NOV-07
Zip:           02124
City:          Dorchester
State:         MA
Created By:    AMORRISO
Created Date:  03-AUG-07
Modified By:   ARISCHER
Modified Date: 24-NOV-07

PL/SQL procedure successfully completed.
```

D) Modify the script created in the preceding exercise (ch16_1c.sql). Change the structure of the zip_rec record so that it contains the total number of students in a given city, state, and zip code. Do not include audit columns such as CREATED_BY and CREATED_DATE in the record structure.

ANSWER: The script should look similar to the following. All changes are shown in bold.

```
-- ch16_1d.sql, version 4.0
SET SERVEROUTPUT ON SIZE 40000
DECLARE
   CURSOR zip_cur IS
      SELECT city, state, z.zip, COUNT(*) students
        FROM zipcode z, student s
       WHERE z.zip = s.zip
       GROUP BY city, state, z.zip;

   zip_rec zip_cur%ROWTYPE;
BEGIN
   OPEN zip_cur;
   LOOP
      FETCH zip_cur INTO zip_rec;
      EXIT WHEN zip_cur%NOTFOUND;

      DBMS_OUTPUT.PUT_LINE ('Zip:      '||zip_rec.zip);
      DBMS_OUTPUT.PUT_LINE ('City:     '||zip_rec.city);
      DBMS_OUTPUT.PUT_LINE ('State:    '||zip_rec.state);
```

```
      DBMS_OUTPUT.PUT_LINE ('Students: '||zip_rec.students);
   END LOOP;
END;
```

In this example, the cursor SELECT statement has been modified so that it returns the total number of students for a given city, state, and zip code. Notice that the ROWNUM restriction has been removed so that the total number of students is calculated correctly. As a result, the buffer size has been changed from 2,000 to 40,000 so that the script does not cause a buffer overflow error.

Consider the partial output retuned by this example:

```
Zip:       07401
City:      Allendale
State:     NJ
Students: 1
Zip:       11373
City:      Amherst
State:     NY
Students: 6
Zip:       48104
City:      Ann Arbor
State:     MI
Students: 1
Zip:       11102
City:      Astoria
State:     NY
Students: 1
Zip:       11105
City:      Astoria
State:     NY
Students: 2
Zip:       11510
City:      Baldwin
State:     NY
Students: 1
Zip:       11360
City:      Bayside
State:     NY
Students: 1
...


PL/SQL procedure successfully completed.
```

Next, assume that, just like in the previous version of the script (ch16_1c.sql), you want to display only four records on the screen. This can be achieved as follows:

```
-- ch16_1e.sql, version 5.0
SET SERVEROUTPUT ON
DECLARE
   CURSOR zip_cur IS
      SELECT city, state, z.zip, COUNT(*) students
        FROM zipcode z, student s
```

```
      WHERE z.zip = s.zip
      GROUP BY city, state, z.zip;


   zip_rec zip_cur%ROWTYPE;
   v_counter INTEGER := 0;
BEGIN
   OPEN zip_cur;
   LOOP
      FETCH zip_cur INTO zip_rec;
      EXIT WHEN zip_cur%NOTFOUND;

      v_counter := v_counter + 1;

      IF v_counter <= 4 THEN
         DBMS_OUTPUT.PUT_LINE ('Zip:      '||zip_rec.zip);
         DBMS_OUTPUT.PUT_LINE ('City:     '||zip_rec.city);
         DBMS_OUTPUT.PUT_LINE ('State:    '||zip_rec.state);
         DBMS_OUTPUT.PUT_LINE ('Students: '||zip_rec.students);
      END IF;
   END LOOP;
END;
```

The SELECT statement defined in the cursor is supported by multiple versions of Oracle. As mentioned previously, starting with 9i, Oracle supports the new ANSI 1999 SQL standard, and the SELECT statement can be modified as follows according to this new standard:

```
SELECT city, state, z.zip, COUNT(*) students
  FROM zipcode z
  JOIN student s
    ON s.zip = z.zip
GROUP BY city, state, z.zip;
```

This SELECT statement uses the ON syntax to specify the join condition between two tables. This type of join becomes especially useful when the columns participating in the join do not have the same name.

BY THE WAY

You will find detailed explanations and examples of the statements using the new ANSI 1999 SQL standard in Appendix C and in the Oracle help. Throughout this book we try to provide examples illustrating both standards; however, our main focus is on PL/SQL features rather than SQL.

16.1.2 **Use User-Defined Records**

In this exercise, you learn more about user-defined records.

Create the following PL/SQL script:

```
-- ch16_2a.sql, version 1.0
SET SERVEROUTPUT ON
DECLARE
   CURSOR zip_cur IS
      SELECT zip, COUNT(*) students
```

```
            FROM student
        GROUP BY zip;

    TYPE zip_info_type IS RECORD
        (zip_code VARCHAR2(5),
         students INTEGER);

    zip_info_rec zip_info_type;
BEGIN
    FOR zip_rec IN zip_cur LOOP
        zip_info_rec.zip_code := zip_rec.zip;
        zip_info_rec.students := zip_rec.students;
    END LOOP;
END;
```

Answer the following questions, and complete the following tasks:

A) Explain the preceding script.

ANSWER: The declaration portion of the script contains the ZIP_CUR cursor, which returns the total number of students corresponding to a particular zip code. Next, it contains the declaration of the user-defined record type, `zip_info_type`, which has two fields, and the actual user-defined record, `zip_info_rec`. The executable portion of the script populates the `zip_info_rec` record using the cursor FOR loop. As mentioned earlier, because `zip_info_rec` is a user-defined record, each record field is assigned a value individually.

B) Modify the script so that `zip_info_rec` data is displayed on the screen for only the first five records returned by the ZIP_CUR cursor.

ANSWER: The script should look similar to the following. Changes are shown in bold.

```
-- ch16_2b.sql, version 2.0
SET SERVEROUTPUT ON
DECLARE
    CURSOR zip_cur IS
        SELECT zip, COUNT(*) students
            FROM student
        GROUP BY zip;

    TYPE zip_info_type IS RECORD
        (zip_code VARCHAR2(5),
         students INTEGER);

    zip_info_rec zip_info_type;
    v_counter INTEGER := 0;
BEGIN
    FOR zip_rec IN zip_cur LOOP
        zip_info_rec.zip_code := zip_rec.zip;
        zip_info_rec.students := zip_rec.students;

        v_counter := v_counter + 1;
        IF v_counter <= 5 THEN
            DBMS_OUTPUT.PUT_LINE ('Zip Code: '||zip_info_rec.zip_code);
```

```
            DBMS_OUTPUT.PUT_LINE ('Students: '||zip_info_rec.students);
            DBMS_OUTPUT.PUT_LINE ('--------------------');
        END IF;
    END LOOP;
END;
```

To display information for the first five records returned by the ZIP_CUR cursor, a new variable, v_counter, is declared. For each iteration of the loop, the value of this variable is incremented by 1. As long as the value of v_counter is less than or equal to 5, the data of the zip_info_rec record is displayed on the screen.

When run, this script produces the following output:

```
Zip Code: 01247
Students: 1
--------------------
Zip Code: 02124
Students: 1
--------------------
Zip Code: 02155
Students: 1
--------------------
Zip Code: 02189
Students: 1
--------------------
Zip Code: 02563
Students: 1
--------------------

PL/SQL procedure successfully completed.
```

C) Modify the script created in the preceding exercise (ch16_2b.sql). Change the structure of the zip_info_rec record so that it also contains the total number of instructors for a given zip code. Populate this new record, and display its data on the screen for the first five records returned by the ZIP_CUR cursor.

ANSWER: The script should look similar to the following. Changes are shown in bold.

```
-- ch16_2c.sql, version 3.0
SET SERVEROUTPUT ON
DECLARE
    CURSOR zip_cur IS
        SELECT zip
          FROM zipcode
         WHERE ROWNUM <= 5;

    TYPE zip_info_type IS RECORD
        (zip_code    VARCHAR2(5),
         students    INTEGER,
         instructors INTEGER);

    zip_info_rec zip_info_type;
```

```
BEGIN
    FOR zip_rec IN zip_cur LOOP
        zip_info_rec.zip_code := zip_rec.zip;

        SELECT COUNT(*)
          INTO zip_info_rec.students
          FROM student
         WHERE zip = zip_info_rec.zip_code;

        SELECT COUNT(*)
          INTO zip_info_rec.instructors
          FROM instructor
         WHERE zip = zip_info_rec.zip_code;

        DBMS_OUTPUT.PUT_LINE ('Zip Code:      '||zip_info_rec.zip_code);
        DBMS_OUTPUT.PUT_LINE ('Students:      '||zip_info_rec.students);
        DBMS_OUTPUT.PUT_LINE ('Instructors:
                              '||zip_info_rec.instructors);
        DBMS_OUTPUT.PUT_LINE ('-------------------');
    END LOOP;
END;
```

Consider the changes applied to this version of the script. In the declaration portion of the script, the cursor SELECT statement has changed so that records are retrieved from the ZIPCODE table rather than the STUDENT table. This change allows you to accurately see the total number of students and instructors in a particular zip code. In addition, because the cursor SELECT statement does not have a group function, the ROWNUM restriction is listed in the WHERE clause so that only the first five records are returned. The structure of the user-defined record type, `zip_info_type`, has changed so that the total number of instructors for a given zip code is stored in the `instructors` field.

In the executable portion of the script are two SELECT INTO statements that populate the `zip_info_rec.students` and `zip_info_rec.instructors` fields, respectively.

When run, this example produces the following output:

```
Zip Code:     00914
Students:     0
Instructors: 0
-------------------
Zip Code:     01247
Students:     1
Instructors: 0
-------------------
Zip Code:     02124
Students:     1
Instructors: 0
-------------------
Zip Code:     02155
Students:     1
Instructors: 0
-------------------
```

```
Zip Code:     02189
Students:    1
Instructors: 0
-------------------
```

PL/SQL procedure successfully completed.

Consider another version of the same script. Here, instead of using two SELECT INTO statements to calculate the total number of students and instructors in a particular zip code, the cursor SELECT statement contains outer joins:

```
-- ch16_2d.sql, version 4.0
SET SERVEROUTPUT ON
DECLARE
   CURSOR zip_cur IS
      SELECT z.zip, COUNT(student_id) students,
             COUNT(instructor_id) instructors
        FROM zipcode z, student s, instructor i
       WHERE z.zip = s.zip (+)
         AND z.zip = i.zip (+)
       GROUP BY z.zip;

   TYPE zip_info_type IS RECORD
      (zip_code    VARCHAR2(5),
       students    INTEGER,
       instructors INTEGER);

   zip_info_rec zip_info_type;
   v_counter INTEGER := 0;
BEGIN
   FOR zip_rec IN zip_cur LOOP
      zip_info_rec.zip_code    := zip_rec.zip;
      zip_info_rec.students    := zip_rec.students;
      zip_info_rec.instructors := zip_rec.instructors;

      v_counter := v_counter + 1;
      IF v_counter <= 5 THEN
         DBMS_OUTPUT.PUT_LINE ('Zip Code:
                              '||zip_info_rec.zip_code);
         DBMS_OUTPUT.PUT_LINE ('Students:
                              '||zip_info_rec.students);
         DBMS_OUTPUT.PUT_LINE ('Instructors: '||
            zip_info_rec.instructors);
         DBMS_OUTPUT.PUT_LINE ('-------------------');
      END IF;
   END LOOP;
END;
```

LAB 16.2
Nested Records

LAB OBJECTIVE

After completing this lab, you will be able to

▶ Use nested records

As mentioned in the introduction to this chapter, PL/SQL allows you to define nested records. These are records that contain other records and collections. The record that contains a nested record or collection is called an enclosing record.

Consider the following code fragment:

FOR EXAMPLE

```
DECLARE
   TYPE name_type IS RECORD
      (first_name VARCHAR2(15),
       last_name  VARCHAR2(30));

   TYPE person_type IS
      (name     name_type,
       street VARCHAR2(50),
       city   VARCHAR2(25),
       state  VARCHAR2(2),
       zip    VARCHAR2(5));

   person_rec person_type;
```

This code fragment contains two user-defined record types. The second user-defined record type, `person_type`, is a nested record type because its field name is a record of the `name_type` type.

Next, consider the complete version of the preceding example:

FOR EXAMPLE

```
DECLARE
   TYPE name_type IS RECORD
      (first_name VARCHAR2(15),
       last_name  VARCHAR2(30));
```

FOR EXAMPLE (continued)

```
   TYPE person_type IS RECORD
      (name    name_type,
       street VARCHAR2(50),
       city   VARCHAR2(25),
       state  VARCHAR2(2),
       zip    VARCHAR2(5));

   person_rec person_type;

BEGIN
   SELECT first_name, last_name, street_address, city, state, zip
     INTO person_rec.name.first_name, person_rec.name.last_name,
          person_rec.street, person_rec.city, person_rec.state,
          person_rec.zip
     FROM student
     JOIN zipcode USING (zip)
    WHERE rownum < 2;

   DBMS_OUTPUT.PUT_LINE ('Name:    '||
      person_rec.name.first_name||' '||person_rec.name.last_name);
   DBMS_OUTPUT.PUT_LINE ('Street: '||person_rec.street);
   DBMS_OUTPUT.PUT_LINE ('City:    '||person_rec.city);
   DBMS_OUTPUT.PUT_LINE ('State:   '||person_rec.state);
   DBMS_OUTPUT.PUT_LINE ('Zip:     '||person_rec.zip);
END;
```

In this example, the person_rec record is a user-defined nested record. Therefore, to reference its field name that is a record with two fields, the following syntax is used:

```
    enclosing_record.(nested_record or nested_collection).field_name
```

In this case, person_rec is the enclosing record because it contains the name record as one of its fields while the name record is nested in the person_rec record.

This example produces the following output:

```
   Name:    James E. Norman
   Street: PO Box 809 Curran Hwy
   City:    North Adams
   State:   MA
   Zip:     01247

   PL/SQL procedure successfully completed.
```

▼ LAB 16.2 EXERCISES

This section provides exercises and suggested answers, with discussion related to how those answers resulted. The most important thing to realize is whether your answer works. You should figure out the implications of the answers and what the effects are of any different answers you may come up with.

16.2.1 **Use Nested Records**

In this exercise, you learn more about nested records.

Create the following PL/SQL script:

```
-- ch16_3a.sql, version 1.0
SET SERVEROUTPUT ON
DECLARE
    TYPE last_name_type IS TABLE OF student.last_name%TYPE
        INDEX BY BINARY_INTEGER;

    TYPE zip_info_type IS RECORD
        (zip          VARCHAR2(5),
        last_name_tab last_name_type);

    CURSOR name_cur (p_zip VARCHAR2) IS
        SELECT last_name
          FROM student
         WHERE zip = p_zip;

    zip_info_rec zip_info_type;
    v_zip         VARCHAR2(5) := '&sv_zip';
    v_counter     INTEGER := 0;
BEGIN
    zip_info_rec.zip := v_zip;

    FOR name_rec IN name_cur (v_zip) LOOP
        v_counter := v_counter + 1;
        zip_info_rec.last_name_tab(v_counter) := name_rec.last_name;
    END LOOP;
END;
```

Answer the following questions, and complete the following tasks:

A) Explain the preceding script.

ANSWER: The declaration portion of the script contains associative array (index-by table) type (`last_name_type`), record type (`zip_info_type`), and nested-user-defined record (`zip_info_rec`) declarations. The field, `last_name_tab`, of the `zip_info_rec` is an associative array that is populated with the help of the cursor, NAME_CUR. In addition, the declaration portion also contains two variables, `v_zip` and `v_counter`. The variable `v_zip` is used to store the incoming value of the zip code provided at runtime. The variable `v_counter` is used to populate the associative array, `last_name_tab`. The executable portion of the script assigns values to the individual record fields, `zip` and `last_name_tab`. As mentioned previously, the `last_name_tab` is an associative array, and it is populated using a cursor FOR loop.

B) Modify the script so that `zip_info_rec` data is displayed on the screen. Make sure that a value of the zip code is displayed only once. Provide the value of 11368 when running the script.

ANSWER: The script should look similar to the following. Changes are shown in bold.

```
-- ch16_3b.sql, version 2.0
SET SERVEROUTPUT ON
DECLARE
   TYPE last_name_type IS TABLE OF student.last_name%TYPE
      INDEX BY BINARY_INTEGER;

   TYPE zip_info_type IS RECORD
      (zip           VARCHAR2(5),
       last_name_tab last_name_type);

   CURSOR name_cur (p_zip VARCHAR2) IS
      SELECT last_name
        FROM student
       WHERE zip = p_zip;

   zip_info_rec zip_info_type;
   v_zip        VARCHAR2(5) := '&sv_zip';
   v_counter    INTEGER := 0;
BEGIN
   zip_info_rec.zip := v_zip;
   DBMS_OUTPUT.PUT_LINE ('Zip: '||zip_info_rec.zip);

   FOR name_rec IN name_cur (v_zip) LOOP
      v_counter := v_counter + 1;
      zip_info_rec.last_name_tab(v_counter) := name_rec.last_name;

      DBMS_OUTPUT.PUT_LINE ('Names('||v_counter||'): '||
         zip_info_rec.last_name_tab(v_counter));
   END LOOP;
END;
```

To display the value of the zip code only once, the DBMS_OUTPUT.PUT_LINE statement

```
DBMS_OUTPUT.PUT_LINE ('Zip: '||zip_info_rec.zip);
```

is placed outside the loop.

When run, this script produces the following output:

```
Enter value for sv_zip: 11368
old  15:    v_zip VARCHAR2(5) := '&sv_zip';
new  15:    v_zip VARCHAR2(5) := '11368';
Zip: 11368
Names(1): Lasseter
Names(2): Miller
Names(3): Boyd
Names(4): Griffen
Names(5): Hutheesing
Names(6): Chatman

PL/SQL procedure successfully completed.
```

C) Modify the script created in the preceding exercise (ch16_3b.sql). Instead of providing a value for a zip code at runtime, populate using the cursor FOR loop. The SELECT statement associated with the new cursor should return zip codes that have more than one student in them.

ANSWER: The script should look similar to the following. Changes are shown in bold.

```
-- ch16_3c.sql, version 3.0
SET SERVEROUTPUT ON SIZE 20000
DECLARE
    TYPE last_name_type IS TABLE OF student.last_name%TYPE
        INDEX BY BINARY_INTEGER;

    TYPE zip_info_type IS RECORD
        (zip           VARCHAR2(5),
        last_name_tab last_name_type);

    CURSOR zip_cur IS
        SELECT zip, COUNT(*)
          FROM student
        GROUP BY zip
        HAVING COUNT(*) > 1;

    CURSOR name_cur (p_zip VARCHAR2) IS
        SELECT last_name
          FROM student
         WHERE zip = p_zip;

    zip_info_rec zip_info_type;
    v_counter      INTEGER;
BEGIN
    FOR zip_rec IN zip_cur LOOP
        zip_info_rec.zip := zip_rec.zip;
        DBMS_OUTPUT.PUT_LINE ('Zip: '||zip_info_rec.zip);

        v_counter := 0;
        FOR name_rec IN name_cur (zip_info_rec.zip) LOOP
            v_counter := v_counter + 1;
            zip_info_rec.last_name_tab(v_counter) :=
              name_rec.last_name;

            DBMS_OUTPUT.PUT_LINE ('Names('||v_counter||'): '||
                zip_info_rec.last_name_tab(v_counter));
        END LOOP;
        DBMS_OUTPUT.PUT_LINE ('----------');
    END LOOP;
END;
```

In the preceding script, you declare a new cursor called `zip_cur`. This cursor returns zip codes that have more than one student in them. Next, in the body of the script, you use nested cursors to populate the `last_name_tab` associative array for each value of the zip code. First, the outer cursor FOR loop populates the `zip` field of the `zip_info_rec` and displays its value on the screen. Then it passes the `zip` field as a parameter to the inner cursor FOR loop that populates the `last_name_tab` table with last names of corresponding students.

Consider partial output from the preceding example:

```
Zip: 06820
Names(1): Scrittorale
Names(2): Padel
Names(3): Kiraly
-------------------
Zip: 06830
Names(1): Dennis
Names(2): Meshaj
Names(3): Dalvi
-------------------
Zip: 06880
Names(1): Miller
Names(2): Cheevens
-------------------
Zip: 06903
Names(1): Segall
Names(2): Annina
-------------------
Zip: 07003
Names(1): Wicelinski
Names(2): Intal
-------------------
Zip: 07010
Names(1): Lopez
Names(2): Mulroy
Names(3): Velasco
Names(4): Kelly
Names(5): Tucker
Names(6): Mithane
-------------------
...

PL/SQL procedure successfully completed.
```

LAB 16.3
Collections of Records

LAB OBJECTIVE

After completing this lab, you will be able to

▶ Use collections of records

In the previous lab you saw an example of a nested record in which one of the record fields was defined as an associative array. PL/SQL also lets you define a collection of records (such as an associative array whose element type is a cursor-based record, as shown in the following example).

FOR EXAMPLE

```
DECLARE
   CURSOR name_cur IS
      SELECT first_name, last_name
        FROM student
       WHERE ROWNUM <= 4;

   TYPE name_type IS TABLE OF name_cur%ROWTYPE
      INDEX BY BINARY_INTEGER;

   name_tab   name_type;
   v_counter INTEGER := 0;
BEGIN
   FOR name_rec IN name_cur LOOP
      v_counter := v_counter + 1;

      name_tab(v_counter).first_name := name_rec.first_name;
      name_tab(v_counter).last_name := name_rec.last_name;

      DBMS_OUTPUT.PUT_LINE('First Name('||v_counter||'): '||
         name_tab(v_counter).first_name);
      DBMS_OUTPUT.PUT_LINE('Last Name('||v_counter||'): '||
         name_tab(v_counter).last_name);
   END LOOP;
END;
```

In the declaration portion of this example, you define the name_cur cursor, which returns the first and last names of the first four students. Next, you define an associative array type whose element type is based on the cursor defined previously using the %ROWTYPE attribute. Then you define an associative array variable and the counter that is used later to reference individual rows of the associative array.

In the executable portion of the example, you populate the associative array and display its records on the screen. Consider the notation used in the example when referencing individual elements of the array:

```
name_tab(v_counter).first_name
```

and

```
name_tab(v_counter).last_name
```

Notice that to reference each row of the array, you use the counter variable, just like in all previous examples. However, because each row of this table is a record, you must also reference individual fields of the underlying record.

This example produces the following output:

```
First Name(1): Fred
Last Name(1): Crocitto
First Name(2): J.
Last Name(2): Landry
First Name(3): Laetia
Last Name(3): Enison
First Name(4): Angel
Last Name(4): Moskowitz

PL/SQL procedure successfully completed.
```

▼ LAB 16.3 EXERCISES

This section provides exercises and suggested answers, with discussion related to how those answers resulted. The most important thing to realize is whether your answer works. You should figure out the implications of the answers and what the effects are of any different answers you may come up with.

16.3.1 Use Collections of Records

In this exercise, you learn more about collections of records.

Complete the following tasks:

A) Modify the script used earlier in this lab. Instead of using an associative array, use a nested table.

ANSWER: The script should look similar to the following. Changes are shown in bold.

```
-- ch16_4a.sql, version 1.0
SET SERVEROUTPUT ON
DECLARE
   CURSOR name_cur IS
      SELECT first_name, last_name
```

```
      FROM student
      WHERE ROWNUM <= 4;

   TYPE name_type IS TABLE OF name_cur%ROWTYPE;

   name_tab name_type := name_type();
   v_counter INTEGER   := 0;
BEGIN
   FOR name_rec IN name_cur LOOP
      v_counter := v_counter + 1;
      name_tab.EXTEND;

      name_tab(v_counter).first_name := name_rec.first_name;
      name_tab(v_counter).last_name := name_rec.last_name;

      DBMS_OUTPUT.PUT_LINE('First Name('||v_counter||'): '||
         name_tab(v_counter).first_name);
      DBMS_OUTPUT.PUT_LINE('Last Name('||v_counter||'): '||
         name_tab(v_counter).last_name);
   END LOOP;
END;
```

In the preceding script, `name_tab` is declared as a nested table. As a result, at the time of its declaration, it is initialized. In other words, `name_tab` is empty but non-null. Furthermore, as soon as the `name_tab` table is initialized, its size must be increased before it can be populated with the next record.

B) Modify the script used earlier in this lab. Instead of using an associative array, use a varray.

ANSWER: The script should look similar to the following. Changes are shown in bold.

```
-- ch16_4b.sql, version 2.0
SET SERVEROUTPUT ON
DECLARE
   CURSOR name_cur IS
      SELECT first_name, last_name
        FROM student
       WHERE ROWNUM <= 4;

   TYPE name_type IS VARRAY(4) OF name_cur%ROWTYPE;

   name_tab name_type := name_type();
   v_counter INTEGER := 0;
BEGIN
   FOR name_rec IN name_cur LOOP
      v_counter := v_counter + 1;
      name_tab.EXTEND;

      name_tab(v_counter).first_name := name_rec.first_name;
      name_tab(v_counter).last_name := name_rec.last_name;

      DBMS_OUTPUT.PUT_LINE('First Name('||v_counter||'): '||
         name_tab(v_counter).first_name);
```

```
        DBMS_OUTPUT.PUT_LINE('Last Name('||v_counter||'): '||
            name_tab(v_counter).last_name);
    END LOOP;
END;
```

In this version of the script, `name_tab` is declared as a varray with four elements. As in the previous version, the collection is initialized and its size is incremented before it is populated with the new record.

Both scripts, ch16_4a.sql and ch16_4b.sql, produce output identical to the original example:

```
First Name(1): Fred
Last Name(1): Crocitto
First Name(2): J.
Last Name(2): Landry
First Name(3): Laetia
Last Name(3): Enison
First Name(4): Angel
Last Name(4): Moskowitz

PL/SQL procedure successfully completed.
```

C) Modify the script used at the beginning of this lab. Instead of using a cursor-based record, use a user-defined record. The new record should have three fields: `first_name`, `last_name`, and `enrollments`. The last field will contain the total number of courses in which a student is currently enrolled.

   ANSWER: The script should look similar to the following. Changes are shown in bold.

```
-- ch16_4c.sql, version 3.0
SET SERVEROUTPUT ON
DECLARE
    CURSOR name_cur IS
        SELECT first_name, last_name, COUNT(*) total
          FROM student
          JOIN enrollment USING (student_id)
        GROUP BY first_name, last_name;

    TYPE student_rec_type IS RECORD
        (first_name  VARCHAR2(15),
         last_name   VARCHAR2(30),
         enrollments INTEGER);

    TYPE name_type IS TABLE OF student_rec_type
        INDEX BY BINARY_INTEGER;

    name_tab name_type;
    v_counter INTEGER := 0;
BEGIN
    FOR name_rec IN name_cur LOOP
        v_counter := v_counter + 1;

        name_tab(v_counter).first_name := name_rec.first_name;
        name_tab(v_counter).last_name := name_rec.last_name;
```

```
        name_tab(v_counter).enrollments := name_rec.total;

        IF v_counter <= 4 THEN
            DBMS_OUTPUT.PUT_LINE('First Name('||v_counter||'): '||
                name_tab(v_counter).first_name);
            DBMS_OUTPUT.PUT_LINE('Last Name('||v_counter||'): '||
                name_tab(v_counter).last_name);
            DBMS_OUTPUT.PUT_LINE('Enrollments('||v_counter||'): '||
                name_tab(v_counter).enrollments);
            DBMS_OUTPUT.PUT_LINE ('--------------------');
        END IF;
    END LOOP;
END;
```

In the declaration portion of the script, the cursor SELECT statement has been modified so that for each student it returns the total number of enrollments. Next, the user-defined record type, student_rec_type, is declared so that it can be used as the element type for the associative array type, name_type.

In the executable portion of the script, the associative array, name_tab, is populated using the cursor FOR loop. Next, the index counter variable, v_counter, is evaluated using the IF-THEN statement so that only the first four records of the index-by table are displayed on the screen.

When run, this script produces the following output:

```
First Name(1): A.
Last Name(1): Tucker
Enrollments(1): 1
--------------------
First Name(2): Adele
Last Name(2): Rothstein
Enrollments(2): 1
--------------------
First Name(3): Adrienne
Last Name(3): Lopez
Enrollments(3): 1
--------------------
First Name(4): Al
Last Name(4): Jamerncy
Enrollments(4): 1
--------------------

PL/SQL procedure successfully completed.
```

▼ TRY IT YOURSELF

In this chapter, you've learned about various types of records, nested records, and collections of records. Here are some projects that will help you test the depth of your understanding:

1) Create an associative array with the element type of a user-defined record. This record should contain the first name, last name, and total number of courses that a particular instructor teaches. Display the records of the associative array on the screen.

2) Modify the script you just created. Instead of using an associative array, use a nested table.

3) Modify the script you just created. Instead of using a nested table, use a varray.

4) Create a user-defined record with four fields: `course_no`, `description`, `cost`, and `prerequisite_rec`. The last field, `prerequisite_rec`, should be a user-defined record with three fields: `prereq_no`, `prereq_desc`, and `prereq_cost`. For any ten courses that have a prerequisite course, populate the user-defined record with all the corresponding data, and display its information on the screen.

The projects in this section are meant to have you use all the skills you have acquired throughout this chapter. The answers to these projects can be found in Appendix D and on this book's companion Web site. Visit the Web site periodically to share and discuss your answers.

Native Dynamic SQL

CHAPTER OBJECTIVES

In this chapter, you will learn about

- ▶ EXECUTE IMMEDIATE statements
- ▶ OPEN-FOR, FETCH, and CLOSE statements

Generally, PL/SQL applications perform a specific task and manipulate a static set of tables. For example, a stored procedure might accept a student ID and return the student's first and last names. In such a procedure, a SELECT statement is known in advance and is compiled as part of the procedure. Such SELECT statements are called static because they do not change from execution to execution.

Now, consider a different type of PL/SQL application in which SQL statements are built on the fly, based on a set of parameters specified at runtime. For example, an application might need to build various reports based on SQL statements where table and column names are not known in advance, or the sorting and grouping of data are specified by a user requesting a report. Similarly, another application might need to create or drop tables or other database objects based on the action specified by a user at runtime. Because these SQL statements are generated on the fly and might change from time to time, they are called *dynamic*.

PL/SQL has a feature called *native dynamic SQL* (dynamic SQL for short) that helps you build applications similar to those just described. The use of dynamic SQL makes such applications flexible, versatile, and concise because it eliminates the need for complicated programming approaches. Native dynamic SQL is more convenient to use than the Oracle-supplied package DBMS_SQL, which has similar functionality. In this chapter you will learn how to create and use dynamic SQL.

LAB 17.1
EXECUTE IMMEDIATE Statements

LAB OBJECTIVE

After completing this lab, you will be able to

▶ Use the EXECUTE IMMEDIATE statement

Generally, dynamic SQL statements are built by your program and are stored as character strings based on the parameters specified at runtime. These strings must contain valid SQL statements or PL/SQL code. Consider the following dynamic SQL statement:

FOR EXAMPLE

```
'SELECT first_name, last_name FROM student WHERE student_id =
:student_id'
```

This SELECT statement returns a student's first and last name for a given student ID. The value of the student ID is not known in advance and is specified with the help of a *bind argument*, `:student_id`. The bind argument is a placeholder for an undeclared identifier, and its name must be prefixed by a colon. As a result, PL/SQL does not differentiate between the following statements:

```
'SELECT first_name, last_name FROM student WHERE student_id =
:student_id'

'SELECT first_name, last_name FROM student WHERE student_id = :id'
```

To process dynamic SQL statements, you use EXECUTE IMMEDIATE or OPEN-FOR, FETCH, and CLOSE statements. EXECUTE IMMEDIATE is used for single-row SELECT statements, all DML statements, and DDL statements. OPEN-FOR, FETCH, and CLOSE statements are used for multirow SELECTs and reference cursors.

BY THE WAY

To improve the performance of dynamic SQL statements you can also use BULK EXECUTE IMMEDI-ATE, BULK FETCH, FORALL, and COLLECT INTO statements. However, these statements are outside the scope of this book and therefore are not covered. You can find detailed explanations and examples of their usage in the online Oracle help.

THE EXECUTE IMMEDIATE STATEMENT

The EXECUTE IMMEDIATE statement parses a dynamic statement or a PL/SQL block for immediate execution. Its structure is as follows (the reserved words and phrases in square brackets are optional):

```
EXECUTE IMMEDIATE dynamic_SQL_string
[INTO defined_variable1, defined_variable2, ...]
[USING [IN | OUT | IN OUT] bind_argument1, bind_argument2,
...][{RETURNING | RETURN} field1, field2, ... INTO bind_argument1,
bind_argument2, ...]
```

$dynamic\_SQL\_string$ is a string that contains a valid SQL statement or a PL/SQL block. The INTO clause contains the list of predefined variables that hold values returned by the SELECT statement. This clause is used when a dynamic SQL statement returns a single row similar to a static SELECT INTO statement. Next, the USING clause contains a list of bind arguments whose values are passed to the dynamic SQL statement or PL/SQL block. IN, OUT, and IN OUT are modes for bind arguments. If no mode is specified, all bind arguments listed in the USING clause are in IN mode. Finally, the RETURNING INTO or RETURN clause contains a list of bind arguments that store values returned by the dynamic SQL statement or PL/SQL block. Similar to the USING clause, the RETURNING INTO clause may also contain various argument modes; however, if no mode is specified, all bind arguments are in OUT mode.

DID YOU KNOW?

When an EXECUTE IMMEDIATE statement contains both USING and RETURNING INTO clauses, the USING clause may specify only IN arguments.

FOR EXAMPLE

```
DECLARE
   sql_stmt VARCHAR2(100);
   plsql_block VARCHAR2(300);
   v_zip VARCHAR2(5) := '11106';
   v_total_students NUMBER;
   v_new_zip VARCHAR2(5);
   v_student_id NUMBER := 151;
BEGIN
   -- Create table MY_STUDENT
   sql_stmt := 'CREATE TABLE my_student '||
            'AS SELECT * FROM student WHERE zip = '||v_zip;
   EXECUTE IMMEDIATE sql_stmt;

   -- Select total number of records from MY_STUDENT table
   -- and display results on the screen
   EXECUTE IMMEDIATE 'SELECT COUNT(*) FROM my_student'
   INTO v_total_students;
   DBMS_OUTPUT.PUT_LINE ('Students added: '||v_total_students);
```

FOR EXAMPLE (continued)

```
-- Select current date and display it on the screen
plsql_block := 'DECLARE '                                   ||
               '   v_date DATE; '                           ||
               'BEGIN '                                     ||
               '   SELECT SYSDATE INTO v_date FROM DUAL; '  ||
               '   DBMS_OUTPUT.PUT_LINE (TO_CHAR(v_date,
                                   ''DD-MON-YYYY''))
               ;'||
               'END;';
EXECUTE IMMEDIATE plsql_block;

-- Update record in MY_STUDENT table
sql_stmt := 'UPDATE my_student SET zip = 11105 WHERE student_id =
            :1 '||
            'RETURNING zip INTO :2';
EXECUTE IMMEDIATE sql_stmt USING v_student_id RETURNING INTO
   v_new_zip;
DBMS_OUTPUT.PUT_LINE ('New zip code: '||v_new_zip);
END;
```

This script contains several examples of dynamic SQL.

First, you create the table MY_STUDENT and populate it with records for a specified value of zip code. It is important to note that the variable v_zip is concatenated with the CREATE statement instead of being passed in as a bind argument. This point is illustrated in the next example.

Second, you select the total number of students added to the MY_STUDENT table and display it on the screen. You use the INTO option with the EXECUTE IMMEDIATE statement because the SELECT statement returns a single row.

Third, you create a simple PL/SQL block in which you select the current date and display it on the screen. Because the PL/SQL block does not contain any bind arguments, the EXECUTE IMMEDIATE statement is used in its simplest form.

Finally, you update the MY_STUDENT table for a given student ID and return a new value of zip code using the RETURNING statement. So, the EXECUTE IMMEDIATE command contains both USING and RETURNING INTO options. The USING option allows you to pass a value of student ID to the UPDATE statement at runtime, and the RETURNING INTO option allows you to pass a new value of zip code from the UPDATE statement into your program.

When run, this example produces the following output:

```
Students added: 4
22-JUN-2003
New zip code: 11105


PL/SQL procedure successfully completed.
```

HOW TO AVOID COMMON ORA ERRORS WHEN USING EXECUTE IMMEDIATE

Consider the simplified yet incorrect version of the preceding example. Changes are shown in bold.

FOR EXAMPLE

```
DECLARE
    sql_stmt VARCHAR2(100);
    v_zip VARCHAR2(5) := '11106';
    v_total_students NUMBER;
BEGIN
    -- Drop table MY_STUDENT
    EXECUTE IMMEDIATE 'DROP TABLE my_student';

    -- Create table MY_STUDENT
    sql_stmt := 'CREATE TABLE my_student '||
                'AS SELECT * FROM student '||
                'WHERE zip = :zip';
    EXECUTE IMMEDIATE sql_stmt USING v_zip;

    -- Select total number of records from MY_STUDENT table
    -- and display results on the screen
    EXECUTE IMMEDIATE 'SELECT COUNT(*) FROM my_student'
    INTO v_total_students;
    DBMS_OUTPUT.PUT_LINE ('Students added: '|| v_total_students);
END;
```

First, you drop the MY_STUDENT table created in the previous version of the example. Next, you re-create the MY_STUDENT table, but in this case, you use a bind argument to pass a value of zip code to the CREATE statement at runtime.

When run, this example produces the following error:

```
DECLARE
*
ERROR at line 1:
ORA-01027: bind variables not allowed for data definition operations
ORA-06512: at line 12
```

DID YOU KNOW?

A CREATE TABLE statement is a data definition statement. Therefore, it cannot accept any bind arguments.

Next, consider another simplified version of the same example that also causes a syntax error. In this version, you pass the table name as a bind argument to the SELECT statement. Changes are shown in bold.

FOR EXAMPLE

```
DECLARE
   sql_stmt  VARCHAR2(100);
   v_zip  VARCHAR2(5) := '11106';
   v_total_students NUMBER;
BEGIN
   -- Create table MY_STUDENT
   sql_stmt := 'CREATE TABLE my_student '||
               'AS SELECT * FROM student '|| 'WHERE zip ='|| v_zip;
   EXECUTE IMMEDIATE sql_stmt;

   -- Select total number of records from MY_STUDENT table
   -- and display results on the screen
   EXECUTE IMMEDIATE 'SELECT COUNT(*) FROM :my_table'
   INTO v_total_students
   USING 'my_student';
   DBMS_OUTPUT.PUT_LINE ('Students added: '|| v_total_students);
END;
```

When run, this example causes the following error:

```
DECLARE
*
ERROR at line 1:
ORA-00903: invalid table name
ORA-06512: at line 13
```

This example causes an error because *you cannot pass names of schema objects to dynamic SQL statements as bind arguments.* To provide a table name at runtime, you need to concatenate this example with the SELECT statement:

```
EXECUTE IMMEDIATE 'SELECT COUNT(*) FROM '||my_table
    INTO v_total_students;
```

As mentioned earlier, a dynamic SQL string can contain any SQL statement or PL/SQL block. However, unlike static SQL statements, a dynamic SQL statement should not be terminated with a semicolon (;). Similarly, a dynamic PL/SQL block should not be terminated with a slash (/). Consider a different version of the same example in which the SELECT statement is terminated with a semicolon. Changes are shown in bold.

WATCH OUT!

If you created the MY_STUDENT table based on the corrected version of the preceding script, you need to drop it before running the following script. Otherwise, the error message generated by the example will differ from the error message shown after the example.

FOR EXAMPLE

```
DECLARE
   sql_stmt VARCHAR2(100);
   v_zip VARCHAR2(5) := '11106';
   v_total_students NUMBER;
BEGIN
   -- Create table MY_STUDENT
   sql_stmt := 'CREATE TABLE my_student '||
               'AS SELECT * FROM student '|| 'WHERE zip = '||v_zip;
   EXECUTE IMMEDIATE sql_stmt;

   -- Select total number of records from MY_STUDENT table
   -- and display results on the screen
   EXECUTE IMMEDIATE 'SELECT COUNT(*) FROM my_student;'
   INTO v_total_students;
   DBMS_OUTPUT.PUT_LINE ('Students added: '|| v_total_students);
END;
```

When run, this example produces the following error:

```
DECLARE
*
ERROR at line 1:
ORA-00911: invalid character
ORA-06512: at line 13
```

The semicolon added to the SELECT statement is treated as an invalid character when the statement is created dynamically. A somewhat similar error is generated when a PL/SQL block is terminated by a slash:

FOR EXAMPLE

```
DECLARE
   plsql_block VARCHAR2(300);
BEGIN
   -- Select current date and display it on the screen
   plsql_block := 'DECLARE '                              ||
                  '   v_date DATE; '                      ||
                  'BEGIN '                                ||
                  '   SELECT SYSDATE INTO v_date FROM DUAL; '||
                  '   DBMS_OUTPUT.PUT_LINE (TO_CHAR(v_date,
                                         ''DD-MON-YYYY''));'||
                  'END;' ;
   EXECUTE IMMEDIATE plsql_block;
END;
```

This example produces the following error message:

```
DECLARE
*
ERROR at line 1:
ORA-06550: line 1, column 133:
PLS-00103: Encountered the symbol "/" The symbol "/" was ignored.
ORA-06512: at line 12
```

PASSING NULLS

In some cases you may need to pass a NULL value to a dynamic SQL statement as a value for a bind argument. For example, suppose you need to update the COURSE table so that the PREREQUISITE column is set to NULL. You can accomplish this with the following dynamic SQL and the EXECUTE IMMEDIATE statement:

FOR EXAMPLE

```
DECLARE
   sql_stmt VARCHAR2(100);
BEGIN
   sql_stmt := 'UPDATE course'||
               '    SET prerequisite = :some_value';
   EXECUTE IMMEDIATE sql_stmt
   USING NULL;
END;
```

However, when run, this script causes the following error:

```
        USING NULL;
            *
   ERROR at line 7:
   ORA-06550: line 7, column 10:
   PLS-00457: expressions have to be of SQL types
   ORA-06550: line 6, column 4:
   PL/SQL: Statement ignored
```

This error is generated because the literal NULL in the USING clause is not recognized as one of the SQL types. To pass a NULL value to the dynamic SQL statement, you should modify this example as follows (changes are shown in bold):

FOR EXAMPLE

```
DECLARE
   sql_stmt VARCHAR2(100);
   v_null VARCHAR2(1);
BEGIN
   sql_stmt := 'UPDATE course'||
               '    SET prerequisite = :some_value';
```

```
EXECUTE IMMEDIATE sql_stmt
    USING v_null;
END;
```

To correct the script, you add an initialized variable v_null and replace the literal NULL in the USING clause with this variable. Because the variable v_null has not been initialized, its value remains NULL, and it is passed to the dynamic UPDATE statement at runtime. As a result, this version of the script completes without any errors.

▼ LAB 17.1 EXERCISES

This section provides exercises and suggested answers, with discussion related to how those answers resulted. The most important thing to realize is whether your answer works. You should figure out the implications of the answers and what the effects are of any different answers you may come up with.

17.1.1 Use the EXECUTE IMMEDIATE Statement

Create the following PL/SQL script:

```
-- ch17_1a.sql, version 1.0
SET SERVEROUTPUT ON
DECLARE
    sql_stmt VARCHAR2(200);
    v_student_id NUMBER := &sv_student_id;
    v_first_name VARCHAR2(25);
    v_last_name VARCHAR2(25);
BEGIN
    sql_stmt := 'SELECT first_name, last_name'||
                '  FROM student'              ||
                ' WHERE student_id = :1';
    EXECUTE IMMEDIATE sql_stmt
    INTO v_first_name, v_last_name
    USING v_student_id;

    DBMS_OUTPUT.PUT_LINE ('First Name: '||v_first_name);
    DBMS_OUTPUT.PUT_LINE ('Last Name:  '||v_last_name);
END;
```

Execute the script, and then complete the following exercises:

A) Explain the preceding script.

ANSWER: The declaration portion of the script declares the string that contains the dynamic SQL statement, and three variables to hold student's ID, first name, and last name, respectively. The executable portion of the script contains a dynamic SQL statement with one bind argument that is used to pass the value of the student ID to the SELECT statement at runtime. The dynamic SQL statement is executed using the EXECUTE IMMEDIATE statement with two options, INTO and USING. The INTO clause contains two variables, v_first_name and v_last_name. These variables contain results returned by the SELECT statement. The USING clause contains the variable v_student_id, which is used to pass a value to the SELECT statement at runtime. Finally, two DBMS_OUTPUT.PUT_LINE statements are used to display the results of the SELECT statement on the screen.

When run, the script produces the following output:

```
Enter value for sv_student_id: 105
old    3:      v_student_id NUMBER := &sv_student_id;
new    3:      v_student_id NUMBER := 105;
First Name: Angel
Last Name:  Moskowitz

PL/SQL procedure successfully completed.
```

B) Modify the script so that the student's address (street, city, state, and zip code) is displayed on the screen as well.

ANSWER: Your script should look similar to the following. Changes are shown in bold.

```
-- ch17_1b.sql, version 2.0
SET SERVEROUTPUT ON
DECLARE
   sql_stmt VARCHAR2(200);
   v_student_id NUMBER := &sv_student_id;
   v_first_name VARCHAR2(25);
   v_last_name VARCHAR2(25);
   v_street VARCHAR2(50);
   v_city VARCHAR2(25);
   v_state VARCHAR2(2);
   v_zip VARCHAR2(5);
BEGIN
   sql_stmt := 'SELECT a.first_name, a.last_name, a.street_address'||
               '      ,b.city, b.state, b.zip'                       ||
               '  FROM student a, zipcode b'                         ||
               ' WHERE a.zip = b.zip'                                ||
               '   AND student_id = :1';
   EXECUTE IMMEDIATE sql_stmt
   INTO v_first_name, v_last_name, v_street, v_city, v_state, v_zip
   USING v_student_id;

   DBMS_OUTPUT.PUT_LINE ('First Name: '||v_first_name);
   DBMS_OUTPUT.PUT_LINE ('Last Name:  '||v_last_name);
   DBMS_OUTPUT.PUT_LINE ('Street:      '||v_street);
   DBMS_OUTPUT.PUT_LINE ('City:        '||v_city);
   DBMS_OUTPUT.PUT_LINE ('State:       '||v_state);
   DBMS_OUTPUT.PUT_LINE ('Zip Code:    '||v_zip);

END;
```

In the preceding script, you declare four new variables—v_street, v_city, v_state, and v_zip. Next, you modify the dynamic SQL statement so that it can return the student's address. As a result, you modify the INTO clause by adding the new variables to it. Next, you add DBMS_OUTPUT.PUT_LINE statements to display the student's address on the screen.

When run, the script produces the following output:

```
Enter value for sv_student_id: 105
old    3:      v_student_id NUMBER := &sv_student_id;
new    3:      v_student_id NUMBER := 105;
```

```
First Name: Angel
Last Name:  Moskowitz
Street:     320 John St.
City:       Ft. Lee
State:      NJ
Zip Code:   07024
```

```
PL/SQL procedure successfully completed.
```

It is important to remember that the order of variables listed in the INTO clause must follow the order of columns listed in the SELECT statement. In other words, if the INTO clause listed variables so that v_zip and v_state were misplaced while the SELECT statement remained unchanged, the scripts would generate an error:

```
SET SERVEROUTPUT ON
DECLARE
    sql_stmt VARCHAR2(200);
    v_student_id NUMBER := &sv_student_id;
    v_first_name VARCHAR2(25);
    v_last_name VARCHAR2(25);
    v_street VARCHAR2(50);
    v_city VARCHAR2(25);
    v_state VARCHAR2(2);
    v_zip VARCHAR2(5);
BEGIN
    sql_stmt := 'SELECT a.first_name, a.last_name, a.street_address'||
                '       ,b.city, b.state, b.zip'                     ||
                ' FROM student a, zipcode b'                         ||
                ' WHERE a.zip = b.zip'                               ||
                '   AND student_id = :1';
    EXECUTE IMMEDIATE sql_stmt
    -- variables v_state and v_zip are misplaced
    INTO v_first_name, v_last_name, v_street, v_city, v_zip, v_state
    USING v_student_id;

    DBMS_OUTPUT.PUT_LINE ('First Name: '||v_first_name);
    DBMS_OUTPUT.PUT_LINE ('Last Name:  '||v_last_name);
    DBMS_OUTPUT.PUT_LINE ('Street:     '||v_street);
    DBMS_OUTPUT.PUT_LINE ('City:       '||v_city);
    DBMS_OUTPUT.PUT_LINE ('State:      '||v_state);
    DBMS_OUTPUT.PUT_LINE ('Zip Code:   '||v_zip);

END;
```

The error message is as follows:

```
Enter value for sv_student_id: 105
old   3:    v_student_id NUMBER := &sv_student_id;
new   3:    v_student_id NUMBER := 105;
DECLARE
*
```

```
ERROR at line 1:
ORA-06502: PL/SQL: numeric or value error
ORA-06512: at line 16
```

This error is generated because the variable v_state can hold up to two characters. However, you are trying to store in it a value of zip code, which contains five characters.

C) Modify the script created in the previous exercise (ch17_1b.sql) so that the SELECT statement can be run against either the STUDENT or INSTRUCTOR table. In other words, a user can specify the table name used in the SELECT statement at runtime.

ANSWER: Your script should look similar to the following. Changes are shown in bold.

```
-- ch17_1c.sql, version 3.0
SET SERVEROUTPUT ON
DECLARE
    sql_stmt VARCHAR2(200);
    v_table_name VARCHAR2(20) := '&sv_table_name';
    v_id NUMBER := &sv_id;
    v_first_name VARCHAR2(25);
    v_last_name VARCHAR2(25);
    v_street VARCHAR2(50);
    v_city VARCHAR2(25);
    v_state VARCHAR2(2);
    v_zip VARCHAR2(5);
BEGIN
    sql_stmt := 'SELECT a.first_name, a.last_name, a.street_address'||
                '       ,b.city, b.state, b.zip'                      ||
                '  FROM '||v_table_name||' a, zipcode b'              ||
                ' WHERE a.zip = b.zip'                                ||
                '   AND '||v_table_name||'_id = :1';
    EXECUTE IMMEDIATE sql_stmt
    INTO v_first_name, v_last_name, v_street, v_city, v_state, v_zip
    USING v_id;

    DBMS_OUTPUT.PUT_LINE ('First Name: '||v_first_name);
    DBMS_OUTPUT.PUT_LINE ('Last Name:  '||v_last_name);
    DBMS_OUTPUT.PUT_LINE ('Street:     '||v_street);
    DBMS_OUTPUT.PUT_LINE ('City:       '||v_city);
    DBMS_OUTPUT.PUT_LINE ('State:      '||v_state);
    DBMS_OUTPUT.PUT_LINE ('Zip Code:   '||v_zip);

END;
```

The declaration portion of the script contains a new variable, v_table_name, which holds the name of a table provided at runtime by the user. In addition, the variable v_student_id has been replaced by the variable v_id because it is not known in advance which table, STUDENT or INSTRUCTOR, will be accessed at runtime.

The executable portion of the script contains a modified dynamic SQL statement. Notice that the statement does not contain any information specific to the STUDENT or INSTRUCTOR tables. In other words, the dynamic SQL statement used by the previous version (ch17_1b.sql)

```
sql_stmt := 'SELECT a.first_name, a.last_name, a.street_address'||
            '       ,b.city, b.state, b.zip'                      ||
```

```
                '   FROM student a, zipcode b'                        ||
                ' WHERE a.zip = b.zip'                                ||
                '   AND student_id = :1';
```

has been replaced by

```
sql_stmt := 'SELECT a.first_name, a.last_name, a.street_address'||
                '       ,b.city, b.state, b.zip'                      ||
                '   FROM '||v_table_name||' a, zipcode b'             ||
                ' WHERE a.zip = b.zip'                                ||
                '   AND '||v_table_name||'_id = :1';
```

The table name (student) has been replaced by the variable v_table_name in the FROM and the WHERE clauses.

DID YOU KNOW?

Note that for the last two versions of the script you have used generic table aliases—a and b instead of s and z or i and z, which are more descriptive. This technique allows you to create generic SQL statements that are not based on a specific table, because you do not always know in advance which table will be used.

This version of the script produces the following output. The first run is against the STUDENT table, and the second run is against the INSTRUCTOR table:

```
Enter value for sv_table_name: student
old   3:    v_table_name VARCHAR2(20) := '&sv_table_name';
new   3:    v_table_name VARCHAR2(20) := 'student';
Enter value for sv_id: 105
old   4:    v_id NUMBER := &sv_id;
new   4:    v_id NUMBER := 105;
First Name: Angel
Last Name:  Moskowitz
Street:     320 John St.
City:       Ft. Lee
State:      NJ
Zip Code:   07024


PL/SQL procedure successfully completed.

Enter value for sv_table_name: instructor
old   3:    v_table_name VARCHAR2(20) := '&sv_table_name';
new   3:    v_table_name VARCHAR2(20) := 'instructor';
Enter value for sv_id: 105
old   4:    v_id NUMBER := &sv_id;
new   4:    v_id NUMBER := 105;
First Name: Anita
Last Name:  Morris
Street:     34 Maiden Lane
City:       New York
State:      NY
Zip Code:   10015


PL/SQL procedure successfully completed.
```

LAB 17.2
OPEN-FOR, FETCH, and CLOSE Statements

LAB OBJECTIVE

After completing this lab, you will be able to

▶ Use OPEN-FOR, FETCH, and CLOSE statements

The OPEN-FOR, FETCH, and CLOSE statements are used for multirow queries or cursors. This concept is very similar to static cursor processing, which you encountered in Chapter 11, "Introduction to Cursors." As in the case of static cursors, first you associate a cursor variable with a query. Next, you open the cursor variable so that it points to the first row of the result set. Then you fetch one row at a time from the result set. Finally, when all rows have been processed, you close the cursor (cursor variable).

OPENING CURSOR

In the case of dynamic SQL, the OPEN-FOR statement has an optional USING clause that allows you to pass values to the bind arguments at runtime. The general syntax for an OPEN-FOR statement is as follows (the reserved words and phrases in brackets are optional):

```
OPEN cursor_variable FOR dynamic_SQL_string
[USING bind_argument1, bind_argument2, ...]
```

$cursor\_variable$ is a variable of a weak REF CURSOR type, and $dynamic\_SQL\_string$ is a string that contains a multirow query.

FOR EXAMPLE

```
DECLARE
   TYPE student_cur_type IS REF CURSOR;
   student_cur student_cur_type;

   v_zip VARCHAR2(5) := '&sv_zip';
   v_first_name VARCHAR2(25);
   v_last_name VARCHAR2(25);
BEGIN
   OPEN student_cur FOR
```

```
    'SELECT first_name, last_name FROM student '|| 'WHERE zip = :1'
  USING v_zip;
...
```

In this code fragment, you define a weak cursor type, `student_cur_type`. Next, you define a cursor variable `student_cur` based on the REF CURSOR type specified in the preceding step. At runtime, the `student_cur` variable is associated with the SELECT statement that returns the first and last names of students for a given value of zip.

FETCHING CURSOR

As mentioned earlier, the FETCH statement returns a single row from the result set into a list of variables defined in a PL/SQL block and moves the cursor to the next row. If a loop is being processed and there are no more rows to fetch, the EXIT WHEN statement evaluates to TRUE, and control of the execution is passed outside the cursor loop. The general syntax for a FETCH statement is as follows:

```
FETCH cursor_variable
 INTO defined_variable1, defined_variable2, ...
EXIT WHEN cursor_variable%NOTFOUND;
```

Adding the previous example, you fetch the student's first and last names into variables specified in the declaration section of the PL/SQL block. Next, you evaluate whether there are more records to process using the EXIT WHEN statement. As long as there are more records to process, the student's first and last names are displayed on the screen. As soon as the last row is fetched, the cursor loop terminates. Changes are shown in bold.

FOR EXAMPLE

```
DECLARE
   TYPE student_cur_type IS REF CURSOR;
   student_cur student_cur_type;

   v_zip VARCHAR2(5) := '&sv_zip';
   v_first_name VARCHAR2(25);
   v_last_name VARCHAR2(25);
BEGIN
   OPEN student_cur FOR
      'SELECT first_name, last_name FROM student '|| 'WHERE zip = :1'
   USING v_zip;

   LOOP
      FETCH student_cur INTO v_first_name, v_last_name;
      EXIT WHEN student_cur%NOTFOUND;

      DBMS_OUTPUT.PUT_LINE ('First Name: '||v_first_name);
      DBMS_OUTPUT.PUT_LINE ('Last Name:  '||v_last_name);
   END LOOP;
...
```

It is important to note that the number of variables listed in the INTO clause must correspond to the number of columns returned by the cursor. Furthermore, the variables in the INTO clause must be type-compatible with the cursor columns.

CLOSING CURSOR

The CLOSE statement disassociates the cursor variable with the multirow query. As a result, after the CLOSE statement executes, the result set becomes undefined. The general syntax for a CLOSE statement is as follows:

```
CLOSE cursor_variable;
```

Now consider the completed version of the example shown previously. Changes are shown in bold.

FOR EXAMPLE

```
DECLARE
   TYPE student_cur_type IS REF CURSOR;
   student_cur student_cur_type;

   v_zip VARCHAR2(5) := '&sv_zip';
   v_first_name VARCHAR2(25);
   v_last_name VARCHAR2(25);
BEGIN
   OPEN student_cur FOR
      'SELECT first_name, last_name FROM student '|| 'WHERE zip = :1'
   USING v_zip;

   LOOP
      FETCH student_cur INTO v_first_name, v_last_name;
      EXIT WHEN student_cur%NOTFOUND;

      DBMS_OUTPUT.PUT_LINE ('First Name: '||v_first_name);
      DBMS_OUTPUT.PUT_LINE ('Last Name:  '||v_last_name);
   END LOOP;
   CLOSE student_cur;

EXCEPTION
   WHEN OTHERS THEN
      IF student_cur%ISOPEN THEN
         CLOSE student_cur;
      END IF;

      DBMS_OUTPUT.PUT_LINE ('ERROR: '||   SUBSTR(SQLERRM, 1, 200));
END;
```

The IF statement in the exception-handling section evaluates to TRUE if an exception is encountered before the cursor processing is completed. In such a case, it is considered a good practice to check and see if a cursor is still open and, if it is, close it. Doing so frees all the resources associated with the cursor before the program terminates.

When run, this example produces the following output:

```
Enter value for sv_zip: 11236
old    5:    v_zip VARCHAR2(5) := '&sv_zip';
new    5:    v_zip VARCHAR2(5) := '11236';
First Name: Derrick
Last Name:  Baltazar
First Name: Michael
Last Name:  Lefbowitz
First Name: Bridget
Last Name:  Hagel


PL/SQL procedure successfully completed.
```

▼ LAB 17.2 EXERCISES

This section provides exercises and suggested answers, with discussion related to how those answers resulted. The most important thing to realize is whether your answer works. You should figure out the implications of the answers and what the effects are of any different answers you may come up with.

17.2.1 Use OPEN-FOR, FETCH, and CLOSE Statements

Create the following PL/SQL script:

```
-- ch17_2a.sql, version 1.0
SET SERVEROUTPUT ON
DECLARE
    TYPE zip_cur_type IS REF CURSOR;
    zip_cur zip_cur_type;

    sql_stmt VARCHAR2(500);
    v_zip VARCHAR2(5);
    v_total NUMBER;

    v_count NUMBER;
BEGIN
    sql_stmt := 'SELECT zip, COUNT(*) total'||
                '  FROM student '          ||
                'GROUP BY zip';

    v_count := 0;
    OPEN zip_cur FOR sql_stmt;
    LOOP
        FETCH zip_cur INTO v_zip, v_total;
        EXIT WHEN zip_cur%NOTFOUND;

        -- Limit the number of lines printed on the
        -- screen to 10
```

```
        v_count := v_count + 1;
        IF v_count <= 10 THEN
            DBMS_OUTPUT.PUT_LINE ('Zip code: '||v_zip||
                                  ' Total: '||v_total);
        END IF;
    END LOOP;
    CLOSE zip_cur;

EXCEPTION
    WHEN OTHERS THEN
        IF zip_cur%ISOPEN THEN
            CLOSE zip_cur;
        END IF;

        DBMS_OUTPUT.PUT_LINE ('ERROR: '||   SUBSTR(SQLERRM, 1, 200));
END;
```

Consider the use of spaces in the SQL statements generated dynamically. In the preceding script, the string that holds the dynamic SQL statement consists of three concatenated strings, where each string is written on a separate line:

```
sql_stmt := 'SELECT zip, COUNT(*) total'||
            '  FROM student '             ||
            'GROUP BY zip';
```

This format of the dynamic SELECT statement is very similar to the format of any static SELECT statement that you have seen throughout this book. However, there is a subtle difference. In one instance, extra spaces have been added for formatting reasons. For example, the FROM keyword is prefixed by two spaces so that it aligns with the SELECT keyword. In another instance, a space has been added to separate a reserved phrase. In this case, a space has been added after the STUDENT table to separate the GROUP BY clause. This step is necessary because after the strings are concatenated, the resulting SELECT statement looks like this:

```
SELECT zip, COUNT(*) total  FROM student GROUP BY zip
```

If no space is added after the STUDENT table, the resulting SELECT statement

```
SELECT zip, COUNT(*) total  FROM studentGROUP BY zip
```

causes this error:

```
ERROR: ORA-00933: SQL command not properly ended

PL/SQL procedure successfully completed.
```

Execute the script, and then complete the following exercises:

A) Explain the preceding script.

ANSWER: In the declaration portion of the script, you define a weak cursor type, `zip_cur_type`, and a cursor variable, `zip_cur`, of the `zip_cur_type` type. Next, you define a string variable to hold a dynamic SQL statement, and two variables, `v_zip` and `v_total`, to hold data returned by the cursor. Finally, you define a counter variable so that only the first ten rows returned by the cursor are displayed on the screen.

In the executable portion of the script, you generate a dynamic SQL statement, associate it with the cursor variable, zip_cur, and open the cursor. Next, for each row returned by the cursor, you fetch values of zip code and total number of students into the variables v_zip and v_total, respectively. Then, you check to see if there are more rows to fetch from the cursor. If there are more rows to process, you increment the value of the counter variable by 1. As long as the value of the counter is less than or equal to 10, you display the row returned by the cursor on the screen. If there are no more rows to fetch, you close the cursor.

In the exception-handling section of the script, you check to see if the cursor is open. If it is, you close the cursor and display an error message on the screen before terminating the script.

When run, the script should produce output similar to the following:

```
Zip code: 01247 Total: 1
Zip code: 02124 Total: 1
Zip code: 02155 Total: 1
Zip code: 02189 Total: 1
Zip code: 02563 Total: 1
Zip code: 06483 Total: 1
Zip code: 06605 Total: 1
Zip code: 06798 Total: 1
Zip code: 06820 Total: 3
Zip code: 06830 Total: 3

PL/SQL procedure successfully completed.
```

B) Modify the script you just created (ch17_2a.sql) so that the SELECT statement can be run against either the STUDENT or INSTRUCTOR table. In other words, a user can specify the table name used in the SELECT statement at runtime.

ANSWER: Your script should look similar to the following. Changes are shown in bold.

```
-- ch17_2b.sql, version 2.0
SET SERVEROUTPUT ON
DECLARE
    TYPE zip_cur_type IS REF CURSOR;
    zip_cur zip_cur_type;

    v_table_name VARCHAR2(20) := '&sv_table_name';
    sql_stmt VARCHAR2(500);
    v_zip VARCHAR2(5);
    v_total NUMBER;

    v_count NUMBER;
BEGIN
    DBMS_OUTPUT.PUT_LINE ('Totals from '||v_table_name||
                          ' table');

    sql_stmt := 'SELECT zip, COUNT(*) total'||
                '  FROM '||v_table_name||' '||
                'GROUP BY zip';

    v_count := 0;
    OPEN zip_cur FOR sql_stmt;
    LOOP
```

```
      FETCH zip_cur INTO v_zip, v_total;
      EXIT WHEN zip_cur%NOTFOUND;

      -- Limit the number of lines printed on the
      -- screen to 10
      v_count := v_count + 1;
      IF v_count <= 10 THEN
         DBMS_OUTPUT.PUT_LINE ('Zip code: '||v_zip||
                              ' Total: '||v_total);
      END IF;
   END LOOP;
   CLOSE zip_cur;

EXCEPTION
   WHEN OTHERS THEN
      IF zip_cur%ISOPEN THEN
         CLOSE zip_cur;
      END IF;

      DBMS_OUTPUT.PUT_LINE ('ERROR: '||   SUBSTR(SQLERRM, 1, 200));
END;
```

In this version of the script, you add a variable, v_table_name, to hold the name of a table provided at runtime. You also add a DBMS_OUTPUT.PUT_LINE table to display a message stating what table the total numbers are coming from. Next, you modify the dynamic SQL statement as follows:

```
sql_stmt := 'SELECT zip, COUNT(*) total'||
            '  FROM '||v_table_name||' '||
            'GROUP BY zip';
```

The variable v_table_name has been inserted in place of the actual table name (STUDENT). Note that you concatenate a space to the variable v_table_name so that the SELECT statement does not cause any errors.

When run, this script produces the following output. The first run is based on the STUDENT table, and the second run is based on the INSTRUCTOR table.

```
Enter value for sv_table_name: student
old    5:    v_table_name VARCHAR2(20) := '&sv_table_name';
new    5:    v_table_name VARCHAR2(20) := 'student';
Totals from student table
Zip code: 01247 Total: 1
Zip code: 02124 Total: 1
Zip code: 02155 Total: 1
Zip code: 02189 Total: 1
Zip code: 02563 Total: 1
Zip code: 06483 Total: 1
Zip code: 06605 Total: 1
Zip code: 06798 Total: 1
Zip code: 06820 Total: 3
Zip code: 06830 Total: 3

PL/SQL procedure successfully completed.
```

```
Enter value for sv_table_name: instructor
old    5:      v_table_name VARCHAR2(20) := '&sv_table_name';
new    5:      v_table_name VARCHAR2(20) := 'instructor';
Totals from instructor table
Zip code: 10005 Total: 1
Zip code: 10015 Total: 3
Zip code: 10025 Total: 4
Zip code: 10035 Total: 1

PL/SQL procedure successfully completed.
```

So far you have seen that values returned by the dynamic SQL statements are stored in individual variables such as `v_last_name` or `v_first_name`. In such cases, you list the variables in the order of the corresponding columns returned by the SELECT statement. This approach becomes somewhat cumbersome when a dynamic SQL statement returns more than a few columns. As a result, PL/SQL allows you to store values returned by the dynamic SELECT statements in the variables of the record type.

Consider the modified version of the script used in this lab. In this version, instead of creating separate variables, you create a user-defined record. This record is then used to fetch data from the cursor and display it on the screen. Changes are shown in bold.

```
SET SERVEROUTPUT ON
DECLARE
   TYPE zip_cur_type IS REF CURSOR;
   zip_cur zip_cur_type;

   TYPE zip_rec_type IS RECORD
      (zip VARCHAR2(5),
       total NUMBER);
   zip_rec zip_rec_type;

   v_table_name VARCHAR2(20) := '&sv_table_name';
   sql_stmt VARCHAR2(500);
   v_count NUMBER;
BEGIN
   DBMS_OUTPUT.PUT_LINE ('Totals from '||v_table_name||
                         ' table');

   sql_stmt := 'SELECT zip, COUNT(*) total'||
               '  FROM '||v_table_name||' '||
               'GROUP BY zip';

   v_count := 0;
   OPEN zip_cur FOR sql_stmt;
   LOOP
      FETCH zip_cur INTO zip_rec;
      EXIT WHEN zip_cur%NOTFOUND;

      -- Limit the number of lines printed on the
      -- screen to 10
      v_count := v_count + 1;
```

```
        IF v_count <= 10 THEN
            DBMS_OUTPUT.PUT_LINE ('Zip code: '||zip_rec.zip||
                                ' Total: '||zip_rec.total);
        END IF;
    END LOOP;
    CLOSE zip_cur;

EXCEPTION
    WHEN OTHERS THEN
        IF zip_cur%ISOPEN THEN
            CLOSE zip_cur;
        END IF;

        DBMS_OUTPUT.PUT_LINE ('ERROR: '||   SUBSTR(SQLERRM, 1, 200));
END;
```

The output is as follows:

```
Enter value for sv_table_name: student
old  10:    v_table_name VARCHAR2(20) := '&sv_table_name';
new  10:    v_table_name VARCHAR2(20) := 'student';
Totals from student table
Zip code: 01247 Total: 1
Zip code: 02124 Total: 1
Zip code: 02155 Total: 1
Zip code: 02189 Total: 1
Zip code: 02563 Total: 1
Zip code: 06483 Total: 1
Zip code: 06605 Total: 1
Zip code: 06798 Total: 1
Zip code: 06820 Total: 3
Zip code: 06830 Total: 3

PL/SQL procedure successfully completed.

Enter value for sv_table_name: instructor
old  10:    v_table_name VARCHAR2(20) := '&sv_table_name';
new  10:    v_table_name VARCHAR2(20) := 'instructor';
Totals from instructor table
Zip code: 10005 Total: 1
Zip code: 10015 Total: 3
Zip code: 10025 Total: 4
Zip code: 10035 Total: 1

PL/SQL procedure successfully completed.
```

▼ TRY IT YOURSELF

This chapter has no Try It Yourself projects. Try It Yourself project 2 in Chapter 19, "Procedures," extends the material on native dynamic SQL and puts it to use within the context of stored procedures.

CHAPTER 18

Bulk SQL

CHAPTER OBJECTIVES

In this chapter, you will learn about

- ▶ The FORALL statement
- ▶ The BULK COLLECT clause

In Chapter 1, "PL/SQL Concepts," you learned that the PL/SQL engine sends SQL statements to the SQL engine, which returns results to the PL/SQL engine. The communication between the PL/SQL and SQL engines is called a context switch. A certain amount of performance overhead is associated with these context switches. However, the PL/SQL language has a number of features that can minimize the performance overhead known as bulk SQL. Generally, if a SQL statement affects four or more rows, bulk SQL may improve performance significantly. Bulk SQL supports batch processing of SQL statements and their results. It consists of two features—the FORALL statement and the BULK COLLECT clause.

LAB 18.1
The FORALL Statement

LAB OBJECTIVE

After completing this lab, you will be able to

▶ Use the FORALL statement

The FORALL statement sends INSERT, UPDATE, or DELETE statements in batches from PL/SQL to SQL instead of one at a time. For example, consider an INSERT statement enclosed in the numeric FOR loop that iterates ten times:

```
FOR i IN 1..10 LOOP
    INSERT INTO table_name
    VALUES (...);
END LOOP;
```

This INSERT statement is sent from PL/SQL to SQL ten times. In other words, ten context switches take place. If you replace the FOR loop with the FORALL statement, the INSERT statement is sent only once from PL/SQL to SQL, yet it is still executed ten times. In this case, there is only one context switch between PL/SQL and SQL.

The FORALL statement has the following structure (the reserved words in brackets are optional):

```
FORALL loop_counter IN bounds_clause
    SQL_STATEMENT [SAVE EXCEPTIONS];
```

where *bounds_clause* is one of the following:

```
lower_limit..upper_limit

INDICES OF collection_name BETWEEN lower_limit..upper_limit

VALUES OF collection_name
```

The FORALL statement has an implicitly defined loop counter variable associated with it. The values of the loop counter variable and the number of loop iterations are controlled by *bounds_clause*, which has three forms. The first form specifies lower and upper limits for the loop counter. This syntax is very similar to the numeric FOR loop. The second form, INDICES OF..., references subscripts of the individual elements of a particular collection. This collection may be a nested table or an associative array that has numeric subscripts.

DID YOU KNOW?

A collection referenced by the INDICES OF clause may be sparse. In other words, some of its elements have been deleted.

The third form of *bounds_clause*, VALUES OF..., references values of the individual elements of a particular collection, which is either a nested table or an associative array.

WATCH OUT!

When you use the VALUES OF option, the following restrictions apply:

▶ If the collection used in the VALUES OF clause is an associative array, it must be indexed by PLS_INTEGER and BINARY_INTEGER.

▶ The elements of the collection used in the VALUES OF clause must be PLS_INTEGER or BINARY_INTEGER.

▶ When the collection referenced by the VALUES OF clause is empty, the FORALL statement causes an exception.

Next, *SQL_STATEMENT* is either a static or dynamic INSERT, UPDATE, or DELETE statement that references one or more collections. Finally, the optional *SAVE EXCEPTIONS* clause allows the FORALL statement to continue even when *SQL_STATEMENT* causes an exception.

Consider the following example that illustrates how the FORALL statement may be used. This example, as well as other examples in this chapter, uses a test table created specifically for this purpose. The rows from the TEST table can be easily inserted, updated, or deleted without affecting the STUDENT schema or violating any integrity constraints.

FOR EXAMPLE

```
CREATE TABLE test (row_num NUMBER, row_text VARCHAR2(10));

DECLARE
    -- Define collection types and variables
    TYPE row_num_type  IS TABLE OF NUMBER        INDEX BY PLS_INTEGER;
    TYPE row_text_type IS TABLE OF VARCHAR2(10)  INDEX BY PLS_INTEGER;

    row_num_tab  row_num_type;
    row_text_tab row_text_type;

    v_total NUMBER;

BEGIN
    -- Populate collections
    FOR i IN 1..10 LOOP
        row_num_tab(i)  := i;
        row_text_tab(i) := 'row '||i;
    END LOOP;
```

FOR EXAMPLE (continued)

```
-- Populate TEST table
FORALL i IN 1..10
   INSERT INTO test (row_num, row_text)
   VALUES (row_num_tab(i), row_text_tab(i));

COMMIT;

-- Check how many rows were inserted in the TEST table
-- and display it on the screen
SELECT COUNT(*)
   INTO v_total
   FROM TEST;

DBMS_OUTPUT.PUT_LINE
   ('There are '||v_total||' rows in the TEST table');
END;
```

As mentioned earlier, when SQL statements are used with FORALL statements, they reference collection elements. So, in this script, you define two collection types as associative arrays and two collections that are populated using the numeric FOR loop. Next, you populate the TEST table with the data from two collections.

When run, this example produces the following output:

```
There are 10 rows in the TEST table

PL/SQL procedure successfully completed.
```

Next, consider another example, which demonstrates the performance gain when you use the FORALL statement. In this example, you compare the execution times of the INSERT statements issued against the TEST table. The first hundred inserts are enclosed by the numeric FOR loop, and the second hundred inserts are enclosed by the FORALL statement.

FOR EXAMPLE

```
TRUNCATE TABLE test;

DECLARE
   -- Define collection types and variables
   TYPE row_num_type  IS TABLE OF NUMBER       INDEX BY PLS_INTEGER;
   TYPE row_text_type IS TABLE OF VARCHAR2(10) INDEX BY PLS_INTEGER;

   row_num_tab  row_num_type;
   row_text_tab row_text_type;

   v_total NUMBER;
```

```
    v_start_time INTEGER;
    v_end_time   INTEGER;

BEGIN
    -- Populate collections
    FOR i IN 1..100 LOOP
        row_num_tab(i)  := i;
        row_text_tab(i) := 'row '||i;
    END LOOP;

    -- Record start time
    v_start_time := DBMS_UTILITY.GET_TIME;

    -- Insert first 100 rows
    FOR i IN 1..100 LOOP
        INSERT INTO test (row_num, row_text)
        VALUES (row_num_tab(i), row_text_tab(i));
    END LOOP;

    -- Record end time
    v_end_time := DBMS_UTILITY.GET_TIME;

    -- Calculate and display elapsed time
    DBMS_OUTPUT.PUT_LINE ('Duration of the FOR LOOP: '||
        (v_end_time - v_start_time));

    -- Record start time
    v_start_time := DBMS_UTILITY.GET_TIME;

    -- Insert second 100 rows
    FORALL i IN 1..100
        INSERT INTO test (row_num, row_text)
        VALUES (row_num_tab(i), row_text_tab(i));

    -- Record end time
    v_end_time := DBMS_UTILITY.GET_TIME;

    -- Calculate and display elapsed time
    DBMS_OUTPUT.PUT_LINE ('Duration of the FORALL statement: '||
        (v_end_time - v_start_time));

    COMMIT;
END;
```

To calculate execution times of the FOR loop and the FORALL statement, you employ the GET_TIME function from the DBMS_UTILITY package that is owned by the Oracle user SYS.

The GET_TIME function returns the current time down to hundredths of a second. Note the output produced by this example:

```
Duration of the FOR LOOP: 3
Duration of the FORALL statement: 0

PL/SQL procedure successfully completed.
```

THE SAVE EXCEPTIONS OPTION

As mentioned previously, the SAVE EXCEPTIONS option enables the FORALL statement to continue even when the corresponding SQL statement causes an exception. These exceptions are stored in the cursor attribute called SQL%BULK_EXCEPTIONS. The SQL%BULK_EXCEPTIONS cursor attribute is a collection of records in which each record consists of two fields, ERROR_INDEX and ERROR_CODE. The ERROR_INDEX field stores the number of the iteration of the FORALL statement during which an exception was encountered, and the ERROR_CODE stores the Oracle error code corresponding to the raised exception.

The number of exceptions that occurred during the execution of the FORALL statement can be retrieved using SQL%BULK_EXCEPTIONS.COUNT. Note that even though the individual error messages are not saved, they can be looked up using the SQLERRM function.

Next, consider an example of the FORALL statement with the SAVE EXCEPTIONS option:

FOR EXAMPLE

```
TRUNCATE TABLE TEST;

DECLARE
   -- Define collection types and variables
   TYPE row_num_type  IS TABLE OF NUMBER       INDEX BY PLS_INTEGER;
   TYPE row_text_type IS TABLE OF VARCHAR2(11) INDEX BY PLS_INTEGER;

   row_num_tab   row_num_type;
   row_text_tab row_text_type;

   -- Define user-defined exception and associated Oracle
   -- error number with it
   errors EXCEPTION;
   PRAGMA EXCEPTION_INIT(errors, -24381);

BEGIN
   -- Populate collections
   FOR i IN 1..10 LOOP
      row_num_tab(i)   := i;
      row_text_tab(i) := 'row '||i;
   END LOOP;

   -- Modify 1, 5, and 7 elements of the V_ROW_TEXT collection
   -- These rows will cause exception in the FORALL statement
   row_text_tab(1) := RPAD(row_text_tab(1), 11, ' ');
```

```
   row_text_tab(5) := RPAD(row_text_tab(5), 11, ' ');
   row_text_tab(7) := RPAD(row_text_tab(7), 11, ' ');


   -- Populate TEST table
   FORALL i IN 1..10 SAVE EXCEPTIONS
      INSERT INTO test (row_num, row_text)
      VALUES (row_num_tab(i), row_text_tab(i));
   COMMIT;

EXCEPTION
   WHEN errors THEN
      -- Display total number of exceptions encountered
      DBMS_OUTPUT.PUT_LINE
         ('There were '||SQL%BULK_EXCEPTIONS.COUNT||' exceptions');

      -- Display detailed exception information
      FOR i in 1.. SQL%BULK_EXCEPTIONS.COUNT LOOP
         DBMS_OUTPUT.PUT_LINE ('Record '||
            SQL%BULK_EXCEPTIONS(i).error_index||' caused error '||i||
            ': '||SQL%BULK_EXCEPTIONS(i).ERROR_CODE||' '||
            SQLERRM(-SQL%BULK_EXCEPTIONS(i).ERROR_CODE));
      END LOOP;
END;
```

In this example, you declare a user-defined exception and associate it with the ORA-24381 exception. This exception occurs when errors are encountered in an array DML statement—which, in this case, is the INSERT statement that uses collection elements.

To cause exceptions, the row_text_tab elements 1, 5, and 7 are expanded to store 11 characters instead of 10, and the exception-handling section is added to handle these errors. In the exception-handling section, you display how many exceptions were encountered by invoking the COUNT method on the SQL%BULK_EXCEPTIONS collection. You also display detailed exception information such as which record number caused an exception and the error message associated with this exception. To display the number of the record that caused an exception, you use the error_index field. To display the error message itself, you employ the SQLERRM function and error_code field. Note that when error_code is passed to the SQLERRM function, it is prefixed by a minus sign.

When run, this script produces the following output:

```
There were 3 exceptions
Record 1 caused error 1: 12899 ORA-12899: value too large for column
(actual: , maximum: )
Record 5 caused error 2: 12899 ORA-12899: value too large for column
(actual: , maximum: )
Record 7 caused error 3: 12899 ORA-12899: value too large for column
(actual: , maximum: )

PL/SQL procedure successfully completed.
```

THE INDICES OF OPTION

As stated previously, the INDICES OF option enables you to loop through a sparse collection. Recall that such a collection may be a nested table or an associative array. The use of the INDICES OF option is illustrated in the following example:

FOR EXAMPLE

```
TRUNCATE TABLE TEST;

DECLARE
    -- Define collection types and variables
    TYPE row_num_type  IS TABLE OF NUMBER        INDEX BY PLS_INTEGER;
    TYPE row_text_type IS TABLE OF VARCHAR2(10) INDEX BY PLS_INTEGER;

    row_num_tab   row_num_type;
    row_text_tab row_text_type;

    v_total NUMBER;
BEGIN
    -- Populate collections
    FOR i IN 1..10 LOOP
        row_num_tab(i)  := i;
        row_text_tab(i) := 'row '||i;
    END LOOP;

    -- Delete 1, 5, and 7 elements of collections
    row_num_tab.DELETE(1); row_text_tab.DELETE(1);
    row_num_tab.DELETE(5); row_text_tab.DELETE(5);
    row_num_tab.DELETE(7); row_text_tab.DELETE(7);

    -- Populate TEST table
    FORALL i IN INDICES OF row_num_tab
        INSERT INTO test (row_num, row_text)
        VALUES (row_num_tab(i), row_text_tab(i));
    COMMIT;

    SELECT COUNT(*)
        INTO v_total
        FROM test;

    DBMS_OUTPUT.PUT_LINE
        ('There are '||v_total||' rows in the TEST table');
END;
```

To make the nested tables sparse, the first, fifth, and seventh elements are deleted. As a result, the FORALL statement iterates seven times, and seven rows are added to the TEST table. This is illustrated by the following output:

```
There are 7 rows in the TEST table

PL/SQL procedure successfully completed.
```

THE VALUES OF OPTION

The VALUES OF option specifies that the values of the loop counter in the FORALL statement are based on the values of the elements of the specified collection. Essentially, this collection is a group of indexes that the FORALL statement can loop through. Furthermore, these indexes do not need to be unique and can be listed in arbitrary order. The following example demonstrates the use of the VALUES OF option:

FOR EXAMPLE

```
CREATE TABLE TEST_EXC (row_num NUMBER, row_text VARCHAR2(50));

TRUNCATE TABLE TEST;

DECLARE
    -- Define collection types and variables
    TYPE row_num_type  IS TABLE OF NUMBER        INDEX BY PLS_INTEGER;
    TYPE row_text_type IS TABLE OF VARCHAR2(11)  INDEX BY PLS_INTEGER;
    TYPE exc_ind_type  IS TABLE OF PLS_INTEGER   INDEX BY PLS_INTEGER;

    row_num_tab  row_num_type;
    row_text_tab row_text_type;
    exc_ind_tab  exc_ind_type;

    -- Define user-defined exception and associated Oracle
    -- error number with it
    errors EXCEPTION;
    PRAGMA EXCEPTION_INIT(errors, -24381);

BEGIN
    -- Populate collections
    FOR i IN 1..10 LOOP
        row_num_tab(i)  := i;
        row_text_tab(i) := 'row '||i;
    END LOOP;

    -- Modify 1, 5, and 7 elements of the V_ROW_TEXT collection
    -- These rows will cause exception in the FORALL statement
    row_text_tab(1) := RPAD(row_text_tab(1), 11, ' ');
    row_text_tab(5) := RPAD(row_text_tab(5), 11, ' ');
    row_text_tab(7) := RPAD(row_text_tab(7), 11, ' ');

    -- Populate TEST table
    FORALL i IN 1..10 SAVE EXCEPTIONS
        INSERT INTO test (row_num, row_text)
```

FOR EXAMPLE (continued)

```
        VALUES (row_num_tab(i), row_text_tab(i));
    COMMIT;

EXCEPTION
    WHEN errors THEN

        -- Populate V_EXC_IND_TAB collection to be used in the VALUES
        -- OF clause
        FOR i in 1.. SQL%BULK_EXCEPTIONS.COUNT LOOP
            exc_ind_tab(i) := SQL%BULK_EXCEPTIONS(i).error_index;
        END LOOP;

        -- Insert records that caused exceptions in the TEST_EXC
        -- table
        FORALL i in VALUES OF exc_ind_tab
            INSERT INTO test_exc (row_num, row_text)
            VALUES (row_num_tab(i), row_text_tab(i));
    COMMIT;
END;
```

In this script, you define the TEST_EXC table, which has the same structure as the TEST table, but with expanded data type sizes. The newly created table is used to store records that cause exceptions when they are inserted into the TEST table. Next, you define the new collection data type `exc_ind_type` as a table of PLS_INTEGER indexed by PLS_INTEGER. This enables you to reference this collection in the VALUES OF clause later.

Next, you modify the first, fifth, and seventh elements of the `row_text_tab` table to cause exceptions in the FORALL statement. Then, in the exception-handling section, you populate the `exc_ind_tab` collection with index values of rows that caused the exceptions. In this example, these index values are 1, 5, and 7, and they are stored in the ERROR_INDEX field of the SQL%BULK_EXCEPTION collection. After `exc_ind_tab` is populated, you use it to iterate through the `row_num_tab` and `row_test_tab` collections again and insert erroneous records in the TEST_EXC tab.

After this script is executed, the TEST and TEST_EXC tables contain the following records:

```
    select * from test;

        ROW_NUM ROW_TEXT
    ---------- ----------
              2 row 2
              3 row 3
              4 row 4
              6 row 6
              8 row 8
              9 row 9
             10 row 10
```

7 rows selected.

```
select * from test_exc;

    ROW_NUM ROW_TEXT
---------- --------------------------------------------------
          1 row 1
          5 row 5
          7 row 7
```

▼ LAB 18.1 EXERCISES

This section provides exercises and suggested answers, with discussion related to how those answers resulted. The most important thing to realize is whether your answer works. You should figure out the implications of the answers and what the effects are of any different answers you may come up with.

18.1.1 Use the FORALL Statement

In this exercise, you create a new table called MY_ZIPCODE that has the same structure as the ZIPCODE table in the STUDENT schema. This table will be used throughout the exercises in this lab. You will populate this table using the FORALL statement. Furthermore, in these exercises you will use various options available for the FORALL statement, such as SAVE EXCEPTIONS, INDICES OF, and VALUES OF.

Create the MY_ZIPCODE table as follows:

```
CREATE TABLE my_zipcode AS
SELECT *
  FROM zipcode
 WHERE 1 = 2;
```

This statement creates an empty MY_ZIPCODE table because the criterion specified in the WHERE clause does not return any records.

Create the following PL/SQL script:

```
-- ch18_1a.sql, version 1.0
SET SERVEROUTPUT ON
DECLARE
   -- Declare collection types
   TYPE string_type IS TABLE OF VARCHAR2(100) INDEX BY PLS_INTEGER;
   TYPE date_type   IS TABLE OF DATE          INDEX BY PLS_INTEGER;

   -- Declare collection variables to be used by the FORALL
   -- statement
   zip_tab      string_type;
   city_tab     string_type;
   state_tab    string_type;
   cr_by_tab    string_type;
   cr_date_tab  date_type;
   mod_by_tab   string_type;
   mod_date_tab date_type;
```

```
      v_counter PLS_INTEGER := 0;
      v_total   INTEGER := 0;

   BEGIN
      -- Populate individual collections
      FOR rec IN (SELECT *
                    FROM zipcode
                   WHERE state = 'CT')
      LOOP
         v_counter := v_counter + 1;
         zip_tab(v_counter)      := rec.zip;
         city_tab(v_counter)     := rec.city;
         state_tab(v_counter)    := rec.state;
         cr_by_tab(v_counter)    := rec.created_by;
         cr_date_tab(v_counter)  := rec.created_date;
         mod_by_tab(v_counter)   := rec.modified_by;
         mod_date_tab(v_counter) := rec.modified_date;
      END LOOP;

      -- Populate MY_ZIPCODE table
      FORALL i in 1..zip_tab.COUNT
         INSERT INTO my_zipcode
            (zip, city, state, created_by, created_date, modified_by,
             modified_date)
         VALUES
            (zip_tab(i), city_tab(i), state_tab(i), cr_by_tab(i),
             cr_date_tab(i), mod_by_tab(i), mod_date_tab(i));
      COMMIT;

      -- Check how many records were added to MY_ZIPCODE table
      SELECT COUNT(*)
        INTO v_total
        FROM my_zipcode
       WHERE state = 'CT';

      DBMS_OUTPUT.PUT_LINE
         (v_total||' records were added to MY_ZIPCODE table');
   END;
```

Answer the following questions and complete the following tasks:

A) Explain the newly created script.

ANSWER: This script populates the MY_ZIPCODE table with records selected from the ZIPCODE table. To enable use of the FORALL statement, it employs seven collections. Note that only two collection types are associated with these collections. This is because the individual collections store only two data types, VARCHAR2 and DATE. The script uses cursor FOR loop to populate the individual collections and then uses them with the FORALL statement to populate the MY_ZIPCODE table. Finally, it checks how many records were added to the MY_ZIPCODE table and displays this on the screen, as shown here:

```
19 records were added to MY_ZIPCODE table

PL/SQL procedure successfully completed.
```

B) Modify the previous version of the script as follows: Select data from the ZIPCODE table for a different state, such as MA. Modify the selected records so that they will cause various exceptions in the FORALL statement. Modify the FORALL statement so that it does not fail when an exception occurs. Finally, display exception details on the screen.

ANSWER: The script should look similar to the following. Changes are shown in bold.

```
-- ch18_1b.sql, version 2.0
SET SERVEROUTPUT ON
DECLARE
    -- Declare collection types
    TYPE string_type IS TABLE OF VARCHAR2(100) INDEX BY PLS_INTEGER;
    TYPE date_type   IS TABLE OF DATE          INDEX BY PLS_INTEGER;

    -- Declare collection variables to be used by the FORALL
    -- statement
    zip_tab        string_type;
    city_tab       string_type;
    state_tab      string_type;
    cr_by_tab      string_type;
    cr_date_tab    date_type;
    mod_by_tab     string_type;
    mod_date_tab   date_type;

    v_counter PLS_INTEGER := 0;
    v_total   INTEGER := 0;

    -- Define user-defined exception and associated Oracle
    -- error number with it
    errors EXCEPTION;
    PRAGMA EXCEPTION_INIT(errors, -24381);

BEGIN
    -- Populate individual collections
    FOR rec IN (SELECT *
                  FROM zipcode
                 WHERE state = 'MA')
    LOOP
        v_counter := v_counter + 1;
        zip_tab(v_counter)      := rec.zip;
        city_tab(v_counter)     := rec.city;
        state_tab(v_counter)    := rec.state;
        cr_by_tab(v_counter)    := rec.created_by;
        cr_date_tab(v_counter)  := rec.created_date;
        mod_by_tab(v_counter)   := rec.modified_by;
        mod_date_tab(v_counter) := rec.modified_date;
    END LOOP;

    -- Modify individual collection records to produce various
    -- exceptions
    zip_tab(1)      := NULL;
    city_tab(2)     := RPAD(city_tab(2), 26, ' ');
    state_tab(3)    := SYSDATE;
```

```
cr_by_tab(4)   := RPAD(cr_by_tab(4), 31, ' ');
cr_date_tab(5) := NULL;

-- Populate MY_ZIPCODE table
FORALL i in 1..zip_tab.COUNT SAVE EXCEPTIONS
    INSERT INTO my_zipcode
        (zip, city, state, created_by, created_date, modified_by,
        modified_date)
    VALUES
        (zip_tab(i), city_tab(i), state_tab(i), cr_by_tab(i),
        cr_date_tab(i), mod_by_tab(i), mod_date_tab(i));
COMMIT;

-- Check how many records were added to MY_ZIPCODE table
SELECT COUNT(*)
  INTO v_total
  FROM my_zipcode
 WHERE state = 'MA';

DBMS_OUTPUT.PUT_LINE
    (v_total||' records were added to MY_ZIPCODE table');

EXCEPTION
    WHEN errors THEN
        -- Display total number of exceptions encountered
        DBMS_OUTPUT.PUT_LINE
            ('There were '||SQL%BULK_EXCEPTIONS.COUNT||' exceptions');

        -- Display detailed exception information
        FOR i in 1.. SQL%BULK_EXCEPTIONS.COUNT LOOP
            DBMS_OUTPUT.PUT_LINE ('Record '||
                SQL%BULK_EXCEPTIONS(i).error_index||' caused error '||i||
                ': '||SQL%BULK_EXCEPTIONS(i).ERROR_CODE||' '||
                SQLERRM(-SQL%BULK_EXCEPTIONS(i).ERROR_CODE));
        END LOOP;

        -- Commit records if any that were inserted successfully
        COMMIT;
END;
```

In this script, you declare a user-defined exception and associate an Oracle error number with it using the EXCEPTION_INIT pragma. Next, you populate individual collections with the cursor FOR loop against the ZIPCODE table, and then you modify them so that they cause exceptions in the FORALL statement. For example, the first record of the `zip_tab` collection is set to NULL. This causes a constraint violation because the ZIP column in the MY_ZIPCODE table has a NOT NULL constraint defined against it. Then, you add the SAVE EXCEPTIONS clause to the FORALL statement and an exception-handling section to the PL/SQL block. In this section, you display the total number of errors encountered, along with detailed exception information. Note the COMMIT statement in the exception-handling section. This statement is added so that records that are inserted successfully by the FORALL statement are committed when control of the execution is passed to the exception-handling section of the block.

When run, this version of the script produces the following output:

```
There were 5 exceptions
Record 1 caused error 1: 1400 ORA-01400: cannot insert NULL into ()
Record 2 caused error 2: 12899 ORA-12899: value too large for
  column (actual: , maximum: )
Record 3 caused error 3: 12899 ORA-12899: value too large for
  column actual: , maximum: )
Record 4 caused error 4: 12899 ORA-12899: value too large for
  column actual: , maximum: )
Record 5 caused error 5: 1400 ORA-01400: cannot insert NULL into ()

PL/SQL procedure successfully completed.
```

C) Modify the previous version of the script as follows: Do not modify records selected from the ZIPCODE table so that no exceptions are raised. Instead, delete the first three records from each collection so that they become sparse. Then modify the FORALL statement accordingly.

ANSWER: This version of the script should look similar to the following. Changes are shown in bold.

```
-- ch18_1c.sql, version 3.0
SET SERVEROUTPUT ON
DECLARE
   -- Declare collection types
   TYPE string_type IS TABLE OF VARCHAR2(100) INDEX BY PLS_INTEGER;
   TYPE date_type   IS TABLE OF DATE          INDEX BY PLS_INTEGER;

   -- Declare collection variables to be used by the FORALL
   -- statement
   zip_tab      string_type;
   city_tab     string_type;
   state_tab    string_type;
   cr_by_tab    string_type;
   cr_date_tab  date_type;
   mod_by_tab   string_type;
   mod_date_tab date_type;

   v_counter PLS_INTEGER := 0;
   v_total   INTEGER := 0;

   -- Define user-defined exception and associated Oracle
   -- error number with it
   errors EXCEPTION;
   PRAGMA EXCEPTION_INIT(errors, -24381);

BEGIN
   -- Populate individual collections
   FOR rec IN (SELECT *
                 FROM zipcode
                WHERE state = 'MA')
   LOOP
      v_counter := v_counter + 1;
```

```
        zip_tab(v_counter)       := rec.zip;
        city_tab(v_counter)      := rec.city;
        state_tab(v_counter)     := rec.state;
        cr_by_tab(v_counter)     := rec.created_by;
        cr_date_tab(v_counter)   := rec.created_date;
        mod_by_tab(v_counter)    := rec.modified_by;
        mod_date_tab(v_counter)  := rec.modified_date;
     END LOOP;

     -- Delete first 3 records from each collection
     zip_tab.DELETE(1,3);
     city_tab.DELETE(1,3);
     state_tab.DELETE(1,3);
     cr_by_tab.DELETE(1,3);
     cr_date_tab.DELETE(1,3);
     mod_by_tab.DELETE(1,3);
     mod_date_tab.DELETE(1,3);

     -- Populate MY_ZIPCODE table
     FORALL i IN INDICES OF zip_tab SAVE EXCEPTIONS
        INSERT INTO my_zipcode
           (zip, city, state, created_by, created_date, modified_by,
            modified_date)
        VALUES
           (zip_tab(i), city_tab(i), state_tab(i), cr_by_tab(i),
            cr_date_tab(i), mod_by_tab(i), mod_date_tab(i));
     COMMIT;

     -- Check how many records were added to MY_ZIPCODE table
     SELECT COUNT(*)
       INTO v_total
       FROM my_zipcode
      WHERE state = 'MA';

     DBMS_OUTPUT.PUT_LINE
        (v_total||' records were added to MY_ZIPCODE table');

EXCEPTION
   WHEN errors THEN
      -- Display total number of exceptions encountered
      DBMS_OUTPUT.PUT_LINE
         ('There were '||SQL%BULK_EXCEPTIONS.COUNT||' exceptions');

      -- Display detailed exception information
      FOR i in 1.. SQL%BULK_EXCEPTIONS.COUNT LOOP
         DBMS_OUTPUT.PUT_LINE ('Record '||
            SQL%BULK_EXCEPTIONS(i).error_index||' caused error '||i||
            ': '||SQL%BULK_EXCEPTIONS(i).ERROR_CODE||' '||
            SQLERRM(-SQL%BULK_EXCEPTIONS(i).ERROR_CODE));
      END LOOP;
```

```
    -- Commit records if any that were inserted successfully
    COMMIT;
END;
```

This version of the script contains two modifications. First, you delete the first three records from each collection. Second, you modify the FORALL statement by replacing the lower and upper limits for the counter variable with the INDICES OF clause.

When run, the script produces the following output:

```
2 records were added to MY_ZIPCODE table

PL/SQL procedure successfully completed.
```

D) Modify the second version of the script, ch18_1b.sql, as follows: Insert records that cause exceptions in a different table called MY_ZIPCODE_EXC.

ANSWER: The MY_ZIPCODE_EXC table may be created as follows:

```
CREATE TABLE MY_ZIPCODE_EXC
   (ZIP            VARCHAR2(100),
    CITY           VARCHAR2(100),
    STATE          VARCHAR2(100),
    CREATED_BY     VARCHAR2(100),
    CREATED_DATE   DATE,
    MODIFIED_BY    VARCHAR2(100),
    MODIFIED_DATE  DATE);
```

Note that even though this table has the same columns as the MY_ZIPCODE table, the column sizes have been increased and all NOT NULL constraints removed. This ensures that records that cause exceptions in the FORALL statements can be inserted into this table.

Next, the script is modified as follows. Changes are shown in bold.

```
-- ch18_1d.sql, version 4.0
SET SERVEROUTPUT ON
DECLARE
    -- Declare collection types
    TYPE string_type  IS TABLE OF VARCHAR2(100)  INDEX BY PLS_INTEGER;
    TYPE date_type    IS TABLE OF DATE           INDEX BY PLS_INTEGER;
    TYPE exc_ind_type IS TABLE OF PLS_INTEGER    INDEX BY PLS_INTEGER;

    -- Declare collection variables to be used by the FORALL
    -- statement
    zip_tab      string_type;
    city_tab     string_type;
    state_tab    string_type;
    cr_by_tab    string_type;
    cr_date_tab  date_type;
    mod_by_tab   string_type;
    mod_date_tab date_type;
    exc_ind_tab  exc_ind_type;

    v_counter PLS_INTEGER := 0;
    v_total   INTEGER := 0;
```

```
   -- Define user-defined exception and associated Oracle
   -- error number with it
   errors EXCEPTION;
   PRAGMA EXCEPTION_INIT(errors, -24381);

BEGIN
   -- Populate individual collections
   FOR rec IN (SELECT *
                 FROM zipcode
                WHERE state = 'MA')
   LOOP
      v_counter := v_counter + 1;
      zip_tab(v_counter)      := rec.zip;
      city_tab(v_counter)     := rec.city;
      state_tab(v_counter)    := rec.state;
      cr_by_tab(v_counter)    := rec.created_by;
      cr_date_tab(v_counter)  := rec.created_date;
      mod_by_tab(v_counter)   := rec.modified_by;
      mod_date_tab(v_counter) := rec.modified_date;
   END LOOP;

   -- Modify individual collection records to produce various
   -- exceptions
   zip_tab(1)     := NULL;
   city_tab(2)    := RPAD(city_tab(2), 26, ' ');
   state_tab(3)   := SYSDATE;
   cr_by_tab(4)   := RPAD(cr_by_tab(4), 31, ' ');
   cr_date_tab(5) := NULL;

   -- Populate MY_ZIPCODE table
   FORALL i in 1..zip_tab.COUNT SAVE EXCEPTIONS
      INSERT INTO my_zipcode
         (zip, city, state, created_by, created_date, modified_by,
          modified_date)
      VALUES
         (zip_tab(i), city_tab(i), state_tab(i), cr_by_tab(i),
          cr_date_tab(i), mod_by_tab(i), mod_date_tab(i));
   COMMIT;

   -- Check how many records were added to MY_ZIPCODE table
   SELECT COUNT(*)
     INTO v_total
     FROM my_zipcode
    WHERE state = 'MA';

   DBMS_OUTPUT.PUT_LINE
      (v_total||' records were added to MY_ZIPCODE table');

EXCEPTION
   WHEN errors THEN
```

```
   -- Populate V_EXC_IND_TAB collection to be used in the VALUES
   -- OF clause
   FOR i in 1.. SQL%BULK_EXCEPTIONS.COUNT LOOP
      exc_ind_tab(i) := SQL%BULK_EXCEPTIONS(i).error_index;
   END LOOP;

   -- Insert records that caused exceptions in the MY_ZIPCODE_EXC
   -- table
   FORALL i in VALUES OF exc_ind_tab
      INSERT INTO my_zipcode_exc
      (zip, city, state, created_by, created_date, modified_by,
       modified_date)
   VALUES
      (zip_tab(i), city_tab(i), state_tab(i), cr_by_tab(i),
       cr_date_tab(i), mod_by_tab(i), mod_date_tab(i));

   COMMIT;
END;
```

In this version of the script, you modify the exception-handling section so that records causing exceptions in the FORALL statement are inserted into the MY_ZIPCODE_EXC table created earlier. First, you populate the collection EXC_IND_TAB with subscripts of records that caused exceptions in the FORALL statement. Then you loop through this collection and insert erroneous records in the MY_ZIPCODE_EXC table. After the script is executed, the MY_ZIPCODE_EXC table contains these records.

LAB 18.2
The BULK COLLECT Clause

LAB OBJECTIVE

After completing this lab, you will be able to

▶ Use the BULK COLLECT clause

The BULK COLLECT clause fetches the batches of results and brings them back from SQL to PL/SQL. For example, consider a cursor against the STUDENT table that returns the student's ID, first name, and last name. After this cursor is opened, the rows are fetched one by one until all of them have been processed. Then this cursor is closed. These steps are illustrated in the following example:

FOR EXAMPLE

```
DECLARE
   CURSOR student_cur IS
      SELECT student_id, first_name, last_name
        FROM student;
BEGIN
   FOR rec IN student_cur LOOP
      DBMS_OUTPUT.PUT_LINE ('student_id: '||rec.student_id);
      DBMS_OUTPUT.PUT_LINE ('first_name: '||rec.first_name);
      DBMS_OUTPUT.PUT_LINE ('last_name:  '||rec.last_name);
   END LOOP;
END;
```

Recall that the cursor FOR loop opens and closes the cursor and fetches cursor records implicitly.

The same task of fetching records from the STUDENT table can be accomplished by employing the BULK COLLECT clause. The difference here is that the BULK COLLECT clause fetches all rows from the STUDENT table at once. Because BULK COLLECT fetches multiple rows, these rows are stored in collection variables.

Consider a modified version of the previous example, in which the cursor processing is replaced by the BULK COLLECT clause:

FOR EXAMPLE

```
DECLARE
-- Define collection type and variables to be used by the
-- BULK COLLECT clause
   TYPE student_id_type IS TABLE OF student.student_id%TYPE;
   TYPE first_name_type IS TABLE OF student.first_name%TYPE;
   TYPE last_name_type  IS TABLE OF student.last_name%TYPE;

   student_id_tab student_id_type;
   first_name_tab first_name_type;
   last_name_tab  last_name_type;

BEGIN
   -- Fetch all student data at once via BULK COLLECT clause
   SELECT student_id, first_name, last_name
     BULK COLLECT INTO student_id_tab, first_name_tab, last_name_tab
     FROM student;

   FOR i IN student_id_tab.FIRST..student_id_tab.LAST
   LOOP
      DBMS_OUTPUT.PUT_LINE ('student_id: '||student_id_tab(i));
      DBMS_OUTPUT.PUT_LINE ('first_name: '||first_name_tab(i));
      DBMS_OUTPUT.PUT_LINE ('last_name:  '||last_name_tab(i));
   END LOOP;
END;
```

This script declares three nested table types and variables. These variables are used to store data returned by the SELECT statement with the BULK COLLECT clause.

DID YOU KNOW?

When nested tables are populated using the SELECT BULK COLLECT INTO statement, they are initialized and extended automatically. Recall that typically a nested table must be initialized prior to its use by calling a constructor function that has the same name as its nested table type. After it has been initialized, it must be extended using the EXTEND method before the next value can be assigned to it.

To display this data, the collections are looped through using a numeric FOR loop. Note how lower and upper limits for the loop counter are specified using the FIRST and LAST methods.

The BULK COLLECT clause is similar to a cursor loop in that it does not raise a NO_DATA_FOUND exception when the SELECT statement does not return any records. As a result, it is considered a good practice to check if a resulting collection contains any data.

Because the BULK COLLECT clause does not restrict the size of a collection and extends it automatically, it is also a good idea to limit the result set when a SELECT statement returns large amounts of data. This can be achieved by using BULK COLLECT with a cursor SELECT and by adding the LIMIT option.

FOR EXAMPLE

```
DECLARE
   CURSOR student_cur IS
      SELECT student_id, first_name, last_name
        FROM student;

-- Define collection type and variables to be used by the
-- BULK COLLECT clause
   TYPE student_id_type IS TABLE OF student.student_id%TYPE;
   TYPE first_name_type IS TABLE OF student.first_name%TYPE;
   TYPE last_name_type  IS TABLE OF student.last_name%TYPE;

   student_id_tab student_id_type;
   first_name_tab first_name_type;
   last_name_tab  last_name_type;

   -- Define variable to be used by the LIMIT clause
   v_limit PLS_INTEGER := 50;

BEGIN
   OPEN student_cur;
   LOOP
      -- Fetch 50 rows at once
      FETCH student_cur
       BULK COLLECT INTO student_id_tab, first_name_tab,
         last_name_tab
      LIMIT v_limit;

      EXIT WHEN student_id_tab.COUNT = 0;

      FOR i IN student_id_tab.FIRST..student_id_tab.LAST
      LOOP
         DBMS_OUTPUT.PUT_LINE ('student_id: '||student_id_tab(i));
         DBMS_OUTPUT.PUT_LINE ('first_name: '||first_name_tab(i));
         DBMS_OUTPUT.PUT_LINE ('last_name:  '||last_name_tab(i));
      END LOOP;

   END LOOP;
   CLOSE student_cur;
END;
```

This script employs a BULK COLLECT clause with the LIMIT option to fetch 50 rows from the STUDENT table at once. In other words, each collection contains, at most, 50 records. To accomplish this, the BULK COLLECT clause is used in conjunction with the cursor loop. Note that in this case, the loop's exit condition is based on the number of records in the collection rather than the `student_cur%NOTFOUND` attribute.

Note how the numeric FOR loop that displays information on the screen has been moved inside the cursor loop. This is done because every new batch of 50 records fetched by the BULK COLLECT replaces the previous batch of 50 records fetched in the previous iteration.

So far you have seen examples of the BULK COLLECT clause fetching data into collections where the underlying elements are simple data types such as NUMBER or VARCHAR2. However, the BULK COLLECT clause can be used to fetch data into collections of records or objects. Collections of objects are discussed in Chapter 23, "Object Types in Oracle." Consider a modified version of the previous example, in which student data is fetched into a collection of user-defined records:

FOR EXAMPLE

```
DECLARE
    CURSOR student_cur IS
        SELECT student_id, first_name, last_name
          FROM student;

    -- Define record type
    TYPE student_rec IS RECORD
        (student_id student.student_id%TYPE,
         first_name student.first_name%TYPE,
         last_name  student.last_name%TYPE);

    -- Define collection type
    TYPE student_type IS TABLE OF student_rec;

    -- Define collection variable
    student_tab student_type;

    -- Define variable to be used by the LIMIT clause
    v_limit PLS_INTEGER := 50;

BEGIN
    OPEN student_cur;
    LOOP
        -- Fetch 50 rows at once
        FETCH student_cur BULK COLLECT INTO student_tab LIMIT v_limit;

        EXIT WHEN student_tab.COUNT = 0;

        FOR i IN student_tab.FIRST..student_tab.LAST
        LOOP
            DBMS_OUTPUT.PUT_LINE
                ('student_id: '||student_tab(i).student_id);
            DBMS_OUTPUT.PUT_LINE
                ('first_name: '|| student_tab(i).first_name);
```

FOR EXAMPLE (continued)

```
            DBMS_OUTPUT.PUT_LINE
                ('last_name:  '|| student_tab(i).last_name);
        END LOOP;

    END LOOP;
    CLOSE student_cur;
END;
```

So far you have seen how to use the BULK COLLECT clause with the SELECT statement. However, often BULK COLLECT is used with the INSERT, UPDATE, and DELETE statements as well. In this case, the BULK COLLECT clause is used in conjunction with the RETURNING clause, as shown here:

FOR EXAMPLE

```
DECLARE
    -- Define collection types and variables
    TYPE row_num_type  IS TABLE OF NUMBER       INDEX BY PLS_INTEGER;
    TYPE row_text_type IS TABLE OF VARCHAR2(10)  INDEX BY PLS_INTEGER;

    row_num_tab  row_num_type;
    row_text_tab row_text_type;

BEGIN
    DELETE FROM TEST
    RETURNING row_num, row_text
    BULK COLLECT INTO row_num_tab, row_text_tab;

    DBMS_OUTPUT.PUT_LINE ('Deleted '||SQL%ROWCOUNT ||' rows:');
    FOR i IN row_num_tab.FIRST..row_num_tab.LAST
    LOOP
        DBMS_OUTPUT.PUT_LINE ('row_num = '||row_num_tab(i)||
            ' row_text = ' ||row_text_tab(i));
    END LOOP;

    COMMIT;
END;
```

This script deletes records from the TEST table created in Lab 18.1. Note that the DELETE statement returns ROW_NUM and ROW_TEXT values using the RETURNING clause. These values are then fetched by the BULK COLLECT clause into two collections, row_num_tab and row_text_tab, which are displayed on the screen.

When run, this script produces the following output:

```
    Deleted 7 rows:
    row_num = 2 row_text = row 2
```

```
row_num = 3 row_text = row 3
row_num = 4 row_text = row 4
row_num = 6 row_text = row 6
row_num = 8 row_text = row 8
row_num = 9 row_text = row 9
row_num = 10 row_text = row 10

PL/SQL procedure successfully completed.
```

Throughout this chapter you have seen how to use the FORALL statement and BULK COLLECT clause. Next, consider an example that combines both. This example is based on the script ch18_1a.sql, which selects some data from the ZIPCODE table and inserts it into the MY_ZIPCODE table. Changes are shown in bold.

FOR EXAMPLE

```
DECLARE
   -- Declare collection types
   TYPE string_type IS TABLE OF VARCHAR2(100) INDEX BY PLS_INTEGER;
   TYPE date_type   IS TABLE OF DATE          INDEX BY PLS_INTEGER;

   -- Declare collection variables to be used by the FORALL statement
   zip_tab      string_type;
   city_tab     string_type;
   state_tab    string_type;
   cr_by_tab    string_type;
   cr_date_tab  date_type;
   mod_by_tab   string_type;
   mod_date_tab date_type;

   v_counter PLS_INTEGER := 0;
   v_total   INTEGER := 0;

BEGIN
   -- Populate individual collections
   SELECT *
     BULK COLLECT INTO zip_tab, city_tab, state_tab, cr_by_tab,
       cr_date_tab, mod_by_tab, mod_date_tab
     FROM zipcode
    WHERE state = 'CT';

   -- Populate MY_ZIPCODE table
   FORALL i in 1..zip_tab.COUNT
      INSERT INTO my_zipcode
         (zip, city, state, created_by, created_date, modified_by,
          modified_date)
      VALUES
         (zip_tab(i), city_tab(i), state_tab(i), cr_by_tab(i),
          cr_date_tab(i), mod_by_tab(i), mod_date_tab(i));
   COMMIT;
```

FOR EXAMPLE (continued)

```
-- Check how many records were added to MY_ZIPCODE table
SELECT COUNT(*)
  INTO v_total
  FROM my_zipcode
 WHERE state = 'CT';

DBMS_OUTPUT.PUT_LINE
    (v_total||' records were added to MY_ZIPCODE table');
END;
```

▼ LAB 18.2 EXERCISES

This section provides exercises and suggested answers, with discussion related to how those answers resulted. The most important thing to realize is whether your answer works. You should figure out the implications of the answers and what the effects are of any different answers you may come up with.

18.2.1 Use the BULK COLLECT Statement

In this exercise, you create various scripts that select and modify data in the MY_INSTRUCTOR table in bulk.

Create the MY_INSTRUCTOR table as follows. If this table already exists, drop it and then re-create it.

```
CREATE TABLE my_instructor AS
SELECT *
  FROM instructor;
```

Complete the following tasks:

A) Create the following script: Select the instructor ID, first name, and last name from the MY_INSTRUCTOR table, and display them on the screen. Note that the data should be fetched in bulk.

ANSWER: This script should look similar to the following:

```
-- ch18_2a.sql, version 1.0
SET SERVEROUTPUT ON;
DECLARE
    -- Define collection types and variables to be used by the
    -- BULK COLLECT clause
    TYPE instructor_id_type IS TABLE OF
        my_instructor.instructor_id%TYPE;
    TYPE first_name_type    IS TABLE OF my_instructor.first_name%TYPE;
    TYPE last_name_type      IS TABLE OF my_instructor.last_name%TYPE;

    instructor_id_tab instructor_id_type;
    first_name_tab     first_name_type;
    last_name_tab      last_name_type;

BEGIN
    -- Fetch all instructor data at once via BULK COLLECT clause
```

```
SELECT instructor_id, first_name, last_name
  BULK COLLECT INTO instructor_id_tab, first_name_tab,
                    last_name_tab
  FROM my_instructor;

FOR i IN instructor_id_tab.FIRST..instructor_id_tab.LAST
LOOP
   DBMS_OUTPUT.PUT_LINE ('instructor_id: '||instructor_id_tab(i));
   DBMS_OUTPUT.PUT_LINE ('first_name:    '||first_name_tab(i));
   DBMS_OUTPUT.PUT_LINE ('last_name:     '||last_name_tab(i));
END LOOP;
END;
```

The declaration portion of this script contains definitions of three collection types and variables. The executable portion of the script populates collection variables using the SELECT statement with the BULK COLLECT clause. Finally, it displays on the screen data stored in the collection variables by looping through them.

When run, this script produces the following output:

```
instructor_id: 101
first_name:    Fernand
last_name:     Hanks
instructor_id: 102
first_name:    Tom
last_name:     Wojick
instructor_id: 103
first_name:    Nina
last_name:     Schorin
instructor_id: 104
first_name:    Gary
last_name:     Pertez
instructor_id: 105
first_name:    Anita
last_name:     Morris
instructor_id: 106
first_name:    Todd
last_name:     Smythe
instructor_id: 107
first_name:    Marilyn
last_name:     Frantzen
instructor_id: 108
first_name:    Charles
last_name:     Lowry
instructor_id: 109
first_name:    Rick
last_name:     Chow
instructor_id: 110
first_name:    Irene
last_name:     Willig


PL/SQL procedure successfully completed.
```

As mentioned previously, the BULK COLLECT clause is similar to the cursor loop in that it does not raise a NO_DATA_FOUND exception when the SELECT statement does not return any rows. Consider deleting all the rows from the MY_INSTRUCTOR table and then executing this script again. In this case the output is as follows:

```
SQL> DELETE FROM my_instructor;
```

10 rows deleted.

```
SQL> SET SERVEROUTPUT ON;
SQL> DECLARE
  2      -- Define collection types and variables to be used by the
  3      -- BULK COLLECT clause
  4      TYPE instructor_id_type IS TABLE OF
         my_instructor.instructor_id%TYPE;
  5      TYPE first_name_type    IS TABLE OF
         my_instructor.first_name%TYPE;
  6      TYPE last_name_type     IS TABLE OF
         my_instructor.last_name%TYPE;
  7
  8      instructor_id_tab instructor_id_type;
  9      first_name_tab    first_name_type;
 10      last_name_tab     last_name_type;
 11
 12  BEGIN
 13      -- Fetch all instructor data at once via BULK COLLECT clause
 14      SELECT instructor_id, first_name, last_name
 15        BULK COLLECT INTO instructor_id_tab, first_name_tab,
              last_name_tab
 16        FROM my_instructor;
 17
 18      FOR i IN instructor_id_tab.FIRST..instructor_id_tab.LAST
 19      LOOP
 20         DBMS_OUTPUT.PUT_LINE ('instructor_id:
                             '||instructor_id_tab(i));
 21         DBMS_OUTPUT.PUT_LINE ('first_name:
                             '||first_name_tab(i));
 22         DBMS_OUTPUT.PUT_LINE ('last_name:
                             '||last_name_tab(i));
 23      END LOOP;
 24  END;
 25  /
```

You see the following error message:

```
DECLARE
*
ERROR at line 1:
ORA-06502: PL/SQL: numeric or value error
ORA-06512: at line 18
```

Note that the error message refers to line 18, which contains a FOR loop that iterates through the collections and displays the results on the screen. Note that the SELECT statement with the BULK

COLLECT clause does not cause any errors. To prevent this error from happening, you can modify the script as follows. Changes are shown in bold.

```
-- ch18_2b.sql, version 2.0
SET SERVEROUTPUT ON;
DECLARE
    -- Define collection types and variables to be used by the
    -- BULK COLLECT clause
    TYPE instructor_id_type IS TABLE OF
        my_instructor.instructor_id%TYPE;
    TYPE first_name_type    IS TABLE OF my_instructor.first_name%TYPE;
    TYPE last_name_type     IS TABLE OF my_instructor.last_name%TYPE;

    instructor_id_tab instructor_id_type;
    first_name_tab    first_name_type;
    last_name_tab     last_name_type;

BEGIN
    -- Fetch all instructor data at once via BULK COLLECT clause
    SELECT instructor_id, first_name, last_name
      BULK COLLECT INTO instructor_id_tab, first_name_tab,
        last_name_tab
      FROM my_instructor;

    IF instructor_id_tab.COUNT > 0 THEN
        FOR i IN instructor_id_tab.FIRST..instructor_id_tab.LAST
        LOOP
            DBMS_OUTPUT.PUT_LINE ('instructor_id:
                            '||instructor_id_tab(i));
            DBMS_OUTPUT.PUT_LINE ('first_name:    '||first_name_tab(i));
            DBMS_OUTPUT.PUT_LINE ('last_name:     '||last_name_tab(i));
        END LOOP;
    END IF;
END;
```

This version of the script contains an IF-THEN statement that encloses the FOR loop. The IF-THEN statement checks if one of the collections is nonempty, thus preventing the numeric or value error.

WATCH OUT!

If you have deleted records from the MY_INSTRUCTOR table, you need to roll back your changes or populate it with the records from the INSTRUCTOR table again before proceeding with the exercise.

B) Modify the newly created script as follows: Fetch no more than five rows at a time from the MY_INSTRUCTOR table.

ANSWER: The script should look similar to the following. Changes are shown in bold.

```
-- ch18_2c.sql, version 3.0
SET SERVEROUTPUT ON;
DECLARE
    CURSOR instructor_cur IS
```

```
   SELECT instructor_id, first_name, last_name
     FROM my_instructor;

-- Define collection types and variables to be used by the
-- BULK COLLECT clause
TYPE instructor_id_type IS TABLE OF
   my_instructor.instructor_id%TYPE;
TYPE first_name_type   IS TABLE OF my_instructor.first_name%TYPE;
TYPE last_name_type    IS TABLE OF my_instructor.last_name%TYPE;

instructor_id_tab instructor_id_type;
first_name_tab    first_name_type;
last_name_tab     last_name_type;

v_limit PLS_INTEGER := 5;
BEGIN
   OPEN instructor_cur;
   LOOP
      -- Fetch partial instructor data at once via BULK COLLECT
      -- clause
      FETCH instructor_cur
       BULK COLLECT INTO instructor_id_tab, first_name_tab,
          last_name_tab
      LIMIT v_limit;

      EXIT WHEN instructor_id_tab.COUNT = 0;

      FOR i IN instructor_id_tab.FIRST..instructor_id_tab.LAST
      LOOP
         DBMS_OUTPUT.PUT_LINE ('instructor_id:
                              '||instructor_id_tab(i));
         DBMS_OUTPUT.PUT_LINE ('first_name:   '||first_name_tab(i));
         DBMS_OUTPUT.PUT_LINE ('last_name:    '||last_name_tab(i));
      END LOOP;
   END LOOP;
   CLOSE instructor_cur;
END;
```

In this version of the script, you declare a cursor against the MY_INSTRUCTOR table. This enables you to do a partial fetch from the MY_INSTRUCTOR table. You process this cursor by fetching five records at a time using the BULK COLLECT clause with the LIMIT option. This ensures that the collection variables contain no more than five records for each iteration of the cursor loop. Finally, to display all the results on the screen, you move the FOR loop inside the cursor FOR loop. This version of the script produces output identical to the first version of the script.

C) Modify the newly created script as follows: Instead of fetching data from the MY_INSTRUCTOR table into individual collections, fetch it into a single collection.

ANSWER: To accomplish this task, the new record type must be declared so that a single collection type can be based on this record type.

This is shown next. Changes are shown in bold.

```
-- ch18_2d.sql, version 4.0
SET SERVEROUTPUT ON;
DECLARE
    CURSOR instructor_cur IS
        SELECT instructor_id, first_name, last_name
            FROM my_instructor;

    -- Define record type
    TYPE instructor_rec IS RECORD
        (instructor_id my_instructor.instructor_id%TYPE,
         first_name    my_instructor.first_name%TYPE,
         last_name     my_instructor.last_name%TYPE);

    -- Define collection type and variable to be used by the
    -- BULK COLLECT clause
    TYPE instructor_type IS TABLE OF instructor_rec;

    instructor_tab instructor_type;

    v_limit PLS_INTEGER := 5;
BEGIN
    OPEN instructor_cur;
    LOOP
        -- Fetch partial instructor data at once via BULK COLLECT
        -- clause
        FETCH instructor_cur
         BULK COLLECT INTO instructor_tab
        LIMIT v_limit;

        EXIT WHEN instructor_tab.COUNT = 0;

        FOR i IN instructor_tab.FIRST..instructor_tab.LAST
        LOOP
            DBMS_OUTPUT.PUT_LINE
                ('instructor_id: '||instructor_tab(i).instructor_id);
            DBMS_OUTPUT.PUT_LINE
                ('first_name:    '||instructor_tab(i).first_name);
            DBMS_OUTPUT.PUT_LINE
                ('last_name:     '||instructor_tab(i).last_name);
        END LOOP;
    END LOOP;
    CLOSE instructor_cur;
END;
```

In this version of the script, you declare a user-defined record type with three fields. Next, you declare a single collection type based on this record type. Then you fetch the results of the cursor into a collection of records that you then display on the screen.

Next, consider another version that also creates a collection of records. In this version, the collection type is based on the row type record returned by the cursor:

```
-- ch18_2e.sql, version 5.0
SET SERVEROUTPUT ON;
DECLARE
   CURSOR instructor_cur IS
      SELECT instructor_id, first_name, last_name
        FROM my_instructor;

   -- Define collection type and variable to be used by the
   -- BULK COLLECT clause
   TYPE instructor_type IS TABLE OF instructor_cur%ROWTYPE;

   instructor_tab instructor_type;

   v_limit PLS_INTEGER := 5;
BEGIN
   OPEN instructor_cur;
   LOOP
      -- Fetch partial instructor data at once via BULK COLLECT
      -- clause
      FETCH instructor_cur
       BULK COLLECT INTO instructor_tab
      LIMIT v_limit;

      EXIT WHEN instructor_tab.COUNT = 0;

      FOR i IN instructor_tab.FIRST..instructor_tab.LAST
      LOOP
         DBMS_OUTPUT.PUT_LINE
            ('instructor_id: '||instructor_tab(i).instructor_id);
         DBMS_OUTPUT.PUT_LINE
            ('first_name:    '||instructor_tab(i).first_name);
         DBMS_OUTPUT.PUT_LINE
            ('last_name:     '||instructor_tab(i).last_name);
      END LOOP;
   END LOOP;
   CLOSE instructor_cur;
END;
```

D) Create the following script: Delete records from the MY_INSTRUCTOR table and display them on the screen.

ANSWER: The script should look similar to the following:

```
-- ch18_3a.sql, version 1.0
SET SERVEROUTPUT ON;
DECLARE
   -- Define collection types and variables to be used by the
   -- BULK COLLECT clause
   TYPE instructor_id_type IS TABLE OF
      my_instructor.instructor_id%TYPE;
```

```
   TYPE first_name_type     IS TABLE OF my_instructor.first_name%TYPE;
   TYPE last_name_type      IS TABLE OF my_instructor.last_name%TYPE;

   instructor_id_tab instructor_id_type;
   first_name_tab    first_name_type;
   last_name_tab     last_name_type;

BEGIN
   DELETE FROM MY_INSTRUCTOR
   RETURNING instructor_id, first_name, last_name
   BULK COLLECT INTO instructor_id_tab, first_name_tab,
      last_name_tab;

   DBMS_OUTPUT.PUT_LINE ('Deleted '||SQL%ROWCOUNT||' rows ');
   IF instructor_id_tab.COUNT > 0 THEN
      FOR i IN instructor_id_tab.FIRST..instructor_id_tab.LAST
      LOOP
         DBMS_OUTPUT.PUT_LINE
            ('instructor_id: '||instructor_id_tab(i));
         DBMS_OUTPUT.PUT_LINE ('first_name:    '||first_name_tab(i));
         DBMS_OUTPUT.PUT_LINE ('last_name:     '||last_name_tab(i));
      END LOOP;
   END IF;
   COMMIT;
END;
```

In this script, you store the instructor ID, first name, and last name in the collections by using the RETURNING option with the BULK COLLECT clause. When run, this script produces the following output:

```
Deleted 10 rows
instructor_id: 101
first_name:    Fernand
last_name:     Hanks
instructor_id: 102
first_name:    Tom
last_name:     Wojick
instructor_id: 103
first_name:    Nina
last_name:     Schorin
instructor_id: 104
first_name:    Gary
last_name:     Pertez
instructor_id: 105
first_name:    Anita
last_name:     Morris
instructor_id: 106
first_name:    Todd
last_name:     Smythe
instructor_id: 107
first_name:    Marilyn
last_name:     Frantzen
```

```
instructor_id: 108
first_name:    Charles
last_name:     Lowry
instructor_id: 109
first_name:    Rick
last_name:     Chow
instructor_id: 110
first_name:    Irene
last_name:     Willig

PL/SQL procedure successfully completed.
```

▼ TRY IT YOURSELF

In this chapter, you've learned about bulk SQL—specifically, the FORALL statement and the BULK COLLECT clause. Here are some projects that will help you test the depth of your understanding.

Before beginning these exercises, create the MY_SECTION table based on the SECTION table. This table should be created empty.

1) Create the following script: Populate the MY_SECTION table using the FORALL statement with the SAVE EXCEPTIONS clause. After MY_SECTION is populated, display how many records were inserted.

2) Modify the script you just created. In addition to displaying the total number of records inserted in the MY_SECTION table, display how many records were inserted for each course. Use the BULK COLLECT statement to accomplish this step. Note that you should delete all the rows from the MY_SECTION table before executing this version of the script.

3) Create the following script: Delete all the records from the MY_SECTION table, and display how many records were deleted for each course. Use BULK COLLECT with the RETURNING option.

The projects in this section are meant to have you use all the skills you have acquired throughout this chapter. The answers to these projects can be found in Appendix D and on this book's companion Web site. Visit the Web site periodically to share and discuss your answers.

Procedures

CHAPTER OBJECTIVES

In this chapter, you will learn about

- ▶ Creating procedures
- ▶ Passing parameters into and out of procedures

All the PL/SQL you have written up to this point has been anonymous blocks that were run as scripts and compiled by the database server at runtime. Now you will begin using modular code. Modular code is a way to build a program from distinct parts (modules), each of which performs a specific function or task toward the program's final objective. As soon as modular code is stored on the database server, it becomes a database object, or subprogram, that is available to other program units for repeated execution. To save code to the database, the source code needs to be sent to the server so that it can be compiled into p-code and stored in the database. This chapter and the next two describe this process. This short chapter introduces stored procedures. Chapter 20, "Functions," covers the basics of stored functions. Chapter 21, "Packages," pulls together all this material.

In Lab 19.1, you will learn more about stored code and how to write the type of stored code known as procedures. In Lab 19.2, you will learn about passing parameters into and out of procedures.

BENEFITS OF MODULAR CODE

A PL/SQL module is any complete logical unit of work. The five types of PL/SQL modules are anonymous blocks that are run with a text script (this is the type you have used so far), procedures, functions, packages, and triggers.

Using modular code offers two main benefits: It is more reusable, and it is more manageable.

You create a procedure either in SQL*Plus or in one of the many tools for creating and debugging stored PL/SQL code. If you are using SQL*Plus, you need to write your code in a text editor and then run it at the SQL*Plus prompt.

BLOCK STRUCTURE

The block structure is common for all the module types. The block begins with a header (for named blocks only), which consists of the module's name and a parameter list (if used).

The declaration section consists of variables, cursors, and subblocks that are needed in the next section.

The main part of the module is the executable section, which is where all the calculations and processing are performed. This section contains executable code such as IF-THEN-ELSE, loops, calls to other PL/SQL modules, and so on.

The last section of the module is an optional exception-handling section, which is where the code to handle exceptions is placed.

ANONYMOUS BLOCK

So far, you have only written anonymous blocks. Anonymous blocks are much like modules, except that anonymous blocks do not have headers. There are important differences, though. As the name implies, anonymous blocks have no name and thus cannot be called by another block. They are not stored in the database and must be compiled and then run each time the script is loaded.

The PL/SQL block in a subprogram is a named block that can accept parameters and that can be invoked from an application that can communicate with the Oracle database server. A subprogram can be compiled and stored in the database. This allows the programmer to reuse the program. It also allows for easier code maintenance. Subprograms are either procedures or functions.

LAB 19.1
Creating Procedures

LAB OBJECTIVES

After completing this lab, you will be able to

▶ Create procedures
▶ Query the data dictionary for information on procedures

A procedure is a module that performs one or more actions; it does not need to return any values. The syntax for creating a procedure is as follows:

```
CREATE OR REPLACE PROCEDURE name
    [(parameter[, parameter, ...])]
AS
    [local declarations]
BEGIN
    executable statements
[EXCEPTION
    exception handlers]
END [name];
```

A procedure may have zero to many parameters, as covered in Lab 19.2. Every procedure has three parts: the header portion, which comes before AS (sometimes you see IS; they are interchangeable); the keyword, which contains the procedure name and parameter list; and the body, which is everything after the AS keyword. The word REPLACE is optional. When REPLACE is not used in the header of the procedure, to change the code in the procedure, you must drop and then re-create the procedure. Because it is very common to change a procedure's code, especially when it is under development, it is strongly recommended that you use the OR REPLACE option.

▼ LAB 19.1 EXERCISES

This section provides exercises and suggested answers, with discussion related to how those answers resulted. The most important thing to realize is whether your answer works. You should figure out the implications of the answers and what the effects are of any different answers you may come up with.

19.1.1 Create Procedures

In this exercise, you run a script that creates a procedure. Using a text editor such as Notepad, create a file that contains the following script:

```
-- ch19_01a.sql
CREATE OR REPLACE PROCEDURE Discount
AS
  CURSOR c_group_discount
  IS
    SELECT distinct s.course_no, c.description
      FROM section s, enrollment e, course c
     WHERE s.section_id = e.section_id
       AND c.course_no = s.course_no
     GROUP BY s.course_no, c.description,
              e.section_id, s.section_id
     HAVING COUNT(*) >=8;
BEGIN
   FOR r_group_discount IN c_group_discount
   LOOP
      UPDATE course
         SET cost = cost * .95
       WHERE course_no = r_group_discount.course_no;
      DBMS_OUTPUT.PUT_LINE
        ('A 5% discount has been given to '||
         r_group_discount.course_no||' '||
         r_group_discount.description
        );
   END LOOP;
END;
```

At a SQL*Plus session, run the previous script

Then answer the following questions:

A) What do you see on the screen? Explain what happens.

ANSWER: The procedure is created. The procedure named Discount is compiled into p-code and stored in the database for later execution. If an error is generated, you must have made a typing mistake. Check the code and recompile.

B) Execute the Discount procedure. How do you accomplish this? What results do you see on the screen?

ANSWER:

```
SQL> EXECUTE Discount
5% discount has been given to 25  Adv. Word Perfect
.... (through each course with an enrollment over 8)
PL/SQL procedure successfully completed.
```

C) The script does not contain a COMMIT. Discuss the issues involved with placing a COMMIT in the procedure, and indicate where the COMMIT could be placed.

ANSWER: Because this procedure does not have a COMMIT, the procedure will not update the database. A COMMIT needs to be issued after the procedure is run if you want the changes to be made. Alternatively, you can enter a COMMIT either before or after the end loop. If you put the COMMIT before the end loop, you are committing the changes after every loop. If you put the COMMIT after the end loop, the changes are not committed until the procedure is near completion. It is wiser to use the second option. This way, you are better prepared to handle errors.

BY THE WAY

If you receive an error in SQL*Plus, enter this command:

    show error

You can also use this command:

    L *start_line_number end_line_number*

to see a portion of the code in order to isolate errors.

19.1.2 **Query the Data Dictionary for Information on Procedures**

Two main views in the data dictionary provide information on stored code. USER_OBJECTS shows you information about the objects, and USER_SOURCE shows you the text of the source code. The data dictionary also has ALL_ and DBA_ versions of these views.

Complete the following tasks:

A) Write a SELECT statement to get pertinent information from the USER_OBJECTS view about the Discount procedure you just wrote. Run the query and describe the results.

ANSWER:

```
SELECT object_name, object_type, status
  FROM user_objects
 WHERE object_name = 'DISCOUNT';
```

The output is as follows:

```
OBJECT_NAME             OBJECT_TYPE      STATUS
--------------------    ---------------  ------
DISCOUNT                PROCEDURE        VALID
```

The status indicates that the procedure was compiled successfully. An invalid procedure cannot be executed.

B) Write a SELECT statement to display the source code from the USER_SOURCE view for the Discount procedure.

ANSWER:

```
SQL> column text format a70
     SELECT TO_CHAR(line, 99)||'>', text
       FROM user_source
     WHERE name = 'DISCOUNT'
```

BY THE WAY

A procedure can become invalid if the table it is based on is deleted or changed. You can recompile an invalid procedure using this command:

    alter procedure *procedure_name* compile

LAB 19.2
Passing Parameters into and out of Procedures

LAB OBJECTIVE

After completing this lab, you will be able to

▶ Use IN and OUT parameters with procedures

Parameters are the means to pass values to and from the calling environment to the server. These are the values that are processed or returned by executing the procedure. The three types of parameter modes are IN, OUT, and IN OUT.

MODES

Modes specify whether the parameter passed is read in or a receptacle for what comes out.

Figure 19.1 illustrates the relationship between parameters when they are in the procedure header versus when the procedure is executed.

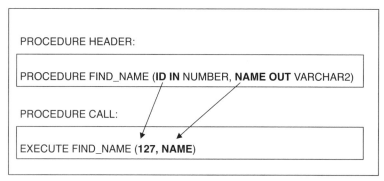

FIGURE 19.1
Matching a procedure call to a procedure header

FORMAL AND ACTUAL PARAMETERS

Formal parameters are the names specified in parentheses as part of a module's header. Actual parameters are the values or expressions specified in parentheses as a parameter list when the module is called. The formal parameter and the related actual parameter must be of the same or compatible datatypes. Table 19.1 explains the three types of parameters.

TABLE 19.1
Three Types of Parameters

MODE	DESCRIPTION	USAGE
IN	Passes a value into the program Constants, literals, expressions Cannot be changed within the program's default mode	Read-only value
OUT	Passes a value back from the program Cannot assign default values Must be a variable A value is assigned only if the program is successful	Write-only value
IN OUT	Passes values in and also sends values back	Has to be a variable

PASSING CONSTRAINTS (DATATYPE) WITH PARAMETER VALUES

Formal parameters do not require constraints in the datatype. For example, instead of specifying a constraint such as VARCHAR2(60), you just say VARCHAR2 against the parameter name in the formal parameter list. The constraint is passed with the value when a call is made.

MATCHING ACTUAL AND FORMAL PARAMETERS

You can use two methods to match actual and formal parameters: positional notation and named notation. Positional notation is simply association by position: The order of the parameters used when executing the procedure matches the order in the procedure's header. Named notation is explicit association using the symbol =>:

```
formal_parameter_name => argument_value
```

In named notation, the order does not matter. If you mix notation, list positional notation before named notation.

Default values can be used if a call to the program does not include a value in the parameter list. Note that it makes no difference which style is used; they function similarly.

▼ LAB 19.2 EXERCISES

This section provides exercises and suggested answers, with discussion related to how those answers resulted. The most important thing to realize is whether your answer works. You should figure out the implications of the answers and what the effects are of any different answers you may come up with.

19.2.1 Use IN and OUT Parameters with Procedures

Create the following text file in a text editor. Run the script at a SQL*Plus session.

```
-- ch19_02a.sql
CREATE OR REPLACE PROCEDURE find_sname
   (i_student_id IN NUMBER,
```

```
   o_first_name OUT VARCHAR2,
   o_last_name OUT VARCHAR2
   )
AS
BEGIN
  SELECT first_name, last_name
    INTO o_first_name, o_last_name
    FROM student
   WHERE student_id = i_student_id;
EXCEPTION
  WHEN OTHERS
  THEN
     DBMS_OUTPUT.PUT_LINE('Error in finding student_id:
        '||i_student_id);
END find_sname;
```

A) Explain what happens in the `find_sname` procedure. What parameters are passed into and out of the procedure? How would you call the procedure? Call the `find_sname` script with the following anonymous block:

```
-- ch19_03a.sql
DECLARE
  v_local_first_name student.first_name%TYPE;
  v_local_last_name student.last_name%TYPE;
BEGIN
  find_sname
    (145, v_local_first_name, v_local_last_name);
  DBMS_OUTPUT.PUT_LINE
    ('Student 145 is: '||v_local_first_name||
     ' '|| v_local_last_name||'.'
    );
END;
```

ANSWER: The procedure takes in a `student_id` using the parameter named `i_student_id`. It passes out the parameters `o_first_name` and `o_last_name`. The procedure is a simple select statement that retrieves the `first_name` and `last_name` from the Student table, where the `student_id` matches the value of `i_student_id`. `i_student_id` is the only in parameter that exists in the procedure. To call the procedure, a value must be passed in for the `i_student_id` parameter.

B) Explain the relationship between the parameters that are in the procedure's header definition versus the parameters that are passed into and out of the procedure.

ANSWER: When calling the procedure `find_sname`, a valid `student_id` should be passed in for `i_student_id`. If it is not a valid `student_id`, an exception is raised. Two variables must also be listed when calling the procedure. These variables, `v_local_first_name` and `v_local_last_name`, are used to hold the values of the parameters that are being passed out. After the procedure has been executed, the local variables have a value and can then be displayed with a DBMS_OUTPUT.PUT_LINE.

▼ TRY IT YOURSELF

In this chapter, you've learned about creating procedures, with and without the use of parameters. Additionally, you've learned about where information and source code for these procedures can be found. Part I of this section contains exercises that cover the basics of procedures. Part 2 extends the material on native dynamic SQL from Chapter 17 and puts it to use within the context of stored procedures.

Part 1

1) Write a procedure with no parameters. The procedure should say whether the current day is a weekend or weekday. Additionally, it should tell you the user's name and the current time. It also should specify how many valid and invalid procedures are in the database.

2) Write a procedure that takes in a zip code, city, and state and inserts the values into the zip code table. It should check to see if the zip code is already in the database. If it is, an exception should be raised, and an error message should be displayed. Write an anonymous block that uses the procedure and inserts your zip code.

Part 2

1) Create a stored procedure based on the script ch17_1c.sql, version 3.0, created in Chapter 17. The procedure should accept two parameters to hold a table name and an ID, and should return six parameters with first name, last name, street, city, state, and zip code information.

2) Modify the procedure you just created. Instead of using six parameters to hold name and address information, the procedure should return a user-defined record that contains six fields that hold name and address information. Note: You may want to create a package in which you define a record type. This record may be used later, such as when the procedure is invoked in a PL/SQL block.

The projects in this section are meant to have you use all the skills you have acquired throughout this chapter. The answers to these projects can be found in Appendix D and on this book's companion Web site. Visit the Web site periodically to share and discuss your answers.

CHAPTER 20

Functions

CHAPTER OBJECTIVES

In this chapter, you will learn about

▶ Creating and using functions

A function that is stored in the database is much like a procedure in that it is a named PL/SQL block that can take parameters and be invoked. There are key differences both in how it is created and how it is used. This short chapter covers the basics of how to create, use, and drop a function. Chapter 21, "Packages," shows you how to extend functions when they are placed in packages.

LAB 20.1
Creating and Using Functions

LAB OBJECTIVES

After completing this lab, you will be able to

▶ Create stored functions

▶ Make use of functions

▶ Invoke functions in SQL statements

▶ Write complex functions

FUNCTION BASICS

Functions are another type of stored code and are very similar to procedures. The significant difference is that a function is a PL/SQL block that returns a single value. Functions can accept one, many, or no parameters, but a function must have a return clause in the executable section of the function. The datatype of the return value must be declared in the header of the function. A function is not a stand-alone executable in the same way a procedure is: It must be used in some context. You can think of it as a sentence fragment. A function has output that needs to be assigned to a variable, or it can be used in a SELECT statement.

FUNCTION SYNTAX

The syntax for creating a function is as follows:

```
CREATE [OR REPLACE] FUNCTION function_name
   (parameter list)
    RETURN datatype
IS
BEGIN
   <body>
   RETURN (return_value);
END;
```

The function does not necessarily have any parameters, but it must have a RETURN value whose datatype is declared in the header, and it must return values for all the varying possible execution streams. The RETURN statement does not have to appear as the last line of the main execution section, and there may be more than one RETURN statement (there should be a RETURN statement for each exception). A function may have IN, OUT, or IN OUT parameters, but you rarely see anything except IN parameters because it is bad programming practice to do otherwise.

FOR EXAMPLE

```
-- ch20_01a.sql ver 1.0
CREATE OR REPLACE FUNCTION show_description
  (i_course_no course.course_no%TYPE)
RETURN varchar2
AS
  v_description varchar2(50);
BEGIN
  SELECT description
    INTO v_description
    FROM course
   WHERE course_no = i_course_no;
   RETURN v_description;
EXCEPTION
  WHEN NO_DATA_FOUND
  THEN
    RETURN('The Course is not in the database');
  WHEN OTHERS
  THEN
    RETURN('Error in running show_description');
END;
```

▼ LAB 20.1 EXERCISES

This section provides exercises and suggested answers, with discussion related to how those answers resulted. The most important thing to realize is whether your answer works. You should figure out the implications of the answers and what the effects are of any different answers you may come up with.

20.1.1 Create Stored Functions

This exercise starts by creating your first function.

A) Put the create script for the function in the preceding example into a text file. Open SQL*Plus, log into the student schema, and run the script from the preceding example. What do you expect to see? Explain the function line by line.

ANSWER: When a function has been compiled without errors, the SQL*Plus session returns the following:

```
Function created.
```

This indicates that the function compiled successfully.

The script creates the function `show_description`. The function heading indicates that it accepts a parameter of the NUMBER datatype, `i_course_no`, and returns a value of VARCHAR2 datatype. The function declares a VARCHAR2(5) variable called `v_description` that is used later on by the RETURN clause. This variable stores the value of the description of the course provided at the run time, and is initialized via the SELECT INTO statement. Once initialized, the value of the `v_description` variable is returned to the calling environment via the RETURN clause. Note the two exceptions employed by the function. The first is the NO_DATA_FOUND exception, the one most likely to occur. The second exception is the OTHERS exception, which is being used as a catchall for any other error that may occur. It is important to note that both exception sections include the RETURN clause as the function must always return a value as the control of the execution is passed to the calling environment after the RETURN clause is issued.

B) Create another function using the following script. Explain what is happening in this function. Pay close attention to the method of creating the Boolean return.

```
-- ch20_01b.sql, version 1.0
CREATE OR REPLACE FUNCTION id_is_good
   (i_student_id IN NUMBER)
   RETURN BOOLEAN
AS
   v_id_cnt NUMBER;
BEGIN
   SELECT COUNT(*)
     INTO v_id_cnt
     FROM student
    WHERE student_id = i_student_id;
   RETURN 1 = v_id_cnt;
EXCEPTION
   WHEN OTHERS
   THEN
      RETURN FALSE;
END id_is_good;
```

ANSWER: The function `id_is_good` is a check to see if the student ID passed in exists in the database. The function takes in a NUMBER datatype (which is assumed to be a student ID) and returns a BOOLEAN value. The function uses the variable `v_id_cnt` as a means to process the data. The SELECT INTO statement determines a total number of students with the ID that was passed in. If the student with such ID is already in the database, the value of `v_id_cnt` is 1. This is because the `student_id` column is the primary key and as such enforces uniqueness on the values stored in it. If the student with provided ID is not in the database, the value of `v_id_cnt` is 0. Note that the SELECT INTO statement does not cause a NO_DATA_FOUND exception as the COUNT(*) function returns 0 for non-existent student ID. Next, the RETURN clause returns TRUE if the value of the `v_id_cnt` is 1 because the expression `1 = v_id_cnt` evaluates to TRUE, and FALSE if the value of the `v_id_cnt` is 0 because the expression `1 = v_id_cnt` evaluates to FALSE. The function will also return FALSE when it encounters an exception.

20.1.2 Make Use of Functions

In this exercise, you will learn how to use the stored functions you created in Exercise 20.1.1.

A) Use the following anonymous block to run the function. When prompted, enter 350. Then try other numbers. What is produced?

```
SET SERVEROUTPUT ON
DECLARE
   v_description VARCHAR2(50);
BEGIN
   v_description := show_description(&sv_cnumber);
   DBMS_OUTPUT.PUT_LINE(v_description);
END;
```

ANSWER: Because the PL/SQL block has a lexical parameter of &cnumber, the user is prompted as follows:

```
Enter value for cnumber:
```

If you enter 350, you see the following:

```
old    4:    v_descript := show_description(&sv_cnumber);
new    4:    v_descript := show_description(350);
Java Developer II
PL/SQL procedure successfully completed.
```

This means that the value for &sv_cnumber has been replaced with 350. The function show_description returns a VARCHAR2 value, which is the course description for the course number that is passed in. The PL/SQL block initializes the v_description value with the return from the show_description function. This value is then displayed with the DBMS_OUTPUT package.

B) Create a similar anonymous block to make use of the function id_is_good. Try running it for a number of different IDs.

ANSWER: The following is one method of testing the id_is_good function:

```
DECLARE
    v_id number;
BEGIN
    v_id := &id;
    IF id_is_good(v_id)
    THEN
        DBMS_OUTPUT.PUT_LINE
            ('Student ID: '||v_id||' is a valid.');
    ELSE
        DBMS_OUTPUT.PUT_LINE
            ('Student ID: '||v_id||' is not valid.');
    END IF;
END;
```

This PL/SQL block evaluates the return from the function and then determines which output to project. Because the function id_is_good returns a Boolean, the easiest way to use this function is to run it and use the result (which will be either TRUE or FALSE) in an IF statement. In this case, if the function id_is_good returns TRUE, the first DBSM_OUTPUT.PUT_LINE statement displays the message stating that the student ID is valid. Similarly, if the function returns FALSE, the second DBMS_OUTPUT.PUT_LINE statement displays the message on the screen stating that the student ID is not valid.

20.1.3 Invoke Functions in SQL Statements

Functions return a single value and can be very useful in a SELECT statement. In this exercise you will learn to use user-defined functions in the SQL statements. This exercise starts by creating your first function that can be used in a SELECT statement.

A) Now you will try another method of using a stored function. Before you type the following SELECT statement, think about what the function show_description is doing. Will this statement produce an error? If not, what will be displayed?

```
SELECT course_no, show_description(course_no)
    FROM course;
```

ANSWER: This SELECT statement is identical to the following SELECT statement:

```
SELECT course_no, description
   FROM course.
```

Functions can be used in a SQL statement. In fact, you have been using them all along and may not have realized it. As a simple example, imagine using the function UPPER in a SELECT statement:

```
SELECT UPPER('bill') FROM DUAL;
```

The Oracle-supplied function UPPER is a function that returns the uppercase value of the parameter that was passed in.

Note that for a user-defined function to be called in a SQL expression, it must be a ROW function, not a GROUP function, and the datatypes must be SQL datatypes. The datatypes cannot be PL/SQL datatypes such as Boolean, table, or record. Additionally, the function is not allowed to have any DML (insert, update, delete).

Note that for you to use a function in a SELECT statement, the function must have a certain level of purity. This is accomplished with the PRAGMA RESTRICT_REFERENCES clause. This is discussed in detail in the next chapter in the context of functions within packages.

20.1.4 **Write Complex Functions**

In this exercise you will create a more complex function. In some cases functions can become elaborate and multifaceted.

A) Create the function using the following script. Before you execute the function, analyze this script and explain line by line what the function does. When could you use this function? Hint: You will use it in the package for the next chapter.

```
-- ch20_01c.sql, version 1.0
CREATE OR REPLACE FUNCTION new_instructor_id
   RETURN instructor.instructor_id%TYPE
AS
   v_new_instid instructor.instructor_id%TYPE;
BEGIN
   SELECT INSTRUCTOR_ID_SEQ.NEXTVAL
     INTO v_new_instid
     FROM dual;
   RETURN v_new_instid;
EXCEPTION
   WHEN OTHERS
   THEN
     DECLARE
        v_sqlerrm VARCHAR2(250) := SUBSTR(SQLERRM,1,250);
     BEGIN
        RAISE_APPLICATION_ERROR(-20003,
           'Error in instructor_id: '||v_sqlerrm);
     END;
END new_instructor_id;
```

ANSWER: This simple function is used to generate a new instructor ID. If the sequence fails to generate a new instructor ID, the function raises an exception.

▼ TRY IT YOURSELF

In this chapter, you have learned about functions. Here are some projects that will help you test the depth of your understanding:

1) Write a stored function called `new_student_id` that takes in no parameters and returns a `student.student_id%TYPE`. The value returned will be used when inserting a new student into the CTA application. It will be derived by using the formula `student_id_seq.NEXTVAL`.

2) Write a stored function called `zip_does_not_exist` that takes in a `zipcode.zip%TYPE` and returns a Boolean. The function will return TRUE if the zip code passed into it does not exist. It will return a FALSE if the zip code does exist. Hint: Here's an example of how this might be used:

```
DECLARE
    cons_zip CONSTANT zipcode.zip%TYPE := '&sv_zipcode';
    e_zipcode_is_not_valid EXCEPTION;
BEGIN
    IF zipcode_does_not_exist(cons_zip)
    THEN
        RAISE e_zipcode_is_not_valid;
    ELSE
        -- An insert of an instructor's record which
        -- makes use of the checked zipcode might go here.
        NULL;
    END IF;
EXCEPTION
    WHEN e_zipcode_is_not_valid
    THEN
        RAISE_APPLICATION_ERROR
            (-20003, 'Could not find zipcode '||
             cons_zip||'.'
            );
END;
```

3) Create a new function. For a given instructor, determine how many sections he or she is teaching. If the number is greater than or equal to 3, return a message saying that the instructor needs a vacation. Otherwise, return a message saying how many sections this instructor is teaching.

The projects in this section are meant to have you use all the skills you have acquired throughout this chapter. The answers to these projects can be found in Appendix D and on this book's companion Web site.

CHAPTER 21

Packages

CHAPTER OBJECTIVES

In this chapter, you will learn about

- ▶ The benefits of using packages
- ▶ Cursor variables
- ▶ Extending the package

A package is a collection of PL/SQL objects grouped under one package name. Packages include procedures, functions, cursors, declarations, types, and variables. Collecting objects into a package offers numerous benefits. In this chapter, you learn what these benefits are and how to take advantage of them.

LAB 21.1
The Benefits of Using Packages

LAB OBJECTIVES

After completing this lab, you will be able to

- ▶ Create package specifications
- ▶ Create package bodies
- ▶ Call stored packages
- ▶ Create private objects
- ▶ Create package variables and cursors

Using packages as a method to bundle your functions and procedures offers numerous benefits. The first is that a well-designed package is a logical grouping of objects such as functions, procedures, global variables, and cursors. All the code (parse tree and pseudocode [p-code]) is loaded into memory (the Shared Global Area [SGA] of the Oracle Server) on the package's first call. This means that the first call to the package is very expensive (it involves a lot of processing on the server), but all subsequent calls result in improved performance. Therefore, packages are often used in applications that use procedures and functions repeatedly.

Packages allow you to incorporate some of the concepts involved in object-oriented programming, even though PL/SQL is not a "true" object-oriented programming language. The PL/SQL package allows you to collect like functions and procedures and give them a context. It also allows you to encapsulate them. Because all the package code has been loaded into memory, you can also write your code so that similar code fragments are placed in the package in a manner that allows multiple procedures and functions to call them. You would want to do this if the logic for the calculation is fairly intensive and you want to keep it in one place.

AN EXAMPLE OF A BASIC CURRENCY CONVERSION

When you have the same calculation written in multiple places, you have a large maintenance job every time the calculation increases in complexity. For example, basic currency conversion is fairly simple. An amount is multiplied by an exchange rate. In actuality, though, currency conversion has become more complex. For example, after the European Union was formed, individual currencies became phased out as each country adopted the euro currency. The European Union then adopted a complex policy on how these "dead" currencies would be converted. This would be important if contracts were set up when the currency was in place and eventually the currency was phased out. If you had an old contract in German deutsche marks, and that amount needed to be converted into U.S. dollars, it needed to go through a process. First the amount was converted from deutsche marks to euros based on the prevailing rate. Then the amount would be rounded based on a standard rounding for deutsche marks to euros, and then it would be converted from euros to dollars at the prevailing rate. If your programs have many places where currency is converted, it would make more sense to encapsulate the conversion process into one function that encompasses this euro scenario. This function could be a public or private function (explained later in this chapter) that all other procedures in the same package make calls to.

Using packages offers an additional level of security. When a user executes a procedure in a package (or stored procedures and functions), the procedure operates with the same permissions as its owner. Packages let you create private functions and procedures, which can be called only from other functions and procedures in the package. This enforces information hiding. The package's structure thus encourages top-down design.

THE PACKAGE SPECIFICATION

The package specification contains information about the package's contents, but not the code for the procedures and functions. It also contains declarations of global/public variables. Anything placed in the declaration section of a PL/SQL block may be coded in a package specification. All objects placed in the package specification are called public objects. Any function or procedure not in the package specification but coded in a package body is called a private function or procedure. When public procedures and functions are called from a package, the programmer writing the "calling" process needs only the information in the package specification. This provides all the required information needed to call one of the procedures or functions within the package. The syntax for the package specification is as follows; note that optional information is enclosed in square brackets:

```
PACKAGE package_name
IS
[declarations of variables and types]
[specifications of cursors]
[specifications of modules]
END [package_name];
```

THE PACKAGE BODY

The package body contains the actual executable code for the objects described in the package specification. The package body contains code for all procedures and functions described in the specification. It also may contain code for objects not declared in the specification. The latter type of packaged object is invisible outside the package and is referred to as hidden. When creating stored packages, you can compile the package specification and body separately. The syntax for the package body is as follows; note that optional information is enclosed in square brackets:

```
PACKAGE BODY package_name
IS
[declarations of variables and types]
[specification and SELECT statement of cursors]
[specification and body of modules]
[BEGIN
executable statements]
```

```
[EXCEPTION
exception handlers]
END [package_name];
```

RULES FOR THE PACKAGE BODY

You must follow several rules in the package body code:

▶ There must be an exact match between the cursor and module headers and their definitions in the package specification.

▶ Do not repeat in the body the declaration of variables, exceptions, types, or constants in the specification.

▶ Any element declared in the specification can be referenced in the body.

REFERENCING PACKAGE ELEMENTS

Use the following syntax when calling packaged elements from outside the package:

```
package_name.element
```

You do not need to qualify elements when they are declared and referenced inside the body of the package or when they are declared in a specification and referenced inside the body of the same package.

▼ LAB 21.1 EXERCISES

This section provides exercises and suggested answers, with discussion related to how those answers resulted. The most important thing to realize is whether your answer works. You should figure out the implications of the answers and what the effects are of any different answers you may come up with.

21.1.1 Create Package Specifications

In this exercise, you learn more about table-based and cursor-based records.

Create the following PL/SQL script:

```
-- ch21_1a.sql
 1   CREATE OR REPLACE PACKAGE manage_students
 2   AS
 3     PROCEDURE find_sname
 4       (i_student_id IN student.student_id%TYPE,
 5        o_first_name OUT student.first_name%TYPE,
 6        o_last_name OUT student.last_name%TYPE
 7       );
 8     FUNCTION id_is_good
 9       (i_student_id IN student.student_id%TYPE)
10       RETURN BOOLEAN;
11   END manage_students;
```

Complete the following tasks, and answer the following questions:

A) Type the preceding code into a text file and run the script in a SQL*Plus session. Explain what happens.

ANSWER: The specification for the package `manage_students` is compiled into the database. The specification for the package indicates that there is one procedure and one function. The procedure, `find_sname`, requires one IN parameter—the student ID—and it returns two OUT parameters—the student's first and last names. The function, `id_is_good`, takes in a single parameter of a student ID and returns a Boolean (true or false). Although the body has not yet been entered into the database, the package is still available for other applications. For example, if you included a call to one of these procedures in another stored procedure, that procedure would compile (but would not execute).

B) If the following script were run from a SQL*Plus session, what would be the result, and why?

```
-- ch21_2a.sql
SET SERVEROUTPUT ON
DECLARE
    v_first_name student.first_name%TYPE;
    v_last_name student.last_name%TYPE;
BEGIN
    manage_students.find_sname
        (125, v_first_name, v_last_name);
    DBMS_OUTPUT.PUT_LINE(v_first_name||' '||v_last_name);
END;
```

ANSWER: The procedure cannot run because the specification for the procedure exists only in the database, not the body. The SQL*Plus session returns the following:

```
ERROR at line 1:
ORA-04068: existing state of packages has been discarded
ORA-04067: not executed, package body
           "STUDENT.MANAGE_STUDENTS" does not exist
ORA-06508: PL/SQL: could not find program
           unit being called
ORA-06512: at line 5
```

C) Create a package specification for a package named `school_api`. The package contains the procedure `discount` from Chapter 19 and the function `new_instructor_id` from Chapter 20.

ANSWER:

```
-- ch21_3a.sql
CREATE OR REPLACE PACKAGE  school_api as
    PROCEDURE discount;
    FUNCTION new_instructor_id
      RETURN instructor.instructor_id%TYPE;
END school_api;
```

21.1.2 Create Package Bodies

In this exercise, you create the body of the `manage_students` and `school_api` packages, which were specified in the preceding section.

FOR EXAMPLE

```
-- ch21_4a.sql
1   CREATE OR REPLACE PACKAGE BODY manage_students
2   AS
3     PROCEDURE find_sname
4       (i_student_id IN student.student_id%TYPE,
5        o_first_name OUT student.first_name%TYPE,
6        o_last_name OUT student.last_name%TYPE
7       )
8     IS
9      v_student_id  student.student_id%TYPE;
10     BEGIN
11        SELECT first_name, last_name
12          INTO o_first_name, o_last_name
13          FROM student
14         WHERE student_id = i_student_id;
15      EXCEPTION
16        WHEN OTHERS
17        THEN
18          DBMS_OUTPUT.PUT_LINE
19      ('Error in finding student_id: '||v_student_id);
20      END find_sname;
21      FUNCTION id_is_good
22        (i_student_id IN student.student_id%TYPE)
23        RETURN BOOLEAN
24      IS
25        v_id_cnt number;
26      BEGIN
27        SELECT COUNT(*)
28          INTO v_id_cnt
29          FROM student
30         WHERE student_id = i_student_id;
31         RETURN 1 = v_id_cnt;
32      EXCEPTION
33      WHEN OTHERS
34      THEN
35        RETURN FALSE;
36      END id_is_good;
37    END manage_students;
```

A) Type the preceding code into a text file and run the script in a SQL*Plus session. Explain what happens.

ANSWER: The specification for the package `manage_students` is compiled into the database. The specification for the package indicates that there is one procedure and one function.

The procedure, find_sname, requires one IN parameter—the student ID—and it returns two OUT parameters—the student's first and last names. The function, id_is_good, takes in a single parameter of a student ID and returns a Boolean (true or false). Although the body has not yet been entered into the database, the package is still available for other applications. For example, if you included a call to one of these procedures in another stored procedure, that procedure would compile (but would not execute).

B) Create a package body for the package named school_api that you created in the previous exercise. This will contain the procedure discount from Chapter 19 and the function new_instructor_id from Chapter 20.

ANSWER:

```
-- ch21_5a.sql
 1 CREATE OR REPLACE PACKAGE BODY school_api AS
 2    PROCEDURE discount
 3    IS
 4       CURSOR c_group_discount
 5       IS
 6       SELECT distinct s.course_no, c.description
 7         FROM section s, enrollment e, course c
 8        WHERE s.section_id = e.section_id
 9        GROUP BY s.course_no, c.description,
10                 e.section_id, s.section_id
11       HAVING COUNT(*) >=8;
12    BEGIN
13       FOR r_group_discount IN c_group_discount
14       LOOP
15       UPDATE course
16          SET cost = cost * .95
17          WHERE course_no = r_group_discount.course_no;
18          DBMS_OUTPUT.PUT_LINE
19             ('A 5% discount has been given to'
20             ||r_group_discount.course_no||'
21             '||r_group_discount.description);
22       END LOOP;
23      END discount_cost;
24     FUNCTION new_instructor_id
25        RETURN instructor.instructor_id%TYPE
26     IS
27        v_new_instid instructor.instructor_id%TYPE;
28     BEGIN
29        SELECT INSTRUCTOR_ID_SEQ.NEXTVAL
30          INTO v_new_instid
31          FROM dual;
32        RETURN v_new_instid;
33     EXCEPTION
34        WHEN OTHERS
35          THEN
36           DECLARE
37              v_sqlerrm VARCHAR2(250) :=
                     SUBSTR(SQLERRM,1,250);
38           BEGIN
```

```
39              RAISE_APPLICATION_ERROR(-20003,
40                'Error in    instructor_id: '||v_sqlerrm);
41          END;
42       END new_instructor_id;
43    END school_api;
```

21.1.3 **Call Stored Packages**

In this exercise, you use elements of the manage_student package in another code block.

FOR EXAMPLE

```
-- ch21_6a.sql
SET SERVEROUTPUT ON
DECLARE
  v_first_name student.first_name%TYPE;
  v_last_name student.last_name%TYPE;
BEGIN
  IF manage_students.id_is_good(&&v_id)
  THEN
    manage_students.find_sname(&&v_id, v_first_name,
        v_last_name);
  DBMS_OUTPUT.PUT_LINE('Student No. '||&&v_id||' is '
      ||v_last_name||', '||v_first_name);
ELSE
   DBMS_OUTPUT.PUT_LINE
   ('Student ID: '||&&v_id||' is not in the database.');
END IF;
END;
```

A) This example displays how a procedure within a package is executed. What results would you expect to see if you ran this PL/SQL block?

ANSWER: This is a correct PL/SQL block for running the function and the procedure in the package manage_students. If an existing student_id is entered, the student's name is displayed. If the ID is not valid, an error message is displayed.

B) Run the script and view the results. How does this compare with what you expected? Explain what the script does line by line.

ANSWER: Initially the following appears:

```
Enter value for v_id:
```

If you enter 145, you see the following:

```
old 5: IF manage_students.id_is_good(&v_id)
new 5: IF manage_students.id_is_good(145)
old  7: manage_students.find_sname(&&v_id, v_first_name,
new  7: manage_students.find_sname(145, v_first_name,
old  9: DBMS_OUTPUT.PUT_LINE('Student No. '||&&v_id||' is '
new 9: DBMS_OUTPUT.PUT_LINE('Student No. '||145||' is '
old 14: ('Student ID: '||&&v_id||' is not in the database.');
new 14: ('Student ID: '||145||' is not in the database.');
Student No. 145 is Lefkowitz, Paul
PL/SQL procedure successfully completed.
```

The function `id_is_good` returns TRUE for an existing `student_id` such as 145. Control then flows to the first part of the IF statement. The procedure `manage_students.find_sname` finds the first and last name for `student_id` 145, which happens to be Lefkowitz, Paul.

C) Create a script that tests the `school_api` package.

ANSWER:

```
-- ch21_7a.sql
SET SERVEROUTPUT ON
DECLARE
    V_instructor_id instructor.instructor_id%TYPE;
BEGIN
    School_api.Discount_Cost;
    v_instructor_id := school_api.new_instructor_id;
    DBMS_OUTPUT.PUT_LINE
        ('The new id is: '||v_instructor_id);
END;
```

21.1.4 **Create Private Objects**

Public elements are elements defined in the package specification. If an object is defined only in the package body, it is private. Private elements cannot be accessed directly by any programs outside of the package. You can think of the package specification as being a "menu" of packaged items that are available to users. Other objects might be working behind the scenes, but they are inaccessible. They cannot be called or utilized in any way. They are available as part of the package's internal "menu" and can be called only by other elements of the package.

A) Replace the last lines of the `manage_students` package specification in ch21_1a.sql with the following, and recompile the package specification:

```
11      PROCEDURE display_student_count;
12    END manage_students;
```

Replace the end of the body with the following, and recompile the package body. Lines 1 through 36 are unchanged from lines 1 through 36 of ch21_4a.sql.

```
37    FUNCTION student_count_priv
38      RETURN NUMBER
39    IS
40      v_count NUMBER;
41    BEGIN
42      select count(*)
43      into v_count
44      from student;
45      return v_count;
46    EXCEPTION
47      WHEN OTHERS
48        THEN
49        return(0);
50    END student_count_priv;
51    PROCEDURE display_student_count
52      is
53      v_count NUMBER;
54    BEGIN
55      v_count := student_count_priv;
```

```
56      DBMS_OUTPUT.PUT_LINE
57        ('There are '||v_count||' students.');
58    END display_student_count;
59  END manage_students;
```

What have you added to the `manage_student` package?

ANSWER: You have added a private function, `student_count_priv`, and a public procedure, `display_student_count`, calling the private function.

B) If you run the following from your SQL*Plus session, what are the results?

```
DECLARE
   V_count NUMBER;
BEGIN
   V_count := Manage_students.student_count_priv;
   DBMS_OUTPUT.PUT_LINE(v_count);
END;
```

ANSWER: If you have decided that a function is to be private, this means that you don't want it to be called as a stand alone function. It should only be called from another function or procedure within the same package. Because the private function, `student_count_priv`, cannot be called from outside the package, you receive the following error message:

```
ERROR at line 1:
ORA-06550: line 4, column 31:
PLS-00302: component 'STUDENT_COUNT_PRIV' must be declared
ORA-06550: line 4, column 3:
PL/SQL: Statement ignored
```

When trying to call the function on its own, it will appear as if the private function does not exist. This is important to keep in mind.

This can be useful when you are writing PL/SQL packages used by other developers. Private elements have no meaning to another developer—that is just calling the public objects in the package. To simplify the package for developers making use of public elements in a package, the developers only need to see the package specification. This way, they know what is being passed into the procedures and functions and what is being returned. They do not need to see the inner workings.

If a number of procedures use the same logic, it may make more sense to put them in a private function called by the procedures. This is also a good method to keep in mind if one calculation will be used in many other procedures in the same package, yet you don't want to expose the calculation publicly. For example, we just created a function to count students. Maybe you have other procedures that will need to make use of this function. For example, a change in the price of all courses may occur as soon as the student count reaches a certain number.

C) If you were to run the following, what would you expect to see?

```
SET SERVEROUTPUT ON
Execute manage_students.display_student_count;
```

ANSWER: This is a valid method of running a procedure. A line is displayed indicating the number of students in the database. Note that the procedure in the package `manage_students` is using the private function `student_count_priv` to retrieve the student count.

Note that if you forget to include a procedure or function in a package specification, it becomes private. On the other hand, if you declare a procedure or function in the package specification, and then you do not define it when you create the body, you receive the following error message:

```
PLS-00323: subprogram or cursor 'procedure_name' is declared in
a package specification and must be defined in the package body
```

D) Add a private function to the `school_api` called `get_course_descript_private`. It accepts a `course.course_no%TYPE` and returns a `course.description%TYPE`. It searches for and returns the course description for the course number passed to it. If the course does not exist or if an error occurs, it returns a NULL.

ANSWER: The complete package specification and body are as follows. Nothing needs to be added to the package specification, because you are adding only a private object.

The package specification for `manage_students` is now as follows:

```
-- ch21_7b.sql
CREATE OR REPLACE PACKAGE manage_students
AS
   PROCEDURE find_sname
     (i_student_id IN student.student_id%TYPE,
      o_first_name OUT student.first_name%TYPE,
      o_last_name OUT student.last_name%TYPE
     );
   FUNCTION id_is_good
     (i_student_id IN student.student_id%TYPE)
     RETURN BOOLEAN;
  PROCEDURE display_student_count;
 END manage_students;
```

The package body for `manage_students` is now as follows:

```
-- ch21_7c.sql
CREATE OR REPLACE PACKAGE BODY manage_students
AS
  PROCEDURE find_sname
    (i_student_id IN student.student_id%TYPE,
     o_first_name OUT student.first_name%TYPE,
     o_last_name OUT student.last_name%TYPE
     )
  IS
   v_student_id  student.student_id%TYPE;
   BEGIN
      SELECT first_name, last_name
        INTO o_first_name, o_last_name
        FROM student
       WHERE student_id = i_student_id;
    EXCEPTION
      WHEN OTHERS
      THEN
        DBMS_OUTPUT.PUT_LINE
     ('Error in finding student_id: '||v_student_id);
    END find_sname;
    FUNCTION id_is_good
```

```
        (i_student_id IN student.student_id%TYPE)
        RETURN BOOLEAN
     IS
       v_id_cnt number;
     BEGIN
       SELECT COUNT(*)
         INTO v_id_cnt
         FROM student
        WHERE student_id = i_student_id;
        RETURN 1 = v_id_cnt;
     EXCEPTION
     WHEN OTHERS
     THEN
        RETURN FALSE;
     END id_is_good;
  FUNCTION student_count_priv
   RETURN NUMBER
  IS
   v_count NUMBER;
  BEGIN
   select count(*)
   into v_count
   from student;
   return v_count;
  EXCEPTION
   WHEN OTHERS
     THEN
     return(0);
  END student_count_priv;
  PROCEDURE display_student_count
   is
   v_count NUMBER;
  BEGIN
   v_count := student_count_priv;
   DBMS_OUTPUT.PUT_LINE
      ('There are '||v_count||' students.');
  END display_student_count;
  FUNCTION get_course_descript_private
     (i_course_no  course.course_no%TYPE)
     RETURN course.description%TYPE
   IS
      v_course_descript course.description%TYPE;
   BEGIN
      SELECT description
        INTO v_course_descript
        FROM course
       WHERE course_no = i_course_no;
      RETURN v_course_descript;
   EXCEPTION
      WHEN OTHERS
```

```
      THEN
          RETURN NULL;
   END get_course_descript_private;
   END manage_students;
```

21.1.5 Create Package Variables and Cursors

The first time a package is called within a user session, the code in the package's initialization section is executed if it exists. This is done only once and is not repeated if the user calls other procedures or functions for that package.

Variables, cursors, and user-defined datatypes used by numerous procedures and functions can be declared once at the beginning of the package specification. Then they can be used by the functions and procedures within the package without having to be declared again.

A) Add a package global variable called `v_current_date` to `student_api`.

ANSWER: Add the following line to the beginning of the package specification:

```
-- ch21_8a.sql
CREATE OR REPLACE PACKAGE  school_api as
   v_current_date DATE;
   PROCEDURE Discount_Cost;
   FUNCTION new_instructor_id
      RETURN instructor.instructor_id%TYPE;
 END school_api;
```

B) Add an initialization section that assigns the current sysdate to the variable `v_current_date`. This variable can then be used in any procedure in the package that needs to make use of the current date.

ANSWER: Add the following to the end of the package body:

```
-- ch21_8b.sql
CREATE OR REPLACE PACKAGE BODY school_api AS
   PROCEDURE discount_cost
   IS
      CURSOR c_group_discount
      IS
      SELECT distinct s.course_no, c.description
        FROM section s, enrollment e, course c
       WHERE s.section_id = e.section_id
      GROUP BY s.course_no, c.description,
               e.section_id, s.section_id
      HAVING COUNT(*) >=8;
   BEGIN
      FOR r_group_discount IN c_group_discount
      LOOP
      UPDATE course
         SET cost = cost * .95
        WHERE course_no = r_group_discount.course_no;
        DBMS_OUTPUT.PUT_LINE
          ('A 5% discount has been given to'
          ||r_group_discount.course_no||'
         '||r_group_discount.description);
      END LOOP;
```

```
  END discount_cost;
FUNCTION new_instructor_id
   RETURN instructor.instructor_id%TYPE
IS
   v_new_instid instructor.instructor_id%TYPE;
BEGIN
   SELECT INSTRUCTOR_ID_SEQ.NEXTVAL
     INTO v_new_instid
     FROM dual;
   RETURN v_new_instid;
EXCEPTION
   WHEN OTHERS
    THEN
     DECLARE
       v_sqlerrm VARCHAR2(250) :=
           SUBSTR(SQLERRM,1,250);
     BEGIN
      RAISE_APPLICATION_ERROR(-20003,
      'Error in    instructor_id: '||v_sqlerrm);
     END;
   END new_instructor_id;
BEGIN
  SELECT trunc(sysdate, 'DD')
    INTO v_current_date
    FROM dual;
END school_api;
```

LAB 21.2
Cursor Variables

LAB OBJECTIVE

After completing this lab, you will be able to

▶ Make use of cursor variables

Up to this point in this book you have seen cursors used to gather specific data from a single SELECT statement. At the beginning of this chapter you learned how to bring a number of procedures into a large program called a package. A package may have one cursor that is used by a few procedures. In this case, each of the procedures that uses the same cursor would have to declare, open, fetch, and close the cursor. In the current version of PL/SQL, cursors can be declared and manipulated like any other PL/SQL variable. This type of variable is called a cursor variable or a REF CURSOR. A cursor variable is just a reference or a handle to a static cursor. It permits a programmer to pass this reference to the same cursor among all the program's units that need access to the cursor. A cursor variable binds the cursor's SELECT statement dynamically at runtime.

Explicit cursors are used to name a work area that holds the information of a multirow query. A cursor variable may be used to point to the area in memory where the result of a multirow query is stored. The cursor always refers to the same information in a work area, whereas a cursor variable can point to different work areas. Cursors are static, but cursor variables can be seen as dynamic because they are not tied to any one query. Cursor variables give you easy access to centralized data retrieval.

You can use a cursor variable to pass the result set of a query between stored procedures and various clients. A query work area remains accessible as long as a cursor variable points to it. So you can freely pass a cursor variable from one scope to another. The two types of cursor variables are strong and weak.

To execute a multirow query, the Oracle server opens a work area called a cursor to store processing information. To access the information, you either name the work area, or you use a cursor variable that points to it. A cursor always refers to the same work area, but a cursor variable can refer to different work areas. Hence, cursors and cursor variables are not interchangeable. An explicit cursor is static and is associated with one SQL statement. A cursor variable can be associated with different statements at runtime. Primarily you use a cursor variable to pass a pointer to query result sets between PL/SQL stored subprograms and various clients, such as a client Oracle Developer Forms application. None of them owns the result set; they simply share a pointer to the query work area that stores the result set. You can declare a cursor variable on the client side, open and fetch from it on the server side, and then continue to fetch from it on the client side.

Cursor variables differ from cursors in the same way that constants differ from variables. A cursor is static; a cursor variable is dynamic. In PL/SQL a cursor variable has a REF CURSOR datatype, where REF stands for reference and CURSOR stands for the class of the object. You will now learn the syntax for declaring and using a cursor variable.

To create a cursor variable, first you need to define a REF CURSOR type, and then you declare a variable of that type.

Before you declare the REF CURSOR of a strong type, you must declare a record that has the datatypes of the result set of the SELECT statement you plan to use (note that this is not necessary for a weak REF CURSOR).

FOR EXAMPLE

```
TYPE inst_city_type IS RECORD
(first_name instructor.first_name%TYPE;
 last_name  instructor.last_name%TYPE;
 city       zipcode.city%TYPE;
 state      zipcode.state%TYPE)
```

Second, you must declare a composite datatype for the cursor variable that is of the type REF CURSOR. The syntax is as follows:

```
TYPE ref_type_name is REF CURSOR [RETURN return_type];
```

ref_type_name is a type specified in subsequent declarations. *return_type* is a record type for a strong cursor; a weak cursor does not have a specific return type but can handle any combination of data items in a SELECT statement. The REF CURSOR keyword indicates that the new type will be a pointer to the defined type. *return_type* indicates the type of SELECT list that the cursor variable eventually returns. The return type must be a record type.

FOR EXAMPLE

```
TYPE inst_city_cur IS REF CURSOR RETURN inst_city_type;
```

A cursor variable can be strong (restrictive) or weak (nonrestrictive). A strong cursor variable is a REF CURSOR type definition that specifies a *return_type*; a weak definition does not. PL/SQL enables you to associate a strong type with type-comparable queries only, whereas a weak type can be associated with any query. This makes a strong cursor variable less error-prone but weak REF CURSOR types more flexible.

These are the key steps for handling a cursor variable:

1. Define and declare the cursor variable.

   Open the cursor variable. Associate the cursor variable with a multirow SELECT statement, execute the query, and identify the result set. An OPEN FOR statement can open the same cursor variable for different queries. You do not need to close a cursor variable before reopening it. Keep in mind that when you reopen a cursor variable for a different query, the previous query is lost. Good programming technique would be to close the cursor variables before reopening them later in the program.

2. Fetch rows from the result set.

   Retrieve rows from the result set one at a time. Note that the return type of the cursor variable must be compatible with the variable named in the INTO clause of the FETCH statement.

   The FETCH statement retrieves rows from the result set one at a time. PL/SQL verifies that the return type of the cursor variable is compatible with the INTO clause of the FETCH statement. For each query column value returned, the INTO clause must have a type-comparable variable. Also, the number of query column values must equal the number of variables. In case of a mismatch in number or type, the error occurs at compile time for strongly typed cursor variables and at runtime for weakly typed cursor variables.

3. Close the cursor variable.

The following is a complete example showing the use of a cursor variable in a package.

FOR EXAMPLE

```
-- ch21_9a.sql
CREATE OR REPLACE PACKAGE course_pkg AS
   TYPE course_rec_typ IS RECORD
      (first_name     student.first_name%TYPE,
       last_name      student.last_name%TYPE,
       course_no      course.course_no%TYPE,
       description    course.description%TYPE,
       section_no     section.section_no%TYPE
      );
   TYPE course_cur IS REF CURSOR RETURN course_rec_typ;
   PROCEDURE get_course_list
      (p_student_id    NUMBER ,
       p_instructor_id NUMBER ,
       course_list_cv IN OUT course_cur);
END course_pkg;
/

CREATE OR REPLACE PACKAGE BODY course_pkg AS
   PROCEDURE get_course_list
```

FOR EXAMPLE (continued)

```
   (p_student_id    NUMBER ,
    p_instructor_id NUMBER ,
    course_list_cv IN OUT course_cur)
 IS
 BEGIN
   IF p_student_id IS NULL AND p_instructor_id
     IS NULL THEN
     OPEN course_list_cv FOR
       SELECT 'Please choose a student-' First_name,
              'instructor combination'   Last_name,
          NULL      course_no,
          NULL      description,
          NULL      section_no
          FROM dual;
   ELSIF p_student_id IS NULL   THEN
     OPEN course_list_cv FOR
       SELECT s.first_name    first_name,
          s.last_name       last_name,
          c.course_no       course_no,
          c.description     description,
          se.section_no     section_no
   FROM   instructor i, student s,
          section se, course c, enrollment e
   WHERE  i.instructor_id = p_instructor_id
     AND  i.instructor_id = se.instructor_id
     AND  se.course_no     = c.course_no
     AND  e.student_id     = s.student_id
     AND  e.section_id     = se.section_id
     ORDER BY  c.course_no, se.section_no;
   ELSIF p_instructor_id IS NULL   THEN
     OPEN course_list_cv FOR
          SELECT i.first_name    first_name,
          i.last_name       last_name,
          c.course_no       course_no,
          c.description     description,
          se.section_no     section_no
   FROM   instructor i, student s,
          section se, course c, enrollment e
   WHERE  s.student_id = p_student_id
     AND  i.instructor_id = se.instructor_id
     AND  se.course_no     = c.course_no
     AND  e.student_id     = s.student_id
     AND  e.section_id     = se.section_id
       ORDER BY  c.course_no, se.section_no;
       END IF;
   END get_course_list;


END course_pkg;
```

You can pass query result sets between PL/SQL stored subprograms and various clients. This works because PL/SQL and its clients share a pointer to the query work area identifying the result set. This can be done in a client program such as SQL*Plus by defining a host variable with a datatype of REF CURSOR to hold the query result generated from a REF CURSOR in a stored program. To see what is being stored in the SQL*Plus variable, use the SQL*Plus PRINT command. Optionally you can have the SQL*Plus command SET AUTOPRINT ON to display the query results automatically.

▼ LAB 21.2 EXERCISES

This section provides exercises and suggested answers, with discussion related to how those answers resulted. The most important thing to realize is whether your answer works. You should figure out the implications of the answers and what the effects are of any different answers you may come up with.

21.2.1 Make Use of Cursor Variables

A) Take a look at the preceding example, script ch21_9a.sql, and explain why the package has two different TYPE declarations. Also explain how the procedure get_course_list uses the cursor variable.

ANSWER: In script ch21_9a.sql, the first TYPE declaration is for the record type course_rec_type. This record type is declared to define the result set of the SELECT statements that will be used for the cursor variable. When data items in a record do not match a single table, it is necessary to create a record type. The second TYPE declaration is for the cursor variable, also known as REF CURSOR. The variable has the name course_cur, and it is declared as a strong cursor, meaning that it can be used for only a single record type. The record type is course_rec_type. The procedure get_course_list in the course_pkg is made so that it can return a cursor variable that holds three different result sets. Each result set is of the same record type. The first type is for when both IN parameters of student ID and instructor ID are null. This produces a result set that is a message, Please choose a student-instructor combination. The next way the procedure runs is if the instructor_id is passed in but the student_id is null. (Note that the logic of the procedure is a reverse negative. Saying in the second clause of the IF statement p_student_id IS NULL means when the instructor_id is passed in.) This runs a SELECT statement to populate the cursor variable that holds a list of all the courses this instructor teaches and the students enrolled in these classes. The last way this can run is for a student_id and no instructor_id. This produces a result set of all the courses the student is enrolled in and the instructors for each section. Also be aware that after the cursor variable is opened, it is never closed until you specifically close it.

B) Create a SQL*Plus variable that is a cursor variable type.

ANSWER:

```
SQL> VARIABLE course_cv REFCURSOR
```

C) Execute the procedure course_pkg.get_course_list, with three different types of variable combinations to show the three possible result sets. After you execute the procedure, display the values of the SQL*Plus variable you declared in question A).

ANSWER: There are three ways to execute this procedure. The first way is to pass a student ID but not an instructor ID:

```
SQL> exec course_pkg.get_course_list(102, NULL, :course_cv);

PL/SQL procedure successfully completed.
```

```
SQL> print course_cv

FIRST_NAME LAST_NAME   COURSE_NO DESCRIPTION            SECTION_NO
---------- ---------- ---------- ---------------------- ----------
Charles    Lowry              25 Intro to Programming            2
Nina       Schorin            25 Intro to Programming            5
```

The next method is to pass an instructor ID but not a student ID:

```
SQL> exec course_pkg.get_course_list(NULL, 102, :course_cv);

PL/SQL procedure successfully completed.

SQL> print course_cv

FIRST_NAME  LAST_NAME   COURSE_NO DESCRIPTION             SECTION_NO
----------- ----------- --------- ----------------------- ----------
Jeff        Runyan             10 Technology Concepts              2
Dawn        Dennis             25 Intro to Programming             4
May         Jodoin             25 Intro to Programming             4
Jim         Joas               25 Intro to Programming             4
Arun        Griffen            25 Intro to Programming             4
Alfred      Hutheesing         25 Intro to Programming             4
Lula        Oates             100 Hands-On Windows                 1
Regina      Bose              100 Hands-On Windows                 1
Jenny       Goldsmith         100 Hands-On Windows                 1
Roger       Snow              100 Hands-On Windows                 1
Rommel      Frost             100 Hands-On Windows                 1
Debra       Boyce             100 Hands-On Windows                 1
Janet       Jung              120 Intro to Java Programming        4
John        Smith             124 Advanced Java Programming        1
Charles     Caro              124 Advanced Java Programming        1
Sharon      Thompson          124 Advanced Java Programming        1
Evan        Fielding          124 Advanced Java Programming        1
Ronald      Tangaribuan       124 Advanced Java Programming        1
N           Kuehn             146 Java for C/C++ Programmers        2
Derrick     Baltazar          146 Java for C/C++ Programmers        2
Angela      Torres            240 Intro to the Basic Language       2
```

The last method is to pass neither the student ID nor the instructor ID:

```
SQL> exec course_pkg.get_course_list(NULL, NULL,  :course_cv);

PL/SQL procedure successfully completed.

SQL>  print course_cv

FIRST_NAME             LAST_NAME               C DESCRIPTION      S
---------------------- ----------------------- - ---------------
Please choose a student-instructor combination
```

D) Create another package called `student_info_pkg` that has a single procedure called `get_student_info`. The `get_student_info` package will have three parameters. The first is `student_id`, the second is a number called `p_choice`, and the last is a weak cursor variable. `p_choice` indicates what information about the student will be delivered. If it is 1, return the information about the student from the STUDENT table. If it is 2, list all the courses the student is enrolled in, with the names of the students who are enrolled in the same section as the student with the `student_id` that was passed in. If it is 3, return the instructor name for that student, with the information about the courses the student is enrolled in.

ANSWER:

```
-- ch21_10a.sql
CREATE OR REPLACE PACKAGE student_info_pkg AS

   TYPE student_details IS REF CURSOR;

   PROCEDURE get_student_info
      (p_student_id    NUMBER ,
       p_choice        NUMBER ,
       details_cv IN OUT student_details);
END student_info_pkg;
/
CREATE OR REPLACE PACKAGE BODY student_info_pkg AS
   PROCEDURE get_student_info
      (p_student_id    NUMBER ,
       p_choice        NUMBER ,
       details_cv IN OUT student_details)
   IS
   BEGIN
     IF p_choice = 1  THEN
       OPEN details_cv FOR
         SELECT s.first_name      first_name,
                s.last_name       last_name,
                s.street_address  address,
                z.city            city,
                z.state           state,
                z.zip             zip
           FROM  student s, zipcode z
          WHERE  s.student_id = p_student_id
            AND  z.zip = s.zip;
     ELSIF p_choice = 2 THEN
       OPEN details_cv  FOR
         SELECT c.course_no       course_no,
                c.description     description,
                se.section_no     section_no,
                s.first_name      first_name,
                s.last_name       last_name
           FROM  student s,  section se,
                 course c, enrollment e
          WHERE  se.course_no     = c.course_no
            AND  e.student_id     = s.student_id
            AND  e.section_id     = se.section_id
```

```
            AND  se.section_id in (SELECT e.section_id
                                   FROM student s,
                                        enrollment e
                                   WHERE s.student_id =
                                         p_student_id
                                     AND  s.student_id =
                                          e.student_id)
        ORDER BY  c.course_no;
      ELSIF p_choice = 3 THEN
        OPEN details_cv FOR
          SELECT i.first_name    first_name,
                 i.last_name     last_name,
                 c.course_no     course_no,
                 c.description   description,
                 se.section_no   section_no
          FROM   instructor i, student s,
                 section se, course c, enrollment e
          WHERE  s.student_id = p_student_id
            AND  i.instructor_id = se.instructor_id
            AND  se.course_no    = c.course_no
            AND  e.student_id    = s.student_id
            AND  e.section_id    = se.section_id
        ORDER BY  c.course_no, se.section_no;
      END IF;
    END get_student_info;

  END student_info_pkg;
```

E) Run the `get_student_info` procedure in SQL*Plus, and display the results.

ANSWER:

```
SQL> VARIABLE student_cv REFCURSOR
SQL> execute student_info_pkg.GET_STUDENT_INFO
     (102, 1, :student_cv);
PL/SQL procedure successfully completed.

SQL>  print student_cv
FIRST_ LAST_NAM ADDRESS            CITY            ST ZIP
------ -------- ------------------ --------------- -- -----
Fred   Crocitto 101-09 120th St.   Richmond Hill   NY 11419

SQL> execute student_info_pkg.GET_STUDENT_INFO
                    (102, 2,  :student_cv);
PL/SQL procedure successfully completed.

SQL> print student_cv
COURSE_NO DESCRIPTION            SECTION_NO FIRST_NAME LAST_NAME
--------- ------------------     ---------- ---------- -----------
       25 Intro to Programming        2 Fred       Crocitto
       25 Intro to Programming        2 Judy       Sethi
       25 Intro to Programming        2 Jenny      Goldsmith
```

```
25 Intro to Programming        2 Barbara    Robichaud
25 Intro to Programming        2 Jeffrey    Citron
25 Intro to Programming        2 George     Kocka
25 Intro to Programming        5 Fred       Crocitto
25 Intro to Programming        5 Hazel      Lasseter
25 Intro to Programming        5 James      Miller
25 Intro to Programming        5 Regina     Gates
25 Intro to Programming        5 Arlyne     Sheppard
25 Intro to Programming        5 Thomas     Edwards
25 Intro to Programming        5 Sylvia     Perrin
25 Intro to Programming        5 M.         Diokno
25 Intro to Programming        5 Edgar      Moffat
25 Intro to Programming        5 Bessie     Heedles
25 Intro to Programming        5 Walter     Boremmann
25 Intro to Programming        5 Lorrane    Velasco

SQL> execute student_info_pkg.GET_STUDENT_INFO
                          (214,  3,    :student_cv);
PL/SQL procedure successfully completed.

SQL> print student_cv
FIRST_NAME LAST_NAME   COURSE_NO  DESCRIPTION               SECTION_NO
---------- ----------- ---------- ------------------------- ----------
Marilyn    Frantzen    120 Intro to Java Programming            1
Fernand    Hanks       122 Intermediate Java Programming        5
Gary       Pertez      130 Intro to Unix                        2
Marilyn    Frantzen    145 Internet Protocols                   1
```

RULES FOR USING CURSOR VARIABLES

▶ Cursor variables cannot be defined in a package specification.

▶ You cannot use cursor variables with remote subprograms on another server, so you cannot pass cursor variables to a procedure that is called through a database link.

▶ Do not use FOR UPDATE with OPEN FOR in processing a cursor variable.

▶ You cannot use comparison operators to test cursor variables for equality, inequality, or nullity.

▶ A cursor variable cannot be assigned a null value.

▶ A REF CURSOR type cannot be used in a CREATE TABLE or VIEW statement, because there is no equivalent datatype for a database column.

▶ A stored procedure that uses a cursor variable can be used only as a query block data source; it cannot be used for a DML block data source. Using a REF CURSOR is ideal for queries that are dependent only on variations in SQL statements, not PL/SQL.

▶ You cannot store cursor variables in an associative array, nested table, or varray.

▶ If you pass a host cursor variable to PL/SQL, you cannot fetch from it on the server side unless you also open it there on the same server call.

LAB 21.3
Extending the Package

LAB OBJECTIVE

After completing this lab, you will be able to

► Extend the package

In this lab you use previously learned concepts to extend the packages you have created and create a new one. Only through extensive exercises will you become more comfortable with programming in PL/SQL. It is very important when writing your PL/SQL code that you carefully consider all aspects of the business requirements. A good rule of thumb is to think ahead and write your code in reusable components so that it will be easy to extend and maintain your PL/SQL code.

▼ LAB 21.3 EXERCISES

This section provides exercises and suggested answers, with discussion related to how those answers resulted. The most important thing to realize is whether your answer works. You should figure out the implications of the answers and what the effects are of any different answers you may come up with.

21.3.1 **Extend the Package**

A) Create a new package specification called `manage_grades`. This package will perform a number of calculations on grades and will need two package level cursors. The first one is for grade types and will be called `c_grade_type`. It will have an IN parameter of a section ID. It will list all the grade types (such as quiz or homework) for a given section that are needed to calculate a student's grade in that section. The return items from the cursor will be the grade type code, the number of that grade type for this section, the percentage of the final grade, and the drop-lowest indicator. First, write a SELECT statement to make sure that you have the correct items, and then write this as a cursor in the package.

ANSWER:

```
-- ch21_11a.sql
CREATE OR REPLACE PACKAGE MANAGE_GRADES AS
   -- Cursor to loop through all grade types for a given section.
      CURSOR  c_grade_type
              (pc_section_id  section.section_id%TYPE,
               PC_student_ID  student.student_id%TYPE)
              IS
        SELECT GRADE_TYPE_CODE,
               NUMBER_PER_SECTION,
```

```
                   PERCENT_OF_FINAL_GRADE,
                   DROP_LOWEST
        FROM   grade_Type_weight
        WHERE  section_id = pc_section_id
          AND section_id IN (SELECT section_id
                               FROM grade
                               WHERE student_id = pc_student_id);
    END MANAGE_GRADES;
```

B) Add a second package cursor to the package `Manage_Grades` called `c_grades`. This cursor will take a grade type code, student ID, and section ID and return all the grades for that student for that section of that grade type. For example, if Alice were registered in "Intro to Java Programming," this cursor could be used to gather all her quiz grades.

ANSWER:

```
-- ch21_11b.sql
CREATE OR REPLACE PACKAGE MANAGE_GRADES AS
    -- Cursor to loop through all grade types for a given section.
        CURSOR   c_grade_type
                   (pc_section_id   section.section_id%TYPE,
                    PC_student_ID   student.student_id%TYPE)
                   IS
          SELECT GRADE_TYPE_CODE,
                 NUMBER_PER_SECTION,
                 PERCENT_OF_FINAL_GRADE,
                 DROP_LOWEST
          FROM   grade_Type_weight
          WHERE  section_id = pc_section_id
            AND section_id IN (SELECT section_id
                                 FROM grade
                                 WHERE student_id = pc_student_id);
    -- Cursor to loop through all grades for a given student
    -- in a given section.
      CURSOR   c_grades
                 (p_grade_type_code
                     grade_Type_weight.grade_type_code%TYPE,
                  pc_student_id   student.student_id%TYPE,
                  pc_section_id   section.section_id%TYPE) IS
          SELECT grade_type_code,grade_code_occurrence,
                 numeric_grade
          FROM    grade
          WHERE   student_id = pc_student_id
          AND     section_id = pc_section_id
          AND     grade_type_code = p_grade_type_code;
    END MANAGE_GRADES;
```

C) Add a procedure to this package specification called `final_grade`. This function will have parameters of student ID and section ID. It will return a number that is that student's final grade in that section, as well as an exit code. You are adding an exit code instead of raising exceptions because this makes the procedure more flexible and allows the calling program to choose how to proceed depending on what the error code is.

ANSWER:

```
-- ch21_11c.sql
CREATE OR REPLACE PACKAGE MANAGE_GRADES AS
    -- Cursor to loop through all grade types for a given section.
        CURSOR  c_grade_type
                   (pc_section_id  section.section_id%TYPE,
                    PC_student_ID  student.student_id%TYPE)
                IS
          SELECT GRADE_TYPE_CODE,
                 NUMBER_PER_SECTION,
                 PERCENT_OF_FINAL_GRADE,
                 DROP_LOWEST
           FROM  grade_Type_weight
          WHERE  section_id = pc_section_id
            AND section_id IN (SELECT section_id
                                 FROM grade
                                WHERE student_id = pc_student_id);
     -- Cursor to loop through all grades for a given student
     -- in a given section.
      CURSOR   c_grades
                  (p_grade_type_code
                      grade_Type_weight.grade_type_code%TYPE,
                   pc_student_id  student.student_id%TYPE,
                   pc_section_id  section.section_id%TYPE) IS
         SELECT grade_type_code,grade_code_occurrence,
                numeric_grade
          FROM   grade
          WHERE  student_id = pc_student_id
          AND    section_id = pc_section_id
          AND    grade_type_code = p_grade_type_code;
    -- Function to calcuate a student's final grade
    -- in one section
        Procedure final_grade
           (P_student_id    IN student.student_id%type,
            P_section_id    IN section.section_id%TYPE,
            P_Final_grade   OUT enrollment.final_grade%TYPE,
            P_Exit_Code     OUT CHAR);
  END MANAGE_GRADES;
```

D) Add the function to the package body. To perform this calculation, you need a number of variables to hold values as the calculation is performed.

This exercise is also a very good review of data relationships among the student tables. Before you begin this exercise, review Appendix B, "Student Database Schema," which lists the student schema and describes the tables and their columns. When calculating the final grade, keep in mind the following:

▶ Each student is enrolled in a course, and this information is captured in the enrollment table.

▶ The enrollment table holds the final grade only for each student enrollment in one section.

▶ Each section has its own set of elements that are evaluated to come up with the final grade.

▶ All grades for these elements (which have been entered, meaning that there is no NULL value in the database) are in the Grade table.

▶ Every grade has a grade type code. These codes represent the grade type. For example, the grade type QZ stands for quiz. The descriptions of each GRADE_TYPE come from the GRADE_TYPE table.

▶ The GRADE_TYPE_WEIGHT table holds key information for this calculation. It has one entry for each grade type that is used in a given section (not all grade types exist for each section).

▶ In the GRADE_TYPE_WEIGHT table, the NUMBER_PER_SECTION column lists how many times a grade type should be entered to compute the final grade for a particular student in a particular section of a particular course. This helps you determine if all grades for a given grade type have been entered, or even if too many grades for a given grade type have been entered.

▶ You also must consider the DROP_LOWEST flag. It can hold a value of Y (yes) or N (no). If the DROP_LOWEST flag is Y, you must drop the lowest grade from the grade type when calculating the final grade. The PERCENT_OF_FINAL_GRADE column refers to all the grades for a given grade type. For example, if homework is 20% of the final grade, and there are five homeworks and a DROP_LOWEST flag, each remaining homework is worth 5%. When calculating the final grade, you should divide the PERCENT_OF_FINAL_GRADE by the NUMBER_PER_SECTION. (That would be NUMBER_PER_SECTION − 1 if DROP_LOWEST = Y.)

Exit codes should be defined as follows:

▶ S: Success. The final grade has been computed. If the grade cannot be computed, the final grade is NULL, and the exit code will be one of the following:

▶ I: Incomplete. Not all the required grades have been entered for this student in this section.

▶ T: Too many grades exist for this student. For example, there should be only four homework grades, but instead there are six.

▶ N: No grades have been entered for this student in this section.

▶ E: A general computation error occurred (exception `when_others`). Having this type of exit code allows the procedure to compute final grades when it can. If an Oracle error is somehow raised by some of the grades, the calling program can still proceed with the grades that have been computed.

To process the calcuation, you need a number of variables to hold temporary values during the calculation. Create all the variables for the procedure final_grade. Leave the main block with the statement NULL; doing so allows you to compile the procedure to check all the syntax for the variable declaration. Explain how each variable will be used.

ANSWER: The student_id, section_id, and grade_type_code are values carried from one part of the program to another. That is why a variable is created for each of them. Each instance of a grade is computed to find out what its percentage of the final grade is. A counter is needed while processing each grade to ensure that enough grades exist for the given grade count. A lowest-grade variable helps hold each grade to see if it is the lowest. When the lowest grade for a given grade type is known, it can be removed from the final grade. Additionally, two variables are used as row counters to ensure that the cursor was opened.

```
-- ch21_11d.sql
CREATE OR REPLACE PACKAGE BODY MANAGE_GRADES AS
      Procedure final_grade
          (P_student_id    IN student.student_id%type,
           P_section_id    IN section.section_id%TYPE,
           P_Final_grade   OUT enrollment.final_grade%TYPE,
           P_Exit_Code     OUT CHAR)
      IS
          v_student_id            student.student_id%TYPE;
          v_section_id            section.section_id%TYPE;
          v_grade_type_code       grade_type_weight.grade_type_code%TYPE;
          v_grade_percent         NUMBER;
          v_final_grade           NUMBER;
          v_grade_count           NUMBER;
          v_lowest_grade          NUMBER;
          v_exit_code             CHAR(1) := 'S';
          v_no_rows1              CHAR(1) := 'N';
          v_no_rows2              CHAR(1) := 'N';
          e_no_grade              EXCEPTION;
      BEGIN
          NULL;
      END;
END MANAGE_GRADES;
```

E) Complete the procedure `final_grade`. Comment each section to explain what is being processed in each part of the code.

ANSWER:

```
-- ch21_11e.sql
CREATE OR REPLACE PACKAGE BODY MANAGE_GRADES AS
      Procedure final_grade
          (P_student_id    IN student.student_id%type,
           P_section_id    IN section.section_id%TYPE,
           P_Final_grade   OUT enrollment.final_grade%TYPE,
           P_Exit_Code     OUT CHAR)
      IS
          v_student_id            student.student_id%TYPE;
          v_section_id            section.section_id%TYPE;
          v_grade_type_code       grade_type_weight.grade_type_code%TYPE;
          v_grade_percent         NUMBER;
          v_final_grade           NUMBER;
          v_grade_count           NUMBER;
          v_lowest_grade          NUMBER;
          v_exit_code             CHAR(1) := 'S';
          v_no_rows1              CHAR(1) := 'N';
          v_no_rows2              CHAR(1) := 'N';
          e_no_grade              EXCEPTION;
      BEGIN
          v_section_id := p_section_id;
          v_student_id := p_student_id;
          -- Start loop of grade types for the section.
```

```
     FOR r_grade in c_grade_type(v_section_id, v_student_id)
     LOOP
-- Since cursor is open it has a result
-- set; change indicator.
         v_no_rows1 := 'Y';
-- To hold the number of grades per section,
-- reset to 0 before detailed cursor loops
         v_grade_count := 0;
         v_grade_type_code := r_grade.GRADE_TYPE_CODE;
-- Variable to hold the lowest grade.
-- 500 will not be the lowest grade.
         v_lowest_grade := 500;
-- Determine what to multiply a grade by to
-- compute final grade. Must take into consideration
-- if the drop lowest grade indicator is Y.
         SELECT (r_grade.percent_of_final_grade /
                 DECODE(r_grade.drop_lowest, 'Y',
                         (r_grade.number_per_section - 1),
                          r_grade.number_per_section
                 ))* 0.01
          INTO  v_grade_percent
          FROM dual;
-- Open cursor of detailed grade for a student in a
-- given section.
         FOR r_detail in c_grades(v_grade_type_code,
                         v_student_id, v_section_id) LOOP
    -- Since cursor is open it has a result
    -- set; change indicator.
             v_no_rows2 := 'Y';
             v_grade_count  := v_grade_count + 1;
    -- Handle the situation where there are more
    -- entries for grades of a given grade type
    -- than there should be for that section.
         If v_grade_count > r_grade.number_per_section THEN
             v_exit_code := 'T';
             raise e_no_grade;
         END IF;
    -- If drop lowest flag is Y, determine which is lowest
    -- grade to drop
         IF  r_grade.drop_lowest = 'Y' THEN
             IF nvl(v_lowest_grade, 0) >=
                     r_detail.numeric_grade
           THEN
                 v_lowest_grade := r_detail.numeric_grade;
             END IF;
         END IF;
    -- Increment the final grade with percentage of current
    -- grade in the detail loop.
         v_final_grade := nvl(v_final_grade, 0) +
                 (r_detail.numeric_grade * v_grade_percent);
```

```
        END LOOP;
        -- Once detailed loop is finished, if the number of grades
        -- for a given student for a given grade type and section
        -- is less than the required amount, raise an exception.
            IF  v_grade_count < r_grade.NUMBER_PER_SECTION THEN
                v_exit_code := 'I';
                raise e_no_grade;
            END IF;
        -- If the drop lowest flag was Y, you need to take
        -- the lowest grade out of the final grade. It was not
        -- known when it was added which was the lowest grade
        -- to drop until all grades were examined.
            IF  r_grade.drop_lowest = 'Y' THEN
                v_final_grade := nvl(v_final_grade, 0) -
                        (v_lowest_grade *  v_grade_percent);
            END IF;
      END LOOP;
    -- If either cursor had no rows, there is an error.
    IF v_no_rows1 = 'N' OR v_no_rows2 = 'N'    THEN
        v_exit_code := 'N';
        raise e_no_grade;
    END IF;
    P_final_grade   := v_final_grade;
    P_exit_code     := v_exit_code;
    EXCEPTION
      WHEN e_no_grade THEN
        P_final_grade := null;
        P_exit_code   := v_exit_code;
      WHEN OTHERS THEN
        P_final_grade := null;
        P_exit_code   := 'E';
  END final_grade;
END MANAGE_GRADES;
```

F) Write an anonymous block to test your `final_grade` procedure. The block should ask for a `student_id` and a `section_id` and return the final grade and an exit code.

ANSWER: It is often a good idea to run a describe command on a procedure to make sure that all the parameters are in the correct order:

```
SQL> desc manage_grades
PROCEDURE FINAL_GRADE
 Argument Name                   Type                   In/Out Default?
 ------------------------------  ---------------------  ------ --------
 P_STUDENT_ID                    NUMBER(8)              IN
 P_SECTION_ID                    NUMBER(8)              IN
 P_FINAL_GRADE                   NUMBER(3)              OUT
 P_EXIT_CODE                     CHAR                   OUT
```

Now that you have the parameters, the procedure can be called:

```
-- ch21_11f.sql
SET SERVEROUTPUT ON
```

```
DECLARE
  v_student_id    student.student_id%TYPE := &sv_student_id;
  v_section_id    section.section_id%TYPE := &sv_section_id;
  v_final_grade   enrollment.final_grade%TYPE;
  v_exit_code     CHAR;
BEGIN
  manage_grades.final_grade(v_student_id, v_section_id,
    v_final_grade, v_exit_code);
  DBMS_OUTPUT.PUT_LINE('The Final Grade is '||v_final_grade);
  DBMS_OUTPUT.PUT_LINE('The Exit Code is '||v_exit_code);
END;
```

If you were to run this for a `student_id` of 102 in section 89, you would get this result:

```
Enter value for sv_student_id: 102
old   2:  v_student_id   student.student_id%TYPE := &sv_student_id;
new   2:  v_student_id   student.student_id%TYPE := 102;
Enter value for sv_section_id: 86
old   3:  v_section_id   section.section_id%TYPE := &sv_section_id;
new   3:  v_section_id   section.section_id%TYPE := 86;
The Final Grade is 89
The Exit Code is S
PL/SQL procedure successfully completed.
```

G) Add a function to the `manage_grades` package specification called `median_grade` that takes in a course number (`p_course_number`), a section number (`p_section_number`), and a grade type (`p_grade_type`) and returns a `work_grade.grade%TYPE`. Create any cursors or types that the function requires.

ANSWER:

```
-- ch21_11g.sql
CREATE OR REPLACE PACKAGE MANAGE_GRADES AS
  -- Cursor to loop through all grade types for a given section.
    CURSOR  c_grade_type
            (pc_section_id  section.section_id%TYPE,
             PC_student_ID  student.student_id%TYPE)
            IS
      SELECT GRADE_TYPE_CODE,
             NUMBER_PER_SECTION,
             PERCENT_OF_FINAL_GRADE,
             DROP_LOWEST
        FROM  grade_Type_weight
       WHERE  section_id = pc_section_id
         AND section_id IN (SELECT section_id
                              FROM grade
                             WHERE student_id = pc_student_id);
    -- Cursor to loop through all grades for a given student
    -- in a given section.
     CURSOR  c_grades
             (p_grade_type_code
                 grade_Type_weight.grade_type_code%TYPE,
              pc_student_id  student.student_id%TYPE,
              pc_section_id  section.section_id%TYPE) IS
```

```
        SELECT grade_type_code,grade_code_occurrence,
               numeric_grade
        FROM   grade
        WHERE  student_id = pc_student_id
        AND    section_id = pc_section_id
        AND    grade_type_code = p_grade_type_code;
  -- Function to calcuate a student's final grade
  -- in one section
    Procedure final_grade
      (P_student_id   IN student.student_id%type,
       P_section_id   IN section.section_id%TYPE,
       P_Final_grade  OUT enrollment.final_grade%TYPE,
       P_Exit_Code    OUT CHAR);
    -- ---------------------------------------------------------
    -- Function to calculate the median grade
     FUNCTION median_grade
        (p_course_number section.course_no%TYPE,
         p_section_number section.section_no%TYPE,
         p_grade_type grade.grade_type_code%TYPE)
       RETURN grade.numeric_grade%TYPE;
    CURSOR c_work_grade
         (p_course_no   section.course_no%TYPE,
          p_section_no section.section_no%TYPE,
          p_grade_type_code grade.grade_type_code%TYPE
          )IS
     SELECT distinct numeric_grade
       FROM grade
      WHERE section_id = (SELECT section_id
                            FROM section
                           WHERE course_no= p_course_no
                             AND section_no = p_section_no)
        AND grade_type_code = p_grade_type_code
      ORDER BY numeric_grade;
    TYPE t_grade_type IS TABLE OF c_work_grade%ROWTYPE
       INDEX BY BINARY_INTEGER;
     t_grade t_grade_type;
   END MANAGE_GRADES;
```

H) Add a function to the `manage_grades` package specification called `median_grade` that takes in a course number (`p_cnumber`), a section number (`p_snumber`), and a grade type (`p_grade_type`). The function should return the median grade (`work_grade.grade%TYPE` datatype) based on those three components. For example, you might use this function to answer the question, "What is the median grade of homework assignments in 'Intro to Java Programming' section 2?" A true median can contain two values. Because this function can return only one value, if the median is made up of two values, return the average of the two.

ANSWER:

```
-- ch21_11h.sql
CREATE OR REPLACE PACKAGE BODY MANAGE_GRADES AS
     Procedure final_grade
        (P_student_id   IN student.student_id%type,
```

```
                P_section_id    IN section.section_id%TYPE,
                P_Final_grade   OUT enrollment.final_grade%TYPE,
                P_Exit_Code     OUT CHAR)
    IS
        v_student_id              student.student_id%TYPE;
        v_section_id              section.section_id%TYPE;
        v_grade_type_code         grade_type_weight.grade_type_code%TYPE;
        v_grade_percent           NUMBER;
        v_final_grade             NUMBER;
        v_grade_count             NUMBER;
        v_lowest_grade            NUMBER;
        v_exit_code               CHAR(1) := 'S';
    --  Next two variables are used to calculate whether a cursor
    --  has no result set.
        v_no_rows1                CHAR(1) := 'N';
        v_no_rows2                CHAR(1) := 'N';
        e_no_grade                EXCEPTION;
    BEGIN
        v_section_id := p_section_id;
        v_student_id := p_student_id;
        -- Start loop of grade types for the section.
          FOR r_grade in c_grade_type(v_section_id, v_student_id)
          LOOP
        -- Since cursor is open it has a result
        -- set; change indicator.
              v_no_rows1 := 'Y';
        -- To hold the number of grades per section,
        -- reset to 0 before detailed cursor loops
              v_grade_count := 0;
              v_grade_type_code := r_grade.GRADE_TYPE_CODE;
        -- Variable to hold the lowest grade.
        -- 500 will not be the lowest grade.
              v_lowest_grade := 500;
        -- Determine what to multiply a grade by to
        -- compute final grade. Must take into consideration
        -- if the drop lowest grade indicator is Y.
              SELECT (r_grade.percent_of_final_grade /
                      DECODE(r_grade.drop_lowest, 'Y',
                                (r_grade.number_per_section - 1),
                                r_grade.number_per_section
                      ))* 0.01
              INTO  v_grade_percent
              FROM dual;
        -- Open cursor of detailed grade for a student in a
        -- given section.
              FOR r_detail in c_grades(v_grade_type_code,
                                v_student_id, v_section_id) LOOP
          -- Since cursor is open it has a result
          -- set; change indicator.
                v_no_rows2 := 'Y';
```

```
                v_grade_count   := v_grade_count + 1;
    -- Handle the situation where there are more
    -- entries for grades of a given grade type
    -- than there should be for that section.
            If v_grade_count > r_grade.number_per_section THEN
                v_exit_code := 'T';
                raise e_no_grade;
            END IF;
    -- If drop lowest flag is Y determine which is lowest
    -- grade to drop
            IF  r_grade.drop_lowest = 'Y' THEN
                IF nvl(v_lowest_grade, 0) >=
                        r_detail.numeric_grade
              THEN
                    v_lowest_grade := r_detail.numeric_grade;
                END IF;
            END IF;
    -- Increment the final grade with percentage of current
    -- grade in the detail loop.
            v_final_grade := nvl(v_final_grade, 0) +
                    (r_detail.numeric_grade * v_grade_percent);
        END LOOP;
    -- Once detailed loop is finished, if the number of grades
    -- for a given student for a given grade type and section
    -- is less than the required amount, raise an exception.
            IF  v_grade_count < r_grade.NUMBER_PER_SECTION THEN
                v_exit_code := 'I';
                raise e_no_grade;
            END IF;
    -- If the drop lowest flag was Y, you need to take
    -- the lowest grade out of the final grade. It was not
    -- known when it was added which was the lowest grade
    -- to drop until all grades were examined.
            IF  r_grade.drop_lowest = 'Y' THEN
                v_final_grade := nvl(v_final_grade, 0) -
                        (v_lowest_grade *  v_grade_percent);
            END IF;
    END LOOP;
-- If either cursor had no rows then there is an error.
IF v_no_rows1 = 'N' OR v_no_rows2 = 'N'    THEN
    v_exit_code := 'N';
    raise e_no_grade;
END IF;
P_final_grade  := v_final_grade;
P_exit_code    := v_exit_code;
EXCEPTION
  WHEN e_no_grade THEN
    P_final_grade := null;
    P_exit_code   := v_exit_code;
  WHEN OTHERS THEN
```

```
            P_final_grade := null;
            P_exit_code    := 'E';
    END final_grade;


FUNCTION median_grade
    (p_course_number section.course_no%TYPE,
     p_section_number section.section_no%TYPE,
     p_grade_type grade.grade_type_code%TYPE)
RETURN grade.numeric_grade%TYPE
    IS
    BEGIN
      FOR r_work_grade
          IN c_work_grade(p_course_number, p_section_number,
                          p_grade_type)
      LOOP
        t_grade(NVL(t_grade.COUNT,0) + 1).numeric_grade :=
          r_work_grade.numeric_grade;
      END LOOP;
      IF t_grade.COUNT = 0
      THEN
        RETURN NULL;
      ELSE
        IF MOD(t_grade.COUNT, 2) = 0
        THEN
          -- There is an even number of work grades. Find the middle
          -- two and average them.
          RETURN (t_grade(t_grade.COUNT / 2).numeric_grade +
                  t_grade((t_grade.COUNT / 2) + 1).numeric_grade
                 ) / 2;
        ELSE
          -- There is an odd number of grades. Return the one in
          -- the middle.
          RETURN t_grade(TRUNC(t_grade.COUNT / 2, 0) +
            1).numeric_grade;
        END IF;
      END IF;
    EXCEPTION
      WHEN OTHERS
      THEN
        RETURN NULL;
    END median_grade;
END MANAGE_GRADES;
```

l) Write a SELECT statement that uses the function `median_grade` and shows the median grade for all grade types in sections 1 and 2 of course 25.

ANSWER:

```
-- ch21_11i.sql
SELECT COURSE_NO,
       COURSE_NAME,
       SECTION_NO,
```

```
            GRADE_TYPE,
            manage_grades.median_grade
                   (COURSE_NO,
                    SECTION_NO,
                    GRADE_TYPE)
                median_grade
FROM
(SELECT DISTINCT
            C.COURSE_NO        COURSE_NO,
            C.DESCRIPTION      COURSE_NAME,
            S.SECTION_NO       SECTION_NO,
            G.GRADE_TYPE_CODE  GRADE_TYPE
FROM SECTION S, COURSE C, ENROLLMENT E, GRADE G
WHERE C.course_no = s.course_no
AND    s.section_id = e.section_id
AND    e.student_id = g.student_id
AND    c.course_no = 25
AND    s.section_no between 1 and 2
ORDER BY 1, 4, 3) grade_source
```

J) What would be the results for all grade types in sections 1 and 2 of course 25?

ANSWER:

```
COURSE_NO COURSE_NAME       SECTION_NO GRADE_TYPE MEDIAN_GRADE
--------- ------------------------------------- ------------
       25 Intro to Programming     1 FI             98
       25 Intro to Programming     2 FI             71
       25 Intro to Programming     1 HM             76
       25 Intro to Programming     2 HM             83
       25 Intro to Programming     1 MT             86
       25 Intro to Programming     2 MT             89
       25 Intro to Programming     1 PA             91
       25 Intro to Programming     2 PA             97
       25 Intro to Programming     1 QZ             71
       25 Intro to Programming     2 QZ             78
```

```
10 rows selected.
```

If you prefer to see the Grade Type Description rather than the Grade Type Code, then you can use the DESCRIPTION column in the GRADE_TYPE table rather then the GRADE_TYPE_CODE, which was used in the previous SQL statement. This would have a result of 'Participation' for PA and 'Midterm' for MT.

▼ TRY IT YOURSELF

In this chapter, you have learned about packages. Here are some projects that will help you test the depth of your understanding:

1) Add a procedure to the `school_api` package called `remove_student`. This procedure accepts a `student_id` and returns nothing. Based on the student ID passed in, it removes the student from the database. If the student does not exist or if a problem occurs while removing the student (such as a foreign key constraint violation), let the calling program handle it.

2) Alter `remove_student` in the `school_api` package body to accept an additional parameter. This new parameter should be a VARCHAR2 and should be called `p_ri`. Make `p_ri` default to R. The new parameter may contain a value of R or C. If R is received, it represents DELETE RESTRICT, and the procedure acts as it does now. If there are enrollments for the student, the delete is disallowed. If a C is received, it represents DELETE CASCADE. This functionally means that the `remove_student` procedure locates all records for the student in all the Student Database tables. It removes them from the database before attempting to remove the student from the student table. Decide how to handle the situation when the user passes in a code other than C or R.

The projects in this section are meant to have you use all the skills you have acquired throughout this chapter. The answers to these projects can be found in Appendix D and on this book's companion Web site. Visit the Web site periodically to share and discuss your answers.

CHAPTER 22

Stored Code

CHAPTER OBJECTIVES

In this chapter, you will learn about

▶ Gathering information about stored code

In Chapter 19 you learned about procedures, in Chapter 20 you learned about functions, and in Chapter 21 you learned about the process of grouping functions and procedures into a package. Now you will learn more about what it means to have code bundled into a package. You can use numerous data dictionary views to gather information about the objects in a package.

Functions in packages are also required to meet additional restrictions to be used in a SELECT statement. In this chapter, you learn what they are and how to enforce them. You will also learn an advanced technique to overload a function or procedure so that it executes different code, depending on the type of the parameter passed in.

LAB 22.1
Gathering Information About Stored Code

LAB OBJECTIVES

After completing this lab, you will be able to

- ▶ Get stored code information from the data dictionary
- ▶ Enforce the purity level with the RESTRICT_REFERENCES pragma
- ▶ Overload modules

Stored programs are stored in compiled form in the database. Information about the stored programs is accessible through various data dictionary views. In Chapter 19, "Procedures," you learned about the two data dictionary views USER_OBJECTS and USER_SOURCE. A few more data dictionary views are useful for obtaining information about stored code. In this lab, you will learn how to take advantage of these.

▼ LAB 22.1 EXERCISES

This section provides exercises and suggested answers, with discussion related to how those answers resulted. The most important thing to realize is whether your answer works. You should figure out the implications of the answers and what the effects are of any different answers you may come up with.

22.1.1 Get Stored Code Information from the Data Dictionary

Complete the following tasks, and answer the following questions:

A) Query the data dictionary to determine all the stored procedures, functions, and packages in the current schema of the database. Also include the current status of the stored code. Write the SELECT statement.

ANSWER: You can use the USER_OBJECTS view you learned about in Chapter 19. This view has information about all database objects in the schema of the current user. Remember, if you want to see all the objects in other schemas that the current user has access to, use the ALL_OBJECTS view. There is also a DBA_OBJECTS view for a list of all objects in the database, regardless of privilege. The STATUS is either VALID or INVALID. An object can change status from VALID to INVALID if an underlying table is altered or privileges on a referenced object have been revoked from the creator of the function, procedure, or package. The following SELECT statement produces the answer you are looking for:

```
SELECT OBJECT_TYPE, OBJECT_NAME, STATUS
FROM   USER_OBJECTS
WHERE  OBJECT_TYPE IN
         ('FUNCTION', 'PROCEDURE', 'PACKAGE',
          'PACKAGE_BODY')
ORDER BY OBJECT_TYPE;
```

B) Type the following script into a text file, and run the script in SQL*Plus. It creates the function `scode_at_line`. Explain the purpose of this function. What is accomplished by running it? When does a developer find it useful?

```
-- ch22_1a.sql
CREATE OR REPLACE FUNCTION scode_at_line
    (i_name_in IN VARCHAR2,
     i_line_in IN INTEGER := 1,
     i_type_in IN VARCHAR2 := NULL)
RETURN VARCHAR2
IS
    CURSOR scode_cur IS
        SELECT text
          FROM user_source
         WHERE name = UPPER (i_name_in)
           AND (type = UPPER (i_type_in)
            OR i_type_in IS NULL)
           AND line = i_line_in;
    scode_rec scode_cur%ROWTYPE;
BEGIN
    OPEN scode_cur;
    FETCH scode_cur INTO scode_rec;
    IF scode_cur%NOTFOUND
        THEN
            CLOSE scode_cur;
            RETURN NULL;
    ELSE
        CLOSE scode_cur;
        RETURN scode_rec.text;
    END IF;
END;
```

ANSWER: The `scode_at_line` function provides an easy mechanism for retrieving the text from a stored program for a specified line number. This is useful if a developer receives a compilation error message referring to a particular line number in an object. The developer can then use this function to find the text that is in error.

The function uses three parameters:

▶ `name_in`: The name of the stored object.

▶ `line_in`: The line number of the line you want to retrieve. The default value is 1.

▶ `type_in`: The type of object you want to view. The default for `type_in` is NULL.

The default values are designed to make this function as easy as possible to use.

BY THE WAY

The output from a call to SHOW ERRORS in SQL*Plus displays the line number on which an error occurred, but the line number doesn't correspond to the line in your text file. Instead, it relates directly to the line number stored with the source code in the USER_SOURCE view.

C) Enter `desc user_errors`. What do you see? In what way do you think this view is useful for you?

ANSWER: This view stores current errors on the user's stored objects. The text file contains the text of the error. This is useful in determining the details of a compilation error. The next exercise walks you through using this view.

```
Name                    Null?       Type
--------------------    --------    -----------
NAME                    NOT NULL    VARCHAR2(30)
TYPE                                VARCHAR2(12)
SEQUENCE                NOT NULL    NUMBER
LINE                    NOT NULL    NUMBER
POSITION                NOT NULL    NUMBER
TEXT                    NOT NULL    VARCHAR2(2000)  ---
```

D) Enter the following script to force an error:

```
CREATE OR REPLACE PROCEDURE FORCE_ERROR
as
BEGIN
    SELECT course_no
    INTO v_temp
    FROM course;
END;
```

Now enter the following:

```
SHO ERR
```

What do you see?

ANSWER:

```
Errors for PROCEDURE FORCE_ERROR:
LINE/COL ERROR
-------- ------------------------------------------
4/4      PL/SQL: SQL Statement ignored
5/9       PLS-00201: identifier 'V_TEMP' must be declared
6/4      PL/SQL: ORA-00904: : invalid identifier
```

E) How can you retrieve information from the USER_ERRORS view?

ANSWER:

```
SELECT line||'/'||position "LINE/COL", TEXT "ERROR"
FROM user_errors
WHERE name = 'FORCE_ERROR'
```

It is important for you to know how to retrieve this information from the USER_ERRORS view, because the `SHO ERR` command shows you only the most recent errors. If you run a script creating a number of objects, you have to rely on the USER_ERRORS view.

F) Enter `desc user_dependencies`. What do you see? How can you make use of this view?

ANSWER: The USER_DEPENDENCIES view is useful for analyzing the impact of table changes or changes to other stored procedures. If tables are about to be redesigned, an impact assessment can be made from the information in USER_DEPENDENCIES. ALL_DEPENDENCIES and DBA_DEPENDENCIES show all dependencies for procedures, functions, package specifications, and package bodies.

```
Name                                 Null?     Type
-----------------------------------  --------  ----
NAME                                 NOT NULL  VARCHAR2(30)
TYPE                                           VARCHAR2(12)
REFERENCED_OWNER                               VARCHAR2(30)
REFERENCED_NAME                      NOT NULL  VARCHAR2(30)
REFERENCED_TYPE                                VARCHAR2(12)
REFERENCED_LINK_NAME                           VARCHAR2(30)
```

G) Enter the following:

```
SELECT referenced_name
FROM user_dependencies
WHERE name = 'SCHOOL_API';
```

Analyze what you see, and explain how it is useful.

ANSWER:

```
REFERENCED_NAME
----------------------------
STANDARD
STANDARD
DUAL
DBMS_STANDARD
DBMS_OUTPUT
COURSE
ENROLLMENT
INSTRUCTOR
INSTRUCTOR
INSTRUCTOR_ID_SEQ
SCHOOL_API
SECTION
```

This list of dependencies for the `school_api` package lists all objects referenced in the package. This includes tables, sequences, and procedures (even Oracle-supplied packages). This information is very useful when you are planning a change to the database structure. You can easily pinpoint the ramifications of any database changes.

H) Enter `desc school_api`. What do you see?

ANSWER:

```
SQL> desc school_api
PROCEDURE DISCOUNT_COST
FUNCTION NEW_INSTRUCTOR_ID RETURNS NUMBER(8)
```

l) Explain what you are seeing. How is this different from the USER_DEPENDENCIES view?

ANSWER: The desc command you have been using to describe the columns in a table is also used for procedures, packages, and functions. The desc command shows all the parameters, with their default values and an indication of whether they are IN or OUT. If the object is a function, the return datatype is displayed. This is very different from the USER_DEPENDENCIES view, which has information on all the objects that are referenced in a package, function, or procedure.

DEPTREE

An Oracle-supplied utility called DEPTREE shows you, for a given object, which other objects are dependent on it. This utility has three pieces. You need to have DBA access to the database to use this utility.

```
Script: utldtree.sql
Procedure: DEPTREE_FILL(type, schema, object_name)
View: ideptree
```

First, run utldtree.sql in your schema. This creates the necessary objects to map the dependencies. The location of utldtree.sql depends on your particular installation, so ask your DBA. The file will be found under the directory that your Oracle server is installed in. This directory is refered to as the ORACLE_HOME. The subdirectory would be as follows:

```
($ORACLE_HOME/rdbms/admin/utldtree.sql)
```

Second, fill the DEPTREE e_temptab table by running DEPTREE_FILL.

Example:

```
SQL> exec DEPTREE_FILL('TABLE', USER, 'COURSE')
```

Finally, look at the DEPTREE information in ideptree view.

Example:

```
SQL> SELECT * FROM ideptree;
```

The result contains the following kind of information:

```
DEPENDENCIES
-------------------------------------------
    FUNCTION STUDENT.SHOW_DESCRIPTION
    PACKAGE BODY STUDENT.SCHOOL_API
    PACKAGE STUDENT.COURSE_PKG
    PACKAGE BODY STUDENT.STUDENT_INFO_PKG
    PROCEDURE STUDENT.FORCE_ERROR
TABLE STUDENT.COURSE
    PROCEDURE STUDENT.DISCOUNT
    PACKAGE BODY STUDENT.MANAGE_STUDENTS
        PACKAGE BODY STUDENT.COURSE_PKG
    PACKAGE BODY STUDENT.COURSE_PKG

10 rows selected
```

22.1.2 Enforce the Purity Level with the RESTRICT_REFERENCES Pragma

The RESTRICT_REFERENCES pragma is now used for backward compatibility only. In Oracle Database versions prior to 8.1.5 (Oracle 8i), programmers used the pragma RESTRICT_REFERENCES to assert a subprogram's purity level (the extent to which it is free of side effects). In subsequent versions, use the hints `parallel_enable` and `deterministic` instead to communicate subprogram purity to the Oracle Database. The pragma RESTRICT_REFERENCES can be removed from code. However, you may keep it for backward compatibility.

Complete the following tasks, and answer the following questions:

A) Add the following function to the `school_api` package specification you created in Chapter 21, "Packages":

```
-- ch22_2a.sql
CREATE OR REPLACE PACKAGE  school_api as
   v_current_date DATE;
   PROCEDURE Discount_Cost;
   FUNCTION new_instructor_id
   RETURN instructor.instructor_id%TYPE;
        FUNCTION total_cost_for_student
            (i_student_id IN student.student_id%TYPE)
        RETURN course.cost%TYPE;
  END school_api;
```

Append to the body so that the new package code is as follows:

```
-- ch22_2b.sql
CREATE OR REPLACE PACKAGE BODY school_api AS
   PROCEDURE discount_cost
   IS
      CURSOR c_group_discount
      IS
      SELECT distinct s.course_no, c.description
        FROM section s, enrollment e, course c
       WHERE s.section_id = e.section_id
       GROUP BY s.course_no, c.description,
                e.section_id, s.section_id
       HAVING COUNT(*) >=8;
   BEGIN
      FOR r_group_discount IN c_group_discount
      LOOP
      UPDATE course
         SET cost = cost * .95
       WHERE course_no = r_group_discount.course_no;
       DBMS_OUTPUT.PUT_LINE
          ('A 5% discount has been given to'
          ||r_group_discount.course_no||'
          '||r_group_discount.description);
      END LOOP;
    END discount_cost;
   FUNCTION new_instructor_id
      RETURN instructor.instructor_id%TYPE
   IS
      v_new_instid instructor.instructor_id%TYPE;
   BEGIN
      SELECT INSTRUCTOR_ID_SEQ.NEXTVAL
```

```
        INTO v_new_instid
        FROM dual;
     RETURN v_new_instid;
  EXCEPTION
    WHEN OTHERS
      THEN
       DECLARE
          v_sqlerrm VARCHAR2(250) :=
             SUBSTR(SQLERRM,1,250);
       BEGIN
         RAISE_APPLICATION_ERROR(-20003,
          'Error in    instructor_id: '||v_sqlerrm);
       END;
  END new_instructor_id;
FUNCTION total_cost_for_student
   (i_student_id IN student.student_id%TYPE)
    RETURN course.cost%TYPE
IS
   v_cost course.cost%TYPE;
BEGIN
   SELECT sum(cost)
     INTO v_cost
     FROM course c, section s, enrollment e
    WHERE c.course_no = s.course_no
      AND e.section_id = s.section_id
      AND e.student_id = i_student_id;
   RETURN v_cost;
EXCEPTION
   WHEN OTHERS THEN
      RETURN NULL;
END total_cost_for_student;
BEGIN
   SELECT trunc(sysdate, 'DD')
     INTO v_current_date
     FROM dual;
END school_api;
```

If you performed the following SELECT statement, what would you expect to see?

```
SELECT school_api.total_cost_for_student(student_id),
      student_id
FROM student;
```

ANSWER: At first glance you might think you would see a list of `student_ids`, with the total cost of the courses they took. But instead you may get the following error (depending on the version of Oracle; in Oracle 11g you do not get this error):

```
ERROR at line 1:
ORA-06571: Function TOTAL_COST_FOR_STUDENT
does not guarantee not to update database
```

Although functions can be used in a SELECT statement, if a function is in a package, it requires some additional definitions to enforce its purity.

A pragma is a special directive to the PL/SQL compiler. You use the RESTRICT_REFERENCES pragma to tell the compiler about the purity level of a packaged function.

To assert the purity level, use this syntax (the meaning of each code will be explained later in this chapter):

```
PRAGMA RESTRICT_REFERENCES
      (function_name, WNDS [,WNPS], [,RNDS] [,RNPS])
```

REQUIREMENTS FOR STORED FUNCTIONS IN SQL

▶ The function must be stored in the database (not in the library of an Oracle tool).

▶ The function must be a row-specific function and not a column or group function.

▶ As for all functions (whether to be used in SQL statements or not), parameters must be in the IN mode.

Numerous function side effects must be considered. Modifying database tables in stored functions may have a ripple effect on queries using the function. Modifying package variables can have an impact on other stored functions or procedures, or in turn on the SQL statement using the stored function. Stored functions in the WHERE clause may subvert the query optimization process. A SQL statement may use a stand-alone function or package function as an operator on one or more columns, provided that the function returns a valid Oracle database type.

A user-defined function may select from database tables or call other procedures or functions, whether stand-alone or packaged. When a function is used in a SELECT statement, it may not modify data in any database table with an INSERT, UPDATE, or DELETE statement, or read or write package variables across user sessions.

The Oracle server automatically enforces the rules for stand-alone functions, but not with a stored function in a package. The purity level of a function in a package must be stated explicitly. This is done using a pragma.

The error message was received because the pragma was not used. You will now learn how to use a pragma.

B) Alter the package specification for `school_api` as follows:

```
-- ch22_2c.sql
CREATE OR REPLACE PACKAGE  school_api as
   v_current_date DATE;
   PROCEDURE Discount_Cost;
   FUNCTION new_instructor_id
   RETURN instructor.instructor_id%TYPE;
        FUNCTION total_cost_for_student
           (i_student_id IN student.student_id%TYPE)
      RETURN course.cost%TYPE;
       PRAGMA RESTRICT_REFERENCES
           (total_cost_for_student, WNDS, WNPS, RNPS);
 END school_api;
```

Now run the SELECT statement from question A). What do you expect to see?

ANSWER: The pragma restriction is added to the package specification. It ensures that the function `total_cost_for_student` meets the required purity restriction for a function to be in a SELECT statement. The SELECT statement now functions properly; it projects a list of the total cost for each student and the student's ID.

RULES FOR USING PRAGMA RESTRICTIONS

▶ You can declare the pragma RESTRICT_REFERENCES only in a package spec or object type spec. You can specify up to four constraints (RNDS, RNPS, WNDS, WNPS) in any order. To call a function from parallel queries, you must specify all four constraints. No constraint implies another. Typically, this pragma is specified for functions. If a function calls procedures, specify the pragma for those procedures as well.

▶ When you specify TRUST, the function body is not checked for violations of the constraints listed in the pragma. The function is trusted not to violate them. Skipping these checks can improve performance.

▶ If you specify DEFAULT instead of a subprogram name, the pragma applies to all subprograms in the package spec or object type spec (including the system-defined constructor for object types). You can still declare the pragma for individual subprograms, overriding the default pragma.

▶ A RESTRICT_REFERENCES pragma can apply to only one subprogram declaration. A pragma that references the name of overloaded subprograms always applies to the most recent subprogram declaration.

▶ The pragma must come after the function declaration in the package specification.

C) What is the purity level of the function `school_api.total_cost_for_student`?

ANSWER: The extent to which a function is free of side effects is its purity level. The function is now very pure. It has the following levels of purity: WNDS means write no database state; that is, it does not make any changes to database tables. WNPS means that the function writes no package state; that is, the function does not alter the values of any package variables. RNPS means that it reads no package state; that is, no package variables are read to calculate the return for the function. There is also an RNDS pragma, which means that no database tables are read. If this is added, the function is too pure for your needs here and cannot be used in a SELECT statement.

Table 22.1 summarizes the codes and their meanings.

TABLE 22.1
Pragma Restrictions

PURITY LEVEL	CODE DESCRIPTION	ASSERTION
WNDS	Writes no database state	No modification of any database table
WNPS	Writes no package state	No modification of any packaged variable
RNDS	Reads no database state	No reading of any database table
RNPS	Reads no package state	No reading of any package variable

D) If you add the following three lines, will the package compile without error?

```
UPDATE STUDENT
   SET Employer = 'Prentice Hall'
   WHERE employer is NULL;
```

So that the entire package body would now look like this:

```
-- ch22_2c.sql
CREATE OR REPLACE PACKAGE BODY school_api AS
   PROCEDURE discount_cost
```

```
   IS
      CURSOR c_group_discount
      IS
      SELECT distinct s.course_no, c.description
        FROM section s, enrollment e, course c
       WHERE s.section_id = e.section_id
       GROUP BY s.course_no, c.description,
               e.section_id, s.section_id
       HAVING COUNT(*) >=8;
   BEGIN
      FOR r_group_discount IN c_group_discount
      LOOP
      UPDATE course
        SET cost = cost * .95
       WHERE course_no = r_group_discount.course_no;
        DBMS_OUTPUT.PUT_LINE
          ('A 5% discount has been given to'
          ||r_group_discount.course_no||'
         '||r_group_discount.description);
      END LOOP;
    END discount_cost;
  FUNCTION new_instructor_id
     RETURN instructor.instructor_id%TYPE
   IS
      v_new_instid instructor.instructor_id%TYPE;
   BEGIN
      SELECT INSTRUCTOR_ID_SEQ.NEXTVAL
        INTO v_new_instid
        FROM dual;
      RETURN v_new_instid;
   EXCEPTION
      WHEN OTHERS
        THEN
         DECLARE
            v_sqlerrm VARCHAR2(250) :=
               SUBSTR(SQLERRM,1,250);
         BEGIN
           RAISE_APPLICATION_ERROR(-20003,
           'Error in    instructor_id: '||v_sqlerrm);
         END;
  END new_instructor_id;
FUNCTION total_cost_for_student
   (i_student_id IN student.student_id%TYPE)
    RETURN course.cost%TYPE
IS
   v_cost course.cost%TYPE;
BEGIN
    SELECT sum(cost)
      INTO v_cost
      FROM course c, section s, enrollment e
```

```
          WHERE c.course_no = s.course_no
            AND e.section_id = s.section_id
            AND e.student_id = i_student_id;
      UPDATE STUDENT
        SET employer = 'Prentice Hall'
       WHERE employer is null;
       RETURN v_cost;
    EXCEPTION
      WHEN OTHERS THEN
          RETURN NULL;
    END total_cost_for_student;
    BEGIN
      SELECT trunc(sysdate, 'DD')
        INTO v_current_date
        FROM dual;
  END school_api;
```

ANSWER: No. You added an update statement and violated the purity level of the pragma restriction WNDS (writes no database state). You receive the following error message when you try to compile the new package:

```
Errors for PACKAGE BODY SCHOOL_API:

LINE/COL ERROR
-------- --------------------------------------------------------------
44/3     PLS-00452: Subprogram 'TOTAL_COST_FOR_STUDENT' violates its
         associated pragmaErrors for PACKAGE BODY SCHOOL_API:
```

22.1.3 Overload Modules

When you overload modules, you give two or more modules the same name. The modules' parameter lists must differ in a manner significant enough for the compiler (and runtime engine) to distinguish between the different versions.

You can overload modules in three contexts:

▶ In a local module in the same PL/SQL block

▶ In a package specification

▶ In a package body

Complete the following tasks:

A) Add the following lines to the package specification of `school_api`. Then recompile the package specification. Explain what you have created.

```
-- ch22_3a.sql
CREATE OR REPLACE PACKAGE  school_api as
    v_current_date DATE;
    PROCEDURE Discount_Cost;
    FUNCTION new_instructor_id
    RETURN instructor.instructor_id%TYPE;
        FUNCTION total_cost_for_student
          (i_student_id IN student.student_id%TYPE)
```

```
        RETURN course.cost%TYPE;
         PRAGMA RESTRICT_REFERENCES
             (total_cost_for_student, WNDS, WNPS, RNPS);
    PROCEDURE get_student_info
         (i_student_id   IN   student.student_id%TYPE,
          o_last_name       OUT student.last_name%TYPE,
          o_first_name      OUT student.first_name%TYPE,
          o_zip             OUT student.zip%TYPE,
          o_return_code  OUT NUMBER);
    PROCEDURE get_student_info
         (i_last_name      IN student.last_name%TYPE,
          i_first_name     IN student.first_name%TYPE,
          o_student_id     OUT student.student_id%TYPE,
          o_zip            OUT student.zip%TYPE,
          o_return_code OUT NUMBER);
    END school_api;
```

ANSWER: No, you have not created Frankenstein; it's just an overloaded procedure. The specification has two procedures with the same name and different IN parameters in both number and datatype. The OUT parameters also differ in number and datatype. This overloaded function accepts either of the two sets of IN parameters and performs the version of the function corresponding to the datatype passed in.

B) Add the following code to the body of the package `school_api`. Explain what is accomplished.

```
-- ch22_4a.sql
CREATE OR REPLACE PACKAGE BODY school_api AS
    PROCEDURE discount_cost
    IS
        CURSOR c_group_discount
        IS
        SELECT distinct s.course_no, c.description
          FROM section s, enrollment e, course c
         WHERE s.section_id = e.section_id
        GROUP BY s.course_no, c.description,
                 e.section_id, s.section_id
        HAVING COUNT(*) >=8;
    BEGIN
       FOR r_group_discount IN c_group_discount
       LOOP
       UPDATE course
          SET cost = cost * .95
         WHERE course_no = r_group_discount.course_no;
         DBMS_OUTPUT.PUT_LINE
            ('A 5% discount has been given to'
            ||r_group_discount.course_no||'
           '||r_group_discount.description);
       END LOOP;
     END discount_cost;
    FUNCTION new_instructor_id
       RETURN instructor.instructor_id%TYPE
```

```
      IS
         v_new_instid instructor.instructor_id%TYPE;
      BEGIN
         SELECT INSTRUCTOR_ID_SEQ.NEXTVAL
           INTO v_new_instid
           FROM dual;
         RETURN v_new_instid;
      EXCEPTION
         WHEN OTHERS
          THEN
           DECLARE
              v_sqlerrm VARCHAR2(250) :=
                  SUBSTR(SQLERRM,1,250);
           BEGIN
             RAISE_APPLICATION_ERROR(-20003,
              'Error in    instructor_id: '||v_sqlerrm);
           END;
      END new_instructor_id;
   FUNCTION total_cost_for_student
      (i_student_id IN student.student_id%TYPE)
       RETURN course.cost%TYPE
   IS
      v_cost course.cost%TYPE;
   BEGIN
      SELECT sum(cost)
        INTO v_cost
        FROM course c, section s, enrollment e
       WHERE c.course_no = s.course_no
         AND e.section_id = s.section_id
         AND e.student_id = i_student_id;
      RETURN v_cost;
   EXCEPTION
      WHEN OTHERS THEN
         RETURN NULL;
   END total_cost_for_student;

   PROCEDURE get_student_info
     (i_student_id   IN  student.student_id%TYPE,
      o_last_name       OUT student.last_name%TYPE,
      o_first_name      OUT student.first_name%TYPE,
      o_zip             OUT student.zip%TYPE,
      o_return_code   OUT NUMBER)
   IS
   BEGIN
      SELECT last_name, first_name, zip
        INTO o_last_name, o_first_name, o_zip
        FROM student
       WHERE student.student_id = i_student_id;
      o_return_code := 0;
```

```
    EXCEPTION
      WHEN NO_DATA_FOUND
      THEN
          DBMS_OUTPUT.PUT_LINE
             ('Student ID is not valid.');
          o_return_code := -100;
          o_last_name := NULL;
          o_first_name := NULL;
          o_zip    := NULL;
    WHEN OTHERS
      THEN
          DBMS_OUTPUT.PUT_LINE
               ('Error in procedure get_student_info');
    END get_student_info;
    PROCEDURE get_student_info
      (i_last_name    IN student.last_name%TYPE,
       i_first_name   IN student.first_name%TYPE,
       o_student_id   OUT student.student_id%TYPE,
       o_zip          OUT student.zip%TYPE,
       o_return_code OUT NUMBER)
    IS
    BEGIN
      SELECT student_id, zip
        INTO o_student_id, o_zip
        FROM student
        WHERE UPPER(last_name)  = UPPER(i_last_name)
        AND UPPER(first_name) = UPPER(i_first_name);
      o_return_code := 0;
    EXCEPTION
      WHEN NO_DATA_FOUND
        THEN
          DBMS_OUTPUT.PUT_LINE
             ('Student name is not valid.');
          o_return_code := -100;
          o_student_id := NULL;
          o_zip    := NULL;
      WHEN OTHERS
        THEN
          DBMS_OUTPUT.PUT_LINE
               ('Error in procedure get_student_info');
    END get_student_info;
      BEGIN
        SELECT TRUNC(sysdate, 'DD')
          INTO v_current_date
          FROM dual;
    END school_api;
```

ANSWER: A single function name, `get_student_info`, accepts either a single IN parameter of `student_id` or two parameters consisting of a student's `last_name` and `first_name`. If a number is passed in, the procedure looks for the student's name and zip code. If it finds them, they are returned, as well as a return code of 0. If they cannot be found, null values are returned, as well as a return code of 100. If two VARCHAR2 parameters are passed in, the procedure searches for the `student_id` corresponding to the names passed in. As with the other version of this procedure, if a match is found, the procedure returns a `student_id`, the student's zip code, and a return code of 0. If a match is not found, the values returned are null and an exit code of –100.

PL/SQL uses overloading in many common functions and built-in packages. For example, TO_CHAR converts both numbers and dates to strings. Overloading makes it easy for other programmers to use your code in an API.

The main benefits of overloading are as follows:

▶ It simplifies the call interface of packages and reduces many program names to one.

▶ Modules are easier to use and therefore are more likely to be used. The software determines the context.

▶ The volume of code is reduced because the code required for different datatypes is often the same.

BY THE WAY

The rules for overloading are as follows:

▶ The compiler must be able to distinguish between the two calls at runtime. Distinguishing between the uses of the overloaded module is what is important, not solely the spec or header.

▶ The formal parameters must differ in number, order, or datatype family.

▶ You cannot overload the names of stand-alone modules.

▶ Functions differing only in RETURN datatypes cannot be overloaded.

C) Write a PL/SQL block using the overloaded function you just created.

ANSWER: A suitable bride for Frankenstein is as follows:

```
DECLARE
    v_student_ID   student.student_id%TYPE;
    v_last_name    student.last_name%TYPE;
    v_first_name   student.first_name%TYPE;
    v_zip          student.zip%TYPE;
    v_return_code NUMBER;
BEGIN
    school_api.get_student_info
        (&&p_id, v_last_name, v_first_name,
         v_zip,v_return_code);
    IF v_return_code = 0
    THEN
      DBMS_OUTPUT.PUT_LINE
         ('Student with ID '||&&p_id||' is '||v_first_name
         ||' '||v_last_name
         );
    ELSE
    DBMS_OUTPUT.PUT_LINE
       ('The ID '||&&p_id||'is not in the database'
       );
```

```
    END IF;
    school_api.get_student_info
        (&&p_last_name , &&p_first_name, v_student_id,
         v_zip , v_return_code);
    IF v_return_code = 0
    THEN
        DBMS_OUTPUT.PUT_LINE
            (&&p_first_name||' '|| &&p_last_name||
             ' has an ID of '||v_student_id
            );
    ELSE
    DBMS_OUTPUT.PUT_LINE
        (&&p_first_name||' '|| &&p_last_name||
         'is not in the database'
         );
    END IF;
END;
```

When you run this code, respond as follows:

```
Enter value for p_id: 149
Enter value for p_last_name: 'Prochaska'
Enter value for p_first_name: 'Judith'
```

It is important to realize the benefits of using a `&&` variable. The value for the variable needs to be entered only once. If you run the code a second time, you are not prompted to enter the value again, because it is now in memory.

Here are a few things to keep in mind when you overload functions or procedures. These two procedures cannot be overloaded:

```
PROCEDURE calc_total (reg_in IN CHAR);
PROCEDURE calc_total (reg_in IN VARCHAR2);
```

In these two versions of `calc_total`, the two different IN variables cannot be distinguished from each other. In the following example, an anchored type (%TYPE) is relied on to establish the datatype of the second calc's parameter:

```
    DECLARE
    PROCEDURE calc (comp_id_IN IN NUMBER)
        IS
    BEGIN ... END;
    PROCEDURE calc
    (comp_id_IN IN company.comp_id%TYPE)
        IS
    BEGIN ... END;
```

PL/SQL does not find a conflict at compile time with overloading even though `comp_id` is a numeric column. Instead, you get the following message at runtime:

```
PLS-00307: too many declarations of '<program>' match this call
```

▼ TRY IT YOURSELF

In this chapter you've learned about stored code. Here are some projects to help you test the depth of your understanding:

1) Add a function to the `school_api` package specification called `get_course_descript`. The caller takes a `course.cnumber%TYPE` parameter, and it returns a `course.description%TYPE`.

2) Create a function in the `school_api` package body called `get_course_description`. A caller passes in a course number, and it returns the course description. Instead of searching for the description itself, it makes a call to `get_course_descript_private`. It passes its course number to `get_course_descript_private`. It passes back to the caller the description it gets back from `get_course_descript_private`.

3) Add a PRAGMA RESTRICT_REFERENCES to `school_api` for `get_course_description` specifying the following: It writes no database state, it writes no package state, and it reads no package state.

The projects in this section are meant to have you use all the skills you have acquired throughout this chapter. The answers can be found in Appendix D and on this book's companion Web site. Visit the Web site periodically to share and discuss your answers.

CHAPTER 23

Object Types in Oracle

CHAPTER OBJECTIVES

In this chapter, you will learn about

▶ Object types
▶ Object type methods

In Oracle, object types are the main ingredient of object-oriented programming. They are used to model real-world tangible entities, such as a student, instructor, or bank account, as well as abstract entities, such as a zip code, geometric shape, or chemical reaction.

In this chapter you will learn how to create object types and how to nest object types within collection types. In addition, you will learn about different kinds of object type methods and their usage.

This chapter is introductory and does not cover more advanced topics such as object type inheritance and evolution, REF modifiers, and object type tables (not to be confused with collections). These topics, along with many others, are covered in the Oracle documentation—specifically, the Database Application Developer's Guide, Object-Relational Features.

LAB 23.1
Object Types

LAB OBJECTIVES

After completing this lab, you will be able to

▶ Use object types
▶ Use object types with collections

Object types generally consist of two parts—attributes (data) and methods (functions and procedures). Attributes are essential characteristics that describe object types. For example, some attributes of the student object type may include first and last names, contact information, and enrollment information. Methods are functions and procedures defined in an object type and are optional. They represent actions that are likely to be performed on the object attributes. For example, some methods of the student object type may include updating student contact information, getting a student name, and displaying student information.

By combining attributes and methods, object types facilitate encapsulation of data with the operations that may be performed on that data, as illustrated in Figure 23.1.

Figure 23.1 shows object type Student. Some of the attributes of the Student object type are Student ID, First Name, Zip, and Enrollment. Some of the methods are Update Contact Info, Get Student ID, and Get Student Name. Figure 23.1 also shows two instances of object types Student 1 and Student 2. The object instance is a value of an object type. In other words, the instances Student 1 and Student 2 of the Student object type contain actual student data so that the Get Student ID method returns student ID 102 for instance Student 1 and 103 for instance Student 2.

BY THE WAY

An object instance is often called an object.

In Oracle, an object type is created with the CREATE OR REPLACE TYPE clause and is stored in the database schema. This means that object types cannot be created within a PL/SQL block or stored subprogram. After an object type has been created and stored in the database schema, a PL/SQL block or subprogram may reference that object type.

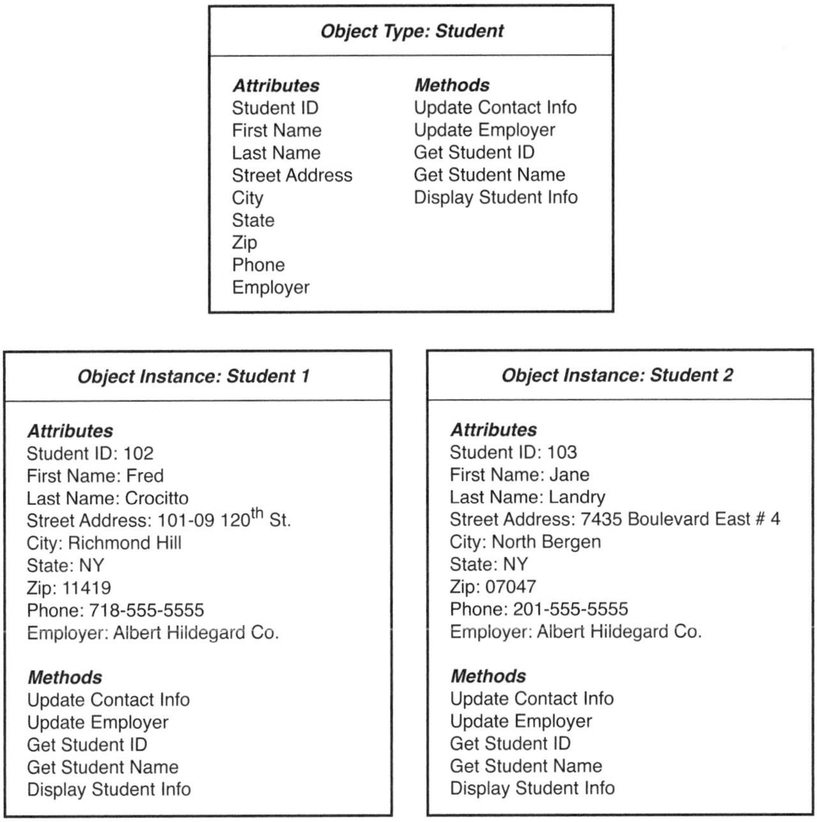

FIGURE 23.1
Object type Student

The general syntax for creating an object type is as follows (the reserved words and phrases in brackets are optional):

```
CREATE [OR REPLACE] TYPE type_name AS OBJECT
   (attribute_name1 attribute_type,
    attribute_name2 attribute_type,
    ...
    attribute_nameN attribute_type,
    [method1 specification],
    [method2 specification],
    ...
    [methodN specification]);
```

```
[CREATE [OR REPLACE] TYPE BODY type_name AS
   method1 body;
   method2 body;
   ...
   methodN body;]
END;
```

Notice that the creation of an object type has two parts: object type specification and object type body. Object type specification contains declarations of attributes and any methods that may be used with that object. ATTRIBUTE_TYPE may be an element PL/SQL type such as NUMBER or VARCHAR2, or a complex user-defined type such as a collection, record, or another object type. The method specification consists of the method type, its name, and any input and output parameters it needs.

Object specification is a required part when creating an object type. Any attributes and methods defined in the object type specification are visible to the outside world (a PL/SQL block, subprogram, or Java application). Object type specification is also called the public interface, and the methods defined in it are called public methods. As mentioned earlier, methods are optional when creating object types. However, if an object type has method specification, it requires an object type body.

The object type body is optional when creating an object type. It contains bodies (executable statements) of the methods defined in the object type specification. In addition, the object type body may contain methods that have not been defined in the object type specification. These methods are private because they are not visible to the outside world. Some types of methods include a constructor, member, and static. Different method types, their usage, and restrictions are discussed in detail in Lab 23.2.

Note that the concepts just explained are very similar to those you learned about in Chapter 21, "Packages." Thus, the rules that apply to the package specification and body mostly apply to the object type specification and body as well. For example, the header of the method defined in the object type specification must match the method header in the object type body.

Consider the following example of the `zipcode_obj_type` object type specification:

FOR EXAMPLE

```
CREATE OR REPLACE TYPE zipcode_obj_type AS OBJECT
   (zip           VARCHAR2(5),
    city          VARCHAR2(25),
    state         VARCHAR2(2),
    created_by    VARCHAR2(30),
    created_date  DATE,
    modified_by   VARCHAR2(30),
    modified_date DATE);
```

Note that this object type does not have any methods associated with it, and its syntax is somewhat similar to the CREATE TABLE syntax.

After this object type has been created, it can be used as shown here:

FOR EXAMPLE

```
DECLARE
   v_zip_obj zipcode_obj_type;
BEGIN
   SELECT zipcode_obj_type(zip, city, state, null, null, null, null)
     INTO v_zip_obj
     FROM zipcode
    WHERE zip = '06883';

   DBMS_OUTPUT.PUT_LINE ('Zip:   '||v_zip_obj.zip);
   DBMS_OUTPUT.PUT_LINE ('City:  '||v_zip_obj.city);
   DBMS_OUTPUT.PUT_LINE ('State: '||v_zip_obj.state);
END;
```

This script defines instance v_zip_obj of the object type zipcode_obj_type. Then it initializes some of the object attributes and displays those values on the screen.

The object attributes are initialized using the SELECT INTO statement. Note how the SELECT clause uses an object type constructor. Recall that you learned about constructors for nested table types in Chapter 15, "Collections." Default constructors for object types are similar in that they are system-defined functions that have the same name as their corresponding object type. In Lab 23.2 you will learn how to define your own constructor functions.

When run, the script produces the following output:

```
   Zip:   06883
   City:  Weston
   State: CT

   PL/SQL procedure successfully completed.
```

UNINITIALIZED OBJECTS

When an object instance is defined, its value is null. This means that not only are its individual attributes null, but the object itself is null as well. The object remains null until its constructor method is called, as shown in the following example:

FOR EXAMPLE

```
DECLARE
   v_zip_obj zipcode_obj_type;
BEGIN
   DBMS_OUTPUT.PUT_LINE ('Object instance has not been initialized');

   IF v_zip_obj IS NULL
   THEN
      DBMS_OUTPUT.PUT_LINE ('v_zip_obj instance is null');
```

FOR EXAMPLE (continued)

```
   ELSE
      DBMS_OUTPUT.PUT_LINE ('v_zip_obj instance is not null');
   END IF;

   IF v_zip_obj.zip IS NULL
   THEN
      DBMS_OUTPUT.PUT_LINE ('v_zip_obj.zip is null');
   END IF;

   -- Initialize v_zip_obj_instance
   v_zip_obj := zipcode_obj_type(null, null, null, null, null, null,
                                 null);
   DBMS_OUTPUT.PUT_LINE ('Object instance has been initialized');

   IF v_zip_obj IS NULL
   THEN
      DBMS_OUTPUT.PUT_LINE ('v_zip_obj instance is null');
   ELSE
      DBMS_OUTPUT.PUT_LINE ('v_zip_obj instance is not null');
   END IF;

   IF v_zip_obj.zip IS NULL
   THEN
      DBMS_OUTPUT.PUT_LINE ('v_zip_obj.zip is null');
   END IF;
END;
```

When run, this script produces the following output:

```
   Object instance has not been initialized
   v_zip_obj instance is null
   v_zip_obj.zip is null
   Object instance has been initialized
   v_zip_obj instance is not null
   v_zip_obj.zip is null

   PL/SQL procedure successfully completed.
```

Note that both the object instance and its attributes are null before the initialization. After the object instance has been initialized with the help of its default constructor, it is not null anymore, even though its individual attributes remain null.

WATCH OUT!

Referencing individual attributes of an uninitialized object instance causes an ORA-06530: Reference to uninitialized composite error:

```
   DECLARE
      v_zip_obj zipcode_obj_type;
```

```
BEGIN
   v_zip_obj.zip := '12345';
END;

DECLARE
*
ERROR at line 1:
ORA-06530: Reference to uninitialized composite
ORA-06512: at line 4
```

Note that this error occurs only when the object type attribute being referenced is a nonnumeric datatype or a numeric datatype that does not have specified precision. This behavior is as follows:

```
CREATE OR REPLACE TYPE obj_type AS OBJECT
   (attribute1 NUMBER(3)
   ,attribute2 VARCHAR2(3));
/
```
Type created.

```
DECLARE
   v_obj obj_type;
BEGIN
   v_obj.attribute1 := 123;

   DBMS_OUTPUT.PUT_LINE ('v_obj.attribute1: '||
      v_obj.attribute1);
END;
/
```
v_obj.attribute1: 123

PL/SQL procedure successfully completed.

```
DECLARE
   v_obj obj_type;
BEGIN
   v_obj.attribute1 := 123;
```
   v_obj.attribute2 := 'ABC';

```
   DBMS_OUTPUT.PUT_LINE ('v_obj.attribute1: '||
      v_obj.attribute1);
```
   DBMS_OUTPUT.PUT_LINE ('v_obj.attribute2: '||
      v_obj.attribute2);

```
END;
/
DECLARE
*
ERROR at line 1:
ORA-06530: Reference to uninitialized composite
ORA-06512: at line 5
```

Note that the first PL/SQL script executes successfully because it does not reference `attribute2`, which is defined as VARCHAR2(3). The second PL/SQL script causes an ORA-06530 error because it references `attribute2`.

As a result, *it is a good practice to always initialize a newly created object type instance.*

COLLECTIONS OF OBJECT TYPES

As mentioned previously, object types and collection types may be nested inside each other. Consider the following collection of zip code objects:

FOR EXAMPLE

```
DECLARE
   TYPE v_zip_type IS TABLE OF zipcode_obj_type
      INDEX BY BINARY_INTEGER;
   v_zip_tab v_zip_type;
BEGIN
   SELECT zipcode_obj_type(zip, city, state, null, null, null, null)
     BULK COLLECT INTO v_zip_tab
     FROM zipcode
    WHERE rownum <= 5;

   FOR i in 1..v_zip_tab.count
   LOOP
      DBMS_OUTPUT.PUT_LINE ('Zip:   '||v_zip_tab(i).zip);
      DBMS_OUTPUT.PUT_LINE ('City:  '||v_zip_tab(i).city);
      DBMS_OUTPUT.PUT_LINE ('State: '||v_zip_tab(i).state);
      DBMS_OUTPUT.PUT_LINE ('----------------------');
   END LOOP;
END;
```

This script declares an associative array of objects. Next, it populates this table of objects using the BULK SELECT statement. Finally, it displays data from the associative array on the screen.

Note how individual object type attributes are referenced by the DBMS_OUTPUT.PUT_LINE statement. Each attribute is prefixed by the table name and row subscript, without any reference to the object type itself.

When run, this example produces the following output:

```
Zip:   00914
City:  Santurce
State: PR
----------------------
Zip:   01247
City:  North Adams
State: MA
----------------------
```

```
Zip:    02124
City:   Dorchester
State: MA
----------------------
Zip:    02155
City:   Tufts Univ. Bedford
State: MA
----------------------
Zip:    02189
City:   Weymouth
State: MA
----------------------

PL/SQL procedure successfully completed.
```

In this example you can see how to populate an associative array of objects with data. PL/SQL also supports selecting the data from a collection of objects. Note that in this case *the collection type should be a nested table or varray type that is created and stored in the database schema* just as its corresponding object type. This is illustrated in the following example:

FOR EXAMPLE

```
CREATE OR REPLACE TYPE v_zip_tab_type IS TABLE OF zipcode_obj_type;
/
DECLARE
   v_zip_tab v_zip_tab_type := v_zip_tab_type();
   v_zip      VARCHAR2(5);
   v_city     VARCHAR2(20);
   v_state    VARCHAR2(2);
BEGIN
   SELECT zipcode_obj_type(zip, city, state, null, null, null, null)
     BULK COLLECT INTO v_zip_tab
     FROM zipcode
    WHERE rownum <= 5;

   SELECT zip, city, state
     INTO v_zip, v_city, v_state
     FROM table(cast(v_zip_tab as v_zip_tab_type))
    where rownum < 2;

   DBMS_OUTPUT.PUT_LINE ('Zip:   '||v_zip);
   DBMS_OUTPUT.PUT_LINE ('City:  '||v_city);
   DBMS_OUTPUT.PUT_LINE ('State: '||v_state);
END;
```

First, this script creates a nested table type, `v_zip_tab_type`, in the student schema. This table type is then used by the preceding PL/SQL block. Creating and storing a nested table type in the STUDENT schema enables you to use TABLE and CAST functions later in the script.

Next, take a closer look at the second SELECT INTO statement. This statement uses CAST and TABLE functions, which essentially enable you to query a nested table of objects as if it were a regular table.

When run, this example produces the following output:

```
Zip:   00914
City:  Santurce
State: PR

PL/SQL procedure successfully completed.
```

▼ LAB 23.1 EXERCISES

This section provides exercises and suggested answers, with discussion related to how those answers resulted. The most important thing to realize is whether your answer works. You should figure out the implications of the answers and what the effects are of any different answers you may come up with.

23.1.1 Use Object Types

In this exercise, you continue exploring object types.

Complete the following tasks:

A) Create object type ENROLLMENT_OBJ_TYPE, which has the following attributes:

```
ATTRIBUTE NAME    DATA TYPE    PRECISION
--------------    ---------    ---------
student_id        NUMBER       8
first_name        VARCHAR2     25
last_name         VARCHAR2     25
course_no         NUMBER       8
section_no        NUMBER       3
enroll_date       DATE
final_grade       NUMBER       3
```

ANSWER: The creation script should look similar to the following:

```
-- ch23_1a.sql, version 1.0
CREATE OR REPLACE TYPE ENROLLMENT_OBJ_TYPE AS OBJECT
   (student_id  NUMBER(8),
    first_name  VARCHAR2(25),
    last_name   VARCHAR2(25),
    course_no   NUMBER(8),
    section_no  NUMBER(3),
    enroll_date DATE,
    final_grade NUMBER(3));
```

B) The following script uses the newly created object type. Execute it and explain the output produced.

```
-- ch23_2a.sql, version 1.0
SET SERVEROUTPUT ON
DECLARE
   v_enrollment_obj enrollment_obj_type;
```

```
BEGIN
    v_enrollment_obj.student_id := 102;
    v_enrollment_obj.first_name := 'Fred';
    v_enrollment_obj.last_name  := 'Crocitto';
    v_enrollment_obj.course_no  := 25;
END;
```

ANSWER: The output of the script should look similar to the following:

```
DECLARE
*
ERROR at line 1:
ORA-06530: Reference to uninitialized composite
ORA-06512: at line 6
```

This version of the script causes an ORA-06530 error because it references individual attributes of the uninitialized object type instance. Before the object attribute can be referenced, the object must be initialized with the help of the constructor method.

C) Modify the script created in the preceding exercise (ch23_2a.sql) so that it does not produce an ORA-06530 error.

ANSWER: The script should look similar to the following. Changes are shown in bold.

```
-- ch23_2b.sql, version 2.0
SET SERVEROUTPUT ON
DECLARE
    v_enrollment_obj enrollment_obj_type;

BEGIN
    v_enrollment_obj :=
        enrollment_obj_type(102, 'Fred', 'Crocitto', 25, null, null,
        null);
END;
```

D) Modify this script (ch23_2b.sql) so that all object attributes are populated with corresponding values selected from the appropriate tables.

ANSWER: The script should look similar to one of the following scripts. Changes are shown in bold.

The first version of the script employs the SELECT INTO statement along with the constructor to initialize other attributes as well. Note that the SELECT INTO statement specifies WHERE criteria for the SECTION_NO in addition to the criteria for the STUDENT_ID and COURSE_NO. This ensures that the SELECT INTO statement does not cause an ORA-01422: exact fetch returns more than requested number of rows error.

```
-- ch23_2c.sql, version 3.0
SET SERVEROUTPUT ON
DECLARE
    v_enrollment_obj enrollment_obj_type;

BEGIN
    SELECT
        enrollment_obj_type(st.student_id, st.first_name, st.last_name,
                            c.course_no, se.section_no, e.enroll_date,
                            e.final_grade)
        INTO v_enrollment_obj
```

```
        FROM student st, course c, section se, enrollment e
       WHERE st.student_id = e.student_id
         AND c.course_no    = se.course_no
         AND se.section_id = e.section_id
         AND st.student_id = 102
         AND c.course_no    = 25
         AND se.section_no = 2;
END;
```

The SELECT statement in the preceding script can be modified according to the ANSI 1999 SQL standard:

```
SELECT enrollment_obj_type(st.student_id, st.first_name,
                           st.last_name, c.course_no, se.section_no,
                           e.enroll_date, e.final_grade)
  INTO v_enrollment_obj
  FROM enrollment e
  JOIN student st
    ON e.student_id = st.student_id
  JOIN section se
    ON e.section_id = se.section_id
  JOIN course c
    ON se.course_no = c.course_no
 WHERE st.student_id = 102
   AND c.course_no    = 25
   AND se.section_no = 2;
```

The preceding SELECT statement uses the ON syntax to specify the join condition between four tables. This type of join becomes especially useful when the columns participating in the join do not have the same name.

BY THE WAY

You will find detailed explanations and examples of the statements using the new ANSI 1999 SQL standard in Appendix C and in the Oracle help. Throughout this book we have tried to provide you with examples illustrating both standards; however, our main focus has remained on PL/SQL features rather than SQL.

The second version of the script uses a cursor FOR loop. This approach eliminates the need for additional criteria against the SECTION_NO.

```
-- ch23_2d.sql, version 4.0
SET SERVEROUTPUT ON
DECLARE
    v_enrollment_obj enrollment_obj_type;

BEGIN
    FOR REC IN (SELECT st.student_id, st.first_name, st.last_name,
                       c.course_no, se.section_no, e.enroll_date,
                       e.final_grade
                  FROM student st, course c, section se, enrollment e
                 WHERE st.student_id = e.student_id
                   AND c.course_no    = se.course_no
```

```
                     AND se.section_id = e.section_id
                     AND st.student_id = 102
                     AND c.course_no   = 25)
     LOOP
        v_enrollment_obj :=
           enrollment_obj_type(rec.student_id, rec.first_name,
                               rec.last_name, rec.course_no,
                               rec.section_no, rec.enroll_date,
                               rec.final_grade);
     END LOOP;
  END;
```

E) Modify one of the scripts created in the previous exercises (use either ch23_2c.sql or ch23_2d.sql) so that attribute values are displayed on the screen.

ANSWER: The script should look similar to the following. All changes are shown in bold.

```
-- ch23_2e.sql, version 5.0
SET SERVEROUTPUT ON
DECLARE
   v_enrollment_obj enrollment_obj_type;

BEGIN
   FOR REC IN (SELECT st.student_id, st.first_name, st.last_name,
                      c.course_no, se.section_no, e.enroll_date,
                      e.final_grade
                 FROM student st, course c, section se, enrollment e
                WHERE st.student_id = e.student_id
                  AND c.course_no   = se.course_no
                  AND se.section_id = e.section_id
                  AND st.student_id = 102
                  AND c.course_no   = 25)
   LOOP
      v_enrollment_obj :=
         enrollment_obj_type(rec.student_id, rec.first_name,
                             rec.last_name, rec.course_no,
                             rec.section_no, rec.enroll_date,
                             rec.final_grade);

      DBMS_OUTPUT.PUT_LINE ('student_id:  '||
         v_enrollment_obj.student_id);
      DBMS_OUTPUT.PUT_LINE ('first_name:  '||
         v_enrollment_obj.first_name);
      DBMS_OUTPUT.PUT_LINE ('last_name:   '||
         v_enrollment_obj.last_name);
      DBMS_OUTPUT.PUT_LINE ('course_no:   '||
         v_enrollment_obj.course_no);
      DBMS_OUTPUT.PUT_LINE ('section_no:  '||
         v_enrollment_obj.section_no);
      DBMS_OUTPUT.PUT_LINE ('enroll_date: '||
         v_enrollment_obj.enroll_date);
```

```
    DBMS_OUTPUT.PUT_LINE ('final_grade: '||
        v_enrollment_obj.final_grade);
  END LOOP;
END;
```

This version of the script produces the following output:

```
student_id:  102
first_name:  Fred
last_name:   Crocitto
course_no:   25
section_no:  2
enroll_date: 30-JAN-07
final_grade:
student_id:  102
first_name:  Fred
last_name:   Crocitto
course_no:   25
section_no:  5
enroll_date: 30-JAN-07
final_grade: 92

PL/SQL procedure successfully completed.
```

23.1.2 Use Object Types with Collections

In this exercise, you continue exploring how object types may be used with collections.

Complete the following tasks:

A) Modify script ch23_2e.sql, created in the preceding exercise. In the new version of the script, populate an associative array of objects. Use multiple student IDs for this exercise—102, 103, and 104.

ANSWER: The script should look similar to the following:

```
-- ch23_3a.sql, version 1.0
SET SERVEROUTPUT ON
DECLARE
   TYPE enroll_tab_type IS TABLE OF enrollment_obj_type
      INDEX BY BINARY_INTEGER;

   v_enrollment_tab enroll_tab_type;

   v_counter integer := 0;

BEGIN
   FOR REC IN (SELECT st.student_id, st.first_name, st.last_name,
                      c.course_no, se.section_no, e.enroll_date,
                      e.final_grade
                 FROM student st, course c, section se, enrollment e
                WHERE st.student_id = e.student_id
                  AND c.course_no   = se.course_no
                  AND se.section_id = e.section_id
                  AND st.student_id in (102, 103, 104))
```

```
LOOP
   v_counter := v_counter + 1;
   v_enrollment_tab(v_counter) :=
      enrollment_obj_type(rec.student_id, rec.first_name,
                          rec.last_name, rec.course_no,
                          rec.section_no, rec.enroll_date,
                          rec.final_grade);

   DBMS_OUTPUT.PUT_LINE ('student_id:  '||
      v_enrollment_tab(v_counter).student_id);
   DBMS_OUTPUT.PUT_LINE ('first_name:  '||
      v_enrollment_tab(v_counter).first_name);
   DBMS_OUTPUT.PUT_LINE ('last_name:   '||
      v_enrollment_tab(v_counter).last_name);
   DBMS_OUTPUT.PUT_LINE ('course_no:   '||
      v_enrollment_tab(v_counter).course_no);
   DBMS_OUTPUT.PUT_LINE ('section_no:  '||
      v_enrollment_tab(v_counter).section_no);
   DBMS_OUTPUT.PUT_LINE ('enroll_date: '||
      v_enrollment_tab(v_counter).enroll_date);
   DBMS_OUTPUT.PUT_LINE ('final_grade: '||
      v_enrollment_tab(v_counter).final_grade);
   DBMS_OUTPUT.PUT_LINE ('------------------');
END LOOP;
END;
```

The preceding script defines an associative array of objects that is populated with the help of the cursor FOR loop. After a single row of the associative array has been initialized, it is displayed on the screen.

Take a closer look at how each row of the associative array is initialized:

```
v_enrollment_tab(v_counter) :=
         enrollment_obj_type(rec.student_id, rec.first_name,
                            rec.last_name, rec.course_no,
                            rec.section_no, rec.enroll_date,
                            rec.final_grade);
```

A row is referenced by a subscript. In this case it is a variable, v_counter. Because each row represents an object instance, it is initialized by referencing the default constructor method associated with the corresponding object type.

When run, the script produces the following output:

```
student_id:  102
first_name:  Fred
last_name:   Crocitto
course_no:   25
section_no:  2
enroll_date: 30-JAN-07
final_grade:
------------------
```

```
student_id:  102
first_name:  Fred
last_name:   Crocitto
course_no:   25
section_no:  5
enroll_date: 30-JAN-07
final_grade: 92
------------------
student_id:  103
first_name:  J.
last_name:   Landry
course_no:   20
section_no:  2
enroll_date: 30-JAN-07
final_grade:
------------------
student_id:  104
first_name:  Laetia
last_name:   Enison
course_no:   20
section_no:  2
enroll_date: 30-JAN-07
final_grade:
------------------
PL/SQL procedure successfully completed.
```

B) Modify the script so that the table of objects is populated using the BULK SELECT INTO statement.

ANSWER: The script should look similar to the following. Changes are shown in bold.

```
-- ch23_3b.sql, version 2.0
SET SERVEROUTPUT ON
DECLARE
   TYPE enroll_tab_type IS TABLE OF enrollment_obj_type
      INDEX BY BINARY_INTEGER;

   v_enrollment_tab enroll_tab_type;

BEGIN
   SELECT
      enrollment_obj_type(st.student_id, st.first_name, st.last_name,
                     c.course_no, se.section_no, e.enroll_date,
                     e.final_grade)
    BULK COLLECT INTO v_enrollment_tab
    FROM student st, course c, section se, enrollment e
   WHERE st.student_id = e.student_id
     AND c.course_no   = se.course_no
     AND se.section_id = e.section_id
     AND st.student_id in (102, 103, 104);

   FOR i IN 1..v_enrollment_tab.COUNT
   LOOP
```

```
        DBMS_OUTPUT.PUT_LINE ('student_id:  '||
            v_enrollment_tab(i).student_id);
        DBMS_OUTPUT.PUT_LINE ('first_name:  '||
            v_enrollment_tab(i).first_name);
        DBMS_OUTPUT.PUT_LINE ('last_name:   '||
            v_enrollment_tab(i).last_name);
        DBMS_OUTPUT.PUT_LINE ('course_no:   '||
            v_enrollment_tab(i).course_no);
        DBMS_OUTPUT.PUT_LINE ('section_no:  '||
            v_enrollment_tab(i).section_no);
        DBMS_OUTPUT.PUT_LINE ('enroll_date: '||
            v_enrollment_tab(i).enroll_date);
        DBMS_OUTPUT.PUT_LINE ('final_grade: '||
            v_enrollment_tab(i).final_grade);
        DBMS_OUTPUT.PUT_LINE ('------------------');
    END LOOP;
END;
```

In this version of the script, the cursor FOR loop has been replaced by the BULK SELECT INTO statement. As a result, the cursor FOR loop is replaced by the numeric FOR loop to display data on the screen. These changes eliminate the need for the variable $v\_counter$, which was used to reference individual rows of the associative array.

When run, this version of the script produces output that is identical to the previous version.

C) Modify the script so that data stored in the table of objects can be retrieved using the SELECT INTO statement as well.

ANSWER: As mentioned previously, for you to select data from a table of objects, the underlying table type must be either a nested table or a varray that is created and stored in the database schema. This is accomplished by the following statement:

```
CREATE OR REPLACE TYPE enroll_tab_type AS TABLE OF
    enrollment_obj_type;
/
```

After the nested table type is created, the script is modified as follows. Changes are shown in bold.

```
-- ch23_3c.sql, version 3.0
SET SERVEROUTPUT ON
DECLARE
    v_enrollment_tab enroll_tab_type;

BEGIN
    SELECT
        enrollment_obj_type(st.student_id, st.first_name, st.last_name,
                            c.course_no, se.section_no, e.enroll_date,
                            e.final_grade)
     BULK COLLECT INTO v_enrollment_tab
     FROM student st, course c, section se, enrollment e
    WHERE st.student_id = e.student_id
      AND c.course_no   = se.course_no
      AND se.section_id = e.section_id
      AND st.student_id in (102, 103, 104);
```

```
FOR rec IN (SELECT *
                FROM TABLE(CAST(v_enrollment_tab AS
                    enroll_tab_type)))
LOOP
    DBMS_OUTPUT.PUT_LINE ('student_id:  '||rec.student_id);
    DBMS_OUTPUT.PUT_LINE ('first_name:  '||rec.first_name);
    DBMS_OUTPUT.PUT_LINE ('last_name:   '||rec.last_name);
    DBMS_OUTPUT.PUT_LINE ('course_no:   '||rec.course_no);
    DBMS_OUTPUT.PUT_LINE ('section_no:  '||rec.section_no);
    DBMS_OUTPUT.PUT_LINE ('enroll_date: '||rec.enroll_date);
    DBMS_OUTPUT.PUT_LINE ('final_grade: '||rec.final_grade);
    DBMS_OUTPUT.PUT_LINE ('------------------');
END LOOP;
END;
```

Note that in this version of the script, the numeric FOR loop is replaced by the cursor FOR loop against the nested table of objects. Note that the DBMS_OUTPUT.PUT_LINE statements are also changed so that they reference records returned by the cursor.

LAB 23.2
Object Type Methods

LAB OBJECTIVE

After completing this lab, you will be able to

▶ Use object type methods

In Lab 23.1 you learned that object type methods are functions and procedures that specify actions that may be performed on the object type attributes and that they are defined in the object type specification. You also have seen how to use default system-defined constructor methods. The constructor is only one of the method types that PL/SQL supports. Some other method types are member, static, map, and order. The method type typically is determined by the actions that a particular method performs. For example, constructor methods are used to initialize object instances, and map and order methods are used to compare and sort object instances.

Often object type methods use a built-in parameter called SELF. This parameter represents a particular instance of the object type. As such, it is available to the methods that are invoked on that object type instance. You will see various examples of the SELF parameter in the following discussions.

CONSTRUCTOR METHODS

As discussed previously, a constructor method is a default method that is implicitly created by the system whenever a new object type is created. It is a function that has the same name as its object type. Its input parameters have the same names and datatypes as the object type attributes and are listed in the same order as the object type attributes. The constructor method returns a new instance of the object type. In other words, it initializes a new object instance and assigns values to the object attributes. Consider the following code fragments, which illustrate calls to the default constructor method for the `zipcode_obj_type` created earlier:

FOR EXAMPLE

```
zip_obj1 := ZIPCODE_OBJ_TYPE('00914', 'Santurce', 'PR', USER, SYSDATE,
                             USER, SYSDATE);

or

zip_obj2 := ZIPCODE_OBJ_TYPE(NULL, NULL, NULL, NULL, NULL,
                             NULL NULL);
```

The first call to the constructor method returns a new instance, `zip_obj1`, of `zipcode_obj_type` with attributes initialized to non-null values. The second call creates a new instance, `zip_obj2`, with NULL attribute values.

Note that both calls produce non-null instances of the `zipcode_obj_type`. *The difference is in the values assigned to the individual attributes.*

In the preceding examples, calls to the default constructor method use positional notation. Recall that positional notation associates values with corresponding parameters by their position in the header of the function, procedure, or, in this case, constructor. Next, consider the call to the default constructor method that uses named notation. Note that in this case, the order of parameters does not correspond to the order of the attributes in `zipcode_obj_type`. Instead, they are referenced by their names:

FOR EXAMPLE

```
zip_obj3 := ZIPCODE_OBJ_TYPE(created_by    => USER,
                             created_date  => SYSDATE,
                             modified_by   => USER,
                             modified_date => SYSDATE,
                             zip           =>'00914',
                             city          => 'Santurce',
                             state         => 'PR');
```

PL/SQL lets you create your own (user-defined) constructors. User-defined constructors offer flexibility that default constructors lack. For example, you may want to define a constructor on the `zipcode_obj_type` that initializes only some of the attributes of the newly created object instance. In this case, the system initializes to NULL any attributes for which you do not specify values. In addition, you can control the number and types of parameters that your constructor may require.

Consider the following example of the user-defined constructors for the `zipcode_obj_type`.

FOR EXAMPLE

Note that before recreating `zipcode_obj_type` you must drop the nested table type `v_zip_tab_type`, created in Lab 23.1, to prevent the following error message:

```
CREATE OR REPLACE TYPE zipcode_obj_type AS OBJECT
*
ERROR at line 1:
ORA-02303: cannot drop or replace a type with type or table
           dependents
```

The nested table type can be dropped as follows:

```
DROP TYPE v_zip_tab_type;
```

The object type can be recreated as shown here:

```
CREATE OR REPLACE TYPE zipcode_obj_type AS OBJECT
   (zip            VARCHAR2(5),
```

```
   city           VARCHAR2(25),
   state          VARCHAR2(2),
   created_by     VARCHAR2(30),
   created_date   DATE,
   modified_by    VARCHAR2(30),
   modified_date  DATE,

   CONSTRUCTOR FUNCTION zipcode_obj_type
      (SELF IN OUT NOCOPY ZIPCODE_OBJ_TYPE, zip VARCHAR2)
   RETURN SELF AS RESULT,

   CONSTRUCTOR FUNCTION zipcode_obj_type
      (SELF IN OUT NOCOPY ZIPCODE_OBJ_TYPE, zip VARCHAR2,
       city VARCHAR2, state VARCHAR2)
   RETURN SELF AS RESULT);
/

CREATE OR REPLACE TYPE BODY zipcode_obj_type AS

CONSTRUCTOR FUNCTION zipcode_obj_type
   (SELF IN OUT NOCOPY zipcode_obj_type, zip VARCHAR2)
RETURN SELF AS RESULT
IS
BEGIN
   SELF.zip := zip;

   SELECT city, state
     INTO SELF.city, SELF.state
     FROM zipcode
    WHERE zip = SELF.zip;

   RETURN;
EXCEPTION
   WHEN NO_DATA_FOUND THEN
      RETURN;
END;

CONSTRUCTOR FUNCTION zipcode_obj_type
   (SELF IN OUT NOCOPY ZIPCODE_OBJ_TYPE, zip VARCHAR2, city VARCHAR2,
    state VARCHAR2)
RETURN SELF AS RESULT
IS
BEGIN
   SELF.zip   := zip;
   SELF.city  := city;
   SELF.state := state;

   RETURN;
END;

END;
/
```

This script overloads two constructor methods for `zip_code_obj_type`. Overloading allows two methods or subprograms to use the same name as long as their parameters differ in either datatypes or their number. In the preceding example, the first constructor method expects two parameters, and the second constructor method expects four parameters.

Both constructors use the default parameter SELF as an IN OUT parameter and as a return datatype in the RETURN clause. As stated previously, SELF references a particular object type instance. Note the use of the NOCOPY compiler hint. This hint typically is used with OUT and IN OUT parameters. By default, OUT and IN OUT parameters are passed by value. This means that the values of the parameters are copied before the subprogram or method is executed. Then, during execution, temporary variables are used to hold values of the OUT parameters. For the parameters that represent complex datatypes such as collections, records, and object type instances, the copying step can add significant processing overhead. By adding a NOCOPY hint, you instruct the PL/SQL compiler to pass OUT and IN OUT parameters by reference and eliminate the copying step.

Next, both constructor methods populate the city, state, and zip attributes. Note how these attributes are referenced using the SELF parameter.

MEMBER METHODS

Member methods provide access to the object instance data. As such, a member method should be defined for each action that object type must perform. For example, you may need to return city, state, and zip code values associated with an object instance to the calling application, as shown in the following example:

FOR EXAMPLE

```
CREATE OR REPLACE TYPE zipcode_obj_type AS OBJECT
   (zip            VARCHAR2(5),
    city           VARCHAR2(25),
    state          VARCHAR2(2),
    created_by     VARCHAR2(30),
    created_date   DATE,
    modified_by    VARCHAR2(30),
    modified_date  DATE,

    CONSTRUCTOR FUNCTION zipcode_obj_type
       (SELF IN OUT NOCOPY ZIPCODE_OBJ_TYPE, zip VARCHAR2)
    RETURN SELF AS RESULT,

    CONSTRUCTOR FUNCTION zipcode_obj_type
       (SELF IN OUT NOCOPY ZIPCODE_OBJ_TYPE, zip VARCHAR2,
        city VARCHAR2, state VARCHAR2)
    RETURN SELF AS RESULT,

    MEMBER PROCEDURE get_zipcode_info
       (out_zip OUT VARCHAR2, out_city OUT VARCHAR2,
        out_state OUT VARCHAR2)
```

```
);
/

CREATE OR REPLACE TYPE BODY zipcode_obj_type AS

CONSTRUCTOR FUNCTION zipcode_obj_type
   (SELF IN OUT NOCOPY zipcode_obj_type, zip VARCHAR2)
RETURN SELF AS RESULT
IS
BEGIN
   SELF.zip := zip;

   SELECT city, state
     INTO SELF.city, SELF.state
     FROM zipcode
    WHERE zip = SELF.zip;

   RETURN;
EXCEPTION
   WHEN NO_DATA_FOUND THEN
      RETURN;
END;

CONSTRUCTOR FUNCTION zipcode_obj_type
   (SELF IN OUT NOCOPY ZIPCODE_OBJ_TYPE, zip VARCHAR2, city VARCHAR2,
    state VARCHAR2)
RETURN SELF AS RESULT
IS
BEGIN
   SELF.zip   := zip;
   SELF.city  := city;
   SELF.state := state;

   RETURN;
END;

MEMBER PROCEDURE get_zipcode_info
   (out_zip OUT VARCHAR2, out_city OUT VARCHAR2, out_state OUT
      VARCHAR2)
IS
BEGIN
   out_zip   := SELF.zip;
   out_city  := SELF.city;
   out_state := SELF.state;
END;

END;
/
```

In this version of the script, you add a member procedure that returns values of zip code, city, and state associated with a particular instance of the `zip_code_obj_type` object type. Note that the reference to the SELF parameter in this procedure is optional, and that the preceding assignment statements can be modified as follows:

```
out_zip   := zip;
out_city  := city;
out_state := state;
```

These statements initialize OUT parameters associated with individual attributes of a particular object instance, just like the statements that include the reference to the SELF parameter.

STATIC METHODS

Static methods are created for actions that do not need to access data associated with a particular object instance. As such, these methods are created for the object type itself and describe actions that are global to that object type. Because static methods do not have access to the data associated with a particular object type instance, they may not reference the default parameter SELF. Consider the following example of the static method that displays zip code information:

FOR EXAMPLE

```
CREATE OR REPLACE TYPE zipcode_obj_type AS OBJECT
    (zip           VARCHAR2(5),
     city          VARCHAR2(25),
     state         VARCHAR2(2),
     created_by    VARCHAR2(30),
     created_date  DATE,
     modified_by   VARCHAR2(30),
     modified_date DATE,

     CONSTRUCTOR FUNCTION zipcode_obj_type
        (SELF IN OUT NOCOPY ZIPCODE_OBJ_TYPE, zip VARCHAR2)
     RETURN SELF AS RESULT,

     CONSTRUCTOR FUNCTION zipcode_obj_type
        (SELF IN OUT NOCOPY ZIPCODE_OBJ_TYPE, zip VARCHAR2,
         city VARCHAR2, state VARCHAR2)
     RETURN SELF AS RESULT,

     MEMBER PROCEDURE get_zipcode_info
        (out_zip OUT VARCHAR2, out_city OUT VARCHAR2,
         out_state OUT VARCHAR2),

     STATIC PROCEDURE display_zipcode_info
        (in_zip_obj IN ZIPCODE_OBJ_TYPE)
);
/

CREATE OR REPLACE TYPE BODY zipcode_obj_type AS
```

```
CONSTRUCTOR FUNCTION zipcode_obj_type
   (SELF IN OUT NOCOPY zipcode_obj_type, zip VARCHAR2)
RETURN SELF AS RESULT
IS
BEGIN
   SELF.zip := zip;

   SELECT city, state
     INTO SELF.city, SELF.state
     FROM zipcode
    WHERE zip = SELF.zip;

   RETURN;
EXCEPTION
   WHEN NO_DATA_FOUND THEN
      RETURN;
END;

CONSTRUCTOR FUNCTION zipcode_obj_type
   (SELF IN OUT NOCOPY ZIPCODE_OBJ_TYPE, zip VARCHAR2, city VARCHAR2,
    state VARCHAR2)
RETURN SELF AS RESULT
IS
BEGIN
   SELF.zip   := zip;
   SELF.city  := city;
   SELF.state := state;

   RETURN;
END;

MEMBER PROCEDURE get_zipcode_info
   (out_zip OUT VARCHAR2, out_city OUT VARCHAR2, out_state OUT
      VARCHAR2)
IS
BEGIN
   out_zip   := SELF.zip;
   out_city  := SELF.city;
   out_state := SELF.state;
END;

STATIC PROCEDURE display_zipcode_info
   (in_zip_obj IN ZIPCODE_OBJ_TYPE)
IS
BEGIN
   DBMS_OUTPUT.PUT_LINE ('Zip: '  ||in_zip_obj.zip);
   DBMS_OUTPUT.PUT_LINE ('City: ' ||in_zip_obj.city);
   DBMS_OUTPUT.PUT_LINE ('State: '||in_zip_obj.state);
END;

END;
/
```

In this version of the script, the static method displays zip code information on the screen. It is important to note that even though this method references data associated with some object instance, this object instance is created elsewhere (such as in another PL/SQL script, function, or procedure) and then passed into this method.

COMPARING OBJECTS

In PL/SQL, element datatypes such as VARCH AR2, NUMBER, and DATE have a predefined order that enables them to be compared to each other or sorted. For example, the comparison operator > determines which variable contains a greater value, and the IF-THEN-ELSE statement evaluates to TRUE, FALSE, or NULL accordingly:

```
IF v_num1 > v_num2 THEN
   -- Do something
ELSE
   -- Do something else
END IF;
```

However, an object type may contain multiple attributes of different datatypes and therefore does not have a predefined order. Then, to be able to compare and sort object instances of the same object type, you must specify how these object instances should be compared and ordered. You can do this using two types of optional member methods—map and order.

MAP METHODS

Map methods compare and order object instances, essentially by mapping an object instance to an element (scalar) datatype such as DATE, NUMBER, or VARCHAR2. This mapping is used to position an object instance on the axis (DATE, NUMBER, or VARCHAR2) used for the comparison.

A map method is a member function that does not accept any parameters and returns an element datatype, as demonstrated in the following example:

FOR EXAMPLE

```
CREATE OR REPLACE TYPE zipcode_obj_type AS OBJECT
   (zip           VARCHAR2(5),
    city          VARCHAR2(25),
    state         VARCHAR2(2),
    created_by    VARCHAR2(30),
    created_date  DATE,
    modified_by   VARCHAR2(30),
    modified_date DATE,

    CONSTRUCTOR FUNCTION zipcode_obj_type
       (SELF IN OUT NOCOPY ZIPCODE_OBJ_TYPE, zip VARCHAR2)
    RETURN SELF AS RESULT,

    CONSTRUCTOR FUNCTION zipcode_obj_type
       (SELF IN OUT NOCOPY ZIPCODE_OBJ_TYPE, zip VARCHAR2,
```

```
        city VARCHAR2, state VARCHAR2)
    RETURN SELF AS RESULT,

    MEMBER PROCEDURE get_zipcode_info
        (out_zip OUT VARCHAR2, out_city OUT VARCHAR2,
        out_state OUT VARCHAR2),

    STATIC PROCEDURE display_zipcode_info
        (in_zip_obj IN ZIPCODE_OBJ_TYPE),

    MAP MEMBER FUNCTION zipcode RETURN VARCHAR2
);
/

CREATE OR REPLACE TYPE BODY zipcode_obj_type AS

CONSTRUCTOR FUNCTION zipcode_obj_type
    (SELF IN OUT NOCOPY zipcode_obj_type, zip VARCHAR2)
RETURN SELF AS RESULT
IS
BEGIN
    SELF.zip := zip;

    SELECT city, state
      INTO SELF.city, SELF.state
      FROM zipcode
     WHERE zip = SELF.zip;

    RETURN;
EXCEPTION
    WHEN NO_DATA_FOUND THEN
        RETURN;
END;

CONSTRUCTOR FUNCTION zipcode_obj_type
    (SELF IN OUT NOCOPY ZIPCODE_OBJ_TYPE, zip VARCHAR2, city VARCHAR2,
    state VARCHAR2)
RETURN SELF AS RESULT
IS
BEGIN
    SELF.zip   := zip;
    SELF.city  := city;
    SELF.state := state;

    RETURN;
END;

MEMBER PROCEDURE get_zipcode_info
    (out_zip OUT VARCHAR2, out_city OUT VARCHAR2, out_state OUT
      VARCHAR2)
```

```
IS
BEGIN
   out_zip   := SELF.zip;
   out_city  := SELF.city;
   out_state := SELF.state;
END;

STATIC PROCEDURE display_zipcode_info
   (in_zip_obj IN ZIPCODE_OBJ_TYPE)
IS
BEGIN
   DBMS_OUTPUT.PUT_LINE ('Zip: '   ||in_zip_obj.zip);
   DBMS_OUTPUT.PUT_LINE ('City: '  ||in_zip_obj.city);
   DBMS_OUTPUT.PUT_LINE ('State: '||in_zip_obj.state);
END;

MAP MEMBER FUNCTION zipcode RETURN VARCHAR2
IS
BEGIN
   RETURN (zip);
END;

END;
/
```

In this version of the script, the map member function returns the value of the `zip` attribute that has been defined as VARCHAR2.

After the map method is added to the object type, the object type instances may be compared or ordered similar to the element datatypes. For example, if V_ZIP_OBJ1 and V_ZIP_OBJ2 are two instances of the ZIPCODE_OBJ_TYPE, they can be compared like this:

```
v_zip_obj1 > v_zip_obj2
```

or

```
v_zip_obj1.zipcode() > v_zip_obj2.zipcode()
```

Note that the second statement uses dot notation to reference the map function.

Consider the following example, which demonstrates how the various object type methods created so far may be used:

FOR EXAMPLE

```
DECLARE
   v_zip_obj1 zipcode_obj_type;
   v_zip_obj2 zipcode_obj_type;
BEGIN
   -- Initialize object instances with user-defined constructor
   -- methods
```

```
    v_zip_obj1 :=
        zipcode_obj_type (zip => '12345',
                              city => 'Some City', state => 'AB');

    v_zip_obj2 := zipcode_obj_type (zip => '48104');

    -- Compare object instances via map methods
    IF v_zip_obj1 > v_zip_obj2
    THEN
        DBMS_OUTPUT.PUT_LINE ('v_zip_obj1 is greater than v_zip_obj2');
    ELSE
        DBMS_OUTPUT.PUT_LINE
            ('v_zip_obj1 is not greater than v_zip_obj2');
    END IF;
END;
```

Note that when user-defined constructors are invoked, the call statements have no reference to the SELF default parameter.

When run, the script produces the following output:

```
    v_zip_obj1 is not greater than v_zip_obj2

    PL/SQL procedure successfully completed.
```

ORDER METHODS

Order methods use a different technique when comparing and ordering object instances. They do not map object instances to an external axis such as NUMBER or DATE. Instead, an order method compares the current object instance with another object instance of the same object type based on some criterion specified in the method.

An order method is a member function with a single IN parameter of the same object type that returns INTEGER as its return type. Furthermore, the method must return a negative number, 0, or a positive number. This number indicates that the object instance referenced by the SELF parameter is less than, equal to, or greater than the object instance referenced by the IN parameter.

DID YOU KNOW?

The map and order methods have the following restrictions:

- ▶ An object type may contain either an order or map method.
- ▶ An object type derived from another object type may not define an order method.

Consider the following example of the order method for the zipcode_obj_type:

FOR EXAMPLE

```
CREATE OR REPLACE TYPE zipcode_obj_type AS OBJECT
   (zip            VARCHAR2(5),
    city           VARCHAR2(25),
    state          VARCHAR2(2),
    created_by     VARCHAR2(30),
    created_date   DATE,
    modified_by    VARCHAR2(30),
    modified_date DATE,

    CONSTRUCTOR FUNCTION zipcode_obj_type
       (SELF IN OUT NOCOPY ZIPCODE_OBJ_TYPE, zip VARCHAR2)
    RETURN SELF AS RESULT,

    CONSTRUCTOR FUNCTION zipcode_obj_type
       (SELF IN OUT NOCOPY ZIPCODE_OBJ_TYPE, zip VARCHAR2,
        city VARCHAR2, state VARCHAR2)
    RETURN SELF AS RESULT,

    MEMBER PROCEDURE get_zipcode_info
       (out_zip OUT VARCHAR2, out_city OUT VARCHAR2,
        out_state OUT VARCHAR2),

    STATIC PROCEDURE display_zipcode_info
       (in_zip_obj IN ZIPCODE_OBJ_TYPE),

    ORDER MEMBER FUNCTION zipcode (zip_obj ZIPCODE_OBJ_TYPE)
    RETURN INTEGER);
/

CREATE OR REPLACE TYPE BODY zipcode_obj_type AS

CONSTRUCTOR FUNCTION zipcode_obj_type
   (SELF IN OUT NOCOPY zipcode_obj_type, zip VARCHAR2)
RETURN SELF AS RESULT
IS
BEGIN
   SELF.zip := zip;

   SELECT city, state
     INTO SELF.city, SELF.state
     FROM zipcode
    WHERE zip = SELF.zip;

   RETURN;
EXCEPTION
   WHEN NO_DATA_FOUND THEN
      RETURN;
END;
```

```
CONSTRUCTOR FUNCTION zipcode_obj_type
   (SELF IN OUT NOCOPY ZIPCODE_OBJ_TYPE, zip VARCHAR2, city VARCHAR2,
    state VARCHAR2)
RETURN SELF AS RESULT
IS
BEGIN
   SELF.zip   := zip;
   SELF.city  := city;
   SELF.state := state;

   RETURN;
END;


MEMBER PROCEDURE get_zipcode_info
   (out_zip OUT VARCHAR2, out_city OUT VARCHAR2, out_state OUT
     VARCHAR2)
IS
BEGIN
   out_zip   := SELF.zip;
   out_city  := SELF.city;
   out_state := SELF.state;
END;


STATIC PROCEDURE display_zipcode_info
   (in_zip_obj IN ZIPCODE_OBJ_TYPE)
IS
BEGIN
   DBMS_OUTPUT.PUT_LINE ('Zip: '  ||in_zip_obj.zip);
   DBMS_OUTPUT.PUT_LINE ('City: ' ||in_zip_obj.city);
   DBMS_OUTPUT.PUT_LINE ('State: '||in_zip_obj.state);
END;


ORDER MEMBER FUNCTION zipcode (zip_obj ZIPCODE_OBJ_TYPE)
RETURN INTEGER
IS
BEGIN
   IF    zip < zip_obj.zip THEN RETURN -1;
   ELSIF zip = zip_obj.zip THEN RETURN  0;
   ELSIF zip > zip_obj.zip THEN RETURN  1;
   END IF;
END;

END;
/
```

In this version of the script, the map member function is replaced by the order member function. Notice that similar to the map method, the order method uses the `zip` attribute as a basis of comparison for the two object type instances.

Consider the following script, which demonstrates how an order method may be used:

```
DECLARE
   v_zip_obj1 zipcode_obj_type;
   v_zip_obj2 zipcode_obj_type;

   v_result    INTEGER;
BEGIN
   -- Initialize object instances with user-defined constructor
   -- methods
   v_zip_obj1 := zipcode_obj_type ('12345', 'Some City', 'AB');
   v_zip_obj2 := zipcode_obj_type ('48104');

   v_result := v_zip_obj1.zipcode(v_zip_obj2);
   DBMS_OUTPUT.PUT_LINE ('The result of comparison is '||v_result);

   IF v_result = 1
   THEN
      DBMS_OUTPUT.PUT_LINE ('v_zip_obj1 is greater than v_zip_obj2');

   ELSIF v_result = 0
   THEN
      DBMS_OUTPUT.PUT_LINE ('v_zip_obj1 is equal to v_zip_obj2');

   ELSIF v_result = -1
   THEN
      DBMS_OUTPUT.PUT_LINE ('v_zip_ob1 is less than v_zip_obj2');
   END IF;
END;
```

In this script, the result of the order method is assigned to the v_result variable, defined as INTEGER. Then, the decision is made based on the value of this variable.

When run, this script produces the following output:

```
The result of comparison is -1
v_zip_ob1 is less than v_zip_obj2

PL/SQL procedure successfully completed.
```

▼ LAB 23.2 EXERCISES

This section provides exercises and suggested answers, with discussion related to how those answers resulted. The most important thing to realize is whether your answer works. You should figure out the implications of the answers and what the effects are of any different answers you may come up with.

23.2.1 Use Object Type Methods

In this exercise, you create various methods for the enrollment_obj_type you created in the exercises portion of Lab 23.1. Note that before proceeding with this exercise, you need to drop the nested table type you created in the preceding lab:

```
DROP TYPE enroll_tab_type;
```

Recall that you created `enrollment_obj_type` as follows:

```
CREATE OR REPLACE TYPE ENROLLMENT_OBJ_TYPE AS OBJECT
    (student_id  NUMBER(8),
     first_name  VARCHAR2(25),
     last_name   VARCHAR2(25),
     course_no   NUMBER(8),
     section_no  NUMBER(3),
     enroll_date DATE,
     final_grade NUMBER(3));
```

Create the following methods for the `enrollment_obj_type`:

A) Create a user-defined constructor method that populates object type attributes by selecting data from the corresponding tables based on the incoming values for student ID, course, and section numbers.

ANSWER: The script should look similar to the following:

```
-- ch23_4a.sql, version 1.0
CREATE OR REPLACE TYPE enrollment_obj_type AS OBJECT
    (student_id  NUMBER(8),
     first_name  VARCHAR2(25),
     last_name   VARCHAR2(25),
     course_no   NUMBER(8),
     section_no  NUMBER(3),
     enroll_date DATE,
     final_grade NUMBER(3),

     CONSTRUCTOR FUNCTION enrollment_obj_type
        (SELF IN OUT NOCOPY enrollment_obj_type, in_student_id NUMBER,
         in_course_no NUMBER, in_section_no NUMBER)
     RETURN SELF AS RESULT);
/

CREATE OR REPLACE TYPE BODY enrollment_obj_type AS

CONSTRUCTOR FUNCTION enrollment_obj_type
    (SELF IN OUT NOCOPY enrollment_obj_type, in_student_id NUMBER,
     in_course_no NUMBER, in_section_no NUMBER)
RETURN SELF AS RESULT
IS
BEGIN
    SELECT st.student_id, st.first_name, st.last_name, c.course_no,
           se.section_no, e.enroll_date, e.final_grade
      INTO SELF.student_id, SELF.first_name, SELF.last_name,
           SELF.course_no, SELF.section_no, SELF.enroll_date,
           SELF.final_grade
      FROM student st, course c, section se, enrollment e
     WHERE st.student_id = e.student_id
       AND c.course_no   = se.course_no
       AND se.section_id = e.section_id
       AND st.student_id = in_student_id
```

```
        AND c.course_no   = in_course_no
        AND se.section_no = in_section_no;


   RETURN;
EXCEPTION
   WHEN NO_DATA_FOUND THEN
        RETURN;
END;
END;
/
```

Take a closer look at the SELECT INTO statement of this constructor method. This statement is very similar to the SELECT INTO statement used in Lab 23.1:

```
SELECT
    enrollment_obj_type(st.student_id, st.first_name, st.last_name,
                        c.course_no, se.section_no, e.enroll_date,
                        e.final_grade)
  INTO v_enrollment_obj
  FROM student st, course c, section se, enrollment e
 WHERE st.student_id = e.student_id
   AND c.course_no   = se.course_no
   AND se.section_id = e.section_id
   AND st.student_id = 102
   AND c.course_no   = 25
   AND se.section_no = 2;
```

Note that the SELECT INTO statement in the constructor body does not reference the system-defined default constructor. Instead, it uses the built-in SELF parameter to reference individual attributes of the current object instance.

You may test the newly added constructor method as follows:

```
SET SERVEROUTPUT ON;
DECLARE
    v_enrollment_obj enrollment_obj_type;
BEGIN
    v_enrollment_obj :=
        enrollment_obj_type(102, 25, 2);

    DBMS_OUTPUT.PUT_LINE ('student_id:
                          '||v_enrollment_obj.student_id);
    DBMS_OUTPUT.PUT_LINE ('first_name:
                          '||v_enrollment_obj.first_name);
    DBMS_OUTPUT.PUT_LINE ('last_name:
                          '||v_enrollment_obj.last_name);
    DBMS_OUTPUT.PUT_LINE ('course_no:
                          '||v_enrollment_obj.course_no);
    DBMS_OUTPUT.PUT_LINE ('section_no:
                          '||v_enrollment_obj.section_no);
    DBMS_OUTPUT.PUT_LINE ('enroll_date:
                          '||v_enrollment_obj.enroll_date);
```

```
    DBMS_OUTPUT.PUT_LINE ('final_grade:
                        '||v_enrollment_obj.final_grade);
END;
```

The test script produces the following output:

```
student_id:  102
first_name:  Fred
last_name:   Crocitto
course_no:   25
section_no:  2
enroll_date: 30-JAN-07
final_grade:

PL/SQL procedure successfully completed.
```

B) Add a member procedure method, GET_ENROLLMENT_INFO, that returns attribute values.

ANSWER: This member procedure method should look similar to the following. Changes are shown in bold.

```
-- ch23_4b.sql, version 2.0
CREATE OR REPLACE TYPE enrollment_obj_type AS OBJECT
    (student_id  NUMBER(8),
     first_name  VARCHAR2(25),
     last_name   VARCHAR2(25),
     course_no   NUMBER(8),
     section_no  NUMBER(3),
     enroll_date DATE,
     final_grade NUMBER(3),
     CONSTRUCTOR FUNCTION enrollment_obj_type
         (SELF IN OUT NOCOPY enrollment_obj_type, in_student_id NUMBER,
          in_course_no NUMBER, in_section_no NUMBER)
     RETURN SELF AS RESULT,

     MEMBER PROCEDURE get_enrollment_ifo
         (out_student_id OUT NUMBER, out_first_name OUT VARCHAR2,
          out_last_name OUT VARCHAR2, out_course_no OUT NUMBER,
          out_section_no OUT NUMBER, out_enroll_date OUT DATE,
          out_final_grade OUT NUMBER))
/

CREATE OR REPLACE TYPE BODY enrollment_obj_type AS

CONSTRUCTOR FUNCTION enrollment_obj_type
    (SELF IN OUT NOCOPY enrollment_obj_type, in_student_id NUMBER,
     in_course_no NUMBER, in_section_no NUMBER)
RETURN SELF AS RESULT
IS
BEGIN
    SELECT st.student_id, st.first_name, st.last_name, c.course_no,
           se.section_no, e.enroll_date, e.final_grade
```

```
          INTO SELF.student_id, SELF.first_name, SELF.last_name,
               SELF.course_no, SELF.section_no, SELF.enroll_date,
               SELF.final_grade
          FROM student st, course c, section se, enrollment e
         WHERE st.student_id = e.student_id
           AND c.course_no   = se.course_no
           AND se.section_id = e.section_id
           AND st.student_id = in_student_id
           AND c.course_no   = in_course_no
           AND se.section_no = in_section_no;

      RETURN;
   EXCEPTION
      WHEN NO_DATA_FOUND THEN
         RETURN;
   END;

   MEMBER PROCEDURE get_enrollment_ifo
      (out_student_id OUT NUMBER, out_first_name OUT VARCHAR2,
       out_last_name OUT VARCHAR2, out_course_no OUT NUMBER,
       out_section_no OUT NUMBER, out_enroll_date OUT DATE,
       out_final_grade OUT NUMBER)
   IS
   BEGIN
      out_student_id  := student_id;
      out_first_name  := first_name;
      out_last_name   := last_name;
      out_course_no   := course_no;
      out_section_no  := section_no;
      out_enroll_date := enroll_date;
      out_final_grade := final_grade;
   END;

   END;
   /
```

C) Add a static method to the `enrollment_obj_type` object type that displays values of individual attributes on the screen.

ANSWER: The script should look similar to the following. Changes are shown in bold.

```
-- ch23_4c.sql, version 3.0
CREATE OR REPLACE TYPE enrollment_obj_type AS OBJECT
   (student_id  NUMBER(8),
    first_name  VARCHAR2(25),
    last_name   VARCHAR2(25),
    course_no   NUMBER(8),
    section_no  NUMBER(3),
    enroll_date DATE,
    final_grade NUMBER(3),
    CONSTRUCTOR FUNCTION enrollment_obj_type
```

```
        (SELF IN OUT NOCOPY enrollment_obj_type, in_student_id NUMBER,
         in_course_no NUMBER, in_section_no NUMBER)
    RETURN SELF AS RESULT,

    MEMBER PROCEDURE get_enrollment_ifo
        (out_student_id OUT NUMBER, out_first_name OUT VARCHAR2,
         out_last_name OUT VARCHAR2, out_course_no OUT NUMBER,
         out_section_no OUT NUMBER, out_enroll_date OUT DATE,
         out_final_grade OUT NUMBER),

    STATIC PROCEDURE display_enrollment_info
        (enrollment_obj enrollment_obj_type))
/

CREATE OR REPLACE TYPE BODY enrollment_obj_type AS

CONSTRUCTOR FUNCTION enrollment_obj_type
    (SELF IN OUT NOCOPY enrollment_obj_type, in_student_id NUMBER,
     in_course_no NUMBER, in_section_no NUMBER)
RETURN SELF AS RESULT
IS
BEGIN
    SELECT st.student_id, st.first_name, st.last_name, c.course_no,
           se.section_no, e.enroll_date, e.final_grade
      INTO SELF.student_id, SELF.first_name, SELF.last_name,
           SELF.course_no, SELF.section_no, SELF.enroll_date,
           SELF.final_grade
      FROM student st, course c, section se, enrollment e
     WHERE st.student_id = e.student_id
       AND c.course_no   = se.course_no
       AND se.section_id = e.section_id
       AND st.student_id = in_student_id
       AND c.course_no   = in_course_no
       AND se.section_no = in_section_no;

    RETURN;
EXCEPTION
   WHEN NO_DATA_FOUND THEN
       RETURN;
END;

MEMBER PROCEDURE get_enrollment_ifo
    (out_student_id OUT NUMBER, out_first_name OUT VARCHAR2,
     out_last_name OUT VARCHAR2, out_course_no OUT NUMBER,
     out_section_no OUT NUMBER, out_enroll_date OUT DATE,
     out_final_grade OUT NUMBER)
IS
BEGIN
    out_student_id  := student_id;
    out_first_name  := first_name;
```

```
    out_last_name    := last_name;
    out_course_no    := course_no;
    out_section_no   := section_no;
    out_enroll_date  := enroll_date;
    out_final_grade  := final_grade;
END;


STATIC PROCEDURE display_enrollment_info
    (enrollment_obj enrollment_obj_type)
IS
BEGIN
   DBMS_OUTPUT.PUT_LINE
      ('student_id: '||enrollment_obj.student_id);
   DBMS_OUTPUT.PUT_LINE
      ('first_name: '||enrollment_obj.first_name);
   DBMS_OUTPUT.PUT_LINE
      ('last_name: '||enrollment_obj.last_name);
   DBMS_OUTPUT.PUT_LINE
      ('course_no: '||enrollment_obj.course_no);
   DBMS_OUTPUT.PUT_LINE
      ('section_no: '||enrollment_obj.section_no);
   DBMS_OUTPUT.PUT_LINE
      ('enroll_date: '||enrollment_obj.enroll_date);
   DBMS_OUTPUT.PUT_LINE
      ('final_grade: '||enrollment_obj.final_grade);
END;


END;
/
```

Recall that static methods are created for actions that do not need to access data associated with a particular object instance. As such, they may not reference the default parameter SELF. Then, to display attribute data associated with some object instance, the instance itself is passed to the method.

The newly created method may be tested as follows:

```
SET SERVEROUTPUT ON;
DECLARE
   v_enrollment_obj enrollment_obj_type;
BEGIN
   v_enrollment_obj := enrollment_obj_type(102, 25, 2);

   enrollment_obj_type.display_enrollment_info (v_enrollment_obj);
END;
```

Note the invocation call to the static method. *The call to the static method is qualified with the object type name, not with the object type instance name.*

The test script produces the following output:

```
student_id:   102
first_name:   Fred
last_name:    Crocitto
```

```
course_no:   25
section_no:  2
enroll_date: 30-JAN-07
final_grade:

PL/SQL procedure successfully completed.
```

D) Add the method to the object type `enrollment_obj_type` so that its instances may be compared and/or sorted. The object instances should be compared based on the values of the `course_no`, `section_no`, and `student_id` attributes.

ANSWER: Recall that for you to compare and sort object instances, their corresponding type must have either map or order methods. For the purposes of this exercise, the map method is added to the type definition as follows. Changes are shown in bold.

```
-- ch23_4d.sql, version 3.0
CREATE OR REPLACE TYPE enrollment_obj_type AS OBJECT
    (student_id  NUMBER(8),
     first_name  VARCHAR2(25),
     last_name   VARCHAR2(25),
     course_no   NUMBER(8),
     section_no  NUMBER(3),
     enroll_date DATE,
     final_grade NUMBER(3),
     CONSTRUCTOR FUNCTION enrollment_obj_type
         (SELF IN OUT NOCOPY enrollment_obj_type, in_student_id NUMBER,
          in_course_no NUMBER, in_section_no NUMBER)
     RETURN SELF AS RESULT,

     MEMBER PROCEDURE get_enrollment_ifo
         (out_student_id OUT NUMBER, out_first_name OUT VARCHAR2,
          out_last_name OUT VARCHAR2, out_course_no OUT NUMBER,
          out_section_no OUT NUMBER, out_enroll_date OUT DATE,
          out_final_grade OUT NUMBER),

     STATIC PROCEDURE display_enrollment_info
         (enrollment_obj enrollment_obj_type),

     MAP MEMBER FUNCTION enrollment RETURN VARCHAR2)
/

CREATE OR REPLACE TYPE BODY enrollment_obj_type AS

CONSTRUCTOR FUNCTION enrollment_obj_type
    (SELF IN OUT NOCOPY enrollment_obj_type, in_student_id NUMBER,
     in_course_no NUMBER, in_section_no NUMBER)
RETURN SELF AS RESULT
IS
BEGIN
    SELECT st.student_id, st.first_name, st.last_name, c.course_no,
           se.section_no, e.enroll_date, e.final_grade
      INTO SELF.student_id, SELF.first_name, SELF.last_name,
           SELF.course_no, SELF.section_no, SELF.enroll_date,
```

```
               SELF.final_grade
        FROM student st, course c, section se, enrollment e
       WHERE st.student_id = e.student_id
         AND c.course_no    = se.course_no
         AND se.section_id = e.section_id
         AND st.student_id = in_student_id
         AND c.course_no    = in_course_no
         AND se.section_no = in_section_no;


    RETURN;
EXCEPTION
   WHEN NO_DATA_FOUND THEN
       RETURN;
END;


MEMBER PROCEDURE get_enrollment_ifo
   (out_student_id OUT NUMBER, out_first_name OUT VARCHAR2,
    out_last_name OUT VARCHAR2, out_course_no OUT NUMBER,
    out_section_no OUT NUMBER, out_enroll_date OUT DATE,
    out_final_grade OUT NUMBER)
IS
BEGIN
   out_student_id  := student_id;
   out_first_name  := first_name;
   out_last_name   := last_name;
   out_course_no   := course_no;
   out_section_no  := section_no;
   out_enroll_date := enroll_date;
   out_final_grade := final_grade;
END;


STATIC PROCEDURE display_enrollment_info
   (enrollment_obj enrollment_obj_type)
IS
BEGIN
   DBMS_OUTPUT.PUT_LINE ('student_id:  '||enrollment_obj.student_id);
   DBMS_OUTPUT.PUT_LINE ('first_name:  '||enrollment_obj.first_name);
   DBMS_OUTPUT.PUT_LINE ('last_name:   '||enrollment_obj.last_name);
   DBMS_OUTPUT.PUT_LINE ('course_no:   '||enrollment_obj.course_no);
   DBMS_OUTPUT.PUT_LINE ('section_no:  '||enrollment_obj.section_no);
   DBMS_OUTPUT.PUT_LINE ('enroll_date: '||enrollment_obj.enroll_date);
   DBMS_OUTPUT.PUT_LINE ('final_grade: '||enrollment_obj.final_grade);
END;


MAP MEMBER FUNCTION enrollment RETURN VARCHAR2
IS
BEGIN
   RETURN (course_no||'-'||section_no||'-'||student_id);
END;


END;
/
```

The newly added function concatenates values stored in the course_no, section_no, and section_id attributes. The resulting string value may now be used to compare different object instances:

```
SET SERVEROUTPUT ON;
DECLARE
   v_enrollment_obj1 enrollment_obj_type;
   v_enrollment_obj2 enrollment_obj_type;
BEGIN
   v_enrollment_obj1 := enrollment_obj_type(102, 25, 2);
   v_enrollment_obj2 := enrollment_obj_type(104, 20, 2);

   enrollment_obj_type.display_enrollment_info (v_enrollment_obj1);
   DBMS_OUTPUT.PUT_LINE ('--------------------');
   enrollment_obj_type.display_enrollment_info (v_enrollment_obj2);

   IF v_enrollment_obj1 > v_enrollment_obj2
   THEN
      DBMS_OUTPUT.PUT_LINE ('Instance 1 is greater than instacne2');
   ELSE
      DBMS_OUTPUT.PUT_LINE
         ('Instance 1 is not greater than instance 2');
   END IF;
END;
```

When run, the test script produces the following output:

```
student_id:  102
first_name:  Fred
last_name:   Crocitto
course_no:   25
section_no:  2
enroll_date: 30-JAN-07
final_grade:
--------------------
student_id:  104
first_name:  Laetia
last_name:   Enison
course_no:   20
section_no:  2
enroll_date: 30-JAN-07
final_grade:
Instance 1 is greater than instance2

PL/SQL procedure successfully completed.
```

▼ TRY IT YOURSELF

In this chapter, you've learned about object types, object type methods, and collections of object types. Here are some projects that will help you test the depth of your understanding:

1) Create the object type `student_obj_type` with attributes derived from the STUDENT table.

2) Add a user-defined constructor function, member procedure, static procedure, and order function methods. You should determine on your own how these methods should be structured.

The projects in this section are meant to have you use all the skills you have acquired throughout this chapter. The answers to these projects can be found in Appendix D and on this book's companion Web site. Visit the Web site periodically to share and discuss your answers.

CHAPTER 24

Oracle Supplied Packages

CHAPTER OBJECTIVES

In this chapter, you will learn about

- ▶ Making use of Oracle-supplied packages to profile PL/SQL, access files, and schedule jobs
- ▶ Making use of Oracle-supplied packages to generate an explain plan and create HTML pages
- ▶ Creating Web pages with the Oracle Web Toolkit

Oracle has built into the Database more than 130 packages that extend what you can achieve with PL/SQL. Usually, each new version of the database comes with new supplied packages. Oracle introduced about 17 new packages in each upgrade to versions 9.2 and 10.0. Oracle 11g had 45 new packages and eight that were updated. These packages offer functionality that you would not be able to achieve with PL/SQL alone. The reason is that the Oracle-supplied packages use the C programming language; this is not something that you can do with ordinary PL/SQL packages. This means that Oracle-supplied packages have full access to the operating system and other aspects of the Oracle Server that are not available to ordinary PL/SQL packages. You are already familiar with the DBMS_OUTPUT package's procedure PUT_LINE, which is used to gather debugging information into the buffer for output. This chapter introduces a few key Oracle supplied packages; you will learn their basic features and how to use them.

LAB 24.1
Making Use of Oracle Supplied Packages to Profile PL/SQL, Access Files, and Schedule Jobs

LAB OBJECTIVES

After completing this lab, you will be able to

- ▶ Access files with UTL_FILE
- ▶ Schedule jobs with DBMS_JOB
- ▶ Submit jobs

PROFILE PL/SQL WITH DBMS_HPROF

In Oracle 11g the package for PL/SQL profiling known previously as DBMS_PROFILER was extended. The Hierarchical Profiler expands DBMS_PROFILER through DBMS_HPROF by adding information about which programs are calling the section of code that is running for a long time. This a tool to locate execution bottlenecks in your stored PL/SQL code. The Profiler indicates how many times each line of code is executed, how long it is executed, and other information.

The DBMS_HPROF package is installed by default. To use it, the DBA must grant execute privileges on the package to the appropriate users and provide a directory on the server to write the profile information to. This will be a text file. You can do this by connecting as SYS (the owner of the package) as follows:

```
GRANT EXECUTE ON dbms_hprof TO public;
CREATE OR REPLACE DIRECTORY profiler_dir AS 'c:/temp';
GRANT READ, WRITE ON DIRECTORY profiler_dir TO public;
```

To analyze the results, the user needs to install the related tables. They can be found in the Oracle home. While logged on as your STUDENT user, run this script to create the tables:

```
@?/rdbms/admin/dbmshptab.sql
```

The first lines are drop tables. If you don't have the tables, you see an error, which you can ignore. The tables DBMSHP_PARENT_CHILD_INFO, DBMSHP_FUNCTION_INFO, and DBMSHP_RUNS are created, as well as the sequence DBMSHP_RUNNUMBER.

The following procedures do not do anything of value; they just call each other. They can be used to show a simple case of utilizing the Profiler:

```
CREATE OR REPLACE PROCEDURE count_student
(p_zip  IN  NUMBER)
AS
 v_count number;
BEGIN
   SELECT COUNT(*)
   INTO V_count
   FROM STUDENT
   where zip = p_zip;
END;

CREATE OR REPLACE PROCEDURE count_instructor
(p_zip  IN  NUMBER)
AS
 v_count number;
BEGIN
   SELECT COUNT(*)
   INTO V_count
   FROM INSTRUCTOR
   where zip = p_zip;
END;

CREATE OR REPLACE PROCEDURE loop_Zipcode
AS
BEGIN
   FOR r in (SELECT * from zipcode) LOOP
      count_student (r.zip);
      count_instructor (r.zip);
   END LOOP;
END;
```

Next you start the Hierarchical Profiler using the START_PROFILING procedure:

```
BEGIN
   DBMS_HPROF.start_profiling (
     location => 'PROFILER_DIR',
    filename => 'profiler.txt');

   loop_Zipcode;

   DBMS_HPROF.stop_profiling;
END;
```

After the profiling is done, you run the ANALYZE function so that the raw data can be analyzed and placed in the appropriate Profiler tables.

```
SET SERVEROUTPUT ON
DECLARE
   l_runid  NUMBER;
```

```
BEGIN
  l_runid := DBMS_HPROF.analyze (
                location   => 'PROFILER_DIR',
                filename   => 'profiler.txt',
                run_comment => 'Test run.');
  DBMS_OUTPUT.put_line('l_runid=' || l_runid);
END;
```

The output shows the runid of the analyze run:

```
l_runid=1
PL/SQL procedure successfully completed
```

This can also be obtained with this SQL:

```
SELECT runid,
       run_timestamp,
       total_elapsed_time,
       run_comment
FROM   dbmshp_runs
ORDER BY runid;

 RUNID RUN_TIMESTAMP                      TOTAL_ELAPSED_TIME RUN_COMMENT
------ -------------------------------- ------------------ -----------
     1 21-MAY-08 11.07.53.468000 PM                138976 Test run.
```

This runid is used to query the DBMSHP_FUNCTION_INFO table as follows:

```
SELECT symbolid,
       owner,
       module,
       type,
       function
FROM   dbmshp_function_info
WHERE  runid = 1
ORDER BY symbolid;

SYMBOLID OWNER   MODULE           TYPE         FUNCTION
-------- ------- ---------------- ------------ -----------------------
       1 STUDENT COUNT_INSTRUCTOR PROCEDURE    COUNT_INSTRUCTOR
       2 STUDENT COUNT_STUDENT    PROCEDURE    COUNT_STUDENT
       3 STUDENT LOOP_ZIPCODE     PROCEDURE    LOOP_ZIPCODE
       4 SYS     DBMS_HPROF       PACKAGE BODY STOP_PROFILING
       5 STUDENT COUNT_INSTRUCTOR PROCEDURE    __static_sql_exec_line6
       6 STUDENT COUNT_STUDENT    PROCEDURE    __static_sql_exec_line6
       7 STUDENT LOOP_ZIPCODE     PROCEDURE    __sql_fetch_line5
```

This output helps you find the SYMBOLID of the top-level procedure. This is LOOP_ZIPCODE, which has a SYMBOLID of **3**. Now this can be used to query the hierarchical information.

```
SET LINESIZE 130
COLUMN name FORMAT A30
COLUMN function FORMAT A25
SELECT RPAD(' ', level*2, ' ') || fi.owner || '.' || fi.module AS name,
       fi.function,
       pci.subtree_elapsed_time,
       pci.function_elapsed_time,
       pci.calls
FROM   dbmshp_parent_child_info pci
       JOIN dbmshp_function_info fi ON pci.runid = fi.runid AND
         pci.childsymid = fi.symbolid
WHERE  pci.runid = 1
CONNECT BY PRIOR childsymid = parentsymid
START WITH pci.parentsymid = 3;
NAME                          FUNCTION                   SUBTREE_ FUNCTION_ CALLS
                                                         ELAPSED_ ELAPSED_
                                                         TIME     TIME

---------------------------   ----------------------     -------- --------- -----
STUDENT.COUNT_INSTRUCTOR      COUNT_INSTRUCTOR              36501      1440    227
STUDENT.COUNT_INSTRUCTOR      __static_sql_exec_line6      35061     35061    227
STUDENT.COUNT_STUDENT         COUNT_STUDENT                65704      1559    227
STUDENT.COUNT_STUDENT         __static_sql_exec_line6      64145     64145    227
STUDENT.LOOP_ZIPCODE          __sql_fetch_line5            34582     34582      3
```

The results display the hierarchy of function calls, along with elapsed times for the function and the subtree as a whole. The dbms_hprof PL/SQL built-in package and the related dbmshp_parent_child_info table are used to help plot the execution and debugging of PL/SQL, revealing the hierarchy of calls to other PL/SQL functions.

ACCESSING FILES WITHIN PL/SQL WITH UTL_FILE

The UTL_FILE package provides text file input and output capabilities within PL/SQL. Oracle introduced the UTL_FILE package with database version 7.3. This means that you can either read input from the operating system files or write to operating system files. This could be useful if you have data from another system that you want to load into the database. For instance, if you have logs from a Web server that you want to place in your data warehouse, the UTL_FILE package would allow you to read the text file logs and then parse them to load the data into the correct tables and columns in the data warehouse. The package also allows you to write data to a file. This is useful if you want to produce logs or capture current information about the database and store it in a text file, or extract data into a text file that another application can process.

It is important to note that this is a server-side text file access. UTL_FILE cannot read binary files. For that, you use the DBMS_LOB package. The files that you access must be mapped to a drive on the server. What directories you can access is controlled by a setting in the INIT.ORA file. You set the drives that can be accessed with the UTL_FILE_DIR initialization parameter.

FOR EXAMPLE

```
UTL_FILE_DIR = 'C:\WORKING\'
```

You can also bypass all server-side security and allow all files to be accessed with the UTL_FILE package using the following setting:

```
UTL_FILE_DIR = *
```

If you do not have access to the INIT.ORA file on the database server, you can query the Data Dictionary to find the value that has been set in your database with the following SQL:

```
SELECT name, value
FROM   V$SYSTEM_PARAMETER
WHERE  name = 'utl_file_dir'
```

BY THE WAY

It is not advisable to allow UTL_FILE access to all files in a production environment. This means that all files, including important files that manage the operation of the database, are accessible. This allows developers to write a procedure that corrupts the database.

The method of using the UTL_FILE file package is to open the text file, process the file by writing to the file and getting lines from the file, and then close the file. If you do not close the file, your operating system will think that the file is in use and will not allow you to write to the file until it is closed. Table 24.1 lists the major functions, procedures, and datatypes in the UTL_FILE packages. Table 24.2 describes the exceptions in this package.

TABLE 24.1
UTL_FILE Functions, Procedures, and Datatypes

FUNCTION, PROCEDURE, OR DATATYPE	DESCRIPTION
FILE_TYPE	The datatype for a file handle.
IS_OPEN	This function has a return datatype of BOOLEAN. It returns true if the file is open and false if the file is closed.
FOPEN	This function opens a file for input or output. The function return value is the form handle in the FILE_TYPE datatype.
	The modes to open a file are R: read mode W: write mode A: append mode
FCLOSE	This procedure closes an open file.
FCLOSE_ALL	This procedure closes all files that are open in the current session. (It is a good idea to place this procedure in your exception to make sure you don't leave any files locked.)

FUNCTION, PROCEDURE, OR DATATYPE	DESCRIPTION
FFLUSH	This procedure takes all the data buffered in memory and writes it to a file.
GET_LINE	This procedure gets one line of text from the opened file and places the text into the OUT parameter of the procedure.
PUT_LINE	This procedure writes a string of text from the IN parameter to the opened file. Afterwards, a line terminator is placed into the text file.
PUT	This procedure is the same as PUT_LINE, except that no line terminator is placed in the open file.
PUTF	This procedure puts formatted text into the opened file.
NEW_LINE	This procedure inserts a new line terminator into the opened text file.

TABLE 24.2
UTL_FILE Exceptions

EXCEPTION NAME	DESCRIPTION
INVALID_PATH	The file location or filename is not valid.
INVALID_MODE	This exception is for FOPEN only. The mode for the OPEN_MODE parameter is not valid.
INVALID_FILEHANDLE	The file handle is not valid.
INVALID_OPERATION	The file could not be opened or operated on in the manner requested.
READ_ERROR	An operating system error prevented the read file operation from occurring.
WRITE_ERROR	An operating system error prevented the write file operation from occurring.
INTERNAL_ERROR	An unspecified PL/SQL error occurred.

The following example demonstrates a procedure that writes to a log file the date, time, and number of users who are currently logged on. In the exercises you will create a more involved procedure that makes use of UTL_FILE. For this example, the user STUDENT needs privileges to access the v$session table. The DBA can grant access to STUDENT as follows:

```
GRANT SELECT ON sys.v_$session TO student;
```

FOR EXAMPLE

```
-- ch24_1a.sql
CREATE OR REPLACE PROCEDURE LOG_USER_COUNT
   (PI_DIRECTORY  IN VARCHAR2,
    PI_FILE_NAME  IN VARCHAR2)
```

FOR EXAMPLE (continued)

```
AS
   V_File_handle   UTL_FILE.FILE_TYPE;
   V_user_count    number;
BEGIN
   SELECT count(*)
   INTO    V_user_count
   FROM    v$session
   WHERE   username is not null;

   V_File_handle  :=
      UTL_FILE.FOPEN(PI_DIRECTORY, PI_FILE_NAME, 'A');
   UTL_FILE.NEW_LINE(V_File_handle);
   UTL_FILE.PUT_LINE(V_File_handle  , '---- User log -----');
   UTL_FILE.NEW_LINE(V_File_handle);
   UTL_FILE.PUT_LINE(V_File_handle  , 'on '||
         TO_CHAR(SYSDATE, 'MM/DD/YY HH24:MI'));
   UTL_FILE.PUT_LINE(V_File_handle  ,
         'Number of users logged on: '|| V_user_count);
   UTL_FILE.PUT_LINE(V_File_handle  , '---- End log -----');
   UTL_FILE.NEW_LINE(V_File_handle);
   UTL_FILE.FCLOSE(V_File_handle);

EXCEPTION
   WHEN UTL_FILE.INVALID_FILENAME THEN
      DBMS_OUTPUT.PUT_LINE('File is invalid');
   WHEN UTL_FILE.WRITE_ERROR THEN
      DBMS_OUTPUT.PUT_LINE('Oracle is not able to write to file');
END;
```

The LOG_USER_COUNT procedure can be executed to log the number of users into the file c:\working\user.log.

FOR EXAMPLE

```
SQL> exec LOG_USER_COUNT('C:\working\', 'USER.LOG');

PL/SQL procedure successfully completed.
```

USER.LOG contents:
```
---- User log -----

on 07/05/03 13:09
Number of users logged on: 1
---- End log -----
```

▼ LAB 24.1 EXERCISES

This section provides exercises and suggested answers, with discussion related to how those answers resulted. The most important thing to realize is whether your answer works. You should figure out the implications of the answers and what the effects are of any different answers you may come up with.

24.1.1 Access Files with UTL_FILE

Complete the following exercises:

A) Create a companion procedure to the sample procedure LOG_USER_COUNT that you just made. Name your new procedure READ_LOG. This procedure will read a text file and display each line using DBMS_OUTPUT.PUT_LINE.

ANSWER: The following PL/SQL creates a procedure to read a file and display the contents. Note that the exception WHEN NO_DATA_FOUND is raised when the last line of the file has been read and there are no more lines to read.

```
CREATE OR REPLACE PROCEDURE READ_FILE
    (PI_DIRECTORY   IN VARCHAR2,
     PI_FILE_NAME   IN VARCHAR2)
AS
    V_File_handle   UTL_FILE.FILE_TYPE;
    V_FILE_Line     VARCHAR2(1024);
BEGIN
    V_File_handle   :=
        UTL_FILE.FOPEN(PI_DIRECTORY, PI_FILE_NAME, 'R');
    LOOP
            UTL_FILE.GET_LINE( V_File_handle , v_file_line);
            DBMS_OUTPUT.PUT_LINE(v_file_line);
    END LOOP;
EXCEPTION
    WHEN NO_DATA_FOUND
            THEN UTL_FILE.FCLOSE(  V_File_handle );
END;
```

B) Run the procedure LOG_USER_COUNT, and then run the procedure READ_LOG for the same file.

ANSWER: Before the procedures are executed, it is important to submit the SQL*Plus command SET SERVEROUTPUT ON.

```
SQL>  EXEC LOG_USER_COUNT('C:\working\', 'User.Log');
SQL>  EXEC READ_FILE('C:\working\', 'User.Log');
```

24.1.2 Schedule Jobs with DBMS_JOB

The Oracle-supplied package DBMS_JOB allows you to schedule the execution of a PL/SQL procedure. It was introduced in PL/SQL version 2.2. DBMS_JOB is an Oracle PL/SQL package provided to users. A job is submitted to a job queue and runs at the specified time. The user can also input a parameter that specifies how often the job should run. A job can consist of any PL/SQL code. As shown in Table 24.3, the DBMS_JOB package has procedures for submitting jobs for scheduled execution, executing a job that has been submitted outside of its schedule, changing the execution parameters of a previously submitted job, suspending a job, and removing jobs from the schedule. The primary reason you would want to use this feature would be to run a batch program during off times when there are fewer users, or to maintain a log.

TABLE 24.3
The Main Procedures in the DBMS_JOB Package

PROCEDURE NAME	DESCRIPTION
SUBMIT	Enters a PL/SQL procedure as a job into the job queue.
REMOVE	Removes a previously submitted PL/SQL procedure from the job queue.
CHANGE	Changes the parameters that have been set for a previously submitted job (description, next run time, or interval).
BROKEN	Disables a job in the job queue.
INTERVAL	Alters the interval set for an existing job in the job queue.
NEXT_DATE	Changes the next time an existing job is set to run.
RUN	Forces the run of a job in the job queue regardless of the job's schedule.

The job queue is governed by the SNP process that runs in the background. This process is used to implement data snapshots as well as job queues. If the process fails, the database attempts to restart the process. The database initialization parameter (set in the INIT.ORA file and viewable in the DBA view V$SYSTEM_PARAMETER) JOB_QUEUE_PROCESSES determines how many processes can start. It must be set to a number greater than 0 (note that the default is 0).

WATCH OUT!

SNP background processes do not execute jobs if the system has been started in restricted mode. It is expected behavior for jobs not to be executed while the database is in restricted mode. However, you can use the ALTER SYSTEM command to turn this behavior on and off as follows:

```
ALTER SYSTEM ENABLE RESTRICTED SESSION;
ALTER SYSTEM DISABLE RESTRICTED SESSION;
```

24.1.3 Submit Jobs

An important first step when submitting jobs to the queue is to be sure that your PL/SQL procedure is valid and executes the way you expect it to run. Before submitting a PL/SQL procedure, make sure you have thoroughly tested the functionality. Job submission assumes that your job is valid. The SUBMIT procedure takes four in parameters and returns one out parameter, as shown in Table 24.4. The out parameter is the job number of the job you have submitted. This job number is also visible in the DBA_JOBS view.

TABLE 24.4
Parameters for the DBMS_JOB.SUBMIT Procedure

PARAMETER NAME	MODE	DESCRIPTION
JOB	OUT	The unique number that identifies the job in the job queue.
WHAT	IN	The PL/SQL procedure and parameters that execute as part of this job.
NEXT_DATE	IN	The next execution date for the job.
INTERVAL	IN	The calculation to compute the next date of the job. This can make use of SYSDATE and any date function.
NO_PARSE	IN	A Boolean indicator as to whether to run the job at job submission. The default is FALSE.

The following example submits the LOG_USER_COUNT procedure (created with ch24_1a.sql) to run every six hours:

FOR EXAMPLE

```
DECLARE
   V_JOB_NO NUMBER;
 BEGIN
   DBMS_JOB.SUBMIT( JOB       => v_job_no,
                    WHAT      => 'LOG_USER_COUNT
                                 (''C:\WORKING\'', ''USER.LOG'');',
                    NEXT_DATE => SYSDATE,
                    INTERVAL  => 'SYSDATE + 1/4 ');
   Commit;
   DBMS_OUTPUT.PUT_LINE(v_job_no);
 END;
```

To see the job in the queue, query the DBA_JOBS view. For STUDENT to be able to perform this query, the DBA needs to perform the following grant:

```
     GRANT SELECT on DBA_JOBS to STUDENT;
```

FOR EXAMPLE

```
SELECT JOB, NEXT_DATE, NEXT_SEC, BROKEN, WHAT
FROM    DBA_JOBS;


JOB   NEXT_DATE NEXT_SEC B WHAT
---- --------- -------- - ----------------------------------------
   1 05-JUL-03 16:56:30 N LOG_USER_COUNT('D:\WORKING', 'USER.LOG');
```

To force job number 1 to run or change, use the RUN or CHANGE procedure. To remove job number 1 from the job queue, use the REMOVE procedure:

FOR EXAMPLE

```
-- execute job number 1
exec dbms_job.run(1);

-- remove job number 1 from the job queue
exec dbms_job.remove(1);

-- change job #1 to run immediately and then every hour of
-- the day
exec DBMS_JOB.CHANGE(1, null, SYSDATE, 'SYSDATE + 1/24 ');
```

After the job fails, it is marked as broken in the job queue. Broken jobs do not run. You can also force a job to be flagged as broken. You may want to do this if you have entered all the parameters correctly but you don't want the job to run its normal cycle while you work on altering one of its dependencies. You can then comment the job again by forcing the broken flag off:

FOR EXAMPLE

```
-- set job 1 to be broken
exec dbms_job.BROKEN(1, TRUE);

-- set job 1 not to be broken
exec dbms_job.BROKEN(1, FALSE);
```

When jobs are running, you see their activity in the view DBA_JOBS_RUNNING. After the run has completed, it no longer is visible in this view.

Complete the following exercises:

A) Create a procedure DELETE_ENROLL that deletes a student's enrollment if there are no grades in the GRADE table for that student and the start date of the section is already one month past.

ANSWER:

```
CREATE or REPLACE procedure DELETE_ENROLL
AS
   CURSOR C_NO_GRADES is

  SELECT st.student_id, se.section_id
   FROM   student st,
          enrollment e,
          section se
  WHERE   st.student_id = e.student_id
  AND     e.section_id  = se.section_id
  AND     se.start_date_time < ADD_MONTHS(SYSDATE, -1)
  AND     NOT EXISTS (SELECT g.student_id, g.section_id
                       FROM   grade g
                       WHERE  g.student_id = st.student_id
                        AND   g.section_id = se.section_id);

   BEGIN
      FOR R in C_NO_GRADES LOOP
         DELETE  enrollment
         WHERE   section_id = r.section_id
         AND     student_id = r.student_id;
      END LOOP;
      COMMIT;
   EXCEPTION
      WHEN OTHERS THEN
         DBMS_OUTPUT.PUT_LINE(SQLERRM);
   END;
```

B) Submit the procedure DELETE_ENROLL to the job queue to execute once a month.

ANSWER:

```
SQL> VARIABLE V_JOB NUMBER
SQL>  EXEC DBMS_JOB.SUBMIT(:v_job, 'DELETE_ENROLL;',SYSDATE,
'ADD_MONTHS(SYSDATE, 1)');

PL/SQL procedure successfully completed
SQL> commit;

Commit complete.

SQL> print v_job

     V_JOB
----------
         2
```

LAB 24.2
Making Use of Oracle-Supplied Packages to Generate an Explain Plan and Create HTML Pages

LAB OBJECTIVE

After completing this lab, you will be able to

▶ Generate an explain plan with DBMS_XPLAN

EXPLAIN PLAN WITH DBMS_XPLAN

The DBMS_XPLAN package became available in Oracle version 9.2. This package helps display the execution plan of a SQL statement that is displayed as the output of the explain plan command. This package displays the output in an easier manner than was possible in prior versions of Oracle. The SQL execution plan and runtime statistics are stored in V$SQL_PLAN. V$SQL and PLAN_STATISTICS are displayed with the DBMS_XPLAN package. The SQL command for creating an explain plan takes this information and populates the PLAN_TABLE. You must know a great deal about query optimization to make use of an explain plan.

BY THE WAY

For details on SQL optimization and how to use the results in an explain plan, see *Oracle SQL by Example*, Third Edition, by Alice Rischert (Prentice Hall PTR, 2004).

The DBMS_XPLAN depends on a table called the PLAN_TABLE. This table holds the results of running an explain plan on a SELECT statement. The DDL to create the PLAN_TABLE is as follows:

```
-- ch24_2a.sql
create table PLAN_TABLE (
        statement_id        varchar2(30),
        plan_id             number,
        timestamp           date,
        remarks             varchar2(4000),
        operation           varchar2(30),
        options             varchar2(255),
        object_node         varchar2(128),
```

```
        object_owner         varchar2(30),
        object_name          varchar2(30),
        object_alias         varchar2(65),
        object_instance      numeric,
        object_type          varchar2(30),
        optimizer            varchar2(255),
        search_columns       number,
        id                   numeric,
        parent_id            numeric,
        depth                numeric,
        position             numeric,
        cost                 numeric,
        cardinality          numeric,
        bytes                numeric,
        other_tag            varchar2(255),
        partition_start      varchar2(255),
        partition_stop       varchar2(255),
        partition_id         numeric,
        other                long,
        distribution         varchar2(30),
        cpu_cost             numeric,
        io_cost              numeric,
        temp_space           numeric,
        access_predicates    varchar2(4000),
        filter_predicates    varchar2(4000),
        projection           varchar2(4000),
        time                 numeric,
        qblock_name          varchar2(30),
        other_xml            clob
    );
```

BY THE WAY

The RDBMS/ADMIN/ subdirectory under your Oracle Home directory always contains the most up-to-date DDL script to create the PLAN_TABLE. You can connect as the SYS DBA to create this table so that it is available to all users. The following statements can be used to create the PLAN_TABLE under the SYS schema and create a public schema and all users to make use of the PLAN_TABLE.

```
SQL> CONN sys/password AS SYSDBA
Connected
SQL> @$ORACLE_HOME/rdbms/admin/utlxplan.sql
SQL> GRANT ALL ON sys.plan_table TO public;
SQL> CREATE PUBLIC SYNONYM plan_table FOR sys.plan_table;
```

By default, if several plans in the plan table match the $statement\_id$ parameter passed to the display table function (the default value is NULL), only the plan corresponding to the last EXPLAIN PLAN command is displayed. Hence, there is no need to purge the plan table after each EXPLAIN PLAN. However, you should purge the plan table regularly (for example, by using the TRUNCATE TABLE command) to ensure good performance in the execution of the DISPLAY table function.

Prior versions of Oracle had a number of options. For example, you could use the SQL*Plus command SET AUTOTRACE TRACE EXPLAIN to generate an immediate explain plan.

FOR EXAMPLE

```
SQL> SET AUTOTRACE TRACE EXPLAIN

  1   SELECT s.course_no,
  2              c.description,
  3              i.first_name,
  4              i.last_name,
  5              s.section_no,
  6              TO_CHAR(s.start_date_time, 'Mon-DD-YYYY HH:MIAM'),
  7              s.location
  8       FROM section s,
  9            course c,
 10            instructor i
 11       WHERE s.course_no    = c.course_no
 12*       AND   s.instructor_id= i.instructor_id

Execution Plan
----------------------------------------------------------
  0        SELECT STATEMENT Optimizer=CHOOSE (Cost=9 Card=78
                                              Bytes=4368)
  1    0    HASH JOIN (Cost=9 Card=78 Bytes=4368)
  2    1     HASH JOIN (Cost=6 Card=78 Bytes=2574)
  3    2       TABLE ACCESS (FULL) OF 'INSTRUCTOR' (Cost=3 Card=10
                                                    Bytes=140)
  4    2       TABLE ACCESS (FULL) OF 'SECTION' (Cost=3 Card=78
                                                 Bytes=1482)
  5    1     TABLE ACCESS (FULL) OF 'COURSE' (Cost=3 Card=30
                                              Bytes=690)
```

You can also generate an explain plan that would be stored in the PLAN_TABLE and then query the results of an explain plan:

FOR EXAMPLE

```
SQL> explain plan for
  2   SELECT s.course_no,
  3              c.description,
  4              i.first_name,
  5              i.last_name,
  6              s.section_no,
  7              TO_CHAR(s.start_date_time,'Mon-DD-YYYY HH:MIAM'),
  8              s.location
  9       FROM section s,
 10            course c,
 11            instructor i
```

```
12      WHERE s.course_no    = c.course_no
13      AND   s.instructor_id= i.instructor_id;

Explained.

-- ch24_2b.sql
select rtrim ( lpad  ( ' ', 2*level )  ||
               rtrim ( operation )     || ' ' ||
               rtrim ( options )       || ' ' ||
               object_name             || ' ' ||
               partition_start         || ' ' ||
               partition_stop          || ' ' ||
               to_char ( partition_id )
             ) the_query_plan
   from plan_table
   connect by prior id = parent_id
   start with id = 0;


THE_QUERY_PLAN
----------------------------------------
  SELECT STATEMENT
    HASH JOIN
      HASH JOIN
       TABLE ACCESS BY INDEX ROWID SECTION
         INDEX FULL SCAN SECT_INST_FK_I
        SORT JOIN
          TABLE ACCESS FULL INSTRUCTOR
       TABLE ACCESS FULL COURSE
```

To make use of the DBMS_XPLAN procedure, use the SELECT * FROM TABLE(DBMS_XPLAN. DISPLAY) command to generate the explain plan:

FOR EXAMPLE

```
SQL> explain plan for
  2   SELECT s.course_no,
  3            c.description,
  4            i.first_name,
  5            i.last_name,
  6            s.section_no,
  7            TO_CHAR(s.start_date_time,'Mon-DD-YYYY HH:MIAM'),
  8            s.location
  9     FROM section s,
 10          course c,
 11          instructor i
 12     WHERE s.course_no    = c.course_no
 13     AND   s.instructor_id= i.instructor_id;
```

```
Explained.
SQL> SELECT * FROM TABLE(DBMS_XPLAN.DISPLAY);

PLAN_TABLE_OUTPUT
-----------------------------------------------------------------------------

-----------------------------------------------------------------------------
| Id  | Operation             | Name        | Rows | Bytes | Cost (%CPU)| Time     |
-----------------------------------------------------------------------------
|   0 | SELECT STATEMENT      |             |   78 |  4368 |    9  (34)| *00:00:01 |
|*  1 |  HASH JOIN            |             |   78 |  4368 |    9  (34)|  00:00:01 |
|*  2 |   HASH JOIN           |             |   78 |  2574 |    6  (34)|  00:00:01 |
|   3 |    TABLE ACCESS FULL| INSTRUCTOR  |   10 |   140 |    3  (34)|  00:00:01 |
|   4 |    TABLE ACCESS FULL| SECTION     |   78 |  1482 |    3  (34)|  00:00:01 |
|   5 |   TABLE ACCESS FULL  | COURSE      |   30 |   690 |    3  (34)|  00:00:01 |
-----------------------------------------------------------------------------

Predicate Information (identified by operation id):
------------------------------------------------

   1 - access("S"."COURSE_NO"="C"."COURSE_NO")
   2 - access("S"."INSTRUCTOR_ID"="I"."INSTRUCTOR_ID")

17 rows selected.
```

▼ LAB 24.2 EXERCISES

This section provides exercises and suggested answers, with discussion related to how those answers resulted. The most important thing to realize is whether your answer works. You should figure out the implications of the answers and what the effects are of any different answers you may come up with.

24.2.1 Generate an Explain Plan with DBMS_XPLAN

Complete the following tasks:

A) Find out if your schema has a table named PLAN_TABLE that matches the DDL in the plan table script ch24_2a.sql. If it does not, use the ch24_2a.sq script to create the PLAN_TABLE.

ANSWER: Describe PLAN_TABLE. If this does not match the values in ch24_2a.sql, run the script.

B) Compute statistics on all tables in your schema using a single SQL statement to generate the command.

ANSWER:

```
SQL> Spool compute.sql
SQL> set pagesize 500
SQL> select 'Analyze table '||table_name||' compute statistics;'
     from user_tables;
```

```
SQL> Spool off
SQL> @compute.sql
```

C) The following SQL statement generates a list of the open sections in courses that the student with an ID of 214 is not enrolled in. Many different SQL statements would produce the same result. Because various inline views are required, it is important to examine the execution plan to determine which plan will produce the result with the least cost to the database. Run the SQL as follows to generate a SQL plan:

```
-- ch24_3a.sql
EXPLAIN PLAN FOR
  SELECT c.course_no      course_no,
         c.description    description,
         b.section_no     section_no,
         s.section_id     section_id,
         i.first_name     first_name,
         i.last_name      last_name
  FROM   course      c,
         instructor i,
         section      s,
        (SELECT
               a.course_no        course_no,
               MIN(a.section_no)  section_no
         FROM (SELECT   count(*)        enrolled,
                        se.CAPACITY     capacity,
                        se.course_no    course_no,
                        se.section_no   section_no,
                        e.section_id    section_id
                FROM section se,
                     enrollment e
                WHERE se.section_id = e.section_id
                  AND e.student_id <> 214
                GROUP BY
                        se.CAPACITY,
                        se.course_no,
                        e.section_id,
                        se.section_no
                HAVING count(*) < se.CAPACITY) a
        GROUP BY
                a.course_no) b
  WHERE c.course_no      = b.course_no
  AND   b.course_no      = s.course_no
  AND   s.section_no     = b.section_no
  AND   s.instructor_id = i.instructor_id;
```

ANSWER: When executed properly, the SQL*Plus session just displays the word `Explained`. If you have another error, the PLAN_TABLE most likely is incorrect.

D) Use the DBMS_XPLAN package to see the execution plan of the SQL statement.

ANSWER:

```
PLAN_TABLE_OUTPUT
--------------------------------------------------------------------------------


--------------------------------------------------------------------------------
| Id  | Operation                  | Name        | Rows  | Bytes | Cost (%CPU)| Time     |
--------------------------------------------------------------------------------
|   0 | SELECT STATEMENT           |             |    12 |   888 |   15  (40)| 00:00:01 |
|*  1 |  HASH JOIN                 |             |    12 |   888 |   15  (40)| 00:00:01 |
|*  2 |   HASH JOIN                |             |    12 |   612 |   12  (42)| 00:00:01 |
|*  3 |    HASH JOIN               |             |    78 |  1950 |    6  (34)| 00:00:01 |
|   4 |     TABLE ACCESS FULL      | INSTRUCTOR  |    10 |   140 |    3  (34)| 00:00:01 |
|   5 |     TABLE ACCESS FULL      | SECTION     |    78 |   858 |    3  (34)| 00:00:01 |
|   6 |    VIEW                    |             |    12 |   312 |    6 (100)| 00:00:01 |
|   7 |     SORT GROUP BY          |             |    12 |   192 |    6  (50)| 00:00:01 |
|   8 |      VIEW                  |             |    12 |   192 |    6 (100)| 00:00:01 |
|*  9 |       FILTER               |             |       |       |           |          |
|  10 |        SORT GROUP BY       |             |    12 |   192 |    6  (50)| 00:00:01 |
|* 11 |         HASH JOIN          |             |   225 |  3600 |    5  (40)| 00:00:01 |
|  12 |          TABLE ACCESS FULL | SECTION     |    78 |   780 |    3  (34)| 00:00:01 |
|* 13 |          INDEX FULL SCAN   | ENR_PK      |   225 |  1350 |    2  (50)| 00:00:01 |
|  14 |   TABLE ACCESS FULL        | COURSE      |    30 |   690 |    3  (34)| 00:00:01 |
--------------------------------------------------------------------------------


   Predicate Information (identified by operation id):
   ---------------------------------------------------

      1 - access("C"."COURSE_NO"="B"."COURSE_NO")
      2 - access("B"."COURSE_NO"="S"."COURSE_NO" AND
                 "S"."SECTION_NO"="B"."SECTION_NO")
      3 - access("S"."INSTRUCTOR_ID"="I"."INSTRUCTOR_ID")
      9 - filter("SE"."CAPACITY">COUNT(*))
     11 - access("SE"."SECTION_ID"="E"."SECTION_ID")
     13 - filter("E"."STUDENT_ID"<>214)


  31 rows selected.
```

E) Generate an alternative SQL that produces the same results, and then examine the explain plan.

ANSWER:

```
  1  EXPLAIN PLAN FOR
  2  SELECT s.course_no, description, s.section_no,
            s.section_id, i.first_name, i.last_name
  3       FROM section s, course c, instructor i
  4          WHERE c.course_no = s.course_no
  5          AND s.instructor_id = i.instructor_id
  6          AND section_id IN
  7           (SELECT MIN(section_id)
  8              FROM section s
  9             WHERE section_id IN
```

```
10                    (SELECT section_id
11                        from enrollment e
12                    GROUP BY section_id
13                    HAVING COUNT(*) <
14                    (SELECT capacity
15                        FROM section
16                        WHERE e.section_id = section_id))
17                    GROUP BY course_no)
18            AND s.course_no NOT IN
19                (SELECT s.course_no
20                    FROM section s, enrollment e
21                    WHERE s.section_id = e.section_id
22                    AND student_id = 214)
23*      ORDER BY s.course_no


Explained.


SQL> select * from table(dbms_xplan.display);


PLAN_TABLE_OUTPUT
-----------------------------------------------------------------------------------------------------
```

Id	Operation	Name	Rows	Bytes	Cost (%CPU)	Time
0	SELECT STATEMENT		1	61	15 (40)	00:00:01
1	SORT ORDER BY		1	61	12 (42)	00:00:01
* 2	FILTER					
3	NESTED LOOPS		1	61	11 (37)	00:00:01
4	NESTED LOOPS		1	38	10 (40)	00:00:01
* 5	HASH JOIN SEMI		1	24	9 (45)	00:00:01
6	TABLE ACCESS FULL	SECTION	4	44	3 (34)	00:00:01
7	VIEW	VW_NSO_2	4	52	6 (100)	00:00:01
8	SORT GROUP BY		4	36	6 (50)	00:00:01
* 9	HASH JOIN		4	36	5 (40)	00:00:01
10	VIEW	VW_NSO_1	4	12	2 (100)	00:00:01
* 11	FILTER					
12	SORT GROUP BY		4	12	2 (50)	00:00:01
13	INDEX FULL SCAN	ENR_SECT_FK_I	226	678	2 (50)	00:00:01
14	TABLE ACCESS BY INDEX ROWID	SECTION	1	5	2 (50)	00:00:01
* 15	INDEX UNIQUE SCAN	SECT_PK	1		1 (100)	00:00:01
16	TABLE ACCESS FULL	SECTION	78	468	3 (34)	00:00:01
17	TABLE ACCESS BY INDEX ROWID	INSTRUCTOR	10	140	2 (50)	00:00:01
* 18	INDEX UNIQUE SCAN	INST_PK	1		1 (100)	00:00:01
19	TABLE ACCESS BY INDEX ROWID	COURSE	30	690	2 (50)	00:00:01
* 20	INDEX UNIQUE SCAN	CRSE_PK	1		1 (100)	00:00:01
21	NESTED LOOPS		1	12	3 (34)	00:00:01
* 22	INDEX RANGE SCAN	ENR_PK	1	6	2 (50)	00:00:01
* 23	TABLE ACCESS BY INDEX ROWID	SECTION	1	6	2 (50)	00:00:01
* 24	INDEX UNIQUE SCAN	SECT_PK	1		1 (100)	00:00:01

```
-----------------------------------------------------------------------------------------------------
```

```
Predicate Information (identified by operation id):
---------------------------------------------------

   2 - filter( NOT EXISTS (SELECT /*+ */ 0 FROM "ENROLLMENT" "E","SECTION" "S" WHERE
               "S"."SECTION_ID"="E"."SECTION_ID" AND LNNVL("S"."COURSE_NO"<>:B1) AND "STUDENT_ID"=214))
   5 - access("SECTION_ID"="$nso_col_1")
   9 - access("SECTION_ID"="$nso_col_1")
  11 - filter(COUNT(*)< (SELECT "CAPACITY" FROM "SECTION" "SECTION" WHERE "SECTION_ID"=:B1))
  15 - access("SECTION_ID"=:B1)
  18 - access("S"."INSTRUCTOR_ID"="I"."INSTRUCTOR_ID")
  20 - access("C"."COURSE_NO"="S"."COURSE_NO")
  22 - access("STUDENT_ID"=214)
  23 - filter(LNNVL("S"."COURSE_NO"<>:B1))
  24 - access("S"."SECTION_ID"="E"."SECTION_ID")


45 rows selected.


- another alternative SQL would be

   1  EXPLAIN PLAN FOR
   2  SELECT * FROM
   3    (
   4        SELECT s.course_no course,
   5               description,
   6        e.section_id sec_id,
   7        section_no,
   8        i.first_name || ' ' || i.last_name i_full_name,
   9        Rank() over (PARTITION BY s.course_no
  10               order by count(e.student_id) ASC,
  11        min(section_no) ASC) as RANK_WITHIN_SEC
  12         FROM section s, enrollment e, course c, instructor i
  13      WHERE s.section_id = e.section_id and
  14            s.instructor_id = i.instructor_id and
  15            c.course_no = s.course_no and
  16           s.course_no not in (SELECT ss.course_no
  17                              FROM section ss, enrollment ee
  18              WHERE ss.section_id = ee.section_id and
  19                      ee.student_id = 214)
  20      GROUP BY s.course_no,
  21             description,
  22        e.section_id,
  23        section_no,
  24        i.first_name || ' ' || i.last_name
  25    )
  26*   WHERE RANK_WITHIN_SEC = 1


Explained.


SQL> select * from table(dbms_xplan.display);
```

```
PLAN_TABLE_OUTPUT
---------------------------------------------------------------------------------------


---------------------------------------------------------------------------------------
| Id  | Operation                       | Name          | Rows | Bytes | Cost (%CPU)| Time     |
---------------------------------------------------------------------------------------
|   0 | SELECT STATEMENT                |               |   14 |  1484 |  32  (38)| 00:00:01 |
|*  1 |  VIEW                           |               |   14 |  1484 |  32 (100)| 00:00:01 |
|*  2 |   WINDOW SORT PUSHED RANK       |               |   14 |   714 |  11  (46)| 00:00:01 |
|   3 |    SORT GROUP BY                |               |   14 |   714 |  11  (46)| 00:00:01 |
|*  4 |     FILTER                      |               |      |       |          |          |
|*  5 |      HASH JOIN                  |               |   14 |   714 |   9  (34)| 00:00:01 |
|   6 |       NESTED LOOPS              |               |   14 |   392 |   6  (34)| 00:00:01 |
|*  7 |        HASH JOIN                |               |    4 |   100 |   6  (34)| 00:00:01 |
|   8 |         TABLE ACCESS FULL       | SECTION       |    4 |    44 |   3  (34)| 00:00:01 |
|   9 |         TABLE ACCESS FULL       | INSTRUCTOR    |   10 |   140 |   3  (34)| 00:00:01 |
|* 10 |        INDEX RANGE SCAN         | ENR_SECT_FK_I |  226 |   678 |   1 (100)| 00:00:01 |
|  11 |       TABLE ACCESS FULL         | COURSE        |   30 |   690 |   3  (34)| 00:00:01 |
|  12 |      NESTED LOOPS               |               |    1 |    12 |   3  (34)| 00:00:01 |
|* 13 |       INDEX RANGE SCAN          | ENR_PK        |    1 |     6 |   2  (50)| 00:00:01 |
|* 14 |       TABLE ACCESS BY INDEX ROWID| SECTION      |    1 |     6 |   2  (50)| 00:00:01 |
|* 15 |        INDEX UNIQUE SCAN        | SECT_PK       |    1 |       |   1 (100)| 00:00:01 |
---------------------------------------------------------------------------------------


Predicate Information (identified by operation id):
---------------------------------------------------

   1 - filter("RANK_WITHIN_SEC"=1)
   2 - filter(RANK() OVER ( PARTITION BY "S"."COURSE_NO" ORDER BY
           COUNT(*),MIN("SECTION_NO"))<=1)
   4 - filter( NOT EXISTS (SELECT /*+ */ 0 FROM "ENROLLMENT" "EE","SECTION" "SS" WHERE
           "SS"."SECTION_ID"="EE"."SECTION_ID" AND LNNVL("SS"."COURSE_NO"<>:B1) AND
           "EE"."STUDENT_ID"=214))
   5 - access("C"."COURSE_NO"="S"."COURSE_NO")
   7 - access("S"."INSTRUCTOR_ID"="I"."INSTRUCTOR_ID")
  10 - access("S"."SECTION_ID"="E"."SECTION_ID")
  13 - access("EE"."STUDENT_ID"=214)
  14 - filter(LNNVL("SS"."COURSE_NO"<>:B1))
  15 - access("SS"."SECTION_ID"="EE"."SECTION_ID")


37 rows selected.
```

In some cases, the explain plan is not what you expect to see. This may be because the SQL was adjusted by having a QUERY RE-WRITE setting turned on. The resulting explain plan is for the SQL that the database rewrote, which is why table alias names may be unfamiliar. Also note that if you have unnamed views inside the SQL, they are given system names, and that is what is referred to in the explain plan.

LAB 24.3
Creating Web Pages with the Oracle Web Toolkit

LAB OBJECTIVE

After completing this lab, you will be able to

▶ Create an HTML page with the Oracle Web Toolkit

Oracle Application Server 11g integrates many technologies required to build and deliver an e-business Web site. Oracle Application Server 11g generates dynamic Web content from PL/SQL procedures and delivers it to a client's Web browser. Oracle Application Server 11g provides the middleware component of the Oracle Internet Platform and delivers and manages applications and data requested by client browsers. The two other components of the Oracle Internet Platform are the Oracle Database 11g and the Oracle Internet Developer Suite.

In June 2000, Oracle released a revamped version of its Application Server called Oracle 9i Application Server. The earlier version had fewer features and was called the Oracle (Web) Application Server (OAS). The OAS was first released in 1995. The last production version of the OAS was released as version 4.0.8.2 in 1999. Oracle stopped supporting the OAS in October 2002 because the new Oracle 9i Application Server had become the standard. The basic functionality of the OAS and the current version of the Oracle Application Server 10g are similar, but the back-end architecture and configuration are considerably different. Oracle Application Server 10g can support a much larger array of technologies and languages. You can generate Web pages using the PL/SQL Web Toolkit with the OAS, but you cannot use PL/SQL Server Pages (PSP).

BY THE WAY

At the time this book was published, Oracle had not yet released Oracle Application Server 11g. Refer to the documentation on Oracle.com when the new version is released for any additional features new to Oracle Application Server 11g.

In Oracle's multitier architecture, Oracle Application Server 10g is the middleware. It incorporates both a Web server and an application server. Oracle Application Server 10g resides between the client and the back-end database, moving application logic from the client. It is the central, middle tier in shared enterprise applications, providing such services as security, message brokering, database connectivity, transaction management, and process isolation.

Oracle Application Server 10g enables users to deploy applications on the Web. Web browsers are "thin" clients that do not need any additional software installation because they are accessing the middle tier through HTTP. The only thing the user needs is a URL to launch the application. A server tier houses the original database so that transaction processing can be optimized on the database. This multitiered model offers great savings in administration and maintenance costs when deploying applications.

The HTTP entry point to Oracle Application Server 10g is the Oracle HTTP Server powered by the Apache Web server. Oracle Application Server 10g functions as both a simple Web server and an application server. The function of a Web server is to translate a URL into a filename on the server and to send that file back to the client's Web browser over the Internet or an intranet. The function of an application server is to run a program or component and to generate dynamic content. This dynamic content results in an HTML file being sent back to the client's browser. The output is the result of running a program or script.

The Oracle HTTP Server functions as an HTTP listener and request dispatcher. Based on the Apache Server, the Oracle HTTP Server is mostly C code that runs on top of the operating system. The Oracle HTTP Server receives HTTP requests from clients and can serve static files from the file system. It routes requests that are not static to other services through modules (such as `mod_plsql`). These modules, often simply called *mods*, are plug-ins to the HTTP Server. A plug-in is a program that extends the functionality of another program, and could be considered a subprogram. The mods are plug-ins that offer native services (such as `mod_ssl`, which handles a Secure Socket Layer). Or they serve as a dispatcher for requests requiring external processes (such as `mod_jserv`, which dispatches requests to the Apache JServ). In addition to the compiled Apache mods provided with Oracle HTTP Server, Oracle has enhanced several of the standard mods and has added Oracle-specific mods such as `mod_plsql`.

The server determines which module to hand the request to based on the URL. The first section of the URL is the name of the server, and the next section is the name of the module. For example, a request for `mod_plsql` has a URL that begins with http://*ServerName*/pls/... . The pls portion indicates to the Oracle HTTP Server that this is a request for the module `mod_plsql`.

The Oracle Application Server 10g Communication Services are responsible for handling requests from the different clients. The Oracle HTTP Server may directly process a portion of the client requests. Other requests may be routed to other components of the Oracle Application Server 10g for processing. Oracle Application Server 10g can be used to support wireless technologies as well, although this book focuses on the HTTP services of Oracle Application Server 10g.

Oracle Application Server 10g provides several features and capabilities that are commonly supplied by separate products. An example of a recent impressive addition to the array of components is Oracle Application Server 10g Unified Messaging. It gives you access to e-mail, voice mail, and faxes from any device, including computers, telephones, personal digital assistants, and pagers. Oracle Application Server 10g is under constant development, so you will see many services being added and modified in the coming years.

THE CLIENT TIER

Clients access PL/SQL Web Applications through a browser using the Web protocol HTTP. Oracle Application Server 10g application components generate HTML, which is returned to the browser and displayed as Web pages. Because Web browsers behave in a similar manner across platforms, and they all read HTML and JavaScript, it does not matter what type of operating system a client's Web browser is operating on.

THE DATABASE TIER

PL/SQL Web Applications are developed as PL/SQL packages and procedures and are stored in an Oracle database. You can access database tables through these packages and present the data as dynamic information in your generated Web pages. First introduced with the Oracle Application Server available with Oracle 8i, Oracle Application Server 10g provides a collection of PL/SQL packages called the PL/SQL Web Toolkit. These packages are also stored in the database and are used in Web-based application packages to generate Web page components and other related functionality.

THE APPLICATION SERVER TIER: THE PL/SQL GATEWAY

The PL/SQL Gateway enables you to call PL/SQL programs from a Web browser. The PL/SQL programs run on the server and return HTML to the browser. Application Server 10g acts as the intermediary between the database and the browser.

ORACLE HTTP SERVER MODULES (MODS)

The compiled Apache modules (called *mods* in this chapter) provided with Oracle HTTP Server support current Internet application technologies to deliver dynamic Web pages. In addition, Oracle has enhanced several of the standard Apache mods and has added Oracle-specific mods. For more information, refer to http://www.apache.org/docs/mod/index.html. The mod that makes use of the Oracle Web Toolkit is `mod_plsql`. This module is an HTTP Server plug-in that dispatches requests for PL/SQL and Java stored procedures to an Oracle database. `mod_plsql` is the most efficient SQL interface for generating HTML. The HTTP Server identifies the request as belonging to this module. Based on the URL from the client, HTTP requests that are identified are handed from the HTTP Server to `mod_plsql`. These requests are then mapped to database stored procedures. The module maintains database connections specified by database access descriptors (DADs).

BY THE WAY

For information on how to configure Oracle Application Server, instruction in HTML and JavaScript, and detailed instructions on how to use the Oracle Web Toolkit (with hundreds of pages of examples), see *Oracle Web Application Programming for PL/SQL Developers* by Susan Boardman, Melanie Caffrey, Solomon Morse, and Benjamin Rosenzweig (Prentice Hall PTR, 2002).

GENERATE HTML FROM THE WEB TOOLKIT WITHOUT ORACLE APPLICATION SERVER 10G

The Oracle Web Toolkit Packages are intended to generate HTML pages over the Internet or an intranet with Oracle Application Server 10g acting as the Web server. In testing mode you can generate the HTML as text files using SQL*Plus. For the purposes of this book, the exercises are done in testing mode. This way, you do not have to address all the setup issues involved with Oracle Application Server 10g, and you can still learn how to make use of this Oracle-supplied package.

WEB TOOLKIT PACKAGES

Table 24.5 briefly describes all the Web Toolkit packages.

TABLE 24.5
Web Toolkit Packages

PACKAGE NAME	DESCRIPTION
HTP	Generates HTML through procedures.
HTF	Generates HTML through functions.
OWA_CACHE	Caches Web pages for improved performance using the PL/SQL Gateway cache.
OWA_COOKIE	Sends and retrieves cookies.
OWA_IMAGE	Creates an image map.
OWA_OPT_LOCK	Handles optimistic locking of data.
OWA_PATTERN	Searches for and replaces values in text strings; pattern matching.
OWA_SEC	Security subprograms.
OWA_TEXT	Other types of string manipulation.
OWA_UTIL	Retrieves environment variables. Redirects users to another site. Other utilities such as printing query results directly in a table.

OVERVIEW OF HTP PROCEDURES

The HTP package is the principal package used to generate HTML. The P or PRN procedure generates HTML in much the same manner as the DBMS_OUTPUT.PUT_LINE procedure takes its IN parameter and generates a display in SQL*Plus. All text in the IN parameter of HTP.P transforms into HTML. Many other procedures generate more complex HTML structures.

Table 24.6 lists some of the commonly used HTP procedures and output. For a comprehensive list of HTP procedures, check Oracle's online documentation.

TABLE 24.6
HTP Procedures

HTP PROCEDURE	OUTPUT
htp.p('<P> text goes here </P>');	<P> text goes here </P>
htp.htmlOpen;	<HTML>
htp.headOpen;	<HEAD>
htp.title('My Title');	<TITLE> My Title<TITLE>
htp.headClose;	</HEAD>
htp.bodyOpen;	<BODY>
htp.header(1, 'My Heading');	<H1> My Heading</H1>
htp.anchor('url', 'Anchor Name', 'Click Here');	<A HREF="url" NAME="Anchor Name"> Click Here</A>
htp.line;	<HR>
htp.bold;	<B></B>
htp.paragraph;	<P>
htp.tableOpen;	<TABLE>
htp.tableCaption;	<CAPTION></CAPTION>
htp.tableRowOpen;	<TR>
htp.tableHeader('Emp ID');	<TH>Emp ID</TH>
htp.tableData('data');	<TD>data</TD>
htp.tableRowClose;	</TR>
htp.tableClose;	</TABLE>
htp.bodyClose;	</BODY>
htp.htmlClose;	</HTML>
htp.script('alert("This is an alert!");','JavaScript');	<SCRIPT LANGUAGE="JavaScript"> alert("This is an alert!"); </SCRIPT>

You can generate a simple Web page by using the procedure in the HTP package:

FOR EXAMPLE

```
CREATE OR REPLACE PROCEDURE my_first_page
  AS
BEGIN
   htp.htmlOpen;
   htp.headOpen;
   htp.title('My First Page');
```

```
    htp.headClose;
    htp.bodyOpen;
    htp.p('Hello world.<BR>');
    htp.bodyClose;
    htp.htmlClose;
EXCEPTION
    WHEN OTHERS THEN
    htp.p('An error occurred on this page.
            Please try again later.');
END;
```

This code generates the following HTML:

```
    <HTML>
    <HEAD>
    <TITLE>My First Page</TITLE>
    </HEAD>
    <BODY>
    Hello world.<BR>
    </BODY>
    </HTML>
```

In testing, the procedure can be executed from the development tool provided with Oracle 11g, called Oracle SQL Developer. This is installed with your Oracle Server. You can find it on the Start menu under *Oracle Home*\Application Development\Oracle SQL Developer. When you start the application, you must connect to the Oracle Database much as you do with SQL*Plus. To work here, you must run your SQL from a SQL file. First you create a new SQL file and associate it with a database connection to your student database. Oracle SQL Developer has three panes, as shown in Figure 24.1. The left side is an object explorer, the top panel on the right is for the code you will execute, and the bottom panel is for seeing the results. To see the results for a PL/SQL Web toolkit procedure, look at the OWA Output tab. Click the comment call out button to display the OWA output. Each time you run new code, you can click the eraser icon to clear it. You can also save the output and open it from Internet Explorer to see how your Web page will appear. The application is slightly different from SQL*Plus. To execute a procedure, you must enclose it in an anonymous block. Figure 24.1 shows that the procedure `my_first_page` was executed from the green triangle; the result appears in the OWA Output tab.

Some procedures such as HTP.HEADER take more than one parameter to generate varieties of similar HTML codes (multiple levels of headers). Other procedures such as HTP.TABLEDATA enclose the IN parameter in all the HTML codes required for a table row in HTML. The next example shows the HTML page that needs to be generated from the database (a list of instructor names). The example after that shows the PL/SQL code that is used to generate the Web page.

FIGURE 24.1
Oracle SQL Developer, with OWA output

FOR EXAMPLE

```
<HTML>
<HEAD>
<TITLE>Instructor List</TITLE>
</HEAD>
<BODY>
<H1>List of Instructors</H1>
The time is          11:36
<TABLE  BORDER=1
BORDERCOLOR="teal" CELLPADDING=5>
<TR>
<TH>First Name</TH>
<TH>Last Name</TH>
</TR>
<TR>
<TD>Rick</TD>
<TD>Chow</TD>
```

```
</TR>
<TR>
<TD>Marilyn</TD>
<TD>Frantzen</TD>
</TR>
<TR>
<TD>Fernand</TD>
<TD>Hanks</TD>
</TR>
<TR>
<TD>Charles</TD>
<TD>Lowry</TD>
</TR>
<TR>
<TD>Anita</TD>
<TD>Morris</TD>
</TR>
<TR>
<TD>Gary</TD>
<TD>Pertez</TD>
</TR>
<TR>
<TD>Nina</TD>
<TD>Schorin</TD>
</TR>
<TR>
<TD>Todd</TD>
<TD>Smythe</TD>
</TR>
<TR>
<TD>Irene</TD>
<TD>Willig</TD>
</TR>
<TR>
<TD>Tom</TD>
<TD>Wojick</TD>
</TR>
</TABLE>
</BODY>
</HTML>
```

FOR EXAMPLE

```
CREATE OR REPLACE PROCEDURE instructor_list IS
   v_string VARCHAR2(100);
   cursor c_instruct is
    SELECT first_name, last_name
    FROM  instructor
```

FOR EXAMPLE (continued)

```
    ORDER  by 2;
BEGIN
   htp.htmlOpen;
   htp.headOpen;
   htp.title('Instructor List');
   htp.headClose;
   HTP.bodyOpen;
   htp.header(1,'List of Instructors');
   HTP.P('The time is           '||to_char(sysdate,'HH:MI'));
   -- Open Table.
   htp.tableOpen('BORDER=1 BORDERCOLOR="teal" CELLPADDING=5');
   htp.tableRowOpen;
   htp.tableHeader('First Name');
   htp.tableHeader('Last Name');
   htp.tableRowClose;
   FOR rec in c_instruct LOOP
     htp.tableRowOpen;
        htp.tableData(rec.first_name);
        htp.tableData(rec.last_name);
     htp.tableRowClose;
   END LOOP;
   htp.tableClose;
   htp.bodyClose;
   htp.htmlClose;
EXCEPTION
   WHEN OTHERS THEN
      HTP.P('An error occurred: '||SQLERRM||'.  Please try again
         later.');
END;
```

HTP VERSUS HTF

Every HTP procedure that generates HTML tags has a corresponding HTF function with identical parameters. The function versions do not directly generate output in your Web page. Instead, they pass their output as return values to the statements that invoked them. Use these functions when you need to nest calls. To learn more about HTF functions, look up the corresponding HTP procedures in the Oracle software documentation. They respond in similar ways.

FOR EXAMPLE

```
htp.tableData (htf.formOpen('pr_update_class')||
              htf.formSubmit()||htf.formClose);
```

This example generates the following:

```
    <TD><FORM ACTION="pr_update_class" METHOD="POST">
    <INPUT TYPE="submit" VALUE="Submit"></FORM></TD>
```

WEB TOOLKIT FRAMESET PROCEDURES

Oracle provides procedures specifically for generating framesets in the HTP package.

Table 24.7 lists some of the commonly used frame-related procedures and their output. For a comprehensive list of HTP procedures, check Oracle's online documentation.

TABLE 24.7
Additional HTP Procedures for Frames and Framesets

HTP PROCEDURE	HTML OUTPUT
`htp.frame('instructors_left_nav', 'instructors_left');`	`<FRAME SRC="instructors_left_nav "NAME="instructors_left">`
`htp.frame('instructors_left_nav', 'instructors_left', '0', '0', 'AUTO', 'Y');`	`<FRAME SRC="instructors_left_nav"NAME="instructors_left"MARGINWIDTH="0"MARGINHEIGHT="0"SCROLLING="AUTO"NORESIZE>`
`htp.framesetOpen(NULL, '125,*');`	`<FRAMESET COLS="125, *">`
`htp.framesetOpen('*,65%', NULL);`	`<FRAMESET ROWS="*,65%">`
`htp.framesetOpen('*,65%');`	`<FRAMESET ROWS="*,65%">`
`htp.framesetClose;`	`</FRAMESET>`
`htp.noframesOpen;`	`<NOFRAMES>`
`htp.noframesClose;`	`</NOFRAMES>`

BY THE WAY

See Chapter 10, "Web Toolkit I: HTML and JavaScript with PL/SQL," of the book *Oracle Web Application Programming for PL/SQL Developers*. Here you will find frame-related Web Toolkit procedures and HTP procedures that can be used to rewrite the htp.frame, `instructors_frame`.

WEB TOOLKIT FORM PROCEDURES

Oracle has supplied a number of procedures for creating form elements. You can use HTP.P with HTML, as you just saw, or you can use the HTP procedures listed in Table 24.8. The resulting HTML is the same, and the performance is unaffected by which one you choose.

TABLE 24.8

Additional HTP Procedures for Forms and Form Elements

HTP PROCEDURE	OUTPUT
`htp.formOpen('show_zipcode');`	`<FORM ACTION="show_zipcode" METHOD="POST">`
`htp.formOpen('show_zipcode', 'GET','main_window',null, 'NAME="my_form"');`	`<FORM ACTION="show_zipcode" METHOD="GET" TARGET="main_window" NAME="my_form">`
`htp.formText('p_name','20');`	`<INPUT TYPE="text" NAME="p_name" SIZE="20">`
`htp.formHidden('p_id','101');`	`<INPUT TYPE="hidden" NAME="p_id"VALUE="101">`
`htp.formCheckbox('cname', 'cvalue');`	`<INPUT TYPE="checkbox" NAME="cname" VALUE="cvalue">`
`htp.formCheckbox('cname', 'cvalue', 'CHECKED');`	`<INPUT TYPE="checkbox" 'CHECKED');NAME="cname" VALUE="cvalue" CHECKED>`
`htp.formRadio('p_salutation', 'Mr.');`	`<INPUT TYPE="radio" NAME= htp.p('Mr.');`
`"p_salutation" VALUE="Mr."> Mr. 'CHECKED'); htp.p('Mrs.');`	`htp.formRadio('p_salutation','Mrs.', <INPUT TYPE="radio" NAME="p_salutation" VALUE="Mrs." CHECKED> Mrs.`
`htp.formSelectOpen('p_salary', 'Select a Salutation:','1');`	`Select a Salutation:<SELECT NAME="p_salary" SIZE="1">`
`htp.formSelectOption('Less than 5000',cattributes => 'VALUE="low"');`	`<OPTION VALUE="low">Less than 5000`
`htp.formSelectOption('5001 to 20000',cattributes => 'VALUE="medium" SELECTED');`	`<OPTION VALUE="medium" SELECTED>5001 to 20000`
`htp.FormSelectOption('Greater than 20000','VALUE="high"');`	`<OPTION VALUE="high">Greater than cattributes => 20000`
`htp.formSelectClose;`	`</SELECT>`
`htp.FormSubmit(null, 'Save', 'cattributes');`	`<INPUT TYPE="submit" VALUE="Save" cattributes>`
`htp.formReset('Reset the Form', 'cattributes');`	`<INPUT TYPE="reset" VALUE="Reset the Form" cattributes>`
`htp.FormClose;`	`</FORM>`

HTML FORMS AS CONTAINERS FOR SENDING DATA

HTML forms are containers for collecting data. The most common tag used in forms, `<INPUT>`, points to the purpose of form elements: to collect user input and send it off for processing. As described in Chapter 5, "Introduction to HTML: Basic Tags, Tables, Frames," of the book *Oracle Web Application Programming for PL/SQL Developers*, the HTML form's ACTION attribute indicates where the form data will be sent, and therefore how it will be acted upon. Without a value for the ACTION attribute, a form does nothing. Similarly, a completed paper job application accomplishes nothing sitting on your desk. You must send it to the employer, who can act upon the data collected in the form. The data collected in an HTML form needs a destination for meaningful action to take place. It is important to consider where form data should be sent, and what the consequences will be.

The values that are collected in HTML form elements must be passed to a program that can handle them. This could be a Common Gateway Interface (CGI) script, Perl script, ASP, or JSP. In the example used here, where all HTML files are being generated by PL/SQL stored procedures by means of Oracle Application Server 10g, another PL/SQL procedure is the action of the HTML form and receives the form's data. PL/SQL can read these incoming values and use them to update a database or help build the next screen the user sees.

It is important to name your HTML form elements because only named form elements are sent to the form handler procedure. If an HTML form element is not given a name, it is not sent to the form handler.

The HTML form handler procedure must have an IN parameter that corresponds to each named form element. These IN parameters must have exactly the same names as the form elements. If a form element is named p_first_name, the form handler procedure must have an IN parameter called p_first_name. The IN parameters must have datatypes that correspond to the type of data being passed in.

WEB TOOLKIT IMAGE PROCEDURES

The Oracle Web Toolkit has a number of procedures to handle HTML image tags. Images that have clickable areas with hyperlinks are handled with HTML image maps. The Oracle Web Toolkit has procedures to handle both server-side HTML image maps and client-side HTML image maps.

BY THE WAY

For information on how to handle HTML images (with extensive examples and exercises), see Chapter 13 of *Oracle Web Application Programming for PL/SQL Developers*.

SERVER-SIDE HTML IMAGE MAPS

In a server-side HTML image map, the image displayed on the client (the HTML file) is a form input of the type IMAGE. This means that when the user clicks the image, the form is submitted. The x- and y-coordinates where the user clicked are received as IN parameters by the form handling procedure. Note that you do not need a Submit button for this type of form. The <INPUT> tag with TYPE="image" is the only required input element in the form. This input type creates an image field on which the user can click and cause the form to be submitted immediately. The coordinates of the selected point are measured in pixels and are returned (along with other contents of the form) in two named value pairs. The x-coordinate is submitted under the name of the field with .x appended, and the y-coordinate with .y appended. Any VALUE attribute is ignored. The image input HTML syntax is as follows:

```
<INPUT TYPE="image" NAME="p_image" SRC="/images/picture1.jpg">
```

The type here is "image". The name is required because this will be the name of the parameter that is being sent to the form's action.

The OWA_IMAGE package has a number of elements for generating this HTML. The preceding example can be generated by using the Oracle-supplied htp.formImage procedure; its syntax is as follows:

```
htp.formImage (cname in varchar2
               csrc in varchar2
               calign in varchar2 DEFAULT NULL
               cattributes in varchar2 DEFAULT NULL);
```

The parameters for this procedure are detailed in Table 24.9. Here is an example (only the first two parameters are passed in here):

```
htp.formImage('v_image','/images/location.gif');
```

It generates the following HTML:

```
<INPUT TYPE="image" NAME="p_image" SRC="/images/location.gif">
```

An HTML form needs a form handler procedure that can be used as the form's action. This procedure must be able to accept what is sent by the image-input item. The IN parameter for the image supplied to the form handler procedure must have the same name as the image input, and a datatype of OWA_IMAGE.POINT, which Oracle supplies. This datatype contains both the X and Y values of a coordinate, so the image has only one IN parameter.

TABLE 24.9
Parameters for the htp.formImage Procedure

PARAMETER	DESCRIPTION
CNAME	The value for the NAME attribute, the name of the parameter to be submitted.
CSRC	The value for the SRC attribute, which specifies the image file.
CALIGN	The value for the ALIGN attribute, which is optional.
CATTRIBUTES	Any other attributes to be included as-is in the tag.

Two more functions in the OWA_IMAGE package can extract the x- or y-coordinate from an OWA_IMAGE.POINT datatype. These functions are OWA_IMAGE.GET_X for the x-coordinate and OWA_IMAGE.GET_Y for the y-coordinate.

Using the OWA_IMAGE.GET_X and OWA_IMAGE.GET_Y functions, the form handler procedure can access the coordinates the user clicked and can work with these numbers.

In the following example, when the user clicks anywhere on the image, a new page appears, showing the x- and y-coordinates where the user clicked. The following example has two procedures called `find_coords`. The first one is `display_image`. It uses the procedure `htp.formImage` to create the image input. The next procedure, `show_cords`, is the action of the `display_image` procedure. This means that the IN parameter named for the image must be the OWA_IMAGE.POINT datatype. The `show_coords` procedure uses the functions OWA_IMAGE.GET_X and OWA_IMAGE.GET_Y to determine the x- and y-coordinates and then displays them on a new Web page.

FOR EXAMPLE

```
CREATE OR REPLACE Package find_coords
AS
  PROCEDURE  display_image;
  PROCEDURE  show_coords (p_image   IN  owa_image.Point);
END find_coords;
/
CREATE OR REPLACE PACKAGE BODY find_coords    AS
PROCEDURE display_image    IS
BEGIN
   htp.headOpen;
   htp.title('Display the Image');
   htp.headClose;
   htp.p('<BODY bgcolor="khaki">');
   htp.header(1,'Find the Coordinates');
   htp.p('Click on the image and you will see the x,y
          coordinates on the next page');
   htp.formOpen('find_coords.show_coords');
   htp.formImage('p_image','/images/location.gif');
   htp.formClose;
   htp.p('</BODY>');
   htp.p('</HTML>');
EXCEPTION
   WHEN OTHERS THEN
      htp.p('An error occurred: '||SQLERRM||'.  Please try again
         later.');
END display_image;
Procedure show_coords
  (p_image IN owa_image.Point)
IS
  x_in NUMBER(4) := owa_image.Get_X(P_image);
  y_in NUMBER(4) := owa_image.Get_Y(P_image);
BEGIN
   htp.headOpen;
   htp.title('Find Your coordinates');
   htp.headClose;
   htp.p('<BODY bgcolor="khaki">');
   htp.header(1,'These are the Coordinates you clicked on:');
   htp.p('<P>
```

FOR EXAMPLE (continued)

```
           You have selected '||x_in||'  as your X coordinate </p>');
   htp.p('<P>
           You have selected '||Y_in||'  as your Y coordinate </p>');
   htp.p('</BODY>');
   htp.p('</HTML>');
EXCEPTION
   WHEN OTHERS THEN
      htp.p('An error occurred: '||SQLERRM||'.  Please try again
         later.');
END ;
END find_coords;
```

The `display_image` procedure creates the following HTML file:

```
<HTML>
<HEAD>
<TITLE>Display the Image</TITLE>
</HEAD>
<BODY bgcolor="khaki">
<H1>Find the Coordinates</H1>
Click on the image and you will see the x,y
coordinates on the next page
<FORM ACTION="find_coords.show_coords" METHOD="POST">
<INPUT TYPE="image" NAME="p_image" SRC="/images/location.gif">
</BODY>
</HTML>
```

CLIENT-SIDE IMAGE MAPS

Two steps are involved in creating a client-side image map in HTML:

1. Set up an image map.

2. Show an image, and use the image map.

You can think of the initial image map as being similar to a JavaScript function that is defined in the beginning of an HTML file and is used later.

CREATE THE IMAGE MAP

The first tag in an image map is <MAP>. This tag must have a NAME attribute, or it cannot be referenced later in the file. The image map contains a number of areas that are each a hyperlink. Each area uses an <AREA> tag. Each <AREA> tag must have a SHAPE attribute to indicate the shape of the area and an HREF attribute to indicate where clicking the map directs the user. The various types of shapes have different sets of coordinates used to define the shape. The coordinates used to define an image map's shape are supplied in the value for the COORDS attribute. The following HTML creates an image map for a square with four inner squares, each one hyperlinking to a different Web page. The shape that is called "default" indicates the hyperlink for any area of the image that is not covered by one of the shapes. The coordinates used here are meaningless and are just used to complete the example.

```
<map name="MyMap">
<area shape="rect" href="first.htm" coords="20,20,70,60">
<area shape="rect" href="second.htm" coords="90,20,140,60">
<area shape="rect" href="third.htm" coords="20,80,70,120">
<area shape="rect" href="fourth.htm" coords="90,80,140,120">
<area shape="default" href="default.htm">
</map>
```

IMAGE MAPS IN PL/SQL

The method to generate this in PL/SQL, using the supplied Oracle packages within the Oracle Web Toolkit, involves the following steps:

1. Name the map.

2. Divide it into clickable areas.

3. Specify the image to be used.

Using PL/SQL, you use the `htp.mapOpen` and `htp.mapClose` procedures to open and close the map definition. You use the `htp.area` procedure to define the areas within the map. Then, when you display the image, you use the `htp.img2` procedure to create the HTML `<IMG>` tag with the corresponding image map. These procedures are described in Table 24.10.

TABLE 24.10
Procedures Used to Create an Image Map

PROCEDURE	RESULTING HTML	DESCRIPTION
`htp.mapOpen('map1');`	`<MAP NAME="map1">` `<AREA SHAPE="rect">`	Names the map.
`htp.area ('0,0,50,50',` `rect,'www.prenhall.com');`	`COORDS="0,0,50,50"HREF=` `"www.prenhall.com">`	Specifies the regions.
`htp.mapClose;`	`</MAP>`	Closes the map.

`htp.img2('MyImage.gif',`
`cismap=>'1',cusemap=>`
`'#map1' );`
	`<IMG SRC="MyImage.gif"`
	`ISMAP USEMAP="#map1">`
		Specifies the image and link to the region.

The ISMAP that is generated in the `<IMG>` tag indicates that this image will use an image map. USEMAP= determines the name of the image map to be used. The image map must have been previously defined in the HTML for the page, or the image map will not function.

At runtime, click the image. The browser processes the coordinates.

▼ LAB 24.3 EXERCISES

This section provides exercises and suggested answers, with discussion related to how those answers resulted. The most important thing to realize is whether your answer works. You should figure out the implications of the answers and what the effects are of any different answers you may come up with.

24.3.1 Create an HTML Page with the Oracle Web Toolkit

In these exercises you create a Web page by using the Oracle-supplied packages known as the Oracle Web Toolkit.

A) Create a PL/SQL procedure that generates the following HTML page:

```
<HTML>
<HEAD>
<TITLE>Section Location Update Form</TITLE>
</HEAD>
<BODY>
<H1>Change Section Location</H1>
<FORM ACTION="update_section"
METHOD="GET">
Section ID:
<INPUT TYPE="text" NAME="p_section" SIZE="8" MAXLENGTH="8"
  VALUE="150">
Course No:
<INPUT TYPE="text" NAME="" SIZE="8" VALUE="120">
<SELECT NAME="p_location" SIZE="10">
<OPTION VALUE=H310>H310
<OPTION VALUE=L206>L206
<OPTION SELECTED  VALUE=L210>L210
<OPTION VALUE=L211>L211
<OPTION VALUE=L214>L214
<OPTION VALUE=L500>L500
<OPTION VALUE=L507>L507
<OPTION VALUE=L509>L509
<OPTION VALUE=L511>L511
<OPTION VALUE=M200>M200
<OPTION VALUE=M311>M311
<OPTION VALUE=M500>M500
</SELECT>
<INPUT TYPE="submit" VALUE="Change the location">
</FORM>
</BODY>
</HTML>
```

ANSWER:

```
CREATE OR REPLACE PROCEDURE section_form IS
   v_string VARCHAR2(100);
   v_section_id  SECTION.section_id%TYPE;
   v_location    SECTION.location%TYPE;    -- Use %TYPE whenever
                                           -- possible.
   v_course_no   SECTION.course_no%TYPE;
   cursor c_location is
```

```
              select distinct location from section
              order by location;
      BEGIN
         SELECT section_id, location, course_no
         INTO v_section_id, v_location, v_course_no
         FROM section
         WHERE section_id=150;
         htp.htmlOpen;
         htp.headOpen;
         htp.title('Section Location Update Form');
         htp.headClose;
         htp.bodyOpen;
         htp.header(1,'Change Section Location');
         htp.FormOpen('update_section', 'GET');
         htp.p('Section ID:');
         htp.formText('p_section', 8, 8,v_section_id);
         htp.p('Course No: ');
         htp.formText( cname=>null, csize=>8,cvalue=>v_course_no);
         htp.FormSelectOpen(cname=>'p_location', nsize=>10);
         FOR rec in c_location LOOP
            IF rec.location = v_location THEN
               htp.FormSelectOption(rec.location,'SELECTED',
                   cattributes=>'VALUE='||rec.location);
            ELSE
              htp.FormSelectOption(rec.location,
                   cattributes=>'VALUE='||rec.location);
           END IF;
         END LOOP;
         htp.FormSelectClose;
         htp.FormSubmit(cvalue=>'Change the location');
         htp.FormClose;
          htp.bodyClose;
          htp.htmlClose;
       EXCEPTION
          WHEN OTHERS THEN
            HTP.P('An error occurred: '||SQLERRM||
                  '.  Please try again later.');
        END;
```

B) Generate an update page for the form action in the last HTML page. This update will be the form handler for the Submit button. It will commit the changes to the database and then refresh the page.

ANSWER:

```
CREATE OR REPLACE PROCEDURE update_section
   (p_section  IN SECTION.section_id%TYPE,
    p_location IN SECTION.location%TYPE)
IS
BEGIN
   UPDATE section
      SET location = p_location
```

```
   WHERE section_id = p_section;
COMMIT;
section_form;
htp.p('The section '||p_section||' is moved to
                '||p_location||'.');
EXCEPTION
  WHEN OTHERS THEN
     HTP.P('An error occurred: '||SQLERRM||'.  Please try again
        later.');
END;
```

BY THE WAY

This chapter does not have a "Try It Yourself" section.

PL/SQL Formatting Guide

This appendix summarizes some of the PL/SQL formatting guidelines used throughout this book. Formatting guidelines are not a required part of PL/SQL, but they act as best practices that facilitate code's quality, readability, and ease of maintenance.

Case

PL/SQL, like SQL, is case-insensitive. The general guidelines here are as follows:

- Use uppercase for keywords (BEGIN, EXCEPTION, END, IF THEN ELSE, LOOP, END LOOP), data types (VARCHAR2, NUMBER), built-in functions (LEAST, SUBSTR), and user-defined subroutines (procedures, functions, packages).

- Use lowercase for variable names as well as column and table names in SQL.

White Space

White space (extra lines and spaces) is as important in PL/SQL as it is in SQL. It is a main factor in providing readability. In other words, you can reveal the program's logical structure by using indentation in your code. Here are some suggestions:

- Put spaces on both sides of an equals sign or comparison operator.

- Line up structure words on the left (DECLARE, BEGIN, EXCEPTION, END, IF and END IF, LOOP and END LOOP). In addition, indent three spaces (using the spacebar, not the Tab key) for structures within structures.

- Put blank lines between major sections to separate them.

- Put different logical parts of the same structure on separate lines even if the structure is short. For example, IF and THEN are placed on one line, whereas ELSE and END IF are placed on separate lines.

Naming Conventions

To prevent conflicts with keywords and column/table names, it is helpful to use the following prefixes:

- `v_variable_name`

- `con_constant_name`

- `i_in_parameter_name`, `o_out_parameter_name`, `io_in_out_parameter_name`

- `c_cursor_name` or `name_cur`

- `rc_reference_cursor_name`

- `r_record_name` or `name_rec`

- `FOR r_stud IN c_stud LOOP...`

- `FOR stud_rec IN stud_cur LOOP`

- `type_name`, `name_type` (for user-defined types)

- `t_table`, `name_tab` (for PL/SQL tables)

- `rec_record_name`, `name_rec` (for record variables)

- `e_exception_name` (for user-defined exceptions)

The name of a package should be the name of the larger context of the actions performed by the procedures and functions contained in the package.

The name of a procedure should describe the action the procedure performs. The name of a function should describe the return variable.

FOR EXAMPLE

```
PACKAGE student_admin
   -- admin suffix may be used for administration.

PROCEDURE remove_student (i_student_id IN student.studid%TYPE);

FUNCTION student_enroll_count (i_student_id student.studid%TYPE)
RETURN INTEGER;
```

Comments

Comments in PL/SQL are as important as in SQL. They should explain the main sections of the program and any major nontrivial logic steps.

Use single-line comments (--) instead of multiline comments (/*). Although PL/SQL treats these comments in the same way, it will be easier for you to debug the code after it is completed, because you cannot embed multiline comments within multiline comments. In other words, you can comment out portions of code that contain single-line comments, but you can't comment out portions of code that contain multiline comments.

Other Suggestions

▶ For SQL statements embedded in PL/SQL, use the same formatting guidelines to determine how the statements should appear in a block.

▶ Provide a comment header that explains the intent of the block and lists the creation date and author's name. Also have a line for each revision, with the author's name, the date, and a description of the revision.

FOR EXAMPLE

The following example shows the aforementioned suggestions. Notice that it also uses a monospaced font (Courier New). This makes formatting easier, because each character takes up the same amount of space. Proportionally spaced fonts can hide spaces and make lining up clauses difficult. Most text and programming editors by default use a monospaced font.

```
REM ********************************************************
REM * filename: coursediscount01.sql            version: 1
REM * purpose:  To give discounts to courses that have at
REM *           least one section with an enrollment of more
REM *           than 10 students.
REM * args:     none
REM *
REM * created by:  s.tashi            date: January 1, 2000
REM * modified by: y.sonam            date: February 1, 2000
REM * description: Fixed cursor, added indentation and
REM *              comments.
REM ********************************************************
DECLARE
   -- C_DISCOUNT_COURSE finds a list of courses that have
   -- at least one section with an enrollment of at least 10
   -- students.
   CURSOR c_discount_course IS
      SELECT DISTINCT course_no
        FROM section sect
       WHERE 10 <= (SELECT COUNT(*)
                      FROM enrollment enr
                     WHERE enr.section_id = sect.section_id
                   );

   -- discount rate for courses that cost more than $2000.00
   con_discount_2000 CONSTANT NUMBER := .90;
```

```
   -- discount rate for courses that cost between $1001.00
   -- and $2000.00
   con_discount_other CONSTANT NUMBER := .95;

   v_current_course_cost course.cost%TYPE;
   v_discount_all NUMBER;
   e_update_is_problematic EXCEPTION;
BEGIN
   -- For courses to be discounted, determine the current
   -- and new cost values
   FOR r_discount_course in c_discount_course LOOP
      SELECT cost
        INTO v_current_course_cost
        FROM course
       WHERE course_no = r_discount_course.course_no;

      IF v_current_course_cost > 2000 THEN
         v_discount_all := con_discount_2000;
      ELSE
         IF v_current_course_cost > 1000 THEN
            v_discount_all :=  con_discount_other;
         ELSE
            v_discount_all := 1;
         END IF;
      END IF;

      BEGIN
         UPDATE course
            SET cost = cost * v_discount_all
          WHERE course_no = r_discount_course.course_no;
      EXCEPTION
         WHEN OTHERS THEN
            RAISE e_update_is_problematic;
      END;   -- end of sub-block to update record
   END LOOP; -- end of main LOOP

   COMMIT;

EXCEPTION
   WHEN e_update_is_problematic THEN
      -- Undo all transactions in this run of the program
      ROLLBACK;
      DBMS_OUTPUT.PUT_LINE
         ('There was a problem updating a course cost.');
   WHEN OTHERS THEN
      NULL;
END;
/
```

Student Database Schema

Table and Column Descriptions

COURSE: Information for a course

COLUMN NAME	NULL	TYPE	DESCRIPTION
COURSE_NO	NOT NULL	NUMBER(8, 0)	The unique course number
DESCRIPTION	NULL	VARCHAR2(50)	The full name of this course
COST	NULL	NUMBER(9,2)	The dollar amount charged for enrollment in this course
PREREQUISITE	NULL	NUMBER(8, 0)	The ID number of the course that must be taken as a prerequisite to this course
CREATED_BY	NOT NULL	VARCHAR2(30)	Audit column—indicates who inserted data
CREATED_DATE	NOT NULL	DATE	Audit column—indicates the date of insertion
MODIFIED_BY	NOT NULL	VARCHAR2(30)	Audit column—indicates who made the last update
MODIFIED_DATE	NOT NULL	DATE	Audit column—date of the last update

SECTION: Information for an individual section (class) of a particular course

COLUMN NAME	NULL	TYPE	DESCRIPTION
SECTION_ID	NOT NULL	NUMBER(8,0)	The unique ID for a section
COURSE_NO	NOT NULL	NUMBER(8,0)	The course number for which this is a section
SECTION_NO	NOT NULL	NUMBER(3)	The individual section number within this course
START_DATE_TIME	NULL	DATE	The date and time when this section meets
LOCATION	NULL	VARCHAR2(50)	The meeting room for the section
INSTRUCTOR_ID	NOT NULL	NUMBER(8,0)	The ID number of the instructor who teaches this section

SECTION: Information for an individual section (class) of a particular course (continued)

COLUMN NAME	NULL	TYPE	DESCRIPTION
CAPACITY	NULL	NUMBER(3,0)	The maximum number of students allowed in this section
CREATED_BY	NOT NULL	VARCHAR2(30)	Audit column—indicates who inserted data
CREATED_DATE	NOT NULL	DATE	Audit column—indicates the date of insertion
MODIFIED_BY	NOT NULL	VARCHAR2(30)	Audit column—indicates who made the last update
MODIFIED_DATE	NOT NULL	DATE	Audit column—date of the last update

STUDENT: Profile information for a student

COLUMN NAME	NULL	TYPE	DESCRIPTION
STUDENT_ID	NOT NULL	NUMBER(8,0)	A unique ID for the student
SALUTATION	NULL	VARCHAR2(5)	This student's title (Ms., Mr., Dr.)
FIRST_NAME	NULL	VARCHAR2(25)	This student's first name
LAST_NAME	NOT NULL	VARCHAR2(25)	This student's last name
STREET_ADDRESS	NULL	VARCHAR2(50)	This student's street address
ZIP	NOT NULL	VARCHAR2(5)	This student's zip code
PHONE	NULL	VARCHAR2(15)	This student's phone number, including area code
EMPLOYER	NULL	VARCHAR2(50)	The name of the company where this student is employed
REGISTRATION_DATE	NOT NULL	DATE	The date this student registered in the program
CREATED_BY	NOT NULL	VARCHAR2(30)	Audit column—indicates who inserted data
CREATED_DATE	NOT NULL	DATE	Audit column—indicates the date of insertion
MODIFIED_BY	NOT NULL	VARCHAR2(30)	Audit column—indicates who made the last update
MODIFIED_DATE	NOT NULL	DATE	Audit column—date of the last update

ENROLLMENT: Information for a student registered for a particular section of a particular course (class)

COLUMN NAME	NULL	TYPE	DESCRIPTION
STUDENT_ID	NOT NULL	NUMBER(8,0)	The ID for a student
SECTION_ID	NOT NULL	NUMBER(8,0)	The ID for a section
ENROLL_DATE	NOT NULL	DATE	The date this student registered for this section

COLUMN NAME	NULL	TYPE	DESCRIPTION
FINAL_GRADE	NULL	NUMBER(3,0)	The final grade given to this student for all the work in this section (class)
CREATED_BY	NOT NULL	VARCHAR2(30)	Audit column—indicates who inserted data
CREATED_DATE	NOT NULL	DATE	Audit column—indicates the date of insertion
MODIFIED_BY	NOT NULL	VARCHAR2(30)	Audit column—indicates who made the last update
MODIFIED_DATE	NOT NULL	DATE	Audit column—date of the last update

INSTRUCTOR: Profile information for an instructor

COLUMN NAME	NULL	TYPE	DESCRIPTION
INSTRUCTOR_ID	NOT NULL	NUMBER(8)	The unique ID for an instructor
SALUTATION	NULL	VARCHAR2(5)	This instructor's title (Mr., Ms., Dr., Rev.)
FIRST_NAME	NULL	VARCHAR2(25)	This instructor's first name
LAST_NAME	NULL	VARCHAR2(25)	This instructor's last name
STREET_ADDRESS	NULL	VARCHAR2(50)	This instructor's street address
ZIP	NULL	VARCHAR2(5)	This instructor's zip code
PHONE	NULL	VARCHAR2(15)	This instructor's phone number, including area code
CREATED_BY	NOT NULL	VARCHAR2(30)	Audit column—indicates who inserted data
CREATED_DATE	NOT NULL	DATE	Audit column—indicates the date of insertion
MODIFIED_BY	NOT NULL	VARCHAR2(30)	Audit column—indicates who made the last update
MODIFIED_DATE	NOT NULL	DATE	Audit column—date of the last update

ZIPCODE: City, state, and zip code information

COLUMN NAME	NULL	TYPE	DESCRIPTION
ZIP	NOT NULL	VARCHAR2(5)	The zip code, unique for a city and state
CITY	NULL	VARCHAR2(25)	The city name for this zip code
STATE	NULL	VARCHAR2(2)	The postal abbreviation for the U.S. state
CREATED_BY	NOT NULL	VARCHAR2(30)	Audit column—indicates who inserted data
CREATED_DATE	NOT NULL	DATE	Audit column—indicates the date of insertion
MODIFIED_BY	NOT NULL	VARCHAR2(30)	Audit column—indicates who made the last update
MODIFIED_DATE	NOT NULL	DATE	Audit column—date of the last update

GRADE_TYPE: Lookup table of a grade type (code) and its description

COLUMN NAME	NULL	TYPE	DESCRIPTION
GRADE_TYPE_CODE	NOT NULL	CHAR(2)	The unique code that identifies a category of grade (such as MT or HW)
DESCRIPTION	NOT NULL	VARCHAR2(50)	The description for this code (such as Midterm or Homework)
CREATED_BY	NOT NULL	VARCHAR2(30)	Audit column—indicates who inserted data
CREATED_DATE	NOT NULL	DATE	Audit column—indicates the date of insertion
MODIFIED_BY	NOT NULL	VARCHAR2(30)	Audit column—indicates who made the last update
MODIFIED_DATE	NOT NULL	DATE	Audit column—date of the last update

GRADE_TYPE_WEIGHT: Information on how the final grade for a particular section is computed; for example, the midterm constitutes 50%, the quiz 10%, and the final examination 40% of the final grade

COLUMN NAME	NULL	TYPE	DESCRIPTION
SECTION_ID	NOT NULL	NUMBER(8)	The ID for a section
GRADE_TYPE_CODE	NOT NULL	CHAR(2)	The code that identifies a category of grade
NUMBER_PER_ SECTION	NOT NULL	NUMBER(3)	How many of these grade types can be used in this section (for example, there may be three quizzes)
PERCENT_OF_FINAL_ GRADE	NOT NULL	NUMBER(3)	The percentage that this category of grade contributes to the final grade
DROP_LOWEST	NOT NULL	CHAR(1)	Is the lowest grade in this type removed when determining the final grade? (Y/N)
CREATED_BY	NOT NULL	VARCHAR2(30)	Audit column—indicates who inserted data
CREATED_DATE	NOT NULL	DATE	Audit column—indicates the date of insertion
MODIFIED_BY	NOT NULL	VARCHAR2(30)	Audit column—indicates who made the last update
MODIFIED_DATE	NOT NULL	DATE	Audit column—date of the last update

GRADE: The individual grades a student received for a particular section (class)

COLUMN NAME	NULL	TYPE	DESCRIPTION
STUDENT_ID	NOT NULL	NUMBER(8)	The ID for a student
SECTION_ID	NOT NULL	NUMBER(8)	The ID for a section
GRADE_TYPE_CODE	NOT NULL	CHAR(2)	The code that identifies a category of grade
GRADE_CODE_ OCCURRENCE	NOT NULL	NUMBER(38)	The sequence number of one grade type for one section. For example, there could be multiple assignments numbered 1, 2, 3, and so on.
NUMERIC_GRADE	NOT NULL	NUMBER(3)	Numeric grade value (such as 70 or 75)
COMMENTS	NULL	VARCHAR2(2000)	Instructor's comments on this grade
CREATED_BY	NOT NULL	VARCHAR2(30)	Audit column—indicates who inserted data
CREATED_DATE	NOT NULL	DATE	Audit column—indicates the date of insertion
MODIFIED_BY	NOT NULL	VARCHAR2(30)	Audit column—indicates who made the last update
MODIFIED_DATE	NOT NULL	DATE	Audit column—date of the last update

GRADE_CONVERSION: Converts a number grade to a letter grade

COLUMN NAME	NULL	TYPE	DESCRIPTION
LETTER_GRADE	NOT NULL	VARCHAR(2)	The unique grade as a letter (A, A–, B+, B, and so on)
GRADE_POINT	NOT NULL	NUMBER(3,2)	The number grade on a scale from 0 (F) to 4 (A)
MAX_GRADE	NOT NULL	NUMBER(3)	The highest grade number that corresponds to this letter grade
MIN_GRADE	NOT NULL	NUMBER(3)	The lowest grade number that corresponds to this letter grade
CREATED_BY	NOT NULL	VARCHAR2(30)	Audit column—indicates who inserted data
CREATED_DATE	NOT NULL	DATE	Audit column—indicates the date of insertion
MODIFIED_BY	NOT NULL	VARCHAR2(30)	Audit column—indicates who made the last update
MODIFIED_DATE	NOT NULL	DATE	Audit column—date of the last update

ANSI SQL Standards

The American National Standards Institute (http://www.ansi.org) first published a standard SQL specification in 1989. The ANSI SQL standard was later revised in 1992, and is often referred to as SQL-92 or SQL-2. This was revised again, giving rise to the latest standard, known as SQL-99. Sometimes it is called SQL-3. Database vendors and third-party software companies have had varying levels of conformance to this standard. Most major database vendors support the SQL-92 standard. Generally what you find is that most vendors have their own extensions to the SQL language. Oracle is no exception. Nonetheless, Oracle has made efforts to maintain the ANSI standard. The reason for this is to provide an easier migration to third-party applications without a need to modify the SQL code. Starting with version 8i, Oracle has introduced a number of enhancements to conform to the SQL-99 standard. This appendix reviews the main enhancements that you see in this book by means of examples. It is important to realize that although many of these features were introduced in Oracle 9i, they have existed in other programming languages. For example, the CASE statement has been a part of Microsoft SQL Server for some time and has been used in COBOL and C since their inception.

JOINs

The 1999 ANSI standard introduced complete JOIN syntax in the FROM clause. The prior method was to list the tables needed in the query in the FROM clause and then define the joins between these tables in the WHERE clause. However, the conditions of the SQL statement are also listed in the WHERE clause. It was decided to enhance this syntax because listing the joins and conditions in the same WHERE clause can be confusing.

The 1999 ANSI join syntax includes cross joins, equijoins, full outer joins, and natural joins.

CROSS JOINS

The CROSS JOIN syntax indicates that you are creating a Cartesian product from two tables. The result set of a Cartesian product usually is meaningless, but it can be used to generate a lot of rows if you need to do some testing. The advantage of the new syntax is that it flags a Cartesian product by having the CROSS JOIN in the FROM clause.

FOR EXAMPLE

Prior to Oracle 9i, you would create a Cartesian product with the following syntax:

```
SELECT *
  FROM instructor, course
```

The new syntax is as follows:

```
SELECT *
  FROM instructor CROSS JOIN
       course
```

The result set from this is 300 rows. This is because the COURSE table has 30 rows and the INSTRUCTOR table has 10 rows. The CROSS JOIN counts all possible combinations, resulting in the 300 rows.

EQUI JOINS

The EQUI JOIN (also called an inner or regular join) syntax indicates the columns that comprise the JOINS between two tables. Prior to Oracle 9i, you would indicate a join condition in the WHERE clause by stating which values in a set of columns from one table are equal to the values in a set of columns from another table.

FOR EXAMPLE

Prior to Oracle 9i, you would join the STUDENT table to the ZIPCODE table as follows:

```
SELECT s.first_name, s.last_name, z.zip, z.city, z.state
  FROM student s, zipcode z
 WHERE s.zip = z.zip
```

The new syntax is as follows:

```
SELECT s.first_name, s.last_name, zip, z.city, z.state
  FROM student s JOIN
       zipcode z USING (zip)
```

The reason for this syntax is that the join condition between the two tables is immediately obvious when you look at the tables listed in the FROM clause. This example is very short, but generally your SQL statements are very long, and it can be time-consuming to find the join conditions in the WHERE clause.

Notice that the ZIP column in the SELECT clause does not have an alias. In the new JOIN syntax, the column that is referenced in the USING clause does not have a qualifier. In the old syntax, if you did not use an alias for column ZIP, as in this version of the SELECT:

```
    SELECT s.first_name, s.last_name, zip, z.city, z.state
      FROM student s, zipcode z
     WHERE s.zip = z.zip
```

Oracle would generate the following error:

ORA-00918: column ambiguously defined

In the new JOIN syntax, if you use a qualifier, as in this example:

```
SELECT s.first_name, s.last_name, z.zip, z.city, z.state
  FROM student s JOIN
       zipcode z USING (zip)
```

Oracle generates the following error:

```
ORA-25154: column part of USING clause cannot have qualifier
```

The new JOIN syntax also allows you to define the join condition using both sides of the join. This is done with the ON syntax. When using the ON syntax for a JOIN, you must use the qualifier. This is also useful when the two sides of the join do not have the same name.

The ON syntax can also be used for three-way joins (or more).

FOR EXAMPLE

```
SELECT s.section_no, c.course_no, c.description,
       i.first_name, i.last_name
  FROM course c
  JOIN section s
    ON (s.course_no = c.course_no)
  JOIN instructor i
    ON (i.instructor_id = s.instructor_id)
```

The syntax for a multiple-table join becomes more complex. Notice that one table is mentioned at a time. The first JOIN lists columns from the first two tables in the ON section. As soon as the third table has been indicated, the second JOIN lists columns from the second and third tables in the ON clause.

NATURAL JOINS

The NATURAL JOIN is another part of the ANSI 1999 syntax that you can use when joining two tables based on columns that have the same name and datatype. The NATURAL JOIN can be used only when all the columns that have the same name in both tables comprise the join condition between these tables. You cannot use this syntax when the two columns have the same name but a different datatype. Another benefit of this join is that if you use the SELECT * syntax, the columns that appear in both tables appear only once in the result set.

FOR EXAMPLE

```
SELECT *
  FROM instructor NATURAL JOIN zipcode
```

The join used here is not only on the ZIP column of both tables, but also on the CREATE_BY, CREATED_DATE, MODIFIED_BY, and MODIFIED_DATE columns.

The student schema does not support the NATURAL JOIN condition, because we have created audit columns that have the same name in each table but are not used in the foreign key constraints among the tables.

OUTER JOINS

INNER JOIN or EQUI JOIN is the result of joining two tables that contain rows where a match occurred on the join condition. It is possible to lose information through an INNER JOIN, because only those rows that match on the join condition appear in the final result set.

The result set of an OUTER JOIN contains the same rows as the INNER JOIN plus rows corresponding to the rows from the source tables where there was no match. The OUTER JOIN has been supported by a number of versions of the Oracle SQL language. It was not a part of the ANSI standard until the 1999 version.

Oracle's OUTER JOIN syntax has consisted of placing a plus sign (+) next to the columns of a table where you expect to find values that do not exist in the other table.

FOR EXAMPLE

```
SELECT i.first_name, i.last_name, z.state
  FROM instructor i, zipcode z
 WHERE i.zip (+) = z.zip
GROUP BY i.first_name, i.last_name, z.state
```

In this example, the result set includes all states that are in the ZIPCODE table. If there is no instructor for a state that exists in the ZIPCODE table, the values of FIRST_NAME and LAST_NAME are blank on output (NULL). This syntax gets more confusing, because it must be maintained if there are more conditions in a WHERE clause. This method can be used on only one side of the outer join at a time.

The new method of OUTER JOINs adopted in Oracle 9i allows the case of an OUTER JOIN on either side or both sides at the same time. (An example would be if some instructors had zip codes that were not in the ZIPCODE table, and you wanted to see all the instructors and all the states in both of these tables.) This task can be accomplished by using the new OUTER JOIN syntax only. This requires the aforementioned JOIN syntax with the addition of new outer join attributes as well. The choice is LEFT/RIGHT/FULL OUTER JOIN. The same OUTER JOIN can now be modified as follows:

```
    SELECT i.first_name, z.state
      FROM instructor i RIGHT OUTER JOIN
           zipcode z
        ON i.zip = z.zip
    GROUP BY i.first_name, z.state
```

The RIGHT indicates that the values on the right side of the JOIN may not exist in the table on the LEFT side of the join. This can be replaced by the word FULL if some instructors have zip codes that are not in the ZIPCODE table.

Scalar Subquery

A scalar row subquery is a single-row subquery. In other words, it returns a single row. If the scalar subquery returns more than one row, it generates an error.

FOR EXAMPLE

```
SELECT city, state,
      (SELECT count(*)
         FROM student s
        WHERE s.zip = z.zip) as student_count
  FROM zipcode z
 WHERE state = 'CT'
```

Answers to the Try It Yourself Sections

Chapter 1, "PL/SQL Concepts"

1) To calculate the area of a circle, you must square the circle's radius and then multiply it by π. Write a program that calculates the area of a circle. The value for the radius should be provided with the help of a substitution variable. Use 3.14 for the value of π. After the area of the circle is calculated, display it on the screen.

ANSWER: The script should look similar to the following:

```
SET SERVEROUTPUT ON
DECLARE
    v_radius NUMBER := &sv_radius;
    v_area NUMBER;
BEGIN
    v_area := POWER(v_radius, 2) * 3.14;
    DBMS_OUTPUT.PUT_LINE
        ('The area of the circle is: '||v_area);
END;
```

In this exercise, you declare two variables, v_radius and v_area, to store the values for the radius of the circle and its area, respectively. Next, you compute the value for the variable v_area with the help of the built-in function POWER and the value of the v_radius. Finally, you display the value of v_area on the screen.

Assume that the number 5 has been entered for the value of the variable v_radius. The script produces the following output:

```
Enter value for sv_radius: 5
old    2:    v_radius NUMBER := &sv_radius;
new    2:    v_radius NUMBER := 5;
The area of the circle is: 78.5

PLSQL procedure successfully completed.
```

2) Rewrite the script ch01_2b.sql, version 2.0. In the output produced by the script, extra spaces appear after the day of the week. The new script should remove these extra spaces.

Here's the current output:

```
Today is Sunday    , 20:39
```

The new output should have this format:

```
Today is Sunday, 20:39
```

ANSWER: The new version of the script should look similar to the following. Changes are shown in bold.

```
SET SERVEROUTPUT ON
DECLARE
    v_day VARCHAR2(20);
BEGIN
    v_day := TO_CHAR(SYSDATE, 'fmDay, HH24:MI');
    DBMS_OUTPUT.PUT_LINE ('Today is '|| v_day);
END;
```

In this script, you modify the format in which you would like to display the date. Notice that the word Day is now prefixed by the letters fm. These letters guarantee that extra spaces will be removed from the name of the day. When run, this exercise produces the following output:

```
Today is Tuesday, 18:54

PLSQL procedure successfully completed.
```

Chapter 2, "General Programming Language Fundamentals"

1) Write a PL/SQL block

   A) That includes declarations for the following variables:

      I) A VARCHAR2 datatype that can contain the string 'Introduction to Oracle PL/SQL'

      II) A NUMBER that can be assigned 987654.55, but not 987654.567 or 9876543.55

      III) A CONSTANT (you choose the correct datatype) that is autoinitialized to the value '603D'

      IV) A BOOLEAN

      V) A DATE datatype autoinitialized to one week from today

   B) In the body of the PL/SQL block, put a DBMS_OUTPUT.PUT_LINE message for each of the variables that received an auto initialization value.

   C) In a comment at the bottom of the PL/SQL block, state the value of your number datatype.

ANSWER: The answer should look similar to the following:

```
SET SERVEROUTPUT ON
DECLARE
    -- A VARCHAR2 datatype that can contain the string
    -- 'Introduction to Oracle PL/SQL'
    v_descript VARCHAR2(35);

    - A NUMBER that allows for the conditions: can be
    - assigned 987654.55 but not 987654.567 or 9876543.55

    v_number_test NUMBER(8,2);

    -- [a variable] autoinitialized to the value '603D'
    v_location CONSTANT VARCHAR2(4) := '603D';
```

```
    -- A BOOLEAN
    v_boolean_test BOOLEAN;

    -- A DATE datatype auto initialized to one week from today

    v_start_date DATE := TRUNC(SYSDATE) + 7;

BEGIN
    DBMS_OUTPUT.PUT_LINE
        ('The location is: '||v_location||'.');
    DBMS_OUTPUT.PUT_LINE
        ('The starting date is: '||v_start_date||'.');
END;
```

2) Alter the PL/SQL block you just created to conform to the following specifications.

   A) Remove the DBMS_OUTPUT.PUT_LINE messages.

   B) In the body of the PL/SQL block, write a selection test (IF) that does the following (use a nested if statement where appropriate):

   I) Checks whether the VARCHAR2 you created contains the course named "Introduction to Underwater Basketweaving."

   II) If it does, put a DBMS_OUTPUT.PUT_LINE message on the screen that says so.

   III) If it does not, test to see if the CONSTANT you created contains the room number 603D.

   IV) If it does, put a DBMS_OUTPUT.PUT_LINE message on the screen that states the course name and the room number that you've reached in this logic.

   V) If it does not, put a DBMS_OUTPUT.PUT_LINE message on the screen that states that the course and location could not be determined.

   C) Add a WHEN OTHERS EXCEPTION that puts a DBMS_OUTPUT.PUT_LINE message on the screen that says that an error occurred.

   ANSWER: The answer should look similar to the following:

```
SET SERVEROUT ON
DECLARE
    -- A VARCHAR2 datatype that can contain the string
    -- 'Introduction to Oracle PL/SQL'
    v_descript VARCHAR2(35);

    -- A NUMBER that allows for the conditions: can be
    - assigned 987654.55 but not 987654.567 or 9876543.55

    v_number_test NUMBER(8,2);

    -- [a variable] auto initialized to the value '603D'
    v_location CONSTANT VARCHAR2(4) := '603D';

    -- A BOOLEAN
    v_boolean_test BOOLEAN;

    -- A DATE datatype autoinitialized to one week from today
    v_start_date DATE := TRUNC(SYSDATE) + 7;
```

```
BEGIN
   IF v_descript = 'Introduction to Underwater Basketweaving'
   THEN
      DBMS_OUTPUT.PUT_LINE ('This course is '||v_descript||'.');

   ELSIF v_location = '603D' THEN

      -- No value has been assigned to v_descript
      IF v_descript IS NOT NULL THEN
         DBMS_OUTPUT.PUT_LINE ('The course is '||v_descript
            ||'.'||' The location is '||v_location||'.');
      ELSE
         DBMS_OUTPUT.PUT_LINE ('The course is unknown.'||
            ' The location is '||v_location||'.');
      END IF;
   ELSE
      DBMS_OUTPUT.PUT_LINE ('The course and location '||
         'could not be determined.');
   END IF;
EXCEPTION
   WHEN OTHERS THEN
      DBMS_OUTPUT.PUT_LINE ('An error occurred.');
END;
```

Chapter 3, "SQL in PL/SQL"

1) Create a table called CHAP4 with two columns; one is ID (a number) and the other is NAME, which is a VARCHAR2(20).

   ANSWER: The answer should look similar to the following:

```
PROMPT Creating Table 'CHAP4'
CREATE TABLE chap4
   (id   NUMBER,
    name VARCHAR2(20));
```

2) Create a sequence called CHAP4_SEQ that increments by units of 5.

   ANSWER: The answer should look similar to the following:

```
PROMPT Creating Sequence 'CHAP4_SEQ'
CREATE SEQUENCE chap4_seq
   NOMAXVALUE
   NOMINVALUE
   NOCYCLE
   NOCACHE;
```

3) Write a PL/SQL block that does the following, in this order:

   A) Declares two variables: one for the `v_name` and one for `v_id`. The `v_name` variable can be used throughout the block to hold the name that will be inserted. Realize that the value will change in the course of the block.

   B) The block inserts into the table the name of the student who is enrolled in the most classes and uses a sequence for the ID. Afterward there is SAVEPOINT A.

C) The student with the fewest classes is inserted. Afterward there is SAVEPOINT B.

D) The instructor who is teaching the most courses is inserted in the same way. Afterward there is SAVEPOINT C.

E) Using a SELECT INTO statement, hold the value of the instructor in the variable v_id.

F) Undo the instructor insertion by using rollback.

G) Insert the instructor teaching the fewest courses, but do not use the sequence to generate the ID. Instead, use the value from the first instructor, whom you have since undone.

H) Insert the instructor teaching the most courses, and use the sequence to populate his or her ID.

Add DBMS_OUTPUT throughout the block to display the values of the variables as they change. (This is a good practice for debugging.)

ANSWER: The script should look similar to the following:

```
DECLARE
    v_name student.last_name%TYPE;
    v_id   student.student_id%TYPE;
BEGIN
  BEGIN
     -- A second block is used to capture the possibility of
     -- multiple students meeting this requirement.
     -- The exception section handles this situation.
     SELECT s.last_name
       INTO v_name
       FROM student s, enrollment e
      WHERE s.student_id = e.student_id
     HAVING COUNT(*) = (SELECT MAX(COUNT(*))
                          FROM student s, enrollment e
                         WHERE s.student_id = e.student_id
                         GROUP BY s.student_id)
     GROUP BY s.last_name;
  EXCEPTION
     WHEN TOO_MANY_ROWS THEN
        v_name := 'Multiple Names';
  END;

  INSERT INTO CHAP4
  VALUES (CHAP4_SEQ.NEXTVAL, v_name);
  SAVEPOINT A;

  BEGIN
     SELECT s.last_name
       INTO v_name
       FROM student s, enrollment e
      WHERE s.student_id = e.student_id
     HAVING COUNT(*) = (SELECT MIN(COUNT(*))
                          FROM student s, enrollment e
                         WHERE s.student_id = e.student_id
                         GROUP BY s.student_id)
     GROUP BY s.last_name;
```

```
EXCEPTION
   WHEN TOO_MANY_ROWS THEN
      v_name := 'Multiple Names';
END;

INSERT INTO CHAP4
VALUES (CHAP4_SEQ.NEXTVAL, v_name);
SAVEPOINT B;

BEGIN
   SELECT i.last_name
     INTO v_name
     FROM instructor i, section s
    WHERE s.instructor_id = i.instructor_id
   HAVING COUNT(*) = (SELECT MAX(COUNT(*))
                        FROM instructor i, section s
                       WHERE s.instructor_id = i.instructor_id
                       GROUP BY i.instructor_id)
   GROUP BY i.last_name;
EXCEPTION
   WHEN TOO_MANY_ROWS THEN
      v_name := 'Multiple Names';
END;

SAVEPOINT C;

BEGIN
   SELECT instructor_id
     INTO v_id
     FROM instructor
    WHERE last_name = v_name;
EXCEPTION
   WHEN NO_DATA_FOUND THEN
      v_id := 999;
END;

INSERT INTO CHAP4
VALUES (v_id, v_name);
ROLLBACK TO SAVEPOINT B;

BEGIN
   SELECT i.last_name
     INTO v_name
     FROM instructor i, section s
    WHERE s.instructor_id = i.instructor_id
   HAVING COUNT(*) = (SELECT MIN(COUNT(*))
                        FROM instructor i, section s
                       WHERE s.instructor_id = i.instructor_id
                       GROUP BY i.instructor_id)
   GROUP BY i.last_name;
```

```
EXCEPTION
  WHEN TOO_MANY_ROWS THEN
     v_name := 'Multiple Names';
END;

INSERT INTO CHAP4
VALUES (v_id, v_name);

BEGIN
   SELECT i.last_name
     INTO v_name
     FROM instructor i, section s
    WHERE s.instructor_id = i.instructor_id
    HAVING COUNT(*) = (SELECT MAX(COUNT(*))
                         FROM instructor i, section s
                        WHERE s.instructor_id = i.instructor_id
                       GROUP BY i.instructor_id)
    GROUP BY i.last_name;
EXCEPTION
   WHEN TOO_MANY_ROWS THEN
       v_name := 'Multiple Names';
END;

INSERT INTO CHAP4
VALUES (CHAP4_SEQ.NEXTVAL, v_name);
END;
```

Chapter 4, "Conditional Control: IF Statements"

1) Rewrite ch04_1a.sql. Instead of getting information from the user for the variable `v_date`, define its value with the help of the function SYSDATE. After it has been determined that a certain day falls on the weekend, check to see if the time is before or after noon. Display the time of day together with the day.

ANSWER: The script should look similar to the following. Changes are shown in bold.

```
SET SERVEROUTPUT ON
DECLARE
   v_day  VARCHAR2(15);
   v_time VARCHAR(8);
BEGIN
   v_day  := TO_CHAR(SYSDATE, 'fmDAY');
   v_time := TO_CHAR(SYSDATE, 'HH24:MI');

   IF v_day IN ('SATURDAY', 'SUNDAY') THEN
      DBMS_OUTPUT.PUT_LINE (v_day||', '||v_time);
      IF v_time BETWEEN '12:01' AND '24:00' THEN
         DBMS_OUTPUT.PUT_LINE ('It''s afternoon');
      ELSE
         DBMS_OUTPUT.PUT_LINE ('It''s morning');
      END IF;
```

```
      END IF;

      -- control resumes here
      DBMS_OUTPUT.PUT_LINE('Done...');
   END;
```

In this exercise, you remove the variable `v_date` that was used to store the date provided by the user. You add the variable `v_time` to store the time of the day. You also modify the statement

```
v_day := TO_CHAR(SYSDATE, 'fmDAY');
```

so that DAY is prefixed by the letters `fm`. This guarantees that extra spaces will be removed from the name of the day. Then you add another statement that determines the current time of day and stores it in the variable `v_time`. Finally, you add an IF-THEN-ELSE statement that checks the time of day and displays the appropriate message.

Notice that two consecutive single quotes are used in the second and third DBMS_OUTPUT.PUT_LINE statements. This allows you to use an apostrophe in your message.

When run, this exercise produces the following output:

```
SUNDAY, 16:19
It's afternoon
Done...

PLSQL procedure successfully completed.
```

2) Create a new script. For a given instructor, determine how many sections he or she is teaching. If the number is greater than or equal to 3, display a message saying that the instructor needs a vacation. Otherwise, display a message saying how many sections this instructor is teaching.

ANSWER: The script should look similar to the following:

```
SET SERVEROUTPUT ON
DECLARE
   v_instructor_id NUMBER := &sv_instructor_id;
   v_total NUMBER;
BEGIN
   SELECT COUNT(*)
     INTO v_total
     FROM section
    WHERE instructor_id = v_instructor_id;

   -- check if instructor teaches 3 or more sections
   IF v_total >= 3 THEN
      DBMS_OUTPUT.PUT_LINE ('This instructor needs '||
         'a vacation');
   ELSE
      DBMS_OUTPUT.PUT_LINE ('This instructor teaches '||
         v_total||' sections');
   END IF;
   -- control resumes here
   DBMS_OUTPUT.PUT_LINE ('Done...');
END;
```

This script accepts a value for the instructor's ID from a user. Next, it checks the number of sections taught by the given instructor. This is accomplished with the help of the SELECT INTO statement. Next, it determines what message should be displayed on the screen with the help of the IF-THEN-ELSE statement. If a particular instructor teaches three or more sections, the condition of the IF-THEN-ELSE statement evaluates to TRUE, and the message This instructor needs a vacation is displayed to the user. In the opposite case, the message stating how many sections an instructor is teaching is displayed. Assume that value 101 was provided at runtime. Then the script produces the following output:

```
Enter value for sv_instructor_id: 101
old    2:    v_instructor_id NUMBER := &sv_instructor_id;
new    2:    v_instructor_id NUMBER := 101;
This instructor needs a vacation

PLSQL procedure successfully completed.
```

3) Execute the following two PL/SQL blocks, and explain why they produce different output for the same value of the variable v_num. Remember to issue the SET SERVEROUTPUT ON command before running this script.

```
-- Block 1
DECLARE
   v_num NUMBER := NULL;
BEGIN
   IF v_num > 0 THEN
      DBMS_OUTPUT.PUT_LINE ('v_num is greater than 0');
   ELSE
      DBMS_OUTPUT.PUT_LINE ('v_num is not greater than 0');
   END IF;
END;


-- Block 2
DECLARE
   v_num NUMBER := NULL;
BEGIN
   IF v_num > 0 THEN
      DBMS_OUTPUT.PUT_LINE ('v_num is greater than 0');
   END IF;
   IF NOT (v_num > 0) THEN
      DBMS_OUTPUT.PUT_LINE ('v_num is not greater than 0');
   END IF;
END;
```

ANSWER: Consider the output produced by the preceding scripts:

```
-- Block1
v_num is not greater than 0

PLSQL procedure successfully completed.

-- Block 2
PLSQL procedure successfully completed.
```

The output produced by Block 1 and Block 2 is different, even though in both examples variable v_num is defined as NULL.

First, take a closer look at the IF-THEN-ELSE statement used in Block 1:

```
IF v_num > 0 THEN
    DBMS_OUTPUT.PUT_LINE ('v_num is greater than 0');
ELSE
    DBMS_OUTPUT.PUT_LINE ('v_num is not greater than 0');
END IF;
```

The condition $v\_num > 0$ evaluates to FALSE because NULL has been assigned to the variable v_num. As a result, control is transferred to the ELSE part of the IF-THEN-ELSE statement. So the message v_num is not greater than 0 is displayed on the screen.

Second, take a closer look at the IF-THEN statements used in Block 2:

```
IF v_num > 0 THEN
    DBMS_OUTPUT.PUT_LINE ('v_num is greater than 0');
END IF;
IF NOT (v_num > 0) THEN
    DBMS_OUTPUT.PUT_LINE ('v_num is not greater than 0');
END IF;
```

The conditions of both IF-THEN statements evaluate to FALSE. As a result, neither message is displayed on the screen.

Chapter 5, "Conditional Control: CASE Statements"

1) Create the following script. Modify the script you created in Chapter 4, project 1 of the "Try It Yourself" section. You can use either the CASE statement or the searched CASE statement. The output should look similar to the output produced by the example you created in Chapter 4.

ANSWER: Consider the script you created in Chapter 4:

```
SET SERVEROUTPUT ON
DECLARE
    v_day  VARCHAR2(15);
    v_time VARCHAR(8);
BEGIN
    v_day  := TO_CHAR(SYSDATE, 'fmDAY');
    v_time := TO_CHAR(SYSDATE, 'HH24:MI');

    IF v_day IN ('SATURDAY', 'SUNDAY') THEN
        DBMS_OUTPUT.PUT_LINE (v_day||', '||v_time);

        IF v_time BETWEEN '12:01' AND '24:00' THEN
            DBMS_OUTPUT.PUT_LINE ('It''s afternoon');
        ELSE
            DBMS_OUTPUT.PUT_LINE ('It''s morning');
        END IF;

    END IF;

    -- control resumes here
    DBMS_OUTPUT.PUT_LINE ('Done...');
END;
```

Next, consider the modified version of the script with nested CASE statements. For illustrative purposes, this script uses both CASE and searched CASE statements. Changes are shown in bold.

```
SET SERVEROUTPUT ON
DECLARE
    v_day  VARCHAR2(15);
    v_time VARCHAR(8);
BEGIN
    v_day  := TO_CHAR(SYSDATE, 'fmDay');
    v_time := TO_CHAR(SYSDATE, 'HH24:MI');

    -- CASE statement
    CASE SUBSTR(v_day, 1, 1)
        WHEN 'S' THEN
            DBMS_OUTPUT.PUT_LINE (v_day||', '||v_time);

            -- searched CASE statement
            CASE
                WHEN v_time BETWEEN '12:01' AND '24:00' THEN
                    DBMS_OUTPUT.PUT_LINE ('It''s afternoon');
            ELSE
                    DBMS_OUTPUT.PUT_LINE ('It''s morning');
            END CASE;
    END CASE;

    -- control resumes here
    DBMS_OUTPUT.PUT_LINE('Done...');
END;
```

In this exercise, you substitute nested CASE statements for nested IF statements. Consider the outer CASE statement. It uses a selector expression

```
SUBSTR(v_day, 1, 1)
```

to check if a current day falls on the weekend. Notice that it derives only the first letter of the day. This is a good solution when using a CASE statement, because only Saturday and Sunday start with S. Furthermore, without using the SUBSTR function, you would need to use a searched CASE statement. Recall that the value of the WHEN expression is compared to the value of the selector. As a result, the WHEN expression must return a similar datatype. In this example, the selector expression returns a string datatype, so the WHEN expression must also return a string datatype.

Next, you use a searched CASE to validate the time of day. Recall that, similar to the IF statement, the WHEN conditions of the searched CASE statement yield Boolean values.

When run, this exercise produces the following output:

```
Saturday, 19:49
It's afternoon
Done...

PLSQL procedure successfully completed.
```

2) Create the following script: Modify the script you created in Chapter 4, project 2 of the "Try It Yourself" section. You can use either the CASE statement or the searched CASE statement. The output should look similar to the output produced by the example you created in Chapter 4.

ANSWER: Consider the script you created in Chapter 4:

```
SET SERVEROUTPUT ON
DECLARE
   v_instructor_id NUMBER := &sv_instructor_id;
   v_total NUMBER;
BEGIN
   SELECT COUNT(*)
     INTO v_total
     FROM section
    WHERE instructor_id = v_instructor_id;

   -- check if instructor teaches 3 or more sections
   IF v_total >= 3 THEN
      DBMS_OUTPUT.PUT_LINE ('This instructor needs '||
         'a vacation');
   ELSE
      DBMS_OUTPUT.PUT_LINE ('This instructor teaches '||
         v_total||' sections');
   END IF;
   -- control resumes here
   DBMS_OUTPUT.PUT_LINE ('Done...');
END;
```

Next, consider a modified version of the script, with the searched CASE statement instead of the IF-THEN-ELSE statement. Changes are shown in bold.

```
SET SERVEROUTPUT ON
DECLARE
   v_instructor_id NUMBER := &sv_instructor_id;
   v_total NUMBER;
BEGIN
   SELECT COUNT(*)
     INTO v_total
     FROM section
    WHERE instructor_id = v_instructor_id;

   -- check if instructor teaches 3 or more sections
   CASE
      WHEN v_total >= 3 THEN
         DBMS_OUTPUT.PUT_LINE ('This instructor needs '||
            'a vacation');
      ELSE
         DBMS_OUTPUT.PUT_LINE ('This instructor teaches '||
            v_total||' sections');
   END CASE;
   -- control resumes here
   DBMS_OUTPUT.PUT_LINE ('Done...');
END;
```

Assume that value 109 was provided at runtime. Then the script produces the following output:

```
Enter value for sv_instructor_id: 109
old    2:     v_instructor_id NUMBER := &sv_instructor_id;
new    2:     v_instructor_id NUMBER := 109;
This instructor teaches 1 sections
Done...


PLSQL procedure successfully completed.
```

To use the CASE statement, the searched CASE statement could be modified as follows:

```
CASE SIGN(v_total - 3)
   WHEN -1 THEN
      DBMS_OUTPUT.PUT_LINE ('This instructor teaches '||
         v_total||' sections');
   ELSE
      DBMS_OUTPUT.PUT_LINE ('This instructor needs '||
         'a vacation');
END CASE;
```

Notice that the SIGN function is used to determine if an instructor teaches three or more sections. Recall that the SIGN function returns –1 if v_total is less than 3, 0 if v_total equals 3, and 1 if v_total is greater than 3. In this case, as long as the SIGN function returns –1, the message This instructor teaches ... is displayed on the screen. In all other cases, the message This instructor needs a vacation is displayed on the screen.

3) Execute the following two SELECT statements, and explain why they produce different output:

```
SELECT e.student_id, e.section_id, e.final_grade, g.numeric_grade,
       COALESCE(g.numeric_grade, e.final_grade) grade
  FROM enrollment e, grade g
 WHERE e.student_id = g.student_id
   AND e.section_id = g.section_id
   AND e.student_id = 102
   AND g.grade_type_code = 'FI';


SELECT e.student_id, e.section_id, e.final_grade, g.numeric_grade,
       NULLIF(g.numeric_grade, e.final_grade) grade
  FROM enrollment e, grade g
 WHERE e.student_id = g.student_id
   AND e.section_id = g.section_id
   AND e.student_id = 102
   AND g.grade_type_code = 'FI';
```

ANSWER: Consider the output produced by the following SELECT statements:

```
STUDENT_ID SECTION_ID FINAL_GRADE NUMERIC_GRADE     GRADE
---------- ---------- ----------- ------------- ----------
       102         86                        85         85
       102         89          92            92         92
```

```
STUDENT_ID SECTION_ID FINAL_GRADE NUMERIC_GRADE      GRADE
---------- ---------- ----------- ------------- ----------
       102         86                         85         85
       102         89          92             92
```

Consider the output returned by the first SELECT statement. This statement uses the COALESCE function to derive the value of GRADE. It equals the value of NUMERIC_GRADE in the first row and the value of FINAL_GRADE in the second row.

The COALESCE function compares the value of FINAL_GRADE to NULL. If it is NULL, the value of NUMERIC_GRADE is compared to NULL. Because the value of NUMERIC_GRADE is not NULL, the COALESCE function returns the value of NUMERIC_GRADE in the first row. In the second row, the COALESCE function returns the value of FINAL_GRADE because it is not NULL.

Next, consider the output returned by the second SELECT statement. This statement uses the NULLIF function to derive the value of GRADE. It equals the value of NUMERIC_GRADE in the first row, and it is NULL in the second row.

The NULLIF function compares the NUMERIC_GRADE value to the FINAL_GRADE value. If these values are equal, the NULLIF function returns NULL. In the opposite case, it returns the value of NUMERIC_GRADE.

Chapter 6, "Iterative Control: Part I"

1) Rewrite script ch06_1a.sql using a WHILE loop instead of a simple loop. Make sure that the output produced by this script does not differ from the output produced by the script ch06_1a.sql.

ANSWER: Consider script ch06_1a.sql:

```
SET SERVEROUTPUT ON
DECLARE
   v_counter BINARY_INTEGER := 0;
BEGIN
   LOOP
      -- increment loop counter by one
      v_counter := v_counter + 1;
      DBMS_OUTPUT.PUT_LINE ('v_counter = '||v_counter);

      -- if EXIT condition yields TRUE exit the loop
      IF v_counter = 5 THEN
         EXIT;
      END IF;

   END LOOP;
   -- control resumes here
   DBMS_OUTPUT.PUT_LINE ('Done...');
END;
```

Next, consider a new version of the script that uses a WHILE loop. Changes are shown in bold.

```
SET SERVEROUTPUT ON
DECLARE
   v_counter BINARY_INTEGER := 0;
BEGIN
   WHILE v_counter < 5 LOOP
```

```
      -- increment loop counter by one
      v_counter := v_counter + 1;
      DBMS_OUTPUT.PUT_LINE ('v_counter = '||v_counter);
   END LOOP;

   -- control resumes here
   DBMS_OUTPUT.PUT_LINE('Done...');
END;
```

In this version of the script, you replace a simple loop with a WHILE loop. It is important to remember that a simple loop executes at least once because the EXIT condition is placed in the body of the loop. On the other hand, a WHILE loop may not execute at all, because a condition is tested outside the body of the loop. So, to achieve the same results using the WHILE loop, the EXIT condition

```
v_counter = 5
```

used in the original version is replaced by the test condition

```
v_counter < 5
```

When run, this example produces the following output:

```
v_counter = 1
v_counter = 2
v_counter = 3
v_counter = 4
v_counter = 5
Done...

PL/SQL procedure successfully completed.
```

2) Rewrite script ch06_3a.sql using a numeric FOR loop instead of a WHILE loop. Make sure that the output produced by this script does not differ from the output produced by the script ch06_3a.sql.

ANSWER: Consider script ch06_3a.sql:

```
SET SERVEROUTPUT ON
DECLARE
   v_counter BINARY_INTEGER := 1;
   v_sum NUMBER := 0;
BEGIN
   WHILE v_counter <= 10 LOOP
      v_sum := v_sum + v_counter;
      DBMS_OUTPUT.PUT_LINE ('Current sum is: '||v_sum);

      -- increment loop counter by one
      v_counter := v_counter + 1;
   END LOOP;

   -- control resumes here
   DBMS_OUTPUT.PUT_LINE ('The sum of integers between 1 '||
                         'and 10 is: '||v_sum);
END;
```

Next, consider a new version of the script that uses a WHILE loop. Changes are shown in bold.

```
SET SERVEROUTPUT ON
DECLARE
   v_sum NUMBER := 0;
BEGIN
   FOR v_counter IN 1..10 LOOP
      v_sum := v_sum + v_counter;
      DBMS_OUTPUT.PUT_LINE ('Current sum is: '||v_sum);
   END LOOP;

   -- control resumes here
   DBMS_OUTPUT.PUT_LINE ('The sum of integers between 1 '||
                         'and 10 is: '||v_sum);
END;
```

In this version of the script, you replace a WHILE loop with a numeric FOR loop. As a result, there is no need to declare the variable $v\_counter$ and increment it by 1, because the loop itself handles these steps implicitly.

When run, this version of the script produces output identical to the output produced by the original version:

```
Current sum is: 1
Current sum is: 3
Current sum is: 6
Current sum is: 10
Current sum is: 15
Current sum is: 21
Current sum is: 28
Current sum is: 36
Current sum is: 45
Current sum is: 55
The sum of integers between 1 and 10 is: 55

PL/SQL procedure successfully completed.
```

3) Rewrite script ch06_4a.sql using a simple loop instead of a numeric FOR loop. Make sure that the output produced by this script does not differ from the output produced by the script ch06_4a.sql.

ANSWER: Recall script ch06_4a.sql:

```
SET SERVEROUTPUT ON
DECLARE
   v_factorial NUMBER := 1;
BEGIN
   FOR v_counter IN 1..10 LOOP
      v_factorial := v_factorial * v_counter;
   END LOOP;
   -- control resumes here
   DBMS_OUTPUT.PUT_LINE ('Factorial of ten is: '||v_factorial);
END;
```

Next, consider a new version of the script that uses a simple loop. Changes are shown in bold.

```
SET SERVEROUTPUT ON
DECLARE
   v_counter     NUMBER := 1;
   v_factorial NUMBER := 1;
BEGIN
    LOOP
      v_factorial := v_factorial * v_counter;

      v_counter := v_counter + 1;
      EXIT WHEN v_counter = 10;
   END LOOP;
   -- control resumes here
   DBMS_OUTPUT.PUT_LINE ('Factorial of ten is: '||v_factorial);
END;
```

In this version of the script, you replace a numeric FOR loop with a simple loop. As a result, you should make three important changes. First, you need to declare and initialize the loop counter, $v\_counter$. This counter is implicitly defined and initialized by the FOR loop. Second, you need to increment the value of the loop counter. This is very important, because if you forget to include the statement

```
v_counter := v_counter + 1;
```

in the body of the simple loop, you end up with an infinite loop. This step is not necessary when you use a numeric FOR loop, because it is done by the loop itself.

Third, you need to specify the EXIT condition for the simple loop. Because you are computing a factorial of 10, the following EXIT condition is specified:

```
EXIT WHEN v_counter = 10;
```

You could specify this EXIT condition using an IF-THEN statement as well:

```
IF v_counter = 10 THEN
   EXIT;
END IF;
```

When run, this example shows the following output:

```
Factorial of ten is: 362880

PL/SQL procedure successfully completed.
```

Chapter 7, "Iterative Control: Part II"

1) Rewrite script ch06_4a.sql to calculate the factorial of even integers only between 1 and 10. The script should use a CONTINUE or CONTINUE WHEN statement.

ANSWER: Recall script ch06_4a.sql:

```
SET SERVEROUTPUT ON
DECLARE
   v_factorial NUMBER := 1;
BEGIN
   FOR v_counter IN 1..10 LOOP
```

```
      v_factorial := v_factorial * v_counter;
   END LOOP;
   -- control resumes here
   DBMS_OUTPUT.PUT_LINE ('Factorial of ten is: '||v_factorial);
END;
```

Next, consider a new version of the script that uses a CONTINUE WHEN statement. Changes are shown in bold.

```
SET SERVEROUTPUT ON
DECLARE
   v_factorial NUMBER := 1;
BEGIN
   FOR v_counter IN 1..10 LOOP
      CONTINUE WHEN MOD(v_counter, 2) != 0;
      v_factorial := v_factorial * v_counter;
   END LOOP;
   -- control resumes here
   DBMS_OUTPUT.PUT_LINE
      ('Factorial of even numbers between 1 and 10 is: '||
       v_factorial);
END;
```

In this version of the script, you add a CONTINUE WHEN statement that passes control to the top of the loop if the current value of $v\_counter$ is not an even number. The rest of the script remains unchanged. Note that you could specify the CONTINUE condition using an IF-THEN statement as well:

```
IF MOD(v_counter, 2) != 0 THEN
   CONTINUE;
END IF;
```

When run, this example shows the following output:

```
Factorial of even numbers between 1 and 10 is: 3840

PL/SQL procedure successfully completed.
```

2) Rewrite script ch07_3a.sql using a simple loop instead of the outer FOR loop, and a WHILE loop for the inner FOR loop. Make sure that the output produced by this script does not differ from the output produced by the original script.

ANSWER: Consider the original version of the script:

```
SET SERVEROUTPUT ON
DECLARE
   v_test NUMBER := 0;
BEGIN
   <<outer_loop>>
   FOR i IN 1..3 LOOP
      DBMS_OUTPUT.PUT_LINE('Outer Loop');
      DBMS_OUTPUT.PUT_LINE('i = '||i);
      DBMS_OUTPUT.PUT_LINE('v_test = '||v_test);
      v_test := v_test + 1;
```

```
      <<inner_loop>>
      FOR j IN 1..2 LOOP
         DBMS_OUTPUT.PUT_LINE('Inner Loop');
         DBMS_OUTPUT.PUT_LINE('j = '||j);
         DBMS_OUTPUT.PUT_LINE('i = '||i);
         DBMS_OUTPUT.PUT_LINE('v_test = '||v_test);
      END LOOP inner_loop;
   END LOOP outer_loop;
END;
```

Next, consider a modified version of the script that uses simple and WHILE loops. Changes are shown in bold.

```
SET SERVEROUTPUT ON
DECLARE
   i INTEGER := 1;
   j INTEGER := 1;
   v_test NUMBER := 0;
BEGIN
   <<outer_loop>>
   LOOP
      DBMS_OUTPUT.PUT_LINE ('Outer Loop');
      DBMS_OUTPUT.PUT_LINE ('i = '||i);
      DBMS_OUTPUT.PUT_LINE ('v_test = '||v_test);
      v_test := v_test + 1;

      -- reset inner loop counter
      j := 1;

      <<inner_loop>>
      WHILE j <= 2 LOOP
         DBMS_OUTPUT.PUT_LINE ('Inner Loop');
         DBMS_OUTPUT.PUT_LINE ('j = '||j);
         DBMS_OUTPUT.PUT_LINE ('i = '||i);
         DBMS_OUTPUT.PUT_LINE ('v_test = '||v_test);
         j := j + 1;
      END LOOP inner_loop;

      i := i + 1;
      -- EXIT condition of the outer loop
      EXIT WHEN i > 3;
   END LOOP outer_loop;
END;
```

Note that this version of the script contains changes that are important due to the nature of the loops that are used.

First, both counters, for outer and inner loops, must be declared and initialized. Moreover, the counter for the inner loop must be initialized to 1 before the inner loop is executed, not in the declaration section of this script. In other words, the inner loop executes three times. It is important not to confuse the phrase *execution of the loop* with the term *iteration. Each execution of the*

WHILE loop causes the statements inside this loop to iterate twice. Before each execution, the loop counter j must be reset to 1 again. This step is necessary because the WHILE loop does not initialize its counter implicitly like a numeric FOR loop. As a result, after the first execution of the WHILE loop is complete, the value of counter j is equal to 3. If this value is not reset to 1 again, the loop does not execute a second time.

Second, both loop counters must be incremented. Third, the EXIT condition must be specified for the outer loop, and the test condition must be specified for the inner loop.

When run, the exercise produces the following output:

```
Outer Loop
i = 1
v_test = 0
Inner Loop
j = 1
i = 1
v_test = 1
Inner Loop
j = 2
i = 1
v_test = 1
Outer Loop
i = 2
v_test = 1
Inner Loop
j = 1
i = 2
v_test = 2
Inner Loop
j = 2
i = 2
v_test = 2
Outer Loop
i = 3
v_test = 2
Inner Loop
j = 1
i = 3
v_test = 3
Inner Loop
j = 2
i = 3
v_test = 3

PL/SQL procedure successfully completed.
```

Chapter 8, "Error Handling and Built-In Exceptions"

1) Create the following script: Check to see whether there is a record in the STUDENT table for a given student ID. If there is not, insert a record into the STUDENT table for the given student ID.

ANSWER: The script should look similar to the following:

```
SET SERVEROUTPUT ON
DECLARE
    v_student_id NUMBER         := &sv_student_id;
    v_first_name VARCHAR2(30) := '&sv_first_name';
    v_last_name  VARCHAR2(30) := '&sv_last_name';
    v_zip          CHAR(5)        := '&sv_zip';
    v_name         VARCHAR2(50);
BEGIN
    SELECT first_name||' '||last_name
      INTO v_name
      FROM student
     WHERE student_id = v_student_id;

    DBMS_OUTPUT.PUT_LINE ('Student '||v_name||' is a valid student');
EXCEPTION
    WHEN NO_DATA_FOUND THEN
       DBMS_OUTPUT.PUT_LINE
          ('This student does not exist, and will be '||
           'added to the STUDENT table');

       INSERT INTO student
          (student_id, first_name, last_name, zip, registration_date,
           created_by, created_date, modified_by, modified_date)
       VALUES
          (v_student_id, v_first_name, v_last_name, v_zip, SYSDATE,
           USER, SYSDATE, USER, SYSDATE);
       COMMIT;
END;
```

This script accepts a value for student's ID from a user. For a given student ID, it determines the student's name using the SELECT INTO statement and displays it on the screen. If the value provided by the user is not a valid student ID, control of execution is passed to the exception-handling section of the block, where the NO_DATA_FOUND exception is raised. As a result, the message This student does not exist ... is displayed on the screen, and a new record is inserted into the STUDENT table.

To test this script fully, consider running it for two values of student ID. Only one value should correspond to an existing student ID. It is important to note that a valid zip code must be provided for both runs. Why do you think this is necessary?

When 319 is provided for the student ID (it is a valid student ID), this exercise produces the following output:

```
Enter value for sv_student_id: 319
old   2:     v_student_id NUMBER := &sv_student_id;
new   2:     v_student_id NUMBER := 319;
Enter value for sv_first_name: John
old   3:     v_first_name VARCHAR2(30) := '&sv_first_name';
new   3:     v_first_name VARCHAR2(30) := 'John';
Enter value for sv_last_name: Smith
old   4:     v_last_name VARCHAR2(30) := '&sv_last_name';
new   4:     v_last_name VARCHAR2(30) := 'Smith';
```

```
Enter value for sv_zip: 07421
old    5:     v_zip CHAR(5) := '&sv_zip';
new    5:     v_zip CHAR(5) := '07421';
Student George Eakheit is a valid student

PLSQL procedure successfully completed.
```

Notice that the name displayed by the script does not correspond to the name entered at runtime. Why do you think this is?

When 555 is provided for the student ID (it is not a valid student ID), this exercise produces the following output:

```
Enter value for sv_student_id: 555
old    2:     v_student_id NUMBER := &sv_student_id;
new    2:     v_student_id NUMBER := 555;
Enter value for sv_first_name: John
old    3:     v_first_name VARCHAR2(30) := '&sv_first_name';
new    3:     v_first_name VARCHAR2(30) := 'John';
Enter value for sv_last_name: Smith
old    4:     v_last_name VARCHAR2(30) := '&sv_last_name';
new    4:     v_last_name VARCHAR2(30) := 'Smith';
Enter value for sv_zip: 07421
old    5:     v_zip CHAR(5) := '&sv_zip';
new    5:     v_zip CHAR(5) := '07421';
This student does not exist, and will be added to the STUDENT table

PLSQL procedure successfully completed.
```

Next, you can select this new record from the STUDENT table as follows:

```
SELECT student_id, first_name, last_name
  FROM student
 WHERE student_id = 555;
```

```
STUDENT_ID FIRST_NAME               LAST_NAME
---------- ------------------------ ----------------
       555 John                     Smith
```

2) Create the following script: For a given instructor ID, check to see whether it is assigned to a valid instructor. Then check to see how many sections this instructor teaches, and display this information on the screen.

   ANSWER: The script should look similar to the following:

```
SET SERVEROUTPUT ON
DECLARE
   v_instructor_id NUMBER := &sv_instructor_id;
   v_name VARCHAR2(50);
   v_total NUMBER;
 BEGIN
   SELECT first_name||' '||last_name
     INTO v_name
     FROM instructor
    WHERE instructor_id = v_instructor_id;
```

```
   -- check how many sections are taught by this instructor
   SELECT COUNT(*)
     INTO v_total
     FROM section
    WHERE instructor_id = v_instructor_id;

   DBMS_OUTPUT.PUT_LINE ('Instructor, '||v_name||
      ', teaches '||v_total||' section(s)');
EXCEPTION
   WHEN NO_DATA_FOUND THEN
      DBMS_OUTPUT.PUT_LINE ('This is not a valid instructor');
END;
```

This script accepts a value for the instructor's ID from a user. For a given instructor ID, it determines the instructor's name using the SELECT INTO statement. This SELECT INTO statement checks to see if the ID provided by the user is a valid instructor ID. If this value is not valid, control of execution is passed to the exception-handling section of the block, where the NO_DATA_FOUND exception is raised. As a result, the message This is not a valid instructor is displayed on the screen. On the other hand, if the value provided by the user is a valid instructor ID, the second SELECT INTO statement calculates how many sections are taught by this instructor.

To test this script fully, consider running it for two values of instructor ID. When 105 is provided for the instructor ID (it is a valid instructor ID), this exercise produces the following output:

```
Enter value for sv_instructor_id: 105
old    2:    v_instructor_id NUMBER := &sv_instructor_id;
new    2:    v_instructor_id NUMBER := 105;
Instructor, Anita Morris, teaches 10 section(s)

PLSQL procedure successfully completed.
```

When 123 is provided for the instructor ID (it is not a valid student ID), this exercise produces the following output:

```
Enter value for sv_instructor_id: 123
old    2:    v_instructor_id NUMBER := &sv_instructor_id;
new    2:    v_instructor_id NUMBER := 123;
This is not a valid instructor

PLSQL procedure successfully completed.
```

Chapter 9, "Exceptions"

1) Create the following script: For a course section provided at runtime, determine the number of students registered. If this number is equal to or greater than 10, raise the user-defined exception e_too_many_students and display an error message. Otherwise, display how many students are in a section.

   ANSWER: The script should look similar to the following:

```
SET SERVEROUTPUT ON
DECLARE
   v_section_id         NUMBER := &sv_section_id;
   v_total_students     NUMBER;
   e_too_many_students EXCEPTION;
```

```
BEGIN
   -- Calculate number of students enrolled
   SELECT COUNT(*)
     INTO v_total_students
     FROM enrollment
    WHERE section_id = v_section_id;

   IF v_total_students >= 10 THEN
      RAISE e_too_many_students;
   ELSE
      DBMS_OUTPUT.PUT_LINE ('There are '||v_total_students||
         ' students for section ID: '||v_section_id);
   END IF;
EXCEPTION
   WHEN e_too_many_students THEN
      DBMS_OUTPUT.PUT_LINE ('There are too many '||
         'students for section '||v_section_id);
END;
```

In this script, you declare two variables, `v_section_id` and `v_total_students`, to store the section ID provided by the user and the total number of students in that section ID, respectively. You also declare a user-defined exception `e_too_many_students`. You raise this exception using the IF-THEN statement if the value returned by the COUNT function exceeds 10. Otherwise, you display the message specifying how many students are enrolled in a given section.

To test this script fully, consider running it for two values of section ID. When 101 is provided for the section ID (this section has more than ten students), this script produces the following output:

```
Enter value for sv_section_id: 101
old   2:     v_section_id        NUMBER := &sv_section_id;
new   2:     v_section_id        NUMBER := 101;
There are too many students for section 101

PL/SQL procedure successfully completed.
```

When 116 is provided for the section ID (this section has fewer than ten students), this script produces different output:

```
Enter value for sv_section_id: 116
old   2:     v_section_id        NUMBER := &sv_section_id;
new   2:     v_section_id        NUMBER := 116;
There are 8 students for section ID: 116

PL/SQL procedure successfully completed.
```

Next, consider running this script for a nonexistent section ID:

```
Enter value for sv_section_id: 999
old   2:     v_section_id        NUMBER := &sv_section_id;
new   2:     v_section_id        NUMBER := 999;
There are 0 students for section ID: 999

PL/SQL procedure successfully completed.
```

Note that the script does not produce any errors. Instead, it states that section 999 has 0 students. How would you modify this script to ensure that when there is no corresponding section ID in the ENROLLMENT table, the message This section does not exist is displayed on the screen?

2) Modify the script you just created. After the exception e_too_many_students has been raised in the inner block, reraise it in the outer block.

ANSWER: The new version of the script should look similar to the following. Changes are shown in bold.

```
SET SERVEROUTPUT ON
DECLARE
    v_section_id       NUMBER := &sv_section_id;
    v_total_students   NUMBER;
    e_too_many_students EXCEPTION;
BEGIN
    -- Add inner block
    BEGIN
        -- Calculate number of students enrolled
        SELECT COUNT(*)
          INTO v_total_students
          FROM enrollment
         WHERE section_id = v_section_id;

        IF v_total_students >= 10 THEN
           RAISE e_too_many_students;
        ELSE
           DBMS_OUTPUT.PUT_LINE ('There are '||v_total_students||
              ' students for section ID: '||v_section_id);
        END IF;
    -- Re-raise exception
    EXCEPTION
       WHEN e_too_many_students THEN
          RAISE;
    END;
EXCEPTION
   WHEN e_too_many_students THEN
      DBMS_OUTPUT.PUT_LINE ('There are too many '||
         'students for section '||v_section_id);
END;
```

In this version of the script, you introduce an inner block where the e_too_many_students exception is raised first and then propagated to the outer block. This version of the script produces output identical to the original script.

Next, consider a different version in which the original PL/SQL block (the PL/SQL block from the original script) has been enclosed in another block:

```
SET SERVEROUTPUT ON
-- Outer PL/SQL block
BEGIN
    -- This block became inner PL/SQL block
```

```
   DECLARE
      v_section_id        NUMBER := &sv_section_id;
      v_total_students    NUMBER;
      e_too_many_students EXCEPTION;
   BEGIN
      -- Calculate number of students enrolled
      SELECT COUNT(*)
        INTO v_total_students
        FROM enrollment
       WHERE section_id = v_section_id;

      IF v_total_students >= 10 THEN
         RAISE e_too_many_students;
      ELSE
         DBMS_OUTPUT.PUT_LINE ('There are '||v_total_students||
            ' students for section ID: '||v_section_id);
      END IF;
   EXCEPTION
      WHEN e_too_many_students THEN
         RAISE;
   END;


EXCEPTION
   WHEN e_too_many_students THEN
      DBMS_OUTPUT.PUT_LINE ('There are too many '||
         'students for section '||v_section_id);
END;
```

This version of the script causes the following error message:

```
Enter value for sv_section_id: 101
old    4:        v_section_id        NUMBER := &sv_section_id;
new    4:        v_section_id        NUMBER := 101;
   WHEN e_too_many_students THEN
        *
ERROR at line 26:
ORA-06550: line 26, column 9:
PLS-00201: identifier 'E_TOO_MANY_STUDENTS' must be declared
ORA-06550: line 0, column 0:
PL/SQL: Compilation unit analysis terminated
```

This occurs because the e_too_many_students exception is declared in the inner block and, as a result, is not visible to the outer block. In addition, the v_section_id variable used by the exception-handling section of the outer block is declared in the inner block as well, and, as a result, is not accessible in the outer block.

To correct these errors, the previous version of the script can be modified as follows:

```
SET SERVEROUTPUT ON
-- Outer PL/SQL block
DECLARE
   v_section_id        NUMBER := &sv_section_id;
   e_too_many_students EXCEPTION;
```

```
BEGIN
   -- This block became inner PL/SQL block
   DECLARE
      v_total_students NUMBER;
   BEGIN
      -- Calculate number of students enrolled
      SELECT COUNT(*)
        INTO v_total_students
        FROM enrollment
       WHERE section_id = v_section_id;

      IF v_total_students >= 10 THEN
         RAISE e_too_many_students;
      ELSE
         DBMS_OUTPUT.PUT_LINE ('There are '||v_total_students||
            ' students for section ID: '||v_section_id);
      END IF;
   EXCEPTION
      WHEN e_too_many_students THEN
         RAISE;
   END;

EXCEPTION
   WHEN e_too_many_students THEN
      DBMS_OUTPUT.PUT_LINE ('There are too many '||
         'students for section '||v_section_id);
END;
```

Chapter 10, "Exceptions: Advanced Concepts"

1) Modify the script you created in project 1 of the "Try It Yourself" section in Chapter 9. Raise a user-defined exception with the RAISE_APPLICATION_ERROR statement. Otherwise, display how many students are in a section. Make sure your program can process all sections.

ANSWER: The script should look similar to the following. Changes are shown in bold.

```
SET SERVEROUTPUT ON
DECLARE
   v_section_id        NUMBER := &sv_section_id;
   v_total_students    NUMBER;
BEGIN
   -- Calculate number of students enrolled
   SELECT COUNT(*)
     INTO v_total_students
     FROM enrollment
    WHERE section_id = v_section_id;

   IF v_total_students >= 10 THEN
      RAISE_APPLICATION_ERROR
         (-20000, 'There are too many students for '||
         'section '||v_section_id);
```

```
      ELSE
         DBMS_OUTPUT.PUT_LINE ('There are '||v_total_students||
            ' students for section ID: '||v_section_id);
      END IF;
END;
```

In this version of the script, you use the RAISE_APPLICATION_ERROR statement to handle the following error condition: If the number of students enrolled in a particular section is equal to or greater than ten, an error is raised. It is important to remember that the RAISE_APPLICATION_ ERROR statement works with the unnamed user-defined exceptions. Therefore, notice that there is no reference to the exception e_too_many_students anywhere in this script. On the other hand, an error number has been associated with the error message.

When run, this exercise produces the following output (the same section IDs are used for this script as well: 101, 116, and 999):

```
Enter value for sv_section_id: 101
old    2:    v_section_id        NUMBER := &sv_section_id;
new    2:    v_section_id        NUMBER := 101;
DECLARE
*
ERROR at line 1:
ORA-20000: There are too many students for section 101
ORA-06512: at line 12


Enter value for sv_section_id: 116
old    2:    v_section_id        NUMBER := &sv_section_id;
new    2:    v_section_id        NUMBER := 116;
There are 8 students for section ID: 116

PL/SQL procedure successfully completed.


Enter value for sv_section_id: 999
old    2:    v_section_id        NUMBER := &sv_section_id;
new    2:    v_section_id        NUMBER := 999;
There are 0 students for section ID: 999

PL/SQL procedure successfully completed.
```

2) Create the following script: Try to add a record to the INSTRUCTOR table without providing values for the columns CREATED_BY, CREATED_DATE, MODIFIED_BY, and MODIFIED_DATE. Define an exception and associate it with the Oracle error number so that the error generated by the INSERT statement is handled.

ANSWER: Consider the following script. Notice that it has no exception handlers:

```
DECLARE
    v_first_name instructor.first_name%type := '&sv_first_name';
    v_last_name  instructor.last_name%type  := '&sv_last_name';
BEGIN
    INSERT INTO instructor
        (instructor_id, first_name, last_name)
```

```
    VALUES
        (INSTRUCTOR_ID_SEQ.NEXTVAL, v_first_name, v_last_name);
    COMMIT;
END;
```

In this version of the script, you are trying to add a new record to the INSTRUCTOR table. The INSERT statement has only three columns: INSTRUCTOR_ID, FIRST_NAME, and LAST_NAME. The value for the column INSTRUCTOR_ID is determined from the sequence INSTRUCTOR_ID_SEQ, and the user provides the values for the columns FIRST_NAME and LAST_NAME.

When run, this script produces the following error message:

```
Enter value for sv_first_name: John
old    2:         '&sv_first_name';
new    2:         'John';
Enter value for sv_last_name: Smith
old    3:         '&sv_last_name';
new    3:         'Smith';
DECLARE
*
ERROR at line 1:
ORA-01400: cannot insert NULL into
  ("STUDENT"."INSTRUCTOR"."CREATED_BY")
ORA-06512: at line 5
```

This error message states that a NULL value cannot be inserted into the column CREATED_BY of the INSTRUCTOR table. Therefore, you need to add an exception handler to the script, as follows. Changes are shown in bold.

```
SET SERVEROUTPUT ON
DECLARE
    v_first_name instructor.first_name%type := '&sv_first_name';
    v_last_name  instructor.last_name%type  := '&sv_last_name';

    e_non_null_value EXCEPTION;
    PRAGMA EXCEPTION_INIT(e_non_null_value, -1400);
BEGIN
    INSERT INTO INSTRUCTOR
        (instructor_id, first_name, last_name)
    VALUES
        (INSTRUCTOR_ID_SEQ.NEXTVAL, v_first_name, v_last_name);
    COMMIT;
EXCEPTION
    WHEN e_non_null_value THEN
        DBMS_OUTPUT.PUT_LINE ('A NULL value cannot be '||
            'inserted. Check constraints on the INSTRUCTOR table.');
END;
```

In this version of the script, you declare a new exception called e_non_null_value. Next, you associate an Oracle error number with this exception. As a result, you can add an exception-handling section to trap the error generated by Oracle.

When run, the new version produces the following output:

```
Enter value for sv_first_name: John
old    2:        '&sv_first_name';
new    2:        'John';
Enter value for sv_last_name: Smith
old    3:        '&sv_last_name';
new    3:        'Smith';
A NULL value cannot be inserted. Check constraints on the
INSTRUCTOR table.

PL/SQL procedure successfully completed.
```

3) Modify the script you just created. Instead of declaring a user-defined exception, add the OTHERS exception handler to the exception-handling section of the block. Then display the error number and the error message on the screen.

ANSWER: The script should look similar to the following. Changes are shown in bold.

```
SET SERVEROUTPUT ON
DECLARE
    v_first_name instructor.first_name%type := '&sv_first_name';
    v_last_name  instructor.last_name%type  := '&sv_last_name';
BEGIN
    INSERT INTO INSTRUCTOR
        (instructor_id, first_name, last_name)
    VALUES
        (INSTRUCTOR_ID_SEQ.NEXTVAL, v_first_name, v_last_name);
    COMMIT;
EXCEPTION
    WHEN OTHERS THEN
        DBMS_OUTPUT.PUT_LINE ('Error code: '||SQLCODE);
        DBMS_OUTPUT.PUT_LINE ('Error message: '||
            SUBSTR(SQLERRM, 1, 200));
END;
```

Notice that as long as the OTHERS exception handler is used, there is no need to associate an Oracle error number with a user-defined exception. When run, this exercise produces the following output:

```
Enter value for sv_first_name: John
old    2:        '&sv_first_name';
new    2:        'John';
Enter value for sv_last_name: Smith
old    3:        '&sv_last_name';
new    3:        'Smith';
Error code: -1400
Error message: ORA-01400: cannot insert NULL into
("STUDENT"."INSTRUCTOR"."CREATED_BY")

PL/SQL procedure successfully completed.
```

Chapter 11, "Introduction to Cursors"

1) Write a nested cursor in which the parent cursor SELECTs information about each section of a course. The child cursor counts the enrollment. The only output is one line for each course, with the course name, section number, and total enrollment.

   ANSWER: The script should look similar to the following:

```
SET SERVEROUTPUT ON
DECLARE
    CURSOR c_course IS
        SELECT course_no, description
          FROM course
         WHERE course_no < 120;

    CURSOR c_enrollment(p_course_no IN course.course_no%TYPE)
    IS
        SELECT s.section_no section_no, count(*) count
          FROM section s, enrollment e
         WHERE s.course_no = p_course_no
           AND s.section_id = e.section_id
         GROUP BY s.section_no;
BEGIN
    FOR r_course IN c_course LOOP
        DBMS_OUTPUT.PUT_LINE
            (r_course.course_no||' '|| r_course.description);

        FOR r_enroll IN c_enrollment(r_course.course_no) LOOP
            DBMS_OUTPUT.PUT_LINE
                (Chr(9)||'Section:  '||r_enroll.section_no||
                ' has an enrollment of: '||r_enroll.count);
        END LOOP;

    END LOOP;
END;
```

2) Write an anonymous PL/SQL block that finds all the courses that have at least one section that is at its maximum enrollment. If no courses meet that criterion, pick two courses and create that situation for each.

   A) For each of those courses, add another section. The instructor for the new section should be taken from the existing records in the instructor table. Use the instructor who is signed up to teach the fewest courses. Handle the fact that, during the execution of your program, the instructor teaching the most courses may change.

   B) Use any exception-handling techniques you think are useful to capture error conditions.

   ANSWER: The script should look similar to the following:

```
SET SERVEROUTPUT ON
DECLARE
    v_instid_min      instructor.instructor_id%TYPE;
    v_section_id_new  section.section_id%TYPE;
    v_snumber_recent  section.section_no%TYPE := 0;
```

```
-- This cursor determines the courses that have at least
-- one section filled to capacity.
CURSOR c_filled IS
   SELECT DISTINCT s.course_no
     FROM section s
    WHERE s.capacity = (SELECT COUNT(section_id)
                          FROM enrollment e
                         WHERE e.section_id = s.section_id);
BEGIN
  FOR r_filled IN c_filled LOOP
     -- For each course in this list, add another section.
     -- First, determine the instructor who is teaching
     -- the fewest courses. If more than one instructor
     -- is teaching the same number of minimum courses
     -- (e.g. if there are three instructors teaching one
     -- course) use any of those instructors.
     SELECT instructor_id
       INTO v_instid_min
       FROM instructor
      WHERE EXISTS (SELECT NULL
                      FROM section
                     WHERE section.instructor_id =
                           instructor.instructor_id
                     GROUP BY instructor_id
                     HAVING COUNT(*) =
                       (SELECT MIN(COUNT(*))
                          FROM section
                         WHERE instructor_id IS NOT NULL
                         GROUP BY instructor_id)
                   )
        AND ROWNUM = 1;

     -- Determine the section_id for the new section.
     -- Note that this method would not work in a multiuser
     -- environment. A sequence should be used instead.
     SELECT MAX(section_id) + 1
       INTO v_section_id_new
       FROM section;

     -- Determine the section number for the new section.
     -- This only needs to be done in the real world if
     -- the system specification calls for a sequence in
     -- a parent. The sequence in parent here refers to
     -- the section_no incrementing within the course_no,
     -- and not the section_no incrementing within the
     -- section_id.
     DECLARE
        CURSOR c_snumber_in_parent IS
           SELECT section_no
             FROM section
```

```
          WHERE course_no = r_filled.course_no
        ORDER BY section_no;
    BEGIN
      -- Go from the lowest to the highest section_no
      -- and find any gaps. If there are no gaps make
      -- the new section_no equal to the highest
      -- current section_no + 1.

      FOR r_snumber_in_parent IN c_snumber_in_parent LOOP
        EXIT WHEN
            r_snumber_in_parent.section_no > v_snumber_recent
              + 1;
            v_snumber_recent := r_snumber_in_parent.section_no
              + 1;
      END LOOP;

      -- At this point, v_snumber_recent will be equal
      -- either to the value preceeding the gap or to
      -- the highest section_no for that course.
    END;
    -- Do the insert.
    INSERT INTO section
      (section_id, course_no, section_no, instructor_id)
    VALUES
      (v_section_id_new, r_filled.course_no, v_snumber_recent,
      v_instid_min);
    COMMIT;
  END LOOP;
EXCEPTION
  WHEN OTHERS THEN
      DBMS_OUTPUT.PUT_LINE ('An error has occurred');
END;
```

Chapter 12, "Advanced Cursors"

This chapter has no "Try It Yourself" section.

Chapter 13, "Triggers"

1) Create or modify a trigger on the ENROLLMENT table that fires before an INSERT statement. Make sure that all columns that have NOT NULL and foreign key constraints defined on them are populated with their proper values.

   ANSWER: The trigger should look similar to the following:

```
CREATE OR REPLACE TRIGGER enrollment_bi
BEFORE INSERT ON ENROLLMENT
FOR EACH ROW
DECLARE
  v_valid NUMBER := 0;
```

```
BEGIN
   SELECT COUNT(*)
     INTO v_valid
     FROM student
    WHERE student_id = :NEW.STUDENT_ID;

   IF v_valid = 0 THEN
      RAISE_APPLICATION_ERROR (-20000,
         'This is not a valid student');
   END IF;

   SELECT COUNT(*)
     INTO v_valid
     FROM section
    WHERE section_id = :NEW.SECTION_ID;

   IF v_valid = 0 THEN
      RAISE_APPLICATION_ERROR (-20001,
         'This is not a valid section');
   END IF;

   :NEW.ENROLL_DATE   := SYSDATE;
   :NEW.CREATED_BY    := USER;
   :NEW.CREATED_DATE  := SYSDATE;
   :NEW.MODIFIED_BY   := USER;
   :NEW.MODIFIED_DATE := SYSDATE;
END;
```

Consider this trigger. It fires before the INSERT statement on the ENROLLMENT table. First, you validate new values for student ID and section ID. If one of the IDs is invalid, the exception is raised, and the trigger is terminated. As a result, the INSERT statement causes an error. If both student and section IDs are found in the STUDENT and SECTION tables, respectively, ENROLL_DATE, CREATED_DATE, and MODIFIED_DATE are populated with the current date, and the columns CREATED_BY and MODIFIED_BY are populated with the current user name.

Consider the following INSERT statement:

```
INSERT INTO enrollment (student_id, section_id)
VALUES (777, 123);
```

The value 777 in this INSERT statement does not exist in the STUDENT table and therefore is invalid. As a result, this INSERT statement causes the following error:

```
INSERT INTO enrollment (student_id, section_id)
*
ERROR at line 1:
ORA-20000: This is not a valid student
ORA-06512: at "STUDENT.ENROLLMENT_BI", line 10
ORA-04088: error during execution of trigger 'STUDENT.ENROLLMENT_BI'
```

2) Create or modify a trigger on the SECTION table that fires before an UPDATE statement. Make sure that the trigger validates incoming values so that there are no constraint violation errors.

ANSWER: The trigger should look similar to the following:

```
CREATE OR REPLACE TRIGGER section_bu
BEFORE UPDATE ON SECTION
FOR EACH ROW
DECLARE
   v_valid NUMBER := 0;
BEGIN
   IF :NEW.INSTRUCTOR_ID IS NOT NULL THEN
      SELECT COUNT(*)
        INTO v_valid
        FROM instructor
       WHERE instructor_id = :NEW.instructor_ID;

      IF v_valid = 0 THEN
         RAISE_APPLICATION_ERROR (-20000,
            'This is not a valid instructor');
      END IF;
   END IF;

   :NEW.MODIFIED_BY    := USER;
   :NEW.MODIFIED_DATE := SYSDATE;
END;
```

This trigger fires before the UPDATE statement on the SECTION table. First, you check to see if there is a new value for an instructor ID with the help of an IF-THEN statement. If the IF-THEN statement evaluates to TRUE, the instructor's ID is checked against the INSTRUCTOR table. If a new instructor ID does not exist in the INSTRUCTOR table, the exception is raised, and the trigger is terminated. Otherwise, all columns with NOT NULL constraints are populated with their respective values.

Note that this trigger does not populate the CREATED_BY and CREATED_DATE columns with the new values. This is because when the record is updated, the values for these columns do not change, because they reflect when this record was added to the SECTION table.

Consider the following UPDATE statement:

```
UPDATE section
   SET instructor_id = 220
 WHERE section_id = 79;
```

The value 220 in this UPDATE statement does not exist in the INSTRUCTOR table and therefore is invalid. As a result, this UPDATE statement when run causes an error:

```
UPDATE section
*
ERROR at line 1:
ORA-20000: This is not a valid instructor
ORA-06512: at "STUDENT.SECTION_BU", line 11
ORA-04088: error during execution of trigger 'STUDENT.SECTION_BU'
```

Next, consider an UPDATE statement that does not cause any errors:

```
UPDATE section
    SET instructor_id = 105
  WHERE section_id = 79;
```

1 row updated.

```
rollback;
```

Rollback complete.

Chapter 14, "Compound Triggers"

1) Create a compound trigger on the INSTRUCTOR table that fires on the INSERT and UPDATE statements. The trigger should not allow an insert or update on the INSTRUCTOR table during off hours. Off hours are weekends and times of day outside the 9 a.m. to 5 p.m. window. The trigger should also populate the INSTRUCTOR_ID, CREATED_BY, CREATED_DATE, MODIFIED_BY, and MODIFIED_DATE columns with their default values.

ANSWER: The trigger should look similar to the following:

```
CREATE OR REPLACE TRIGGER instructor_compound
FOR INSERT OR UPDATE ON instructor
COMPOUND TRIGGER

    v_date DATE;
    v_user VARCHAR2(30);

BEFORE STATEMENT IS
BEGIN
    IF RTRIM(TO_CHAR(SYSDATE, 'DAY')) NOT LIKE 'S%' AND
        RTRIM(TO_CHAR(SYSDATE, 'HH24:MI')) BETWEEN '09:00' AND '17:00'
    THEN
        v_date := SYSDATE;
        v_user := USER;
    ELSE
        RAISE_APPLICATION_ERROR
            (-20000, 'A table cannot be modified during off hours');
    END IF;

END BEFORE STATEMENT;

BEFORE EACH ROW IS
BEGIN
    IF INSERTING THEN
        :NEW.instructor_id := INSTRUCTOR_ID_SEQ.NEXTVAL;
        :NEW.created_by    := v_user;
        :NEW.created_date  := v_date;

    ELSIF UPDATING THEN
        :NEW.created_by    := :OLD.created_by;
```

```
     :NEW.created_date   := :OLD.created_date;
   END IF;

   :NEW.modified_by    := v_user;
   :NEW.modified_date  := v_date;

END BEFORE EACH ROW;

END instructor_compound;
```

This compound trigger has two executable sections, BEFORE STATEMENT and BEFORE EACH ROW. The BEFORE STATEMENT portion prevents any updates to the INSTRUCTOR table during off hours. In addition, it populates the `v_date` and `v_user` variables that are used to populate the CREATED_BY, CREATED_DATE, MODIFIED_BY, and MODIFIED_DATE columns. The BEFORE EACH ROW section populates these columns. In addition, it assigns a value to the INSTRUCTOR_ID column from INSTRUCTOR_ID_SEQ.

Note the use of the INSERTING and UPDATING functions in the BEFORE EACH ROW section. The INSERTING function is used because the INSTRUCTOR_ID, CREATED_BY, and CREATED_DATE columns are populated with new values only if a record is being inserted in the INSTRUCTOR table. This is not so when a record is being updated. In this case, the CREATED_BY and CREATED_DATE columns are populated with the values copied from the OLD pseudorecord. However, the MODIFIED_BY and MODIFIED_DATE columns need to be populated with the new values regardless of the INSERT or UPDATE operation.

The newly created trigger may be tested as follows:

```
SET SERVEROUTPUT ON
DECLARE
   v_date VARCHAR2(20);
BEGIN
   v_date := TO_CHAR(SYSDATE, 'DD/MM/YYYY HH24:MI');
   DBMS_OUTPUT.PUT_LINE ('Date: '||v_date);

   INSERT INTO instructor
      (salutation, first_name, last_name, street_address, zip, phone)
   VALUES
      ('Mr.', 'Test', 'Instructor', '123 Main Street', '07112',
      '2125555555');

   ROLLBACK;
END;
/
```

The output is as follows:

```
Date: 25/04/2008 15:47

PL/SQL procedure successfully completed.
```

Here's the second test:

```
SET SERVEROUTPUT ON
DECLARE
   v_date VARCHAR2(20);
```

```
BEGIN
   v_date := TO_CHAR(SYSDATE, 'DD/MM/YYYY HH24:MI');
   DBMS_OUTPUT.PUT_LINE ('Date: '||v_date);

   UPDATE instructor
      SET phone = '2125555555'
    WHERE instructor_id = 101;

   ROLLBACK;
END;
/
```

The output is as follows:

```
Date: 26/04/2008 19:50
DECLARE
*
ERROR at line 1:
ORA-20000: A table cannot be modified during off hours
ORA-06512: at "STUDENT.INSTRUCTOR_COMPOUND", line 15
ORA-04088: error during execution of trigger 'STUDENT.INSTRUCTOR_COM-
POUND'
ORA-06512: at line 7
```

2) Create a compound trigger on the ZIPCODE table that fires on the INSERT and UPDATE statements. The trigger should populate the CREATED_BY, CREATED_DATE, MODIFIED_BY, and
MODIFIED_DATE columns with their default values. In addition, it should record in the STATISTICS
table the type of the transaction, the name of the user who issued the transaction, and the date
of the transaction. Assume that the STATISTICS table has the following structure:

```
Name                              Null?    Type
-------------------------------   -------- ----
TABLE_NAME                                 VARCHAR2(30)
TRANSACTION_NAME                           VARCHAR2(10)
TRANSACTION_USER                           VARCHAR2(30)
TRANSACTION_DATE                           DATE
```

ANSWER: The trigger should look similar to the following:

```
CREATE OR REPLACE TRIGGER zipcode_compound
FOR INSERT OR UPDATE ON zipcode
COMPOUND TRIGGER

   v_date DATE;
   v_user VARCHAR2(30);
   v_type VARCHAR2(10);

BEFORE STATEMENT IS
BEGIN
   v_date := SYSDATE;
   v_user := USER;
END BEFORE STATEMENT;
```

```
BEFORE EACH ROW IS
BEGIN
   IF INSERTING THEN
      :NEW.created_by   := v_user;
      :NEW.created_date := v_date;

   ELSIF UPDATING THEN
      :NEW.created_by   := :OLD.created_by;
      :NEW.created_date := :OLD.created_date;
   END IF;

   :NEW.modified_by   := v_user;
   :NEW.modified_date := v_date;

END BEFORE EACH ROW;

AFTER STATEMENT IS
BEGIN
   IF INSERTING THEN
      v_type := 'INSERT';

   ELSIF UPDATING THEN
      v_type := 'UPDATE';
   END IF;

   INSERT INTO statistics
      (table_name, transaction_name, transaction_user,
       transaction_date)
   VALUES ('ZIPCODE', v_type, v_user, v_date);

END AFTER STATEMENT;

END zipcode_compound;

UPDATE zipcode
   SET city = 'Test City'
 WHERE zip  = '01247';
```

1 row updated.

```
SELECT *
  FROM statistics
 WHERE transaction_date >= TRUNC(sysdate);
```

TABLE_NAME	TRANSACTION_NAME	TRANSACTION_USER	TRANSACTION_DATE
ZIPCODE	UPDATE	STUDENT	24-APR-08

```
ROLLBACK;
```

Rollback complete.

Chapter 15, "Collections"

1) Create the following script: Create an associative array (index-by table), and populate it with the instructor's full name. In other words, each row of the associative array should contain the first name, middle initial, and last name. Display this information on the screen.

ANSWER: The script should look similar to the following:

```
SET SERVEROUTPUT ON
DECLARE
    CURSOR name_cur IS
        SELECT first_name||' '||last_name name
          FROM instructor;

    TYPE name_type IS TABLE OF VARCHAR2(50)
        INDEX BY BINARY_INTEGER;
    name_tab name_type;

    v_counter INTEGER := 0;
BEGIN
    FOR name_rec IN name_cur LOOP
        v_counter := v_counter + 1;
        name_tab(v_counter) := name_rec.name;

        DBMS_OUTPUT.PUT_LINE ('name('||v_counter||'): '||
            name_tab(v_counter));
    END LOOP;
END;
```

In the preceding example, the associative array `name_tab` is populated with instructors' full names. Notice that the variable `v_counter` is used as a subscript to reference individual array elements. This example produces the following output:

```
name(1): Fernand Hanks
name(2): Tom Wojick
name(3): Nina Schorin
name(4): Gary Pertez
name(5): Anita Morris
name(6): Todd Smythe
name(7): Marilyn Frantzen
name(8): Charles Lowry
name(9): Rick Chow

PL/SQL procedure successfully completed.
```

2) Modify the script you just created. Instead of using an associative array, use a varray.

ANSWER: The script should look similar to the following. Changes are shown in bold.

```
SET SERVEROUTPUT ON
DECLARE
    CURSOR name_cur IS
        SELECT first_name||' '||last_name name
          FROM instructor;
```

```
    TYPE name_type IS VARRAY(15) OF VARCHAR2(50);
    name_varray name_type := name_type();

    v_counter INTEGER := 0;
BEGIN
    FOR name_rec IN name_cur LOOP
        v_counter := v_counter + 1;
        name_varray.EXTEND;
        name_varray(v_counter) := name_rec.name;

        DBMS_OUTPUT.PUT_LINE ('name('||v_counter||'): '||
            name_varray(v_counter));
    END LOOP;
END;
```

In this version of the script, you define a varray of 15 elements. It is important to remember to initialize the array before referencing its individual elements. In addition, the array must be extended before new elements are added to it.

3) Modify the script you just created. Create an additional varray, and populate it with unique course numbers for the courses that each instructor teaches. Display the instructor's name and the list of courses he or she teaches.

ANSWER: The script should look similar to the following:

```
SET SERVEROUTPUT ON
DECLARE
    CURSOR instructor_cur IS
        SELECT instructor_id, first_name||' '||last_name name
          FROM instructor;

    CURSOR course_cur (p_instructor_id NUMBER) IS
        SELECT unique course_no course
          FROM section
         WHERE instructor_id = p_instructor_id;

    TYPE name_type IS VARRAY(15) OF VARCHAR2(50);
    name_varray name_type := name_type();

    TYPE course_type IS VARRAY(10) OF NUMBER;
    course_varray course_type;

    v_counter1 INTEGER := 0;
    v_counter2 INTEGER;
BEGIN
    FOR instructor_rec IN instructor_cur LOOP
        v_counter1 := v_counter1 + 1;
        name_varray.EXTEND;
        name_varray(v_counter1) := instructor_rec.name;

        DBMS_OUTPUT.PUT_LINE ('name('||v_counter1||'): '||
            name_varray(v_counter1));
```

```
      -- Initialize and populate course_varray
      v_counter2 := 0;
      course_varray := course_type();
      FOR course_rec in course_cur (instructor_rec.instructor_id)
      LOOP
         v_counter2 := v_counter2 + 1;
         course_varray.EXTEND;
         course_varray(v_counter2) := course_rec.course;

         DBMS_OUTPUT.PUT_LINE ('course('||v_counter2||'): '||
            course_varray(v_counter2));
      END LOOP;
      DBMS_OUTPUT.PUT_LINE ('===========================');
   END LOOP;
END;
```

Consider the script you just created. First, you declare two cursors, INSTRUCTOR_CUR and COURSE_CUR. COURSE_CUR accepts a parameter because it returns a list of courses taught by a particular instructor. Notice that the SELECT statement uses the function UNIQUE to retrieve distinct course numbers. Second, you declare two varray types and variables, `name_varray` and `course_varray`. Notice that you do not initialize the second varray at the time of declaration. Next, you declare two counters and initialize the first counter only.

In the body of the block, you open INSTRUCTOR_CUR and populate `name_varray` with its first element. Next, you initialize the second counter and `course_varray`. This step is necessary because you need to repopulate `course_varray` for the next instructor. Next, you open COURSE_CUR to retrieve corresponding courses and display them on the screen.

When run, the script produces the following output:

```
name(1): Fernand Hanks
course(1): 25
course(2): 120
course(3): 122
course(4): 125
course(5): 134
course(6): 140
course(7): 146
course(8): 240
course(9): 450
===========================
name(2): Tom Wojick
course(1): 10
course(2): 25
course(3): 100
course(4): 120
course(5): 124
course(6): 125
course(7): 134
course(8): 140
course(9): 146
course(10): 240
===========================
```

```
name(3): Nina Schorin
course(1): 20
course(2): 25
course(3): 100
course(4): 120
course(5): 124
course(6): 130
course(7): 134
course(8): 142
course(9): 147
course(10): 310
===========================
name(4): Gary Pertez
course(1): 20
course(2): 25
course(3): 100
course(4): 120
course(5): 124
course(6): 130
course(7): 135
course(8): 142
course(9): 204
course(10): 330
===========================
name(5): Anita Morris
course(1): 20
course(2): 25
course(3): 100
course(4): 122
course(5): 124
course(6): 130
course(7): 135
course(8): 142
course(9): 210
course(10): 350
===========================
name(6): Todd Smythe
course(1): 20
course(2): 25
course(3): 100
course(4): 122
course(5): 125
course(6): 130
course(7): 135
course(8): 144
course(9): 220
course(10): 350
===========================
```

```
name(7): Marilyn Frantzen
course(1): 25
course(2): 120
course(3): 122
course(4): 125
course(5): 132
course(6): 135
course(7): 145
course(8): 230
course(9): 350
===========================
name(8): Charles Lowry
course(1): 25
course(2): 120
course(3): 122
course(4): 125
course(5): 132
course(6): 140
course(7): 145
course(8): 230
course(9): 420
===========================
name(9): Rick Chow
===========================
name(10): Irene Willig
===========================

PL/SQL procedure successfully completed.
```

As mentioned, it is important to reinitialize the variable $v\_counter2$ that is used to reference individual elements of $course\_varray$. When this step is omitted and the variable is initialized only once, at the time of declaration, the script generates the following runtime error:

```
name(1): Fernand Hanks
course(1): 25
course(2): 120
course(3): 122
course(4): 125
course(5): 134
course(6): 140
course(7): 146
course(8): 240
course(9): 450
name(2): Tom Wojick
DECLARE
*
ERROR at line 1:
ORA-06533: Subscript beyond count
ORA-06512: at line 33
```

Why do you think this error occurs?

4) Find and explain the errors in the following script:

```
DECLARE
   TYPE varray_type1 IS VARRAY(7) OF INTEGER;
   TYPE table_type2  IS TABLE OF varray_type1 INDEX BY
      BINARY_INTEGER;

   varray1 varray_type1 := varray_type1(1, 2, 3);
   table2  table_type2  := table_type2(varray1,
                                       varray_type1(8, 9, 0));

BEGIN
   DBMS_OUTPUT.PUT_LINE ('table2(1)(2): '||table2(1)(2));

   FOR i IN 1..10 LOOP
      varray1.EXTEND;
      varray1(i) := i;
      DBMS_OUTPUT.PUT_LINE ('varray1('||i||'): '||varray1(i));
   END LOOP;
END;
```

ANSWER: This script generates the following errors:

```
   table2 table_type2 := table_type2(varray1, varray_type1(8, 9, 0));
                     *
ERROR at line 6:
ORA-06550: line 6, column 26:
PLS-00222: no function with name 'TABLE_TYPE2' exists in this scope
ORA-06550: line 6, column 11:
PL/SQL: Item ignored
ORA-06550: line 9, column 44:
PLS-00320: the declaration of the type of this expression is
incomplete or malformed
ORA-06550: line 9, column 4:
PL/SQL: Statement ignored
```

Notice that this error refers to the initialization of `table2`, which has been declared as an associative array of varrays. Recall that associative arrays are not initialized prior to their use. As a result, the declaration of `table2` must be modified. Furthermore, an additional assignment statement must be added to the executable portion of the block:

```
DECLARE
   TYPE varray_type1 IS VARRAY(7) OF INTEGER;
   TYPE table_type2  IS TABLE OF varray_type1 INDEX BY
     BINARY_INTEGER;

   varray1 varray_type1 := varray_type1(1, 2, 3);
   table2  table_type2;
BEGIN
   -- These statements populate associative array
   table2(1) := varray1;
   table2(2) := varray_type1(8, 9, 0);
```

```
   DBMS_OUTPUT.PUT_LINE ('table2(1)(2): '||table2(1)(2));

   FOR i IN 1..10 LOOP
      varray1.EXTEND;
      varray1(i) := i;
      DBMS_OUTPUT.PUT_LINE ('varray1('||i||'): '||varray1(i));
   END LOOP;
END;
```

When run, this version produces a different error:

```
table2(1)(2): 2
varray1(1): 1
varray1(2): 2
varray1(3): 3
varray1(4): 4
DECLARE
*
ERROR at line 1:
ORA-06532: Subscript outside of limit
ORA-06512: at line 15
```

Notice that this is a runtime error that refers to `varray1`. This error occurs because you are trying to extend the varray beyond its limit. `varray1` can contain up to seven integers. After initialization, it contains three integers. As a result, it can be populated with no more than four additional integers. So the fifth iteration of the loop tries to extend the varray to eight elements, which in turn causes a `Subscript outside of limit` error.

It is important to note that there is no correlation between the loop counter and the EXTEND method. Every time the EXTEND method is called, it increases the size of the varray by one element. Because the varray has been initialized to three elements, the EXTEND method adds a fourth element to the array for the first iteration of the loop. At the same time, the first element of the varray is assigned a value of 1 through the loop counter. For the second iteration of the loop, the EXTEND method adds a fifth element to the varray while the second element is assigned a value of 2, and so forth.

Finally, consider the error-free version of the script:

```
DECLARE
   TYPE varray_type1 IS VARRAY(7) OF INTEGER;
   TYPE table_type2  IS TABLE OF varray_type1 INDEX BY
      BINARY_INTEGER;

   varray1 varray_type1 := varray_type1(1, 2, 3);
   table2  table_type2;
BEGIN
   -- These statements populate associative array
   table2(1) := varray1;
   table2(2) := varray_type1(8, 9, 0);

   DBMS_OUTPUT.PUT_LINE ('table2(1)(2): '||table2(1)(2));
```

```
FOR i IN 4..7 LOOP
   varray1.EXTEND;
   varray1(i) := i;
END LOOP;

-- Display elements of the varray
FOR i IN 1..7 LOOP
   DBMS_OUTPUT.PUT_LINE ('varray1('||i||'): '||varray1(i));
END LOOP;
END;
```

The output is as follows:

```
table2(1)(2): 2
varray1(1): 1
varray1(2): 2
varray1(3): 3
varray1(4): 4
varray1(5): 5
varray1(6): 6
varray1(7): 7

PL/SQL procedure successfully completed.
```

Chapter 16, "Records"

1) Create an associative array with the element type of a user-defined record. This record should contain the first name, last name, and total number of courses that a particular instructor teaches. Display the records of the associative array on the screen.

ANSWER: The script should look similar to the following:

```
SET SERVEROUTPUT ON
DECLARE
   CURSOR instructor_cur IS
      SELECT first_name, last_name,
             COUNT(UNIQUE s.course_no) courses
        FROM instructor i
        LEFT OUTER JOIN section s
          ON (s.instructor_id = i.instructor_id)
      GROUP BY first_name, last_name;

   TYPE rec_type IS RECORD
      (first_name      instructor.first_name%type,
       last_name       instructor.last_name%type,
       courses_taught NUMBER);

   TYPE instructor_type IS TABLE OF REC_TYPE
INDEX BY BINARY_INTEGER;
```

```
      instructor_tab instructor_type;

      v_counter INTEGER := 0;
BEGIN
   FOR instructor_rec IN instructor_cur LOOP
      v_counter := v_counter + 1;

      -- Populate associative array of records
      instructor_tab(v_counter).first_name :=
         instructor_rec.first_name;
      instructor_tab(v_counter).last_name :=
         instructor_rec.last_name;
      instructor_tab(v_counter).courses_taught :=
         instructor_rec.courses;

      DBMS_OUTPUT.PUT_LINE ('Instructor, '||
         instructor_tab(v_counter).first_name||' '||
         instructor_tab(v_counter).last_name||', teaches '||
         instructor_tab(v_counter).courses_taught||' courses.');
   END LOOP;
END;
```

Consider the SELECT statement used in this script. It returns the instructor's name and the total number of courses he or she teaches. The statement uses an outer join so that if a particular instructor is not teaching any courses, he or she will be included in the results of the SELECT statement. Note that the SELECT statement uses the ANSI 1999 SQL standard.

BY THE WAY

You will find detailed explanations and examples of the statements using the new ANSI 1999 SQL standard in Appendix C and in the Oracle help. Throughout this book we have tried to provide examples illustrating both standards; however, our main focus is on PL/SQL features rather than SQL.

In this script, you define a cursor against the INSTRUCTOR and SECTION tables that is used to populate the associative array of records, `instructor_tab`. Each row of this table is a user-defined record of three elements. You populate the associative array using the cursor FOR loop. Consider the notation used to reference each record element of the associative array:

```
instructor_tab(v_counter).first_name
instructor_tab(v_counter).last_name
instructor_tab(v_counter).courses_taught
```

To reference each row of the associative array, you use the counter variable. However, because each row of this table is a record, you must also reference individual fields of the underlying record. When run, this script produces the following output:

```
Instructor, Anita Morris, teaches 10 courses.
Instructor, Charles Lowry, teaches 9 courses.
Instructor, Fernand Hanks, teaches 9 courses.
Instructor, Gary Pertez, teaches 10 courses.
Instructor, Marilyn Frantzen, teaches 9 courses.
Instructor, Nina Schorin, teaches 10 courses.
Instructor, Rick Chow, teaches 1 courses.
```

```
Instructor, Todd Smythe, teaches 10 courses.
Instructor, Tom Wojick, teaches 9 courses.

PL/SQL procedure successfully completed.
```

2) Modify the script you just created. Instead of using an associative array, use a nested table.

ANSWER: The script should look similar to the following. Changes are shown in bold.

```
SET SERVEROUTPUT ON
DECLARE
    CURSOR instructor_cur IS
        SELECT first_name, last_name,
               COUNT(UNIQUE s.course_no) courses
          FROM instructor i
          LEFT OUTER JOIN section s
            ON (s.instructor_id = i.instructor_id)
        GROUP BY first_name, last_name;

    TYPE rec_type IS RECORD
        (first_name      instructor.first_name%type,
         last_name       instructor.last_name%type,
         courses_taught NUMBER);

    TYPE instructor_type IS TABLE OF REC_TYPE;
    instructor_tab instructor_type := instructor_type();

    v_counter INTEGER := 0;
BEGIN
    FOR instructor_rec IN instructor_cur LOOP
        v_counter := v_counter + 1;
        instructor_tab.EXTEND;

        -- Populate associative array of records
        instructor_tab(v_counter).first_name :=
           instructor_rec.first_name;
        instructor_tab(v_counter).last_name :=
           instructor_rec.last_name;
        instructor_tab(v_counter).courses_taught :=
           instructor_rec.courses;

        DBMS_OUTPUT.PUT_LINE ('Instructor, '||
           instructor_tab(v_counter).first_name||' '||
           instructor_tab(v_counter).last_name||', teaches '||
           instructor_tab(v_counter).courses_taught||' courses.');
    END LOOP;
END;
```

Notice that the `instructor_tab` must be initialized and extended before its individual elements can be referenced.

3) Modify the script you just created. Instead of using a nested table, use a varray.

   ANSWER: The script should look similar to the following:

```
SET SERVEROUTPUT ON
DECLARE
   CURSOR instructor_cur IS
      SELECT first_name, last_name,
             COUNT(UNIQUE s.course_no) courses
        FROM instructor i
        LEFT OUTER JOIN section s
          ON (s.instructor_id = i.instructor_id)
       GROUP BY first_name, last_name;

   TYPE rec_type IS RECORD
      (first_name      instructor.first_name%type,
       last_name       instructor.last_name%type,
       courses_taught NUMBER);

   TYPE instructor_type IS VARRAY(10) OF REC_TYPE;
   instructor_tab instructor_type := instructor_type();

   v_counter INTEGER := 0;
BEGIN
   FOR instructor_rec IN instructor_cur LOOP
      v_counter := v_counter + 1;
      instructor_tab.EXTEND;

      -- Populate associative array of records
      instructor_tab(v_counter).first_name :=
         instructor_rec.first_name;
      instructor_tab(v_counter).last_name :=
         instructor_rec.last_name;
      instructor_tab(v_counter).courses_taught :=
         instructor_rec.courses;

      DBMS_OUTPUT.PUT_LINE ('Instructor, '||
         instructor_tab(v_counter).first_name||' '||
         instructor_tab(v_counter).last_name||', teaches '||
         instructor_tab(v_counter).courses_taught||' courses.');
   END LOOP;
END;
```

This version of the script is almost identical to the previous version. Instead of using a nested table, you are using a varray of 15 elements.

4) Create a user-defined record with four fields: `course_no`, `description`, `cost`, and `prerequisite_rec`. The last field, `prerequisite_rec`, should be a user-defined record with three fields: `prereq_no`, `prereq_desc`, and `prereq_cost`. For any ten courses that have a prerequisite course, populate the user-defined record with all the corresponding data, and display its information on the screen.

ANSWER: The script should look similar to the following:

```
SET SERVEROUTPUT ON
DECLARE
   CURSOR c_cur IS
      SELECT course_no, description, cost, prerequisite
        FROM course
       WHERE prerequisite IS NOT NULL
         AND rownum <= 10;

   TYPE prerequisite_type IS RECORD
      (prereq_no   NUMBER,
       prereq_desc VARCHAR(50),
       prereq_cost NUMBER);

   TYPE course_type IS RECORD
      (course_no          NUMBER,
       description        VARCHAR2(50),
       cost               NUMBER,
       prerequisite_rec PREREQUISITE_TYPE);

   course_rec COURSE_TYPE;
BEGIN
   FOR c_rec in c_cur LOOP
      course_rec.course_no := c_rec.course_no;
      course_rec.description := c_rec.description;
      course_rec.cost := c_rec.cost;

      SELECT course_no, description, cost
        INTO course_rec.prerequisite_rec.prereq_no,
             course_rec.prerequisite_rec.prereq_desc,
             course_rec.prerequisite_rec.prereq_cost
        FROM course
       WHERE course_no = c_rec.prerequisite;

      DBMS_OUTPUT.PUT_LINE ('Course: '||
         course_rec.course_no||' - '||
         course_rec.description);
      DBMS_OUTPUT.PUT_LINE ('Cost: '|| course_rec.cost);
      DBMS_OUTPUT.PUT_LINE ('Prerequisite: '||
         course_rec.prerequisite_rec. prereq_no||' - '||
         course_rec.prerequisite_rec.prereq_desc);
      DBMS_OUTPUT.PUT_LINE ('Prerequisite Cost: '||
         course_rec.prerequisite_rec.prereq_cost);
      DBMS_OUTPUT.PUT_LINE
         ('======================================');
   END LOOP;
END;
```

In the declaration portion of the script, you define a cursor against the COURSE table; two user-defined record types, `prerequisite_type` and `course_type`; and user-defined record, `course_rec`. It is important to note the order in which the record types are declared. The `prerequsite_type` must be declared first because one of the `course_type` elements is of the `prerequisite_type`.

In the executable portion of the script, you populate `course_rec` using the cursor FOR loop. First, you assign values to `course_rec.course_no`, `course_rec.description`, and `course_rec.cost`. Next, you populate the nested record, `prerequsite_rec`, using the SELECT INTO statement against the COURSE table. Consider the notation used to reference individual elements of the nested record:

```
course_rec.prerequisite_rec.prereq_no,
course_rec.prerequisite_rec.prereq_desc,
course_rec.prerequisite_rec.prereq_cost
```

You specify the name of the outer record followed by the name of the inner (nested) record, followed by the name of the element. Finally, you display record information on the screen.

Note that this script does not contain a NO_DATA_FOUND exception handler even though there is a SELECT INTO statement. Why do you think this is the case?

When run, the script produces the following output:

```
Course: 230 - Intro to the Internet
Cost: 1095
Prerequisite: 10 - Technology Concepts
Prerequisite Cost: 1195
====================================
Course: 100 - Hands-On Windows
Cost: 1195
Prerequisite: 20 - Intro to Information Systems
Prerequisite Cost: 1195
====================================
Course: 140 - Systems Analysis
Cost: 1195
Prerequisite: 20 - Intro to Information Systems
Prerequisite Cost: 1195
====================================
Course: 142 - Project Management
Cost: 1195
Prerequisite: 20 - Intro to Information Systems
Prerequisite Cost: 1195
====================================
Course: 147 - GUI Design Lab
Cost: 1195
Prerequisite: 20 - Intro to Information Systems
Prerequisite Cost: 1195
====================================
Course: 204 - Intro to SQL
Cost: 1195
Prerequisite: 20 - Intro to Information Systems
Prerequisite Cost: 1195
====================================
```

```
Course: 240 - Intro to the BASIC Language
Cost: 1095
Prerequisite: 25 - Intro to Programming
Prerequisite Cost: 1195
=====================================
Course: 420 - Database System Principles
Cost: 1195
Prerequisite: 25 - Intro to Programming
Prerequisite Cost: 1195
=====================================
Course: 120 - Intro to Java Programming
Cost: 1195
Prerequisite: 80 - Programming Techniques
Prerequisite Cost: 1595
=====================================
Course: 220 - PL/SQL Programming
Cost: 1195
Prerequisite: 80 - Programming Techniques
Prerequisite Cost: 1595
=====================================

PL/SQL procedure successfully completed.
```

Chapter 17, "Native Dynamic SQL"

This chapter has no "Try It Yourself" section.

Chapter 18, "Bulk SQL"

Before beginning these exercises, create the MY_SECTION table based on the SECTION table. This table should be created empty.

The MY_SECTION table can be created as follows:

```
CREATE TABLE my_section AS
SELECT *
  FROM section
 WHERE 1 = 2;
```

Table created.

Specifying this criterion guarantees the creation of an empty table.

1) Create the following script: Populate the MY_SECTION table using the FORALL statement with the SAVE EXCEPTIONS clause. After MY_SECTION is populated, display how many records were inserted.

   ANSWER: The script should look similar to the following:

```
SET SERVEROUTPUT ON
DECLARE
   -- Declare collection types
```

```
   TYPE number_type IS TABLE of NUMBER INDEX BY PLS_INTEGER;
   TYPE string_type IS TABLE OF VARCHAR2(100) INDEX BY PLS_INTEGER;
   TYPE date_type   IS TABLE OF DATE INDEX BY PLS_INTEGER;

   -- Declare collection variables to be used by the FORALL statement
   section_id_tab      number_type;
   course_no_tab       number_type;
   section_no_tab      number_type;
   start_date_time_tab date_type;
   location_tab        string_type;
   instructor_id_tab   number_type;
   capacity_tab        number_type;
   cr_by_tab           string_type;
   cr_date_tab         date_type;
   mod_by_tab          string_type;
   mod_date_tab        date_type;

   v_counter PLS_INTEGER := 0;
   v_total   INTEGER := 0;

   -- Define user-defined exception and associated Oracle
   -- error number with it
   errors EXCEPTION;
   PRAGMA EXCEPTION_INIT(errors, -24381);

BEGIN
   -- Populate individual collections
   FOR rec IN (SELECT *
                 FROM section)
   LOOP
      v_counter := v_counter + 1;
      section_id_tab(v_counter)      := rec.section_id;
      course_no_tab(v_counter)       := rec.course_no;
      section_no_tab(v_counter)      := rec.section_no;
      start_date_time_tab(v_counter) := rec.start_date_time;
      location_tab(v_counter)        := rec.location;
      instructor_id_tab(v_counter)   := rec.instructor_id;
      capacity_tab(v_counter)        := rec.capacity;
      cr_by_tab(v_counter)           := rec.created_by;
      cr_date_tab(v_counter)         := rec.created_date;
      mod_by_tab(v_counter)          := rec.modified_by;
      mod_date_tab(v_counter)        := rec.modified_date;
   END LOOP;

   -- Populate MY_SECTION table
   FORALL i in 1..section_id_tab.COUNT SAVE EXCEPTIONS
      INSERT INTO my_section
         (section_id, course_no, section_no, start_date_time,
          location, instructor_id, capacity, created_by,
          created_date, modified_by, modified_date)
```

```
      VALUES
         (section_id_tab(i), course_no_tab(i), section_no_tab(i),
          start_date_time_tab(i), location_tab(i),
          instructor_id_tab(i), capacity_tab(i), cr_by_tab(i),
          cr_date_tab(i), mod_by_tab(i), mod_date_tab(i));
   COMMIT;

   -- Check how many records were added to MY_SECTION table
   SELECT COUNT(*)
     INTO v_total
     FROM my_section;

   DBMS_OUTPUT.PUT_LINE
      (v_total||' records were added to MY_SECTION table');

EXCEPTION
   WHEN errors THEN
      -- Display total number of exceptions encountered
      DBMS_OUTPUT.PUT_LINE
         ('There were '||SQL%BULK_EXCEPTIONS.COUNT||' exceptions');

      -- Display detailed exception information
      FOR i in 1.. SQL%BULK_EXCEPTIONS.COUNT LOOP
         DBMS_OUTPUT.PUT_LINE ('Record '||
            SQL%BULK_EXCEPTIONS(i).error_index||' caused error '||i||
            ': '||SQL%BULK_EXCEPTIONS(i).ERROR_CODE||' '||
            SQLERRM(-SQL%BULK_EXCEPTIONS(i).ERROR_CODE));
      END LOOP;

      -- Commit records if any that were inserted successfully
      COMMIT;
END;
```

This script populates the MY_SECTION table with records selected from the SECTION table. To enable use of the FORALL statement, it employs 11 collections. Note that only three collection types are associated with these collections. This is because the individual collections store only three datatypes—NUMBER, VARCHAR2, and DATE.

The script uses a cursor FOR loop to populate the individual collections and then uses them with the FORALL statement with the SAVE EXCEPTIONS option to populate the MY_SECTION table. To enable the SAVE EXCEPTIONS options, this script declares a user-defined exception and associates an Oracle error number with it. This script also contains an exception-handling section where a user-defined exception is processed. This section displays how many exceptions were encountered in the FORALL statement as well as detailed exception information. Note the COMMIT statement in the exception-handling section. This statement is added so that records that are inserted successfully by the FORALL statement are committed when control of the execution is passed to the exception-handling section of the block.

When run, this script produces the following output:

```
78 records were added to MY_SECTION table

PL/SQL procedure successfully completed.
```

2) Modify the script you just created. In addition to displaying the total number of records inserted in the MY_SECTION table, display how many records were inserted for each course. Use the BULK COLLECT statement to accomplish this step. Note that you should delete all the rows from the MY_SECTION table before executing this version of the script.

ANSWER: The new version of the script should look similar to the following. Changes are shown in bold.

```
SET SERVEROUTPUT ON
DECLARE
   -- Declare collection types
   TYPE number_type IS TABLE of NUMBER INDEX BY PLS_INTEGER;
   TYPE string_type IS TABLE OF VARCHAR2(100) INDEX BY PLS_INTEGER;
   TYPE date_type   IS TABLE OF DATE INDEX BY PLS_INTEGER;

   -- Declare collection variables to be used by the FORALL statement
   section_id_tab       number_type;
   course_no_tab        number_type;
   section_no_tab       number_type;
   start_date_time_tab date_type;
   location_tab         string_type;
   instructor_id_tab    number_type;
   capacity_tab         number_type;
   cr_by_tab            string_type;
   cr_date_tab          date_type;
   mod_by_tab           string_type;
   mod_date_tab         date_type;
   total_recs_tab       number_type;

   v_counter PLS_INTEGER := 0;
   v_total   INTEGER := 0;

   -- Define user-defined exception and associated Oracle
   -- error number with it
   errors EXCEPTION;
   PRAGMA EXCEPTION_INIT(errors, -24381);

BEGIN
   -- Populate individual collections
   FOR rec IN (SELECT *
                 FROM section)
   LOOP
      v_counter := v_counter + 1;
      section_id_tab(v_counter)       := rec.section_id;
      course_no_tab(v_counter)        := rec.course_no;
      section_no_tab(v_counter)       := rec.section_no;
      start_date_time_tab(v_counter) := rec.start_date_time;
      location_tab(v_counter)         := rec.location;
      instructor_id_tab(v_counter)    := rec.instructor_id;
      capacity_tab(v_counter)         := rec.capacity;
      cr_by_tab(v_counter)            := rec.created_by;
      cr_date_tab(v_counter)          := rec.created_date;
```

```
        mod_by_tab(v_counter)          := rec.modified_by;
        mod_date_tab(v_counter)        := rec.modified_date;
    END LOOP;

    -- Populate MY_SECTION table
    FORALL i in 1..section_id_tab.COUNT SAVE EXCEPTIONS
        INSERT INTO my_section
            (section_id, course_no, section_no, start_date_time,
             location, instructor_id, capacity, created_by,
             created_date, modified_by, modified_date)
        VALUES
            (section_id_tab(i), course_no_tab(i), section_no_tab(i),
             start_date_time_tab(i), location_tab(i),
             instructor_id_tab(i), capacity_tab(i), cr_by_tab(i),
             cr_date_tab(i), mod_by_tab(i), mod_date_tab(i));
    COMMIT;

    -- Check how many records were added to MY_SECTION table
    SELECT COUNT(*)
      INTO v_total
      FROM my_section;

    DBMS_OUTPUT.PUT_LINE
        (v_total||' records were added to MY_SECTION table');

    -- Check how many records were inserted for each course
    -- and display this information
    -- Fetch data from MY_SECTION table via BULK COLLECT clause
    SELECT course_no, COUNT(*)
      BULK COLLECT INTO course_no_tab, total_recs_tab
      FROM my_section
    GROUP BY course_no;

    IF course_no_tab.COUNT > 0 THEN
        FOR i IN course_no_tab.FIRST..course_no_tab.LAST
        LOOP
            DBMS_OUTPUT.PUT_LINE
            ('course_no: '||course_no_tab(i)||
             ', total sections: '||total_recs_tab(i));
        END LOOP;
    END IF;

EXCEPTION
    WHEN errors THEN
        -- Display total number of exceptions encountered
        DBMS_OUTPUT.PUT_LINE
            ('There were '||SQL%BULK_EXCEPTIONS.COUNT||' exceptions');

        -- Display detailed exception information
        FOR i in 1.. SQL%BULK_EXCEPTIONS.COUNT LOOP
```

```
      DBMS_OUTPUT.PUT_LINE ('Record '||
         SQL%BULK_EXCEPTIONS(i).error_index||' caused error '||i||
         ': '||SQL%BULK_EXCEPTIONS(i).ERROR_CODE||' '||
         SQLERRM(-SQL%BULK_EXCEPTIONS(i).ERROR_CODE));
   END LOOP;

   -- Commit records if any that were inserted successfully
   COMMIT;
END;
```

In this version of the script, you define one more collection, `total_recs_tab`, in the declaration portion of the PL/SQL block. This collection is used to store the total number of sections for each course. In the executable portion of the PL/SQL block, you add a SELECT statement with a BULK COLLECT clause that repopulates `course_no_tab` and initializes `total_recs_tab`. Next, if the `course_no_tab` collection contains data, you display course numbers and the total number of sections for each course on the screen.

When run, this version of the script produces the following output:

```
78 records were added to MY_SECTION table
course_no: 10, total sections: 1
course_no: 20, total sections: 4
course_no: 25, total sections: 9
course_no: 100, total sections: 5
course_no: 120, total sections: 6
course_no: 122, total sections: 5
course_no: 124, total sections: 4
course_no: 125, total sections: 5
course_no: 130, total sections: 4
course_no: 132, total sections: 2
course_no: 134, total sections: 3
course_no: 135, total sections: 4
course_no: 140, total sections: 3
course_no: 142, total sections: 3
course_no: 144, total sections: 1
course_no: 145, total sections: 2
course_no: 146, total sections: 2
course_no: 147, total sections: 1
course_no: 204, total sections: 1
course_no: 210, total sections: 1
course_no: 220, total sections: 1
course_no: 230, total sections: 2
course_no: 240, total sections: 2
course_no: 310, total sections: 1
course_no: 330, total sections: 1
course_no: 350, total sections: 3
course_no: 420, total sections: 1
course_no: 450, total sections: 1

PL/SQL procedure successfully completed.
```

3) Create the following script: Delete all the records from the MY_SECTION table, and display how many records were deleted for each course as well as individual section IDs deleted for each course. Use BULK COLLECT with the RETURNING option.

ANSWER: This script should look similar to the following:

```
SET SERVEROUTPUT ON;
DECLARE
   -- Define collection types and variables to be used by the
   -- BULK COLLECT clause
   TYPE section_id_type IS TABLE OF my_section.section_id%TYPE;

   section_id_tab section_id_type;

BEGIN
   FOR rec IN (SELECT UNIQUE course_no
                 FROM my_section)
   LOOP
      DELETE FROM MY_SECTION
       WHERE course_no = rec.course_no
      RETURNING section_id
      BULK COLLECT INTO section_id_tab;

      DBMS_OUTPUT.PUT_LINE ('Deleted '||SQL%ROWCOUNT||
         ' rows for course '||rec.course_no);

      IF section_id_tab.COUNT > 0 THEN
         FOR i IN section_id_tab.FIRST..section_id_tab.LAST
         LOOP
            DBMS_OUTPUT.PUT_LINE
               ('section_id: '||section_id_tab(i));
         END LOOP;
         DBMS_OUTPUT.PUT_LINE ('==============================');
      END IF;
      COMMIT;
   END LOOP;
END;
```

In this script you declare a single collection, `section_id_tab`. Note that there is no need to declare a collection to store course numbers. This is because the records from the MY_SECTION table are deleted for each course number instead of all at once. To accomplish this, you introduce a cursor FOR loop that selects unique course numbers from the MY_SECTION table. Next, for each course number, you DELETE records from the MY_SECTION table, returning the corresponding section IDs and collecting them in `section_id_tab`. Next, you display how many records were deleted for a given course number, along with individual section IDs for this course.

Note that even though the collection `section_id_tab` is repopulated for each iteration of the cursor loop, there is no need to reinitialize it (in other words, empty it). This is because the DELETE statement does this implicitly.

Consider the partial output produced by this script:

```
Deleted 1 rows for course 10
section_id: 80
===============================
Deleted 4 rows for course 20
section_id: 81
section_id: 82
section_id: 83
section_id: 84
===============================
Deleted 9 rows for course 25
section_id: 85
section_id: 86
section_id: 87
section_id: 88
section_id: 89
section_id: 90
section_id: 91
section_id: 92
section_id: 93
===============================
Deleted 5 rows for course 100
section_id: 141
section_id: 142
section_id: 143
section_id: 144
section_id: 145
===============================
Deleted 6 rows for course 120
section_id: 146
section_id: 147
section_id: 148
section_id: 149
section_id: 150
section_id: 151
===============================
Deleted 5 rows for course 122
section_id: 152
section_id: 153
section_id: 154
section_id: 155
section_id: 156
===============================
...

PL/SQL procedure successfully completed.
```

Chapter 19, "Procedures"

PART 1

1) Write a procedure with no parameters. The procedure should say whether the current day is a weekend or weekday. Additionally, it should tell you the user's name and the current time. It also should specify how many valid and invalid procedures are in the database.

ANSWER: The procedure should look similar to the following:

```
CREATE OR REPLACE PROCEDURE current_status
AS
    v_day_type CHAR(1);
    v_user     VARCHAR2(30);
    v_valid    NUMBER;
    v_invalid  NUMBER;
BEGIN
    SELECT SUBSTR(TO_CHAR(sysdate, 'DAY'), 0, 1)
      INTO v_day_type
      FROM dual;

    IF v_day_type = 'S' THEN
        DBMS_OUTPUT.PUT_LINE ('Today is a weekend.');
    ELSE
        DBMS_OUTPUT.PUT_LINE ('Today is a weekday.');
    END IF;
    --
    DBMS_OUTPUT.PUT_LINE('The time is: '||
        TO_CHAR(sysdate, 'HH:MI AM'));
    --
    SELECT user
      INTO v_user
      FROM dual;
    DBMS_OUTPUT.PUT_LINE ('The current user is '||v_user);
    --
    SELECT NVL(COUNT(*), 0)
      INTO v_valid
      FROM user_objects
     WHERE status = 'VALID'
       AND object_type = 'PROCEDURE';
    DBMS_OUTPUT.PUT_LINE
        ('There are '||v_valid||' valid procedures.');
    --
    SELECT NVL(COUNT(*), 0)
      INTO v_invalid
      FROM user_objects
     WHERE status = 'INVALID'
       AND object_type = 'PROCEDURE';
```

```
    DBMS_OUTPUT.PUT_LINE
        ('There are '||v_invalid||' invalid procedures.');
END;


SET SERVEROUTPUT ON
EXEC current_status;
```

2) Write a procedure that takes in a zip code, city, and state and inserts the values into the zip code table. It should check to see if the zip code is already in the database. If it is, an exception should be raised, and an error message should be displayed. Write an anonymous block that uses the procedure and inserts your zip code.

ANSWER: The script should look similar to the following:

```
CREATE OR REPLACE PROCEDURE insert_zip
  (I_ZIPCODE IN zipcode.zip%TYPE,
   I_CITY    IN zipcode.city%TYPE,
   I_STATE   IN zipcode.state%TYPE)
AS
   v_zipcode zipcode.zip%TYPE;
   v_city    zipcode.city%TYPE;
   v_state   zipcode.state%TYPE;
   v_dummy   zipcode.zip%TYPE;
BEGIN
   v_zipcode := i_zipcode;
   v_city    := i_city;
   v_state   := i_state;
--
   SELECT zip
     INTO v_dummy
     FROM zipcode
    WHERE zip = v_zipcode;
--
   DBMS_OUTPUT.PUT_LINE('The zipcode '||v_zipcode||
       ' is already in the database and cannot be'||
       ' reinserted.');
--
EXCEPTION
   WHEN NO_DATA_FOUND THEN
      INSERT INTO ZIPCODE
      VALUES (v_zipcode, v_city, v_state, user, sysdate,
              user, sysdate);
   WHEN OTHERS THEN
      DBMS_OUTPUT.PUT_LINE ('There was an unknown error '||
         'in insert_zip.');
END;


SET SERVEROUTPUT ON
BEGIN
  insert_zip (10035, 'No Where', 'ZZ');
END;
```

```
BEGIN
   insert_zip (99999, 'No Where', 'ZZ');
END;


ROLLBACK;
```

PART 2

1) Create a stored procedure based on the script ch17_1c.sql, version 3.0, created in Lab 17.1 of Chapter 17. The procedure should accept two parameters to hold a table name and an ID and should return six parameters with first name, last name, street, city, state, and zip code information.

ANSWER: The procedure should look similar to the following. Changes are shown in bold.

```
CREATE OR REPLACE PROCEDURE get_name_address
    (table_name_in    IN VARCHAR2
    ,id_in             IN NUMBER
    ,first_name_out OUT VARCHAR2
    ,last_name_out  OUT VARCHAR2
    ,street_out     OUT VARCHAR2
    ,city_out       OUT VARCHAR2
    ,state_out      OUT VARCHAR2
    ,zip_out        OUT VARCHAR2)
AS
    sql_stmt VARCHAR2(200);
BEGIN
    sql_stmt := 'SELECT a.first_name, a.last_name, a.street_address'||
                '       ,b.city, b.state, b.zip'                      ||
                ' FROM '||table_name_in||' a, zipcode b'             ||
                ' WHERE a.zip = b.zip'                                ||
                '   AND '||table_name_in||'_id = :1';
    EXECUTE IMMEDIATE sql_stmt
    INTO first_name_out, last_name_out, street_out, city_out,
         state_out, zip_out
    USING id_in;
END get_name_address;
```

This procedure contains two IN parameters whose values are used by the dynamic SQL statement and six OUT parameters that hold data returned by the SELECT statement. After it is created, this procedure can be tested with the following PL/SQL block:

```
SET SERVEROUTPUT ON
DECLARE
    v_table_name VARCHAR2(20) := '&sv_table_name';
    v_id         NUMBER := &sv_id;
    v_first_name VARCHAR2(25);
    v_last_name  VARCHAR2(25);
    v_street     VARCHAR2(50);
    v_city       VARCHAR2(25);
    v_state      VARCHAR2(2);
    v_zip        VARCHAR2(5);
```

```
BEGIN
   get_name_address (v_table_name, v_id, v_first_name, v_last_name,
                     v_street, v_city, v_state, v_zip);

   DBMS_OUTPUT.PUT_LINE ('First Name: '||v_first_name);
   DBMS_OUTPUT.PUT_LINE ('Last Name:  '||v_last_name);
   DBMS_OUTPUT.PUT_LINE ('Street:     '||v_street);
   DBMS_OUTPUT.PUT_LINE ('City:       '||v_city);
   DBMS_OUTPUT.PUT_LINE ('State:      '||v_state);
   DBMS_OUTPUT.PUT_LINE ('Zip Code:   '||v_zip);
END;
```

When run, this script produces the following output. The first run is against the STUDENT table, and the second run is against the INSTRUCTOR table.

```
Enter value for sv_table_name: student
old   2:     v_table_name VARCHAR2(20) := '&sv_table_name';
new   2:     v_table_name VARCHAR2(20) := 'student';
Enter value for sv_id: 105
old   3:     v_id NUMBER := &sv_id;
new   3:     v_id NUMBER := 105;
First Name: Angel
Last Name:  Moskowitz
Street:     320 John St.
City:       Ft. Lee
State:      NJ
Zip Code:   07024


PL/SQL procedure successfully completed.

Enter value for sv_table_name: instructor
old   2:     v_table_name VARCHAR2(20) := '&sv_table_name';
new   2:     v_table_name VARCHAR2(20) := 'instructor';
Enter value for sv_id: 105
old   3:     v_id NUMBER := &sv_id;
new   3:     v_id NUMBER := 105;
First Name: Anita
Last Name:  Morris
Street:     34 Maiden Lane
City:       New York
State:      NY
Zip Code:   10015


PL/SQL procedure successfully completed.
```

2) Modify the procedure you just created. Instead of using six parameters to hold name and address information, the procedure should return a user-defined record that contains six fields that hold name and address information. Note: You may want to create a package in which you define a record type. This record may be used later, such as when the procedure is invoked in a PL/SQL block.

ANSWER: The package should look similar to the following. Changes are shown in bold.

```
CREATE OR REPLACE PACKAGE dynamic_sql_pkg
AS
   -- Create user-defined record type
   TYPE name_addr_rec_type IS RECORD
      (first_name VARCHAR2(25),
       last_name  VARCHAR2(25),
       street     VARCHAR2(50),
       city       VARCHAR2(25),
       state      VARCHAR2(2),
       zip        VARCHAR2(5));

   PROCEDURE get_name_address (table_name_in  IN VARCHAR2
                              ,id_in          IN NUMBER
                              ,name_addr_rec OUT name_addr_rec_type);
END dynamic_sql_pkg;
/

CREATE OR REPLACE PACKAGE BODY dynamic_sql_pkg AS

PROCEDURE get_name_address (table_name_in  IN VARCHAR2
                           ,id_in          IN NUMBER
                           ,name_addr_rec OUT name_addr_rec_type)
IS
   sql_stmt VARCHAR2(200);
BEGIN
   sql_stmt := 'SELECT a.first_name, a.last_name, a.street_address'||
               '        ,b.city, b.state, b.zip'                    ||
               '  FROM '||table_name_in||' a, zipcode b'           ||
               ' WHERE a.zip = b.zip'                              ||
               '   AND '||table_name_in||'_id = :1';
   EXECUTE IMMEDIATE sql_stmt
   INTO name_addr_rec
   USING id_in;
END get_name_address;

END dynamic_sql_pkg;
/
```

In this package specification, you declare a user-defined record type. The procedure uses this record type for its OUT parameter, name_addr_rec. After the package is created, its procedure can be tested with the following PL/SQL block (changes are shown in bold):

```
SET SERVEROUTPUT ON
DECLARE
   v_table_name VARCHAR2(20) := '&sv_table_name';
   v_id NUMBER := &sv_id;
   name_addr_rec DYNAMIC_SQL_PKG.NAME_ADDR_REC_TYPE;
```

```
BEGIN
    dynamic_sql_pkg.get_name_address (v_table_name, v_id,
                                      name_addr_rec);

    DBMS_OUTPUT.PUT_LINE ('First Name: '||name_addr_rec.first_name);
    DBMS_OUTPUT.PUT_LINE ('Last Name:  '||name_addr_rec.last_name);
    DBMS_OUTPUT.PUT_LINE ('Street:     '||name_addr_rec.street);
    DBMS_OUTPUT.PUT_LINE ('City:       '||name_addr_rec.city);
    DBMS_OUTPUT.PUT_LINE ('State:      '||name_addr_rec.state);
    DBMS_OUTPUT.PUT_LINE ('Zip Code:   '||name_addr_rec.zip);

END;
```

Notice that instead of declaring six variables, you declare one variable of the user-defined record type, `name_addr_rec_type`. Because this record type is defined in the package DYNAMIC_SQL_PKG, the name of the record type is prefixed with the name of the package. Similarly, the name of the package is added to the procedure call statement.

When run, this script produces the following output. The first output is against the STUDENT table, and the second output is against the INSTRUCTOR table.

```
Enter value for sv_table_name: student
old   2:    v_table_name VARCHAR2(20) := '&sv_table_name';
new   2:    v_table_name VARCHAR2(20) := 'student';
Enter value for sv_id: 105
old   3:    v_id NUMBER := &sv_id;
new   3:    v_id NUMBER := 105;
First Name: Angel
Last Name:  Moskowitz
Street:     320 John St.
City:       Ft. Lee
State:      NJ
Zip Code:   07024

PL/SQL procedure successfully completed.

Enter value for sv_table_name: instructor
old   2:    v_table_name VARCHAR2(20) := '&sv_table_name';
new   2:    v_table_name VARCHAR2(20) := 'instructor';
Enter value for sv_id: 105
old   3:    v_id NUMBER := &sv_id;
new   3:    v_id NUMBER := 105;
First Name: Anita
Last Name:  Morris
Street:     34 Maiden Lane
City:       New York
State:      NY
Zip Code:   10015

PL/SQL procedure successfully completed.
```

Chapter 20, "Functions"

1) Write a stored function called `new_student_id` that takes in no parameters and returns a `student.student_id%TYPE`. The value returned will be used when inserting a new student into the CTA application. It will be derived by using the formula `student_id_seq.NEXTVAL`.

ANSWER: The function should look similar to the following:

```
CREATE OR REPLACE FUNCTION new_student_id
RETURN student.student_id%TYPE
AS
   v_student_id student.student_id%TYPE;
BEGIN
   SELECT student_id_seq.NEXTVAL
     INTO v_student_id
     FROM dual;
   RETURN(v_student_id);
END;
```

2) Write a stored function called `zip_does_not_exist` that takes in a `zipcode.zip%TYPE` and returns a Boolean. The function will return TRUE if the zip code passed into it does not exist. It will return a FALSE if the zip code does exist. Hint: Here's an example of how this might be used:

```
DECLARE
    cons_zip CONSTANT zipcode.zip%TYPE := '&sv_zipcode';
    e_zipcode_is_not_valid EXCEPTION;
BEGIN
    IF zipcode_does_not_exist(cons_zip)
    THEN
       RAISE e_zipcode_is_not_valid;
    ELSE
       -- An insert of an instructor's record which
       -- makes use of the checked zipcode might go here.
       NULL;
    END IF;
EXCEPTION
   WHEN e_zipcode_is_not_valid THEN
       RAISE_APPLICATION_ERROR
          (-20003, 'Could not find zipcode '||cons_zip||'.');
END;
```

ANSWER: The function should look similar to the following:

```
CREATE OR REPLACE FUNCTION zipcode_does_not_exist
   (i_zipcode IN zipcode.zip%TYPE)
RETURN BOOLEAN
AS
   v_dummy char(1);
BEGIN
   SELECT NULL
     INTO v_dummy
```

```
   FROM zipcode
  WHERE zip = i_zipcode;

   -- Meaning the zipcode does exit
   RETURN FALSE;
EXCEPTION
   WHEN OTHERS THEN
      -- The select statement above will cause an exception
      -- to be raised if the zipcode is not in the database.
      RETURN TRUE;
END zipcode_does_not_exist;
```

3) Create a new function. For a given instructor, determine how many sections he or she is teaching. If the number is greater than or equal to 3, return a message saying that the instructor needs a vacation. Otherwise, return a message saying how many sections this instructor is teaching.

ANSWER: The function should look similar to the following:

```
CREATE OR REPLACE FUNCTION instructor_status
   (i_first_name IN instructor.first_name%TYPE,
    i_last_name  IN instructor.last_name%TYPE)
RETURN VARCHAR2
AS
   v_instructor_id instructor.instructor_id%TYPE;
   v_section_count NUMBER;
   v_status        VARCHAR2(100);
BEGIN
   SELECT instructor_id
     INTO v_instructor_id
     FROM instructor
    WHERE first_name = i_first_name
      AND last_name = i_last_name;

   SELECT COUNT(*)
     INTO v_section_count
     FROM section
    WHERE instructor_id = v_instructor_id;

   IF v_section_count >= 3 THEN
      v_status :=
         'The instructor '||i_first_name||'  '||
          i_last_name||' is teaching '||v_section_count||
         ' and needs a vaction.';
   ELSE
      v_status :=
         'The instructor '||i_first_name||'  '||
          i_last_name||' is teaching '||v_section_count||
         ' courses.';
   END IF;
   RETURN v_status;
EXCEPTION
   WHEN NO_DATA_FOUND THEN
```

```
      -- Note that either of the SELECT statements can raise
      -- this exception
      v_status :=
          'The instructor '||i_first_name||'  '||
          i_last_name||' is not shown to be teaching'||
          ' any courses.';
      RETURN v_status;
   WHEN OTHERS THEN
      v_status :=
          'There has been in an error in the function.';
      RETURN v_status;
END;
```

Test the function as follows:

```
SELECT instructor_status(first_name, last_name)
  FROM instructor;
/
```

Chapter 21, "Packages"

1) Add a procedure to the `student_api` package called `remove_student`. This procedure accepts a `student_id` and returns nothing. Based on the student ID passed in, it removes the student from the database. If the student does not exist or if a problem occurs while removing the student (such as a foreign key constraint violation), let the calling program handle it.

   ANSWER: The package should be similar to the following:

```
CREATE OR REPLACE PACKAGE student_api AS
    v_current_date DATE;

    PROCEDURE discount;

    FUNCTION new_instructor_id
    RETURN instructor.instructor_id%TYPE;

    FUNCTION total_cost_for_student
        (p_student_id IN student.student_id%TYPE)
    RETURN course.cost%TYPE;
    PRAGMA RESTRICT_REFERENCES
        (total_cost_for_student, WNDS, WNPS, RNPS);

    PROCEDURE get_student_info
        (p_student_id   IN student.student_id%TYPE,
         p_last_name    OUT student.last_name%TYPE,
         p_first_name   OUT student.first_name%TYPE,
         p_zip          OUT student.zip%TYPE,
         p_return_code OUT NUMBER);

    PROCEDURE get_student_info
        (p_last_name    IN student.last_name%TYPE,
         p_first_name   IN student.first_name%TYPE,
```

```
      p_student_id  OUT student.student_id%TYPE,
      p_zip         OUT student.zip%TYPE,
      p_return_code OUT NUMBER);

  PROCEDURE remove_student
      (p_studid IN student.student_id%TYPE);
END student_api;
/
CREATE OR REPLACE PACKAGE BODY student_api AS

PROCEDURE discount
IS
   CURSOR c_group_discount IS
      SELECT distinct s.course_no, c.description
        FROM section s, enrollment e, course c
       WHERE s.section_id = e.section_id
       GROUP BY s.course_no, c.description,
               e.section_id, s.section_id
      HAVING COUNT(*) >=8;
BEGIN
   FOR r_group_discount IN c_group_discount LOOP
      UPDATE course
         SET cost = cost * .95
       WHERE course_no = r_group_discount.course_no;

      DBMS_OUTPUT.PUT_LINE
         ('A 5% discount has been given to'||
          r_group_discount.course_no||' '||
          r_group_discount.description);
   END LOOP;
END discount;

FUNCTION new_instructor_id
RETURN instructor.instructor_id%TYPE
IS
   v_new_instid instructor.instructor_id%TYPE;
BEGIN
   SELECT INSTRUCTOR_ID_SEQ.NEXTVAL
     INTO v_new_instid
     FROM dual;
   RETURN v_new_instid;
EXCEPTION
   WHEN OTHERS THEN
      DECLARE
         v_sqlerrm VARCHAR2(250) := SUBSTR(SQLERRM,1,250);
      BEGIN
         RAISE_APPLICATION_ERROR
            (-20003, 'Error in instructor_id: '||v_sqlerrm);
      END;
END new_instructor_id;
```

```
FUNCTION get_course_descript_private
   (p_course_no  course.course_no%TYPE)
RETURN course.description%TYPE
IS
   v_course_descript course.description%TYPE;
BEGIN
   SELECT description
     INTO v_course_descript
     FROM course
    WHERE course_no = p_course_no;
   RETURN v_course_descript;
EXCEPTION
   WHEN OTHERS THEN
      RETURN NULL;
END get_course_descript_private;


FUNCTION total_cost_for_student
   (p_student_id IN student.student_id%TYPE)
RETURN course.cost%TYPE
IS
   v_cost course.cost%TYPE;
BEGIN
   SELECT sum(cost)
     INTO v_cost
     FROM course c, section s, enrollment e
    WHERE c.course_no = c.course_no
      AND e.section_id = s.section_id
      AND e.student_id = p_student_id;
   RETURN v_cost;
EXCEPTION
   WHEN OTHERS THEN
      RETURN NULL;
END total_cost_for_student;


PROCEDURE get_student_info
   (p_student_id   IN  student.student_id%TYPE,
    p_last_name   OUT student.last_name%TYPE,
    p_first_name  OUT student.first_name%TYPE,
    p_zip         OUT student.zip%TYPE,
    p_return_code OUT NUMBER)
IS
BEGIN
   SELECT last_name, first_name, zip
     INTO p_last_name, p_first_name, p_zip
     FROM student
    WHERE student.student_id = p_student_id;
   p_return_code := 0;
EXCEPTION
   WHEN NO_DATA_FOUND THEN
      DBMS_OUTPUT.PUT_LINE ('Student ID is not valid.');
```

```
         p_return_code := -100;
         p_last_name := NULL;
         p_first_name := NULL;
         p_zip := NULL;
   WHEN OTHERS THEN
      DBMS_OUTPUT.PUT_LINE
         ('Error in procedure get_student_info');
END get_student_info;

PROCEDURE get_student_info
   (p_last_name    IN student.last_name%TYPE,
    p_first_name   IN student.first_name%TYPE,
    p_student_id  OUT student.student_id%TYPE,
    p_zip          OUT student.zip%TYPE,
    p_return_code OUT NUMBER)
IS
BEGIN
   SELECT student_id, zip
     INTO p_student_id, p_zip
     FROM student
    WHERE UPPER(last_name) = UPPER(p_last_name)
      AND UPPER(first_name) = UPPER(p_first_name);
   p_return_code := 0;
EXCEPTION
   WHEN NO_DATA_FOUND THEN
      DBMS_OUTPUT.PUT_LINE ('Student name is not valid.');
         p_return_code := -100;
         p_student_id := NULL;
         p_zip := NULL;
   WHEN OTHERS THEN
      DBMS_OUTPUT.PUT_LINE
         ('Error in procedure get_student_info');
END get_student_info;

PROCEDURE remove_student
   (p_studid IN student.student_id%TYPE)
IS
BEGIN
   DELETE
     FROM STUDENT
    WHERE student_id = p_studid;
END;

BEGIN
   SELECT trunc(sysdate, 'DD')
     INTO v_current_date
     FROM dual;
END student_api;
/
```

2) Alter `remove_student` in the `student_api` package body to accept an additional parameter. This new parameter should be a VARCHAR2 and called `p_ri`. Make `p_ri` default to R. The new parameter may contain a value of R or C. If R is received, it represents DELETE RESTRICT, and the procedure acts as it does now. If there are enrollments for the student, the delete is disallowed. If a C is received, it represents DELETE CASCADE. This functionally means that the `remove_student` procedure locates all records for the student in all the tables. It removes them from the database before attempting to remove the student from the student table. Decide how to handle the situation when the user passes in a code other than C or R.

ANSWER: The package should look similar to the following:

```
CREATE OR REPLACE PACKAGE student_api AS
   v_current_date DATE;

   PROCEDURE discount;

   FUNCTION new_instructor_id
      RETURN instructor.instructor_id%TYPE;

   FUNCTION total_cost_for_student
      (p_student_id IN student.student_id%TYPE)
   RETURN course.cost%TYPE;
   PRAGMA RESTRICT_REFERENCES
      (total_cost_for_student, WNDS, WNPS, RNPS);

   PROCEDURE get_student_info
      (p_student_id   IN   student.student_id%TYPE,
       p_last_name    OUT student.last_name%TYPE,
       p_first_name   OUT student.first_name%TYPE,
       p_zip          OUT student.zip%TYPE,
       p_return_code OUT NUMBER);

   PROCEDURE get_student_info
      (p_last_name    IN student.last_name%TYPE,
       p_first_name   IN student.first_name%TYPE,
       p_student_id   OUT student.student_id%TYPE,
       p_zip          OUT student.zip%TYPE,
       p_return_code OUT NUMBER);

   PROCEDURE remove_student
      (p_studid IN student.student_id%TYPE,
       p_ri     IN VARCHAR2 DEFAULT 'R');
END student_api;
/

CREATE OR REPLACE PACKAGE BODY student_api AS

PROCEDURE discount
IS
   CURSOR c_group_discount IS
      SELECT distinct s.course_no, c.description
        FROM section s, enrollment e, course c
```

```
        WHERE s.section_id = e.section_id
        GROUP BY s.course_no, c.description,
                 e.section_id, s.section_id
        HAVING COUNT(*) >=8;
BEGIN
    FOR r_group_discount IN c_group_discount LOOP
        UPDATE course
           SET cost = cost * .95
         WHERE course_no = r_group_discount.course_no;

        DBMS_OUTPUT.PUT_LINE
            ('A 5% discount has been given to'||
             r_group_discount.course_no||' '||
             r_group_discount.description);
    END LOOP;
END discount;


FUNCTION new_instructor_id
RETURN instructor.instructor_id%TYPE
IS
    v_new_instid instructor.instructor_id%TYPE;
BEGIN
    SELECT INSTRUCTOR_ID_SEQ.NEXTVAL
      INTO v_new_instid
      FROM dual;
    RETURN v_new_instid;
EXCEPTION
    WHEN OTHERS THEN
        DECLARE
           v_sqlerrm VARCHAR2(250) := SUBSTR(SQLERRM,1,250);
        BEGIN
           RAISE_APPLICATION_ERROR
               (-20003, 'Error in instructor_id: '||v_sqlerrm);
        END;
END new_instructor_id;


FUNCTION get_course_descript_private
    (p_course_no course.course_no%TYPE)
RETURN course.description%TYPE
IS
    v_course_descript course.description%TYPE;
BEGIN
    SELECT description
      INTO v_course_descript
      FROM course
     WHERE course_no = p_course_no;
    RETURN v_course_descript;
EXCEPTION
    WHEN OTHERS THEN
        RETURN NULL;
```

```
    END get_course_descript_private;

FUNCTION total_cost_for_student
    (p_student_id IN student.student_id%TYPE)
RETURN course.cost%TYPE
IS
    v_cost course.cost%TYPE;
BEGIN
    SELECT sum(cost)
      INTO v_cost
      FROM course c, section s, enrollment e
     WHERE c.course_no = c.course_no
       AND e.section_id = s.section_id
       AND e.student_id = p_student_id;
    RETURN v_cost;
EXCEPTION
    WHEN OTHERS THEN
        RETURN NULL;
END total_cost_for_student;

PROCEDURE get_student_info
    (p_student_id   IN  student.student_id%TYPE,
     p_last_name    OUT student.last_name%TYPE,
     p_first_name   OUT student.first_name%TYPE,
     p_zip          OUT student.zip%TYPE,
     p_return_code OUT NUMBER)
IS
BEGIN
    SELECT last_name, first_name, zip
      INTO p_last_name, p_first_name, p_zip
      FROM student
     WHERE student.student_id = p_student_id;
    p_return_code := 0;
EXCEPTION
    WHEN NO_DATA_FOUND THEN
        DBMS_OUTPUT.PUT_LINE ('Student ID is not valid.');
        p_return_code := -100;
        p_last_name := NULL;
        p_first_name := NULL;
        p_zip := NULL;
    WHEN OTHERS THEN
        DBMS_OUTPUT.PUT_LINE
            ('Error in procedure get_student_info');
END get_student_info;

PROCEDURE get_student_info
    (p_last_name    IN student.last_name%TYPE,
     p_first_name   IN student.first_name%TYPE,
     p_student_id  OUT student.student_id%TYPE,
     p_zip          OUT student.zip%TYPE,
     p_return_code OUT NUMBER)
```

```
IS
BEGIN
   SELECT student_id, zip
     INTO p_student_id, p_zip
     FROM student
    WHERE UPPER(last_name) = UPPER(p_last_name)
      AND UPPER(first_name) = UPPER(p_first_name);
   p_return_code := 0;
EXCEPTION
   WHEN NO_DATA_FOUND THEN
      DBMS_OUTPUT.PUT_LINE
         ('Student name is not valid.');
      p_return_code := -100;
      p_student_id := NULL;
      p_zip := NULL;
   WHEN OTHERS THEN
      DBMS_OUTPUT.PUT_LINE
         ('Error in procedure get_student_info');
END get_student_info;

PROCEDURE remove_student
   -- The parameters student_id and p_ri give the user an
   -- option of cascade delete or restrict delete for
   -- the given student's records
   (p_studid IN student.student_id%TYPE,
    p_ri     IN VARCHAR2 DEFAULT 'R')
IS
   -- Declare exceptions for use in procedure
   enrollment_present EXCEPTION;
   bad_pri EXCEPTION;
BEGIN
   -- R value is for restrict delete option
   IF p_ri = 'R' THEN
      DECLARE
         -- A variable is needed to test if the student
         -- is in the enrollment table
         v_dummy CHAR(1);
      BEGIN
         -- This is a standard existence check.
         -- If v_dummy is assigned a value via the
         -- SELECT INTO, the exception
         -- enrollment_present will be raised.
         -- If the v_dummy is not assigned a value, the
         -- exception no_data_found will be raised.
         SELECT NULL
           INTO v_dummy
           FROM enrollment e
          WHERE e.student_id = p_studid
            AND ROWNUM = 1;
```

```
                -- The rownum set to 1 prevents the SELECT
                -- INTO statement raise to_many_rows
                -- exception.
                -- If there is at least one row in the enrollment
                -- table with a corresponding student_id, the
                -- restrict delete parameter will disallow the
                -- deletion of the student by raising
                -- the enrollment_present exception.
                RAISE enrollment_present;
            EXCEPTION
                WHEN NO_DATA_FOUND THEN
                    -- The no_data_found exception is raised
                    -- when there are no students found in the
                    -- enrollment table. Since the p_ri indicates
                    -- a restrict delete user choice the delete
                    -- operation is permitted.
                    DELETE FROM student
                     WHERE student_id = p_studid;
            END;
        -- When the user enters "C" for the p_ri
        -- he/she indicates a cascade delete choice
        ELSIF p_ri = 'C' THEN
            -- Delete the student from the enrollment and
            -- grade tables
            DELETE FROM enrollment
             WHERE student_id = p_studid;

            DELETE FROM grade
             WHERE student_id = p_studid;

            -- Delete from student table only after corresponding
            -- records have been removed from the other tables
            -- because the student table is the parent table
            DELETE FROM student
             WHERE student_id = p_studid;
        ELSE
            RAISE bad_pri;
        END IF;
    EXCEPTION
        WHEN bad_pri THEN
            RAISE_APPLICATION_ERROR
                (-20231, 'An incorrect p_ri value was '||
                 'entered. The remove_student procedure can '||
                 'only accept a C or R for the p_ri parameter.');

        WHEN enrollment_present THEN
            RAISE_APPLICATION_ERROR
                (-20239, 'The student with ID'||p_studid||
                 ' exists in the enrollment table thus records'||
                 ' will not be removed.');
```

```
END remove_student;

BEGIN
    SELECT trunc(sysdate, 'DD')
      INTO v_current_date
      FROM dual;
END student_api;
```

Chapter 22, "Stored Code"

1) Add a function to the `student_api` package specification called `get_course_descript`. The caller takes a `course.cnumber%TYPE` parameter, and it returns a `course.description%TYPE`.

ANSWER: The package should look similar to the following:

```
CREATE OR REPLACE PACKAGE student_api AS
    v_current_date DATE;

    PROCEDURE discount;

    FUNCTION new_instructor_id
    RETURN instructor.instructor_id%TYPE;

    FUNCTION total_cost_for_student
        (p_student_id IN student.student_id%TYPE)
    RETURN course.cost%TYPE;
    PRAGMA RESTRICT_REFERENCES
        (total_cost_for_student, WNDS, WNPS, RNPS);

    PROCEDURE get_student_info
        (p_student_id   IN student.student_id%TYPE,
         p_last_name    OUT student.last_name%TYPE,
         p_first_name   OUT student.first_name%TYPE,
         p_zip          OUT student.zip%TYPE,
         p_return_code OUT NUMBER);

    PROCEDURE get_student_info
        (p_last_name    IN student.last_name%TYPE,
         p_first_name   IN student.first_name%TYPE,
         p_student_id  OUT student.student_id%TYPE,
         p_zip          OUT student.zip%TYPE,
         p_return_code OUT NUMBER);

    PROCEDURE remove_student
        (p_studid IN student.student_id%TYPE,
         p_ri     IN VARCHAR2 DEFAULT 'R');

    FUNCTION get_course_descript
        (p_cnumber course.course_no%TYPE)
    RETURN course.description%TYPE;
END student_api;
```

2) Create a function in the `student_api` package body called `get_course_description`. A caller passes in a course number, and it returns the course description. Instead of searching for the description itself, it makes a call to `get_course_descript_private`. It passes its course number to `get_course_descript_private`. It passes back to the caller the description it gets back from `get_course_descript_private`.

ANSWER: The package body should look similar to the following:

```
CREATE OR REPLACE PACKAGE BODY student_api AS

PROCEDURE discount
IS
   CURSOR c_group_discount IS
      SELECT distinct s.course_no, c.description
        FROM section s, enrollment e, course c
       WHERE s.section_id = e.section_id
       GROUP BY s.course_no, c.description,
                e.section_id, s.section_id
       HAVING COUNT(*) >=8;
BEGIN
   FOR r_group_discount IN c_group_discount LOOP
      UPDATE course
         SET cost = cost * .95
       WHERE course_no = r_group_discount.course_no;

      DBMS_OUTPUT.PUT_LINE
         ('A 5% discount has been given to'||
          r_group_discount.course_no||' '||
          r_group_discount.description);
   END LOOP;
END discount;

FUNCTION new_instructor_id
RETURN instructor.instructor_id%TYPE
IS
   v_new_instid instructor.instructor_id%TYPE;
BEGIN
   SELECT INSTRUCTOR_ID_SEQ.NEXTVAL
     INTO v_new_instid
     FROM dual;
   RETURN v_new_instid;
EXCEPTION
   WHEN OTHERS THEN
      DECLARE
         v_sqlerrm VARCHAR2(250) := SUBSTR(SQLERRM,1,250);
      BEGIN
         RAISE_APPLICATION_ERROR
            (-20003, 'Error in instructor_id: '||v_sqlerrm);
      END;
END new_instructor_id;
```

```
FUNCTION get_course_descript_private
   (p_course_no   course.course_no%TYPE)
RETURN course.description%TYPE
IS
   v_course_descript course.description%TYPE;
BEGIN
   SELECT description
     INTO v_course_descript
     FROM course
    WHERE course_no = p_course_no;
   RETURN v_course_descript;
EXCEPTION
   WHEN OTHERS THEN
      RETURN NULL;
END get_course_descript_private;


FUNCTION total_cost_for_student
   (p_student_id IN student.student_id%TYPE)
RETURN course.cost%TYPE
IS
   v_cost course.cost%TYPE;
BEGIN
   SELECT sum(cost)
     INTO v_cost
     FROM course c, section s, enrollment e
    WHERE c.course_no = c.course_no
      AND e.section_id = s.section_id
      AND e.student_id = p_student_id;
   RETURN v_cost;
EXCEPTION
   WHEN OTHERS THEN
      RETURN NULL;
END total_cost_for_student;


PROCEDURE get_student_info
   (p_student_id   IN student.student_id%TYPE,
    p_last_name    OUT student.last_name%TYPE,
    p_first_name   OUT student.first_name%TYPE,
    p_zip          OUT student.zip%TYPE,
    p_return_code OUT NUMBER)
IS
BEGIN
   SELECT last_name, first_name, zip
     INTO p_last_name, p_first_name, p_zip
     FROM student
    WHERE student.student_id = p_student_id;
   p_return_code := 0;
EXCEPTION
   WHEN NO_DATA_FOUND THEN
      DBMS_OUTPUT.PUT_LINE ('Student ID is not valid.');
```

```
         p_return_code := -100;
         p_last_name   := NULL;
         p_first_name  := NULL;
         p_zip         := NULL;

   WHEN OTHERS THEN
      DBMS_OUTPUT.PUT_LINE
         ('Error in procedure get_student_info');
END get_student_info;

PROCEDURE get_student_info
   (p_last_name    IN student.last_name%TYPE,
    p_first_name   IN student.first_name%TYPE,
    p_student_id  OUT student.student_id%TYPE,
    p_zip         OUT student.zip%TYPE,
    p_return_code OUT NUMBER)
IS
BEGIN
   SELECT student_id, zip
     INTO p_student_id, p_zip
     FROM student
    WHERE UPPER(last_name)  = UPPER(p_last_name)
      AND UPPER(first_name) = UPPER(p_first_name);
   p_return_code := 0;
EXCEPTION
   WHEN NO_DATA_FOUND THEN
      DBMS_OUTPUT.PUT_LINE ('Student name is not valid.');
      p_return_code := -100;
      p_student_id  := NULL;
      p_zip         := NULL;

   WHEN OTHERS THEN
      DBMS_OUTPUT.PUT_LINE
         ('Error in procedure get_student_info');
END get_student_info;

PROCEDURE remove_student
   -- The parameters student_id and p_ri give the user an
   -- option of cascade delete or restrict delete for
   -- the given student's records
   (p_studid IN student.student_id%TYPE,
    p_ri     IN VARCHAR2 DEFAULT 'R')
IS
   -- Declare exceptions for use in procedure
   enrollment_present EXCEPTION;
   bad_pri EXCEPTION;
BEGIN
   -- The R value is for restrict delete option
   IF p_ri = 'R' THEN
      DECLARE
```

```
      -- A variable is needed to test if the student
      -- is in the enrollment table
      v_dummy CHAR(1);
   BEGIN
      -- This is a standard existence check.
      -- If v_dummy is assigned a value via the
      -- SELECT INTO, the exception
      -- enrollment_present will be raised.
      -- If the v_dummy is not assigned a value, the
      -- exception no_data_found will be raised.
      SELECT NULL
        INTO v_dummy
        FROM enrollment e
       WHERE e.student_id = p_studid
         AND ROWNUM = 1;

      -- The rownum set to 1 prevents the SELECT
      -- INTO statement raise to_many_rows exception.
      -- If there is at least one row in the enrollment
      -- table with a corresponding student_id, the
      -- restrict delete parameter will disallow
      -- the deletion of the student by raising
      -- the enrollment_present exception.
      RAISE enrollment_present;
   EXCEPTION
      WHEN NO_DATA_FOUND THEN
         -- The no_data_found exception is raised
         -- when no students are found in the
         -- enrollment table.
         -- Since the p_ri indicates a restrict
         -- delete user choice, the delete operation
         -- is permitted.
         DELETE FROM student
          WHERE student_id = p_studid;
   END;
-- When the user enters "C" for the p_ri
-- he/she indicates a cascade delete choice
ELSIF p_ri = 'C' THEN
   -- Delete the student from the enrollment and
   -- grade tables
   DELETE FROM enrollment
    WHERE student_id = p_studid;

   DELETE FROM grade
    WHERE student_id = p_studid;

   -- Delete from student table only after
   -- corresponding records have been removed from
   -- the other tables because the student table is
   -- the parent table
```

```
        DELETE
          FROM student
         WHERE student_id = p_studid;
    ELSE
        RAISE bad_pri;
    END IF;
EXCEPTION
    WHEN bad_pri THEN
        RAISE_APPLICATION_ERROR
            (-20231, 'An incorrect p_ri value was '||
             'entered. The remove_student procedure can '||
             'only accept a C or R for the p_ri parameter.');

    WHEN enrollment_present THEN
        RAISE_APPLICATION_ERROR
            (-20239, 'The student with ID'||p_studid||
             ' exists in the enrollment table thus records'||
             ' will not be removed.');
END remove_student;

FUNCTION get_course_descript
    (p_cnumber course.course_no%TYPE)
RETURN course.description%TYPE
IS
BEGIN
    RETURN get_course_descript_private(p_cnumber);
END get_course_descript;

BEGIN
    SELECT trunc(sysdate, 'DD')
      INTO v_current_date
      FROM dual;
END student_api;
```

3) Add a PRAGMA RESTRICT_REFERENCES to `student_api` for `get_course_description` specifying the following: It writes no database state, it writes no package state, and it reads no package state.

ANSWER: The package should look similar to the following:

```
CREATE OR REPLACE PACKAGE student_api AS
    v_current_date DATE;

    PROCEDURE discount;

    FUNCTION new_instructor_id
    RETURN instructor.instructor_id%TYPE;

    FUNCTION total_cost_for_student
        (p_student_id IN student.student_id%TYPE)
        RETURN course.cost%TYPE;
```

```
   PRAGMA RESTRICT_REFERENCES
      (total_cost_for_student, WNDS, WNPS, RNPS);

   PROCEDURE get_student_info
      (p_student_id   IN student.student_id%TYPE,
       p_last_name    OUT student.last_name%TYPE,
       p_first_name   OUT student.first_name%TYPE,
       p_zip          OUT student.zip%TYPE,
       p_return_code  OUT NUMBER);

   PROCEDURE get_student_info
      (p_last_name    IN student.last_name%TYPE,
       p_first_name   IN student.first_name%TYPE,
       p_student_id   OUT student.student_id%TYPE,
       p_zip          OUT student.zip%TYPE,
       p_return_code  OUT NUMBER);

   PROCEDURE remove_student
      (p_studid IN student.student_id%TYPE,
       p_ri     IN VARCHAR2 DEFAULT 'R');

   FUNCTION get_course_descript
      (p_cnumber course.course_no%TYPE)
   RETURN course.description%TYPE;
   PRAGMA RESTRICT_REFERENCES
      (get_course_descript,WNDS, WNPS, RNPS);
END student_api;
/
```

Chapter 23, "Object Types in Oracle"

1) Create the object type `student_obj_type` with attributes derived from the STUDENT table.

ANSWER: The object type should look similar to the following:

```
CREATE OR REPLACE TYPE student_obj_type AS OBJECT
   (student_id         NUMBER(8),
    salutation         VARCHAR2(5),
    first_name         VARCHAR2(25),
    last_name          VARCHAR2(25),
    street_address     VARCHAR2(50),
    zip                VARCHAR2(5),
    phone              VARCHAR2(15),
    employer           VARCHAR2(50),
    registration_date  DATE,
    created_by         VARCHAR2(30),
    created_date       DATE,
    modified_by        VARCHAR2(30),
    modified_date      DATE);
/
```

After this object type is created, it can be used as follows:

```
SET SERVEROUTPUT ON
DECLARE
   v_student_obj student_obj_type;
BEGIN
   -- Use default contructor method to initialize student object
   SELECT student_obj_type(student_id, salutation, first_name,
             last_name, street_address, zip, phone, employer,
             registration_date, null, null, null, null)
     INTO v_student_obj
     FROM student
    WHERE student_id = 103;

   DBMS_OUTPUT.PUT_LINE ('Student ID: '||v_student_obj.student_id);
   DBMS_OUTPUT.PUT_LINE ('Salutation: '||v_student_obj.salutation);
   DBMS_OUTPUT.PUT_LINE ('First Name: '||v_student_obj.first_name);
   DBMS_OUTPUT.PUT_LINE ('Last Name: ' ||v_student_obj.last_name);
   DBMS_OUTPUT.PUT_LINE
       ('Street Address: '||v_student_obj.street_address);
   DBMS_OUTPUT.PUT_LINE ('Zip: '    ||v_student_obj. zip);
   DBMS_OUTPUT.PUT_LINE ('Phone: '   ||v_student_obj.phone);
   DBMS_OUTPUT.PUT_LINE ('Employer: '||v_student_obj.employer);
   DBMS_OUTPUT.PUT_LINE
       ('Registration Date: '||v_student_obj.registration_date);
END;
/
```

The output is as follows:

```
Student ID: 103
Salutation: Ms.
First Name: J.
Last Name: Landry
Street Address: 7435 Boulevard East #45
Zip: 07047
Phone: 201-555-5555
Employer: Albert Hildegard Co.
Registration Date: 22-JAN-03

PL/SQL procedure successfully completed.
```

2) Add user-defined constructor function, member procedure, static procedure, and order function methods. You should determine on your own how these methods should be structured.

ANSWER: The newly modified student object should be similar to the following:

```
CREATE OR REPLACE TYPE student_obj_type AS OBJECT
   (student_id          NUMBER(8),
    salutation          VARCHAR2(5),
    first_name          VARCHAR2(25),
    last_name           VARCHAR2(25),
    street_address      VARCHAR2(50),
    zip                 VARCHAR2(5),
```

```
phone              VARCHAR2(15),
employer           VARCHAR2(50),
registration_date DATE,
created_by         VARCHAR2(30),
created_date       DATE,
modified_by        VARCHAR2(30),
modified_date      DATE,

CONSTRUCTOR FUNCTION student_obj_type
    (SELF IN OUT NOCOPY STUDENT_OBJ_TYPE,
     in_student_id  IN NUMBER,    in_salutation IN VARCHAR2,
     in_first_name  IN VARCHAR2, in_last_name  IN VARCHAR2,
     in_street_addr IN VARCHAR2, in_zip        IN VARCHAR2,
     in_phone       IN VARCHAR2, in_employer   IN VARCHAR2,
     in_reg_date    IN DATE,     in_cr_by      IN VARCHAR2,
     in_cr_date     IN DATE,     in_mod_by     IN VARCHAR2,
     in_mod_date    IN DATE)
RETURN SELF AS RESULT,

CONSTRUCTOR FUNCTION student_obj_type
    (SELF IN OUT NOCOPY STUDENT_OBJ_TYPE,
     in_student_id IN NUMBER)
RETURN SELF AS RESULT,

MEMBER PROCEDURE get_student_info
    (student_id  OUT NUMBER,    salutation OUT VARCHAR2,
     first_name  OUT VARCHAR2, last_name  OUT VARCHAR2,
     street_addr OUT VARCHAR2, zip        OUT VARCHAR2,
     phone       OUT VARCHAR2, employer   OUT VARCHAR2,
     reg_date    OUT DATE,     cr_by      OUT VARCHAR2,
     cr_date     OUT DATE,     mod_by     OUT VARCHAR2,
     mod_date    OUT DATE),

STATIC PROCEDURE display_student_info
    (student_obj IN STUDENT_OBJ_TYPE),

ORDER MEMBER FUNCTION student
    (student_obj STUDENT_OBJ_TYPE)
RETURN INTEGER);
/

CREATE OR REPLACE TYPE BODY student_obj_type AS

CONSTRUCTOR FUNCTION student_obj_type
    (SELF IN OUT NOCOPY STUDENT_OBJ_TYPE,
     in_student_id  IN NUMBER,    in_salutation IN VARCHAR2,
     in_first_name  IN VARCHAR2, in_last_name  IN VARCHAR2,
     in_street_addr IN VARCHAR2, in_zip        IN VARCHAR2,
     in_phone       IN VARCHAR2, in_employer   IN VARCHAR2,
     in_reg_date    IN DATE,     in_cr_by      IN VARCHAR2,
```

```
       in_cr_date      IN DATE,        in_mod_by       IN VARCHAR2,
       in_mod_date     IN DATE)
RETURN SELF AS RESULT
IS
BEGIN
   -- Validate incoming value of zip
   SELECT zip
     INTO SELF.zip
     FROM zipcode
    WHERE zip = in_zip;

   -- Check incoming value of student ID
   -- If it is not populated, get it from the sequence
   IF in_student_id IS NULL THEN
      student_id := STUDENT_ID_SEQ. NEXTVAL;
   ELSE
      student_id := in_student_id;
   END IF;

   salutation        := in_salutation;
   first_name        := in_first_name;
   last_name         := in_last_name;
   street_address    := in_street_addr;
   phone             := in_phone;
   employer          := in_employer;
   registration_date := in_reg_date;

   IF in_cr_by IS NULL THEN created_by := USER;
   ELSE                     created_by := in_cr_by;
   END IF;

   IF in_cr_date IS NULL THEN created_date := SYSDATE;
   ELSE                       created_date := in_cr_date;
   END IF;

   IF in_mod_by IS NULL THEN modified_by := USER;
   ELSE                      modified_by := in_mod_by;
   END IF;

   IF in_mod_date IS NULL THEN modified_date := SYSDATE;
   ELSE                        modified_date := in_mod_date;
   END IF;

   RETURN;
EXCEPTION
   WHEN NO_DATA_FOUND THEN
      RETURN;
END;
```

```
CONSTRUCTOR FUNCTION student_obj_type
   (SELF IN OUT NOCOPY STUDENT_OBJ_TYPE,
    in_student_id IN NUMBER)
RETURN SELF AS RESULT
IS
BEGIN
   SELECT student_id, salutation, first_name, last_name,
          street_address, zip, phone, employer,
          registration_date, created_by, created_date,
          modified_by, modified_date
     INTO SELF.student_id, SELF.salutation, SELF.first_name,
          SELF.last_name, SELF.street_address, SELF.zip,
          SELF.phone, SELF.employer, SELF.registration_date,
          SELF.created_by, SELF.created_date,
          SELF.modified_by, SELF.modified_date
     FROM student
    WHERE student_id = in_student_id;

   RETURN;
EXCEPTION
   WHEN NO_DATA_FOUND THEN
      RETURN;
END;

MEMBER PROCEDURE get_student_info
   (student_id  OUT NUMBER,    salutation OUT VARCHAR2,
    first_name  OUT VARCHAR2, last_name  OUT VARCHAR2,
    street_addr OUT VARCHAR2, zip        OUT VARCHAR2,
    phone       OUT VARCHAR2, employer   OUT VARCHAR2,
    reg_date    OUT DATE,     cr_by      OUT VARCHAR2,
    cr_date     OUT DATE,     mod_by     OUT VARCHAR2,
    mod_date    OUT DATE)IS
BEGIN
   student_id  := SELF.student_id;
   salutation  := SELF.salutation;
   first_name  := SELF.first_name;
   last_name   := SELF.last_name;
   street_addr := SELF.street_address;
   zip         := SELF.zip;
   phone       := SELF.phone;
   employer    := SELF.employer;
   reg_date    := SELF.registration_date;
   cr_by       := SELF.created_by;
   cr_date     := SELF.created_date;
   mod_by      := SELF.modified_by;
   mod_date    := SELF.modified_date;
END;
```

```
STATIC PROCEDURE display_student_info
   (student_obj IN STUDENT_OBJ_TYPE)
IS
BEGIN
   DBMS_OUTPUT.PUT_LINE ('Student ID: '||student_obj.student_id);
   DBMS_OUTPUT.PUT_LINE ('Salutation: '||student_obj.salutation);
   DBMS_OUTPUT.PUT_LINE ('First Name: '||student_obj.first_name);
   DBMS_OUTPUT.PUT_LINE ('Last Name: ' ||student_obj.last_name);
   DBMS_OUTPUT.PUT_LINE
       ('Street Address: '||student_obj.street_address);
   DBMS_OUTPUT.PUT_LINE ('Zip: '      ||student_obj.zip);
   DBMS_OUTPUT.PUT_LINE ('Phone: '    ||student_obj.phone);
   DBMS_OUTPUT.PUT_LINE ('Employer: '||student_obj.employer);
   DBMS_OUTPUT.PUT_LINE
       ('Registration Date: '||student_obj.registration_date);
END;

ORDER MEMBER FUNCTION student (student_obj STUDENT_OBJ_TYPE)
RETURN INTEGER
IS
BEGIN
   IF    student_id < student_obj.student_id THEN RETURN -1;
   ELSIF student_id = student_obj.student_id THEN RETURN  0;
   ELSIF student_id > student_obj.student_id THEN RETURN  1;
   END IF;
END;

END;
/
```

This student object type has two overloaded constructor functions, member procedure, static procedure, and order function methods.

Both constructor functions have the same name as the object type. The first constructor function evaluates incoming values of student ID, zip code, created and modified users, and dates. Specifically, it checks to see if the incoming student ID is null and then populates it from STUDENT_ID_SEQ. Take a closer look at the statement that assigns a sequence value to the STUDENT_ID attribute. The ability to access a sequence via a PL/SQL expression is a new feature in Oracle 11g. Previously, sequences could be accessed only by queries. It also validates that the incoming value of zip exists in the ZIPCODE table. Finally, it checks to see if incoming values of the created and modified user and date are null. If any of these incoming values are null, the constructor function populates the corresponding attributes with the default values based on the system functions USER and SYSDATE. The second constructor function initializes the object instance based on the incoming value of student ID using the SELECT INTO statement.

The member procedure GET_STUDENT_INFO populates out parameters with corresponding values of object attributes. The static procedure DISPLAY_STUDENT_INFO displays values of the incoming student object on the screen. Recall that static methods do not have access to the data associated with a particular object type instance. As a result, they may not reference the default parameter SELF. The order member function compares two instances of the student object type based on values of the `student_id` attribute.

The newly created object type may be tested as follows:

```
DECLARE
   v_student_obj1 student_obj_type;
   v_student_obj2 student_obj_type;

   v_result INTEGER;
BEGIN
   -- Populate student objects via user-defined constructor method
   v_student_obj1 :=
      student_obj_type (in_student_id  => NULL,
                        in_salutation  => 'Mr.',
                        in_first_name  => 'John',
                        in_last_name   => 'Smith',
                        in_street_addr => '123 Main Street',
                        in_zip         => '00914',
                        in_phone       => '555-555-5555',
                        in_employer    => 'ABC Company',
                        in_reg_date    => TRUNC(sysdate),
                        in_cr_by       => NULL,
                        in_cr_date     => NULL,
                        in_mod_by      => NULL,
                        in_mod_date    => NULL);

   v_student_obj2 := student_obj_type(103);

   -- Display student information for both objects
   student_obj_type.display_student_info (v_student_obj1);
   DBMS_OUTPUT.PUT_LINE ('=================================');
   student_obj_type.display_student_info (v_student_obj2);
   DBMS_OUTPUT.PUT_LINE ('=================================');

   -- Compare student objects
   v_result := v_student_obj1.student(v_student_obj2);
   DBMS_OUTPUT.PUT_LINE ('The result of comparison is '||v_result);

   IF v_result = 1 THEN
      DBMS_OUTPUT.PUT_LINE
         ('v_student_obj1 is greater than v_student_obj2');

   ELSIF v_result = 0 THEN
      DBMS_OUTPUT.PUT_LINE
         ('v_student_obj1 is equal to v_student_obj2');

   ELSIF v_result = -1 THEN
      DBMS_OUTPUT.PUT_LINE
         ('v_student_obj1 is less than v_student_obj2');
   END IF;

END;
/
```

The output is as follows:

```
Student ID: 403
Salutation: Mr.
First Name: John
Last Name: Smith
Street Address: 123 Main Street
Zip: 00914
Phone: 555-555-5555
Employer: ABC Company
Registration Date: 24-APR-08
================================
Student ID: 103
Salutation: Ms.
First Name: J.
Last Name: Landry
Street Address: 7435 Boulevard East #45
Zip: 07047
Phone: 201-555-5555
Employer: Albert Hildegard Co.
Registration Date: 22-JAN-03
================================
The result of comparison is 1
v_student_obj1 is greater than v_student_obj2

PL/SQL procedure successfully completed.
```

Chapter 24, "Oracle Supplied Packages"

This chapter has no "Try It Yourself" section.

INDEX

D

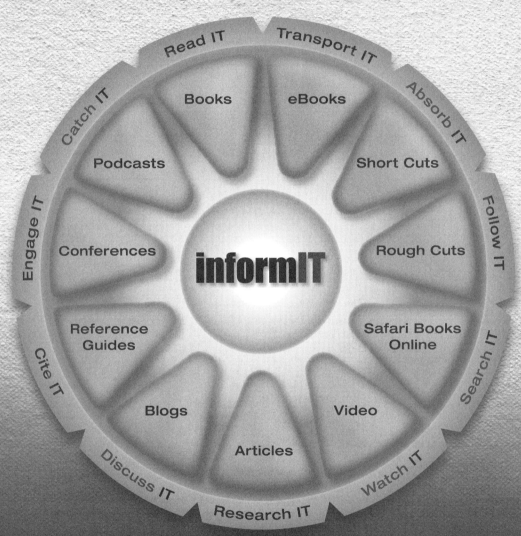

FREE Online Edition

Your purchase of **Oracle® PL/SQL™ by Example** includes access to a free online edition for 45 days through the Safari Books Online subscription service. Nearly every Prentice Hall book is available online through Safari Books Online, along with over 5,000 other technical books and videos from publishers such as Addison-Wesley Professional, Cisco Press, Exam Cram, IBM Press, O'Reilly, Que, and Sams.

SAFARI BOOKS ONLINE allows you to search for a specific answer, cut and paste code, download chapters, and stay current with emerging technologies.

Activate your FREE Online Edition at
www.informit.com/safarifree

> **STEP 1:** Enter the coupon code: QWRGJGA.

> **STEP 2:** New Safari users, complete the brief registration form.
> Safari subscribers, just login.

If you have difficulty registering on Safari or accessing the online edition,
please e-mail customer-service@safaribooksonline.com